Human Rights and the Third World

Human Rights and the Third World

Issues and Discourses

Edited by Subrata Sankar Bagchi and Arnab Das

LEXINGTON BOOKS
Lanham • Boulder • New York • Toronto • Plymouth, UK

Published by Lexington Books
An imprint of Rowman & Littlefield
4501 Forbes Boulevard, Suite 200, Lanham, Maryland 20706
www.rowman.com

10 Thornbury Road, Plymouth PL6 7PP, United Kingdom

Copyright © 2013 by Lexington Books
First paperback edition 2014

All rights reserved. No part of this book may be reproduced in any form or by any electronic or mechanical means, including information storage and retrieval systems, without written permission from the publisher, except by a reviewer who may quote passages in a review.

British Library Cataloguing in Publication Information Available

Library of Congress Cataloging-in-Publication Data

The hardback edition of this book was previously cataloged by the Library of Congress as follows:

Human rights and the Third World : issues and discourses / edited bu Subrata Sankar Bagchi and Arnab Dis
  p. cm.
  Includes bibliographical references and index.
  1. Human rights—Developing countries. 2. Human rights—Cross-cultural studies.
I. Bagchi, Subrata Sankar, 1965– II. Das, Arnab, 1963–
  JC599.D44H84 2013
  323.09172'4—dc23   2012034491

ISBN 978-0-7391-7735-8 (cloth : alk. paper)
ISBN 978-0-7391-9798-1 (pbk. : alk. paper)
ISBN 978-0-7391-7736-5 (electronic)

∞™ The paper used in this publication meets the minimum requirements of American National Standard for Information Sciences—Permanence of Paper for Printed Library Materials, ANSI/NISO Z39.48-1992.

Printed in the United States of America

Contents

Acknowledgments		vii
Introduction: Human Rights and the Third World: Issues and Discourse *Subrata Sankar Bagchi and Arnab Das*		1

Part I Global Human Rights Standards and the Third World

1) Universal Claim and Postcolonial Realities: The Deep Unease over Western-Centered Human Rights Standards in the Global South — *Marie-Luisa Frick* — 17
2) The Impossible Dream: Global Realization of the Human Right to Development—Now! — *Clarence J. Dias* — 31
3) Development and Environmental Issues vis-à-vis Current Perspectives of Human Rights — *Aniruddha Mukhopadhyay and Sayan Bhattacharya* — 59
4) Human Rights and Corruption: Indonesian Case for Reconciling Universalism and Relativism — *Agus Wahyudi* — 81

Part II Politics of Human Rights from Third World Perspectives

5) Human Rights and Indigenous Self-Government: The Taiwanese Experience — *Scott Simon and Awi Mona (Chih-Wei Tsai)* — 99
6) Colonial Continuities, Neoliberal Hegemony and Adivasi (Original Dweller) Space: Human Rights as Paradox and Equivocation in Contexts of Dispossession in India — *Dip Kapoor* — 123
7) Hindutva Politics – Impact on Human Rights — *Ram Puniyani* — 145

Part III Rights of the Marginalized

8) Human Rights Violations in India: Exploring the Societal Roots of Marginality — *Debi Chatterjee* — 165
9) Media, Cultural Rights and the Third World — *Pranta Pratik Patnaik* — 179
10) The Fault Lines in Soviet-Style Accommodation of Minority Rights in Ethiopia — *Semahagn Gashu* — 193
11) Human Rights and the Third World Other — *Subrata Sankar Bagchi* — 215

Part IV Rights for Children and Genders

12) Culture and Issues of Rights to the Eyes of the Indians with 'Other' Self-Identities of Sexuality and Gender 235
    Arnab Das and Pawan Dhall
13) Roots and Shoots of Female Feticide in Pockets of India—Lending Voice to the Voiceless 265
    Tushar Kanti Saha

Part V Rights of the Disabled and Health

14) The Rights of People Living with Disability from the Third World Perspective: The Zimbabwean Context 287
    Francis Machingura
15) Disability in the Third World: A Critical Mapping of the Indian Scenario 309
    Anuradha Saibaba Rajesh
16) "People's Health in People's Hands"—A Goal Ever-Elusive? 331
    Satyabrata Chakrborty

Part VI Expanding Frontiers of Human Rights

17) Human Rights and Information Society: Problematizing India 353
    Dipankar Sinha
18) Biotechnology and Human Rights 371
    Subhasis Mukhopadhyay

    Index 393

    Notes on Contributors 415

Acknowledgments

When we started planning this edited volume on the Third World discourses of human rights we thought that it would not be a particularly onerous set of tasks. After all, the editors only have to identify a set of topics for discussion, enlist one or more authorities on the topics to write essays, provide some substantive feedback on each of the drafts, and then assemble the finals drafts and ship them off to the publisher. But the reality of doing it turned out to be much more challenging than originally anticipated. Not only is there usually insufficient space to cover all of the topics relevant to the broader area of research, but it is rarely possible to include as authors all of the accomplished scholars in the area. Thus, decisions have to be made about coverage and authorship. Moreover, once these matters have been settled, there is the challenge of coaxing the targeted authors to write the first drafts of the designated chapters within a limited span of time. And finally, there is the seemingly endless task of badgering the authors to revise their chapters in accordance with the central theme of the volume, which may be quite extensive, and to submit their revised drafts in a timely manner. The responsibility of preparing camera-ready form for publication further added the drudgery involved with this task.

We experienced all of these challenges in editing this volume, with some being much more time-consuming than initially anticipated. Such editorial challenges notwithstanding, we prevailed. And we did so not only because of our belief in the utility of the volume for scholars and students of human rights, but also because of the commitment and assistance of a number of individuals, to whom we owe a measure of gratitude. Foremost among the individuals are the chapter authors themselves, most of whom found the idea of the volume to be as important as we did. Obviously, if they had not stuck with us, tolerating our frequent badgering and coming through in the end, this volume would not have seen the light of day.

We also acknowledge the acquisition editor Amy King of Lexington Books who accepted our proposal of publishing this volume. Priyadarsini Sengupta and Yajnaseni Chakarborty also warrant thanks for their assistance in copy editing some of the essays. We are also thankful to Suman Hajra who helped us to prepare a detailed index of the book. We also express our gratitude to following institutes for varying degree of support: Bangabasi Evening College, Centre for the Study of Social Exclusion and Inclusive Policy and Department of Anthropology of the University of Calcutta.

Finally, we gratefully acknowledge permission to use the following previously published material:

Chapter 6, "Colonial Continuities, Neoliberal Hegemony and Adivasi (Original Dweller) Space: Human Rights as Paradox and Equivocation in Contexts of Dispossession in India" by Dip Kapoor is reprinted by permission of, and was first published by, SAGE Publications Ltd. *Journal of Asian and African Studies* 47(4)/August 2012: London.

A portion of chapter 16, "'People's Health in People's Hands'—A Global Ever-Elusive?" by Satyabrata Chakraborty, was reprinted from *Democracy and Democratization in the 21st Century* (2011) edited by Basu, et al. Har-Anand Publications: New Delhi. Reprinted by permission of Jadavpur University

Subrata Sankar Bagchi
Arnab Das

INTRODUCTION

Human Rights and the Third World: Issues and Discourses
Subrata Sankar Bagchi and Arnab Das

The universalistic nature of human rights requires a set of legal and normative standards for the entire mankind as the people across the world are eligible to enjoy certain rights irrespective of their ethnic, cultural, religious, linguistic and other identities. This notion of human rights is linked to the Western liberal notion of the rights of each and every individual in the society. More than 1000 years of Western history can be traced back as the background of the development of this liberal notion.

The British charter of Magna Carta, Hobbesian assault on the divine basis of 'natural rights', Kantian doctrine of the 'universality of state law based on equality, freedom, autonomy of the citizen or American Declaration of Independence and French Declaration of the Rights of Man and its Citizens, Rousseau's view on social contract based on the protection of rights of each citizen, Paine's doctrine on secular natural rights—all these and many other important chapters of Western history are considered as the defining moments in shaping this liberal notion (Bagchi 2009).

However, the actual formalization of the notion of universality of human rights has a relatively recent origin, i.e. with the establishment of United Nations after World War II and the adoption of Universal Declaration of Human Rights (UDHR). The trauma of the Second World War essentially prompted the world leaders to formulate the UDHR immediately after the War. Though the importunate goal of the declaration of UDHR in 1948 was to prevent another holocaust in the West, it highlighted the universality and the centrality of individual freedom which is the sine qua non of the long history of Western liberalism. After the adoption of UDHR we find the dramatic proliferation of human rights organizations, treaties, covenants, and resolutions.

The consequences of the declaration of UDHR and other major international human rights provisions have been marked by the most dramatic level of political emancipation through decolonization when within the two decades after the War, practically all of Asia's and Africa's nations got independence from their colonial rulers. From human rights point of view this rapid decolonization process had greatly shifted the focus from the struggle against the violation of rights by the colonizers to spread positive and liberal visions of human rights in the decolonized countries in the post–war era. Thus the international human rights regimes, rights declarations and monitoring bodies have been regarded as having emancipatory effects in the young democracies in the decolonized countries. The erstwhile colonizers, in most cases, took more initiatives to introduce the Western–style democratic institutions and its attendant human rights values to the former colonies.

However, the responses to these human rights measures in the Third World countries have been remarkably varied. The diverse socio–cultural backgrounds of the people of these countries sometimes lead to the rejection of all that are Western including the human rights values and the different historical vicissitudes experienced by these countries after their independence. Thus the Western liberal view on rights of each and every individual in the society was challenged and alternative views on the 'collective rights' for the wellbeing and preservation of the society started to emerge in the human rights discourses in the Third World. These alternative views, opposing the universalistic nature of human rights, cannot be traced back to a common source or a common tradition. These views reflected a variety of concerns, values and objectives which include the protection of traditional communities where morality tends to be directed toward the wellbeing of the society as a whole rather than that of each and every individual in the society (Tharoor 1990) and degree of conformity to these traditions by the entire society is required. These countries prioritize the collective duties and rights to protect wellbeing of the society as a whole as they fear that the prioritization of individual rights at the expense of social values would lead to a Western style breakdown of social order and family structure and an erosion of traditional values in that society. Sometime, the foreign policies of many of the Third World countries are also guided by a political realism which prevents a particular country to criticize the internal affairs of a sovereign country. We have seen such situations like the issue of violation of human rights in the India–controlled Kashmir that has remained a domestic affair of India for many years, and the international trade interests which prevent a particular country to take any drastic step against human rights violation in another country as we see India's growing trade with military junta in Burma. Though many of these concerns reflect the feelings of the citizens living in the traditional societies as the entire Third World needs culturally relative discourses to protect and promote both the human rights and cultural diversities in these countries (Bagchi 2009), there are cases where some of these views are regularly being used by the ruling elites to protect their own interests which include amassing astounding wealth through oppression.

Although these Third World perspectives are derived from different origins and traditions they all converged to a single agendum, i.e. the opposition of the liberal view on the protection of the rights of the each and every individual in a society. These alternative perspectives gained importance from the late 1960s and 1970s when the Third World countries started expressing their concerns on the rights of self-determination and culture–specific development models in opposition to the internationally recognized universalistic development models which were based on the liberal notion of individual rights. Many of these differences were discussed during the United Nations World Conference on Human Rights in 1993 held in Vienna immediately after the end of Cold War. Some international human rights agencies like Amnesty International was scathingly critical on some of the views aired in the conference and opined that it served "to reopen issues closed 50 years ago" (The Guardian June 22, 1993: 8). The conference came out with the 'Vienna Declaration and Plan of Action (VDPA 1993)' which apart from reaffirming the human rights as relevant and universal standard also recognized human rights as indivisible, interdependent and interrelated. Thus the Part I, Para 5 of 'Vienna Declaration and Plan of Action (VDPA 1993)' states "All human rights are universal, indivisible and interdependent and interrelated. The international community must treat human rights globally in a fair and equal manner, on the same footing, and with the same emphasis. While the significance of national and regional particularities and various historical, cultural and religious backgrounds must be borne in mind, it is the duty of States, regardless of their political, economic and cultural systems, to promote and protect all human rights and fundamental freedoms." Problems like poverty, social exclusion, minority groups, indigenous people, child labor, enforced disappearances etc. which were more prevalent in the Third World countries were not always seen in direct conjunction with human rights and were discussed and consequently motions were adopted on all these issues. VDPA also recommended the General Assembly the establishment of a High Commissioner for Human Rights "for the promotion and protection of all human rights" and the post of United Nations High Commissioner for Human Rights was subsequently created by the General Assembly on December 1993. VDPA is the mark of an unprecedented consensus on human rights among the member nations immediately after the Cold War. While it established the interdependence of democracy, economic development, and human rights it also ended a Cold War separation of Civil and Political Rights (CPR) from Economic Social and Cultural Rights (ESCR) advocating the indivisible, interdependent, and interrelated nature of human rights. For the first time in the post-Second World War history Third World concerns were addressed to and incorporated in a UN Declaration although in a universalistic framework of human rights.

Human Rights Perspectives from Asia, Africa and Latin America

The culturally relative nature of human rights is now being by and large accepted by a growing number of experts and policymakers and these people are now trying to seek commonalities within these immense varieties so that some generalizations can be made. Asian perspectives on human rights also bear the testimonies to cultural relativism as the perspectives change according to the priorities like subsistence or political freedoms or applicability of universal human rights notions in an Asian conservative society; for example, the Hindu society is bound by the roles and duties framed by the caste system where inequality is inherent in the society legitimized by the age-old customs. In the

Hindu society even the intellectual properties of food are used to protect social position (Appadurai 1981). Hence the question of protecting the rights of the vulnerable groups is more urgent than the individual where the self-respect of these groups is to be asserted. If one wants to understand the proper way of ameliorating the strict caste and gender situation, the primary areas of social deprivation and also of greatest unawareness, one has to systematically study the impact of the factors like raising of awareness, outside contact, education, economic opportunities, etc. (Franke and Chasin 1989; Menscher 1974). A culture–specific ethnographic approach on human rights may be developed where civil, political and cultural rights might have combined with other rights like right to food, rights against poverty and inequality and other socioeconomic rights (Joshi 1986; Khare 1991) which might lead to resisting the existing order (Yamane, 1982). The spate of terrorism and insurgent violence in the last two decades has also redefined the concept of human rights in many of the Asian countries where the authorities, in the pretext of saving its citizens from these 'menaces', advocate a limited form of rights and imposed a lot of duties without associated rights to its citizens and imposed various repressive laws which can detain people for longer time without any trial. The so-called 'encounter killings' are also common in many of these Asian countries. These laws and encounters are often being used by the authority to smother the dissent voices within the countries. The resurgence of Islamic militants in various countries like Pakistan and Afghanistan have also resulted regular breaching of violation of the rights of people living in these countries both by their own governments as well as by the transnational forces sometimes in collusion of the national armies.

Universalistic notions of human rights have also been transgressed when the question of its applicability came to Africa as the prime concern of most of the African people has always been how to get rid of the vicious circle of poverty and development rather than individual freedom. The perils of colonial rule on the African political system have long been accused for the collapse of the African society as we find in the study of Evans Pritchard (1940) on African political system. In this study we find that Europeans had diminished the authority of the chiefs and made them puppets of colonial rule where the tribes had the tradition of strong chiefs. On the other hand, Europeans created some omnipotent chiefs among the tribes which had no system of centralized authority in the form of a strong chief for the sake of their rule. The result devastated much of the African people as the traditional political system weakened and an alternative political system was imposed on the people who could not accept this European intervention. As Evans Pritchard (1940: 89) said "Africans, do not analyse their social system; they live it." The roots of much of the present maladies of Africa can be found in the European intervention in the societies of the African people and the indiscriminately drawn borders between the countries leading to partitioning of the same population in two or three countries like Hutus and Tutsis. After the Second World War, African countries started to gain their own sovereignties and the leaders from the decolonized countries in Africa immediately faced ethnic conflict and ecological deterioration along with abject poverty. The priorities before the African countries were to alleviate poverty, prevent large scale ethnic riots and arrest further ecological deterioration. Thus after decades of debates they later came up with their own regional charter known as African (Banjul) Charter on Human and Peoples Rights (1981 [1986]) where they stressed on rights of the "peoples" (meaning nations and not component ethnic groups) not individuals to come out of spiraling poverty and underdevelopment in Africa (Howard 1985, 1986, 1992; Shepherd 1990; Welch and Meltzer 1984). The aftermath of the adoption of this declaration saw an acrimonious debate between the universal autonomous individuals with rights and community rights as the African scholars played down the need of individual rights and "achieved" personhood (Gyeke 1992; Nyansi 1989) and it witnessed a reinvigoration of the argument of 'man as a social being performing his/her social roles and thus his/her rights should be seen in terms of his/her social unit not individually (Adegbit 1968; Legesse 1980). Although there are severe critiques of this African philosophy as the critics argue that the exploitation and deprivation are socially structured in Africa for generations and if one cannot break this vicious cycle (Howard 1985, 1986) one can definitely be torn between these contradictory discourses on human rights in Africa. However, after a closer look at the situation of the continent one cannot miss various crises on human rights like the lack of protection and increased vulnerability of women and children, presence of slavery, bonded/forced labor, genocide, ethnocide, chronic hunger and the recent proliferation of rights abuses in the name of Islamic Sharia laws in some African nations. Human rights scholars should also study the recent upsurge of pro–democracy movements in the Arab world, both in Africa and Asia, as intense debates have raged in these countries on the nature of these movements due to the involvement of the religious fundamentalists in some of these movements. All these issues must urgently be taken up and without the proper understanding of the African 'Others' these efforts would meet the same consequences that of most of the past and the present efforts.

Latin American human rights issues are as varied as the other two Third World continents. The most impending rights issues in Latin America are the rights of the indigenous people to land, culture and self-determination and abuses against the native peoples by the state authorities (Davis 1984, 1988; Guidieri, Pellizzi and Tambiah 1988; Smith 1990). Various authoritarian regimes, backed sometimes by the West, have been accused of being ruthless against the various rights of the indigenous people as well as the middle class citizens, mostly the political dissidents (Lewellyn 1985). Spiraling poverty and the lack of other basic amenities for the overwhelming majority of the Latin American people also featured frequently in the discourses of human rights of the continent (Smith 1990, 1991). Latin American human rights perspectives have also been compounded by various factors like the fragmentation of indigenous identities by postcolonial notion of sovereignty, religious fundamentalism, ultra–leftist resistance movements, dilemma in priorities on the rights of collectivities over the individuals and effects of various development projects run by different national and international development agencies on the land and subsistence rights of the native population. Only micro-level inclusive understandings on the various perception of rights in different cultural settings could uncluttered the colonial, religious as well as ultra–leftist jinxes to the realization of rights of both the indigenous as well as other citizens of Latin America.

Outline of the Volume

This edited volume has six separate sections. Each section is engaged in critical analyses of diverse aspects of human rights from Third World perspectives. The first section deals with the standards of human rights in the global context, accosting various issues and how the Third World nations are positioned with regard to certain basic human rights issues. This section begins with the chapter written by Marie-Luisa Frick where she argues that from an early stage of Western civilization documents like the US Declaration (1776) and French Declaration (1789) have been considered as having universal applicability, irrespective of national boundaries which ultimately culminated in the forming of UDHR IN 1948. But with the new balance of power tilted toward the global South, the perceived consensus on the universality of a single human rights standard for the entire world is disintegrating with the gradual augmentation of a general feeling of unease over the issue of "coloniality of knowledge" perceived through the discourses of human rights. According to Frisk, the Third World nations are particularly opposed to the Western–centered human rights standards which put individual rights ahead of the collective wellbeing of a society. Drawing examples of this opposition from various parts of the Third World like Asian values debate, blasphemy laws in Pakistan, Ecuador's recent constitution, anti–homosexuality bill in Uganda, Frisk argued that though one can not deny the deep rift between the West and the Third World the quest for true universality of human rights should continue "with respect for cultural alterity as well as for one's own ethical ideals".

The next chapter of this section, written by Clarence J. Dias, compares historically the right to development, as a "third generation" human rights in the United Nations system and within India's Constitution, laws, policies and programs over the past 25 years. Diaz argues that both Colonial and Cold War conceptual baggage has contributed to the constant impediment of understanding, recognition and realization of the development as a right. The right to development also became a pawn of the Cold War by East–West divide, North–South divide and breach of promise of the developed world to developing countries by way of "official development assistance" (ODA). Later the "victims" of development in the nongovernmental sector in developing countries, appearing before the drafting group had very clear notions of what they wanted from recognition of a human right to development. Diaz also argues that the Right to Development as a Human Right offers a redefinition of the very concept and rationale of development, development as an "inalienable" "human right" of "every human person" and "all peoples", whereby a human person is the central subject of development vis-à-vis the main participant and beneficiary of development. States have the duty to take steps, individually and collectively, to formulate international development policies with a view to facilitating the full realization of the right to development. Diaz describes how the Third Working Group on the Rights to Development of UN Human Rights Commission came under extreme pressure from the Western group, and especially the United States, to virtually abandon the Declaration on the Right to Development. In spite of all resistances, a human rights–based approach to development embodies all of the normative principles contained in the right to development, which has become a programming tool for development cooperation. Since 1995, at the World Summit on Social Development a new rhetoric has been developed on the need to privatize development and allow corporations to play a significant role in social development as a part of Corporate Social Responsibility (CSR), which is essentially the deliberate inclusion of public interest into corporate decision-making, and the honoring of a triple bottom line: People, Planet, Profit. Diaz concludes that the right of peoples to self-determination and to sovereign control over their resources and their future is the core of the right to development and the governments cannot yield their prerogatives to "the invisible hand of the market".

The third chapter, jointly written by Aniruddha Mukhopadhyay and Sayan Bhattacharya, interrogates how the evolution of human society has posed serious questions to the human rights concerning economic, social and cultural levels. The study initiates critically to answer why ecologically rich regions of the globe are economically poor. It discusses the problems of the usage of resources, distribution systems and access to safe and secured environment. The authors argue that with the advancement of civilization and development, degradation of environment happened with the simultaneous violation of human rights. Development has not ensured the basic universal rights to food, water, energy, shelter, etc. although the concept of sustainable development has the potential to accommodate the basic components of human rights. Sustainable human development is   directed towards the promotion of human dignity and security of all kinds of human rights like economic, social, cultural, civil, political, etc. So far as the protection of nature is concerned, authors contend, there is always a philosophical conflict between the developed and developing nations. The developed world stresses more on the protection of nature, while the developing world emphasizes more on social justice. Protection of nature is not possible without safeguarding the basic rights of the biomass dependent 'common people', who are sometimes referred to as 'ecosystem people'.

The fourth chapter, dealing with a debatable nexus between corruption and human rights, is written by Agus Wahyudi. Wahyudi examines both the violative perspectives ("mainstream views") of corruption as "it disables the state from meeting its obligation to respect, fulfill and protect the human rights of its citizen" as well as the perspectives of other scholars ("non–mainstream views") who refuse to accept corruption as a human rights violating factor. Drawing examples from Indonesia, Wahyudi argues the New Order Suharto's idea of state perfectionism resulting in an authoritarian rule, actually contributed to a culture of corruption in Indonesia; and the liberal notions of universality of civil and political rights has been applied to understand the corruption and violations of human rights in the nation. But this notion, Wahyudi contends, is not capable in entirety to comprehend "the true nature of violations and political corruptions in Indonesia". Wahyudi concludes that a balance is necessary in the human rights discourses between the "pretentious and unrealistic universalism" and a "paralyzing cultural relativism".

The second section of this volume concentrates on how the rights issues have been politicized in different parts of the Third World and how it featured in the political discourses in the Third World countries. The first chapter, jointly penned by Scott Simon and Awi Mona, analyzes the problems of the rights of the indigenous people in Taiwan which constitutes 2.2 percent of the total population and living in Taiwan for at least 6000 years before the Chinese settlement. This chapter argues that Taiwan was one of the first nations to recognize and adopt UNDRIP (United Nations Declaration on the Rights of Indigenous Peoples), ILO's Indigenous and Tribal Peoples Convention C107 and passed the *Basic Law on Indigenous Peoples* in 2005. But the proposed indigenous autonomy law (Bill–12300) in Taiwan to give an effective self-government to the indigenous population has been created without any effective participation of indigenous peoples and the indigenous authority has been "minimized to exclude regulatory authority over the land, policing, and juridical powers". Thus they conclude that without a true recognition of inherent sovereignty of the indigenous people in Taiwan, which is true for the entire Third World, the rights discourses mean very little to the indigenous people and they will continue to feel the same sense of deprivation as they used to feel during the colonial rule.

The next chapter of this section, written by Dip Kapoor, engages in post-colonial discourses on the politics of human rights as institutionalized by the state. Citing examples from research he conducted among the Adivasis (Indian equivalence of Indigenous people) in the Indian province of Orissa, Kapoor argues that this "estatized" form of human rights can not help in realizing the rights of the precariously placed Adivasis in India who are facing wide-scale development displacement and dispossession due to the advent of neoliberal economy. Kapoor argues that the non–institutionalized human rights can help us in transgressing "the hegemonic hijacking of construction, interpretation and mis/application of rights in the wider interests of an Advasi and indigenous politics for pluri–nationalism and coexistence" though it might face problems like legitimization from the state and the "constant challenge by the imperial and colonial project of a globalizing capitalism".

The last chapter of this section delves into one of the most widespread problems in recent decades in India as well as in many parts of South Asia, i.e. communalism, which means in the subcontinent as promoting violence against the religious minorities by a section of people from the majority religion. Written by Ram Puniyani, one of the most renowned human rights activists and a relentless advocate against communalism in South Asia, this examines how the political paradigm changed in India from the 1980s when the word Hindutva (the identity of being a Hindu) became popular thanks to the Hindu "fascist" Nationalist organizations like Rashtriya Swayamsevak Sangh (RSS) which thrived on the Ram Temple movement. Puniyani argues that RSS and the other Hindu Nationalist organizations like Bhartiya Janta Party, Vishwa Hindu Parishad, Bajrang Dal etc. were instrumental in propagating communal hatred against the religious minorities through the politics of Hindutva; and committed various anti–minority acts like the demolition of a mosque built by the Mughal–ruler Babar, rioting and killing Muslim minorities in the Indian province of Gujarat, anti Christian violence in the Indian province of Orissa, etc. In this essay he further discusses the concept of religion based nationalism and the abolition of secular values actually go against the perception of pluralism, democracy and rights for the weaker sections like dalits, women, Adivasis and minorities.

The third section of this volume deals with the rights of the marginalized section of population in the Third World. The first chapter of this section is written by Debi Chatterjee and discusses how social marginalization causes a huge section of Indian population to remain excluded from the basic goods and services, thereby itself tantamount to the violation of human rights. Chatterjee also explains how the age-old brahminical order and its attendant patriarchy resulted in the deep-rooted inegalitarian social order in India which caused to expose the lower castes, tribal people, women and the religious minorities to a form of oppression for generations which is beyond human dignity. She also argues that more than fifty years of independence and parliamentary democratic exercises resulted in several legislations making these discriminations widespread; and hence without basic changes in the social structure one can not expect any major changes in the lives of the marginalized section of population in India.

The second chapter in this section discusses the role of media in ensuring the cultural rights of marginalized people. Writer of this essay Pranta Pratik Patnaik, citing examples from the Indian state of Orissa, states that the Oriya television channels have indulged in the politics of creating and defining an Oriya culture and identity by promoting cultural stereotypes which are basically common in the coastal region of Orissa and "reinforcing the prevailing stereotypes and existing power structure". The same media are now involved in the legitimization of the project from the Korean POSCO steel company and neglecting the struggle of the people to save their agricultural land and cultural identity. Patnaik argues that the perception of universalizing the measures to safeguard cultural rights is inadequate and is incapable of fighting various injustices perpetrated on the marginalized people as witnessed in Orissa.

In the next chapter of this section the writer Semahagn Gashu argues that one can appreciate the ethnic federal structure of Ethiopia which has recognized the rights of Ethiopia's nationalities to self-determination, including secession. But according to Gashu, this Soviet–style model has failed, as it lacks democratic exercise, political consensus, legitimacy and a proper perception of state sovereignty based on 'Ethiopian' identity 'nations, nationalities and peoples'. The rights of the minority groups have not been properly realized due to various reasons like the lack of federal structure threatening the survival of state and social cohesion; inconsistent and confusing definition and distinction between people based on ethnic criteria; lack of emphasis on cultural, historical and social ties among the ethnic groups, resulting in a resurrection of already weak ethnic identities; domination of some ethnic groups over other ethnic groups; repression of the federal government based on the military might on the minorities; absence of consensus on the mode of accommodation of minority rights; lack of democratic set-up within the country which prevent the free operation of news media and rights–based NGOs; lack of resources to the regional administrative units and the like. All these contributed to some serious violation of minority rights as witnessed in the Ogaden and Gambella Regional State of the country. Thus Gashu contends that the protection of minority rights in Ethiopia will only be possible if the nation can alleviate the aforesaid maladies which can only be possible with the installation of a genuine pluralistic notion of democracy and a political consensus on the mode of accommodation of minority rights.

The last chapter of this section is written by Subrata Sankar Bagchi, one of the editors of this volume. Bagchi describes how the present human rights discourses have been marked by the deep North–South divide on the issue of prioritization of rights of each and every individual in the society in the West vis-à-vis collective rights to preserve the culture and wellbeing of a society in the Third World. Bagchi argues that the alternative perspectives of human rights sometimes require absolute conformity with the prevailing social norms which often ends up in stifling the voice of the vulnerable and marginalized individuals and sections of a population. Thus human rights discourses in the Third World should find mechanism to incorporate the "authentic self-expression of the Third World Other" to ensure the rights of the minorities and vulnerable marginalized people in the Third World. Bagchi concludes "that a dialogue should be immediately opened in the human rights discourses which will go beyond the Spivakian contention of deliberate act of speaking by the subaltern (Other). Instead we should attempt to *listen* to the Third World Other in many ways by which they communicate so that their authentic self-expressions can be included in the human rights discourses for the Third World".

The fourth section of this volume is on the rights of children and genders. The section starts with the chapter jointly authored by Arnab Das (one of the editors of this volume) and Pawan Dhall. It starts by portraying the problems of sexual diversity in Indian context right from the ground of conceptualizing it in terms of paradigm shift from essentialist to constructivist and performative understanding. The ethnographic terrain is emphasized for exploring the culturally sensitive understanding of sexual diversity and particularly MSM (men who have sex with men) constructs and practices around the world and particularly in India. The study of the complex diversity reaches out to the linkages among (I) Backdrop of present claims of action claims, (II) different frameworks of understanding same–sex scenario in India, (III) the diverse categories of MSM in India, (IV) use of femininity and masculinity in MSM population of India, (V) the scenario of activism for justice, rights, legislature in context of civil society. All these issues help constituting the pivot of the problems in dealing with the rights and justice to the MSM population in India. Otherwise, the authors argue, chances are that the communities will play into the hands of the system that perpetrates omnipresent structural violence as status quo will be only too happy to see the threat posed by gender and sexual diversity dissipated by wasteful rivalry.

The second chapter of this section is on female feticide in India which is a widespread practice in some parts of India even today. Written by Tushar Kanti Saha, this essay describes the status of declining women in modern India which is suffering from "missing women" syndrome due to a trend of daughter aversion and son preference. This is due to the fact that the sons are still seen as the treasure of a family since they stay with the family and contribute to family earning while daughters are perceived as economic burden due to the prevalent dowry system in India. The most outrageous fallout of this trend is the surreptitious detection of the sex of embryo and medical termination of the pregnancy if the embryo is found to be a female one which is a brazen violation of violence against women. Sometimes the girls are even killed at a tender age by the family to get rid of the huge economic burden caused due to the marriage of the girls. Despite various legislations to stop the acts like female feticide and female infanticide and other such violative acts like child marriage, child abuse and child prostitution, etc. the violations against the girl child are happening in various parts of India continually. Saha concludes that to prevent these violations the requisite acts should be appropriately amended. Indian government should also take sincere initiatives to create a comprehensive national data base for births and deaths, to modernize the marriage registration system and initiate some corrective mechanism like tightening the relevant Indian Penal Codes, levying a small marriage registration fee for insurance cover to the future children of the newly married couples.

The fifth section of this volume deals with the rights of the disabled and health rights in the Third World. The first chapter is on the problems of the persons living with disability in Zimbabwe. The author of this article Francis Machingura describes how the discrimination against disabled persons is institutionalized in the Zimbabwean society like blaming the mother of the disabled, stigma, fears, myths and misconceptions associated with disabilities in the country. Discriminatory religious teachings and beliefs from the Churches are often blamed for the institutionalization of discrimination against the people living with disability in that country. Machingura argues that it is the poor persons living with disability, particularly the rural poor, who are the hardest hit as they face the maximum brunt of the socially constructed hostile environment against the disabled persons in Zimbabwe. Persons with disability face discrimination in almost every aspect of life like education, employment, health care, free movement, getting vital information, being part of society, making choices, freedom of marriage and religion. Machingura concludes that this deep-rooted discriminatory social attitude and values against the disabled will only change by social and political means when it would be coupled with the international initiatives.

The next chapter in this section, written by Anuradha Saibaba Rajesh, overviews the disability discourses in India. As we know that the paradigm of disability has now shifted from the medicinal and welfare model to the rights framework in India along with the rest of the world with the United Nations Convention on Rights of Persons with Disabilities 2007 and the July 2009 General Assembly resolution on "Realizing the Millennium Development Goals for Persons with Disabilities through the implementation of the World Programme of Action concerning Disabled Persons and the Convention on the Rights of Persons with Disabilities". Saibaba observes that disability remains a tabooed issue in the Third World and in India it has been tremendously influenced by religious and cultural dogma along with the contributory factors like poverty, illiteracy, lack of nutrition, etc. Disabled people are discriminated against in all walks of life like education, employment, health care, cultural and family lives; despite the Indian Constitution having several provisions against such discriminations. Saibaba argues that the enactment of *Persons with Disabilities (Equal Opportunities, Full Participation and Protection of Rights) Act 1995* along with such other legislations and the establishment of the Office of Disability Commissioner could not prevent these discriminations. This chapter calls for looking beyond paternalism and social protection and instead we should consider the persons with disability as the equal citizens of this country.

The last chapter of this section is on the sticky issue of the right to health and healthcare in a Third World country like India. The writer of this chapter Satyabrata Chakraborty elucidates how the right to health is a composite issue as per the UDHR which includes medical care as well as non–medical components like food, clothing, housing, necessary social services, right to security in the event of unemployment, sickness, disability, widowhood, old age and lack of livelihood. Health is an important component of development recognized by international communities and is inextricably bound with the democratic set-up of the country. Chakraborty observes that though the Constitution of India has enshrined right to health as one of the fundamental rights and became a signatory of Alma-Ata Declaration on health rights, there is an immense gap between the efforts of government in the health sector and the realization of the right to health of its citizens resulting in an awfully inadequate state of health for the poor and vulnerable section of population. Chakraborty argues by citing one example from the work of a voluntary organization in the Sundarbans area in rural West Bengal that the minimal realization of the right to health is possible in a Third World country like India only with a participatory model where people become aware of their right to health and organize themselves to ensure the realization of that right.

The last section of this volume is on some emerging aspects of human rights. The first chapter of this section, authored by Dipankar Sinha, seeks to engage the readers with an unconventional and under–researched theme on the linkage between human rights and the Information Society. India, especially by virtue of being the "largest democracy in the world", figures prominently in the global scenario. But what often remains out of sight, both in conceptual and practical terms, is that the vital and sensitive question of the (ab)use of human rights is often directly and indirectly linked to the nature and status of Information Society because of the quantity of raw information and it is the 'information culture' that goes a long way to determine to what degree human rights can be established and sustained, that too in the Indian society which is highly diverse and inequitable. Avoiding a dominant but reductionist focus on human rights per se, the essay seeks to explain the interplay of various forces that contribute to an 'incomplete' and 'distorted' information society in India, and it ultimately advocates a people–centric everyday orientation in approaching the problem and its solution. In the specific content of India the essay explains, with the metaphorical question—Is the glass half full or half empty?— to bring out the binary division between statism and activism that seems to be determining the fate of the Indian society and its people. In the process of elaboration the essay reveals—taking into account but going beyond the problems associated with the state's attitude toward human rights—the constraints of human rights activism. This constitutes the basis of Sinha's argument that with the coming of the market the human rights scenario in India has become all the more complex, especially with the commodification of information. In the ultimate analysis Sinha reposes faith in the existing 'little' information societies—based on local knowledge, local resource and local skill. Providing some concrete instances, he argues that notwithstanding the fact that these little versions have their own limitations and constraints they are the ones which can be relied upon to broadening the horizons and democratizing the foundation of the human rights scenario in India. The content of the essay has many reflections which extend beyond the boundaries of India to be relevant to the Third World societies.

In the last chapter of this section Subhasis Mukhopadhyay, an eminent Biotechnologist in India, takes up the issue of a different aspect of biotechnology which invades in the privacy of the body and soul of people violating human rights. Nowadays, many Third World countries like India have state-of-the-art biotechnological programs and devices recognized by the international communities but its citizens face the maximum brunt of the human rights abuses with the help of advanced biotechnology as many of these countries use these biotechnological inventions against its own citizens without any ethical dilemma. Mukhopadhyay argues that only a collective wisdom both from the individual nations and the international community will be able to solve this yawning ethical gap between the indiscriminate use of biotechnology and the wellbeing of a society.

Together the volume's authors struggle with the controversial questions on human rights and the volume strives to find some Third World perspectives on human rights. This volume opens up a discursive space in the human rights discourse and endeavors to address a few unresolved questions in human rights citing issues and problems from different countries in the Third World—

a) Whether alternative perspectives should be taken as the standard for human rights in the Third World countries?
b) Should there be a universalistic notion of rights for Homo sapiens or are we talking about two diametrically opposite trends and standards of human rights for the same species?
c) How far can these Third World perspectives of human rights ensure the protection of the minorities and the vulnerable sections of population particularly the women and children within the Third World?
d) Can these alternative perspectives help in fighting the Third World problems like poverty, hunger, corruption, despotism, social exclusion like the caste system in India, communalism and the like?
e) Can there be reconciliation between the Third World perspectives and the Western perspective of human rights?

References

Adegbite, L.O., 1968. African Attitudes to the International Protection of Human Rights. *International Protection of Human Rights*, edited by A. Eide and H. Shue, 60–81. New York: Interscience.

Appadurai, A., 1981. Gastro-politics in Hindu South Asia. *American Ethnologist* 8, No. 3: 494–511.

Bagchi, S.S., ed. 2009. *Expanding Horizons of Human Rights*. New Delhi: Atlantic.

Davis, S., 1984. International Strategies for the Protection of Human Rights of Indigenous Peoples. *Cultural Survival Quarterly* 8, no. 4: 64–65.

———. 1988. *Land Rights and Indigenous Peoples. The Role of the Inter-American Commission on Human Rights*. Cambridge, Mass: Cultural Survival.

Evans-Pritchard, E. E., 1940. T*he Nuer: A Description of the Modes of Livelihood and Political Institutions of a Nilotic People*. Oxford: Clarendon Press.

Franke, R. and B. Chasin, 1989. Kerala: Radical Reform as Development in an Indian State. *Food First Development Rep*. No. 6. San Francisco: Inst. Food Dev. Policy.

Guidieri, R., F. Pellizzi and S. Tambiah, eds. 1988. *Ethnicites and Nations. Processes of Interethnic Relations in Latin America, Southeast Asia, and the Pacific*. Houston: Rothco Chanel.

Gyeke, K., 1992. Person and Community in African Thought. *Person and Community*, edited by Kwasi Wiredu and Kwame Gyekye, 231–46. Washington D.C.: The Council for Research in Values and Philosophy.

Howard, R., 1985. The Full Belly Thesis: Should Economic Rights Take Priority Over Civil and Political Rights? Evidence from Sub–Saharan Africa. *Human Rights Quarterly* 5: 467–90.

———. 1986. *Human Rights in Commonwealth Africa*. Totowa: Rowman and Littlefield.

———. 1992. *Dignity, Community, and Human Rights*. Totowa: Rowman and Littlefield.

Ismaelillo, ed. 1982. *Native Peoples in Struggle: Cases from the Fourth Russell Tribunal*. Bombay: ERIN.

Joshi, B., 1986. *Untouchable!* London: Zed.

Khare, R., 1991. *The Issue of Right to Food among the Hindus. Notes and Comments. Human Rights to Food*: Religious Promise and Practice Lecture Series, Brown University.

Legesse, A., 1980. "Human Rights in African Political Culture." In *The Moral Imperative of Human Rights: A World Survey*, edited by E. Thompson, 81–108. Washington, DC: University Press of America.

Lewellyn, T.C., 1985. Structures of Terror. A Systems Analysis of Repression in El Salvador. *Human Rights and Third World Development*, edited by G.W. Shepherd and V.P. Nanda, 45–63. Westport, Conn: Greenwood.

Menscher, J.P., 1974. The Caste System Upside Down, or the Not–so–mysterious East. *Current Anthropology* 15: 469–93.

Nyansi, J.M., 1989. The Ontological Significance of "I" and "we" in African Philosophy. *I. We. and body. 1st Joint symposium of Philosophers from Africa and from the Netherlands at Rotterdam on March 10, 1989,* edited by H. Kimmerle, 13–23. Amsterdam: Verlag B. R. Gruner.

Shepherd, G.W. and M. Ankipo, eds. 1990. *Emerging Human Rights: The African Political Economic Context.* Westport, Conn: Greenwood.

Smith, C.A., 1990. *Guatemalan Indians and the State.* Austin: University of Texas Press.

———. 1991. Maya Nationalism. *Report on the Americas* 25, no. 3: 29–33.

Tharoor, S., 1990. "Universality of Human Rights and Their Relevance to Developing Countries." *Nordic Journal of International Law.* 59, no. 2/3: 139–152.

The Guardian (22nd June 1993): 8

VPDA http://www.unhchr.ch/huridocda/huridoca.nsf/a.conf.157.23.en (accessed August 4, 2011).

Welch, C.E. and R. Meltzer, eds. 1984. *Human Rights and Development in Africa.* Albany: State Univ. New York.

Yamane, H., 1982. Human Rights for the People of Asia. *Human Rights Teach* 3: 18–22.

CHAPTER 1

Universal Claim and Postcolonial Realities: The Deep Unease over Western–Centered Human Rights Standards in the Global South

Marie-Luisa Frick

At the time the first human rights declarations were framed in the United States (1776) and France (1789) and the expansion of the European civilization was aspiring to its peak, the norms and values contained in these documents were considered to be universal to the effect that they were both deemed stemming from a universal human nature and applying to all human beings irrespectively of nationality. When after the Second World War the Universal Declaration of Human Rights (UDHR) was passed by the General Assembly of the United Nations (1948) under the auspices of the United States, the rights stipulated again were proclaimed to be independent from regional or cultural frameworks, despite reservations made by several countries with socialist or Islamic orientation. Today's trend towards globalization and a shift of power from the *West* to newly industrialized countries in the *global South*, make it increasingly obvious that the claim whereupon the classical human rights values and norms are universal or even constitute a consensus of mankind, dashes against postcolonial realities that reject the West's hegemony in moral and political terms. How *universal* the Western conception of human rights *de facto* is can be easily guessed when looking at additional or competing human rights declarations, such as the African [Banjul] Charta on Human and Peoples' Rights (1981) or the Cairo Declaration on Human Rights in Islam (1990). In this contribution I would like to outline the fault lines pervading the human rights discourse between the *West* and the *global South* and analyze to what extent they are grounded in mutual misconceptions, power, political ambitions or profound value conflicts.

Rigid Dichotomies?

Before starting my analysis, I would like to put in perspective the relation between Western societies and their human rights thinking and practice and the societies of the global South, i.e. nations of Central and South America, Africa and Asia. It would constitute a gross falsification of reality to draw the picture of homogenous Western human rights thinking opposed to or challenged by a likewise homogenous human rights understanding of non–Western countries. On the contrary, reality is far more complex. Just as much considerable support for Western human rights standards exists all over the world—including countries whose regimes vehemently refuse them—there also exists obvious discomfort within Western societies regarding the interpretation and range of specific human rights norms, e. g. the right to freedom of speech, the right to marry and found a family. Today in Europe and North America this discomfort primarily is based on religious reservations vis-à-vis the alleged unbound freedom of man proclaimed by the secular–liberal human rights tradition. Only if bound to truth, so Pope Benedict XVI., a prominent critic of what he termed the tyranny of modern societies' relativism, true freedom can unfold. Unrestricted freedom or human rights, respectively, would constantly threaten to override the basic human rights of others—especially in case of unborn children deprived of their dignity and right to life by the modern *right* to reproductive self-determination (cf. Ratzinger 2005). Similar anxiety is uttered, for example, by Patriarch Alexy II., the primate of the Russian Orthodox Church, in his address to the Council of Europe where he makes the diagnosis of "a break between human rights and morality" (Patriarch Alexy II. 2007). This break, so Patriarch Alexy II., comes to the fore "in a new generation of rights that contradict morality, and [...] human rights [..] used to justify immoral behavior" (ibid.).

Against the background of such widespread unease over secular and liberal human rights discourses, it should become clear that the focus of this contribution is not laid on the global South for its alleged intrinsic unease over Western human rights, but rather for the overall issue of *Human Rights from Third World Perspective*.

General Unease Over Western–Centered Human Rights Standards: The "Coloniality of Knowledge"

In the course of decolonization countries of the global South may have (re–) gained political autonomy, but hardly any economic independence, and—according to many—still less independence from Western epistemic hegemony. From the eurocentric perspective, the Western way to see the world, to interpret man's being, to organize social relationships and the political sphere was regarded superior to all other traditions and in this alleged superiority the legitimacy was found to impose it on others. It was, however, not only this ethnocentric mentality of superiority, which conditioned the overall influence of European culture and which just as well can be found in all other great cultural traditions. Above all, the scientific–technological–military supremacy of the European powers contributed to spreading their culture. It is therefore not surprising that as soon as this domination based on power and—enough times—brute force began to erode, the return to domestic resources in matters of religion, arts and education gained in importance. The epistemic tradition of the West, its materialistic science, its legal tradition, its anthropology, etc., increasingly suffered the loss of universality—the idea of human rights being no exemption.

The claim to universality and the ambition to present the human rights formulated in the UDHR as *supracultural* may have been intended to serve the higher goal of humanity, i.e. the acceptance of certain unalienable rights, but, nevertheless, can not fade out the historical fact that the idea of human rights emerged in the European modern era in the course of the Enlightenment with its specific notions of *social contract, natural rights* and popular sovereignty which not only constituted a departure from former European traditions and beliefs, but also from the traditions and beliefs of the entire previous mankind. Thus, the concept of human rights is imbedded in a set of ideas, assumptions and demands that are contingent insofar as they are the product of a specific civilization at a specific period in time.[1] But, if human rights as a concept are the product of a specific culture, this implies "difference, boundaries, particularity" (de Sousa Santos 2007a: 6). So the question arises: "How can human rights be both cultural and a global politics?" (ibid.).

Today, the universalization of Western human rights standards is frequently opposed precisely with reference to their actual relativity. Combined with universalism, i. e. the claim to universal validity, for some this relativity is sheer intolerable. "[T]he perceived universalism in the human rights approaches", Bagchi is convinced, "is sometimes endangering various forms of cultural diversities and local innovations" (Bagchi 2009: 9). Makau Mutua argues: "The official human rights corpus, which issues from European predicates, seeks to supplant all other traditions while rejecting them. It claims to be the only genius of the good society" (Mutua 2002: xi). Western human rights standards, so Mutua, conceptually can not be divided from liberal democracy and in trying to impose their human rights thinking on others, Western countries inevitably espouse a peculiar form of government which might have little local support and, hence, not the legitimacy required. Ultimately, this implicit "political agenda" (ibid.: 1) of the human rights project would be used to justify (military) interventions. Mutua explicitly criticizes the West's "pathology of the savior mentality" (ibid.: 6) regarding Third World countries that should be abandoned. To claim true universality, according to him, the "the participation of all societies and cultural milieus must be required" (ibid.: xi).

The claim to universality, according to Boaventura de Sousa Santos, has not just since the shift of hegemonic balance at the end of the Cold War lost its persuasive power; rather, already the great project of the UDHR lacked the universality it stressed for the declaration "was drafted without the participation of the majority of the peoples of the world" (de Sousa Santos 2007a: 13). In particular, it suffered, he argues, from the "exclusive recognition of individual rights, with the sole exception of the collective rights to self-determination [...]; [and from] the priority given to civil and political rights over economic, social and cultural rights" (ibid.: 13f). Accepting that different human communities possess varied worldviews and that there are "no complete knowledges" (de Sousa Santos et al. 2007: xvii) would enable us to finally overcome the "coloniality of knowledge" (ibid.: xlix). Otherwise, human rights would "tend to operate as a globalized localism, a form of globalization from above" (de Sousa Santos, 2007a: 11).

Against this imposition from above, ministers and representatives from Asian states preparing for the UN World Conference on Human Rights in Vienna 1993 have objected in their "Bangkok Declaration". They repeatedly emphasized the "principles of respect for national sovereignty, territorial integrity and noninterference in the internal affairs of States" and stressed "that the promotion of human rights should be encouraged by cooperation and consensus and not through confrontation and the imposition of incompatible values" (Ministers and Representatives of Asian Sates 1993). They asked for respect concerning "regional particularities and various historical, cultural and religious backgrounds" and also warned against using human rights as an "instrument of political pressure" (ibid.). Taking the same line, former Malaysian president Mohammad Mahathir argues: "The West assumes that any idea coming out from them is perfect and must be accepted by the whole world. And yet they must know that ideas like socialism, communism, republicanism, and all kinds of isms, came out from the West, and today the West rejects this as wrong. How do we know their ideas about democracy, about human rights, will not be rejected in the future?" (Mahathir 2001).

From a philosophical point of view, the argument that human rights to a large part constitute a Western, local heritage and therefore in their current style should not be universalized and imposed on others, is incomplete and hence, somewhat problematic. However, the problem of this argument is not that it is relativistic. Rather, it gives no reason *why* such a universalization or imposition has to be forborne. The sheer fact that the modern human rights corpus is not universally accepted in totality can not serve as a foundation for the normative claim of relativism simply because there is no such easy bridge from *is* to *ought*, as we learned from David Hume. The implicit reason for human rights relativism first and foremost seems to be a motive of *fairness*: If Western societies have to admit that *their* human rights notion is particularistic to the effect that it is imbedded in their specific world view which is one out of many in a multicultural, globalizing world, they would have to ask themselves how they can justify bothering other societies with Western human rights. To insist that there can be no justification due to their *de facto* relativity is begging the question simply because universal acceptance or approval does not say anything about the quality of norms or values. Imagine, for example, the practice of slavery which until recently, i.e. circa 200 years ago, has been common to nearly all human societies over a period of thousands of years. Can one, from the prevalence of slavery, deduce its legitimacy? Of course not! It is exactly in this manner representatives of Western countries could concede the particularity (of some) of their human rights norms and at the same time wish and work for their universalization— without lacking the due respect for their adversaries who do precisely not stand on shakier ground in epistemic terms. Those hypothetic Westerners might very well be aware of the factual relativity of their world view and consider it fair to tolerate equally relative systems of belief, but at the same time be convinced it is by far more unjust to tolerate certain severe human rights violations.

Furthermore, the value of a specific idea or concept can not be determined with reference to its origin. Such an approach would constitute a genetic fallacy. In other words: Just because the idea of human rights emerged in the West that does not mean it is necessarily futile or even wrong for other peoples. If it was, to the same degree Western science and technology would be futile for the rest of the World.

From this it follows, that in order to decide whether or to what extent Western human rights standards should be universally applied, one has to move to the level of their material content. This approach will also draw the attention to the practical unease over Western–centered human rights standards and might help to explain in what regard exactly they meet with disapproval in the global South.

Specific Unease over Western–Centered Human Rights Standards: The Primacy of the Individual

After having outlined in brief the general unease over the quasi–colonial paternalism of Western countries vis-à-vis countries of the global South when it comes to human rights, I now would like to focus on the question what precisely in the Western understanding of human rights fuels the discontentment of its critics. For this purpose I will analyze the specific unease over Western–centered human rights standards in four short case studies.

1. "Asian Values": Opportune Pretence for Authoritarian Rule or Cure to Western Societies' Excessive Individualism?

During the last decade of the 20th century so-called Asian values were the height of fashion in theoretical disputes about the universality or relativity, respectively, of human rights norms and their underlying values. Against the background of a rapid economic growth—which was not interrupted until the 1997/8 financial crisis—the Asian *tiger* and *dragon* nations "could arrogantly sneer at the West for its decadence and economic decline" (Wai-Teng Leong, 2008: 121). Their increasing self-awareness led to what Mahathir called "a fundamental cultural shift" (Mahathir, 1999: 45) which fostered the overcoming of colonialism's "psychological burden" and "shackles of mental servitude" (ibid.: 14, 68) as well as the promise of "a new age" (ibid.: 12). Mahathir explained: "Under colonial rule, many of us in Asia were taught and came to fear that our values and ways were second-rate. But the emergence of Asia as a major player in the global economy proved to us that Asian values are not inferior simply because they are Asian" (ibid.: 68). This "Asian exceptionalism argument" (Wai-Teng Leong 2008: 129) functions on the basis of the assumption of a substantial difference between Western and Asian societies combined with the conviction that this difference was positive for the latter and serving them well. Not surprisingly, the *return* to values assumed to be typically *Asian*—more aptly Confucian/Islamic—and hence more appropriate for countries like Malaysia, Singapore, Indonesia or China did not leave unaffected their relationship to classical human rights. Just like democracy, human rights should not be applied to Asian countries without adding to them an "Asian flavour" (ibid.: 43). Actually, this Asian taste can be described in many ways. Former Singaporean president Lee Kuan Yew, for example, outlined it by highlighting the principles of placing society above oneself, stressing racial and religious harmony and resolving major issues through consensus rather than contention (cited in Geiger/Kieserling, 2001: 133ff.). The easiest way, however, to explain this sort of Asian flavored human rights reasoning is to call it a profound aversion to individualism and unrestricted individual rights. Something regarded a distinctive feature of Western civilization: "In Europe and America, there may well be much greater pluralism and so-called freedom of the press, but in Asia it has been, and it will continue to be, the good of the many rather than the selfishness of the few or the individual that is treasured" (Mahathir, 1999: 44). Asian societies, according to Mahathir, place greater emphasis on the family, the community and would not accept "absolute personal freedom" (ibid.: 69): "Fulfilling your responsibilities towards your family and your community comes before your right to claim individual privileges" (ibid.).

Not only to Westerners themselves but also to everyone familiar with everyday reality in Western countries the immediate question arises as to the adequacy of the description of Western individualism opposed to Asian communitarism. Of course the conceptual framework of the classical human rights corpus developed in Western modernity from the renaissance onwards *is* individualistic insofar as it is the individual who is the bearer of rights since it is the individual who has to make sense of his or her being, choose among rivaling ways of living and finally realize himself or herself, respectively. And it is always the individual who is exposed to violations of his or her freedom, body or bare life. But does this conceptual primacy of the individual lead to a virtually dissolution of society as a whole as some critics of *Western* human rights admonish? In mainstream Western society the "intrinsic balance", Chandra Muzaffar supposes, "between rights and responsibilities, rights and relationships, rights and roles has been eroded by an obsession with rights" (Muzaffar 2002: 46f.). Mahathir too identifies the "cult of the individual" with the alleged downgrade of Western civilization: "Hence, Western societies today are riddled with single-parent families, with homosexuality, with cohabitation, [...] and disrespect for others" (Mahathir 1999: 78).

To be sure, axiological differences do exist between different societies in different parts of the world, but can anybody seriously doubt that Europeans, for example, have no true sense for the importance of community cohesion when evidentially European societies are supporting their increasing masses of senior citizens with a substantial part of their economic wealth? Who can really maintain that family solidarity is the value of a specific region or culture when in fact the brotherly embrace or the advice of a mother is beneficial anywhere in the world and the domestic conflicts arising from differences in interests bother families from Asia over Africa to the Americas in equal measure.[2] Hence, the assumption suggests itself that the Asian values or Asian exceptionalism argument in its descriptive form rather is an occidentalistic parody of the West and far from an accurate depiction of the world we live in. The question, "does freedom give an individual the right to do whatever he or she wishes, regardless of the consequences for the rest of society?" (Mahathir 1999: 72) is not only raised by people critical of Western human rights standards but also subject to heated discussions within Western societies themselves. Within the concept and practice of human rights obviously the possibility of fundamental tensions exists between the interests of the individual on the one side, and the interests of society on the other. And this tension is not dissolved in Western societies by automatically ranking the individual's desires above society's just as Asian societies do not necessarily negate all individual claims with reference to social harmony. Approaching this issue in such a simplistic manner obstructs the view on the fact that in terms of a human rights weighing of individual interests against the interests of the collective the question is not either-or, but the one of the proper balance. Imagine for example the human right to freedom from torture as formulated in Art. 5 UDHR (UN 1948). Although not uncontested nowadays, the rationale behind this precise human right is the idea that the interest of society to convict somebody of a crime—no matter how strong this interest or how outrageous the crime might be—can never prevail over the interest of the individual in question not to suffer boundless pain forcing him to confess or make up a confession.

If now Asian societies in case of some human rights, such as the right to freedom of speech or the right to freedom of assembly, would want to (slightly) shift the balance from the individual's interest to the needs of society, they could very well do so as long as the human right in question is not totally annihilated. Such an approach which may be named relativistic universalism (the norm is universal, the concrete materialization is left to individual societies or cultures) is also adopted by Jack Donnelly who argues that "that international human rights norms are sufficiently broad to accommodate most Asian desires for more communitarian practices" (Donnelly 1999: 76). Hence, it could be argued, for example, that in countries like Malaysia or Singapore where inter–religious harmony is quite fragile, the right to discuss religious subjects in public could be restricted since for the people living there peace and security are simply more important than a *right to taunt*.

In light of the lack of plausibility of Asian values clearly distinguishable from Western values one could raise the question whether the intention behind the Asian values argument might have been directed at something else. This suggestion is put forward, for example, by Ann Kent. She is convinced that first and foremost the Asian values debate was a mere pretence by certain governments "to achieve legitimization of their authoritarian rule at a time when authoritarian communist regimes in Europe were crumbling. It was also designed to ward off threat of cultural, political, and social change posed by an increasingly globalized world" (Kent 2008: 83). A telling example for this sort of strategic exceptionalism is the People's Republic of China (PRC) and its relationship to international human rights. Whereas China prides itself on major progress regarding the human rights situation in the country and declares to be committed to the "full realization of human rights" (cf. PRC 2010), violations of basic rights with reference to the higher end of a "harmonious society" are a daily occurrence. This idea of societal harmony—absorbed from the Confucian concept of social order envisioned to be dependent on "a complex set of interlocking, hierarchical, social roles and relations centered on filial piety and loyalty" (Donnelly 1999: 79)—is regularly applied in order to stifle criticism against the Chinese government and the Communist Party of China, respectively. Though the Chinese regime officially emphasizes that "citizens have the right to make criticism and suggestions" (PRC 2010), this right obviously ceases as soon as it fails to be *constructive*, i.e. based on the intention to improve minor deficits of a system perfect in principle—as can be seen in case of Liu Xiaobo, winner of the Noble Peace Prize 2010. The decision of the Nobel Committee to award the prize to him "for his long and non-violent struggle for fundamental human rights in China" (The Norwegian Nobel Committee 2010) provoked harsh criticism on part of Chinese officials. The spokeswoman of the Chinese foreign ministry stated: "All policies in China are for the interest of the majority. We will not change [...] because of the interference of some clowns who are anti–China" (cited in Branigan 2010). Freedom of speech, China announced, "does not mean one can say whatever one wants" (Guo 2010) and that there would exist higher principles than civil and political rights, first and foremost "the protection of national security, public order or public health or morals" (ibid.).

From a genuine human rights perspective unspoiled by political thirst for power it is a clear-cut issue: "The Chinese claim [..] that 'individuals must put the state's rights before their own' [...] is incompatible with any plausible conception of human rights" (Donnelly 1999: 114). Blocking demands for basic human rights—inside as well as outside China—with reference to social–political stability and national sovereignty has already been a popular strategy of authoritarian regimes in the past and apparently seems to work well also with modern–day China—at least as long as the Chinese people unreservedly agree that—"a harmonious and stable society is the fundamental requirement to protect Chinese people's human rights" (Zhang 2010).

2. Freedom of Speech Vs. Right to Murder? Pakistan's Blasphemy Laws

The tension between classical human rights and the Islamic world view (cf. Frick 2010)—though not insurmountable—likewise concerns the unease over Western individualism. In orthodox Islamic reasoning the Ummah, i.e. the community of believers, is far more important than the single Muslim whose terrestrially wellbeing may even be scarified in order to guarantee the flourishing of *God's true religion* (Brohi 1982: 48). "Collectivity", the jurist and former minister of Pakistan, A. K. Brohi, argues, "has a special sanctity attached to in Islam. All Quranic prayers are in the plural and the value of prayers offered by an individual is greater if he goes [...] to join a bigger gathering of his brethren [...] (ibid.: 48). But this tension has roots reaching beyond the material (individualistic) content of human rights: Contested is also the *nature* of human rights as manmade laws claiming universal, eternal validity whereas such qualities according to many Muslims can only be granted to the laws of God. Muzaffar explains: "In the main stream contemporary Western human rights tradition, it is the individual human being who is the source of rights—and values from which these rights are resumed to be derived. It is the individual who possesses rights. It is the individual who is the arbiter of right and wrong, of good and evil. The individual is the ultimate measure of all things" (Muzaffar 2002: 84).

Thus it comes as no surprise that individual rights or claims, respectively, easily conflict either with the rights of God (Maududi 1960: 166) or the wants and interests of the Ummah. The latter could be observed recently in Pakistan where opponents and proponents of the severe blasphemy laws which prescribe punishments for *insulting* Islam, its places of worship, its holy book or its prophet ranging from monetary penalty to death penalty. When in 2010 the Christian woman Asia Bibi was accused of defaming Mohammed Pakistan faced worldwide criticism for her arrest. In the course of the events, Salman Taseer, the Governor of Punjab and a critic of the blasphemy laws, was killed by a man claiming to be proud of this deed intended to bring to justice the *enemies* of his religion. In a press statement Pakistan's influential opposition party, Jamaat-e-Islami, vindicated the murder by stating that "the Muslims' love and attachment for the Holy Prophet (pbuh) was natural and unlimited and any Muslim worth the name could not tolerate blasphemy of the Prophet (pbuh), as had been proved by this incident" (Jamaat-e-Islami Pakistan 2011). They also criticized the government for trying "only to please their masters in the west" and thereby trampling on the feelings of Pakistan's Muslim majority. The unease over Western human rights standards from this perspective arises from the unwillingness to accept that the (secular) human rights corpus by no means bows to orthodox versions of Islamic law and in this way approves of all kinds of behavior that—from a religious perspective—might be called *sinful* or *criminal*. This sort of conflict also exists in case of the prohibition of apostasy with exactly the same underlying clash of hierarchies: the interest of the individual to speak her mind—in the case of Asia Bibi to state that Jesus, not Mohammed, is the *true* savior—or to choose *and* change his religion; the interest of the Ummah in terms of intactness in the broadest sense on the other. Can there be any way of solving this conflict without taking sides? From a human rights perspective—which is not inherently anti–Islamic or anti–religious—the right to freedom of religion in principle is open to compromise and is not absolute. It does not allow for human sacrifice, for example (Donnelly 1999: 133). On the other hand, restricting the free choice of religious beliefs per definition runs contrary to the right to freedom of religion and can never be justified with reference to the *true* nature of Islam. This claim simply can not have any significance for the perspective of human rights which has to acknowledge all religions equally without taking sides. In Bibi's case of the infringement of the right to freedom of speech, too, partiality can not be expected from a human rights point of view: they either have to be valid for all or none. Those (Pakistani) Muslims who feel offended by others openly rejecting their assertion of Mohammed's prophecy are not only at war with Western human rights standards, but finally with humankind as such that can not be imagined without its fundamental condition of plurality.

3. "Rights of Nature": The Better Human Rights? Ecuador's 2008 Constitution

Another sort of discomfort with human rights standards of the West can be registered when moving from Asia to South America. Although here too the individualistic nature of classical human rights is challenged, it is not individualistic claims against a collective that are rejected in cases where the latter is prioritized over the former. Rather, the notion of an individual autonomous vis-à-vis creation in its totality is contested. The reason lies in different definitions of identity possessed by many indigenous peoples to whom the idea of nature as external to society and as a *resource* is entirely alien (de Sousa Santos 2007: xxxvi).

For a very long time this cosmic consciousness of universal relations and interdependences among man and other *soulful* beings, such as animals, plants, but also rivers or soil, was oppressed and nearly eliminated by the European colonial counter–conception in terms of an anthropocentric, rights–based political framework. Today, the recollection of epistemic traditions is set in motion in many countries of Latin America. A telling example of this process is Ecuador. Its constitution, passed in 2008, is remarkable insofar as it not only acknowledges rights of the people, but also *rights of nature*. The rights of *Pachamama*, as they are called, refer to the indigenous concept of a motherly Goddess pervading the entire cosmos. Art. 71 of the Ecuadorian constitution declares: "Nature or Pachamama, where life is reproduced and actualized, has the right to be respected comprehensively in her existence, persistence and regeneration of her vital cycles, structure, functions and processes in evolution" (Republic of Ecuador 2008). According to this guarantee, the state is obliged to prevent or eliminate any consequences of severe or permanent damage to the environment, such as in case of the exploitation of non–renewable natural resources. Reflecting the Ecuadorian approach the question arises as to what is effectively gained for the people living in Ecuador by attributing special rights to *Mother Nature*? On the other hand, one could reformulate the question the other way round when reflecting the so-called third generation of human rights, i.e. collective rights, such as the right to a clean and healthy environment. What is effectively gained by granting the right to a healthy and clean environment to people? Imagine, for example, a large-scale contamination of soil and water due to toxics from a gold mine. People living there and insisting on their right to a clean and healthy environment could be replied: 'Of course you have this right, but you have no right to a *particular* clean living environment and so you may very well actualize your right by moving away from here to a another place offering better living conditions.' By enforcing the rights of nature instead, it turns out that what really are protected in actual fact are the human rights of the people. In this regard, the concept of Pachamama is by no means rivaling Western human rights standards, but rather corrects their inefficiency when it comes to *indirect* violations of vital interests. From the perspective of Western human rights standards the rights of individuals to life, bodily integrity or as well a healthy environment would still be satisfied if all the inhabitants of earth would live on one single intact continent whereas the rest of the planet was descending into toxic waste.

From the Pachamama anthropological point of view, this is just not satisfactory because in the end the single human being and the ecosystem are *one*. It is from this understanding that the Ecuadorian constitution affirms the celebration of nature "of which we are part and which is vital to our existence" (ibid.).

4. No Human Right to Be Gay? Uganda's Anti–Homosexuality Bill

For a final short case study on the unease over Western–centered human rights standards in the global South we are moving to Africa where in Uganda the dispute continues about a newly introduced bill penalizing homosexuality even prescribing the death penalty as maximum punishment. The bill, not yet enacted, caused a storm of protest from Western countries worried about the life and security of Uganda's gay and lesbians in particular after Ugandan newspapers published the names of suspected homosexuals or even headlined: "Hang them" (cf. Karimi 2010). Those sympathizing with the tightening of Uganda's anti–homosexuality laws regularly argue that homosexuality is not a human right (cf. Mubangizi 2010). The question whether or not discrimination based on someone's sexual orientation to the same degree contradicts human rights standards as does the discriminations based on sex, color or religious affiliation for example, is the root of recurring tensions between Western countries and countries of the global South. In this regard, the African, Caribbean and Pacific Group of States (ACP) laments "profound divergences" within its partnership with the European Union (EU) when it comes to the issue of homosexuality. The EU demands that the prohibition of discrimination based on sexual orientation should be integrated into the EU–ACP Cotonou agreement. However, the ACP insists on respect for cultural differences and "urgently appeal[s] to the European Union to refrain from any attempts to impose its values which are not freely shared in the framework of the ACP–EU Partnership" (ACP Parliamentary Assembly 2010).

In Uganda, the man behind the anti–homosexuality bill is MP David Bahati. In an interview he defended his anti–gay engagement with reference to his intention "to protect the children of Uganda" and "to defend the tradition of family in Uganda" (Bahati 2010). Like Bahati many Ugandans are convinced that gay men "recruit" young people and "target other people's children because they don't have their own to enlist" (Mubangizi 2010). From a genuine human rights perspective, the question suggests itself why—if one really intends to protect children from sexual abuse which is indeed highly urgent—the bill in question is not directed against child molesters or active pedophiles? And why female homosexuals should be affected by the proposed laws as well since they are barely known for child molestation? Thus, this implausible line of argumentation indicates that the protection of children is a mere pretence. The actual reasons might be found in the religious orientation of Uganda's anti–gay warriors who—at least in case of Bahati—are cross–linked with (US)—evangelicals. In the above–mentioned interview Bahati finally—being cornered by the interviewer—*admits* that the gravest reason in support of the new bill was that homosexuality "is not part of God's law" (Bahati 2010). Hence, the situation is quite similar to the Islamic opposition to certain human rights. Of course people drawn to same–sex relationships can not claim a human right to be applauded for their way of life since many people simply believe that their behavior is *wrong* and in that case it is their right to freedom of speech to articulate their disapproval. On the other hand, gays and lesbians—just like anybody else—should be granted the right not to be put to death or imprisoned for life just because a devoted believer condemns their sexual behavior that, besides, in no way affects him in *his* basics rights. In other words: A universal human right to enforce one's personal morals upon others would plunge the world into chaos and never–ceasing war.

Conclusion

In this contribution I tried to outline the general as well as specific unease over Western–centered human rights standards in countries of the global South in the context of their post–colonial emancipation. As far as the criticism of Western countries' coloniality of knowledge is concerned, fallacies in anti–Western/anti–human rights argumentation could be exhibited as well as the possibility of a respectful handling of human rights dissensions. In four case studies the specific unease over the Western individualistic, anthropocentric, or secular human rights concept has been illustrated and examined. Whereas a general objection against international human rights on the basis of religious dogmatism or the construction of *intrinsic* cultural values proved unsustainable, the possibility of a fertile enculturation of certain human rights has been emphasized. Especially the case of rights of nature enhancing the protective power of classical human rights gives proof of the fact that not all types of criticism are actually inimical to or insignificant for contemporary mainstream human rights standards. Not least because of this finding, the global discourse on human rights and the quest for true universality must continue—with respect both for alterity and one's own ethical ideals.

References

ACP Parliamentary Assembly, 2010. *Declaration of the 21st Session of the ACP Parliamentary Assembly on the peaceful co-existence of religions and the importance given to the phenomenon of homosexuality in the ACP–EU Partnership.* http://www.europarl.europa.eu/meetdocs/2009_2014/documents/droi/dv/201/201011/20101129_10declaration_en.pdf (accessed January 12, 2011).

Bagchi, S. S., ed. 2009. *Expanding Horizons of Human Rights.* New Delhi: Atlantic.

Bahati, D., 2010. Interviewed by Rachel Maddow. http://maddowblog.msnbc.msn.com/_news/2010/12/09/5616533-the-david-bahati-interview (accessed January 12, 2011).

Branigan, T., 2010. Eighteen More Countries Refuse to Attend Nobel Peace Prize Ceremony. *The Guardian,* 2010. http://www.guardian.co.uk/world/2010/dec/07/china-nobel-peace-prize-clowns (accessed January 12, 2011).

Brohi, A., 1982. The Nature of Islamic Law and the Concept of Human Rights. *Human Rights in Islam,* edited by International Commission of Jurists /

University of Kuwait and Union of Arab Lawyers, 43–60. Kuwait: International Commission of Jurists.

Donnelly, J., 1999. Human Rights and Asian Values: A Defense of 'Western' Universalism. *The East Asian Challenge for Human Rights*, edited by Joanne R. Bauer & Daniel A. Bell, 60–87. Cambridge: Cambridge University Press.

———. 2003. *Universal Human Rights in Theory and Practice.* Ithaca: Cornell University Press.

Frick, M-L., 2010. Ummah's Rights or Human Rights? Universalism, Individualism and Islamic Ethics in the 21st Century. *American Journal of Islamic Social Sciences,* 27, no. 3 (July 2010): 1–23.

Geiger, K. F. and Kieserling, M., eds. 2001. *Asiatische Werte. Eine Debatte und ihr Kontext.* München: Westphälisches Dampfboot.

Guo, J. *Nobel Peace Prize not International Community Voice,* 2010. http://www.china.org.cn/opinion/2010-11/01/content_21245946.htm (accessed January 12, 2011).

Jamaat-e-Islami Pakistan, *Taseer Himself Responsible for Murder,* 2011. http://jamaat.org/site/general_detail/news/1748 (accessed January 12, 2011).

Karimi, F., 2010. Uganda Newspaper Publishes 'Gay List'. Calls For Their Hanging." *CNN,* 2010. http://edition.cnn.com/2010/WORLD/africa/10/20/uganda.gay.list/index.html (accessed January 12, 2011).

Kent, A., 2008. Chinese Values and Human Rights. *Human Rights in Asia. A Reassessment of the Asian Values Debate,* edited by Leena Avonius and Damien Kingsbury, 83–97. New York: Plagrave Macmillan.

Kingsbury, D., 2008. Universalism and Exceptionalism in Asia. *Human Rights in Asia. A Reassessment of the Asian Values Debate,* edited by Leena Avonius and Damien Kingsbury, 19–39. New York: Plagrave Macmillan.

Mahathir, M., 1999. *A New Deal for Asia.* Selangor: Pelanduk Publications.

———. 2001. "Interview." *Commanding Heights.* http://www.pbs.org/wgbh/commandingheights/shared/minitextlo/int_mahathirbinmohamad.html (accessed January 12, 2011).

Maududi, S. A. A., 1960. *Towards Understanding Islam.* Lahore: Islamic Publications Limited.

Ministers and Representatives of Asian States, *Final ("Bangkok") Declaration of the regional meeting for Asia of the World Conference on Human Rights,* 1993. http://law.hku.hk/lawgovtsociety/Bangkok%20Declaration.htm (accessed January 12, 2011).

Mutua, M., 2002. *Human Rights. A Political and Cultural Critique.* Philadelphia: University of Philadelphia Press.

Muzaffar, C., 2002. *Rights, Religion and Reform.* London: Routledge Curzon.

Mubangizi, M., 2010. *Homosexuality is not a Right,* The Observer. Retrieved on 11 January 2010.

Norwegian Nobel Committee, 2010. *The Nobel Peace Prize for 2010. Press Release.* http://nobelprize.org/nobel_laureates/2010/press.html (accessed January 12, 2011).

Patriarch Alexy II. *Address to the Parliamentary Assembly of the Council of Europe.* http://orthodoxeurope.org/page14/128.aspx#1 (accessed December 21, 2010).
People's Republic of China, *White Paper, 2010.* www.gov.cn/english/official/2010-09/26/content_1709982.htm (accessed January 12, 2011).
———. 2010. *What's Behind "Enshrining" Liu Xiaobo?* http://www.china.org.cn/world/2010-12/09/content_21508165.htm (accessed January 12, 2011).
Ratzinger, J., 2005. *Werte in Zeiten des Umbruchs.* Freiburg: Herder.
Republic of Ecuador, *Constitution,* 2008. http://pdba.georgetown.edu/ Constitutions/Ecuador/ecuador08.html#mozTocId822446 (accessed January 12, 2011).
de Sousa Santos, B., ed. 2007. *Another Knowledge is possible. Beyond Northern Epistemologies.* London: Verso.
———. 2007a. Human Rights as an Emancipatory Script? Cultural and Political Conditions. *Another Knowledge is possible. Beyond Northern Epistemologies,* edited by Boaventura de Sousa Santos, 3–40. London: Verso.
de Sousa Santos, B. J. A. Nunes and M. P. Meneses, 2007. Introduction. Opening up the Canon of Knowledge and Recognition of Difference. *Another Knowledge is possible. Beyond Northern Epistemologies,* edited by Boaventura de Sousa Santos, xix–lxii. London: Verso.
United Nations Organization, *Universal Declaration of Human Rights,* 1948. http://www.un.org/en/documents/udhr/ (accessed January 12, 2011).
Wai-Teng Leong, L. 2008. From 'Asian Values' to Singapore Exceptionalism. *Human Rights in Asia. A Reassessment of the Asian Values Debate,* edited by Leena Avonius and Damien Kingsbury, 121–240. New York: Plagrave Macmillan.
Zhang, D. 2010. Not a Noble Way of Involving China. *China Daily,* 2010. http://www.chinadaily.com.cn/opinion/2010-2/08/content_11667718.htm (accessed December 21, 2010).

Notes

1. That does not imply, however, that because of its European place of birth in terms of the history of ideas human rights necessarily are totally alien to other cultural traditions. Whereas non-Western cultural traditions did not develop a genuine concept of human rights, i. e. the idea that everyone without exception is entitled to certain individual rights, just because he or she is human, they do not lack (religious-)ethical resources able to pave the way for the idea of human rights as well as concrete human rights norms. But to call them some sort of (rudimentary) "human rights" is misleading, for it constitutes a confusion of human rights with ethical values or humanistic achievements. Jack Donnelly emphasizes in this regard: "Nothing is gained by confusing human rights with justice, fairness, limited government, or any other values or practices" (Donnelly 2003: 87).

2. Of course, one could quote examples of Western teenaged mothers whose drug addicted boyfriends beat to death their infants. But if we stick to the description of individual cases, we could also mention the examples of Asian parents casting out their offspring because of disability or change of religious affiliation. One can easily see how childish it is in the end, to claim superiority by drawing to that sort of *arguments.*

CHAPTER 2

THE IMPOSSIBLE DREAM: GLOBAL REALIZATION OF THE HUMAN RIGHT TO DEVELOPMENT—NOW!

Clarence J. Dias

I

Conceptual Baggage Threatening the Survival and Development of the Paradigm of Universal Human Rights

From its very birth in the Charter of the United Nations,[1] the paradigm of universal human rights has struggled to survive what might euphemistically be termed "conceptual baggage" (but what candidly should be called "conceptual garbage") that keeps intruding its way into the consensual articulation and global implementation of a paradigm of universal human rights. This conceptual baggage, has been wittingly or unwittingly produced and reproduced by a few but influential, vocal and articulate human rights scholars and intellectuals (Baxi 1987) and has been securely stored and incessantly recycled by a few highly visible, but not necessarily highly representative, transparent or participatory human rights NGOs and activists, throughout the World: be it first, second, third or fourth (Baxi 2007a). The conceptual baggage has been a product of an unholy historical alliance between a Colonial father (Raghavan 1990)[2] and a Cold War mother.[3]

Thanks to the success of the UN Decade on Decolonization, the world has, substantially succeeded in decolonization and self-determination of territory, although colonization has not yet been fully eliminated (Robie 1989 and Robie 1992). But, formidable tasks lie ahead in terms of decolonization of minds (Friere 2000) and self-determination of peoples.[4] Implementation and realization of the human right to development can contribute significantly to both such tasks. But this requires full acceptance of the right to development as a human right and the conceptual baggage, alluded to above, is a major obstacle to such full acceptance.

Colonial governments have been loathe to recognize the concept that human rights are universal and inherent in the human person—in all human persons. Colonial governance has been premised on a concept of equality wherein some people are more equal than others; and on the assumption that it is the prerogative of the State to bestow human rights on such categories of persons as they choose. India's national independence struggle challenged such colonial view of human rights with its stirring motto, "Swaraj is my birthright, and I shall have it!" But in the post–colonial era, neo–colonial attitudes towards human rights have been forged, favoring a State–centered paradigm of human rights. Human rights have been equated with legal rights, to be bestowed by the state, protected solely by state authorities and fulfilled only at the whim of the state. Human rights accountability has not generally been extended to non–state actors, except in a reluctant few instances such as domestic violence against women.

The UN Decade of Decolonization witnessed the era of the Cold War between the world's two Superpowers. The Cold War brought with it additional baggage, cluttering up the paradigm of universal human rights. In the capitalist block of First World countries, the contention has gained sway that the only real human rights to be granted recognition are civil and political rights of individuals. In the communist block of Second World countries, the contention has gained sway that the only real human rights to be granted recognition are collective economic, social and cultural rights. However, the holistic paradigm of human rights contained in the Charter of the UN and the Universal Declaration of Human Rights stresses that human rights are universal, indivisible, interrelated and interdependent (Dias 1995a and Dias 1998) (Baxi 1999a). The practice of human rights on the part of governments has however, degenerated into one of selectivity and double standards (Dias 1994).

Both the above sets of Colonial and Cold War conceptual baggage continue to impede understanding, recognition and realization of the right development, as human rights.

II

The Negotiation, Drafting and Adoption Processes of the UN Declaration on the Right to Development

In the mid 1980's an intergovernmental drafting group was created by the UN to draft a legal instrument which would articulate the concept of the right to development. The originator of the concept of the right to development was Keba M'Baye (M'Baye 1972). Other early support for the right came from scholars such as Upendra Baxi (Baxi 1998) and Phillip Alston (Alston 1988).

From the very outset, different Member States of the UN had very different (often contradictory) views as to why it was important to recognize a right to development and also as to what the normative context of such right might be. First, there was an East–West divide. The Communist bloc of countries, ably led by Poland, were using the occasion to get clear international reaffirmation of economic, social and cultural rights (both individual and collective) as universal human rights. Thereby, they were seeking recognition of the progress that those countries had made in realizing economic; and social rights. The group of developed Western states, stridently led by the United States, was strongly opposed to such a move and instead, sought to reassert the primacy of civil and political rights of individuals against the state, claiming that such rights were the only true human rights. The right to development became a pawn of the Cold War.

Second, there was a North–South divide. Mainly as a result of the UN Decade on Decolonization, a large number of newly independent States had come into existence and joined the ranks of the United Nations. These former colonies of the Western developed countries were seeking to be "compensated' for the substantial resources that had been stolen from them, by their colonial masters during the decades of colonial rule. Moreover, they claimed that existing international systems of trade, finance and investment were causing a continuation of the flow of wealth and resources from the developing countries to the developed countries (through adverse terms of trade, through the operation of the intellectual property rights system, and later through debt–servicing arrangements).

Moreover, the developed countries had pledged that they would aspire to provide 1 percent of their gross national product to the developing countries by way of "Official Development Assistance" (ODA). But this promise turned out to be honored much more in breach, than in observance, reminding one of the definitions under Common Law of the legal concept of fraud: "a promise made with no intent to perform".

The developed countries, for their part, had legitimate grievances about corruption and bad governance in developing countries, resulting in the ineffective use of the development assistance that had indeed been provided (IBON 2007). They cited numerous examples of aid being siphoned off into private, Swiss bank accounts of the leaders of certain developing countries.

Into this highly contentious situation came another set of actors and advocates, this time from the nongovernmental sector. They described themselves as the "victims" of development (Baxi 1994a). In many counties of the developing world, development as practiced, had overtaken poverty as the single largest cause of human rights denials, violations and abuses.

As the work of the drafting group on the right to development began to enter its final phase, two nongovernmental human rights organizations[5] brought to Geneva, representatives from (and advocates of) some dozen communities in Asia who had been victims of what the late Ernest Feder termed "perverse development" (Feder 1983 and Dias 1981). During a day-long dialogue with the drafting group on the right to development, they narrated what had been done to them in the name of development. They asked, "What relief, redress and remedies would be meaningful for them? What lessons were there to be learned and heeded in the future?"

From India came stories of hundreds of thousands of people suffering permanent disability as a result of the world's worst industrial disaster, in Bhopal; and of hundreds of thousands of tribal people who faced being flooded out of their homes and lands as a result of the construction of large, multi-purposes dams in the Narmada Valley.

From Thailand came stories of thousands of victims of floods, resulting from reckless deforestation to sell timber to Japan; and of subsistence fisher folk whose livelihood was eliminated by the excessive practice of tiger prawn–focused aquaculture.

From the Philippines came stories of thousands of slum dwellers facing eviction and forced resettlement as a result of the development of the Tondo foreshore; and of the population of the island of Marinduque, being slowly but inevitably, poisoned as a result of the operations of single, copper–mining multinational.

Exploitation of women in free trade zones (and in garment factories within such zones); exploitation of migrant workers from the Philippines; of children in India, Pakistan and Nepal forced to work in harmful, health–damaging factories; trafficking in women and children (and even in the organs of children)—these and other real-life cases were placed before the drafting group.

These "victims" of development, appearing before the drafting group had very clear notions of what they wanted from recognition of a human right to development and they let the drafting group know, in no uncertain terms.

III

The UN Declaration on the Right to Development: A Textual Analysis

In 1986 the UN General Assembly Declaration explicitly reaffirmed, the existence of a human right to development.[6] It went further and elaborated the content of the right as well as the specific obligations for States and Governments (both individually and collectively) that flow from the right.

The UN Declaration on the Right to Development tries to accommodate all of the interest groups identified in the preceding section of this article. But in trying to please them all, the Declaration is far from an ideal legal instrument (Dias et. al. 1999).

However, it does:

a. Reaffirm a human right to development which addresses, rather well, the concerns of the "victims of development" (for whom the issue now is one of effective implementation of the Declaration);
b. Prescribe normative principles about how development is to be undertaken which if adhered to, would allay concerns of donor countries regarding corruption and misuse of development assistance; and
c. Recognize a right of States to development cooperation (although it does so in the most vague and general terms).

The Right to Development as a Human Right

The Declaration makes three major contributions to clarifying the relationship between development and human rights.

First it provides a normative redefinition of the very concept and rationale of development. It defines "development" as "a comprehensive economic, social, cultural and political process, which aims at the constant improvement of the wellbeing of the entire population and of all individuals" "in which all human rights and fundamental freedoms can be fully realized" (Preamble).

Second, it affirms that development is an "inalienable" "human right" of "every human person" and "all peoples", by virtue of which they are entitled to participate in, contribute to, and enjoy economic, social, cultural and political development, in which all human rights and fundamental freedoms can be fully realized (Article 1.1).

Third, it prescribes certain normative principles about how development is to be undertaken. The development process is to be one which assures to "every person and to all peoples" "active, free and meaningful participation in development" and the right to "fair distribution" of the benefits from development. The human person is the central subject of the development process and development policy should, therefore, make the human being the main participant and beneficiary of development (Preamble).

The Human Right to Development of Individuals and Peoples

The right to development is an inalienable human right of every human person and all peoples (Article 1.1).

a. Every human person and all peoples are entitled to participate in, contribute to, and enjoy economic, social, cultural and political development, in which all human rights and fundamental freedoms can be fully realized (Article 1.1).
b. The human person is the central subject of the development process and the main participant and beneficiary of development (Article 2.1 and Preamble).
c. Every human person and all peoples are entitled to free and meaningful participation in development (Preamble). This is the most explicit articulation of a human right to participation in UN human rights law (Dias et. al. 1999).
d. Every human person and all peoples are entitled to the fair distribution of benefits resulting from development (Preamble).

Duties of the State (Individually)

a. States have the duty to take steps, individually and collectively, to formulate international development policies with a view to facilitating the full realization of the right to development (Article 4.1).
b. States have the right and the duty to formulate appropriate national development policies that aim at the constant improvement of the wellbeing of the entire population and of all individuals, on the basis of their active, free and meaningful participation in development and in the fair distribution of the benefits resulting there from (Article 2.3).

Duties of the State (Collectively)

The Declaration prescribes certain duties upon States the most notable of which are: the duty "to ensure full exercise and progressive enhancement of the right to development" (Article 10), the duty to "undertake at the national level, all necessary measures for the realization of the right to development" (Article 4), and the duty not to discriminate on the basis of "race, sex, language or religion" (Article 6.1). States also have the duty to cooperate with each other in ensuring development and eliminating obstacles to development.

Legally–binding Nature of the Declaration on the Right to Development

The Declaration is a codification of existing human rights law contained in other UN human rights treaties. As set out in the Declaration, the right to development comprises several component rights which are already contained in legally–binding instruments. Key among the component rights are:
a. The right to self-determination
b. The right of nondiscrimination
c. The right of participation.

Thus, there is no doubt, today, that the right to development is not a mere pipe dream or ideological slogan. It is a human right guaranteed by international law.

IV

The Declaration on the Right to Development within the UN: Twenty Five Years of the Little Done and the Vast yet to be Done

The Declaration on the Right to Development explicitly states that, "Steps should be taken to ensure the full exercise and progressive enhancement of the right to development, including the formulation, adoption and implementation of policy, legislative and other measures at the national and international level" (Article 10). However, an analysis and assessment below, of the steps taken thus far at the international level, leave one with a significant sense of unease.

The Right to Development and the UN Global Conferences on Development

Beginning with the Rio Conference on Environment and Development in 1992, the UN has held a series of global conferences (at the level of Heads of States and Governments) on various aspects of development. Each Conference has adopted, by consensus, a Declaration and Program of Action. Each Conference has been followed up by a review process at 5, 10 and 15 year intervals respectively. The right to development, as detailed in the Declaration on the Right to Development, has been repeatedly reiterated and further elaborated, by consensus, at several of these Conferences.

By common agreement, governments, development agencies and nongovernmental organizations (international, regional and national), made sure that the right to development figured prominently on the agenda of the Vienna World Conference on Human Rights in 1993. The Vienna World Conference was preceded by several national, regional and thematic consultations and Preparatory Conferences, all of which expressly addressed various issues relating to the right to development (Dias and Gilles 1993, Dias 1994 and Dias et. al. 1999). The Vienna Declaration and Programme of Action, makes it clear that "the promotion and protection of all human rights (including the right to development) and fundamental freedoms must be considered as a priority objective of the United Nations in accordance with its purposes and principles, in particular the purpose of international cooperation" (Article 5).

In similar vein, the Programme of Action adopted by the Cairo International Conference; Commitment 1 of the Copenhagen Declaration and Programme of Action of the World Summit on Social Development (March 1995); the Beijing Platform for Action adopted by the Fourth World Conference on Women and Development (September 1995) all reaffirm that the right to development is a "universal and inalienable right and an integral part of fundamental human rights."[7]

Global Consultation on the Right to Development as a Human Right

After the Declaration on the Right to Development was adopted by the General Assembly, the Commission on Human Rights examined the question of the means of implementing it at the national and international levels. With this in mind, it organized (in 1990) a global consultation on the implementation of the right to development (UNCHR 1990). The Consultation clarified the content of the right to development; identified obstacles to the implementation of the right and made recommendations to overcome such obstacles (Barsh 1991). Unfortunately, the valuable work of the Consultation, which remains relevant even two decades later, remains, largely ignored by governments and development agencies alike.

The UN Human Rights Commission Working Groups and Task Force on the Right to Development:

Pursuant to the Vienna World Conference on Human Rights, the UN Human Rights Commission has organized three successive Working Groups on the Right to Development.

The First Working Group was set up in 1993 with a mandate:
a. To identify obstacles to the implementation and realization of the Declaration on the Right to Development, on the basis of information furnished by Member States and other appropriate sources; and
b. To recommend ways and means towards the realization of the right to development by all States".

The Group met five times, identified obstacles, formulated proposals, recommendations and remedies. But it could not reach a consensus to adopt a final Report.[8] However, it did recommend to the Commission on Human Rights that the work be pursued by an intergovernmental group of experts.

Accordingly, in 1996 the Commission set up a Second Working Group with a mandate to elaborate concrete and practical measures for the implementation and promotion of the right to development. The Group held two sessions, and produced a Report which was widely criticized by governments for varied reasons. The countries of Europe (in particular France, Italy and the Netherlands) found the final report "well balanced." The countries of Latin America (Brazil, Cuba and Mexico, most notably) deplored the fact that the report had not accorded sufficient attention to the international dimensions of the right to development (UNCHR 1998a). At the end of its term, all that the Second Group could agree upon was to adopt the suggestion for a global strategy for the promotion and implementation of the right to development and recommend the creation of a follow-up mechanism for implementing the Declaration on the Right to Development.

Taking into account the difficulties encountered by the first two working groups in attempting to achieve significant progress on this question, the Commission on Human Rights, in 1998, set up a new intergovernmental working group, this time open-ended,[9] with the mandate:

a. To monitor and review progress made in the promotion and implementation of the right to development at the national and international levels, providing recommendations thereon and further analyzing obstacles to its full enjoyment.
b. To review reports and any other information submitted by States, United Nations agencies, other relevant international organizations and nongovernmental organizations on the relationship between their activities and the right to development (UNCHR 1998b).

This Third Working Group could meet for the first time only in 2000, upon the election of its Chair. From its inception however, the meetings have become the scene of confrontations between various interest groups over the conception and the vision of the right to development, or even the idea of development in and of itself. Melik Özden, director of the Human Rights Program of the Europe–Third World Centre (CETIM) has provided a concise and precise summary of the diverse stands taken at the meetings of the Third Working Group (Ozden 2008).

For the G77,[10] conditions favorable to the realization of the right to development and sustainable efforts at the national level are largely dependent upon effective international cooperation and a favorable economic environment.

The Latin American and Caribbean Group[11] deplore an international climate unfavorable to the realization of the right to development: dependence on basic commodities, trade rules, etc. It calls for cooperation and the financing of development based on multilateral agreement.

For the African Group and the Like Minded Group,[12] the obstacles to international cooperation are an unjust and unequal international order, the marginalization of the South in key decision-making processes, the burden of external debt, and obstacles to market access for countries of the South.

The European Union considers national responsibility the cornerstone of development. Good governance is essential for sustainable development and the eradication of poverty. Further, the European Union insists on conditions being attached to their cooperation.

The United States believes that measures taken at the national level are fundamental for realizing the right to development. It keeps reiterating its claim that there is no consensus on the right to development (having been the sole country to have voted against the 1986 UN Declaration on the Right to Development).

a. For Japan, the notion of "compulsory" international cooperation poses a problem, since such cooperation is not "automatic".
b. For Switzerland, respect for, and implementation of, human rights are compulsory, but international cooperation should be based on good faith.
c. According to Egyptian position, it is not sufficient to cancel or restructure the debt, but measures must be taken to assure that the vicious cycle does not perpetuate itself.
d. For Australia, the Doha Declaration (adopted in November 2001 at the WTO summit in Doha) is a contribution to the realization of the right to development.
e. India and Pakistan contest the universal position. India deplores the non–respect of the exception clauses in the WTO agreements, and Pakistan calls for revision of the agreement on Trade–Related Aspects of Intellectual Property Rights.
f. Iran and Cuba denounce the obstacles to the right to development created by embargos and unilateral coercive measures.

There thus remains a wide divergence of views and positions (Piron 2002 and Kirchmeier 2006). The Third Working Group has come under extreme pressure from the Western group, and especially the United States, to virtually abandon the Declaration on the Right to Development. The achievements of the Group continue to be disappointing, especially in view of the fact that the Group has now become virtually permanent, with its mandate regularly extended, by the Human Rights Commission, and now by the new Human Rights Council.

Moreover, the Commission also authorized, in 2004, the creation of a High Level Task Force within the working group, to support it in its work (UNHRC 2004a). The Task Force is chaired by Stephen Marks who has written extensively on the right to development (Marks 2003a, Marks 2003b and Marks 2004). Like the working group's mandate, that of this subgroup has been regularly extended since its inception to date. The High Level Task Force comprises five members as well as "high level" representatives from institutions and organizations in the areas of trade, development and finance who participate with the status of "experts": UNDP, UNICEF, IMF, WTO and the World Bank. The Task Force has therefore, attracted criticism as to its composition and also as to its mandate. The Task Force's mandate is the analysis of:

a. obstacles and challenges to the implementation of the Millennium Development Goals from the point of view of the right of development;

b. studies of social impact at the national and international level in the areas of trade and development;
c. best practices in the implementation of the right to development (UNHRC 2004b).

Some criticism has been heard, within the working group, concerning the efforts of the Task Force. The feeling is growing, that the creation of the Task Force may well be a distraction.[13]

The Independent Expert on the Right to Development

In 1999, the Chair of the Commission on Human Rights appointed a "high level" independent expert in the person of Arjun Sengupta (India) to help the Working Group in its efforts, particularly in conducting a study on "the current state of progress in the implementation of the right to development." The Independent Expert, although an economist of great distinction, needed time to familiarize himself with the international human rights system: its laws, mechanisms and procedures.

The Independent Expert produced six reports, some of which are problematic, while others hold promise largely unfulfilled (Sengupta 1999 to 2004). The reports of the Independent Expert have largely failed to focus either conceptually or empirically on implementation of the right to development nationally, internationally or regionally. The Independent Expert proposed implementing the program through a "development compact" between countries concerned and representatives of the international community, the major donors and the international financial institutions. The concept of a "development compact" is vague, ephemeral and, probably, illusory. Moreover, the Independent Expert repeatedly overlooked the hostility, expressed in both the Working Groups and the Task Force, to the role and involvement of the international financial institutions in the process; since they were widely viewed as one of the major obstacles to implementation of the right to development.

Initially, the Independent Expert chose to define the right to development as a right to process: the right to a process of development that allows the realization of all basic rights and freedoms. The Declaration however is unambiguous in defining the right to development as a human right in and of itself and the Vienna Declaration reaffirms the right to development as a "universal and inalienable right and an integral part of fundamental human rights." Upendra Baxi provided a lucid elaboration of the significance of such definitional differences in a lecture aptly titled, "Development as a human right or as political largesse? Does it make any difference?" (Baxi 2007c). Thus, the position of the Independent Expert has been criticized, from various angles, by almost all countries.

Moreover, to facilitate the realization of the process in a step-by-step manner, the Independent Expert proposed starting with three rights: the right to food, the right to primary health and the right to primary education. But if a country preferred to choose other rights first, "that could be accommodated without any difficulty into the program". This proposal of the Independent Expert lacks appreciation of the holistic nature of universal human rights and their indivisibility, interdependence and interrelatedness. Moreover, it invited human rights trade offs, selectivity and double standards. Once again, the Independent Expert exposed himself to strong, and utterly justified, criticism.

The reports of the Independent Expert do not adequately address the collective dimension of the right and the systemic and structural impediments to its realization. Issues of accountability and governance at global or national levels are absent in the reports. However, the Independent Expert has also left behind a body of writings, other than official reports, which enables a critical appraisal of his thinking on the right to development (Sengupta 2000a, 2002b, 2003c, and Saloman and Sengupta 2003a). It is only towards the end of his mandate that the Independent Expert began to examine national experiences in developing countries.[14]

Two quotes fairly sum up the contribution of the UN Working Group (and are just as pertinent in respect of the Independent Expert, and the High-Level Task Force) on implementing the right to development.

Political differences made the work of the first working group more than difficult, and resulted in low productivity within this body (Kirchmeier 2006: 18).

The three successive working groups have not been able to produce any significant progress in the implementation of the right to development. Worse, there is a regression in many Western countries which go so far as to question the consensus of Vienna, even if they do not say so officially—except for the United States (Ozden 2008: 21).

V

Realizing the Human Right to Development at National Level: The Roles of Rights–Holders, Governments, and Development Agencies

Implementing Human Rights: A Division of Labor at National and International Levels

The dismal record of the UN at implementing its Declaration on the Right to Development can be attributed to a failure to appreciate that the right to development is a human right. Every human right carries with it four correlative duties: the duty to respect; the duty to protect; the duty to promote; and the duty to fulfill. Moreover, there are a number of tasks and functions that must be performed to fulfill these duties. Some of these tasks and functions are more appropriately performed at the international level, others at the national level, and still others at both levels. Over the years, a practical pattern of division of labor has evolved, and continues to evolve.

The task of norms and standard–setting usually commences at the international level, and creates need for incorporation and harmonization of such human rights standards at the national level. So far as the right to development is concerned, initial standard–setting has taken place in the UN Declaration on the Right to Development, but further work lies ahead to secure transparency and accountability of global governance of development (including "fair distribution of the benefits there from"). National incorporation of the standards contained in the Declaration, involve creating a national enabling legal environment that ensures transparency, accountability, nondiscrimination, inclusion, participation, access and effective remedies.

The task of implementation of human rights standards is primarily undertaken at the national level, with a right and responsibility for international provision of technical, technological, financial and human resources needed for such implementation. The roles of a human rights–based approach and of corporate social responsibility in implementing the right to development at the national level, are examined in sections that follow.

The tasks of respecting and protecting human rights at national level involve monitoring of both implementation and violation of human rights standards and this is usually performed simultaneously at national and international levels. National human rights institutions, national and local NGOs and national protective mechanisms for those vulnerable and at risk are complimented and reinforced by treaty–body reporting, Special Procedures and the Universal Periodic Review at the international level. The human right to development entitles all victims and potential victims of development to the full range of such institutions and mechanisms, both national and international.

The task of enforcement of human rights standards requires the sanctioning of violators and the provision of timely and effective remedies and redress to victims. Both these tasks take place primarily nationally through transparent, accountable and participatory governance institutions, a rule of law–based justice system, and appropriate and effective programs of capacity building. But here again, as far as the human right to development is concerned, there are complimentary roles to be played at the international level to ensure the human rights accountability of corporations, and "the international mobilization of shame", especially in relation to universal crimes that carry with them universal jurisdiction.

Finally, there is the important task of promotion of awareness about human rights standards so that awareness leads to asserting and claiming such rights. National governmental and nongovernmental organizations as well as their international counterparts have long been active in human rights education and awareness–raising programs regarding the right to development (PDHRE no date, Dias 1989, Dias 1993b, Dias 1995b, Dias 1999).

The Right to Development: Many Claimants by Perceived Rights–Holders

Over the years, many interest groups have invoked the right to development, some more successfully than others, to advance their claims and interests. A list of claimants (by no means exhaustive) includes:
a. Indigenous peoples and other ethnic groups presenting the claim to move form decolonization of territory to self-determination of peoples. But, as Upendra Baxi explicitly documents, in such struggles for autonomy, one person's freedom-fighter gets labeled another's terrorist! (Baxi 2006).

b. The right to development was invoked, in this sense, by the Maori people of New Zealand to renegotiate the Treaty of Waitangi (which governs their status and rights). Their claim was upheld by the highest court of the land in New Zealand (Greig 2010).
c. The poor, claiming that the right to development not only mandates, but necessitates effective poverty–alleviation development programs. It has been similarly invoked by those adversely affected by structural adjustment programs to support their claims for effective "safety nets".
d. Bilateral and multilateral agencies, to support programs of good governance and democracy on the basis that transparency and accountability are essential components of the right to development.
e. Environmentalists, concerned about the environmental footprint of development and its impacts on inter-generational justice, who claim that the right to "fair distribution of the benefits of development" necessitates that all development activity must be environmentally sustainable.
f. Proponents of sustainable human development, who maintain that the right to development provides a normative basis for Nobel laureate Amartya Sen's ground-breaking conceptualization of development as being more than economic development, requiring the meeting of "entitlements" and the enhancement of "capabilities." (Sen 1981 and Sen 1999).
g. Women, struggling against exclusion from and discrimination in development, and the feminization of poverty.
h. Jurists, propounding international "duties sans frontiers" to cooperate on international development (ICHRP n.d.).
i. Multilateral and bilateral development assistance agencies, to justify their adoption of a human rights–based approach to development.

The Human Rights–Based Approach to Development: Implications for National and International Development Agencies (Both Governmental and Nongovernmental).

Just before the new millennium, two events helped put the right to development back on center stage, in the global agenda of cooperation. In 1997, the program of reform launched by the then UN Secretary-General, Kofi Anan designated human rights as cutting across each of the four substantive fields of the Secretariat's work program: peace and security; economic and social affairs; development cooperation; and humanitarian affairs. In 1998, UNDP adopted its policy of "Integrating Human Rights with Sustainable Human Development". Since then, almost all bilateral development agencies have joined the UN system in "adopting a human rights based approach to development."[15] The key elements of a human rights–based approach to development include:

a. The requirement that the values, principles and standards of human rights permeate the entire process of development programming: from situational analysis and assessment through to program design, implementation and evaluation;

b. A focus in setting development priorities on those most marginalized and excluded in society since their human rights are most widely denied or left unfulfilled;
c. The requirement that those targeted by development are empowered;
d. The identification of duty–bearers and the empowerment of rights–holders;
e. Non–discrimination and participation;
f. Transparency and accountability

Thus, a human rights–based approach to development embodies all of the normative principles contained in the right to development. The right to development has become a programming tool for development cooperation (Van Weerelt 2001).

Governance: The Enabling Legal Environment for Implementing the Right to Development:

As far back as 1995, the Copenhagen Declaration and Programme of Action of the World Summit on Social Development urged governments to adopt an enabling legal environment for social development (Dias 1981:2 and Dias 1988). Obviously, what this entails will vary from country to country (WDR 2002, Thio 2009, HDSA 1999, APF 2001 and Singh 2007). For example, in India this has entailed:

a. Enacting right to information legislation and creating institutions such as Commissions of Enquiry and offices of the ombudsman to secure transparency and accountability.
b. Creation of a duty to disclose assets of public officials, including judges, to ensure that credibility prevails over corruption.
c. National and State Human Rights Commissions and Special Commissions on Women and on Children and Youth to perform tasks ranging from complaints–handling and fact–finding, to human rights capacity building, human rights scrutiny of draft legislation and preparation of human rights–related law reform proposals.
d. National and State Commissions on Legal Aid and reform of judicial procedures seek to improve access to justice (Baxi 1980).
e. Participatory governance at local (panchayat) level (Kapoor 2010) and reservations policies for elective and public office to remedy long-standing, exclusionary practices impacting on women as well as "scheduled castes, scheduled tribes and other backward classes".

These measures are far from free of limitations and shortcomings. But they represent a good–faith attempt at developing an enabling legal environment (GOI 2010). The contribution of civil society and nongovernmental organizations has been immense. But, there is little room for complacency. On her recent visit to India, the UN Special Rapporteur on Human Rights Defenders cautioned that there are indications that space for civil society action may be narrowing.[16]

VI

Realizing the Human Right to Development at National Level: The Roles of Corporations–National and Multinational

Corporations and Realization of the Right to Development

Since 1995, at the World Summit on Social Development we began to hear rhetoric from some governments, and the UN, about the need to privatize development and allow corporations to play a significant role in social development." (Dias 1995c). Caught in a debt trap, of their own making, developing country governments were forced by the IMF and World Bank into privatizing development, through Structural Adjustment Programs (SAPs) which, in reality, are indeed SAPs: programs of systematically administered pauperization. This was followed by a decade of historically unparalleled aggressive promotion of economic globalization through the implementation of neoliberal policies almost everywhere in the world (Baxi 1999c), and accompanied by an epidemic of acute development assistance fatigue (both bilateral and multilateral); opening up the field for multinational and national corporations to become virtually the lead "vehicles for social development." But the dictum of Lord Acton that, "Power corrupts; and absolute power corrupts absolutely" is inescapable (Acton 1907). Especially when power is unaccompanied by accountability, as the now defunct Enron and Union Carbide; and the soon to be defunct Exxon and TEPCO[17] will have inscribed on their respective tombstones.

In light of the context sketched above, two tasks are vital if the human right to development is not to be relegated to the dustbin of history:
a. Corporations must be held fully, and expeditiously accountable for all of the adverse human rights impacts that result from their activities and conduct (Wright 2010) even if this involves speaking softly, and carrying a big stick.
b. Communities affected by the activities of corporations must have all of their human rights fully respected, protected, promoted, and fulfilled.[18]

Thus far, there have been four UN (and one UN–supported) initiatives responsive to these twin tasks:

a) The Code of Conduct Initiative of the UN Center on Transnational Corporation

This initiative was stillborn. The post–NIEO mobilization of the power of global capital ensured that any Code of Conduct governing multinational corporations would be stifled at birth, emboldening the execution of the death penalty on the only UN entity mandated to deal with transnational corporations, The year 1991 saw the terminal closure of the UN Center on Transnational Corporations, and therewith, the Code of Conduct approach towards transnational corporations, which would only survive, on a non–binding basis, under OECD auspices.

b) *The UN Global Compact initiative of the UN Secretary-General*

This initiative was born at Davos, raising a presumption of illegitimacy. However, largely because the diplomatic skills, commitment, and access to human expertise of former Secretary-General Kofi Annan, the Global Compact has evolved and progressed from being yet another corporate exercise in self-promotion (Deva 2006) to becoming an invaluable precedent in moving from voluntarism, to self-compulsion and external monitoring.

The UN Global Compact asks companies to adopt a set of core values in the areas of human rights, labor standards, the environment and anti–corruption. These values are set out in ten principles which enjoy universal consensus and are derived from:

- The Universal Declaration of Human Rights
- The International Labor Organization's Declaration on Fundamental Principles and Rights at Work
- The Rio Declaration on Environment and Development
- The United Nations Convention Against Corruption

The two principles relating to human rights are: Businesses should support and respect the protection of internationally–proclaimed human rights, and make sure that they are not complicit in human rights abuses. Companies participate in the Global Compact on a purely voluntary basis and in its early days, the Global Compact was criticized as being little more than a vehicle for corporate "blue-washing" by using participation in the Global Compact, and its logo for public relations purposes. Today, the Global Compact seeks to advance universal principles on human rights, labor, environment and anti–corruption through the active engagement of the corporate community, in cooperation with civil society and representatives of organized labor. The initiative does not monitor or measure participants' performance. Nevertheless, with the aim of assuring that the integrity of the Global Compact is safeguarded at all times, the Secretary-General has adopted three integrity–measures, dealing respectively with:

Failure to Communicate Progress: The Global Compact's policy on communicating progress asks participants to communicate annually to all stakeholders their progress in implementing the ten principles of the Global Compact. If a participant fails to communicate its progress by the deadline, it will be listed as "non–communicating" on the Global Compact website. If a further year passes without the submission of a communication of progress (COP), the company will be de–listed.

Allegations of Systematic or Egregious Abuses: When a matter is presented in writing to the Global Compact Office, the Office will use its judgment to filter out prima facie frivolous allegations. If an allegation of systematic or egregious abuse is found not to be prima facie frivolous, the Global Compact Office will forward the matter to the participating company concerned, requesting written comments, which should be submitted directly to the party raising the matter, with a copy to the Global Compact Office. If, as a result of the process outlined above, and based on the review of the nature of the matter submitted and the responses by the participating company, the continued listing of the participating company on the Global Compact website is considered to be detrimental to the reputation and integrity of the Global Compact, the Global Compact Office reserves the right to remove that company from the list of participants and to so indicate on the Global Compact website.

Misuse of Association with the UN and/or Global Compact: The use of the United Nations name and emblem and any abbreviation thereof is reserved for official purposes of the Organization in accordance with General Assembly resolution 92(I) of 7 December 1946. That resolution expressly prohibits the use of the United Nations name and emblem for commercial purposes or in any other manner without the prior authorization of the Secretary-General, and recommends that Member States take the necessary measures to prevent the unauthorized use thereof.

The Norms of the UN Sub-Commission on Human Rights on Business and Human Rights[19]

The Preamble to the Norms states that even though States have the primary responsibility to promote, secure the fulfillment of, ensure respect of and protect human rights, transnational corporations and other business enterprises, as organs of society, are also responsible for promoting and securing the human rights set forth in the Universal Declaration of Human Rights. It further states that transnational corporations and other business enterprises, their officers and persons working for them are also obligated to respect generally–recognized responsibilities and norms contained in United Nations treaties and other international instruments.[20]

The Norms set out the General Obligation that transnational corporations and other business enterprises have the obligation to promote, secure the fulfillment of, ensure respect of and protect human rights recognized in international as well as national law. They then go on to list obligations relating to several human rights, notably: the right to equal opportunity and non–discriminatory treatment; the right to security of persons and a detailed set of rights of workers. It also details obligations relating to consumer protection and to protection of the environment.

After these Norms were adopted a study was undertaken by the UN Sub-Commission on human rights (UN Sub-Commission 2004) regarding monitoring and implementation of the Norms. It was decided that for a trial period, companies on a purely voluntary basis, could agree to be monitored by the Office of the High Commissioner for Human Rights, as to their compliance with the Norms. As such, the Norms represent a very promising initiative. But unfortunately, they have been put on hold, pending the final Report of the Special Representative of the UN Secretary-General on Business and Human Rights.

The Special Representative of the UN Secretary-General on Business and Human Rights (SRSG)

The appointment of John Ruggie, a scholar of considerable credentials, as the Special Representative of the UN Secretary-General on Business and Human Rights was welcomed, initially, by both human rights activists and corporate accountability proponents. But disappointment and concern rapidly set in and in May 2007, a coalition of some of the most influential and credible international NGOs[21] were prompted to convene a Corporate Accountability Strategy meeting in New York to assess, and strategize how to deal with the work of the SRSG.[22]

There were many causes for concern: the attitude of the SRSG towards the Norms of the UN Sub-Commission on Human Rights; the SRSG's clear preference for voluntary initiatives and corporate social responsibility over corporate civil and criminal liability under law; the absence of consultations with social movements, grassroots organizations and local NGOs; and the lack of a victim's perspective (Joint NGO Intervention 2007). Through strategizing, advocacy, engagement with the UN system and lobbying the SRSG, the Coalition has been able to make an impact on the SRSG and the Human Rights Council, on the issue of human rights accountability of corporations.

The SRSG continues his preference for voluntary initiatives and has recently issued Guidelines on Company–based Grievance Mechanisms.[23] But he is also focusing on assessment and reform of company law and securities law.[24] He has decided to take up the issue of extra–territorial jurisdiction.[25] Home states have been promoting investments abroad (extra–territorially, if you will) often in conflict–affected regions where bad things are known to happen. In the view of the SRSG, this does no favors to victims of corporate–related human rights abuse; to host governments that may lack the capacity for dealing with the consequences; to companies that may face operational disruptions or find themselves in a lawsuit for the next decade; or to the home country whose own reputation is on the line.

The SRSG has developed what he terms as the "protect, respect and remedy" framework for better managing business and human rights challenges. The Framework rests on three pillars: the state duty to protect against human rights abuses by third parties; the corporate responsibility to respect human rights, which in essence means to act with due diligence to avoid infringing on the rights of others; and greater access for victims to effective remedy, judicial and non-judicial.

The Framework represents an encouraging start but some caveats are called for.:

a. Regarding the first pillar, the State duty to protect: the reality is often one of skewed power relations and some host States may well need protection themselves, against powerful and giant corporate behemoths.
b. Regarding the second pillar, the corporate responsibility to respect human rights: voluntary approaches do have their place. But if, in themselves, they are not enough to ensure against corporate disrespect of human rights, then

accountability must come into play, including through enforcement of appropriate corporate civil and criminal liability.
c. Regarding the third pillar, access for victims to effective remedy, judicial and non-judicial: such access must be not only effective but timely as well and must be not only reactive, but proactive as well to prevent victimization, multiple victimization and re–victimization.

Corporate Social Responsibility: From Corporate Public Relations to Corporate Public Accountability.

Corporate Social Responsibility (CSR) is essentially the deliberate inclusion of public interest into corporate decision-making, and the honoring of a triple bottom line: People, Planet, Profit. The practice of CSR is subject to much debate. Proponents argue that there is a strong business case for CSR, since corporations benefit in multiple ways by operating with a perspective broader than their own short-term profits. Critics argue that CSR distracts from the fundamental economic role of businesses; that it is nothing more than superficial window-dressing; and that it is an attempt to preempt the role of governments as a watch-dog over powerful multinational corporations.

CSR is a voluntary initiative and begins usually with a corporation declaring its corporate social responsibility policy and then developing programs, practices, management and implementation structures, and timetables and methods for reporting to the public. However, recently home countries of corporations are issuing national CSR policies issuing recommendations to their corporate citizens doing business both at home and abroad. The SRSG has recently conducted an informative study of such national CSR policies in 29 member states of the UN who have responded to a survey sent out by the OHCHR (SRSG 2010).

Efforts to secure the more effective implementation of CSR have taken the form of independent, third-party performance monitoring and, if so called for, appropriate action by State regulatory authorities. To provide a flavor of how CSR works in practice, we summarize a case study focusing on India's Tata group of companies (FIAN 2008).

The Tata conglomerate is a business dynasty that has had more influence in India than any other company. The corporation, is comprised of 98 companies in seven business sectors, operates in 54 countries, with a total revenue of USD 28.8 billion in the year 2006-7 (FIAN 2008: 6).

The Tata Group adopted a Code of Conduct of its own that is applicable to all its members. The Code states that "A Tata company: shall not undertake any project that will have an adverse impact on the social and cultural life patterns of it's (the nation's) citizens, shall be committed to be a good corporate citizen by actively assisting in the improvement of the quality of life of the people in the communities in which it operates, with the objective of making them self-reliant, shall not treat these activities as optional ones, but shall strive to incorporate them as an integral part of its business plan. Tata companies are encouraged to develop social accounting systems and to carry out social audits of their operations." (FIAN 2008: 28).

Tata, a member of the UN Global Compact, has endorsed the Sullivan Principles and the Global Reporting Initiative. However, the FIAN case study focusing on three sites of Tata corporate activity has produced irrefutable evidence (FIAN 2008: 17-24) of:

a. Massacre of Adivasis at Kalinga Nagar, Orissa. All the information about the massacre was gathered during the days following the massacre when various fact-finding missions from national human rights organizations and tribal advocacy groups, as well as national and international media came to document the tragic occurrence. They spoke to involved persons and issued several fact-finding reports and media articles.

b. Massive land eviction and state repression of Adivasis in Bastar, Chhattisgarh. At least 1,500 Adivasi families face eviction from their lands due to the planned construction of the Tata steel plant. Apart from the loss of their land and livelihood resources, the local population is confronted with severe violence from state repression, from the Naxalites (a Maoist movement), and a state-sponsored counter-movement under the name "Salwa Judum" which the state calls a spontaneous peoples' movement.

c. The setting up of a car factory, causing large-scale land evictions in Singur, West Bengal. More than 30,000 people were evicted from their land and livelihood resources when the state government acquired their agricultural lands for the construction of an industrial car plant of Tata Motors.

The following set of recommended actions provides a prime example of how CSR policies combined with independent monitoring and regulatory action based on international and national human rights law can "enforce" CSR and thereby, help realize the right to development in India.

With regard to the cases of Bastar, Kalinga Nagar and Singur, the Tata Group should:

- ensure that adequate compensation is paid to all people who have been subjected to expropriation.
- install community grievance procedures and extend the operations of Community Development and Social Welfare Departments to the respective areas.
- ensure that the cases of violence, torture and arbitrary killing in relation to protests against its operation are investigated and that damages are paid to the victims.
- implement regular human rights impact assessments in the areas.

With regard to all present and future operations, the Tata Group should:

- develop and implement regular human rights impact assessment prior to installing and during the running of each operation.
- ensure, in accordance with the finding of its human rights impact assessments, that they do not get involved with or become complicit in government oppression of peaceful protests, and in this regard, consider acceding to the "Voluntary Principles on Security and Human Rights."
- extend the operations of Community Development and Social Welfare Departments to all areas where they operate.

- take seriously all of the Corporate Social Responsibility commitments it has made and report fully, in each of the initiatives, on progress, as well as on problems in implementing human rights (FIAN 2008: 34-35).

VII

Realizing the Human Right to Development at National Level: The Roles of Peoples, and Communities

The right of peoples to self-determination and to sovereign control over their resources and their future is the core of the right to development. This is why governments, the main actors in the realization of the right to development, cannot yield their prerogatives to "the invisible hand of the market". Both host and home governments must discharge their obligation to govern in a transparent, accountable and just manner, at all levels from top to bottom. Both host and home governments must fully discharge their duty to protect.

In 1948, the start of the first development decade, disparity between the richest and the poorest countries in the world was at a ratio of 10:1. In 1960, the ratio was 30:1. In 1989, after fifty years of development activity, the ratio was 60:1. By 1998, with economic globalization well underway, the ratio was 99:1; and by the year 2001, it had exceeded 1000:1. Enough is enough!

Realizing the human right to development is no longer an impossible dream.[26] Today, it is a non-negotiable priority and necessity (Baxi 1994b), well within our individual reach and our collective grasp—"A man's reach, should exceed his grasp. Else what's a heaven for?" (Browning 1971: 15).

References

Acton, Lord J., 1907. *Historical Essays and Studies, by Baron John Emerich Edward Dalberg-Acton.* Edited by John Neville Figgis and Reginald Vere Laurence. London: Macmillan.

Alston, P., 1988. Making space for new Human Rights: The case of the Right to Development. *Harvard* Human *Rights Yearbook* 1: 3–40.

APF (Asia-Pacific Forum of NHRIs), 2001. *The Role of NHRIS and Other Mechanisms in Promoting and Protecting ESCR,* Workshop Conclusions and Recommendations, Bangkok (July, 2001).

Barsh, R., 1991. The right to development as a human right: Results of the Global Consultation. *Human Rights Quarterly* 13: 322–328.

Baxi, U., 1980. Taking Suffering Seriously: Social Action Litigation in the Supreme Court of India. *Delhi Law Review,* 8 & 9 (1979–1980): 91–116.

———. 1987. From Human Rights to the Right to Be Human: Some Heresies. *The Right to be Human* edited by U. Baxi, G. Sen, and J. Fernandes, 185–190. New Delhi: Lancer International in association with Indian International Center.

———. 1994a. *Inhuman Wrongs and Human Rights: Unconventional Essays.* New Delhi: Har Anand.

———. 1994b. *Mambrino's Helmet?: Human Rights for a Changing World.* New Delhi: Har Anand.

———. 1998. The Development of the Right to Development. *Human Rights: New Dimensions and Challenges*, edited by J. Symonides, 99–116. Hants: Dartmouth.

———. 1999a. Voices of Suffering, Fragmented Universality and the Future of Human Rights. *The Future of International Human Rights* edited by B. Weston and S. Marks, 101–56. New York: Ardsley Transnational Publishers.

———. 1999b. Human Rights: Between Suffering and Market. *Global Social Movements*, edited by R. Cohen and S. Rai, 32–45. London, Altheone.

———. 1999c. *The Unreason of Globalization and the Reason of Human Rights.* Mumbai: Dept. of Sociology, University of Mumbai. Book, Vol. 1 in a series/set.

———. 2005. Market Fundamentalisms: Business Ethics at the Altar of Human Rights. *Human Rights Law Review* 5: 1–26.

———. 2006. *The Development of the Right to Development amidst the 'War of Terror' and the 'War on Terror': Unconventional Essays.* New Delhi: Oxford University Press.

———. 2007a. *Human Rights in a Post-human World: Critical Essays.* New Delhi: Oxford University Press.

———. 2007b. Failed De-Colonization and the Future of Social Rights. *Social Rights* edited by D. Barkarz and A. Gross, 1110–1112. Oxford: Oxford University Press.

———. 2007c. Development as a Human Right or as Political Largesse? Does it Make Any Difference? *Founders Day Lecture* [Working Paper].

Browning, R., 1971. *The Complete Works*, Ohio, Ohio University Press.

Deva, S., 2006. Global Compact: A Critique of the U.N.'S 'Public–Private' Partnership for Promoting Corporate Citizenship. *Syracuse Journal of International Law and Comparative Policy* (Fall): 107–117.

Dias, C., 1981. Realizing the Right to Development: the Importance of Legal Resources. *Development, Human Rights and the Rule of Law,* edited by International Commission of Jurists, 67–75. Geneva, International Commission of Jurists.

———. 1988. *Human Rights, Legal Resources for Development. In Law, Human Rights and Legal Services: A Neglected Field of Development Cooperation.* New York: Friedrich-Naumann-Stiftung.

———. ed. 1989. Initiating *Human Rights Education at the Grassroots: Asian Experience.* Thailand: ACFOD (Asian Cultural Forum on Development).

———. 1993a. Development, Democracy and Human Rights: An Asian NGO Perspective. *Development, Democracy and the Global Realization of all Human Rights* edited by North–South Institute, Canada, 103–112. Ottawa: North–South Institute.

———. 1993b. Rural Development, Grassroots Education and Human Rights: Some Asian Perspectives. *Human Rights in the Twenty–First Century: A Global Challenge,* edited by K. Mahoney and P. Mahoney, 174–191. Netherlands: Martinus Nijhoff Publishers.

———. 1994. Relationships between Human Rights NGOs in the Third World. *Human Rights* edited by. K. P. Saksena, 61–191. New Delhi: Institute for World Congress on Human Rights.

———. 1994. Governance, Democracy and Conditionality: NGO Positions and Roles. *Governance, Democracy and Conditionality: What Role for NGOs?* edited by A. Clayton, 32–41. Oxford: Oxford University Press.

———. 1995a. The Universality of Human Rights. *Law and Society Trust Review*, (September): 6–9.

———. 1995b. Human Rights Education as a Strategy for Development. *Human Rights Education,* edited by R. Claude, 51–63. Baltimore: Baltimore University.

———. 1995c. The UN and Development: Business as Usual. *Development and Cooperation*, no. 3: 135–150.

———. 1998. Indivisibility. *Cinquenta Anos Declaracao,* edited by International Relations Research Institute, 129–145. Brazil: Universal Dos Direttos Humanos.

———. 1999. The Role of NGOs in the Protection and Promotion of Human Rights in Asia. *Human Rights of Migrant Workers: Agenda for NGOs,* edited by Graziano Battistella, 85–111. Scalabrini Migration Center: Manila.

Dias, C., Y. Danieli and E. Stamatopooulou, eds. 1999. *The Universal Declaration of Human Rights: Fifty Years and Beyond,* New York: Baywood Publishing Company.

Dias, C. and D. Gilles, 1993. *Human Rights Democracy and Development.* Montreal: International Centre for Human Rights and Democratic Development.

Dias, C. and S. Leckie, 1996. *Human Development and Shelter: A Human Rights Perspective.* Human Development Report Office, UNDP, Occasional Papers, Special Issue, Habitat II Conference (June).

Feder, E., 1988. *Perverse Development.* Philippines: Foundation for Nationalist Studies.

FIAN., 2008. *Governments, Corporations and Human Rights in India: the House of Tata.* Germany: FIAN International.

Freire, P., 2000. *Pedagogy of the Oppressed.* 30th Anniversary Edition. London: Continuum Books.

GOI, (Government of India, Planning Division), 2010. *Notes on the Functioning of Various Divisions.* New Delhi GOI.

Greig, E., 2010. *The Maori Right to Development and New forms of Property.* Dissertation submitted at the University of Otago.

Halperin, M. and D. Scheffer and P. Small, 1992. *Self-Determination in the New World Order.* New York: Carnegie Endowment for International Peace.

HDSA (Human Development in South Asia), 1999. *Human Development in South Asia 1999: The Crisis of Governance.* Oxford: Oxford University Press.

IBON., 2007. *International. Primer on Development and Aid Effectiveness.* Philippines: IBON.

ICHRP (The International Council on Human Rights Policy) (n.d.) *Duties Sans Frontiers: Human Rights and Social Justice.* www.ichrp.org (accessed July 20, 2011).

Joint NGO Intervention, 2007. Joint NGO Intervention at the UN Human Rights Council in response to the Report of the Special Representative on Human Rights and Business (2007). http://www.escr-net.org (accessed July 20, 2011).

Kapoor, V., 2010. *Human Rights Based Approach to Development and People's Empowerment through Participatory Governance: A Critical Examination of Panchayati Raj Institutions in India.* www2.lse.ac.uk/human-Rights/.../kapoorAug2010.pdf (accessed July 20, 2011).

Kirchmeier, F., 2006. The Right to Development: Where do we stand? The State of the Debate on the Right to Development. *Occasional Paper*, New York: Friedrich Ebert Stiftung.

Marks, S., 2003a. *The Human Rights Framework for Development: Seven Approaches.* Cambridge: Harvard University.

———. 2003b. *Obstacles to the Right to Development.* Cambridge: Harvard University.

———. 2004. The Human Right to Development: Between Rhetoric and Reality. Harvard Human Rights Journal no.17: 139–168.

M'Baye, K., 1972. Le droit au developpement comme un droit de l'homme. *Revue internationale des droits de l'homme*, V: 1–34.

Ozden, M., 2008. The Right to Development: Current state of the debates held at the U.N. on the implementation of the historic Declaration adopted in this regard by the General Assembly of the United Nations on 4 December 1986. Brochure prepared for CETIM.

Peoples Decade for Human Rights Education, (n.d.) Human Rights and Development. www.pdhre.org (accessed July 20 2011).

Piron, L., 2002. *The Right to Development.* A review of the current state of the debate for the Department for International Development, ODI.

Raghavan, C., 1990. *Recolonization: Gatt, the Uruguay Round and the Third World.* London: Zed Books.

Robie, D., 1989. *Blood on their Banner: Nationalist Struggles in the South Pacific.* London: Zed Books.

Robie, D., 1992. *Tu Galala: Social Change in the Pacific.* Wellington: Wellington Books.

Sen, A., 1981. *Poverty and Famines. An Essay on Entitlement and Deprivation.* Oxford: Oxford University Press.

———. 1999. *Development as Freedom.* Oxford: Oxford University Press.

Sengupta, A., 1999. *First Report of the Independent Expert on the Right to Development.* UN Doc. E/CN.4/1999/WG.18/2.

———. 2000a. *Second Report of the Independent Expert on the Right to Development.* U.N. Doc. A/55/306.

——— 2000b. *The Right to Development as Human Right.* Cambridge: The Francis Xavier Bagnoud Center (FXBC).

———. 2001. *Third Report of the Independent Expert on the Right to Development.* UN Doc. E/CN.4/2001/WG.18/2.
———. A., 2002a. *Fourth Report of the Independent Expert on the Right to Development.* UN Doc. E/CN.4/2002/WG.18/2.
———. 2002b. "On the Theory and Practice of the Right to Development" *Human Rights Quarterly*, 24, No. 4 (November): 837–889.
———. 2003a. *Fifth Report of the Independent Expert on the Right to Development: Framework for Development Cooperation and the Right to Development.* UN Doc. E/CN.4/2003/WG.18/6.
———. 2003b. *Preliminary Study of the Independent Expert on the Right to Development on the Impact of International Economic and Financial Issues on the Enjoyment of Human Rights.* UN Doc. E/CN.4/2003/WG.18/2.
———. 2003c. *Development Cooperation and the Right to Development.* Cambridge: FXBC.
———. 2004. *Sixth Report of the Independent Expert on the Right to Development: Implementing the Right to Development in the Current Global Context.* UN Doc. E/CN.4/2004/WG.18/2.
Singh, R. (Chief Minister, Government of Chhattisgarh), 2007. To the 54th meeting of the National Development Council, December 19.
SRSG, 2010. *Survey of State Corporate Social Responsibility Policies–Summary of Key Trends* (June). www.reports-and-materials.org/Ruggie-survey-re-state-csr-policies.pdf (accessed July 20 2011).
Thio, L., 2009. Unpacking the Human Right to Development: The 2007 ASEAN Charter and Legal Empowerment Trajectories. *ANLEP Working Paper* No. 1 (May).
UNCHR. *Global Consultation on the Right to Development as a Human Right.* January 1990, E/CN.4/1990Rev.1
———. 1996. *Report of the Working Group on the Right to Development on its Fifth Session.* E/CN.4/1996/24.
———. 1998a. *Report of Group of Experts on the Right to Development.* E/CN.4/1998/29.
———. 1998b. *Resolution 1998/72, § 10.,* http://www.unhchr.ch (accessed July 20, 2011)
———. 2002a. *Report of the open-ended Working Group on the Right to Development on its Third Session.* E/CN.4/2002/28/Rev.
———. 2002b. *Report of the open-ended Working Group on the Right to Development on its Third Session.* E/CN.4/2002/28/Rev, §118.
UNGA., 1986. *Declaration on the Right to Development, Adopted by UN General Assembly Resolution.* 41/128 of 4 December.
UNHRC, 2004a. *Resolution 2004/7 of the Human Rights Council.*
———. 2004b. *Report of the Working Group on the Right to Development on its Fifth Session, § 49.* E/CN.4/2004/23.
UN Sub-Commission on the Promotion and Protection of Human Rights, 2003. *Norms on the Responsibilities of Transnational Corporations and Other Business Enterprises with Regard to Human Rights, U.N. Doc. E/CN.4/Sub.2/2003/38/Rev.2.*

UN Sub-Commission on the Promotion and Protection of Human Rights, 2004. *Study on Policies for Development in a Globalizing World: What can Human Rights Approach Contribute?* 25 UN Doc. E/CN.4/Sub.2/2004/18.

Van Weerelt, P., 2001. The Right to Development as a Programming Tool for Development Cooperation. *The Poverty of Human Rights: Human Rights and the Eradication of Poverty*, Chapter 10, 25–167. London: Zed Books.

WDR (World Development Report), 2002. *Building Institutions: Complement, Innovate, Connect, and Compete.* Washington: The World Bank.

Wright, M., 2010. Corporations and Human Rights: A Survey of the Scope and Patterns of Alleged Corporate-Related Human Rights Abuse. Appended to SRSG John Ruggie's Report to the Human Rights Council (A/HRC/8/5).

Notes

1. In the Preamble itself, the Charter of the United Nations states, "We the peoples of the United Nations ... reaffirm faith in fundamental human rights, in the dignity and worth of the human person, in the equal rights of men and women and of nations large and small ..."

2. Bilateral development aid, tied all too often with conditionalities of a geopolitical nature, is a thinly disguised form of neo-colonization. Development through trade, under the prevailing international regime of trade, investment and finance provides a vehicle for recolonization.

3. In the era of the Cold War, hegemony was bi-polar: the US bloc and the Soviet bloc. Thereafter, single super power hegemony has provoked new divisions within the UN and resulted in the formation of Groups, whose positions towards the right to development are examined later in the text.

4. Self-determination, contrary to frequent misconception, is not synonymous with secession. It is synonymous with autonomy. The early literature on self-determination by Western scholars focuses mainly on self-determination of territory, while that by Soviet scholars focuses mainly on self-determination of peoples.

5. The author, heading the International Center for Law in Development, worked in partnership with the Secretary-General of the International Commission of Jurists to facilitate this interaction.

6. The Declaration was adopted by 146 countries. One country, the United States, cast a negative vote. Eight countries abstained: Denmark, Finland, the Federal Republic of Germany, Iceland, Israel, Japan, Sweden and the United Kingdom.

7. Article 1(10) Vienna Declaration, Principle 3, Cairo Programme of Action, Commitment 1(n) Copenhagen Declaration and Article 213 Beijing Platform of Action).

8. Opposition to the Report centered on its proposal for cooperation and dialogue between the World Bank and human rights programs. As the expert from Malaysia put it, "the international financial institutions (including the World Bank) have been identified as themselves being obstacles to the realization of the right to development, and of economic, social and cultural rights, owing to the effects of their structural adjustment policies."

9. This Group is open to participation by all member states of the UN.

10. The Group currently comprises 130 member countries. http://www.g77.org .

11. One of the five official U.N. regional groups.

12. Comprising of Algeria, Bangladesh, Belarus, Bhutan, China, Cuba, Egypt, India, Indonesia, Malaysia, Myanmar, Nepal, Pakistan, Philippines, Sri Lanka, Sudan, Vietnam and Zimbabwe.

13. It would not occur to this Task Force, for example, to examine the recent Latin American initiative called the Bolivarian Alternative for the Americas (ALBA). Yet this initiative offers a real hope and draws implicitly on the right to development. ALBA establishes the bases of a new form of integration, founded not on capitalist values of profit and pillage by transnational corporations but based on cooperation, solidarity and complementariness. Currently, four countries have joined this initiative: Bolivia, Cuba, Nicaragua and Venezuela. Ecuador participates in some of its projects and is studying the possibility of joining. For further details, see the CETIM written statement on ALBA to the fourth session of the Human Rights Council: http://www.cetim.ch/en/interventions_details.

14. This was mainly done in partnership with the François-Xavier Bagnoud Center (FXBC) for Health and Human Rights, Harvard School of Public Health in a research project that commissioned several country studies.

15. In 2003, all UN development agencies adopted *The Human Rights Based Approach to Development Cooperation - Towards a Common Understanding among UN Agencies.* Popularly known as *the Common Understanding,* It sets out 3 basic principles of a human rights-based approach to development:
- All programs of development co-operation, policies and technical assistance should further the realization of human rights.
- Human rights standards contained in, and principles derived from, international human rights instruments guide all development cooperation and programming, in all sectors and in all phases of the programming process.
- Development cooperation contributes to the development of the capacities of 'duty-bearers' to meet their obligations and/or of 'rights-holders' to claim their rights.

16. Press conference of the UN Special Rapporteur on the situation of human rights defenders, Margaret Sekaggya, at the end of her first fact-finding mission to India (from 10-21 January 2011) New Delhi, January 21, 2011.

17. TEPCO is the Tokyo Electric Power Company. Exxon spills, Carbide kills. Enron self-destructs, fortunately, on the verge of its enormously destructive and enormously profitable energy development project in India.

18. This remains an impossible dream unless the human right to development is instantly implemented and progressively realized.

19. The *Norms* were adopted by the Sub-Commission in August 2003 but since the Human Rights Commission did not adopt them, the Special Representative of the UN Secretary-General on Business and Human Rights (SRSG), John Ruggie is of the view that they have no legal – not even soft law – value, and therefore, he refers to them as the "Draft Norms" in his 2007 Report, and subsequently. However, the view of the SRSG is, to say the least, highly contentious.

20. The Preamble lists some 19 treaties including all the human rights treaties and the 4 Geneva Conventions (with their Protocols) as well as several Declarations, including the Declaration on the Right to Development.

21. Coalition members included: Amnesty International, Human Rights Watch, the International Commission of Jurists, and the International Federation for Human Rights, Rights and Accountability in Development and ESCR-Net via its Corporate Accountability Working Group.

22. Participants included WEDO, US, Earth Rights International, Friends of the Earth International, Action Aid International, Oxfam International and FORUM-Asia.

23. Five companies are running year-long pilot projects to test the guidance that the SRSG has developed for company-based grievance mechanisms. They are Cerrejon Coal, Colombia; Esquel Group, Hong-Kong based garment manufacturer with operations in Vietnam; Hewlett Packard and two of its suppliers in China; Sakhalin Energy in Russia; and Tesco, the retailer, piloting a grievance mechanism in its South African fresh fruit supply chain.

24. This work has been assisted by 19 law firms from around the world that have examined whether corporate law facilitates or impedes company recognition of human rights and identifies possibilities for policy and legal reform.

25. The SRSG refers to this issue as "the elephant in the room that polite people have preferred not to talk about".

26. Joe Darion, in his lyrics for the Broadway musical Man of La Mancha, based on the Cervantes novel Don Quixote, describes the impossible dream as: To fight, the unbeatable foe ... to right the unrightable wrong ... to fight without question or pause ... to be willing to go into hell for a heavenly cause ... to strive with one's last ounce of courage ... to reach the unreachable star.

CHAPTER 3

Development and Environmental Issues vis-à-vis Current Perspectives of Human Rights

Aniruddha Mukhopadhyay and Sayan Bhattacharya

The terms 'development' and 'environment' have become buzzwords nowadays. Development has become an integral part of civilization and technological advancement. Environment on the other hand comprises our surroundings that include the social, political, historical, economic, cultural, philosophical and religious dimensions as well. Human footprints on the globe may be as old as the human species itself, but the last few decades witnessed changes to an unprecedented level. There are three phases of human civilization, namely, agricultural, industrial and information technology based globalized civilization. In all the above mentioned phases man has become an agent that has modified his immediate environment which gives him physical sustenance and affords him the opportunity for intellectual, moral, social and spiritual growth. Since ancient age, man has developed the capacity to modify the face of the earth. During the course of evolution of the human race, civilization has transformed the environment in countless ways and on an unprecedented scale. Use of fire, domestication of animals and early agricultural practices are the major steps to modify the already existing conditions. During the last two centuries, the human society has tremendously used energy, raw materials, marginalized people and transported commodities over huge distances and generated an enormous amount of wastes—mostly hazardous, culminating in the destruction of the equilibrium of the environment (Conkin 2007). Human intelligence and intellect, if used wisely as per the laws of nature, can bring natural, social and cultural equilibrium and it can help to enhance the quality of life. If the same power is wrongly used, it can make incalculable harm to the society in general and the environment in particular. Moreover, population explosion has currently raised many issues like depletion of resources, waste generation, massive extinction of flora and fauna and the degradation of the quality of human life. The quality of life is being influenced by both the multiplying poor and the consumerist rich section of the society.

Environment and Rights: Global Retrospect

The fundamental backbones of human existence on the earth are life, livelihoods, culture and society. Hence their maintenance and development is a fundamental human right. Destruction and misuse of resources and degradation of the environment is a violation of human rights. Human rights recognize the dignity inherent in every person both as an individual and a community, regardless of his or her particular nationality, race, ethnicity, religion, gender, sexuality, class or any other affiliation. The most fundamental principle of the human rights system is that of nondiscrimination, as laid down in the Universal Declaration of Human Rights adopted and proclaimed by the United Nations General Assembly in 1948: "Everyone is entitled to all the rights and freedoms set forth in this Declaration, without distinction of any kind, such as race, color, sex, language, religion, political or other opinion, national or social origin, property, birth or other status."

The foremost priority of human rights is to protect life, personal security, and the physical integrity and dignity of affected populations. These can be carried out by population protection against the negative impacts of natural hazards, against violence (including gender based) and corruption. The other priority is connected with the basic needs of life such as access to adequate food, sanitation, shelter, clothing and essential health services. The other social, cultural and economic rights include education, property, livelihood and work. The civil and political rights include electoral rights, freedom of movement, assembly, association and religion (Clapham 2007).

Over the years, the international community has increased its awareness on the relationship between environmental degradation and human rights abuses. In the last half of the twentieth century, four key themes emerged from the collective concerns and aspirations of the world community: peace, freedom, development, and environment (National Research Council, 1999). Environmental degradation transcends political boundaries and is of critical importance to the preservation of world peace and security. The protection of the environment is internationalized, while the global environmental issues have become a concern of the international community. In 1972, the United Nations Conference on the Environment and Development (UNCED) made a direct link between the environment and the rights to healthy life. Ten years later, the World Charter on Nature explicitly referred to the right of access to information and the right to participate in environmental decision-making (National Research Council, 1999). And a decade after that, in 1992, the Rio Declaration acknowledged the right to a healthy and productive life in harmony with nature and the right of access to environmental information and of public participation in environmental decision-making. Recently, however, the 2002 World Summit on Sustainable Development in Johannesburg simply acknowledged the consideration being given to the possible relationship between environment and human rights (World Summit on Sustainable Development 2002).

Sustainable human development today has become the theme of development vis-à-vis environment, both in terms of process and outcome. It can only be achieved through the gradual integration and realization of the basic human rights, fundamental human freedoms and environmental justice. Development planning integrates technology, infrastructure and use of natural resources and finally consumption patterns remain as the major indicator. Therefore it is important to evaluate and make development decisions which structurally culminate to a more futuristic and sustainable society.

Environmental Issues and Human rights

1. Water and Human Rights

The hydrological cycle of the globe can be referred to as water democracy that is a system of distributing water for all the living beings. Clean, safe water is a basic requirement in our daily life. Water is needed not only for drinking but also for agriculture and industry to provide food and basic hygiene, supporting health and preventing disease. Providing water is absolutely essential for a country's development objectives—job creation, food security, GDP growth and social goals including poverty reduction (UNESCO 2009). In 2002, the World Health Organization estimated that 1.1 billion people (17 percent of the global population) lacked access to safe water resources, and 2.6 billion people (42 percent of the global population) lacked access to improved sanitation, which is the primary cause of water contamination and waterborne diseases" (WHO 2004). Every year in developing countries an estimated 3 million people die prematurely from water–related diseases. The largest proportion of these deaths are among infants and young children, followed by women from poor rural families who lack access to safe water and improved sanitation (UNESCO 2009).

Global consumption of water is doubling every 20 years, more than twice the rate of human population growth. At present more than one billion people on earth lack access to fresh drinking water. By the year 2025 the demand for freshwater is expected to rise to 56 percent above what currently available water can deliver, if current trends persist (Barlow, 2003). Many of the world's major industries are highly water intensive. In many areas, agriculture is also irrigation intensive. Such irrigations need a huge amount of water. Deforestation, destruction of wetlands, unsustainable use of pesticides and fertilizers and climate change are affecting the fragile water resources of the earth tremendously. India has the highest volume of annual groundwater extraction in the world, and in most parts of it, groundwater extraction is twice the rate of annual recharge (Barlow 2003).

A region where renewable fresh water availability is below 1700 cubic meters/capita/annum is a 'water stress' region, and one where availability falls below 1000 cubic meters/capita/annum is termed as water scarce region (Falkenmark 1992). The annual per capita availability of renewable freshwater in India has reduced from around 5,277 cubic meters in 1955 to 2,464 cubic meters in 1990. Considering the projected increase in population by the year 2025, the per capita availability is likely to drop to below 1,000 cubic meters and India will face severe water scarcity (The Energy and Resources Institute 1993). Interestingly, the annual average rainfall in India is 4000 billion cubic meters, but the annual water requirement of India is only 450 billion cubic meters (Rao 1995). It clearly indicates that the main problems of Indian water resources are mismanagement and unsustainable use of water, which, in turn, is making the whole situation paradoxical.

Potential human right issues can arise from lack of safe water. For example, environmental refugees often can't get proper access to safe water and sanitation. Lack of access to safe water in the vicinity of the home can affect the health and education of women and children (WHO 2000). Many children usually carry water from distant sources rather than going to school, which impairs their right to an education. Most of the women and girl children in Rajasthan, India, spend a considerable amount of time of their life for collecting water. On an average, a rural woman walks more than 14000 km./year for searching and collecting water. In the remote rural areas of Rajasthan, men generally migrate to urban areas in search of work because the chances of agricultural prosperity are significantly low in those water scarce regions. Women spend most of their time in collecting water, and little time is generally left for other productive works (Shiva 2005).

On the other hand, the story is just the reverse for the developed areas of the world. The richest parts of the world, mainly the industrialized nations, account for 86 percent of consumption of all goods including water. North Americans use 1,280 cubic meters of water/person/year; Europeans use 694; South Americans use 311; whereas in Asia and Africa, the figures are 535 and 186 respectively (UNESCO 2009).

Civilization is becoming more and more dependent on irrigated land for growing food. Scarcity of fresh water affects the food security issues. In water stressed areas, particularly in the tropics, the FAO estimated that temperature rise because of global warming can increase evapotranspiration which can increase salinity in the soil and water. The reduction of the overall availability of water for irrigation would limit the possibility to extend irrigated areas for agriculture in future. In addition to the water scarcity on arid lands, salinity will also affect soil productivity adversely (Parry et. al. 2007). The intensity of groundwater use, partly encouraged by subsidized rural electrification, has led to the emergence of many groundwater-dependent economies—that are facing serious threats from aquifer depletion and pollution related problems (UNESCO 2009).

The concepts of water footprints and virtual water are often used to describe the relations between water management, international trade and policies. Water footprint is defined as the total volume of fresh water used for production of goods and services consumed by the individual or community. On the other hand, virtual water is referred to the amount of water used for the production of goods or services, and is a tool for determining the movement of water through international trade. Water is mainly a local issue, although it becomes a regional issue where rivers or lakes cross national boundaries. It is the virtual water that actually makes it a global issue in terms of production and consumption. Countries with water shortages can import water–intensive goods and services, while water–abundant countries can increase the economic strength by using the crisis (UNESCO 2009).

The growth in water consumption is highest in the richest agricultural and industrial areas, where the resources to buy water are readily available with rich farmers and industrialists. This increase in consumption will be satisfied through the market dynamics often at the cost of the poor who cannot afford the increased water tariffs.

The diminishing quality of water supplies, water tax, privatization and strict environmental effluent standards are compelling industries to increase their water efficiency. Industrial water productivity is a general indicator of efficiency and performance in water use. In emerging market economies industrial demand for water is rising with rapid growth in manufacturing output, so water use efficiency should be increased accordingly to maintain the equilibrium (UNESCO 2009).

Vulnerability to pollution is generally linked to an aquifer's accessibility. Shallow aquifers generally suffer from agrochemicals, domestic and industrial waste pollution. Major water pollutants include microbes (like intestinal pathogens and viruses), nutrients (like phosphates and nitrates), heavy metals and metalloids (like arsenic, lead, mercury), organic chemicals (like DDT, lubricants, industrial solvents), oil, sediments and heat. Virtually all industrial and goods–producing activities generate pollutants as unwanted by-products. Globally, the most prevalent water quality problem is eutrophication, because of high–nutrient loads in surface water bodies, which substantially impairs beneficial uses of water. Major nutrient sources include agricultural runoff, domestic sewage, industrial effluents and atmospheric inputs from fossil fuel burning and bush fires. Lakes and reservoirs are particularly affected by eutrophication because of their complex hydrodynamics, relatively longer water residence times and their role as an integrating sink for pollutants from their drainage basins (Carnea 1996).

Heavy metals can contaminate the aquifer and subsequently can bioaccumulate in the tissues of humans and other organisms. For example, more than 100 million people are living in the arsenic affected districts of India and Bangladesh; nine districts out of 19 in West Bengal, 78 blocks and around 3150 villages are affected with arsenic–contaminated groundwater (Chakraborti et. al. 2002). The use of arsenic contaminated groundwater for irrigation purposes in crop fields elevates arsenic concentration in surface soil and in the plants grown in those areas (Meharg and Rahman 2003).

Mercury and lead from industrial activities, mining and landfill leachates also affect human health. In Japan, mercury toxicity caused minamata disease which killed and impaired several thousand people. Minamata disease is a poisoning disease of central nervous system developed among the inhabitants who routinely had large quantities of fishes and shellfishes in which methylmercury compound had been absorbed directly through the gills or through the intestinal tracts or been accumulated at high concentrations by food chains after discharge from chemical plant to the sea and rivers (Ministry of Environment, Govt. of Japan 2006).

Groundwater systems are very vulnerable freshwater resources and prone to contamination. Pollutants can take years to reach the aquifers, but, once it reaches the water source, it is very difficult and costly to remove the pollutants. More than 80 percent of sewage in developing countries is discharged without proper treatment which can pollute the river systems, lakes and coastal water bodies (UNESCO 2009).

Community based water management policies such as rainwater harvesting, checking dam construction, sustainable watershed management, integrated river basin management and irrigation efficiency are far better and sustainable alternatives to water privatization. These actions also can respect the human rights as well (Agarwal and Narain 1997).

Large scale deforestation for dams and canals can lead to imbalances in the ecosystems. Following the construction of dams, the aquatic life is generally severely affected. Changes in water velocity, water chemistry, temperature and turbidity disturb the free passage of fishes. Weeds often spread in irrigation reservoirs. These, in turn, can spread diseases among human beings and cattle. Constructions of dams on many rivers make them lifeless; can reduce the flow as well (Shiva 2003). Thus, the rivers become incapable of withstanding the increasing pollution load. As most of the civilizations depend on the rivers for their social, biological and economic benefits, it can lead to degradation of the quality of human life. Soil erosion and degradation is another significant effect caused by dam construction, mainly because of water logging and salinity. Construction of dams can eminently affect the livelihood of the tribal population. Dams are usually constructed in remote forest and hill areas where most of the indigenous and tribal people live. The sudden influx of modern technologies, destruction and modification of the natural systems and the ultimate displacement and resettlement can cause social, cultural and economic collapse in the indigenous communities (Shiva 2003).

Another shortcoming of estimating dam–related displacement is that only reservoir displacement is generally taken into account by the government officials. Large dam projects can displace people in a number of ways including due to associated canal construction, downstream impacts, treatment of catchment area, compensatory afforestation, secondary displacement strategies and due to related conservation schemes like sanctuaries and national parks establishment. When all the factors are considered for evaluation, it can lead to much larger figures of displacement. Estimates of displacement also fail to consider the effect of the rise in water level as the reservoir begins to silt up. As a result of the submergence area being larger than originally estimated, larger numbers of people are displaced than previous estimations. Further, people resettled on the edges of the reservoir may be forced to move repeatedly as the water rises to submerge the new settlements. A review by the World Bank published that on an average, 13,000 people are displaced for each new dam construction in modern scenario (Cernea 1996). By this estimate, more than 39 million people have been displaced so far due to construction of over 3000 large dams. So, the estimates of only two million people in India till 1990 have been displaced by all dams shown by the official reports are vastly inaccurate (Gleich 1999).

To solve the growing water crisis, one of the possible solutions that has been proposed and has been implemented is privatization of water, which in effect leads to treatment of water as a commodity. But the administrations are consciously overlooking the complexities of the water management systems that are deeply integrated in the social, political and economical structures. On the other hand, water has become big business for global corporations. It has limitless markets in the changing scenario of growing water demand and water scarcity. Numerous case studies around the world highlight the other ills of water privatization such as poor quality of water, unsustainable water mining and lack of transparency and accountability (UNESCO 2009). The privatization of water has already happened in several developed countries and is being pushed in many developing countries through structural adjustment policies (Barlow, 2003). Water privatization will invariably increase the price of this common property resource because there are hidden costs involved in water collection, purification and distribution. The corporations will recover their costs by exploiting the consumers. It has been argued that privatization will help to reduce unsustainable water use and will promote water conservation. The price hikes will make water unaffordable to the poor (Barlow 2003). Another possible threat of water privatization is the unsustainable water extraction by the water corporations for maximizing profits and subsequent destruction of water bodies and aquifers. As for example, indiscriminate mining of groundwater by a multinational soft drink giant in Andhra Pradesh, Tamilnadu and Kerala has resulted severe threats to the local water resources. They are extracting one million liter of groundwater per day which is destroying the balance of the local ecosystems and human societies. Many wells are dried up and also become contaminated (with excessive calcium and magnesium) in the adjoining areas of the soft drink bottling factory in Kerala. The company's usage of agricultural land for non-agricultural purposes is also questionable. A study of World Wildlife Federation in 2001 showed that the bottled water industries use 1.5 million tons of plastic every year, and after disposal, these bottles release toxic chemicals in the environment (Barlow 2003). Privatization by definition eliminates public control of the resource in question. Public control of water is essential not only because of water is necessary for survival and human fulfillment, but also because of the severe and ever–worsening water crisis that the world is faced with. Corporations may compromise on water quality in order to reduce costs and for increasing profits. In India, the drinking water and soft drink industries have been shown to have high pesticide levels in their products. In 2003, the New Delhi, India based Centre for Science and Environment showed that some of the soft drinks that were being sold in India contained lindane, DDT, malathion and other deadly pesticides which can cause cancer and can affect the immune systems (Mathur, Johnson and Kumar 2003). Privatization can also favor bulk water exports as control over water is transferred from local communities to global corporations, which will have disastrous ecological and environmental consequences. Many crops and vegetables need a large amount of water for their growth and production. For example, in India, production of one kilo of Basmati rice requires 4200 liters of water, for long duration coarse rice it is 2500 liters and for wheat the amount is 700 liters (Shiva 2003). Water pricing and privatization will inevitably increase the price of the major crops and vegetables all around the world, which, in turn, can adversely affect another human right issue of food security. While government management of water resources is partly responsible for the water crisis we face today, privatization will at best compound the problem.

2. Human Rights and Climate Change

In the past few decades scientists have assembled considerable amount of data which speak in favour of the causes and projected impacts of the growing concern of climate change. United Nations Framework Convention on Climate Change (UNFCC) defines climate change as "a change of climate which is attributed directly or indirectly to human activity that alters the composition of the global atmosphere and which is in addition to natural climate variability observed over comparable time periods" (Parry et. al. 2007).

Global average surface temperature of the earth has increased by about $0.74^{\circ}C$ over the last century. The 1980s and 1990s were the warmest decades since accurate records began in the late 1800s (Garvey 2009). The latest warning from a group of scientists from NASA is "2005 was the warmest year on record since the end of last major ice age nearly 12000 years ago" (Nair 2009).

In many dimensions, climate change can affect the basic human rights as follows:

1. *The right to safe life:* Direct impacts of climate change include the increased incidents of natural disasters, while indirect impacts include poorer standards of health, nutrition, access to clean drinking water and susceptibility to disease.

2. *The right to develop and welfare*: The anthropogenic climate change has its long lasting impacts on food and water security, earth's landmass, weather patterns and the destruction of ecosystems, which, in turn can affect the basic rights develop and welfare.

3. *The right to natural resources and property:* Climate change may result in the loss of natural resources and properties without compensation (specifically in coastal areas), and may also have an effect on land uses as a result of changing weather patterns.

4. *The right to education and health:* Climate change driven natural disasters prevent many from continuation of education. Climate change is likely to increase mortality from malnutrition, heat stress and infectious diseases worldwide. These factors can collectively affect the human health to a large extent.

5. *The right to food and nutrition:* Climate change can affect food security by reducing availability, changing access, worsening the stability and supply and affecting the utilization. Moreover, the effects on agricultural production will strike the human population at its question of survival.

6. *The right to water:* Climate change can change the components of the hydrological cycle and hydrological systems such as changing rainfall patterns and intensity. Changes in distribution can deprive some communities for whom water is more precious than the others.

7. *The rights of the Indigenous People*: According to the Intergovernmental Panel for Climate Change report, the communities who live in marginal lands and whose livelihoods are highly dependent on natural resources are among the most

vulnerable to climate change (Parry et. al. 2007). Biodiversity loss as a result of adverse impacts of climate change will affect the indigenous people in a multidimensional way, such as depriving them of important food sources and reducing their ability to cope with pests and diseases with the help of medicinal plants.

We can observe several noticeable changes in the earth, which, in turn can support the effects of climate change on human society and on the basic human rights. As for example, one of the many warning signals of global warming is the changes in the ice caps due to melting, thinning, shrinking, retreating, freezing and disappearing (Nair, 2009). Settlements in mountain regions are at enhanced risk of floods caused by melting glaciers. In parts of Central Asia, regional increases in temperature will increase mudflows and avalanches that could adversely affect human settlements (Afiazova 1997). In the past century, sea level rise has occurred at a mean rate of 1.8 mm per year (Douglas 1997), but the recent satellite data revealed that the rate has been changed from 1993 onwards (2.8 ± 0.4 to 3.1 ± 0.7 mm. per year) (Mirza 2003). Although it is clear that human population can live, survive, and flourish in extreme climates from the Arctic to the Sahara, if the predictable extremes of the local climate are exceeded, problems will occur. Sea level rise could also displace many shore-based populations; it is estimated that a sea level rise of just 200 mm could create 740,000 homeless people in Nigeria (Parry et al. 2007). Many small islands have poorly developed infrastructure and limited resources, and often small island populations are dependent on marine resources to meet their protein needs. So, climate change could completely change the social and economic conditions of the islands. Sea level rise will also destroy about 40 to 50 percent of the world's coastal wetlands by 2080 (Nair, 2009). World Bank has reported that sea level rise in Bangladesh can destroy up to 16 percent of land, supporting 13 percent of population and producing 12 percent of the current GDP (Afiazova 1997). In Bangladesh, three extreme floods have occurred in the last two decades, and in 1998 about 70 percent of the country's area was inundated (Parry et al. 2007). A World Bank report in 1994 concluded that human activities in the deltas can cause the areas to sink much faster than any predicted rise to sea level, thus can increase their vulnerability to storms and floods (Afiazova 1997). Sea level rise in the Nile delta can change the water quality, can affect many freshwater fishes, can increase the salinity of the groundwater and also can inundate the fertile agricultural lands. Rising sea levels will threaten coastal aquifers. Reports are showing that the underdeveloped countries that emit very low carbon are affected most due to the effect of climate change (Parry et. al. 2007).

A warmer climate will accelerate the hydrological cycle; can alter the intensity and timing of rainfall. Warm air can hold more moisture and can increase evaporation of surface moisture, which in turn can intensify rainfall and snowfall events. So, intensity of flood will also increase. If there is deficiency of moisture in the soil, solar radiation will increase the temperature, which could contribute to longer and more severe droughts (Parry et al. 2007). In a number of studies, it has been proved that global warming and decline in rainfall may reduce net recharge and can affect groundwater levels. Decrease in winter precipitation would reduce the total seasonal precipitation being received during December-

February, and can impose greater water stress. Intense rain for few days will result in increased frequency of floods and the monsoon rain would also be lost as direct runoff, thus can decrease the groundwater recharging potential (Mall et. al. 2006). Increased rainfall amounts and intensities will lead to greater rates of soil erosion. In India, Pakistan, Nepal and Bangladesh, rapid urbanization and industrialization, population growth and inefficient water use are the main causes of water crisis which is further aggravated by changing climate and its adverse impacts on demand, supply and water quality.

A large number of deaths due to heat waves—mainly among the poor, aged people and laborers such as rural daily wage earners, agricultural workers and rickshaw pullers have been reported in Andhra Pradesh, Orissa and elsewhere in India during the past five years (Lal 2002). Diarrhoeal diseases and outbreaks of other infectious diseases (e.g., cholera, hepatitis, malaria, dengue fever) have been reported to be influenced by climate–related factors. Exposure to heat can be a significant risk factor for cerebral infarction and cerebral ischemia during the summer months (Honda et. al. 1995). Epidemiological data collected in Brisbane, Australia from 1996 to 2001 shows that respiratory–and cardiovascular–related hospital admissions and mortality were elevated when both temperature and Particulate Matter concentrations increased (Ren et. al. 2006). The combination of air pollutants and allergen production linked to climate change may enhance allergic disease and asthma incidences in vulnerable individuals, especially children, infants, and asthmatics (Epstein 2006).

In some regions, changes in temperature and precipitation can increase the frequency and severity of fire events. Toxic gaseous and particulate air pollutants are released into the atmosphere, which can significantly contribute to acute and chronic illnesses of the respiratory system. Pollutants from forest fires can affect air quality for thousands of kilometers (Hoyt et. al. 2004, Sapkota et. al. 2005).

The World Health Organization (WHO) says global warming could lead to a major increase in insect–borne diseases in Britain and Europe. In April 2008, it was reported by the World Health Organization that, as a result of increased temperatures, malaria is appearing in the highland areas of Papua New Guinea, where it has always been too cold for disease–spreading mosquitoes. Endemic morbidity and mortality due to diarrhoeal disease primarily associated with floods and droughts are expected to rise in East, South and South–East Asia due to projected changes in the hydrological cycle associated with global warming (Maslin et. al. 2004). Increases in coastal water temperature would exacerbate the abundance and/or toxicity of cholera in South Asia. There is a strong corelation between increase in sea surface temperature and sea level and the annual severity of cholera epidemics in Bangladesh. Warmer sea–surface temperatures of South and South–East Asia would support higher phytoplankton blooms, which are excellent habitats for survival and spread of infectious bacterial diseases such as cholera (Pascual et. al. 2002).

In general, increased warmth and moisture will enhance transmission of diseases (Maslin et. al. 2004). Mathematical models proved that by 2080, the potential exposure of people by mosquitoes could increase by 2-4 percent (Douglas

1997). An empirical model projected that the population at risk of dengue fever will be larger in India and China (Hales et. al. 2002).

Future climate change is expected to have considerable impacts on natural resource systems, which, in turn, can lead to instability and conflict, often followed by displacement of people and changes in occupancy and migration patterns (Barnett, 2003). The production losses due to climate change may drastically increase the problem of poverty, food insecurity and malnutrition in several developing countries in Asia (Wang 2006).

Climate can be a factor in an area's comparative advantage for economic production and growth. Not only can climate affect an area's own economic patterns; it can also affect the competitive position of its markets and competitors, and thus affect prospects for local employment and individual livelihoods. For example, in 2003 the heat wave in Western Europe affected settlements and economic services in a variety of ways. Economically, it created stress on health, water supplies, and food storage and energy systems. In smaller locations, particularly developing countries, it was estimated with high confidence that, in the year of the extreme event, short-run damages could amount to more than 25 percent GDP (Parry et. al. 2007). The Intergovernmental Panel on Climate Change (IPCC) provides evidence that global insured and uninsured property losses currently amount to over $40 billion per annum compared to just $4 billion per annum (all in real terms) some 50 years ago.

Sustainable development has become part of all climate change policy discussions at the global level. It is 'the development that meets the needs of the present without compromising the ability of future generations to meet their own needs' (WCED, 1987). Environmental conservation for sustainability of natural resources is not a luxury but a necessity when considering long-term economic growth and development, particularly in the least developed countries. Linking the concept of sustainable development to climate change provides an opportunity to explore long-term societal responses to global environmental change, which, in turn, can conserve human rights as a whole.

3. Human Rights, Food Security and Health

The productive and diverse environment and its natural wealth, which are used for food provision, are becoming increasingly degraded. According to World Health Organization, The enjoyment of the highest attainable standard of health is one of the fundamental rights of every human being (WHO 2005). But the fundamental rights of food are continuously being perturbed by the malfunctioning of the Public Distribution System, especially in India. The ecological footprints of the human society are continuously shrinking the dimensions of food security. The colonial powers invested little in the food production systems of the developing countries, and by independence, their populations were growing at significantly high rates. By the mid–1960s, hunger and malnutrition were widespread, especially in Asia, which increase the dependency on food aid from rich countries. With the change of time, income growth, globalization, urbanization, high energy prices, shifting diets and climate change are transforming food consumption, production and markets. The overall issue of food and health is very broad, covering all aspects of food safety including pesticides, veterinary drug issues (e.g. antibiotics, hormones), transgenic plants and various contaminants like heavy metals or mycotoxins. The global food crisis is affecting the structures of the human society severely. It is pushing millions of people into poverty and malnutrition, and subsequently deprives the people in one of the basic and primary human rights. The inequitable distributions of food, land, and other productive resources, as well as low or income are the controlling factors for poverty, hunger and malnutrition. Recent increases in the prices of the main agricultural commodities have increased the number of hunger affected people from 850 million to 963 million all over the world (UNESCO 2009).

The undernourishment associated with missing macronutrients or micronutrients in poor–quality diets is even more widespread than the undernourishment indicated by underweight alone, in both the developed and developing world (WHO 2005). Millions of people are also suffering from one or more vitamin and mineral deficiencies. These results in shorter life spans, frequent illnesses, or reduced physical and mental abilities (WHO 2005). More than three-quarters of poor people in developing countries live in rural areas, and most of them depend directly or indirectly on agriculture for their livelihoods. It is ironical that most of the people affected by food insecurity live in rural areas where food is produced. The so-called 'green revolution' that introduced technological packages, based on industrial production methods in high potential areas, increased national food production but failed to reach the hungry and even exacerbated hunger at local levels. Paradoxically, only 43 percent of the cereal produced all over the world is available for human consumption; the rest is lost because of harvest and post–harvest distribution and use of cereal for animal feed (UNESCO 2009). Between September 2007 and March 2008 the price of wheat, corn, rice and other cereals increased in an average of 41 percent on the international market (UNESCO 2009).The price hikes have reduced the affordability of poor people and have inhibited the ability of the third world countries to supply food for their populations. In underdeveloped poor societies where male children are more highly valued than female, girls and boys are subject to different feeding practices and food intakes. Changes in food economy can aggravate this problem in future.

Aquaculture, freshwater and marine fisheries supply about 10 percent of the total calorie intake of world populations. The fisheries of the world have declined since 1980s because of habitat damage, pollution, and climate change. Eutrophication is a major threat to freshwater and coastal marine fisheries, the sources of which are the agricultural runoff and sewage disposal. It significantly affects the undernourished coastal population, who generally survive on marine resources (UNESCO 2009). For many people, particularly in India, wetlands are considered as the main source for their livelihood. Local people use food products from the wetland bioresources which can satisfy the nutritional requirement of those poor people. Destruction of wetlands for construction purposes can deprive those people from accessing the natural reservoir of water and food resources (Ghosh 2005).

Globally, economic growth in emerging and developing countries will continue to lead to changing dietary patterns, with staple foods of vegetable origin being replaced by proteins of animal origin. These increase demand for crops used as animal feedstock disproportionately. The demand for ready-to-cook and ready-to-eat foods is increasing in urban areas, particularly in metropolitan cities. These foods do not always have the same nutritional value as fresh or home-made food, and have a higher environmental footprint (energy consumption for manufacturing, pollution and depletion of resources etc.) (UNEP 2009).

Another way of using nature as a resource is through the genetic reprogramming of the nature itself. Herbicide resistant cotton, vitamin rich rice, pest resistant potatoes, infection free fish—all are the examples of increasing outputs and consumption by means of genetic remodeling. Genetically Modified Foods (or GM foods) are foods derived from genetically modified organisms. Genetically Modified Organisms are produced by specific changes introduced into their DNA by genetic engineering techniques. The term GM foods or GMOs (genetically-modified organisms) is most commonly used to refer to crop plants developed for human or animal consumption by the applications of molecular biology techniques. These plants have been modified in the laboratory to enhance desired traits such as increased resistance to herbicides or improved nutritional content. The enhancement of desired traits has traditionally been undertaken through breeding, but conventional plant breeding methods can be very time consuming and are often not very accurate. Genetic engineering, on the other hand, can create plants with the exact desired trait very rapidly and with great accuracy. Researchers are focusing on traits like allowing crops to cope with water stress, temperature variation, salinity etc. These advances have the potential to improve both the resilience of crops (to climate change and land degradation) and their sustainability. But, there is a growing concern that introducing foreign genes into food plants may have an unexpected and negative impact on human health. Additionally, the new varieties of genetically modified seeds can increase the price of seeds, which can raise the question of affordability of the poor farmers of the developing countries. The introduction of terminator gene technology (plants that have been genetically modified to render seeds sterile at harvest) has deprived the farmers from their basic rights and subsequently has affected the economic structure of the society. These new technologies have triggered many questions regarding bioethics, human rights and food security, and most of them remain unanswered (Smith 2007).

Crop diversity has declined in many parts of the earth over the last century due to mechanization, as mechanization requires farms to have uniform crop types, structure and management practices. The genetic diversity of crops has declined with industrial agriculture. Although hundred of edible plant species have been important in traditional crop systems, today only three crops—Rice, Wheat and Maize provide 60 percent of our plant based diet worldwide (FAO 2002). Among the 8,000 traditional rice varieties of China, which were grown in 1949, only 50 remained in 1970. Modern varieties have supplanted traditional varieties for 70 percent of the world's corn, 75 percent of Asian rice, and half of the wheat in Africa, Latin America, and Asia. In 1950, India had 30,000 wild varieties of rice, but by 2015, only 50 varieties are expected to remain (Fowler and Mooney 1990). The area under diverse traditional food crops has declined substantially too, replaced by monocultures of exotic cash crops. The advent of hybrid seeds, chemical fertilizers, bore wells, and government loans have provoked many farmers to do gambling on cash crops like cotton and sugarcane—and the outcomes were not positive (Lumb 1988).

The right to food is a perfect example of the indivisibility, interdependence, and interconnectedness of economic and social rights. A rights–based approach for ensuring food security is advantageous on many levels. It supports the human rights law of nondiscrimination and equality; it supports a number of other basic human rights, such as the right to the highest attainable standard of health; and it significantly enhances human dignity and democracy. But fulfilling one's need for food in the biological sense is different from fulfilling one's right to food. If people have no chance to influence what and how they were being fed, if they are provided with prepackaged rations or capsules, their right to adequate food will not be fulfilled, even if they get all the nutrients necessary for their bodies. Human rights are mainly about upholding human dignity, not about meeting the basic physiological needs. Understanding food systems in modern socio-cultural context may be essential for designing sustainable food production and marketing for adequate human consumption.

Unfortunately, in India and other developing nations, National food security did not translate into nutrition security due to lack of effective research on nutritional security or on availability of a balanced diet comprising cereals and millets, pulses, vegetables and fruits, and animal products. Food security is closely interlinked with many other related disciplines such as water, biotechnology, nutrition, climatology, etc. There is need for much greater inter-disciplinary research work across various institutes and researchers, possibly through collaborative research symposia, seminars and long term projects. This will help generate more valuable and effective inputs for food security. Several areas should be better understood, tested and implemented by the officials before nutrition can fully serve in the frontline as a promoter of economic, social, and cultural rights. First, transparency in nutrition data should be maintained in all records. Common people must have the opportunities to claim their legal human rights related to the right to adequate food from the relevant duty holders and administrators, in both government and private sectors. Furthermore they must have the right to complain to appropriate institutions about violations of rights that are essential for their food security and nutritional wellbeing. Ultimately, food sovereignty should be maintained for establishing sustainable food security. This is the right of each nation and its people to maintain and develop its own capacity and freedom to produce people's basic food, whilst respecting environmental, social and cultural diversity.

4. Human Rights and Biodiversity

In terms of resource use, there are two categories of communities in the world. The ecosystem people are those who depend on the natural environment for satisfying most of their material needs. In contrast, biosphere people command recourses from anywhere in the world, and are not dependent on the local resources for their survival (Dasmann 1984). Here lies the anthropocentric philosophy of sustainability and consumerism. In India, around 70 percent of the population directly depends on land–based occupations, forests, wetlands and marine habitats for ecological livelihoods and cultural sustenance. Because of this close interdependence of humans and their environment, the culture of societies is greatly influenced by their environment.

It is not only humans that are affected because of unsustainable activities, but all other life forms on the earth too. The concept of environment, when explained in terms of biological rights, must also respect the right of other species to survive on this planet. There are millions of species of plants, animals, and microorganisms in the biosphere, and each has a value of its own, a role to play in a vast, complex web of interdependent connections. Human existence and survival is ultimately dependent upon the existence of other organisms. This range of species, the habitats they live in, and the internal genetic diversity they display, is called biological diversity or biodiversity. Such diversity is part of our daily lives and livelihoods, constituting resources upon which families, communities, nations and future generations depend. Biodiversity has numerous uses in agriculture, medicine, food and industry. It helps to maintain ecological balance and evolutionary processes, and has spiritual, cultural, aesthetic and recreational values. Its loss will eventually lead to the degradation of environmental human rights.

For satisfying the increasing food demands of our society, large-scale farming has caused the loss not only of wild plant and animal genetic resources, but has also influenced the ecosystem structure due to intensive use of pesticides and herbicides. Plant genetic resources are essential for agricultural sustainability and food security. FAO estimates that humans have used 10,000 species for food throughout the history of civilization. Only 120 cultivated species provide around 90 percent of our food resources globally (FAO 2002). The present unsustainable consumption pattern has its deleterious impact on the genetic viability of these cultivated species. From the early 1980s, there was a growing concern about the degradation of tropical forest and the question of survival of the indigenous communities living in those areas. The Stern Review estimates that forests store more than 4,500 gigatons of carbon, which is more than the total amount of carbon in remaining oil stocks and more than the amount of carbon currently held in the atmosphere (Stern 2006). The review concluded that maintaining biodiversity and controlling deforestation could provide one of the least expensive strategies for reducing emissions, and should be an essential tool for climate change mitigation policies (Stern 2006).

Forest–based goods and services are central to the economic, social, and cultural rights of hundreds of millions of people around the world. The World Bank estimates that 90 percent of the 1.2 billion people living in extreme poverty depend on forest resources for some part of their livelihood (World Bank, 2004). Forests are also important to the maintenance of cultural identity. In East Kalimantan, Indonesia, research conducted with local communities identified and documented more than 2100 forest species with 3642 different uses, including food, traditional medicine, hunting equipment, construction materials, and culturally-significant ornamentations. More than a hundred of these species had no known substitute for the particular use (Sheil et. al. 2001). Despite the importance of forests and the indigenous communities living in them, forest communities are often denied access to forest resources. In many countries, there is a rich history of repressive measures taken by both State and non-state actors to control forest access and use. Disruption of forest ecosystems will in turn lead to disruption in the provision of forest-based ecosystem goods and services (like timber, fuel wood, forage, fruits, medicines, and materials for handicrafts) which are often of particular importance to poor communities in developing countries. Forest-based ecosystem services include cultural, spiritual, and aesthetic services, as well as hydrological, pollination, and pest control services which are also important to the context of national economics (Reid, 2005). The degradation of forest ecosystems and associated resilience to the impacts of climate change will reduce forest-based incomes. Particularly, the impact of climate change on forests will also make the forest communities more vulnerable to natural disasters such as forest fires, landslides, and floods and can generate environmental refugees beyond carrying capacity.

Transnational companies are now searching profit in the rich biological resources of the developing world. With the help of the local indigenous peoples, they try to locate biological materials that have medicinal values, study their beneficial properties in the laboratory and patent the resources as their own invention. Biopiracy is defined as "the illegal appropriation of life—microorganisms, plants and animals (including humans)—and the traditional cultural knowledge that accompanies it" (Shiva 1997). The biotechnological corporations have been able to extract and patent the genes from these plants and thus claim the plants for themselves. Corporate patents do not recognize or compensate the indigenous people who are the main conservators of those resources. Indigenous communities, over the centuries, have identified and classified plants native to their lands and found their beneficial characteristics. But, the tribes do not have access to legal information that would protect their plants and cultural knowledge nor do they have the finances to obtain them (Shiva 1997). Therefore, Indigenous Peoples face an uphill battle in protecting their plants and cultural knowledge. The loss of forests and genetic material combined with the money making incentives for corporations increase the need for protection of Indigenous communities' land, plants and cultural knowledge. Moreover, with the introduction of the genetically modified crops and high yielding varieties, the local crop varieties are being lost and out-competed. The farmer's rights to choose the desired crops have become difficult to implement. Furthermore, the patenting of gene sequences and biotechnology techniques with broad applications means that developing countries in particular may be excluded from affordable access to technologies that they urgently need.

Human Rights, Sustainable Development and Social Justice

When the World Commission on Environment and Development presented their 1987 report, 'Our Common Future', they tried to balance the conflict between environment and development by establishing the concept of sustainable development. Sustainable development is development which meets the needs of the present without compromising the ability of future generations to meet their own needs. In fact, it speaks about the intergenerational equity of resources. There were three quite distinct ideas about what should be developed: people, economy, and society. In 2002, in the World Summit on Sustainable Development, it was mentioned that "Globalization has added a new dimension to these challenges. The rapid integration of markets, mobility of capital and significant increases in investment flows around the world has opened new challenges and opportunities for the pursuit of sustainable development. But the benefits and costs of globalization are unevenly distributed, with developing countries facing special difficulties in meeting this challenge.....We are determined to ensure that our rich diversity, which is our collective strength, will be used for constructive partnership for change and for the achievement of the common goal of sustainable development" (World Summit on Sustainable Development 2002). Much of the early literature focused on economic development, with productive sectors providing employment, desired consumption, and wealth. More recently, attention has shifted to human development, including an emphasis on values and goals, such as increased life expectancy, education, equity, and opportunity. Sustainable development is a far more sophisticated concept that challenges the conventional school of thought and recognizes the reality that quality of life depends on economic, social and environmental improvement at the same time not at the expense of each other. Conservation and development need not be in perpetual conflict, but can, and perhaps must co-exist. The concept of sustainable development aims to achieve this. Economic growth is critical to development, especially in developing countries like India. The only caveat is that if economic growth is needed to realize development, it should be of sustainable growth mode and thus should not result in the depletion of capital or environmental assets beyond the rate of regeneration of these assets (Himesh 2001).

The concrete challenges of sustainable development are at least as heterogeneous and complex as the diversity of human societies and natural ecosystems around the world. Sustainable development demands restructuring of neoclassical economic structure that is based on open-ended consumption of material resources and growth (Himesh 2001). Incorporation of ecological concerns into industrialization is an innovative, effective, and efficient strategy for enhancing the competitive edge of our industrial sector in the fast changing global market and economic scenario, with greatest concern for environment than ever before (Himesh 2002).

Human rights and sustainable human development are interdependent and mutually reinforcing concepts. Sustainable human development seeks to expand choices for all people—women, men and children, current and future generations—while protecting the natural systems on which all life depends. Thus sustainable human development aims to eliminate poverty, promote human dignity and rights, and provide equitable opportunities for all through good governance, thereby promoting the realization of economic, social, cultural, civil and political rights. The promotion of human rights is of particular relevance in the context of globalization and its potential for excluding and marginalizing weak members of the international community and people with limited resources. The 1986 UN Declaration on the Right to Development states that development is a human right. That proclamation was strengthened by the Declaration of the 1993 UN World Conference on Human Rights, which says that "the right to development is an inalienable human right and an integral part of fundamental human freedoms." This view was confirmed at the UN global conferences on population and development (Cairo) and women (Beijing) and at the World Summit on Social Development (Copenhagen). Indeed, poverty is a violation of human rights (Roy 2005). Poverty and inequality can undermine human rights by fueling social unrest and violence and increasing the precariousness of social, economic and political rights. Likewise, people's access to and control over productive resources is often determined by a country's legal framework and institutions. Like human rights, poverty and sustainable livelihoods are multifaceted and complex, involving both material factors (meeting basic needs) and nonmaterial ones (rights, participation, human dignity and security). Because of these links, programming in poverty and sustainable livelihoods can benefit from broadening the focus to include human rights. Civic and social education will help people better understand their rights and increase their choices and income–earning capacity. At the same time, developing and implementing equal opportunity laws will empower people to gain more equitable access to productive resources.

Climate change will hamper sustainable development as it increases the pressures on natural resources and the environment associated with rapid urbanization, industrialization and economic development. In order to reduce the effect of climate change, we need to include climate–proofing concepts in national and international development initiatives. In recent times cities have become the places of urban environmental degradation and resource depletion, which is proving to be costly to generations present and future. Sustainable urban development should be done by the development of the urban areas and protection of the environment by maintaining the equity in employment, shelter, basic services, social infrastructure and transportation. Basic services like water, waste, energy, and transportation should be ensured in a way that it can satisfy the principles of sustainable development. In order to be economically efficient a city needs to reduce production costs, e.g. costs of receiving inputs and distributing outputs (Parry et. al. 2007).

Implementation of ecological knowledge and activities into industrialization and consumerism is an innovative and effective strategy in modern society which can promote sustainability. It can trigger the new sustainable areas of industrialization, which can be equally competitive and ecologically sound. Conservation and development need not be in perpetual conflict, but co-exist with our sustainable outlooks (Himesh 2001).

According to the United Nations, a human rights–based approach to development is a conceptual framework for the process of human development that is normatively based on international human rights standards and operationally directed to promoting and protecting human rights. In its essence, a rights–based approach integrates the norms, standards and principles of the international human rights system into the plans, policies and processes of development. Accountability at all levels combined with productive participation by the poor at various decentralized levels can help us to find a new perspective of development.

Conclusion

With time, the examples of population explosion and natural resource crises in our society remind us about Charles Darwin's theory and Malthusian theory of population. The occurrence of increasing numbers of individuals in limited space will inevitably create competition and conflicts, both in social and biological dimensions. Till now, we cannot comprehend the proper meaning of 'enough'; so the seeds of consumerism are spreading among individuals, and are simultaneously destroying the roots of natural and social security.

With the advancement of civilization and development, environment has become affected to a considerable extent. Environmental degradation has raised the uncomfortable questions about the concept of development itself. With environmental degradations, a large section of people has become marginalized and their lives and livelihood has faced grave concerns. It is an unfortunate observation that the fruits of development have not reached to everyone. But development is achieved by the use of the common goods. Development as expected has increased consumerism in a small section of the society, but as expected, it has degraded and depleted natural resources. And more importantly, development has violated the basic rights of human community. It is a need of the hour to secure the right to safe food, water, air and all other natural ingredients in particular and environment in general. Though a lot of regulations, acts and laws have been enacted here and there, the same is not enough to protect the rights of human beings. It is important to raise the general awareness of the common people about their basic rights. Then only the people will come to understand how their rights are being violated. Knowledge about development and environment is not enough; rather the upsurge of the common people and pushing the principles of human rights are extremely important. An endeavor should be encouraged on behalf of the international, national, regional and local authorities to respect, restore and recharge the basic rights of the human, both as an individual and a collective entity.

References

Afiazova, R.K., 1997. Climate Change Impact on Mud Flow Formation in Trans-Ili-Alatay Mountains. *Hydrometeorology and Ecology* 3: 12–23.

Agarwal A., and S. Narain, 1997. *Dying Wisdom. Rise, Fall and Potential of India's Traditional Water Harvesting Systems.* New Delhi: Centre for Science & Environment (CSE).

Barlow, M., 2003. *Blue Gold–The Fight to Stop the Corporate Theft of the World's Water.* New Delhi: Leftword Books.

Barnett, J., 2003. Security and Climate Change. *Global Environmental Change* 13, no. 1: 7–17.

Cernea, M. M., 1996. Public Policy Responses to Development Induced Population Displacement. *Economic and Political Weekly* (June 15): 1515–1523.

Chakraborti, D., M.M Rahman,. K. Paul, U.K. Chowdhury, M.K. Sengupta, D. Lodh, C.R. Chanda, K.C. Saha, and S.C. Mukherjee, 2002. Arsenic calamity in the Indian subcontinent: what lessons have been learned? *Talanta* 58, no. 4: 3–22.

Clapham, A., 2007. *Human rights: A Very Short Introduction.* New York: Oxford University Press.

Clarke, R. and J. King, 2009. *The Atlas of Water.* London: Earthscan.

Conkin, P. K., 2007. *The State of the Earth-environmental Challenges on the Road to 2100.* India: University Press.

Dasmann, R. F., 1984. *Environmental Conservation.* New York: John Wiley and Sons.

Douglas, B. C., 1997. Global Sea Rise: A Redetermination. *Surveys in Geophysics* 18, no. 2/3: 279–292.

Energy and Resources Institute, 1996. *State of India's Environment (A Quantitative Analysis).* Report No. 1995EE52.

Epstein, P.R., 2007. Climate Change and Human Health. *The New England Journal of Medicine* 353, no. 14: 1433–1436.

Falkenmark, M. and C. Widstrand, 1992. *Population and Water Resources: A Delicate Balance.* (Population Bulletin 47). Washington, DC: Population Reference Bureau (PRB).

Food and Agriculture Organization (FAO), 2011. World Food Summit News. http:// www.fao.org/worldfoodsummit/english/newsroom/news/6460-en.html (accessed April 7, 2011).

Fowler, C. and P.R. Mooney, 1990. *Shattering: Food, Politics, and the Loss of Genetic Diversity.* Tucson: University of Arizona Press.

Garvey, J., 2009. *The Ethics of Climate Change–Right or Wrong in a Warming World.* New York: Continuum International Publishing Group.

Ghosh, D., 2005. *Ecology and Traditional Wetland Practices.* Kolkata: Worldview Press.

Gupta, A., R. Singh, R.S. Singh and L.S. Rathore, 2006. Water Resources and Climate Change: An Indian Perspective. *Current Science* 90, no. 12: 1610–1626.

Hales, S. N., de Wet, J. Maindonald, and A. Woodward, 2002. Potential Effect of Population and Climate Changes on Global Distribution of Dengue Fever: An Empirical Model. *Lancet* 360, no. 9336: 830–834.

Himesh, S., 2002. Dilemma of Development and Environment: A Perspective. *Current Science* 80, no. 9: 1101–1102.

Honda,Y., M. Ono, I. Uchiyama and A. Sasaki, 1995. Relationship between Daily High Temperature and Mortality in Kyushu, Japan. *Japanese Journal of Public Health* 42, no. 4: 260–268.

Hoyt, K.S. and A.E. Gerhart, 2004. The San Diego County Wildfires: Perspectives of Health Care. *Disaster Management and Response* 2, no. 2: 46–52.

Lal, M., 2002. *Global Climate Change: India's Monsoon and Its Variability.* Final Report under Country Studies Vulnerability and Adaptation Work Assignment with Stratus Consulting's Contract of the U.S. Environmental Protection Agency.

Lumb, L., 1988. Crops of Truth: conserving agricultural biodiversity in Andhra Pradesh, India. *Science from the Developing World.* IDRC Reports. http://www.idrc.ca/reports (accessed July 3, 2011).

Mall, R.K., A. Gupta, R. Singh, R.S. Singh and L.S. Rathore, 2006. Water Resources and Climate Change: An Indian Perspective. *Current Science* 90, no. 12: 1610–1626.

Maslin, M., 2004. *Global Warming: A Very Short Introduction.* USA: Oxford University Press.

Mathur, H.B., S. Johnson, A. Kumar, 2003. *Analysis of Pesticide Residues in Soft Drinks.* Centre for Science and Environment, New Delhi.

Meharg A.A. and M.M. Rahman, 2003. Arsenic Contamination in Bangladesh Paddy Field Soils: Implication for Rice Contribution to Arsenic Consumption. *Environmental Science and Technology* 37, no. 2: 229–234.

Ministry of the Environment, Government of Japan, 2006. *Annual Report on the Environment in Japan.* http://www.env.go.jp/en/wpaper/2006/index.html (accessed June 6, 2011).

Mirza, M.M.Q., 2003. Three Recent Extreme Floods in Bangladesh: A Hydrometeorological Analysis. *Natural Hazards* 28: 35–64.

National Research Council, Policy Division, Board on Sustainable Development, 1999. *Our Common Journey: A Transition toward Sustainability.* Washington: National Academy Press.

Nair, P.S.G., 2009. *Earth in Peril.* India: Publication Division.

Parry, M.L., O.F. Canziani, J.P. Palutikof and C.E. Hanson, eds. 2007. *IPCC Forth Assessment Report: Climate Change 2007.* New York: Cambridge University Press.

Pascual, M., M.J. Bouma and A.P. Dobson, 2002. Cholera and Climate: Revisiting the Quantitative Evidence. *Microbes and Infections* 4, no. 2: 237–245.

Rao, K.L., 1995. *India's Water Wealth.* India: Orient Longman.

Reid, W.V., 2005. *Millenium Ecosystem Assessment 2005. Ecosystems and Human Well-Being: Synthesis.* Washington, DC: Island Press.

Ren, C.Z. and S.L. Tong, 2006. Temperature Modifies The Health Effects of Particulate Matter in Brisbane, Australia. *International Journal of Biometeorology* 51, no. 2: 87–96.

Roy, S., 2005. *Environmental Science.* Kolkata: New Central Book Agency.

Sapkota, A., J.M. Symons, J. Kleissl, L. Wang, M.B. Parlange, J. Ondov, P.N. Breysse, G.B. Diette, P.A. Eggleston and T.J. Buckley, 2005. Impact of the 2002 Canadian Forest Fires on Particulate Matter Air Quality in Baltimore City *Environmental Science and Technology* 39, no. 1 (2005): 24–32.

Sheil, D., R.K. Puri, I. Basuki, M. Van Heist, Saefuddin, Rukmiyati, M.A. Sardjono, I. Samsoedin, K.D. Sidiyasa, Chrisandini, E. Permana, E.M Angi, F. Gatzweiler, B. Johnson and A. Wijaya, 2001. Exploring Biological

Diversity, Environment and Local People's Perspectives in Forest Landscapes: Methods for a Multidisciplinary Landscape Assessment. *Centre for International Forestry Research, Indonesia.* http://www.cifor.cgiar.org/nc/online-library/browse/view-publication/publication/ 1021.html (accessed April 25, 2011).

Shiva, V., 1997. *Biopiracy: The Plunder of Nature and Knowledge.* New Delhi: Research Foundation for Science, Technology and Ecology.

———. 2005. *Water and women: A Report by Research Foundation for Science, Technology and Ecology for National Commission for Women.* New Delhi: Navdanya.

Shiva, V. and K. Jalees, 2003. *The Impact of the River Linking Project.* New Delhi: Navdanya.

Smith, J. M., 2007. *Genetic Roulette: The Documented Health Risks of Genetically Engineered Foods.* India: Other India Press.

Stern, N., 2006. *The Economics of Climate Change: The Stern Review.* Cambridge: Cambridge University Press.

UNESCO, 2009. World Water Assessment Programme. *The United Nations World Water Development Report 3: Water in a Changing World.* http://www.unesco.org/water/wwap/wwdr/wwdr3/pdf/WWDR3_Water_in_a_Changing_World.pdf (accessed July 2, 2011).

Wang, X., F. Chen, and Z. Dong, 2006. The Relative Role of Climatic and Human Factors in Desertification in Semiarid China. *Global Environmental Change* 16, no. 1: 48–57.

World Bank, 2004. *Sustaining Forests: A Development Strategy.* Washington, DC: World Bank.

WCED, 1987. *Our Common Future (Report of the World Commission on Environment and Development).* New York: Oxford University Press.

World Health Organization, 2000. Global Water Supply and Sanitation Assessment 2000 Report. http://www.who.int/water_sanitation_health/monitoring/jmp2000.pdf (accessed July 12, 2011).

———. 2004. Water Sanitation and Hygiene Linked to Health. http://www.who.int/water_sanitation_health/publications/ facts2004/en/ (accessed March 23, 2011).

———. 2005. Health and Human Rights. http://www.who.int/hhr/en/ (accessed April 22, 2011).

World Summit on Sustainable Development, 2002. Draft Political declaration submitted by the president of the summit. 2002. http://www.rrcap.unep.org/wssd/Political%20declaration_4%20Sep%2002.pdf (accessed April 5, 2011).

CHAPTER 4

Human Rights and Corruption: Indonesian Case for Reconciling Universalism and Relativism

Agus Wahyudi

The links between human rights and corruption have widely attracted scholarly attention in the last few years. Yet, even until recently, the relationship between human rights and corruption seems to remain debatable. We may identify two opposing views in this regard. On the one hand, the mainstream views, articulated by various contemporary human rights activists and scientists, suggest that corruption violates human rights, or that corruption disables a state from meeting its obligation to respect, fulfill and protect the human rights of its citizens (Eigen 2004: 1; Kumar 2002; Anukansai 2010). On the other hand, the non–mainstream ones, reflected in the works of some political scientist, cultural studies and economics insist that corruption can be a good thing, and does not necessarily violate human rights (see Gathii 2007: 7–14).

Thus, it will be submitted that the corruption and human rights nexus is more complicated than one might have realized. The contentious nature of human rights itself, reflected for instance in the apparently misleading, yet noticeable distinction between the universality and the relativity of human rights (see Chowdhry 2004: 229; Donnelly 1984), may add further complexities in any effort to develop a common and acceptable understanding of the relationship between human rights and corruption. In the first place, the denial of the very idea of universality of rights has been perceived by those who champion it from both East and West, as concealing, in the words of Richard Falk, "a propaganda ploy by leaders [in many Asian and African countries] who seek to shield their abusive behavior from criticism" (Falk 2004: 18). This certainly suggests no trivial accusation as political corruption has been more rampant in recent years in non–Western countries than the Western ones. However, from the perspective of those who defend "Asian Values" or "Islamic Values," claim such as the universality of human rights is no more than Western countries' efforts to preserve their self-interest and perpetuate their dominant power. This would mean that, debates of the values of human rights "actually mask a competition for power" (Van Ness 1999: 12; Muzaffar 1999: 28), and may also imply that rampant corruption currently marks the life of many Third World countries, or developing is impossible to be fairly conceived without an understanding of the roles played by the West.

The aims of this essay are twofold. First, it is intended to critically examine the above two conflicting views of the human rights and corruption nexus, and to consider which one is more plausible. Second, attempting to reconstruct an understanding of their relationships, this essay will draw a lesson from the phenomena of political corruption in Indonesia, a country that despite has undergone profound political and administrative changes since the heyday of the Asian values debates, and has enjoyed the significant political backing to human rights, is noted to persistently oppose to human rights (Asplund 2009: 28).

This essay will be divided into two parts. In the first part, it will discuss some exemplary writings that represent both "mainstream and non–mainstream views" of the human rights and corruption nexus, and it will be argued that the mainstream views are more plausible than the non–mainstream ones as the former is better able to explain the relationship between human rights and corruption by considering both instrumental and intrinsic justifications than the latter. In the second part, looking at the phenomena of political corruption in Indonesia, this essay will show how a dominant liberal human rights discourse—which among other envisions the universality of human rights and give a priority to the civil and political rights—is applicable for understanding the corruptions and the violations of human rights in Indonesia. This has to do in particular with the Indonesian 'New Order' government receptions of a perfectionist state that had contributed to the culture of corruption and the violation of human rights. However, it will also be demonstrated that the liberal human rights discourse is less able to capture the true nature of human rights violations and political corruptions in Indonesia.

Mainstream and Non–Mainstream Views

Three points may need a clarification before discussing the mainstream and non–mainstream views with regard to the human rights and corruption nexus, and before assessing which one is more plausible. The three concepts covering "the general meaning of human rights"; "the definition of corruption"; and "the concepts of instrumental and intrinsic justifications" will be discussed respectively.

First, the general meaning of human rights. Human rights refer to the notion of "what is in the Universal Declaration of Human Rights (UDHR)" (cited in Donnelly 2003: 22), that is, a document adopted by the United Nations General Assembly on December 10, 1948 which contains a short but substantial list of rights considered by some academics as "the most important legal documents in the history of the world" (cited in Feng 2004: 2). While the list of human rights can be understood as minimal standard, that is, focus only on "areas of great injustice", and that "they can hope to be supported by very reasons of universal appeal, to be of high priority, and to resist claims of national and cultural autonomy" (Nickel 2007: 3), another important related value of it should be recognized and this relates to the notion that "all human rights are embedded in a social context and have important social dimensions" (Donnelly 2003: 25). This means, as Donnelly explains, "the very ideas of respecting and violating human rights rest on the idea of the individual as part of a larger social enterprise" (Donnelly 2003: 26). These general descriptions may suggest a crucial meaning of what the values that are covered and not covered in the terms of human rights.

Clearly, there are now three "generations" of rights that mark the international human rights regimes which according to Linda Butenhoff consist of the *first generation* (we call it the dominant discourse) which is comprised of civil and political rights; the second generation which specifies economic, social and cultural rights; and a *third generation*, which emphasizes people's rights and groups rights, particularly on their right to self-determination and the right to development (cited in Van Ness 1999: 9). What seems to be crucial for an understanding of the values of human rights is also the fact that from the UDHR emerged two U.N. covenants—the International Covenant on Economic, Social and Cultural Rights (ICESCR), and the International Covenant on Civil and Political Rights (ICCPR)—that codified human rights into binding international treaties, and it is these covenant, along with two optional protocol that "comprise what is now known as the International Bill of Rights" (Feng 2004: 2).

The above distinction of human rights principles was not without controversy as they involved the forms of politically state interests. Today, however, the world accepts the doctrine that, as Article 5 of the 1993 Vienna Declaration puts it, "All human rights are universal, indivisible and interdependent and interrelated" (cited in Donnelly 2003: 27), even though this doctrine was regularly challenged during the Cold War, with the U.S. refusing to guarantee most economic and social rights, and the U.S.S.R. and many commentators of the Third World countries equally adamant in refusing most civil and political rights, and as a consequence, the international Bill of Human Rights was then divided into two treaties. As it is widely known, relying on the principles of free market capitalism as its justification, the U.S. still rejects to ratify the ICESCR. A part from this, the adoption of the 1993 Vienna declaration was taken as a sign of progress in repairing the division of economic and political rights into separate categories of human rights, even though it is fully realized that "significant issues in this research field remain such as the blatant discrepancy between theory and practice, and what enforcement mechanism are necessary to close this gap" (Donnelly 2003: 27; Feng 2004: 3).

Second, the definition of corruption. It may not be surprising, yet it is worth noting that "there is no universally accepted definition of corruption" (Terracino 2008: 5), and that "the term of 'corruption' can be used in various ways" (Anukansai 2010: 6). However, corruption is often understood, using the most used definition of corruption adopted by non-governmental organization, *Transparency International* as "the abuse of entrusted power for private gain" (cited in Terracino 2008: 5).

According to Terracino, as corruptions also occur not only in the public sector but also in the private sectors, the above definition of corruption can also be translated as "the abuse of entrusted power both in private and public sectors for private gain", suggesting that this definition should and can be further specified in order "to analyze when and how different corrupt practices entail a violation of human rights" and therefore he suggests to accept the legal definition of corruption by adding a further condition to ensure that "the person in a position of power who is accused of corruption must be acting contrary to the law" (Terracino 2008: 6). The problem with this definition, however, is that corruption as such in legal terms does not exist as a crime both at the international and national level, and corruption is used generally as a term to group certain criminal acts which correspond to the general notion of an abuse of entrusted power (Terracino 2008: 6)

Similar to the above definition, in this essay, corruption will be understood in terms of power relations that suggest any "abuse of power", and thus it is assumed that corruption would never exist if there were no abuse of power (cf Anukansai 2010: 7). In the context of domestic corruption, abuse of power could refer to "the abuse of function of the state authority which is defined as 'the performance of or failure to perform an act in violation of the law by a public officials in the discharge of his or her functions, for purpose of obtaining an undue advantage for himself or herself or for another person or entity'" (cited in Anukansai 2010: 7: see also ICHRP 2009).

An understanding of corruption within the broader context of power relations may help to understand the very nature of corruption, given that from power relations perspective, "corruption is an activity carried out by individual or groups who gain access to power" and "it is asymmetric power relation which determines who controls whom and by what means" (Anukansai 2010: 7). As the purposes of this essay is to understand, among others, a link between the practices of corruption and the violation of human rights in a country like Indonesia, the above definition of corruption as power relation may serve to understand the nature of corruption and how corruption may relate to a violation of human rights. The core of corruption acts in this sense can take various forms, which according to Terracino (2008: 7) include bribery, embezzlement, trading in influence, abuse of functions, and illicit enrichment.

Third, the notion of instrumental and intrinsic justifications. In some cases, defending human rights can be done by suggesting that respecting human rights is important to achieve certain goods, including common good. Thus, for example, by respecting and defending human rights, a country can escape from being the target of international criticisms, and may achieve certain international standing and integrity. But there is something odd in seeing and justifying human rights in this way, because like in the case of democracy, "many people would argue that we should favor democracy even if it turned out that democratic systems were less good than others at achieving common good" (Wolff 2006: 76), and so with Jonathan Wolff, this essay attempts to differentiate between *instrumental justification,* that is, by considering if human rights and anti-corruptions acts can be a way of achieving something else one values, and *intrinsic justifica-*

tion, that is, by questioning if there is something *intrinsically* good about human rights and anti-corruption acts, or that they are good even if it is not able always to achieve desirable consequences. In what follows, we are going to discuss some exemplars of the mainstream and non–mainstream views pertinent to the human rights and corruption nexus, in order to have a sense of its plausibility with respect to these two justifications.

As has already been mentioned, mainstream views refer to those who hold that the link between corruption and human rights is necessarily positive, and insist that corruption is a violation of human rights, while non–mainstream views refer to those who believe that the link between corruption and human rights is not always as such a positive and clear-cut as it may seem, and according to this view, corruption can be a good thing and does not necessarily violate human rights. There are various examples represented this mainstream view. Peter Eigan, Chairman of Transparency International, for example, notes that "corruption leads to a violation of human rights in at least three respects: corruption perpetuates discrimination, corruption prevents the full realization of economic, social, and cultural rights, and corruption leads to the infringement of numerous civil and political rights" (Eigen 2004: 1). Other similar views also underline such corruption and human rights nexus, suggesting that since basic human rights and liberties come under threat, and social and economic contract become unpredictable because of corruption acts, therefore, "corruption affects both civil and political rights, as well as economic, social, and cultural rights" (Pilapitiya 1998: 9–10; see also Feng 2004; Kumar 2002; Anukansai 2010). In a more modest way, however, Mary Robinson, executive director of the Ethical Globalization Initiative and Former U.N. High Commissioner for Human Rights is also noted as saying in Transparency International *Global Corruption Report 2004* that the relationship between human rights and corruption demands further consideration, suggesting that if human rights violations and corruption are linked, then respecting human rights could serve as an important aid in the anti-corruption movement (cited in Feng 2004: 6). To get a deeper sense of this mainstream position, the work of Thusita Pilapitiya "The impact of Corruption on the Human Rights based Approach to Development" (UNDP, September 2004), and a piece written by Kanokkan Anukansai, "Corruption: The Catalyst of Violation of Human Rights" (2010) will be discussed.

In her attempt to explain the link between corruption and human rights, Pilapitiya, Program Analyst (Legal), UNDP Sri Lanka, uses Human Rights Based Approach to Development (HRBA) which is defined as "a conceptual framework for the process of human development that is normatively based on international human rights standards and operationally directed to promoting and protecting human rights" (Pilapitiya 2004: 4). While showing that this approach contains some important elements to include "express linkages to right, accountability, empowerment, participation, and attention to disadvantaged groups", she insists that "the results envisaged by the HRBA cannot be achieved" because of *corruption*, which affects the poor disproportionately, due to their powerlessness to change the status quo and inability to pay bribes (Pilapitiya 2004: 4). So what she sees is that while the United Nations agreed that human rights must be mainstreamed into all development programs, yet the HRBA literature does not explicitly consider corruption, and corruption literature does not discuss its impact on HRBA, and suggests that the issue needs to be directly tackled if HRBA is to be credible and effective.

> If the duty bearers are corrupt, none of the three points [of HRBA main points formulated by UN in 2004] can be achieved. If the duty bearers in the justice sector are corrupt, this is even more serious, as the justice sector is tasked with upholding and protecting the rights of the rights holders. Whether corruption is need based (as in the case of poorly paid low level officials who need the bribe to pay for food or schooling) or greed based (as in more highly paid officials who don't need the bribe to survive), this will have the effect of making HRBA redundant. (Pilapitiya 2004: 7)

While recognizing that HRBA neither has an impact on all causes of corruption, nor succeeds in the presence of corruption, yet she notes that corruption indeed has negative impact to development. Quoting the Seoul findings on 11th International Anti-corruption Conference, May 2003, that condemned "corruption as immoral, unjust and repugnant to the ideal of humanity enshrined in the Universal Declaration of Human Right", and that "confirmed the conviction that all human beings have a basic human right to live in a corruption-free society", she further reiterates the notion that "large scale corruption should be designated a crime against humanity, as for many around the world it falls into the same category as torture, genocide and other crimes against humanity that rob humans of human dignity" (Pilapitiya 2004: 9).

Kanokkan Anukansai, a program manager of Transparency Thailand, also seeks to clarify the interconnection between corruption and human rights, but instead of seeking a connection between corruption and the broader issue of development, Anukansi addresses a conceptual linkage between the two and he sees corruption as the catalyst to violate human rights. Anukansai explains his findings into four propositions. First, corruption for him is "about power, power relation and abuse of power", suggesting that "relationship between corruption and violation of human rights is framed by this unequal power relation" and thus "human rights are subjected to violation when power is abused by corrupt practices", while admitting that "not all forms of human rights violation result from corruption" (Anukansai 2010: 7). Second, the forms the human rights violation as a harmful consequence of corruption takes can be direct or indirect. Direct violation is "when some corrupts acts are deliberately used as a means to violate a right and thus it takes the place when corruption itself is a part of the violation" (Anukansai 2010: 8), while indirect violation is "when corruption becomes a necessary condition for human rights violation" or "when corruption is seen as an origin of subsequent human right violation" and thus one can see this "causes deteriorating effects but it is not an act of human rights violation itself" (Anukansai 2010: 10). Third, in a situation when the abuse of power in a large scale is the source of problem, "grand and endemic corruption heightens massive human rights violation, conflict and violence" (Anukansai 2010: 11). Anukansai points at the conflict in Niger Delta, where authority have been extremely corrupt and so "with endemic corruption, the conflict and violence will cease to end" and "will inevitable result in ongoing violations of human rights in various forms" (Anukansai 2010: 11). Fourth and lastly, corruption exacerbates human right violations and exploitations. Because of the nature of a power relation perspective, Anukansai notes "corrupt people who possess higher status and power will attempt to maintain their position of power", and so people who are vulnerable and lacking power under their domination will be easily oppressed by them, and "in this sense, corruption is an instrument that helps to define, sustain, expand or reduce the social order on the basis of unequal power between the powerful and the powerless" (Anukansai 2010: 13). So, Anukansai concludes that the ways in which corruption leads to human rights violation explain the relationship between human rights and corruption, and the two are closely interconnected.

> Acts of corruption can directly and indirectly violate human rights and especially exacerbate violation of human rights of the disadvantaged. These two acts are complimentary. Reducing one helps to lessen the others. To resolve one issue could possible lead to another issue. Therefore, anti-corruption measures need a human right perspective. Similarly effective human rights protection measures need to incorporate and integrate anti-corruption measures as well (Anukansai 2010: 14).

So, it is plausible to accept the notions that corruption violates human rights and that the needs to respect and uphold human rights value are seriously threatened by the very corrupt acts. The matter proves to be very serious especially when the so called human rights violators are state institutions or agents of state, and so, corruptions by the state officials, which sometimes are done in collaboration with international agents, endanger the needs to respect and uphold the human rights values. However, the fact remains that unlike the position generally held by this mainstream view, progress in the fight against corruption has not received blanket support from the worldwide academic community.

We can now go on to consider the second, non mainstream views. One of the exemplars of this non–mainstream view that is going to be taken into account is the work of Samuel Huntington. In his "Political Order in Changing Societies" (1968), he suggested that the phenomena of corruption in the context of many modernizing countries is "part not so much the result of the deviance of behavior from accepted norms as it is the deviance of norms from the established patterns of behavior" (1968: 60). As corruption for him refers to "behavior of public officials which deviates from accepted norms in order to serve private ends", corruption correlated "reasonably well with rapid social and economic modernization" (Huntington, 1968: 59) and is by no means "inimical to growth and development in the 1960's and 1970's" (Gathii 2007: 12). As Huntington (1968) notes:

> Just as the corruption produced by the expansion of political participation helps integrate new groups into the political system, so also the corruption produced by the expansion of governmental regulation may help stimulate economic development. Corruption may be one way of surmounting tradi-

tional laws or bureaucratic regulations which hamper economic development (Huntington 1968: 68)

Furthermore, in explaining why modernization breed, corruption, Huntington noted that this correlates with the following factors, first, modernization involves a change in the basic values of the society, and this "means the gradual acceptance by groups within the society of universalistic and achievement-based norms, the emergence of loyalties and identifications of individuals and groups with the nation-state, and the spread of the assumption that citizens have equal rights against the state and equal obligation to the state" (Huntington 1968: 60). Second, corruption is also a consequence of modernization since the latter creates new sources of wealth and power, and the relation of which to politics is undefined by the dominant traditional norms of society and on which the modern norms are not yet accepted by the dominant groups within the society (Huntington 1968: 61). Thirdly, corruption was also encouraged by the changes the modernization produces on the output side of the political system, adding that the initial adherence to modern values by a group in a transitional country often takes an extreme form (Huntington 1968: 61). According to Huntington, this fanatical anticorruption mentality has ultimate effects similar to those of corruption itself which together challenge the autonomy of politics: one substituting private goals for public ones, and the other replacing political values with technical ones (Huntington 1968: 63). Huntington suggested, therefore, that reducing corruption in a society "often involves both a scaling down of the norms thought appropriate for the behavior of public officials and at the same time changes in the general behaviors of such officials in the direction of those norms" (Huntington 1968: 63).

As James Thuo Gathii has observed, corruption for Huntington "was important for purpose of national integration as it was for stimulating economic development," even though, according to Gathii, Huntington predicated his hope on the false optimism of the future of newly independent countries becoming developed as a matter of course, while Gathii also expresses his concern with regard to the supports for Huntington unacceptable ideas,

> This optimism was buoyed by the fact that the U.S. had experienced speedy growth as a result of similar corruption in the 1870's and 1880's particularly at the state level with the emerging giant railroad and utility corporations. Other leading scholars such as Joseph S. Nye supported this view giving it further credibility. Even scholars from a Marxist orientation overlooked corruption premising their hopes on Africa's future less to the history of medieval Europe than to the "successful" economic planning that had turned the Soviet Union into a great power within a very short period of time (Gathii 2007: 13).

According to Gathii, while corruption may have led to the emergence of an entrepreneurial class in medieval Europe and in gilded-age era of the U.S., corruption may not and did not necessarily lead to the same consequences in sub-Saharan Africa, and quoting Pranab Bardhan argument, Gathii notes that in developing countries, corruption feeds upon itself for a number of reasons. First, because it is beneficial for both the payee and the payer. Second, because it is so entrenched that it becomes a self-fulfilling prophecy and third, because once corruption takes root in a society it is hard to eliminate or win back trust (Gathii 2007: 13–14).

With Gathii, this paper suggests that such a view advanced by Pranab Bardhan is a much more nuanced understanding of the persistence of corruption, as it does not presume that a one-time anti-corruption campaign or a simple reversal of corrupt behavior will eliminate corruption, while it does not also presume that corruption in societies where it is endemic is there to stay. And as we will see latter in the next part, this also implies an important notion that anti-corruption measures ought to combine human rights and constitutionalism with broad public support in order to be effective.

A point worth underlining here is that while the non–mainstream views of the corruption and human rights nexus such as that defended by Huntington may give an impression of stressing the *instrumental* justification of the corruption and human rights nexus, that is, focused merely on analyzing the effects of corruption on the development in modernizing countries, one can see that it is "the mainstream views" such as those advanced by Thusita Pilapitiya, and Kanokkan Anukansai, that arguably have greater hope for taking into account the intrinsic justifications, as they are premised on the notion that there is connection between corruption and human rights, and so, it is reasonable to assume that there is a greater possibility to develop an argument of intrinsic justification, that is, by questioning if there is something *intrinsically* good about human rights and anti-corruption acts, or that whether they are good even if it is not able always to achieve desirable consequences. As the next part of this paper attempts to show, there is a value for seeing the human rights and corruption nexus in this way. In what follows we are going to consider the deeper roots of the practices of corruption and the violations of human rights in Indonesia especially under the New Order government which arguably lays on the fact that Indonesia had embraced state perfectionism, represented in the idea of integralism (Negara Integralistik), which was crucial in influencing the fundamental spirit of 1945 Indonesian Constitution. We are going to see how this state perfectionism might have provided a fertile ground for the culture of political corruption and human rights violations in Indonesia especially under the New Order State, before finally discussing the ability of a dominant liberal human rights discourse to capture the true nature of human rights violations and corruptions in Indonesia.

Corruption in Indonesia: Perfectionist State and a Dominant Liberal Human Rights Discourse

As the data drawn from Corruption Perception Index indicate a definite correlation between corruption and human rights abuses, it is perhaps relevant to take Indonesia into account with regard to the discussion of corruption and human rights. For one thing, Indonesia is noted to have a reputation as one of the most corrupt countries in the world, which Transparency International reported in

2010 that Indonesia is ranked 110th out of 178 countries in the Corruption Perception Index 2010 (TI 2010).

Political corruptions[1] in Indonesia have a long and complicated history, while the persistence of the rampant corruption poses not only a serious challenge to the country but also warrant a plausible explanation of its basic causes, and some indeed had attempted to explain the mechanism by which corruption occurred and has become widespread in Indonesia (McLeod 2000; King 2000; Hart 2001). Moreover, while many see that authoritarian regime in Indonesia has gone since the downfall of President Suharto in May 21, 1998, and so one might suppose that the process of implementing human rights in the country would be more promising, there remained a strong indication that "opposition to human rights still persist", and some even believe that "there seem to be deeper processes that tend to work against a liberal convergence of values in the region" (Asplund 2009: 28). Thus, the opposition to human rights in Indonesia remains to be an issue, and this may account for the nature of current rampant corruption in Indonesia.

Let us look deeper into how Indonesia's state was imagined since its inception. Knut D. Asplund in his "Resistance to Human Rights in Indonesia: Asian Values and Beyond" (2009) notes that individual freedom tends to be little emphasized in the Indonesian human rights discourse, while he states that "despite a somewhat indifferent attitude towards "individuals freedom", Indonesian are no stranger to "freedom" *merdeka* (or *kebebasan*) which is the equivalent term in Indonesia" (Asplund 2009: 31). As Asplund further explains,

> [t]he idea that freedom is an important prerequisite for a good life has long been well established in Indonesia. The term has, however, come to be as regularly associated with political freedom; that of smaller communities relative autonomy versus larger kingdoms, but particularly freedom stemming from the emancipation of colonized people, or process of national liberation...[and] although not equally potent, the first of "individual freedom"; "individual" also has strong connotations insinuating individualism. In some circles in Indonesia, individualism is perceived as characteristically western trait; a life stance able to find foothold only within a society where the link between the person and community has been cut. The "individual" is thus someone who is not complying norms in a given place, someone who is not bound by the village's unwritten rules, someone who has escaped and threatens the social order (Asplund 2009: 32).

Asplund's explanations about the meaning of freedom and individualism may not completely reflect the contemporary Indonesian political culture, but his insistence on the values of communitarianism and the idea of good that are supposed to characterize the Indonesian political culture may have well described the deeper nature of Indonesia's old Constitution, and this would serve well to understand the deeper roots of opposition to human rights in Indonesia. I will argue that the development of Indonesian political culture has been influenced by the idea of state perfectionism (or teleologism/communitarianism) that had dominated the state's construction in general and of Indonesian state–civil society relation in particular.

Focusing particularly on the debates of the formation of Indonesian Constitution, I will point to two choices available with regard to the values underlying considerations of the Indonesia state formation; liberalism on the hand one, and communitarianism on the other hand. Liberalism defends the importance of "state–neutrality", or "neutral state" which means that a state should not "justify its action on the basis of the intrinsic superior or inferiority of conception of the good life, and which does not deliberately attempt to influence people judgments of the value of these different conception", while the communitarianism defends the idea of "a perfectionist state", because it is assumed that people makes mistakes about the good life, so the state has the responsibility to teach its citizens about a virtuous life, with its corollary that "people are not free…to choose their own conception of the good life, at least not without being penalized by society" (Kymlicka 1990: 205).

As alluded to earlier, the establishment of the Indonesian state reflects the rivalry of the above two fundamental values, even though one may argue that the spirit of the original Indonesian Constitution, known as the 1945 Constitution i.e. *Undang-Undang Dasar (UUD) Republik Indonesia* in 1945, was very much shaped by communitarian assumptions, rather than liberal ones. An architect of the UUD 1945, Supomo, introduced the idea of organicist state or integralistic state in the Constitution, and rejected the very idea of separation of power and checks and balances, and paying not much attention to the danger of "the accumulation of all power in the same hand" and ignoring the need to consider, as Madison in the United State once puts it, the "auxiliary precautions". Thus, in comparison to those of the considerations that have inspired the formation of US Constitution, the underlying consideration of Indonesian Constitution was starkly different. While attention to communitarianism may not completely be absence in the case of the formation of U.S. Constitution,[2] and while the U.S. founding fathers believed that the legal restrain of conflict among political interests could be achieved by the creation of separate and distinct departments, and so political practices built into the Constitution would sustain restrained inter–branch conflict, the formation of Indonesian state Constitution seems to have been built on a very different assumption. Unlike those of the US, Indonesian founding fathers were very much preoccupied with the issue of goodness, such as the questions about "principles of state" or "dasar Negara" (the state basis). The implication of Soepomo's philosophical conception has been widely known. As a defender of the organicism or integralism, he suggested that the task of the state was "not to guarantee the interest of either individuals or groups, but rather to protect the interests of the whole society". The state according to Soepomo was coterminous with "the social order as a whole", in which "all groups, all parts and all members are bound tightly to one another to form organic unity in society" (Bourchier 1996: 78–79). While Soepomo's organicism or integralism rejected all the notions of *separation of powers* and *check balances* known in the democratic constitutional orders, he suggested that the Indonesian State should be established in accordance with the Indonesian social structure and character, so the Indonesian state must base itself on the integralist *statesidee,* in which the state unites with the entire people and stands above all groups in every field of endeavor and so, it is unsurprising that Soepomo rejected the idea of safeguard to protect individuals from abuse of power and the need for human rights protection.

Supomo's integralistic state is deliberately mentioned here since it was very influential especially after being regenerated by the New Order Suharto government in the mid 1980s, to describe what is called "nilai-nilai asli" (the original values) that shaped "kepribadian Indonesia" (Indonesian identity) even though the claim of "integralistic state" to underlie the Indonesian original values has been strongly refuted by scholars (Bourchier 1996). Such a theory of the good (perfectionism, teleologism or communitarism) may continue to influence the thinking and behavior of some contemporary Indonesian leaders and people alike, but the point I want to make here is that it is this kind of value that embedded so deeply within the Indonesian culture and norms that accounts for the very constraints of reform directed against corruption and the violations of human rights in Indonesia, but also explain the deeper roots by which Indonesia government may have mistakenly overemphasized the values of relativism and tended to undermine the universality of human rights principles. Arguably, it was such a claim of uniqueness and relativism that was used to justify the model of state during the New Order Suharto government era and that had resulted in the rampant corruptions and the violations of human rights.

Now, a point that I wanted to suggest is that treating human rights by merely emphasizing the relativist discourse of it is mistaken, but it is equally wrong to see human rights as universal in its application. On the hand one, in the case of Indonesia under the New Order Suharto leadership, the idea of integralism or "integralitic state" (Negara integralistik), as mentioned previously, had a practical function by which some forms of repression and abuse of power were perpetrated in clear defiance of the international covenant and human rights principles, while it also represented a stumbling block by which Indonesian people were less able to exercise their rights effectively. Thus it was then not so surprising why corruptions were pervasive under Suharto's authoritarian regime (see McLeod 2000). Part of the reason perhaps was that, as Anwar Ibrahim noted, "authoritarian rule more often than not has been used as masquerade for kleptocracies, bureaucratic incompetence, and worst of all, for unbridled nepotism and corruption" (cited in Donnelly 2003: 110).

On the other hand, an argument that human rights is universal in its application, is beneficial to all people, and thus is—and should be—exportable, represents "a dominant liberal human rights discourse," and it is equally mistaken. As Geeta Chowdhry explains, "it is universal only in pretension, not in practice", besides "international human rights are a ruse for the exercise of realpolitik as the US (and the West) emerge as the leader of human rights," and thus, for a postcolonialist like Geeta Chowdhry, it is essential for scholars to advance human rights that is "historically grounded and "context specific", while at the same time also "locate their analysis...in the imperial juncture" (Chowdhry 2004: 230–233). Similarly, despite noting the hegemonic influences and sustainability of core international human rights principles and values, Sheila Nair also suggests that a dominant liberal human rights discourse "suffers its own erasures although it renders human rights as universal, timeless and inclusionary" (Nair 2004: 256), adding that "a postcolonial rereading of human rights discourse allows us to….shows how human rights abuses are shaped by both contemporaneous and historical conditions" (Nair 2004: 260).

Following postcolonial scholars like Chowdhry and Nair, this essay attempts to balance "relativist" and "universalist" analyses by showing how an authoritarian rule, such as Suharto, retains relativist position to secure his own power, while it also considers an alternative, postcolonial aspiration to investigate how regimes of power, like those of a dominant liberal human right discourse" enables and produces certain kinds of human rights practices and abuses. Thus, even though the "liberal human rights discourse" has been arguably applicable to the cases of human rights violations and of the rampant corruption in Indonesia, it will be shown that this dominant liberal discourse is less able to capture the true nature of human rights violations and corruptions in Indonesia. There are at least two illustrations for this.

First, it is unfair, if not fully unthinkable, to separate the current practices of corruption in Indonesia from the roles played by the Western, external powers. Like many developing and third world countries, Indonesia not only suffered from colonialism, but also has inherited a culture of corruption for a long time before its independence in 1945. As some commentators note, even under the Dutch colonial administration, there were the bureaucratic traditions that not actually open to insight from ordinary citizens (Scott 2002: 123–38), and even there had already been a collusion between its business interests and colonial administrations (Quah 1999: 483–94). This does not mean to suggest that the current widespread corruption in Indonesian should be attributed solely to its colonial past or that it has become the sole responsibility of Western powers, given that there was a time when the traditional corruption in Indonesia was eroded especially when there was an increasing critical attitude against the corrupt bureaucratic behaviors during the postwar era (Quah 1999: 486). However, suffice it to say that the unusually aberrant characteristics that marked the current Indonesian public bureaucrats and leaders must also be related to various factors including the Western dominant power. As Rajeswary Ampalavanar Brown points out, there was the paradoxical role played by the IMF, World Bank, and IFC in shaping the organization and regulation of the Indonesian bureaucracy since 1980, in which "they became part of the problem" (Brown 2006: 955), and this assessment may underline the many critical views against the liberal discourse on human rights such as spoken by Noam Chomsky and Mahathir Mohamad that "the liberal discourse is comprised by its complicity with capital, which significantly reworks its political implications" (cited in Nair 2004: 258).

Second, the dominant liberal human rights discourse fails in considering states' authority in determining the human rights and corruption eradication agenda and how they determine the agenda in accordance with domestic challenges and situations. In this connection, Sheila Nair gives an illustration of "the establishment of official and government—appointed human rights commission" which functions as legitimacy for a government being accused of violation of human rights despite its stated purpose to address the problem of human rights (Nair 2004: 257). The same phenomenon applies with regard to such institution as "Corruption Eradication Team" (Team Pemberantasan Korupsi) which was created in June 1968 under the Indonesian Suharto government, but was "ineffective because its efforts were blocked by influential men in the regime (Quah 1999: 486). While Indonesia in the post authoritarian's regime still believe in the efficacies of such institutions to address its domestic human rights and corruption issues, the development of such institutions reflect the very inadequacy of the liberal human rights model as states' adherence to this model has been very uneven and unpredictable (cf Nair 2004: 257).

Finally, another example of how a dominant liberal human rights discourse has misleadingly assumed is that democracy, which guarantees respect for people rights, must be translated into some forms of political decentralization. This may be in line with conventional wisdom that generally takes the incentive for corruption as being correlated with some types of government structure, and thus the formula offered is that "the more centralized the government, the more 'fused' political power in it, and the less access that the press has to government, the more likely that corrupt official will survive attempts to prosecute them" (cited in Kristiansen and Ramli 2006: 207–33; see also Henry 2010: 133; Blair 2000: 21–29 and Breton 1996).

Even though it does make sense to suggest that "countries with more political rights and civil liberties should have lower level of corruption", however "democracy does not guarantee clean government" (Shen and Williamson 2005: 329). In the case of Indonesia, the drives toward decentralization have been quite strong especially after 1998 because of the sentiment against the highly centralized political and economic system under the authoritarian's Suharto rule (see, e.g. Firman 2009; Kristiansen and Pratikno 2006; Kristiansen et al. 2009). However, against this mistaken development, various recent studies suggest that in practice the policy of decentralization in Indonesia has little positive impact for the fight against corruptions and tended to reactivated "money politics" and undemocratic practices at local level, and so with decentralization corruption problems have become larger and more destructive because this "has facilitated regional government official to maximize their own individual gains with small risks of control and sanctions," and so, in the words of MacIntyre, "the country now suffers from hundreds of little Suharto's" (MacIntyre 2003: 519). While this would imply that "decentralization may need to be context specific, and some socio-economic conditions may have been overlooked in the eagerness to make devolution reforms in Indonesia" (Kristiansen and Pratikno 2006: 519), this peculiar problem of decentralization and the increase of decentralization of corruption also suggest that the liberal human rights discourse has failed to capture the true nature of corruption in Indonesia.

Conclusion

This essay has examined the two views pertinent to human rights and corruption nexus, and it has been argued that the mainstream view is more plausible than the non–mainstream one. The rampant political corruption and human rights violations in a country seem to have to do with deeper values that may be used to justify its political culture and institutions. In the case of the New Order Suharto's authoritarian rule, this was rooted in the idea of state perfectionism, and this has arguably been responsible for the explanation of rampant political corruption and human rights abuses in Indonesia.

This by no means suggests that a dominant liberal human rights discourse, which, among others envisions the universality of human rights and gives a priority to the civil and political rights, is without a problem and limitation. Following postcolonial scholars like Chowdhry and Nair, this essay has attempted to balance "relativist" and "universalist" analyses by showing how an authoritarian rule, such as that of Suharto Indonesia, had retained relativist position to secure his own power, while it also considers an alternative, postcolonial aspiration to investigate how regimes of power, like that of a dominant liberal human right discourse enables and produces certain kinds of human rights practices and abuses. With this, we have attempted to find a balance between a pretentious and unrealistic universalism on the one hand, and a paralyzing cultural relativism, on the other hand, and at least, to recognize that there seems to be a way, to bridge the gap between the Western perceptions and non-Western ones with regard to the issues of human rights and corruption.

References

Anukansai, K., 2010. Corruption: The Catalyst of Violation of Human Rights. *National Anti-Corruption Commission,* 2010. http://www.nacc.go.th/images/journal/kanokkan.pdf (accessed November 17, 2010).

Asplund, K. D., 2009. Resistance to Human Rights in Indonesia: Asian Values and Beyond. *Asia-Pacific Journal on Human Rights and the Law,* 10, no.1: 27–47.

Blair, H., 2000. Participation and Accountability at the Periphery: Democratic Local Governance in Six Countries. *World Development* 28, no. 1: 21–39.

Bourchier, D., 1996. *Lineages of Organicist Political Thought in Indonesia.* (Unpublished doctoral dissertation). Monash University, Australia.

Breton, A., 1996. *Competitive Governments: An Economic Theory of Politics and Public Finance.* New York: Cambridge University Press.

Brown, R. A., 2006. Indonesian Corporations, Cronyism, and Corruption. *Modern Asian Studies,* 40, no. 4: 953–992.

Chowdhry, G., 2004. Postcolonial Interrogations of Child Labor: Human Rights, Carpet Trade, and Rugmark in India. *Power, Poscolonialism and International Relations: Reading Race, Gender, and Class,* edited by Getta Chowdhry and Sheila Nair, 225–253. London and New York: Routledge.

Dallmayr, F., 2002. 'Asian Values' and Global Human Rights. *Philosophy East and West* 52, no. 2 (April): 173–189.

Donnelly, J., 1984. Cultural Relativism and Universal Human Rights. *Human Rights Quarterly* 6 no. 4 (November): 400–419.

———. 2003. *Universal Human Rights in Theory and Practice Second Edition.* Ithaca: Cornell University Press.

Eigen, P., 2004. Corruption is a Human Rights Issue. *Paper for the 2004 Business and Human Rights Seminar*, (December 9). http://www.bhrseminar.org/2004%20Documents/ Peter_Eigen_09.12.04.doc (accessed November 17, 2010).

Falk, R., 2004. Think again: Human Rights. *Foreign Policy* (March/April). http://www.foreignpolicy.com/articles/2004/03/01/think_again_human_rights (accessed November 17, 2010).

Feng, K., 2010. The Human Rights Implications of Corruption: An Alien Tort Claims-Act Based Analysis. *Wharton Research School Scholar Journal* (2004, April 24). http://repository.upenn.edu/Wharton_research_scholars/6 (accessed November 17).

Firman, T., 2009. Decentralization Reform and Local-Government Proliferation in Indonesia: Towards a Fragmentation of Regional Development. *Review of Urban and Regional Development Studies (RURDS)* 21, no. 2/3 (July/November): 143–157.

Gathii, J.T., 2007. Defining the Relationship between Corruption and Human Rights. *Albany Law School Research Paper*, 33 (July 28–29). http://papers.ssrn.com/sol3/papers.cfm?abstract_id=1342649 (accessed November 17, 2010).

Hart, N. H., 2001. Anti-corruption Strategies in Indonesia. *Bulletin of Indonesian Economic Studies* 37, no. 1: 65–82.

Henry, N., 2010. *Public administration and public affairs*. New Delhi: PHI Learning Private Limited.

Huntington, S. P., 1986. *Political Order in Changing Society*. New Haven: Yale University Press.

ICHR and Transparency International, 2009. Corruption and Human Rights: Making the Connection. *International Council on Human Rights Policy*. http://www.ichrp.org/files/reports/40/131_web.pdf (accessed November 17, 2010).

Kausikan, B., 1993. Asia's Different Standard. *Foreign Policy* 92 (September 22) 24–41. http://www.highbeam.com/doc/1G1-14397463.html (accessed November 17, 2010).

King, D.Y., 2000. Corruption in Indonesia: A Curable Cancer? *Journal of International Affairs*, 53, no. 2: 603–624. http://www.accessmylibrary.com/article-1G1-62361356/corruption-indonesia-curable-cancer.html (accessed November 17, 2010).

Kristiansen, S. and Y. Pratikno, 2006. Decentralizing Education in Indonesia. *International Journal of Educational Development* 26 no. 5: 513–531.

Kristiansen, S. and M. Ramli, 2006. Buying an Income: The Market for Civil Service Positions in Indonesia. *Contemporary Southeast Asia* 28 no. 2: 207–33.

Kristiansen, S., A. Dwiyanto, A. Pramusinto, and E. A. Putranto, 2009. Public Sector Reforms and Financial Transparency: Experiences from Indonesian Districts. *Contemporary Southeast Asia* 31, no. 1: 64–87.

Kumar, C.R., 2002. Corruption and Human Rights: The Human Rights to Corruption Free-Service, Some Constitutional and International Perspective.

Frontline, India's National Magazine 19 (14–27 September). http://www.frontlineonnet.com/fl1919/19190780.htm (accessed November 17, 2010).

Kymlicka, W., 1990. *Contemporary political philosophy: An introduction.* Oxford: Clarendon Press.

MacIntyre, A., 2003. Institutions and the Political Economy of Corruption in Developing Countries. *Asia-Pacific School of Economics and Management, Australian National University,* 2003. http://www.cdi.anu.edu.au/_research/1998-004/research_publications/research_downloads/ StanfordCorruption paper.pdf (accessed November 17, 2010).

McLeod, R.H., 2000. Soeharto's Indonesia: A Better Class of Corruption. *The Indonesian Quarterly* 7, no. 2: 99–112. http://epress.anu.edu.au/agenda/007/02/7-2-A-1.pdf (accessed November 17, 2010).

Muzaffar, C., 1999. From Human Rights to Human Dignity. *Debating Human Rights: Critical Essays from the United States and Asia,* edited by Peter Van Ness, 25–31. New York: Routledge.

Nair, S., 2004. Human Rights and Postcoloniality: Representing Burma. *Power, Postcolonialism and International Relations: Reading Race, Gender and Class,* edited by Geeta Chowdhry and Sheila Nair, 254–284. New York and London: Routledge.

Nickel, J. W., 2007. *Making Sense of Human Rights.* Second Edition. Oxford: Blackwell Publishing.

Pilapitiya, T., 2004. The Impact of Corruption on the Human Rights Based Approach to Development. *UNDP Oslo Government Center* (September). http: //www.undp.org/oslocentre/docs05/Thusitha_final.pdf (accessed November 17, 2010).

Quah, J.S.T., 1999. Corruption in Asian countries: Can it be Minimized? *Public Administration Review* 59, no. 6: 483–94.

Rajagopal, B., 1999. Corruption, Legitimacy and Human Rights: The Dialectic of the Relationship. *Connecticut Journal of International Law* 14, no. 2: 1–11.

Scott, J.C., 2002. Handling Historical Comparisons Cross-Nationally. *Political Corruption: Concepts and Contexts,* edited by A.J. Heidenheimer and M. Johnston, 123–38. New Jersey: Transaction Publishers.

Shen, C., and J.B. Williamson, 2005. Corruption, Democracy, Economic Freedom and State Strength a Cross-National Analysis. *International Journal of Comparative Sociology* 46, no. 4 (August): 327–345.

Terracino, J.B., 2008. Corruption as a Violation of Human Rights. *International Council on Human Rights Policy.* http://papers.ssrn.com/sol3/papers.cfm?abstract_id=1107918# (accessed 11/17/2010).

Transparency International, 2010. *Corruption perceptions index 2010 Results.* http://www.transparency.org/policy_research/surveys_indices/cpi/2010/resu lts (accessed November 17, 2010).

Van Ness, P., 1999. Introduction. *Debating Human Rights: Critical Essays from the United States and Asia,* edited by Peter Van Ness, 1–21. New York: Routledge.

Wolff, J., 2006. *An Introduction to Political Philosophy.* Revised Edition, Oxford: Oxford University Press.

Notes

1. Political corruption is one among various classifications of corruption that has important human rights implications, and by political corruption it means "political leaders use the control and authority bestowed upon them on behalf of the general public interest for their personal benefit" (Feng 2004: 9).

2. Since the very beginning American founding fathers, like James Madison, clearly considered the value of the Judeo-Christian conception of human nature, in which they believe that because their "fallen" status mankind's virtue too often gave way to unpredictable passion and interests neglectful of the liberties of others.

CHAPTER 5

Human Rights and Indigenous Self-Government: The Taiwanese Experience

Scott Simon and Awi Mona (Chih-Wei Tsai)

The United Nations Declaration on the Rights of Indigenous Peoples (UNDRIPs) was adopted by the UN General Assembly on September 13, 2007, with 144 states in favour, 11 abstentions. Only four states (Australia, Canada, New Zealand, and the United States) voted against UNDRIPs, and all of them subsequently decided to support the Declaration. Although UNDRIPs lacks the binding force and enforcement mechanisms of a Convention, this document reflecting more than two decades of international indigenous activism at the UN now serves as a moral compass for policy makers and indigenous rights advocates around the world. UNDRIPs, composed of 46 articles, is based on the fundamental right of self-determination. Article 3 states that "indigenous peoples have the right to self-determination." Article 4 stipulates that: "Indigenous peoples, in exercising their right to self-determination, have the right to autonomy or self-government in matters relating to their internal and local affairs, as well as ways and means for financing their autonomous functions" (United Nations 2007). All other rights, like human rights in general, are based on this fundamental *right of self-determination*. Indigenous peoples have this basic collective human right based on the recognition that they have suffered from historical injustice arising from colonization and dispossession of their lands. A critical reflection of "autonomy" or "self-government," taking into account different historical and social contexts, is thus important for both the advancement of indigenous rights and for a social scientific understanding of the global human rights movement of indigenism (Niezen 2003).

In Asia, only Japan, the Philippines, and the Republic of China on Taiwan recognized quickly in the wake of UNDRIPs that the Declaration applies to populations within their territories, and require domestic legal changes. Taiwan, which as a non-member of the UN General Assembly, could not even vote on

UNDRIPs, announced through the cabinet-level Council of Indigenous Peoples (CIPs) that Taiwan's indigenous policy accords with UNDRIPs. This declaration of the CIPs did not emerge from nowhere. Although the majority of Taiwan's population has historical roots in China, some 500,000 indigenous people (2.2 percent of the total population) are Austronesians, related to other peoples of the Pacific and Indian Ocean, and whose ancestors inhabited Taiwan for at least 6000 years before any Chinese settlement. Due to their continued presence on their island, and a history of different legal institutions from the mainstream Han (Chinese) population, especially different property rights regimes, Taiwan's Austronesian peoples quickly adopted an identity as indigenous and were recognized as such by the state. Taiwan, which held China's seat in the UN at the time, even signed one of the first international conventions dealing with indigenous rights, when they adopted the International Labour Organization (ILO) Indigenous and Tribal Peoples Convention C107 in 1962 (Iwan 2005: 33).

Taiwan has an autonomous grassroots indigenous rights movement since the 1980s (Allio 1998a, Stainton 1995) and a constitutional quota for indigenous legislators since 1991 (Allio 1998b, Iwan 2005)—both sources of political change in Taiwan and of delegations to events related to the UN Permanent Forum on Indigenous Issues. Over the past decades, as part of wider international trends, indigenous rights gained momentum in Taiwan, progressing from a 1999 presidential campaign promise, to cabinet-level discussions of indigenous provisions in a new constitution (Simon 2006, Xianfa Yuanzhu Minzu Zhengce Zhixian Tuidong Xiaozu 2005), and subsequently the 2005 passing of a *Basic Law on Indigenous Peoples*. Indigenous self-government or autonomy, one of the main demands of the indigenous social movement since its first days, has emerged as one of the main goals. The ROC Legislative Yuan, as of the writing of this chapter in January 2011, is currently studying the drafting of a bill on indigenous self-government. This will affect primarily the 14 tribes currently recognized by the government, especially if, as expected, self-government institutions will be established at the larger tribal, rather than community level.

Indigenous rights are by no means the imposition of external "universal" norms on the Third World. In fact, much of the impetus for indigenous rights has come from the Third World, beginning with Latin American initiatives at the International Labour Organization (ILO) to replace the more state-centric and assimilationist C107 with C169, the *Indigenous and Tribal Peoples Convention*, in 1989 (ILO 1989). This work, which according to ILO conventions, included input from labour unions as well as state representatives, provided the model for civil society contributions to the United Nations Permanent Forum on Indigenous Issues (UNPFII) and the writing of UNDRIPs.[1] UNDRIPs is thus unique among UN human rights instruments because it has been drafted with the participation of indigenous representatives themselves, and many of them from the Third World. It remains to be seen how it will contribute to a global reformulation of human rights.

The preamble of UNDRIPs recognizes that the situation of indigenous peoples varies from region to region according to various historical and cultural backgrounds; and that these differences should be taken into consideration. The study of these differences through case studies thus promises new insights on the global meaning of indigenous rights in particular and of human rights in general. Indigenous self-government, as the basis for all other rights promised by UN-DRIPs, is clearly the most pressing issue. Taiwan is a relatively understudied case, but, like others, one in which the recognition of indigenous rights is a rocky road with obstacles as well as significant steps forward. Considering the diversity of Taiwan's indigenous peoples and different colonial experiences, we find it useful to focus in this chapter exclusively on the Truku and Seediq peoples. We explore the following issues. How has indigenous self-government been framed in Taiwan by civil society and state actors? How are these initiatives influenced by historical factors unique to Taiwan? What obstacles remain? What lessons can be learned for other groups in the Third World from the experience of Taiwan's indigenous peoples?

Inherent Sovereignty: The Core Issue

Discussions of indigenous autonomy are often grounded in the concept of inherent sovereignty, the claim that indigenous peoples have inherent, natural rights to self-determination that have not been extinguished by colonization and encroachment on their lands. In terms of political philosophy, it is useful for heuristic purposes to identify a spectrum of possible positions on the issue of indigenous sovereignty. At one end of the spectrum is the international "constitutionalism" of James Tully, who, picking up on the theme of the *Haudensosaunee* Two Row Wampum Treaty, argues that indigenous nations have never abandoned their sovereignty. In North America, he argues, the history of treaty making gave "rise to a constitutional association of interdependence and protection, but not to discontinuity or subordination to a single sovereign" (Tully 1995: 126). Indigenous peoples thus possess natural, or inherent, sovereignty by virtue of being human, and this was not extinguished by the arrival of the nation–state. At the other end of the spectrum, Tom Flanagan calls indigenous sovereignty a "fiction," especially because indigenous peoples historically had no states, had no political continuity in the same locations, and have in treaties effectively recognized the sovereignty of the Crown (Flanagan 2008: 23–24). For him, inherent sovereignty is "only a rhetorical turn of phrase. It may produce domestic political results by playing on guilt or compassion, but it has no effect in international law or....in domestic law" (Flanagan 2008: 61). In Canada, he argues, the best indigenous leaders can hope for is constitutionally-protected self-government, like that of provinces and other local governments, that preserves the integrity of the Canadian state (Flanagan 2008: 87). UNDRIP seems closer to Flanagan's philosophy. The only mention of sovereignty in the entire document is Article 46, which protects "the territorial or political unity of sovereign and independent States" (United Nations 2007).

The concept of inherent sovereignty in Taiwan is expressed through the

Chinese *ziran zhuquan*, 自然主權, which was first proposed in a partnership agreement between DPP candidate Chen Shui-bian and leaders of Taiwan indigenous tribes during his 2000 electoral campaign. Article 1 of the *New Partnership Agreement between Indigenous Peoples and the Taiwanese Government* stated that the government shall recognize the indigenous inherent sovereignty. As President, Chen, on October 19, 2002, reconfirmed the agreement, which henceforth became an official document defining the guiding principles of government policy. The Executive Yuan pledged to ensure that indigenous peoples would have the tools to become self-sufficient and self-governing by recognizing indigenous rights to land and self-government. After being re-elected for a second term in 2004, President Chen declared that the government would commit to a nation-to-nation relationship with indigenous tribes and add a special indigenous chapter to the R.O.C. Constitution. These actions started a new indigenous rights dialogue between indigenous peoples and the Taiwan (R.O.C.) government. Finally, a milestone accomplishment for indigenous rights was reached when the Legislative Yuan passed the *Basic Law on Indigenous Peoples* in 2005. The idea of indigenous inherent sovereignty was incorporated in article 20, which stipulates that the government recognizes indigenous land and natural resources rights. The legal reasoning for this article shows that the definition of "indigenous peoples" affirms indigenous nations exist prior to any other political regimes, thus states must universally respect existing indigenous territorial and jurisdictional rights, as well as other derived indigenous land and natural resources rights (Legislative Yuan 2005).

Alternatively speaking, both the Truku and Seediq peoples' governing authority are revealed in the historical practice of territorial recognition. From a linguistic perspective, the eastern Seediq peoples' living area, i.e. their possession of the land, called *"drhilang"*. The meaning of *"drhilang"* embraces the exclusive control and exercise of authority over the specific territory; and is an integral part of the Seediq customary law of Gaya. Based on Shou-chen Liao's findings, different Gaya tribes and sub-Gaya groups have their own particular territory (Masaw, 1998: 23). The Seediq peoples traditionally conceptualized this territorial regime by using the term *"Drhilang* [the name of the Gaya group]." (Ibid.) For example, "Drhiling Gluban" refers to the territory of Gluban. At a higher level, "Drhiling Seediq" refers to the Seediq Gaya tribe's territory, which was made up by a number of sub-Gaya groups. In a legal sense, the highest-level pre–colonial Seediq polity was more like a confederation of different local Gaya groups which placed its highest governing authority in the tribal council composed of elders of equal stature. Since the sub-Gaya group (*alang*) was the most important unit of political autonomy, on difficult mountainous terrain that separated groups for most of the year, these confederations were subject to processes of fission as well as fusion. Looking back historically, the non–recognition of indigenous rights and lack of legal entitlement to indigenous self-government have gradually devastated indigenous communities and social structures. Taiwan's contemporary indigenous policy, based on the principle of indigenous self-government of the *Basic Law*, has broken new ground in the government's relationship with indigenous peoples because it promises to make tribal confederations into legal persons capable of negotiating the terms of self-government with the state.

Autonomy and Self-government in Taiwan: a Historical Path

Self-government was by no means unknown to the Seediq and Truku peoples before colonialism. As high mountain tribes, they were largely left alone by the Qing Dynasty Chinese state that slowly expanded its reach across the island's plains between 1683 and 1895. The Qing, in fact, even labelled maps of the island as areas of *shoufan* (lit. "cooked savages," who had submitted to Qing political institutions), and *shengfan* (lit. "raw savage," who maintained their own political institutions).[2] The Seediq and Truku peoples, like the closely related Atayal, were what political anthropologist Wei Hwei-lin (1965) classified as a "quasi-horde," or egalitarian society, in which temporary community leaders emerged according to their demonstrated ability for immediate needs. In general, they lived in small autonomous groups of around 50 people, in which all political decisions were made by consultation with the elders (*ludan*) in the name of the sacred law of *Gaya*. Although they did not create states or other formal high-level political institutions, they created confederation–like political links in the same river systems with other related communities (Masaw 1998: 23). The general pattern, as documented by Japanese survey anthropologists, was that they formed alliances and exchanged wives with communities along the same river valleys. This political system, remembered fondly by Seediq and Truku elders was described by Japanese survey anthropologist Kojima as "egalitarian, autonomous and republican. If one can say that they constitute a political body, one can say that they are a democratic system without equal" (Kojima 1996 [1915]: 235). This political autonomy, however, came to an end as the Japanese extended modern state institutions across the island.

Japan, which annexed Taiwan in 1895 under the provisions of the Sino-Japanese Treaty of Shimonoseki, was the first power to pacify all of Taiwan's indigenous peoples and subjugate them to state control. Inspired by American models of Indian policy, Japanese administrators forced indigenous communities to settle in fixed reserve forests and take up agriculture (Fujii 1997: 151), effectively living as state wards in contrast with the Chinese inhabitants who enjoyed private property rights. At the same time, they declared all forests, rivers, and mountains to be state property, thus making it possible for the Japanese to develop the camphor and other resources of the mountain forests (Tavares 2005). The major appropriation of indigenous territory was the seizure of forest commons by the colonial department of forestry through the promulgation of the Regulation of Nation Forest Management and Camphor Production in 1896. These lands are still vested in the Forestry Department of the current ROC administration. The colonial state also established formal chiefdoms and band councils that were ultimately under Japanese authority (Masaw 1998: 49). In spite of the obvious drawbacks to Japanese colonial rule, participation in these new institutions also created new goals for real self-determination within the state system. In 1945, Japanese rule of Taiwan was replaced by that of the Republic of China; Gao Yisheng of the Tsou tribe advocated that the island's indigenous peoples form one single autonomous district as part of a democratic Taiwan. Gao, who mobilized Tsou participation in 1947 demonstrations against ROC misrule, including an attack on the Chiayi airport, was arrested and finally executed in 1954 (Harrison 2001 : 63–66).[3]

In the 1945 *Plan for Taking Administration of Taiwan* (*Taiwan jieguan jihua*, 臺灣接管計畫), while civil war was still raging in China, the ROC government simply declared that the "savage tribes" (*fanzu*, 蕃族) would have the same rights to self-determination and autonomy (*zijue zizhi*, 自決自治) as all other Chinese minorities (Fujii 2001 : 156). The first concrete change in indigenous governance was to transfer indigenous affairs from the police to the Civil Administration Division (*Minzhengting*, 民政廳) of the Taiwan provincial government. Following the Republican ideology of the Three Principles of the People, the new government promised the indigenous people, now known as "mountain compatriots" (*shandi tongbao*, 山地同胞), a tri-pronged policy of economic development, status as peoples, and local autonomy. The declared goal was to "protect" the indigenous people while simultaneously assimilating them to the norms of other districts (Taiwan Shengzhengfu Minzhengting 1954: 6). In implementation, local autonomy meant the creation of thirty mountain townships and 159 villages with the institutions of primary schools, clinics, police stations, and administration offices. In the new electoral system, only mountain compatriots could become township magistrates. In contrast with the non–indigenous people, who experienced a land-to-the-tiller land reform, indigenous land remained state property, with indigenous individuals gaining only the right to buy and sell usufruct rights to reserve land to other indigenous individuals. All of the mountains and forests that had been declared state land by the Japanese were placed under the control of the incoming state. As for the political status of Indigenous peoples, quotas were established for provincial and national legislative bodies. The new administrative systems created a new indigenous elite dependent on the ruling KMT, the Chinese Nationalist Party, but was otherwise not substantive self-government (Rudolph 2003: 89–91). Under this administrative framework, and still under Martial Law, it was not yet possible for indigenous peoples to reclaim control of lands lost during a half-century of Japanese colonization.

In 1983, a group of anthropologists at Academia Sinica, charged with evaluating the human rights situation of Taiwan's indigenous peoples, demanded a legal status of indigenous autonomy (Li, et.al. 1983: 50). For the next decade, autonomy was a rallying cry for the indigenous social movement, which made demands to return lost land, as well as to rectify names. The land return movement included protests against mining companies (Simon 2002), national parks (Huang & Chang 2001), and other encroachments on indigenous territory, both on reserve land and on the wider traditional territories. In the first name rectification movement (*zhengming yundong*, 正名運動), indigenous activists demanded that the term "mountain compatriot" be replaced with "indigenous people." In 1994, the term "indigenous people" (*yuanzhumin*, 原住民) was included in a series of constitutional revisions. In 1997, following the 1996 creation of the Council of Indigenous Peoples, this was further revised to "indigenous peoples" (Allio 1998b: 47). The new constitutional amendment stated that, "The government shall, in accordance with the will of the peoples, protect the status and political participation of indigenous peoples," specifically in regard to education and culture, transportation and irrigation, health, economics and land, and social welfare.[4] This legal phrasing seemed to indicate that *peoples* would have rights to autonomy, and that autonomy would include greater control over land. In 1999, KMT legislator Cai Zhong-han of the Amis tribe thus proposed the first of several draft bills for the creation of indigenous autonomous zones (Huang 2008).

As democratization accelerated in the 1980s and 1990s, the newly-formed opposition Democratic Progressive Party (DPP) picked up the *Leitmotiv* of indigenous autonomy. In 1999, Chen Shui-bian signed the *New Partnership Agreement between Indigenous Peoples and the Taiwanese Government*. This document, which promised autonomy to large territorially–based tribes, was signed by Igung Shiban on behalf of the Truku and Presbyterian minister Watan Jiro for the Seediq. Ideas of indigenous autonomy were nourished by two closely related intellectual currents: the social justice theology of the Presbyterian Church of Taiwan (PCT) and the international indigenous people's movement. The PCT, in fact, had played a leading role in 1984 in the creation of Taiwan's first self-organized indigenous NGO, the Alliance of Taiwanese Aborigines (ATA) (Allio 1998a, Rudolph 2003: 86–87). In 1991, the ATA participated in the Working Group on Indigenous Peoples in Geneva (Rudolph 2003: 144, Allio 1998c: 58–60), the first of many UN meeting on indigenous issues. Through these networks, Taiwanese indigenous activists were able to introduce the most progressive goals and strategies to Taiwan.

Further progress was made during the DPP presidency from 2000 to 2008. In 2000, the CIP began studying examples of indigenous rights internationally, with the goal of proposing a law on autonomy. The resulting *Law of Indigenous Autonomous Zones* (*yuanzhu minzu zizhiqu fa*, 原住民族自治區法) with 104 articles defined all aspects of autonomy, but was reduced to 15 articles in the official version of June 3, 2003. Debates were moved to the Legislative Yuan, and four indigenous legislators (KMT or affiliated independents) proposed their own versions (Jin 2005). In the absence of a compromise, no law was passed. In 2004, however, the CIP held a series of workshops on how to incorporate indigenous rights into a new constitution, and autonomy was an important issue (Simon 2007, Xianfa Yuanzhu Minzu Zhengce Zhixian Tuidong Xiaozu 2005). On January 21, 2005, the KMT–dominated Legislative Yuan adopted the *Basic Law on Indigenous Peoples* (*yuanzhu minzu jibenfa*, 原住民族基本法). Article

4 stipulated that, "The government shall guarantee the equal status and development of self-governance of indigenous peoples and implement indigenous peoples' autonomy in accordance with the will of indigenous peoples. The relevant issues shall be stipulated by laws" (ROC Executive Yuan 2005). Article 5 required that the state provide budgets to develop autonomy, and Article 6 gave the Office of the President the power to resolve conflicts between indigenous groups and local governments. Throughout this legal history, one consensus emerged: indigenous peoples have the right to establish autonomous zones with their own governing institutions, territories, and budgets. The relevant law, however, has yet to be passed. It is thus not clear if indigenous peoples will regain control of traditional territories. It is also unclear if they will gain substantial autonomy as a co-constitution of a multi-national society, as envisioned by Tully's idea of indigeneity, or a legally protected local self-government on the order of municipalities, in terms similar to those outlined by Tom Flanagan.

Autonomy and Natural Resource Management

As popularized by the film *Avatar*, control of natural resources is a central issue in indigenous rights. Over millennia, indigenous peoples have continued to develop a profound interdependent relationship with their land, natural resources and territory. Though all human society invariably organized to a particular region, the most important characteristic of indigenous peoples attributes to their sacred relationship with the land and natural resources (Groves 1996: 128). For indigenous peoples, their interdependent relationship with the land is the foundation of spiritual and cultural worldviews. As Erica-Irene A. Daes stated, "The relationship with the land and all living things is at the core of indigenous societies." (Daes, 2001: 13) In other words, within traditional indigenous society, land and natural resources provide the basis of indigenous social recognition and identity; further to serve as the tribal spiritual and cultural distinctions. (Weaver, 1996) Therefore, land and natural resources have been universally affirmed to be the core values of indigenous cultures, and incorporated into international human rights conventions and instruments.[5]

For these reasons, Article 32 of UNDRIPs declares that 1) indigenous peoples have the right to determine and develop priorities for resource use on their lands and territories; 2) states must consult and cooperate in good faith with indigenous peoples for free, informed consent prior to approval of any resource exploitation on indigenous land; and 3) states shall provide mechanisms for redress and take appropriate measures to mitigate adverse impacts of such resource use (United Nations 2007). Taiwan's *Basic Law*, similarly has provisions for free, prior and informed consent for resource use. Article 21 says:

> The government or private party shall consult indigenous peoples and obtain their consent or participation, and share with indigenous peoples benefits generated from land development, resource utilization, ecology conservation and academic research in indigenous people's regions. In the event that the gov-

ernment, laws or regulations impose restrictions on indigenous peoples' utilization of their land and natural resources, the government shall first consult with indigenous peoples or indigenous persons and obtain their consent. A fixed proportion of revenues generated in accordance with the preceding two paragraphs shall be allocated to the indigenous peoples' development fund to serve as returns or compensations (ROC Executive Yuan 2005).

As for indigenous individuals, Article 19 of Taiwan's *Basic Law* permits them to hunt wild animals, collect wild plants and fungi, collect minerals, rocks and soils, and utilize water resources; albeit only under the conditions that these are non-profit seeking activities for the sole purposes of traditional culture, ritual or self-consumption (ROC Executive Yuan 2005). These issues are closely related, and derive from indigenous autonomy. Obviously, Article 21 can be implemented only if relevant self-government institutions exist *as legal persons* that can give or withdraw consent. In the absence of self-governing institutions, indigenous communities find themselves in situations in which their traditional lands as well as reserves are used for mining projects, tourist developments, tea plantations, national parks, and other forms of natural resource exploitation approved by township offices and various government ministries in the past; yet indigenous individuals are arrested for collecting rocks or trapping animals on the same lands. Many individuals find it unjust that mining companies, with township approval, can "legally" appropriate agricultural land or excavate entire hillsides (see Simon 2002), but individuals are arrested and face fines if they collect and polish river rocks for sale to tourists. Hunting and trapping practices are especially salient to indigenous men, who enjoy hunting, even in cases where it is only a leisure activity for workers returning from the cities. Early evaluations of Taiwan's indigenous human rights situation thus saw the criminalization of hunting as a reason for concern about indigenous rights (Zhongguo renquan xiehui 1987: 313). Furthermore, hunting in Seediq and Truku culture is intrinsically a ritual event that mediates relations between the living and the dead, as well as between humans and animals. Yet, to this day, hunting is illegal in national parks, trapping is illegal everywhere, and townships are only beginning to develop procedures by which individuals can apply for hunting permission for cultural activities. It remains difficult for indigenous men to hunt legally, even though the sharing of game meat is a fundamental aspect of Gaya (Simon 2009).

These issues can be difficult to resolve because of epistemological and ontological differences between indigenous stakeholders and non-indigenous state actors (Nadasdy 2003). Non-indigenous planners often mistakenly assume that indigenous people will inevitably urbanize and abandon rural practices such as hunting and trapping (Asch 1990). Many Canadian communities have thus tried to resolve these issues through co-management institutions. The 1975 *James Bay and Northern Québec Agreement* (JBNQA), for example, recognized the Grand Council of the Crees (GCC) as having negotiating power with the government, even as local band councils retained great autonomy. Québec and the Cree also established the Québec-Cree Hunting Trapping and Fishing Coordinating Committee (HTFCC) to give the two parties equal participation in policy decisions regarding wildlife use and conservation (Salisbury 1986, Scott 2005). In spite of good intentions, however, such institutions risk marginalizing indigenous perspectives, especially if an understanding of "tradition" in the use of Traditional Ecological Knowledge leads to a disregard for indigenous perspectives on "modern" activities such as mining or forestry (Nadasdy 2003: 121). In James Bay, for example, these assumptions have led to inadequate Cree control over forestry (Feit and Beaulieu 2001), which continues to leave forests open to "development" by outsiders and creates conflicts with non-indigenous sports hunters (Scott and Jeremy 2001). Taiwan can surely learn much from the successes, but perhaps even more from the failures, of these precedents.

On paper, Taiwan's provisions for consent over natural resource exploitation are even more strongly in favor of indigenous sovereignty than the standards set by UNDRIPs, or practices in Canada. Whereas in UNDRIPs, indigenous peoples determine their development priorities and states must consult with them "in good faith," there is still room for states to develop without that consent as long as redress is given and attempts are made to mitigate negative impacts. The JBNQA likewise gave the Québec government the "right to develop" over all but 1.3% of traditional Cree territory, the part that had been set aside for permanent settlements (Mulrennen and Scott 2001: 80–81). Taiwan's *Basic Law* requires that states and private parties not only consult with indigenous peoples, but also "*obtain* their consent or participation." The problem is that neither the state nor private parties such as mining companies can consult indigenous self-government bodies with the power to give consent. Township governments must, by their nature as elected powers, represent non-indigenous as well as indigenous constituents. Indigenous NGOs, even those created in preparation for eventual indigenous self-government, do not have the legal mandate to make such decisions. In the absence of formal institutions such as the GCC or even the HTFCC, indigenous communities in Taiwan are thus even less able than their counterparts in Canada to assert their rights to evaluate natural resource use projects, give consent, or manage wildlife. The political discourse on indigeneity in Taiwan underwent a transition from a "New Partnership" with indigenous peoples in 2000 to a "government-to-government relationship" in 2004. It was acknowledged that indigenous peoples have constitutional rights to represent themselves in negotiations with the government. Nevertheless, given the blurry content of the *Basic Law* and the uncertainty of political development, indigenous rights developments are mainly pursued on the political front and rely on often undependable compassion of the courts in Taiwan. The key issue remains that, in the absence of a self-government law, indigenous peoples do not yet exist as legal persons.

Judicial Issues

For a long time, there has been a conflict between indigenous legal construction, or ontology, and the state–based justice administration. Within the overarching constitutional principle of substantial equality and multiculturalism, a series of legal reforms for indigenous rights has been advocated from the grassroots indigenous community. Starting from the preservation and protection of indigenous hunting cultures, article 20 of the Statute For Controlling Firearms, Ammunition, and Weapons was revised in 2001 to the decriminalization of indigenous possession and use of hunting gun. Furthermore, in recognizing indigenous traditional rituals, article 21–1 of the Wildlife Act was added to allow indigenous cultural needs for hunting wild game through a process of application and review by township officials. In addition, for safeguarding indigenous basic subsistence and traditional livelihoods, Article 15 of the Forestry Act was amended to incorporate indigenous traditional use and utilization of forestry products within indigenous traditional territory. The aforementioned three regulations are centered on the protection of indigenous traditional livelihoods and culture performances in accordance with their customary laws. However, these regulations have posed certain requirements upon indigenous peoples to fulfill for their realization of these rights. Taking Article 15 (4) of the Forestry Act as an example, there exists three requirements for the realization of indigenous gathering right. First, the gathering activity must be conducted within indigenous traditional territory. Second, these forest products must be gathered for indigenous traditional living needs. And third, the gathering activity shall be part of indigenous traditional cultures. However, in the eyes of western–based National laws of Taiwan, these core concepts have been identified as indeterminate legal concepts (*ein Stück offengelassener Gesetzgebung*) needing substantiation through by-laws making. This, in turn, practically becomes a derogation clause for the indigenous rights' implementations, as the relevant by-laws and procedures are not uniformly implemented. For example, indigenous hunters—for whom the act of hunting is intrinsically a personal ritual linking them to nature, the ancestors, and Gaya—must apply to township officials to hunt a limited number of only certain animals in order to hunt legally as part of a collective ritual invented for that purpose. The new laws, although framed in terms of indigenous rights and multiculturalism, still conflict with Gaya. In actual practice, hunting "rituals," in the few villages that have tried to implement this law, are often tourist spectacles; whereas hunters following Gaya are prosecuted.

Retroactively speaking, indigenous people in Taiwan have endured racism and subaltern status in the social hierarchy for the past century. After four decades of an authoritarian regime and the lifting of Martial law, large-scale conflicts have become less frequent. Unfortunately, as they have decreased, domestic "legal violence" has risen in the ignorance of indigenous rights by the executive branches and justice departments, which constitute serious violations of fundamental indigenous human rights protected by international human rights law and domestic *Basic Law*. This chapter has demonstrated how domestic and international indigenous rights' developments have converged significantly on the protection of indigenous rights by recognizing and approving their guardianship over the land and natural resources (Anaya & Williams 2001: 42–53; Scheinin 2004). More importantly, international law affirms indigenous spiritual relationship with their land, and the embeddedness of indigenous beliefs, customs, traditions, and cultures (Gilbert, 2006: 139). Furthermore, indigenous peoples have formed multifaceted connections with their traditional territory and natural resources, including spiritual, cultural, economic and social dimensions,[6] all of which have contributed to the formation of indigenous peoples' customary legal systems pertaining to accommodating indigenous rights.[7]

In a similar context, Taiwan's *Basic Law* concludes in Article 30 with the declaration that:

> The government shall respect tribal languages, traditional customs, cultures and values of indigenous peoples in dealing with indigenous affairs, making laws or implementing judicial and administration remedial procedures, notarization, mediation, arbitration or any other similar procedure for the purpose of protecting the lawful rights of indigenous peoples. In the event that an indigenous person does not understand the Chinese language, an interpreter who speaks the tribal language shall be provided. For the purpose of protecting indigenous peoples' rights and access to the judiciary, indigenous peoples' court or tribunal may be established (ROC Executive Yuan 2005).

Quantitatively speaking, Tay-Sheng Wang (2003) in the research on the establishment of an indigenous land court had compiled and analyzed 1999 onward indigenous lawsuits concerning the reserve land system. Based on Wang's findings, the most contentious cases were litigated between indigenous and non-indigenous people, followed by litigation between indigenous people. Nevertheless, it is worth noting that, there exist a large number of litigations between the state administrative organs and indigenous people (Ibid.: 42). In addition, Wang's research is also concerned with the criminalization of indigenous customary uses of traditional territory and natural resources; the most commonly seen cases include violations of *Utilization and Transfer of Reserved Mountainous Land* (山坡地保育利用條例), *Soil and Water Conservation Act* (水土保持法), *Forestry Act* (森林法), *Statute For Controlling Firearms, Ammunition, And Weapons* (槍砲彈藥刀械管制條例), *Fisheries Act* (漁業法), and *Wildlife Conservation* (野生動物保育法). Wang's research findings confirmed that indigenous peoples are foreign to the state's laws, and testified colonial dispossessions of indigenous peoples in its modern form. The 2005 Smangus case would just tell the story.

In September 2005, three Atayal tribal members, who cut down and removed a fallen tree, were arrested by the police and charged by the prosecutor for the illegal taking of state forest products. However in actuality, their collecting areas were within their traditional territory. In addition, they were conducting traditional subsistence practices in accordance with customary law. Moreover, the Atayal collecting and gathering practices are integral to their lives, rituals, cultures and have been incorporated into their customary laws. All of these have been proven to fulfill indigenous rights requirements prescribed in the *Basic Law*. Nevertheless, the Atayal cultural claims presented before the District court and the High court were all been denied. The position with respect to indigenous ownership claims of resources was immediately contested. The High Court did not specifically deal with the question of legitimacy of indigenous traditional territory and ownership of resources, but merely considered the implementation of legislation governing forestry land. But the effectiveness and validity of the *Basic Law* was not determined by the District and High Courts in Smangus. It was until nearly five years later when the Supreme Court would conclusively set out, in asserting a constitutional value to substantive equality and multiculturalism, a framework for the confirmation of indigenous rights. On the Supreme Court's reasoning in Smangus, indigenous traditional customs have their roots in history and cultural distinction. For the purposes of substantive equality and sustainable development, taking the perspectives of multiculturalism and cultural relativism, it is a constitutional interest to protect indigenous rights within indigenous traditional territory, which form an integral part of traditional cultures in accordance with the principle of proportionality.[8]

Taiwan did not experience indigenous claims for traditional territory litigation until Smangus, as indigenous Taiwanese became more politically active after the enactment of the *Basic Law*. Although the *Basic Law* recognizes the rights of indigenous communities, the fact remains that the *Basic Law* was not, at least in the mind of the governmental agencies, designed to be a forum for the elaboration of rights of indigenous peoples. In actual practices, indigenous claims for traditional territory and inchoate rights often imply claims of collective rights. These claims are in many respects at odds with many of the norms recognized by the domestic and international laws regimes, which aims to secure rights for individuals. From the standpoint of cultural relativism and indigenous self-determination, how to harmonize, within the liberal multiculturalism structure, the constitutionality of individual rights and the cultural integrity and identity of indigenous collective rights is the main concern of indigenous self-government. It is entrenched in the preamble of the UNDRIPs:

> Recognizing the urgent need to respect and promote the inherent rights of indigenous peoples which derive from their political, economic and social structures and from their cultures, spiritual traditions, histories and philosophies, especially their rights to their lands, territories and resources (United Nations 2007).

The void in the current legal and administrative system in Taiwan has been filled with the Supreme Court and High Court's approval of the *Basic Law on Indigenous Peoples*, which spells out such indigenous justice system in a comprehensive manner and thus provides substance and meaning to the provisions of the *Basic Law* for indigenous customary rights. That being said, indigenous calls for independent and culturally-competent justice systems have been made repeatedly in public discussions as one important feature to indigenous self-government, which purports to be one solution to most of the problems with the present legal system. According to international jurisprudence of indigenous rights, it is fair to say that under the *Basic Law* indigenous peoples enjoy legitimatized rights to exercise their customary law and legal institutions through the implementation of self-government.

The Proposed New Autonomy Law

The rights of indigenous peoples have assumed a prominent place in international human rights discourse since the Second World War. Especially since the 1970s, there has been a steady normative development of indigenous rights under international law. S. James Anaya, the UN Special Rapporteur on the Situation of Human Rights and Fundamental Freedoms of Indigenous Peoples, demonstrates that while historical trends in international law largely facilitated colonization of indigenous peoples and their lands, the development of modern international human rights law has modestly responded to indigenous peoples' aspirations to survive as distinct communities in control of their own destinies (Anaya, 2008) The UN, the OAS, and the ILO have all instituted, or are in the process of approving, various international human rights instruments to build a legal framework concerning the rights of indigenous peoples. Within the past decades, these have inspired significant advancements in Taiwan's indigenous human rights advocacy, engendering a reformed system for indigenous movements to further claim their self-government right.

The ROC government has repeatedly stated its commitment to implement indigenous self-government right in a number of official pronouncements, as well as through negotiation and legislation. The former DDP government proposed twice indigenous peoples' self-government bills to the legislation in 2003 and 2007, but with no concrete results. While campaigning in 2008, President Ma Ying-jeou proposed to implement indigenous self-government by phases "on a trial basis" in his indigenous policy White Paper. For this purpose, the current KMT government put forward its draft bill for indigenous self-government on September 23, 2010. According to the Council of Indigenous Peoples, the implementation of indigenous self-government consists of three legislative principles: minimum impact to the existing governance system（對現況影響最小化）, maximizing indigenous rights protection（原住民族權益維護最大化）, and implementing indigenous self-government by phases（分階段實施自治願景）. Further, in order to assure the administrative systems' feasibility and to avoid dispensable controversy, indigenous self-government has to be based on the following three "NOs": (1) No modifications to the existing local government's administrative zonings.（不變動現行各地方自治團體行政區域）; (2) No alterations to the existing local government's administrative authority（不變更現行各地方自治團體機關權限）; and (3) No changes to the existing rights of non-indigenous individuals within autonomous region（不影響自治區域內非原

住民個人既有權益). The 2010 Indigenous Self-government Bill is divided into five chapters, which are composed of 83 articles. Other than the part I on general principles and part V on supplementary provision, the draft includes detail regulatory density on the establishment of indigenous autonomous zones (原住民族自治區之設立), rights and obligations of indigenous autonomous zones' citizens (自治區民之權利及義務), indigenous self-government authority (自治區之民族自治事項), by-laws making authority and procedure (自治法規之制(訂)定), organization and operation of indigenous autonomous legislative and administrative branches (自治區立法機關與行政機關之組織與運作), and general guidelines on indigenous autonomous fiscal arrangements (自治區的財政規範及紀律). What the government had proposed in actuality consists of three principles, i.e. "overlapping administrative districts" (空間合一), "divisions of administrative authorities" (權限分工), and "partnership for general services (事務合作)", which serve as the legal bases to structure relationships between indigenous self-government and local administrative systems.

Looking back in history, since the inception of the modern nation–state and the reception of the western legal system in Taiwan under subsequent Japanese and Chinese states, indigenous policy-making and institutional framing was perceived as derived from the exclusive authority of the state. In this way, the indigenous right to self-government can be jeopardized by the compulsory imposition of alien cultures and rules (Daes 1996). In most cases, the indigenous peoples of Taiwan have not been consulted and have not participated in the making of the ROC Constitution or legislation relevant to indigenous peoples. Indigenous individuals have participated as legislators and members of the National Assembly, but their rights derive from ROC citizenship and not from recognition as representatives of indigenous nations. This political reality is particularly pertinent in the case of the newly drafted bill of proposed autonomy law for indigenous peoples.

To get directly to the point, the newly proposed indigenous autonomy law (Bill–12300) was created without the effective participation of indigenous peoples and without acquiring aboriginal "free, prior and informed consent". By unilaterally imposing legislation that has a direct impact on indigenous peoples, the very existence of the Bill–12300 is contrary to the international norm of indigenous self-determination. Two controversial issues that await further negotiation and clarification are how the government should deal with indigenous claims to land and self-government, and how indigenous self-government should be implemented.

An examination of the Bill–12300 shows the government's policy of self-government is not based on the recognition of any inherent right of indigenous peoples to freely determine their political status and economic, social and cultural development. While international human rights law has been relatively consistent in recognizing indigenous self-government as an inherent right, the languages of articles 9–19 the Bill–12300, which contains the establishment procedures, seems to imply the contrary. The most critical issue revealed from public deliberations is that the initiation of indigenous self-government will be subject to local government approval and through review by the central government. These obstacles are being created in spite of the fact that indigenous self-government right is entrenched within the ROC Constitution and 2005 *Basic Law on Indigenous Peoples*. Article 4 of the *Basic Law* reads, "The government shall guarantee the equal status and development of self-governance of indigenous peoples and implement indigenous people's self-government in accordance with the will of indigenous peoples. The relevant issues shall be enacted by laws" (ROC Executive Yuan 2005). This article shall be understood as denoting that the ROC state has very little discretion and must defer to the will of indigenous peoples to carry out self-government.

Nonetheless, legislative records and historical policy implementations have been inconsistent with the expectations of the indigenous peoples. The ambiguity of the text leaves the government a wide range of discretion to limit the indigenous right to self-government. Based on the context of additional article 10 of the ROC Constitution and the *Basic Law*, the legal authority of indigenous governance is anticipated to be exercised under the policy based on a delegation of power from the central political authorities. The *Basic Law* and the Bill–12300 recognize the "will" of indigenous peoples, but not an inherent right to self-government. By expressing their will to self-government, indigenous peoples shall be delegated power from the state to exercise this "will." This is contrary to existing international legal instruments and practices supporting the proposition that indigenous peoples possess at minimum a right to self-government over their internal affairs. This inherent right exists in customary international law and is not open for debate. The ambivalent language used in the current format is contrary to the principle of the indigenous right of self-government.

In addition, according to Bill–12300, indigenous peoples do not enjoy the exclusive authority to make and enforce by-laws on their land. In order to create an effective government, the power of indigenous self-government includes "legislative competence, or the authority to make laws, executive capacity to execute the laws and carry on public administration, and judicial jurisdiction to resolve disputes.... Internal legal authority, however, is not always enough to make a government effective. Another important factor is the degree to which other powerful governments and institutions recognize and accept what is done by the government" (Chartrand 2006: 15). In the context of the Bill–12300, a by-law can only be made by the absolute legal authority of the central government through legislation or authorization. The language used in the Bill–12300 further undermines the value of indigenous right to self-government by making the self-government right subject to some future actions by the state in enacting laws to effectuate this "will" of the indigenous people. Indigenous peoples may only assume the decision-making authority delegated by the government. If such delegated powers are not given to indigenous peoples, they will not be able to exercise them.

Moreover, the Bill–12300 provides that a number of specific by-laws of governance should be enacted by the central government. According to UNDRIPs, it is fundamental to the indigenous right of self-government that the right applies to all aspects of indigenous life. The preamble to UNDRIP declares:

> Convinced that control by indigenous peoples over developments affecting them and their lands, territories and resources will enable them to maintain and strengthen their institutions, cultures and traditions, and to promote their development in accordance with their aspirations and needs (United Nations 2007).

International law recognizes that indigenous peoples have the right to control issues regarding health, housing, education, social welfare, and economic development, etc. Given UNDRIP's framework, there is enormous scope for the Declaration to empower indigenous peoples in a variety of arenas. The Bill–12300, on the other hand, fails to provide for a sufficiently broad right of self-government. In spite of its abstract recognition of indigenous rights over the fundamental issues of education, housing, traditional knowledge, economic development, health, and self-government, these provisions employ language that creates an option for the government to decide when to act or not to act because of the aforementioned three principles of "overlapping administrative districts" （空間合一）, "divisions of administrative authorities" （權限分工）, and "partnership for general services （事務合作）".

Public criticisms against Bill–12300 show concern that indigenous authority is minimized to exclude regulatory authority over the land, policing, and juridical powers. For instance, Article 20, Paragraph 1 of the *Basic Law* recognizes that indigenous peoples have the right to land. In order to solve various indigenous land claims, the government needs to establish a special committee under the *Basic Law*. However, article 20, paragraph 2 of the Basic Law states that "[t]he organization and other related matters of the committee shall be enacted by law." The most critical problem is that no provision in Bill–12300 empowers indigenous rights to land and natural resources as enshrined in the Basic Law.

It is against the fundamental notion of self-government to unilaterally impose laws on indigenous peoples without their participation and consent. Since the legal authority of indigenous self-government lies with the central government, the government has the last say, which implies that indigenous peoples may not have a just and feasible self-government right. Under the current design of the relationship between the indigenous peoples and the government, the right to self-government has been downgraded to merely being an extended arm of the government, which delivers social services. Indigenous governments will not even have the rights of municipalities to make by-laws, as proposed by Canadian conservative Tom Flanagan. In the absence of a true recognition of inherent sovereignty in Taiwan, discourses of "indigenous rights" and "multiculturalism" provide mere window dressing to the continuation of what many indigenous people perceive as colonial rule.

Conclusion

In his discussions on the effective governance of Indian tribal government, Joseph P. Kalt states that, "[t]he evidence is overwhelming that political self-rule is the only policy that has enabled at least some tribes to break out of a twentieth-century history of federal government-dominated decision-making that yields social, cultural, and economic destruction. (Kalt 2006: 184)" Indigenous self-government is an empowerment process, which may be defined as a process which enhances the ability of disadvantaged individuals or groups to challenge and change existing power relationships that place them in subordinate economic, social and political positions (Agarwal 1996; Kymlicka 1995).

As domestic dependent nations, right to self-government has been guaranteed to American Indian nations in hundreds of treaties, statutes, court decisions, and executive orders in American jurisprudence.[9] Likewise, aboriginal and treaty rights of Canadian First Nations are protected by section 35(1) of the Canadian Constitution (Morse 1997: 1042). Also, the principle of indigenous self-government as an inherent right has been considered on numerous occasions by Canadian courts.[10] Unlike American Indians and Canadian First Nations, indigenous peoples in Taiwan have neither made treaties with colonial settlers nor have any constitutionally-protected rights been adequately implemented and enforced. In addition, the ROC courts, unlike Canadian courts, have not recognized indigenous rights to land or self-government, except insofar as such rights are given by the ROC legislation.

Taiwan's Bill-12300, although phrased in the terminology of indigenous autonomy, is not really an expression of an indigenous inherent right to self-government as a specific form of their right to self-determination articulated by UNDRIPs, ILO C169, and the International Covenant on Civil and Political Rights. Self-government relies on the support of the indigenous peoples for its effectiveness. Under the current version of Bill-12300, indigenous rights to self-governance and autonomous power are strictly circumscribed and reserved for central and/or local government authority. It is an imposed system ultimately controlled by the state. In other words, the Bill-12300 is, in its current form, a legal measure directed at indigenous peoples, in which indigenous peoples only retain delegated powers at central and local governments' discretions. In short, the fundamental goal of the Bill-12300 is the legal entrenchment into indigenous territory of the entire ROC legal system. This premise is completely contrary to the notion of self-government espoused in international human rights laws. If the Bill-12300 is to meet the minimum standard of indigenous self-government set by international human rights instruments and the Basic Law, it is necessary for the ROC government to cede power, authority, responsibility, and accountability to indigenous peoples.

References

Agarwal, B., 1996 *Comment on Equity Equality and Empowerment*. Washington: International Food Policy Research Institute.

Allio, F., 1998a. La construction d'un espace politique austronésien. *Perspectives Chinoises* 47 (mai / juin): 54–62.

———. 1998b. Les Austronésiens dans la course électorale. *Perspectives chinoises* 50 (novembre / décembre): 46–48.

Anaya, S. J., 2008. The Human Rights of Indigenous Peoples, in the Light of the New Declaration, and the Challenge of Making Them Operative. *Report of the Special Rapporteur on the Situation of Human Rights and Fundamental Freedoms of Indigenous Peoples* (SJ Anaya), UN Doc. A/HRC/9/9 (5 August).

Anaya, S. James & Robert A. Williams, Jr., 2001. "The Case of Awas Tingni v. Nicaragua: A New Step in the International Law of Indigenous Peoples." *Harvard Human Rights Journal* 14: 33–86.

Asch, M., 1990. The Future of Hunting and Trapping and Economic Development in Alberta's North: Some Facts and Myths about Inevitability. *Proceedings of the Fort Chipewyan and Fort Vermilion Bicentennial Conference*, edited by Patricia A. McCormack and R. Geoffrey Ironside, 25–29. Edmonton: Boreal Institute for Northern Studies.

Brown, M., 2004. *Is Taiwan Chinese? The Impact of Culture, Power, and Migration on Changing Identities*. Stanford: Stanford University Press.

Chartrand, Paul L.A.H., 2006. *International Expert Group Meeting on the Millennium Development Goals, Indigenous Participation and Good Governance* (11–13 January) PFII/2006/WS.3/4, New York: U.N. Permanent Forum on Indigenous Issues. http://www.un.org/esa/socdev/unpfii/documents/workshop_MDG_chartrand.doc (accessed March 6, 2011).

Daes, Erica-Irene A., 1996. The Right of Indigenous Peoples to 'Self-Determination' in the Contemporary World Order. *Self-Determination: International Perspectives*, edited by Donald Clark & Robert Williamson, 47–57. New York: St. Martin's Press.

———. 2001. *Indigenous Peoples and Their Relationship to Land. Final Working Paper*. Geneva: Sub-Commission on the Promotion and Protection of Human Rights.

Feit, Harvey A. and Robert, B. 2001. Voices from a Disappearing Forest: Government, Corporate and Cree Participatory Forestry Management Practices. *Aboriginal Autonomy and Development in Northern Québec and Labrador*, edited by Colin H. Scott, 119–148. Vancouver: UBC Press.

Flanagan, T., 2008. *First Nations, Second Thoughts* (2nd edition). Montréal: McGill- Queens University Press.

Fujii, S. 藤井志津枝, 1997. *Lifan: Riben Zhili Taiwan de Jice: Meiyou Paohuo de Zhanzheng* 理蕃：日本治理台灣的計策 沒有砲火的戰爭(一) [Ruling Savages: Japanese Governace on Taiwan – A War without Gunfire, Volume 1]. Taipei: Wenyingtang 臺北市： 文英堂出版社.

_____. 2001. *Taiwan Yuanzhuminshi : Zhengcepian (san).* 臺灣原住民史：政

策篇 （三）. [Taiwan aboriginal history: Policy section, 3] Nantou : Taiwan Wenxian guan 南投：臺灣文獻館.
Gilbert, J., 2006. *Indigenous Peoples' Land Rights under International Law: From Victims to Actors*. Ardsley, N.Y.: Transnational Publishers.
Groves, R., 1996. Territoriality and Aboriginal Self-Determination: Options for Pluralism in Canada. *Law & Anthropology* 8: 123–146.
Harrison, H., 2001. Changing Nationalities, Changing Ethnicities: Taiwan Indigenous Villages in the Years after 1946. *In Search of the Hunters and their Tribes : Studies in the History and Culture of the Taiwan Indigenous People*, edited by David Faure (dir.), 50–78. Taipei : Shung Ye Museum of Formosan Aborigines.
Huang, Shu-min 黃樹民., 2008. "Quanqiuhua yu Taiwan yuanzhumin jiben zhengce zhi bianqian ye xiankuang 全球化與台灣原住民基本政策之變遷與現況". Conference on "Social Change and Policy Assessments of Taiwanese Indigenous Peoples, 1983–2008," Institute of Ethnology, Academia Sinica, Taipei (30 May).
Huang,Yueh-Wen 黃躍雯 and Chang, Chang-Yi 張長義., 2001. Guojia yu shehui de hudong: guojia gongyuan de jianzhi yu Taiwan yuanzhumin de zhizu yishi 國家與社會的互動：國家公園的建制與台灣原住民的自主意識." [Interaction between State and Society: The Establishment of National Park and the Awareness of Autonomy of the Aborigines]. Dili xuebao 地理學報, No. 30: 1–18.
Iwan Nawi 黃鈴華., 2005. *Taiwan Yuanzhu Minzu Yundong de Guihui Luxian* 台灣原住民族運動的國會路線. [Taiwan Indigenous Movement at the National Legislative Yuan] Taipei : Guojia Zhanwang Wenjiao Jijinhui 臺北：國家展望文教基金會.
Jin, Huang-jie 金煌傑., 2005. *Taiwan yuanzhu minzu zizhi yiti tantao : Zizhifa ge caoan zhi bijiao yu pipan* 臺灣原住民族自治議題探討：自治法個草案之比較與批判 [Study on the Indigenous Self-government in Taiwan: comparative and critical approaches to draft laws], MA thesis, National Donghua University Institute of Indigenous Development Hualien. http://etd.lib.ndhu.edu.tw/theses// available/etd-0713105-135019/unrestricted/etd-0713105-135019.pdf (accessed 4 June 2008).
Kalt, Joseph P., 2006. Constitutional Rule and the Effective Governance of Native Nations. *American Indian Constitutional Reform and the Rebuilding of Native Nations*, edited by Eric D. Lemont, 191–212. Austin, TX: University of Texas Press.
Kojima Yoshimichi 小島由道., 1996[1915]. *Fanzu Xiguan Diaocha Baogao Shu, Di yi juan, Taiyazu* 番族慣習調查報告書，第一卷，泰雅族 [Investigation of the Custom of the Aboriginal in Taiwan, Vol. 1, Atayal], translated by the Institute of Ethnology, Academia Sinica. Taipei: Academia Sinica Institute of Ethnology.
Kymlicka, W., 1995. *Multicultural Citizenship: A Liberal Theory of Minority*

Rights. Oxford University Press.
Li, Yih-yüan, et.al. 李亦園, 1983. *Shandi xingzheng zhengce zhi yanjiu yu pinggu baogaoshu* 山地行政政策之研究與評估報告書 [Research and Evaluation Report on Mountainous Adminstration Policy]. Nantou : Taiwan sheng zhengfu minzheng ting 南投：臺灣省政府民政廳.
Liao, Shou-chen., 1998. *Taiya Zu de Shehui Zuzhi* 泰雅族的社會組織[*Social organization of the Atayal tribe*]. Hualien: Tzu Chi College of Humanities and Social Sciences.
Masaw M., 1998. *Taiya Zu de Shehui Zuzhi* 泰雅族的社會組織[Social organization of the Atayal tribe]. Hualien : Tzu Chi University Research Center on Aboriginal Health.
Morse, B. W., 1997. Permafrost Rights: Aboriginal Self-Government and the Supreme Court in R. v. Pamajewon. [1997] *McGill L.J.*: 1011.
Mulrennen, M. E. and Colin, H. S. 2001. Aboriginal Rights and Interests in Canadian Northern Seas. *Aboriginal Autonomy and Development in Northern Québec and Labrador*, edited by C. H. Scott, 78–97. Vancouver: UBC Press.
Nadasdy, P., 2003. *Hunters and Bureaucrats: Power, Knowledge and Aboriginal–State Relations in the Southwest Yukon*. Vancouver: UBC Press.
Niezen, R., 2003. *The Origins of Indigenism: Human Rights and the Politics of Identity*. Berkeley: University of California Press.
ROC Executive Yuan., 2005. *Basic Law on Indigenous Peoples*. Taipei: Executive Yuan. http://law.moj.gov.tw/eng/LawClass/LawAll.aspx?PCode=D0130003 (accessed April 16, 2012)
Rudolph, M., 1993. *Die Prostitution der Frauen der taiwanesischen Bergminderheiten : historische, sozio-kulturelle und kultur-psychologische Hintergründe*. Hamburg : LIT Verlag.
_____. 2003. *Taiwans multi-ethnische Gesellschaft und die Bewegung der Ureinwohner: Assimilation oder kulturelle Revitalisierung?* Hamburg: LIT Verlag.
Salisbury, R., 1986. *A Homeland for the Cree*. Montréal: McGill-Queen's University Press.
Scheinin, M., 2004. "Indigenous Peoples' Land Rights under the International Covenant on Civil and Political Rights." Paper presented at *Torkel Oppsahls minneseminar*, Norwegian Centre for Human Rights, University of Oslo (April). http://www.galdu.org/govat/doc/ind_peoples_land_rights.pdf (accessed February 14, 2011)
Scott, C. H., ed. 2001. *Aboriginal Autonomy and Development in Northern Québec and Labrador*. Vancouver: UBC Press.
_____. 2005. "Co-Management and the Politics of Aboriginal Consent to Resource Development: The Agreement Concerning a New Relationship between Le Gouvernement du Québec and the Crees of Québec." In *Canada, the State of the Federation 2003: Reconfiguring Aboriginal–State Relations*, edited by Michael Murphy, 133–163. Montréal: McGill-Queen's University

Press.

Scott, C. H. and Jeremy, W. 2001. "Conflicts between Cree Hunting and Sport Hunting: Co-Management Decision Making at James Bay." In *Aboriginal Autonomy and Development in Northern Québec and Labrador*, edited by C. H. Scott, 149–174. Vancouver: UBC Press.

Schulte-Tenckhoff, I., 1997. *La question des peuples autochtones*. Bruxelles : Bruylant.

Simon, S., 2002. "The Underside of a Miracle: Industrialization, Land, and Taiwan's Indigenous Peoples," *Cultural Survival Quarterly* 26, no. 2: 64–67.

_____. 2006. Taiwan's Indigenized Constitution: What Place for Aboriginal Formosa? *Taiwan International Studies Quarterly* 2, no. 1: 251–270.

_____. 2007. Paths to Autonomy: Aboriginality and the Nation in Taiwan. *The Margins of Becoming. Identity and Culture in Taiwan*, edited by Carsten Storm et Mark Harrison (dir.), 221–240. Wiesbaden, Harrassowitz.

_____. 2009. Indigenous Peoples and Hunting Rights. *Confronting Discrimination and Inequality in China: Chinese and Canadian Perspectives*, edited by Errol P. Mendes and Sakunthala Srighanthan, 405–421. Ottawa: University of Ottawa Press.

Stainton, M., 1995. *Return our Land: Counterhegemonic Presbyterian Aboriginality in Taiwan*, MA, Social Anthropology, York University, Toronto.

Tavares, A. C., 2005. "The Japanese Colonial State and the Dissolution of the Late Imperial Frontier Economy in Taiwan, 1886–1909." *Journal of Asian Studies* 64 No. 2: 361–385.

Tully, J., 1995. *Strange Multiplicity: Constitutionalism in an Age of Diversity*. Cambridge: Cambridge University Press.

United Nations., 2007. *United Nations Declaration on the Rights of Indigenous Peoples*. New York: UN General Assembly. http://www.un.org/esa/socdev/unpfii/documents/DRIPS_en.pdf (accessed January 3, 2011).

Wang, Tay-Sheng 王泰升., 2003. *Yuanzhumin baoliudi tudi zhuanshu fating shezhi yanjiu* 原住民保留地土地專屬法庭設置研究[Research on the Establishment of Aboriginal Courts in Taiwan]. Taipei: Council of Indigenous Peoples, Executive Yuan.

Wei, Hwei-chin 衛惠林., 1965. Taiwan tuzu shehui de buluo zuzhi yu quanwei zhidu 臺灣土著社會的部落組織與權威制度 [Tribal organization and authoritative system of Taiwan aboriginal society]. *Kaogu renleixue kan* 考古人類學刊 25–26: 71–92.

Weaver, J., 1996. *Defending Mother Earth: Native American Perspectives on Environmental Justice*. Maryknoll, N.Y.: Orbis Books.

Xianfa Yuanzhu Minzu Zhengce Zhixian Tuidong Xiaozu., 2005. 憲法原住民族政策制憲推動小組[Task Force on drafting constitutional indigenous policy] *Yuanzhu minzu xianfa zhuanzhang huiyi shilu* 原住民族憲法專章會議實錄. [Minutes of the Meetings on the Indigenous Special Clause in the Constitution]. Taipei: Indigenous Peoples Council.

Zhongguo renquan xie hui., 1987. 中國人權協會[Chinese Association for Human Rights] (ed.). *Taiwan tuzhu de chuantong shehui wenhua yu renquan xiankuang* 臺灣土著的傳統社會文化與人權現況[Taiwan Indigenous Peoples' traditional society, culture and human rights conditions]. Taipei : Dajia chubanshe 大佳出版社.

Notes

1. For a history of the UN work on indigenous peoples, see Schulte-Tenckhoff 1997.

2. For a history of the Qing expansion on Taiwan from an indigenous perspective, see Brown 2004 and Shepherd 1993.

3. For more information on this incident and indigenous relations with the ROC security apparatus, see Williams 2005.

4. The official English translation of Article 10 of the Additional Articles of the ROC Constitution: "The State shall, in accordance with the will of the ethnic groups, safeguard the status and political participation of the aborigines. The State shall also guarantee and provide assistance and encouragement for aboriginal education, culture, transportation, water conservation, health and medical care, economic activity, land, and social welfare, measures for which shall be established by law. The same protection and assistance shall be given to the people of the Penghu, Kinmen, and Matsu areas." (http://english.president.gov.tw/Default.aspx?tabid=1037#10). For unknown reasons, the English translation does not capture the crucial legal difference in Chinese between yuanzhuminzu (indigenous peoples) and yuanzhumin (indigenous people). See Lin 2000 for the constitutional dilemmas of indigenous Taiwan.

5. Article 25 of the UNDRIPs, "Indigenous peoples have the right to maintain and strengthen their distinctive spiritual relationship with their traditionally owned or otherwise occupied and used lands, territories, waters and coastal seas and other resources and to uphold their responsibilities to future generations in this regard." Also see article 13.1 of the ILO C169, "governments shall respect the special importance for the cultures and spiritual values of the peoples concerned of their relationship with the lands or territories, or both as applicable, which they occupy or otherwise use, and in particular the collective aspects of this relationship."

6. *Ilmari Länsman et al. v. Finland* (Communication 511/1992), Views adopted: 26 October 1994, Report of the Human Rights Committee, Vol. II, GAOR, Fiftieth Session, Suppl. No. 40 (A/50/40): 66–76; *Apirana Mahuika et al. v. New Zealand* (Communication No. 547/1993), Views adopted 27 October 2000, Report of the Human Rights Committee, Vol. II, UN doc. A/56/40 (Vol. II): 11–29.

7. Article 34 of the UNDRIPs, "Indigenous peoples have the right to promote, develop and maintain their institutional structures and their distinctive customs, spirituality, traditions, procedures, practices and, in the cases where they exist, juridical systems or customs, in accordance with international human rights standards"; Article 40 of the UNDRIPs, "Indigenous peoples have the right to access to and prompt decision through just and fair procedures for the resolution of conflicts and disputes with States or other

parties, as well as to effective remedies for all infringements of their individual and collective rights. Such a decision shall give due consideration to the customs, traditions, rules and legal systems of the indigenous peoples concerned and international human rights"; Article 8 of the ILO C169, "1. In applying national laws and regulations to the peoples concerned, due regard shall be had to their customs or customary laws. 2. These peoples shall have the right to retain their own customs and institutions, where these are not incompatible with fundamental rights defined by the national legal system and with internationally recognized human rights. Procedures shall be established, whenever necessary, to resolve conflicts which may arise in the application of this principle. 3. The application of paragraphs 1 and 2 of this Article shall not prevent members of these peoples from exercising the rights granted to all citizens and from assuming the corresponding duties. Article 9 of the ILO C169, "1. To the extent compatible with the national legal system and internationally recognized human rights, the methods customarily practiced by the peoples concerned for dealing with offences committed by their members shall be respected. 2. The customs of these peoples in regard to penal matters shall be taken into consideration by the authorities and courts dealing with such cases".

8. 最高法院 98 年台上字第 7210 號刑事判決指出：「原住民族之傳統習俗，有其歷史淵源與文化特色，為促進各族群間公平、永續發展，允以多元主義之觀點、文化相對之角度，以建立共存共榮之族群關係，尤其在原住民族傳統領域土地內，依其傳統習俗之行為，在合理之範圍，予以適當之尊重，以保障原住民族之基本權利。」

9. See e.g. Treaty with the Delaware Nation, 1778, 7 Stat. 13; Cherokee Nation v. Georgia, 30 U.S. (5 Pet.) 1 (1831); Indian Self-Determination and Education Assistance Act (25 U.S.C. 450 et seq.).

10. Campbell v. British Columbia, (2000) 189 D.L.R. (4th) 333; *Mitchell, supra* note.

CHAPTER 6

Colonial Continuities, Neoliberal Hegemony and Adivasi (Original Dweller) Space: Human Rights as Paradox and Equivocation in Contexts of Dispossession in India[1]

Dip Kapoor

> The 'new' nations of Asia and Africa somewhat understandably insisted that the right to self-determination extended only to situations of 'classic colonialism', available to their 'peoples' only once in history: to determine their collective status as sovereign states within the meaning of international law. That right once exercised was extinguished for all times; this presumed that the 'logic' of colonialism, which made all sorts of different peoples, cultures, and territories vessels of imperial unity, should continue in the post-colony. (Baxi 2002: 36)

According to the United Nation (UN)'s working group on indigenous populations and the International Work Group for Indigenous Affairs (IWGIA), problems faced by indigenous peoples of Asia include 'plundering of resources', 'forced relocation' and 'forced integration of indigenous peoples into market economies' (Eversol, McNeish and Cimadamore 2005: 32; Fisher 1999). These problems have been exacerbated in the post–1991 New Economic Policy (NEP) environment in India (Baviskar 2005; Fernandes 2006; Ghosh 2006; Kapoor 2011; McMichael 2010; Mehta 2009; Menon and Nigam 2007; Oliver-Smith 2010; Patnaik 2007; Prasad 2004; Ray and Katzenstein 2005; Sanyal 2010) where the key neoliberal response to the Adivasi[2] as a state-defined category of impoverished peoples in need of inclusion and amelioration or what amounts to a political exercise in exclusive governmentality and socio-economic control (Ghosh 2006; Kapoor 2010), has been to enable processes of displacement, dispossession or market assimilation (Cameron and Palan 2004; Padel and Das 2010).

Subsequently, while Adivasis constitute 8% of the Indian population (or 80 million or more people belonging to some 612 scheduled tribes), they account for 40% of Development-Displaced Persons (DDPs). In the state of Orissa (the context of the research base for this paper), which is home to 62 groups numbering eight million or more people where Adivasis make up 22% of the population, they account for 42% of DDPs (Fernandes 2006; Hussain 2008). According to some estimates, dams, mining, industries and parks have displaced 21.3 million people between 1951 and 1990 (prior to the neoliberal-turn in the Indian economy and the establishment of special economic zones, or SEZs, that have accelerated this process) of which 40% were Adivasi and 20% were Dalit (or scheduled castes) peoples (Nag 2001). The government of India acknowledged 15.5 million displaced persons when it finally drafted a national rehabilitation policy in 1994, of which 75% are/were still awaiting 'rehabilitation' (Bharati 1999: 20).

Development-displacement and dispossession of Adivasi and rural subalterns (including Dalits) continues to proliferate while India remains a signatory to the International Labour Organization (ILO) Convention No. 169 (and several other inter/national human rights and legal commitments) that require governments to recognize indigenous 'rights of ownership and possession ... over the lands, which they traditionally occupy', while further stipulating that

> indigenous peoples have the right to decide their own priorities for the process of development as it affects their lives, beliefs, institutions and spiritual well-being and the lands they occupy or otherwise use, and to exercise control, to the extent possible, over their own economic, social and cultural development. (Hannum 2003: 88)

A UN document entitled 'The Practice of Forced Evictions: Comprehensive Human Rights Guidelines on Development Based Displacement' states that evictions constitute a prima facie violation of a wide range of internationally recognized human rights, while a 1990 UN document ('Global Constitution on the Realization of the Right to Development as a Human Right') explicitly recognizes 'that the most destructive and prevalent abuses of indigenous rights are a direct consequence of development strategies that fail to respect the fundamental rights of self-determination' (Das 2001: 86). Indigenous peoples have finally, after persisting over a 30-year period, secured ratification (including more recent 'partial' endorsement by the United States [US], Canada, Australia and New Zealand) for the United Nations Declaration of the Rights of Indigenous Peoples (UNDRIP; November 2007).

This paper attempts to make sense of these processes of ongoing Adivasi development displacement and dispossession despite the proliferation of various human rights instruments and guarantees that should in effect supposedly pre-empt such continued colonization and neoliberal exploitation of Adivasi space. The proposition advanced here is that a political analysis of human rights as a politics of imperialism and colonial continuity in contexts of development-displacement and dispossession of Adivasi provides a compelling explanation for why human rights-based approaches to address the coloniality of the contemporary neoliberal project (or what Peruvian political-sociologist Anibal Quijano [2000: 215] has referenced as the *coloniality of power* being expressed through a globalizing capitalism) remains paradoxical at best and/or equivocal by design. Such human rights deployments, whether as paradox or as *necessary* equivocation in hegemonic designs, require close scrutiny in the *Age of Rights* (Henkin 1990) when, 'for many in the west, human rights discourse has emerged as the sole language of resistance to oppression and emancipation in the Third World' (Rajagopal 2003: 172). Furthermore, such scrutiny is also warranted given that some observers have pointed to the symbiotic relationship between human rights and imperialism, suggesting that 'Empire's powers of intervention might best be understood as beginning not directly with its weapons of lethal force but rather with its moral instruments' such as those 'global, regional, and local organizations that are dedicated to relief work and the protection of human rights' (Hardt and Negri 2000: 35–36); that is, international human rights activism as a form of high moral imperialism in the service of empire. According to Randall Williams (2010), there is an urgent need to re-examine the politics of human rights given the 'ascendancy of rights as the privileged discourse for the symbolic articulation of international justice in an era of advanced global capitalism' (xv), especially since the demise of state-socialisms in the late 1980s. Reading the politics of the Zapatistas in Chiapas, Mexico, Williams (2010) describes their attempt to construct another way of practicing politics as a turn away from a statist-rights defined approach and as 'a refusal to accept any modified project of modernity that reproduces the colonial capitalist divisions of humanity' (xxiv).

Having acknowledged these dubious links between human rights and colonialism and imperialism, human rights simultaneously offer an albeit problematic ethico-political-legal space and a derivative-politics/discourse for Adivasi/other rural subaltern social movement politics addressing continued colonization and neoliberal hegemony (imperialism). The paper subsequently alludes to the relatively limited potential of official/estatized human rights (as opposed to movement-generated conceptions of human rights which are briefly referenced) for Adivasi and rural subaltern movements that seek to deploy these state human rights mechanisms for redress and the *delivery of human rights* (Stammers 2009) in the age of imperialism (Boron 2005; Chomsky 1998; Evans 1998; Hardt and Negri 2000; Harvey 2003; Mookerjea 2011; Williams 2010).

These insights are developed from funded research exploring and contributing towards Adivasi (Kondh, Saora and Panos/Dalits) social movement learning (Kapoor 2009a, 2009b) between 2006 and 2009 in South Orissa (Gajapati district) that has addressed the politics of the Adivasi-Dalit Ektha Abhijan (ADEA) movement (which encompasses 120 villages or some 20,000 people) and translocal Adivasi/subaltern activism in Orissa (Kapoor 2011); the author's engagements with Adivasi movement activism in South Orissa since the early 1990s; and pertinent theoretical and secondary literatures concerning Adivasi and/or the politics of human rights. The academic project addressed here seeks to avoid an anthropologization of Adivasi (Kapoor and Shizha 2010; Tuhiwai-Smith 1999) as objects of knowledge-production for efficient statecraft or for purposes advancing the reproduction of capital (Kapoor and Jordan 2009); the attempt is to objectify, scrutinize and expose the processes and institutions of continuous colonial domination and neoliberal (imperial) penetration and exploitation of Adivasi and rural subalterns, including related hegemonic constructions and deployments of human rights in-service of this project.

Towards a Political Appreciation of State–Institutionalization of Rights and the Politics of Human Rights in Contexts of Development-Displacement: Colonialism, Neoliberalism and Adivasi Dispossession in the 'Post-Colony'

Popular conceptions of human rights are often associated with the international system that was initiated in 1948 as the Universal Declaration of Human Rights (UNDHR). As noted by Neil Stammers (2009: 116), in contrast to a process whereby human rights have arisen out of various social struggles and then been institutionalized, the construction of the international human rights system was an institutionalized process from the outset: an institutionalized process between elite actors at the level of the inter-state system. Critics of this institutionalization have pointed out the western and Eurocentric bias of the UNDHR in terms of the foundational values and ethics embedded in the declaration (e.g. primary commitment to liberal-individualism), in turn serving the wider political-economic and cultural interests of capital and powerful western states (Evans 1998), despite the shaping influence of non-western states and anti-colonial critics like Gandhi and Nkrumah (Ishay 2004). Randall William's (2010) analysis points to the predictability of such an arrangement once we shift our analytical perspective from one that assumes that colonialism and imperialism is a *problem for* international law and human rights to one that 'grasps their mutually constitutive relationship' (William 2010: xx). China Mieville's (2005: 293) Marxist analysis of international law, similarly argues that international law and human rights, in fact, '*assumes imperialism*' (italics added). According to this line of thinkers, the rise to prominence of international human rights regimes needs to be understood keeping in mind the context of the post–war era and the advance of global capitalism driven by the ascendance of US imperial power (economic and military) and the reconfiguration of global power under the aegis of 'the collective imperialism of the triad of the US, Europe (west of the Polish frontier) and Japan' (Amin 2006). Williams (2010) points out the need to recognize that the post–war re-formation of international institutions

> did not constitute a break with the historical structures of colonial violence but instead was part and parcel of an imperialist-directed reorganization of relations within and between contemporary state and social formations: the colonial, the neocolonial, and the neoimperial. (Williams 2010: xxl)

The post–1991 (new economic policy) opening-up of the Indian political-economy to the historical development and reproduction of capital advanced by the imperial collective, arguably, makes the Indian state a complicit actor in this project with associated implications for similar deployments of an institutionalized human rights apparatus.

Estatized–Human Rights and the Politics of Institutionalization

The institutionalization of human rights thus conceived have served to not only propagate a postcolonial capitalist development project in the post–colony but, by being located in the very structure of power of the state (given the associated conception of *delivery of human rights by the state*–see Stammers, 2009), seriously constrained the possibility of using human rights to challenge the power of the state. Indeed, the power of *eminent domain* or the power that the Indian state may exercise over all land within its territory and the law related to the compulsory acquisition of land for a *public purpose* (Ramanathan 2009: 133, italics in original) with a wide open interpretation of *what exactly constitutes public purpose* or *for which public* is pertinent here in relation to development displacement and dispossession of Adivasi for state-corporate projects (e.g. mining in Orissa) as appeals to relevant human rights enshrined in covenants, conventions and constitutional schedules/provisions by Adivasi social movements/struggles becomes 'a matter solely for executive determination and statement, and, is therefore, non-justiciable'. In fact

> the endorsement of the *eminent domain* power of the state in the early constitutional years of independent India was assisted by jurisprudence that developed around the colonial Land Acquisition Act of 1894 . . .it has also not been tempered by altered notions of the relationship between citizens and the state which independence from colonial power may well be expected to bring in its wake. (Ramanathan 2009: 133–134)

Thus, as noted by Stammers (2009: 115), the 'institutionalization of human rights within modern nation states has resulted in understandings, approaches and policies with respect to human rights which are often deeply ambiguous in relation to power'.

The institutionalization of human rights in state power and mechanisms for redress was also largely predicated on the assumption that the people's right to self-determination enshrined in article 21 of the UNDHR, which states that 'the will of the people shall be the basis of the authority of government' (Rajagopal 2003: 192–193), was to be understood exclusively as a right of national self-determination for independent statehood during the time of national anti-colonial struggles, as Third World states accepted human rights because there was an understanding that this would expand the ambit of the state and the sphere of governance. Such a truncated notion of the right to self-determination, or what Richard Falk (2000: 102) describes as a 'sanction that only repudiates alien rule at the level of the state', effectively precludes similar appeals to self-determination by Adivasi peoples and internal minorities subsequently failing to provide a similar rights mechanism for such struggles against various forms of internal colonization (see related quote by Uppendra Baxi at the commencement of this paper), thereby negating what Falk (2000: 97) calls a potentially 'powerful mobilizing instrument with which to resist involuntary governance', as in the case of development-dispossession of Adivasi and rural subalterns; that is, 'neo-colonialism is born just when the practices of the right to self-determination seem to succeed [national decolonization in the post–war period]' (Baxi 2002: 26). Or in the words of a Kondh Adivasi elder, 'We fought the British thinking that we will be equal in the independent India' (interview, January 2007). Even at the international level, some observers have noted that 'the wider human rights network does not see development aimed at integrating indigenous peoples into the national society as a human rights violation' (Blaser, Feit and McRae 2004: 6). That is, the ability of indigenous organizations to call on human rights groups to further indigenous projects is limited (Choudry 2007) since the later tend to view the state's integrationist agenda as being legitimate, as long as the development state follows the model of the developed countries and avoids the most flagrant violations of human rights in executing its projects.

The institutionalization of human rights within state power not only limits (or renders relatively ineffective) Adivasi people's recourse to such rights when questioning the actions of the state in relation to the dispossession of Adivasi: the content and reach of human rights is also subject to state-corporate monopolization and definition. For instance, in contexts of Adivasi development displacement and dispossession (neocolonial appropriations of space and peoples) for accelerated neoliberal-inspired economic growth projects (exploitation of Adivasi land, labor and ecology in the pursuit of profit), fundamental relationships between violence and human rights discourse can be assessed to determine which types of violence are recognized as 'violations' by the human rights discourse and which are not and why. As Balakrishnan Rajagopal (2003: 173) puts it, 'does human rights discourse have a theory of violence and how does this theory relate to development?'

His own analysis suggests that the 'estatization of human rights' and the role of the state in the realization of human rights is, as Upendra Baxi explains, 'a discourse concerning justified violence' (quoted in Rajagopal 2003: 174). Human rights discourse, then, is not based on a theory of non-violence but it approves certain forms of violence and disapproves certain other forms. Pertinent to the Adivasi context of development displacement, dispossession and colonization, Rajagopal (2003: 195) suggests that, while the mass deportation of 1.5 million people from Phnom Penh by the Khmer Rouge in 1975 is considered a crime against humanity, 'the mass eviction/ deportation of 33 million development refugees from their homes due to development projects such as dams, by the Indian government, is simply seen as a social cost (if at all) of development'. He concludes that such selective blindness around certain forms of violence can be explained by the pathological link between human rights and models of the state in the economy that are derived/embedded in the development discourse; that is:

> human rights discourse ... remains aloof from the 'private' violence of the market on individuals and communities. This tendency has become more pronounced in an era of globalization and privatization wherein the march of the market is celebrated unreservedly ... In essence, economic violence – that is, violence caused by the market – is treated as out of bounds of human rights

law, even as it attempts to assert itself as the sole liberatory discourse in the Third World. (Rajagopal 2003: 196)

It follows that the biggest myth, then, is that human rights is an anti-state discourse or an unambiguous avenue for Adivasi resistance to neoliberal state-market-led displacement, dispossession and continued colonization or what Jack Donnelly (1989: 188) has referenced as 'development repression' in the contemporary Indian scenario. In the words of a Jhodia Adivasi with regard to violence and resistance to the Kashipur bauxite mine in Rayagada, South Orissa, that has now clocked some 17 years:

> People were questioning why after so many years of protesting for a school and a health centre which is not available in a 35km radius, they are now building a police station in Kuchipadar village instead!
>
> ... There were at least 5,000 of us when they fired. I too was one of 12 injured (pointing to scar on the thigh) but I never spoke up for fear of police retaliation. I have endured my lot in poverty and silence and could not get treated but we will never back down ... even in Chilika, after Tatas got shut down by the Supreme Court decision because they violated the Coastal Regulation Zone with their aquaculture project, their mafias came and destroyed people's fishing boats ... it seems we act non-violently and use the law and the courts but they always respond with customary violence and break their own laws ... signatures of 'consent' for the project (in Kashipur) were sometimes taken at gun point and under heavy police presence and after 'consenting' we were forcibly fed meat and liquor. (Focus group notes, February 2008)

Frantz Fanon's (1963/2004) theorization of violence is instructive here in relation to necessary Adivasi political responses to market and colonial violence and the related blindness of an estatized–human rights recourse to the same while simultaneously advocating for civility and nonviolence as axiomatic principles for any response considered by Adivasi or other aggrieved groups. Violence, as Fanon saw it, is the *sine qua non* of imperialism and colonialism and, in his conception, the totalizing nature of colonial violence must not only be challenged by the absolute violence of decolonization but such a confrontation also carries with it an obligation to take sides; that is, an injunction to affirm the material praxis of anti-colonial violence as a necessary and strategic response to colonial violence in contrast to approaches that, once more, place the colonial burden on the colonized by the immediate demand for truth and reconciliation (Williams 2010: xxviii). Perhaps echoing an element of Fanon's analysis, Adivasi leaders share the following:

> They are fighting against those who have everything and nothing to lose. We will persist and as long as they keep breaking their own laws – this only makes it easier for us! (Focus group notes, February 2008)
>
> The movement is here to fight collectively (*sangram*) to save (*raksha*) the forests and to protect our way of life. (Focus group notes, February 2007)

> We, who have been lying low for so many years, are now actively tightening our belts (*onta bhirunchanti*) ... (Focus group notes, January 2007)

State-sanctioned market violence and the selective blindness of a human rights regime predominantly wedded to neoliberal market-developmental interests also enlists a racist-colonial ploy once used to justify British colonialism in India (and to downplay the threat to British rule posed by anti-colonial movements) against Adivasi (and related rural subaltern, including Dalits) struggles in order to play down this threat to unjust state–market neoliberal rule today. Essentialist and racist views pertaining to the duality of modern India/ns (with moral/caste–race superiority) and Adivasi traditionalism and backwardness (inferiority) are frequently marshaled to justify development repression of Adivasi as expressed by Evans-Pritchard in 1965 in relation to Indian anti-colonial movements:

> we are rational, primitive peoples, pre-logical, living in a world of dreams and make believe, of mystery and awe; we are capitalist, they are communists; we are monogamous, they are promiscuous; we are monotheists, they are fetishists, animists, pre-animist or what have you and so on. (As cited in Rajagopal 2003: 179)

In the words of a Kondh Adivasi woman leader of the ADEA in South Orissa:

> The *sarkar* (government) and their workers think that we Adivasis do not know anything and we are good for nothing ... That is why they think they do not need to ask us anything before going ahead. That's why they think they can put their pressure and power on us (*shakti a bong prayogo karanti*). So they are selling our forests, they are selling our water and they are selling our land and maybe they will sell us also. (Interview notes, February, 2007)

Or, as a Dalit leader of the ADEA puts it, 'where we live, they call this area *ad-husith* (akin to an Adivasi–Dalit "pest infestation"); we are condemned to the life of the *ananta paapi* (eternal sinners), as *colonkitha* (dirty/black/stained), as *ghruniya* (despised and hated)' (Interview notes, February, 2007).

As Evans (1998: 4) has also noted, when rights are construed as 'power over people, expressed in exclusionary practices that deny the full participation of those who fail to support the interests of the dominant group'—that is, when rights are concerned with establishing and maintaining the moral claims that legitimate particular interests such as neoliberal state–market interests or religious conservative casteist interests in the Adivasi or Dalit context (Prasant and Kapoor 2010)—such exclusions are often justified on the basis of an alleged lack of rational or moral capacity of excluded groups to engage in decision-making processes or the simple prejudiced assertion that such groups are 'mad' (Keeley 1990).

Hegemony and the Subversion of Human Rights Commitments: Controlling Realities

In Gramscian terms (Gramsci 1971), in a bid to secure the right to exercise social and political control that binds the ruler and the ruled in a consensual order that legitimates power, the hegemon or neoliberal Indian state or corporate–state nexus utilizes human rights rhetoric (made evident in numerous examples cited in this paper of state duplicity in delivering rights to Adivasi and rural subalterns around development displacement and dispossession) as part of a process of socialization to enhance control based on might with that based on right, in order to secure its intellectual and moral leadership; that is, the human rights commitment of an increasingly corporatized Indian state can be convincingly construed as an instrument in the exercise of hegemonic control by the corporate state, as different and potentially resistant groups like the Adivasi are encouraged to accept an order characterized by a common social–moral language, namely human rights and citizenship, 'that expresses a singular version of reality informing with its spirit all forms of thought and behaviour' (Evans 1998: 5). While *dominance without hegemony* (Guha 1997) is always a reality in Adivasi contexts of dispossession (e.g. for a chronology of state–corporate violence in the service of mining market fundamentalism in Orissa, including the macabre spectacle of the dismemberment of the hands of six Adivasi killed by the police after police firing on unarmed protestors on 2 January 2006 in the case of anti-Tata Steel protests in Kalinganagar, see the coverage of www.sanhati.org regarding Kalinganagar or for anti-bauxite mining activism-related intimidation and violence, see Das and Das 2006), the use of force is always a costly affair, both in ethico-political (as 'public relations') and material terms. Subsequently, Gramsci's proposition that coercion alone cannot guarantee the long term success of a hegemon and that hegemony requires and signifies the building of a (false) consensus around a set of values (e.g. expressed as human rights) that support the hegemon's interests, remains instructive to some degree in relation to an Adivasi–state–market–civil society politics of dispossession and displacement, especially when Adivasi *seem to have accepted such development*. The hegemon exercises control through a combination of might and the legitimation of right, the highest form of hegemony being exercised when the hegemon's values (e.g. all forms of legitimate political expression are boiled down to a human rights-based Eurocentric or 'Third World-elitist-politics') are accepted as 'common sense' (Evans 2005: 17–18; Gramsci 1971).

More importantly, as Randall Williams (2010) suggests, regardless of whether Adivasi accept elite values/conceptions and political conceptions (e.g. estatized international human rights), by being encouraged (e.g. by international non-governmental organizations [INGOs]) or compelled (by the state) to resort to a state-sanctioned and administered human rights-based politics, they effectively enter in to a dependent politics whose rules and possibilities are dictated by the state; that is, a realm of depoliticization (or a sanitized 'civil society' politics) that has little to no room for a more militant brand of politics for decolonization (see point made in relation to Fanon) in response to the daily violence of colonial control which characterizes processes of displacement and dispossession (Kapoor 2009c; Nandy 2008). Or, in Balakrishnan Rajagopal's terms, 'the institutionalization of human rights helps to manage mass resistance' (2003: 53).

In understanding the working of human rights and hegemonic propensities alluded to by Evans (1998), an examination of several examples of human rights duplicity and contradiction would help to begin to substantiate the case and lend credence to the argument that human rights provisions are merely part of the state's arsenal in securing hegemonic control over the populace (by offering them rights in a bid to secure the moral right to govern) while all the while simultaneously usurping these rights in the service of securing the dominant interests of a global and national corporate–consumer class/caste elite as is being suggested.

Since the first notification to recognize scheduled tribes in India in 1950 and the Indian commitment to indigenous/tribal peoples expressed through the ILO and other international covenants and conventions, according to a report on the Draft National Policy on Tribals by the Asian Centre for Human Rights (ACHR), 'non-implementation of these laws and adoption of laws and procedures to negate these legal protections has had an adverse impact on indigenous people' (ACHR 2005: 2). The report notes that 'contradictory legal provisions and failure to implement or translate constitutional provisions in to reality' (Ibid: 4) continue to undermine indigenous assertions as self-determined peoples. For instance, and as pointed out in this report, while the fifth schedule of the constitution and the Provisions of the Panchayat's Act (Extension to the Scheduled Areas; 1996) or PESA, 'recognize the ownership rights of indigenous peoples to their traditional lands recognized as Protected Areas' (Ibid: 4), such assertions are undermined by forest laws that confer 'usufruct rights' to use minor forest products without a right to ownership and subject to a 'whimsical no damage to the forest' determination by forest officials (Ibid: 5). In the words of a Kondh Adivasi man,

> The government and the companies come and take away truckloads of bamboo. The forests which our ancestors nurtured (*banchaye chonti*) is getting destroyed by these outsiders (*bahari ko lok*). When these things happen, the forest guards give them protection and, when we have needs, they ask us if we have paid our royalty or have you paid your taxes on the tamarind trees—we are taxed for each of these trees. When they take truck loads of sal, timbers, bamboos and the paper mills exploit this for their business—how can they say the Adivasis are destroying the forests? We depend on forests for life, the business people (*vyavasahi*) and the government are destroying them for their own profit (*labho*). (Interview notes, February 2007)

When it comes to forced or illegal evictions (euphemistically referred to as 'displacement' in official parlance), the report of the ACHR notes several such contradictions between protections under the fifth and sixth schedules of the constitution (or commitments under the international covenants on civil and political rights and economic, social and cultural rights) on the one hand and specific acts such as the Forest Conservation Act (1980), the Wild Life (Protection)

Act (1972) and the Land Acquisition Act (1894). The latter has been instrumental in the eviction of indigenous and tribal peoples for more than a century and, until recently, had no provisions for resettlement and rehabilitation (R&R), not to mention right to free, prior and informed consent. Some studies have demonstrated, for instance, that there is practically no evidence of consultation of the Gram Sabha by the state (despite said stipulations in PESA) when it comes to land acquisition and/or R&R packages, not to mention that the latter is not even recognized as a right under the constitution of India (Bandopadhya 2004; Das 2001).

Under the Indian Forest Act (1927) and the Forest Conservation Act (FCA; 1980), cultivable lands that existed prior to both acts are being categorized as encroachment areas. For instance, the National Commission on Scheduled Castes and Tribes has noted that, as a result of the FCA (1980), some 148,000 people (mainly tribals) occupying 184,000 hectares of land in forest areas in the state of Madhya Pradesh suddenly became encroachers on 24 October 1980, and thus liable to eviction (ACHR 2005). Under the recent Scheduled Tribes and Other Traditional Forest Dwellers (Recognition of Forest Rights) Act–or FRA–(2006), hailed in some quarters as a victory by people's movements in the struggle for Adivasi autonomy and sovereignty as the act appears to recognize the Adivasi way of life, there is now a growing scepticism in some quarters that this is yet another 'law and "new welfare model" used by the state to retain its authority, power and supremacy over resources, alienate people from their land and way of life, and create and sustain capital markets' (Ramdas 2009: 72). While the FRA recognizes community and customary rights to the forest and confers power to the communities to protect forests in accordance with their own modes of conservation, the Ministry of Tribal Welfare and the Forest Department have interpreted these provisions as a license to sanction export/urban market oriented mono/cash-crop rubber, coffee, and fruit plantations in conjunction with the National Rural Employment Guarantee Scheme (NREGS), whereby tribals are reduced to being a source of cheap labor for these so-called tribal development schemes (Kapoor 2010).

Now tribals can cultivate their lands with dignity and without any fear. Tribals can plant rubber plants, mango, cashew nut, orange, lime, or palm oil as per local conditions. The state government would also develop lands in tribal areas and the tribals will be paid daily wages under the NREGS program though they are working on their own land (Ramdas 2009: 69).

The 'free choice' between palm oil and coffee mono-crop for markets is ironic to say the least, as Adivasi agriculture (indigenous choice of crops) focused on food for families is being viewed by the Forest Departments (for instance) as 'encroachment' and being met with considerable aggression to evict Adivasi/forest dwelling communities from their homelands across the country (see World Rainforest Movement Bulletin 135, October 2008, for a disturbing analysis of atrocities committed by state agents against Adivasi/Dalit women, while allegedly implementing the FRA):

> when FRA and PESA is actually supposed to strengthen the hands of Adivasi

communities and local Gram Sabhas to decide on whether or not to implement mono-crop plantations or any other programmes that might threaten to displace Adivasi production, cultures, ecosystems, knowledge and ways. The claim on the state, that continues to fall on deaf ears, is to recognize Adivasi ways of living and being as a political right and not as an essentialized-inferiority in need of protection and welfare from a self-appointed guardian or paternalistic state. (Kapoor 2010: 28–29).

In the words of a Kondh woman:

> The Forest Department comes and asks us to create a Forest Protection Committee (*jungle surakshya manch*). Protection from whom should I ask? . . . We do not cooperate because they really do not care about the forest! We need to protect the forest from them! (Interview notes, January 2007, village D).

Such examples of consistent and widespread legal/rights contradictions and duplicity in relation to forced/illegal evictions, forest and land rights, lends credence to the argument that human rights commitments serve hegemonic aspirations of the state and the dominant interests that inform state partiality to elite projects that contradict the wellbeing of Adivasi despite these various so-called protective provisions.

In their analysis of neoliberal impacts on land policies and processes of land alienation, Pimple and Sethi (2005: 239) conclude that 'under the application of neoliberal land policies . . . traditional occupiers of land under customary law confront the prospect and reality of becoming illegal encroachers on land they have cultivated and sustained for generations' (see earlier reference to example from Madhya Pradesh re: the same). They identify some key strategies and approaches employed by the neoliberal state to accomplish this: (1) originally practiced by the British in the 1800s, reservation of forests whereby large tracts of land are declared as reserved or protected forests and cultivable and wasteland areas and these demarcated territories are declared to be out of bounds (leads to eviction unless a cheap source of labor is required to work the land/forest); (2) leasing of forests to industrialists for timber felling, regeneration, agribusiness, mining, and tourism ventures; (3) land alienation enabled by the Land Acquisition Amendment Act, which simplifies the procedures for the acquisition of land by state-controlled or state-owned enterprises on the grounds of serving the public purpose; and (4) the Wild Life (Protection) Act (1972) 'which has been used to define the tribal as the enemy of ecology and the outsider/environmentalist as protector' (Ibid: 242), as tribals are displaced from lands and forests demarcated as national parks and sanctuaries and even grudging concessions such as licenses that permit limited access are challenged by some environmentalists (conservationists).

> Even today you will find there is not enough cultivable land available for our people because they have taken it away . . . They have the power of *dhana* (wealth) and *astro-shastro* (armaments). They have the power of of artificial laws and rules (*kruthrima ain*)—they created these laws to maintain their own interests. (Adivasi leader of the ADEA, interview notes, February 2007) There

is communal conflict around land and forests because the political powers, in order to keep their control and access to these vital resources, are promoting division and hatred among the communities (Domb, Kondh and Saora). Our communities once had equal access to land and forests, which today is being controlled by these outside methods of the *sarkar* (government) and the *vyaparis* (business classes) and upper castes (Brahmins). They want to perpetuate their ways and ideas among us and always keep us divided. We are all poor classes (*garib sreni*) and land and forest are vital for our survival. And if they succeed in controlling them, they also end up controlling our lives. As has the case over the ages, they want us to live in disharmony and difference so that they can be the rulers (*shashaks*) all the time. So they have done this. (Adivasi elder, interview notes, February 2007)

The likelihood of such displacement and dispossession increasing, regardless of the state-institutionalized legal/human rights 'protections' (or blindness) regarding the same, is real and on-going as noted in relation to what is being referred to as the global *land grab*; that is, the purchase or lease of large tracts of land by wealthier, food insecure nations and private investors from mostly poor, developing countries in order to produce crops for export. According to the International Food Policy Research Institute (IFPRI), foreign investors sought or secured between 37 million and 49 million acres of farmland in the developing world between 2006 and 2009 (Daniel and Mittal 2009). Such market-driven neoliberal policy prescriptions around land markets, and development and poverty alleviation are actively promoted by the World Bank, a central agent and global architect of imperial control, which sees similar opportunity in addressing climate change (Ramdas 2009); that is, it is deemed to be an investment opportunity that will assist communities to use forests as a means for moving out of poverty, suggesting that local ownership offers opportunities to capitalize on forest assets, an approach being pursued through the bank's short-term financing from the BioCarbon Fund to mobilize small/marginal farmers to raise plantations of tree species with high rates of carbon sequestration in their lands, from which they will earn income from carbon credits. According to Ramdas (2009: 72), 'The powerful convergence of global climate change policies and neoliberal markets appears to be an overriding force that is shaping current environment and forest policy in India ... All initial evidence points towards the displacement of Adivasi subjectivities and livelihoods'. The Indigenous People's Declaration on Climate Change (The Anchorage Declaration 2009) exposes sustainable development dispossession of Adivasi and indigenous peoples globally, while still appealing to 'human rights':

> We, Indigenous People challenge States to abandon false solutions to climate change that negatively impact Indigenous People's rights, lands, air, oceans, forests, territories and waters. These include . . . agro-fuels, plantations and market based mechanisms such as carbon trading, the Clean Development Mechanism and forest offsets. The human rights of Indigenous Peoples to protect our forests and forest livelihoods must be recognized, respected and ensured. (As cited in Kapoor 2010: 28)

The preceding examples and arguments have been used to demonstrate the active, premeditated and non-accidental (consistent pattern) nature of the subversion of Adivasi and indigenous human and legal rights around displacement/dispossession, forest and land-related issues and the related implications for Adivasi's exercising sovereign control over their own ways/development processes as affirmed in the fifth and sixth schedules of the Indian constitution. There is good and ample reason to believe that state-institutionalized human/legal rights discourse in India have been used by the corporatized and developmentalist state to advance colonial controls and neoliberal and dominant religious conservative interests in relation to the Adivasi place (or active exclusion) in the contemporary Indian polity, subsequently raising critical questions in relation to the limitations of a human rights-based state-institutionalized politics of justice/redress with respect to displacement and dispossession of Adivasi and other marginalized rural subaltern communities.

Colonial Continuities, Neoliberal-Hegemony and the Re-Politicization (?) of Human Rights: Concluding Reflections

If, at some level, the modernist purpose of rights and related notions of citizenship are to create the conditions for individuals and peoples to lead a dignified and peaceful life, then the promise of non-institutionalized human rights lies in its potential to stimulate political struggles (movements and movement-defined conceptions of human rights or other political possibilities thereof?; Kapoor 2011) that transgress the hegemonic hijacking of the construction, interpretation and mis/application of rights in the wider interests of an Adivasi and indigenous politics for pluri-nationalism and co-existence (Kapoor and Shizha 2010; Meyer and Alvarado 2010), while being against colonization and imperial appropriations of peoples, cultures, lands and ecology. The Eurocentric and state-centric institutionalized conception of human rights/legal codings, as discussed, are mostly constitutive of (or re-shaped in the interests of) the project of colonialism and today's neoliberal hegemonic project (imperialism), with limited prospects for deployment by Adivasi/indigenous peoples who are compelled (when engaging in *real politik*) to resort to this mostly derived politics/discursive formation to repeat what has always already been said before. A human rights discourse is deemed *necessary* in order to enhance the prospects of becoming audible in imperial/metropolitan society.

If there is an Adivasi conception of something akin to 'human rights', it probably resides in an affirmation of a way/state of being that is under constant challenge by the imperial and colonial project of a globalizing capitalism. At a global level, a statement by Via Campesina (the largest peasant-indigenous people's network of movements) expresses the claim as follows:

> No agrarian reform is acceptable that is based only on land redistribution. We believe that the new agrarian reform must also include a cosmic vision of the territories of communities of peasants, the landless, indigenous peoples, rural workers, fisher-folk, nomadic pastoralists, tribal, afro-descendents, ethnic minorities, and displaced peoples, who base their work on the production of food

and who maintain a relationship of respect and harmony with Mother Earth and the oceans. (Via Campesina 2006)

In Adivasi terms from the South Orissa region, a manifesto developed by 13 Adivasi-Dalit-landless peasants and displaced peoples' movement organizations express their claim as follows:

> We, the people's movements present here representing people's struggles from South and coastal Orissa have discussed and debated our issues and are hereby resolved to stand as a broad-based platform known as Lok Adhikar Manch (LAM) in support of the following manifesto [people's statement]:
>
> (1) We are communities dependent on natural resources like land, forest and water, which are more than resources for us—our life system depends on them. Our way of life, beliefs, knowledge and values have historically and as it is today revolve around our natural surroundings. More than at any point of time in our lives as traditional communities, today we feel pressurized and pushed hard to give up our ways and systems and give way to unjust intrusions by commercial, political and religious interests for their development and domination (*shemano koro prabhavo abom unathi*). We have been made to sacrifice, we have been thrown out throughout history by these dominant groups and forces for their own comfort and for extending their way of life while we have been made slaves, servants and subordinates (*tolualoko*). Our natural systems have taught us that each of us is important, each of our communities are important and we are an integrated part of the natural order we live in. At this critical juncture, we resolve to work together to protect ourselves, our interests, our natural bases (*prakrutic adhar*) and fight against any unjust appropriation of our natural habitations by commercial and state developmentalist interests. The manner in which industrialization is taking place (especially mining and dam projects), displacing the sons and daughters of the soil, destroying our resource and life base: we collectively oppose it in the future. We have nothing to gain from liberalization (*mukto bojaro*), privatization (*ghoroi korono*) and globalization (*jagothi korono*), which are talked about today. We want to live the way we know how to live among our forests, streams, hills and mountains and water bodies without culture, traditions and whatever that is good in our society intact. We want to define change and development for ourselves (*amo unathi abom parivarthonoro songhya ame nirupono koribako chaho*). We are nature's friends (*prakruthi bandhu*), so our main concern is preserving nature and enhancing its influence in our lives. (LAM statement, field notes, April 2009)

While the conceptions of the claims are clear, the issue is one of politics and possibility thereof around moving from where we are to where we need to be. Drawing on the work of Frantz Fanon, Randal Williams (2010) alludes to the pitfalls and cul-de-sacs of the recourse to a human rights-based politics in colonial circumstances by any anti-colonial formation (in this case, an Adivasi/indigenous challenge) or by euphoric advocates for a human rights-based approach to these political conundrums:

> Fanon offered, well beyond what was specific to the conditions of colonialism proper (and wholly relevant for today), a critical set of political directives de-

veloped out of the relative certainty that any strategic appropriation of dominant structures and forms in the course of struggle must reckon with the corrupted histories of those same forms after the achievement of their tactical ends. This enduring lesson should trouble, albeit in different ways, any non-dialectical advocacy of human rights or decolonization, insofar as any readily available 'way' out of the structures of domination is, both, likely at the same time, a 'way' back in. In the case of human rights, for example, inserting the formal equality of the universal human into structures of violence regulated by domestic and international law subjects any 'successful' appropriation of juridical terms to swift and effective counterappropriation. (Williams 2010: xxix)

Acknowledgment

The author acknowledges the assistance of the Social Sciences and Humanities Research Council of Canada (SSHRC) for this research in to 'Learning in Adivasi (original dweller) social movements in India' through a Standard Research Grant (2006–2009). Reflections and grounded discussions in this paper are both informed by this research.

References

Amin, S., 2006. *Beyond US Hegemony? Assessing the Prospects for a Multipolar World.* New York: Zed Books.

Asian Centre for Human Rights (ACHR), 2005. Promising Picture or Broken Future? Commentary and Recommendations on the Draft National Policy on Tribals of the Government of India. www.achrweb.org (accessed September 28, 2011).

Bandopadhya, D., 2004. Rayagada Story Retold: Destitutes of Development. *Economic and Political Weekly* 39, no. 5 (January): 3250.

Bandyopadhyay, J. and V. Shiva, 1990. Asia's Forests and Asia's Cultures. *Lessons for the Rainforest* edited by S. Head and R. Hienzman, 66–77. San Francisco, CA: Sierra Club Books.

Barnes, R., A. Gray.and B. Kingsbury, eds. 1995. *Indigenous Peoples of Asia.* Ann Arbor, MI: Association for Asian Studies.

Baviskar A., 2005. Red in Tooth and Claw? Looking for Class in Struggles over Nature. *Social Movements in India: Poverty, Power and Politics* edited by R. Ray and M. Katzenstein, 161–178. Lanham, MD: Rowman and Littlefield.

Baxi U., 2002. *The Future of Human Rights.* Oxford: Oxford University Press.

Bharati, S., 1999. Human Rights and Development Projects in India. *The PRP Journal of Human Rights* 3, no. 4: 20.

Blaser, M., H. Feit and G. McRae, eds. 2004. *In the Way of Development: Indigenous Peoples, Life Projects and Globalization.* London: Zed Books.

Boron, A., 2005. *Empire and Imperialism: A Critical Reading of Michael Hardt and Antonio Negri.* London: Zed Books.

Cameron, A. and R. Palan, 2004. *The Imagined Economies of Globalization.* London: Sage.

Chomsky. N., 1988. The United States and the Challenge of Relativity. *Human*

Rights Fifty Years On: A Reappraisal, edited by T. Evans, 26–56. Manchester: Manchester University Press.

Choudry, A., 2007. Transnational Activist Coalition Politics and the De/Colonization of Pedagogies of Mobilization: Learning From Anti-Neoliberal Indigenous Movement Articulations. *International Education* 37 no. 1: 97–112.

Daniel, S. and A. Mittal, 2009. *The Great Land Grab: The Rush for the World's Farmland Threatens Food Security for the Poor*. Oakland, CA: Oakland Institute.

Das, J., 2001. *Human Rights and Indigenous Peoples*. New Delhi: APH Publishing House.

Das, A. and V. Das, 2006. *Chronicle of a Struggle and Other Writings*. Kashipur, Rayagada, Orissa: Agragamee Publications.

Donnelly, J., 1989. *Universal Human Rights in Theory and Practice*. Ithaca, NY: Cornell University Press, 1989.

Evans, T., 1998. *Human Rights Fifty Years On: A Reappraisal*. Manchester: Manchester University Press.

———. 2005. *The Politics of Human Rights: A Global Perspective*. London: Pluto Press.

Eversol, R., J. McNeish, J. and A. Cimadamore, eds. 2005. *Indigenous Peoples and Poverty: An International Perspective*. London: Zed Books.

Falk, R., 2000. *Human Rights Horizons*. London and New York: Routledge.

Fanon, F., 2004 [1963]. *The Wretched of the Earth* (Richard Philcox, trans.). New York: Grove Press.

Fernandes, W., 2006. Development Related Displacement and Tribal Women. *Tribal Development in India: The Contemporary Debate*, edited by G. Rath, 112–132. New Delhi: Sage.

Fisher, W., 1999. Going Under: Indigenous People and the Struggles against Big Dams: Introduction. *Cultural Survival Quarterly* 23, no. 3: 29–32.

Ghosh, K., 2006. Between Global Flows and Local Dams: Indigenousness, Locality and the Transnational Sphere in Jharkhand, India. *Cultural Anthropology* 21, no. 4: 501–534.

Gramsci, A., 1971. *Selections from Prison Notebooks* (Q Hoare and G Howell, eds and trans). London: Lawrence & Wishart.

Guha, R., 1988. Ideological Trends in Indian Environmentalism. *Economic and Political Weekly* 23, no. 49: 80–92.

———. 1997. *Dominance without Hegemony: History and Power in Colonial India*. New York: Harvard University Press.

Hannum, H., 2003. Indigenous Rights." In *International Human Rights in the 21st Century: Protecting the Rights of Groups*, edited by G. Lyons and J. Mayall, 72–99. Lanham, MD: Rowman and Littlefield.

Hardt, M. and A. Negri, 2000. *Empire*. Cambridge, MA: Harvard University Press.

Harvey, D., 2003. *The New Imperialism*. London: Oxford University Press.

Henkin, L., 1990. *The Age of Rights*. New York: Columbia University Press.

Hussain, M., 2008. *Interrogating Development: State, Displacement and*

Popular Resistance on North Eastern India. New Delhi: Sage.
Ishay, M., 2004. *The History of Human Rights.* Berkeley, CA: University of California Press.
Kamat, S., 2001. Anthropology and Global Capital: Rediscovering the Noble Savage. *Cultural Dynamics* 13, no. 1: 29–51.
Kapoor, D., 2009a. Participatory Academic Research (par) and People's Participatory Action Research (PAR): Research, Politicization and Subaltern Social Movements (SSMs) in India. *Education, Participatory Action Research and Social Change: International Perspectives*, edited by D. Kapoor and S. Jordan, 29–44. New York: Palgrave Macmillan.
———. 2009b. Subaltern Social Movement Learning: Adivasis (Original Dwellers) and the Decolonization of Space in India. *Education, Decolonization and Development: Perspectives from Asia, Africa and the Americas*, edited by D. Kapoor, 7–38. Rotterdam: Sense Publishers.
———. 2009c. Adivasi (Original Dwellers) in the Way Of State-Corporate Development: Development Dispossession and Learning in Social Action for Land and Forests in India. *McGill Journal of Education* 44, no. 1: 55–78.
———. 2010. Learning from Adivasi (Original Dweller) Political-Ecological Expositions of Development: Claims on Forests, Land and Place in India. *Indigenous Knowledge and Learning in Asia/Pacific and Africa: Perspectives on Development, Education and Culture* edited by D. Kapoor and E. Shizha, 17–34. New York: Palgrave Macmillan.
———. 2011. Subaltern Social Movement (SSM) Post-Mortems of Development in India: Locating Translocal Activism and Radicalism. *Journal of Asian and African Studies* 46, no. 2: 130–148.
Kapoor, D. and S. Jordan, 2009. Introduction: International Perspectives on Education, PAR, and Social Change. *Education, Participatory Action Research and Social Change: International Perspectives*, D. Kapoor and S. Jordan, 1–11. New York: Palgrave Macmillan.
Kapoor, D. and E. Shizha, eds. 2010. *Indigenous Knowledge and Learning in Asia/Pacific and Africa: Perspectives on Development, Education and Culture.* New York: Palgrave Macmillan.
Keeley, J., 1990. Towards a Foucauldian Analysis of International Regimes. *International Organization* 44, no. 1: 83–105.
McMichael, P., ed. 2010. *Contesting Development: Critical Struggles for Social Change.* New York: Routledge.
McNeish, J. and R. Eversole, 2005. Overview: The right to Self-determination. *Indigenous Peoples and Poverty: An International Perspective*, edited by R. Eversole, J. McNeish and A. Cimadamore, 97–107. London: Zed.
Mehta, L., ed. 2009. *Displaced by Development: Confronting Marginalization and Gender Injustice.* New Delhi: Sage.
Menon, N. and A. Nigam, 2007. *Power and Contestation: India Since 1989.* London: Zed Books.
Meyer, L. and M. Alvarado, eds. 2010. *New World of Indigenous Resistance: Noam Chomsky and Voices from North, South and Central America.* San

Francisco, CA: City Lights Books.
Mieville, C., 2005. *Between Equal Rights: A Marxist Theory of International Law*. Chicago, IL: Hay Market Books.
Mookerjea, S., 2011. On Learning How to Liberate the Common: Subaltern Biopolitics and the Endgame of Neoliberalism. *Critical Perspectives on Neoliberal Globalization, Development and Education in Africa and Asia*, edited by D. Kapoor, 51–68. Rotterdam: Sense Publishers,
Nag, S., 2001. Nationhood and Displacement in the Indian Subcontinent. *Economic and Political Weekly* 36, no. 51 (March 1): 4753–4760.
Nandy, A., 2008. *Romancing the State: And the Fate of Dissent in the Tropics*. New York: Oxford University Press.
Oliver-Smith, A., 2010. *Defying Displacement: Grassroots Resistance and the Critique of Development*. Austin, TX: University of Texas Press.
Padel, F. and S. Das, 2010. *Out of This Earth: East India Adivasis and the Aluminium Cartel*. New Delhi: Orient Blackswan.
Patnaik, U., 2007. *The Republic of Hunger and Other Essays*. Gurgaon: Three Essays Collective.
Pimple, M. and M. Sethi, 2005. Occupation of land in India: Experiences and challenges. *Reclaiming Land: The Resurgence of Rural Movements in Africa, Asia and Latin America*, edited by S. Moyo and P. Yeros, 235–256. London: Zed.
Prasad, A., 2003. *Against Ecological Romanticism: Verrier Elwin and the Making of an Anti-Modern Tribal Identity*. New Delhi: Three Essays Collective.
———. 2004. *Environmentalism and the Left: Contemporary Debates and the Future Agendas in Tribal Areas*. New Delhi: Left Word Books.
Prasant, K. and D. Kapoor, 2010. Learning and Knowledge Production in Dalit Social Movements in Rural India. *Learning from the Ground Up: Global Perspectives on Social Movements and Knowledge Production*, edited by A. Choudry and D. Kapoor, 193–210. NY: Palgrave Macmillan.
Quijano, A., 2000. Coloniality of power and eurocentrism in Latin America. *International Sociology* 15, no. 2: 215–232.
Rajagopal, B., 2003. *International Law from Below: Development, Social Movements and Third World Resistance*. Cambridge: Cambridge University Press.
Ramanathan, U., 2009. A Word on Eminent Domain. *Displaced by Development: Confronting Marginalization and Gender Injustice* edited by L. Mehta, 133–145. New Delhi: Sage Publications.
Ramdas, S., 2009. Women, Forest Spaces and the Law: Transgressing the Boundaries. *Economic and Political Weekly* 64, no. 44: 65–73.
Ray, R. and M. Katzenstein, 2005. *Social Movements in India: Poverty, Power and Politics*. Lanham, MD: Rowman & Littlefield.
Sanyal, K., 2010. *Rethinking Capitalist Development: Primitive Accumulation, Governmentality and Postcolonial Capitalism*. New Delhi: Routledge.
Stammers, N., 2009. *Human Rights and Social Movements*. New York: Pluto Press.

Tuhiwai-Smith, L., 1999. *Decolonizing Methodologies*. London: Zed Books.
Via Campesina, 2006. Sovranita Alimentare, Final Declaration. http://viacampesina.org/main_en/index.php?option=com_content&task=view&id=180&Itemid=27 (accessed September 4, 2011).
Williams, R., 2010. *The Divided World: Human Rights and its Violence*. Minneapolis, MN: University of Minnesota Press.

Notes

1. This chapter is reprinted by permission of, and was first published by, SAGE Publications Ltd. in the *Journal of Asian and African Studies* 47(4)/August 2012: London. The author and publisher are grateful to Sage for granting permission.

2. Adivasi is a claim to indigenous location as 'original dwellers' or first (mulo nivasi or 'root people' is the expression used by Kondh Adivasi research participants in this study) inhabitants vis-à-vis later arrivals. In keeping with the UN and the Declaration of the Rights of Indigenous Peoples, self-definition is consistent with recognition for the self-determination of indigenous peoples and the usage in this paper is in keeping with this understanding. Adivasi is also understood in terms of what may well be the common historical and contemporary experience of most indigenous peoples including: being original inhabitants of a land later colonized by others; non-dominant sectors of society with unique ethnic identities and cultures; strong ties to land and territory; experiences or threats of dispossession from ancestral territory; the experience of being subjected to culturally foreign governance and institutional structures; and the threat of assimilation and loss of identity vis-à-vis a dominant society (McNeish and Eversole 2005: 5). This being said, the designation in the Indian and Asian contexts (estimated to be the spatial container for 70% of the world's indigenous peoples) in general is vigorously contested given that: (1) governments in Asia (including India) do not recognize the category (with the exception of the Philippines); (2) indigenous could often mean prior rather than original peoples given the multiple waves of colonization and migration in Asia/India; (3) dissident ethnic/caste groups (e.g. Dalits/scheduled castes in India) sandwiched between indigenous and non-indigenous peoples obscure such claims by demanding indigenous status as well (e.g. given ameliorative and other perceived or real advantages of scheduled tribe status which is the state-category/taxonomy for Adivasi in relation to a politics of exclusive governmentality – see Ghosh 2006 for a critique of such ethno-racist statecraft); and (4) indigenous peoples of Asia (post colony) do not have the clarity of definition afforded to indigenous peoples of the settler colonies of North America, Australia and New Zealand where the indigenous category came in to existence vis-à-vis western European colonialism (Barnes, Gray and Kingsbury 1995). Archana Prasad (2003: 28) refers to the 'original peoples = forest dwelling' argument as a 'creation myth of the original inhabitant' citing historical evidence/records to suggest that forest-dwelling status/location happened largely as a result of marginalization of tribals by caste Hindu peasants in central India and 'their sedentization in to forests by the British land settlements'; that is, the permanent settlement of agricultural and zamindari lands (feudal arrangements) by the British ensured that the movement of tribals between the highlands and plains was stopped forever. That said, in terms of the politics of representation, the Adivasi/indigenous category troubles the real and representational left-politics (Kamat 2001; Prasad 2004) of class struggle by disaggregating the preferred category of peasant (compels a peasantization of Adivasi – see Kapoor 2011 for this discussion). Left-academic politics also obscures/dismisses (either as pure caricature/representational politics or as mere British colonial invention) Adivasi claims to being 'original peoples' in

the necessary interests of addressing the real politik of class struggle aimed at the very forces (including a conservative saffron politics that dismisses Adivasi as 'jungle peoples' or, conversely, pragmatically enlists Adivasi in a divisive caste politics aimed at scheduled castes/Dalits) that displace and dispossess Adivasi and/or peasant alike. Gandhian-environmentalist (Bandopadhyay and Shiva 1990) politics of representation are also similarly critiqued by Guha (1988: 83–84) and others (Prasad 2003, 2004) for their attempts to deploy the Adivasi (forest/original peoples positioning and aranya sanskriti or forest culture as embodying a living-critique of development) to set up an ideological counterpoint to development (caricaturing) which excludes the Adivasi as a conscious subjects of their own history, while Alpa Shah (2010: 130) refers to the same tendency as 'eco-incarceration'. This politics of representation adds to the complexity of definition and location of Adivasi (original dwellers) in India.

CHAPTER 7

Hindutva Politics—Impact on Human Rights

Ram Puniyani

During last three decades India has witnessed a strange political scene. The language of political interaction has been made to shift away from the struggles and travails of the poor and exploited i.e. issues revolving around bread, butter, shelter, housing, health and education (the problems of this world). The issues supposed to be related to 'faith' have been imposed on society. We are witness to newer dangers to society, to democratic and secular values in the form of communalism, communal violence and rise of new social political forces basing themselves on 'Religion' in the political arena. We have been hearing a word called Hindutva from last three decades or so. As per Biju Mathew "Hindutva is Nationalist Ideology, based on the Modern day version of intolerant Centralized Hinduism, It has nothing to do with historical tradition of spiritual practices that we call Hinduism. Such a chauvinist-centralized Hinduism–Hindutva has been brought to the forefront by a group of Organizations called as Sangh Parivar (Sangh Family Consisting of Rashtriya Swayam Sevak Sangh... (Mathew n.d.)

Though this Hindutva ideology was rooted in certain social segments from last many decades, its social visibility has been much more prominent in the last few decades. On first thought it gives the impression as if it is some sort of religion. As we will see it derives its name from Hindu Religion but it is a political ideology akin to the Islamist political ideology. This political ideology has raised afresh, the questions of nationality, community, identity and host of other issues in the social space. The Hindutva movement presents itself for building a strong nation based on the tenets of `Hindu Dharma', Hindu Rashtra (Hindu Nation). There are many notions attached to this word and we need to understand the meaning of this. But this is a newer set of value system, which has found sympathy amongst a section of population. We need to understand as to which segment of society is behind this political movement.

While pursuing its political agenda, the Hindutva movement has brought to fore a number of precepts, which have found acceptance amongst some sections of society. It has popularized a new version of History, which looks at the past through the parameter of religion alone. Also the major political force, which is the vehicle of Hindutva politics, the RSS has been spreading this version of history from last many decades. Today large section of media does accept this version of History. It, in a way has become part of 'social common sense'. We need to elaborate that RSS–Hindutva politics has nothing to do with Hindu religion as such, it is part of social agenda of a section of society totally opposed to the democratic and Human rights of weaker sections of society.

Rashtriya Swayamsevak Sangh

Hindutva movement is being spearheaded by a plethora of organizations, the patriarch of which is Rashtriya Swayamsevak Sangh (RSS), the real controller of all other organizations. It was founded in 1925. It was founded in the backdrop which needs to be understood in detail. In 1920 with the entry of Mahatma Gandhi into the political arena, the dynamics of the anti-British movement got tremendously galvanized. He brought in to the struggle the people of all religions, castes and creed. The elite–upper caste domination in the Congress started declining. At this time the upper castes, and the elite landlord section, *Jamindari* elements and *bania's* in particular, in order to reassert their hegemony on the social political and social scene came up with the idea of a Religion based National organization, the RSS.

Slightly prior to this Savarkar had put forward the idea of 'Hindutva as the basis for politics, which stood for Nationalism based on Hinduism.' (Puniyani 2000: 51) At that time the Non-Brahman movement was peaking itself and was threatening to shake the very social power of Jamindar-Brahmin nexus. At international level the race based Nationalism of Nazis (Germany) and Fascists (Italy) was on the ascendance. This was the main inspiration for the political ideas 'Nationalism' of RSS. "German National pride has now become the topic of the day. To keep up the purity of the nation and its culture, Germany shocked the world by her purging the country of the Semitic races—the Jews. National pride at its highest has been manifested here. Germany has also shown to the world how well nigh impossible it is for races and cultures having differences going to the roots to be assimilated into one united whole, a good lesson for us in India to learn and profit by." (Golwalkar 1939: 27)

Marzia Casolari, an Italian researcher who has done work on roots of Hindu Nationalism concludes that "(a) the main historical organizations and leaders of Hindu Nationalism had a distinctive and sustained interest in fascism and Nazism; (b) fascist ideological influences on Hindu Nationalism were present and relevant; (c) to a certain extent, these influences were channeled through direct contacts between Hindu nationalists and members of the Italian fascist state."(Casolari, 2000, 37) RSS decided to keep aloof from day to day to day political struggles and began to train the young boys into the doctrine of Hindu Rashtra. As per this core ideology of RSS "Hindus and Hindus alone, constitute the Indian Nation, since they are the original inhabitants and sole creators of its society and culture. Hinduism is uniquely catholic and tolerant and hence superior to other faiths, ...The subsequent entry and takeover by foreigners created an illusion that India was a land of many different and equal cultures....Only a 'truly secular' Hindu Rashtra will afford protection to non-Hindus"(Basu et. al. 1993: 37).

Even when the whole country was coming forward to struggle against British colonialism, "...RSS identified Muslims rather than the British as the primary enemy of Hindu Rashtra and refrained itself from anti colonial struggle. As its ideal is an 'imagined' Hindu nation, a nation exclusively for Hindus, it attempts to construct a Hindu identity by projecting the Muslims as principal enemy of Hindu nation" (Kanungo 2002: 21).

Bharatiya Janata Party (BJP) is its political wing, Vishwa Hindu Parishad (VHP), is the organization translating Hindutva political agenda on the emotive, religious ground, Bajrang Dal is a group of youth, who are active on the streets. Vanavasi Kalyan Ashram is engaged in promoting 'Hindu norms' amongst Adivasis and Rashtrasevika Samiti is its women's wing. In addition there are other organizations like Saraswati Shishu Mandirs, which inculcate the young minds with its social, cultural and political understanding. These all are collectively called as Sangh Parivar (SP).

The initial concern of Hindutva movement (RSS and Hindu Mahasabha) was to counter the politics of Muslim League and to influence the Congress in pro–Hindu direction. RSS was mainly focusing on Shakhas (Branches), training volunteers for Hindutva movement and Hindu Mahasabha was taking part in electoral politics. After independence the number of cadres of RSS increased, Hindu Mahasabha gradually went into oblivion. One of the ex-pracharak of RSS, Nathuram Godse, murdered Mahatma Gandhi in 1948, following which RSS was banned for some time. Meanwhile RSS volunteers kept on infiltrating in army, bureaucracy media and educational institutions. The number of RSS volunteers went on increasing and multiple RSS controlled organizations started coming up.

RSS undertook mainly the campaigns of ban-cow slaughter in earlier period (1960s) but the response was lukewarm. It became very visible with its anti-communist noises during India–China war and projected 'Nationalist, Patriotic' fervor. Its political wing Jan Sangh undertook the campaign 'Indianize Muslims' (late 1960s). Meanwhile the ideology spread by RSS and the increasing urbanization process were the key factor in the increasing intensity of communal violence.

RSS gained higher respectability Jayprakash Narayan's anti-Congress movement (1974); its political wing joined Janata Party, and came to power, got vital ministries (External affairs, Information and broadcasting etc.) and used the opportunity to further enter the bureaucracy. It left the Janata Party on the issue of duel membership; there was a demand from other components of Janata Party that former members of Jan Sangh leave the RSS. And so either they should leave RSS or the Janata Party. It did not want to leave the RSS, Janata Party broke and Jan Sangh reemerged as BJP, Bharatiya Janata Party, on the plank of 'Gandhian Socialism'.

The period of early 1980s saw a great turmoil in the society. Initially the event of conversion of some Dalits to Islam was given a great projection as the threat of Islam engulfing India. In 1984 the operation Blue Star (Indian army entering golden temple to evacuate the temple from the occupation of Khalistani militants) was followed by the assassination of Indira Gandhi by her body guards. This was followed by massive anti-Sikh pogrom in which many a Congress workers led the assaulting mobs. During this pogrom the RSS ideologue wrote a document subtly supporting Rajiv Gandhi's turning blind eye to the ongoing anti-Sikh pogroms (Nanaji Deshmukh 1984). Later to appease the Muslim fundamentalists Rajiv Gandhi got a bill passed in the Lok Sabha to reverse the Shah Bano verdict granting maintenance to her by the Supreme Court. In the same superficial and opportunist style he went on to get the locks of Babri Masjid opened. This was due to the pressure of the agitation of VHP "By then, however, the VHP-led sadhus and Sants, having tasted victory by forcing the Rajiv Gandhi Government to allow shilanyas at the disputed site in Ayodhya, had decided to carry on the movement..." (Chatterjee 1996: 97)

Both the fundamentalist streams, Hindu and Muslim were on the ascendance. The opening of the locks emboldened the Hindu Fundamentalists and now the sections of Muslim leadership started feeling insecure on the Babri masjid issue. Opening of the locks of Babri Masjid gave a fillip to the SP and BJP decided to take up the Ram Janmbhumi issue.

In 1990 due to his own compulsions vis-à-vis the politics of Devi Lal, V.P. Singh cleaned the dust of Mandal Commission report and decided to implement it. This implementation of Mandal Commission recommendations intensified the backlash of upper castes, which rallied around SP (Sangh Parivar) in a big way and the Rath Yatra got a tremendous response from these sections of society. With the Kar Seva of Dec. 6, the SP's political wing became politically more powerful getting more seats in the Lok Sabha and also coming to power in various state assemblies.

The presence of religion in social and political space was not significant in first few decades of India's independence. The political formation of religion in politics is RSS which "was conceived primarily as the egalitarian vanguard of the 'Hindu Rashtra' (Hindu Nation),its leaders' conception of ideal society continued to be based on the Varna (caste) system.(Jaffrelot 2010: 23) RSS remained a fairly insignificant formation till quite late. Through its 'quiet' work it did keep on training young boys into the Hindutva doctrine. Hindutva doctrine is the crystallized ideology of Hindu Communal politics. Historically development of concept of Hindutva ...comes in succession on the construction of Brahmanism as Hinduism and this Brahmanical Hinduism then forming the base for Hindutva politics. Savarkar began to articulate the ideology of Hindu elite (zamindars, Brahmins, kings) by integrating Brahmanical Hinduism with nationalism, calling it Hindutva which further showed the way to building the Hindu Rashtra. His key sentence was "Hinduize all politics and militarize all Hindudom." (Puniyani 2000) This ideology asserts that India is a Hindu Nation and here Christians and Muslims are aliens. There is no place of 'Western' concepts like Secularism and Democracy in Hindu nation as Hinduism itself is the most 'secular' and tolerant religion. This ideology aims to bring in Hindu Rashtra in India and so far it has been consolidated on the hatred of Muslims, Christians and 'Western concepts'.

It did go in to create a number of 'children' organizations, meant to bring in the Hindu Rashtra by working in different fields of society. Before independence this ideology was the rival to Muslim communal ideology. After 1950s it kept communalizing the social space, receiving due provocation's from either the remnant Muslim communalism here or from the assertive postures of Pakistan on Kashmir issue, from across the border. The communalization of society resulted in the communal riots, which began in a big way from 1960's and these riots went on assuming more menacing proportions over a period of time. The most ghastly of which, were to be seen in the decades of 1980s, "The decade of eighties proved to be quite disastrous from communal violence point of view. This decade was most dangerous decade as riot after riot took place right from 1981 to 1990. A major communal violence erupted in Biharsharif (Bihar) in 1981; two major riots took place in 1982 in Meerut, Banaras and Nellie in Assam…" (Engineer 2006: 41). Post–Babri demolition riots being amongst the worst as for as their impact on the psyche of minorities is concerned. Talking in the same breath one has to take note of the 'new' enemy of this ideology. From 1996 this ideology's followers have been paying 'special' attention to another minority about which they were 'just theorizing' so far, the Christians. "In 1996 there were seven cases of anti-Christian violence, in 1997 it went up to 24 and in 1998 the violent acts were more than 120 in number. These included attacking Churches, burning Bibles, intimidating Missionaries to 'Quit India', and the most horrific of all the burning of Father Graham Stewart Stains along with his two sons, while they were sleeping in a jeep on the night of 22nd–23 Jan 1999." (Puniyani 2010: 46)

The 'real' strength of this ideology started picking up in the social and political arena after the development model pursued so far resulted in the rise of vast sections of middle classes. The lopsided development on one hand resulted in the rise of rich farmers and on the other of vast mass of landless peasantry totally bereft of any support system. In cities it got compounded by the rising unemployment and under-employment due to rise of small-scale industries, which act as suppliers and subcontractors to the main industries. These type of industries result in the proliferation of small but prosperous industrialists on one hand and that of the workers whose living conditions are abysmal and wages are very close to the poverty line on the other. It also results in the rise of affluent professional groups. These middle sections have the peculiar type of existential anxieties; they are the one who have been the strongest supporters of the communal ideology. This is the sector, which has shown strong presence in the social space since the 1980s.

Hindutva: What is it?

Hinduism is a collation of multiple religious traditions developed in Indian sub continent. While the religious streams were diverse in themselves the culture of people was equally diverse. Religion is only one of the markers of culture of the people while there are so many other components of culture which are similar amongst people of different religion in the same region. We can not equate religion with culture. This is so very well exemplified in the cultural similarities between Hindus and Muslims for example in Kerala. Also the culture of a Kerala Muslim and a Bangladeshi Muslim is so very different.

Hindutva as a term came in usage mainly from the second decade of 20th century. There is some vague mention of this term in 19th century as well, but it did not have a broad usage. This term began in the backdrop of consolidation of Brahmanism into Hinduism. Savarkar was the one to initially formulate the politics of Hindutva, "the Aryans who settled in India at the dawn of history already formed a nation, now embodied in the Hindus ...Hindus are bound together not only by the tie of the love they bear to a common fatherland and by the common blood that courses through their veins and keeps our hearts throbbing and our affection warm but also by the tie of the common homage we pay to our great civilization, our Hindu culture."(Savarkar 1923: 94) Thus "Hindutva according to him rests on three pillars: geographical unity, racial features and common culture." (Jaffrelot 1993: 26). He further went on to elaborate the criterion for who is a Hindu? According to him all those who regard this land as their fatherland and holy land are the only ones who are Hindus and thereby the people to whom this land belongs. This led to the automatic interpretations that the Christians and the Muslims, whose holy places are in Jerusalem and Mecca, are not on par with the 'Hindus' who own this country. Initiating the theorizing of the 'doubting of patriotism of Muslims', Savarkar posits, "but besides culture the tie of common holy land has at times proved stronger than the chains of a motherland. Look at Mohammedans: Mecca to them is a sterner reality than Delhi or Agra" (Savarkar 1923: 108). This development of the concept of Hindutva comes in succession to the construction of *Brahmanism* as Hinduism and this Brahmanical Hinduism then forming the base for Hindutva politics. Savarkar began to articulate the ideology of Hindu elite (zamindars, Brahmans, kings) by integrating Brahmanical Hinduism with nationalism, calling it Hindutva, which further showed the way for building the Hindu Rashtra.

These concepts were further refined and given the parallel projection by M. S. Golwalkar the second supremo (*Sarsanghchalak*) of RSS, an organization formed in 1925, ostensibly aimed to train young boys in 'Hindu Culture'. Its ideology was based on Brahmanical Hinduism; Hindutva and it aspired for the formation of Hindu Rashtra. This body which began as exclusively upper caste Hindu male organization (and continues to be so despite some sprinkling of low castes and a rare show piece in the form of a Muslim or a Christian) concentrated in indoctrinating adolescent boys in the 'hate other' (Muslim) ideology and began slowly consolidating in different parts of cow belt to begin with Golwalkar drawing heavily from Nazi ideology went on to elaborate the ideas on Nation, *Hindu Rashtra*, in his book '*We or our Nationhood defined*' and '*Bunch of Thoughts*'. He was forthright in his criticism of Nationalism of Congress, and its 'amazing' theory that the nation is composed of all those who for one reason or the other happen to live at the time in a country. For Golwalkar racial factor in nationhood is crucial and he goes on to propound, "To keep up the purity of Race and its culture, Germany shocked the world by her purging the country of Semitic races, the Jews. Race pride at its highest has been manifested here. Germany has also shown how well nigh impossible it is for races and cultures having differences going to the root, to be assimilated in to one united whole, a good lesson for us in *Hindustan* to learn and profit by" (Golwalkar 1938: 27). He is very candid in showing the other races and those belonging to 'foreign' religions their place, "The foreign races in Hindustan must either adopt the Hindu culture and language, must learn to respect and hold in reverence Hindu religion, must entertain no ideas but those of glorification of the Hindu race and culture or may stay in the country wholly subordinated to the Hindu nation claiming nothing, deserving no privileges, far less any preferential treatment not even citizens rights." (Golwalkar 1938: 52)

Thus Hindutva is a political and not religious category. Hindutva is a brew of (Brahmanical) Hinduism with Nationalism, i.e. politics of Hindu Religious Nationalism, i.e. Political movement for Hindu Rashtra.

Hindutva and Culture

The politics of Hindutva asserts that the Hindu nation has existed for 8,000 to 10,000 years and Hindustan has been in possession of Hindus for at least that length of time. Also, that in India for its proper running the majority community, the Hindus, should have a dominant role. Both these assertions are at the root of Hindutva movement and both of these contradict the Indian ethos and culture. Despite various theories about the origin of Aryans one can roughly say that their original abode was somewhere in the northwest, from where they migrated to different areas and on way they went on interacting with different cultures in Iran, Afghanistan and Indian subcontinent. The flowering of social life was a product of interaction of the Aryans and the native tribes. Though this also resulted in the caste system and other social evils, the interaction mainly resulted in growth of interactive culture.

As a reaction against many social evils, Buddhism came up as a religion, which had wide popularity amongst the untouchables and some other sections of society. This development came as a corrective to the uninhibited growth of social evils, and went a long way to enrich Indian culture. This culture was further enriched by arrival and spread of Islam (through Arab merchants in South and Mughal rulers in north) and Christianity (through traders again, through Malabar Coast and through missionaries coming during the British rule). Thus India had been a vast social field developing, progressing and marching forward with the interaction of multiple cultural streams. During the rule of Mughals the syncretic culture reached its heights with development of Bhakti and Sufi sects. Both these were very popular amongst the people for the simplicity of their appeals, and unity of their message. People like Kabir, Nanak and Tukaram contributed their soul to the richness of the life of society. All this is a part of Indian ethos, which in nutshell can be ascribed to different facets of Indian syncretic culture, which stands on the principles of love for all fellow beings, respect for others faith, tolerance for others' religion and equal treatment to followers of different paths.

In contrast Hindutva politics is based on upper caste ethos, and aims at the hegemony of one section of society, one type of religion over the whole society. It theorizes the subjugation of minorities to the upper caste ethos. It does away with the affirmative action needed for the protection and furtherance of the interests of disadvantaged sections of society. Hindutva contradicts the Indian ethos and syncretic culture and is a total break from the 'spirit' of Indian-ness.

Comparing the Concepts of Hinduism and Hindutva

Hinduism and Hindutva are not the same. As we have seen above Hinduism is a religion which has multiple streams the most dominant of which is the Brahmanical one. Hindutva includes not only religion, race language but also geographical territory. In practice it was the politics of feudal elements in pre-independence times and now it represents the political agenda of upper caste/upper class elite.

Table I: Comparing Hinduism and Hindutva

Hinduism	Hindutva
(1) A collation of multiple traditions like Brahmanism—Shramanism-Tantra, Kabir, Tukaram, Nanak	(1) Politics of Hindu elite, drawing from Brahmanical Hinduism.
(2) Brahmanism is based on ethos of Caste system	(2) Brew of Brahmanical Hinduism and Nationalism
(3) Brahmanism was projected as the Hinduism initially in 6–10 century, then in early 19th century, Brahmanical Hinduism was projected to be synonymous with Hinduism.	(3) Aims at Hindu Rashtra based on Brahmanical Hinduism
(4) Shramanic traditions: there were constant rebellion: attempt to escape the clutches of Brahmanism: Conversion to Buddhism (early times and now after the lead given by Ambedkar).	(4) Led initially by Brahmins: Banias: even now dominant Leadership is from upper castes.
(5) 'Dharma' is caste based religious duties.	(5) Political expression through Sangh Parivar now, earlier Hindu Mahasabha and RSS.
(6) Sanitization process being spear-head by SP–Holy deity: Ram, Holy book: Gita, clergy: Shankaracharyas etc.	(6) A mix of fundamentalism and fascism (see later table)
(7) Its proponents claim it to be tolerant and catholic. cf: Earlier its attitude to shudras cf: Now its attitude to Muslims	(7) VHP bring in the stink of fundamentalism in the essentially fascist politics of RSS, BJP and Bajrang Dal.

Table II: Similarities and Differences between Hindutva and Fascism

Hindutva	Fascism
Similarities:	
(1) It got strengthened in post-Mandal Period: after fearing the assertion of Lower castes.	Came up and became strong in the wake of powerful workers movement
(2) Projects 'National' interests over the interests of the people.	Same
(3) Has the seeds of expansionism; Concept of 'Akhand Bharat' (undivided India, including Pakistan, Myanmar, Bangladesh and Sri Lanka)	Expansionist: attacked neighboring Countries on the ground that they were part of earlier German empire
(4) Targeting Muslims as the cause of the ills of the country	Targeted Jews as the cause of ills Of the country.
(5) Glorification of the past.	Same
(6) Oppressive to workers (produce for nation, do not bother about your rights), Dalits (oppose Mandal in a subtle way of demand for meritocracy), women (they should be ideal wives and mothers), minorities (they should subjugate themselves to Hindu culture).	Oppressive to Jews, (subjected them to physical elimination), Communists/workers (physical violence to reduce their strength), women (their place is in the kitchen, church and they primary role is in rearing children).
(7) Post Babri demolition resulted in Social space full of Terror and anti-human rights, 'pro'-national Hysteria.	The regime implemented its Pogrom through creation of mass Hysteria.
(8) Urbanized middle class and rich peasants/upper castes and some backward castes: the main support base.	Urban middle class and landed Aristocracy: the main social base.
Differences	
(1) Long gestation period: Successful communalization of Social space in 'cow belt' region; Success in polarization of upper Castes only after implementation of Mandal Commission.	Quick ascendancy to power on the anti-Jew plank.
(2) Medium range social crisis from mid 1980's: rising unemployment, increasing poverty.	Severe post World War economic crisis.

Table III: Comparing Hindutva and Fundamentalism

Hindutva	Fundamentalism
Targeting against liberal ethos of the society	Same
Imposition of retrograde social values selectively culled out from religious texts.	Same
Swadeshi is the "economic policy'	Anti imperialist noises
Built around (Gita, Vedas), Ram and Acharyas	Based on Semitic religion–Holy book, Holy daily and clergy
Harping on traditional orthodox beliefs	Same
Projection of women as ideal mothers	Women under patriarchal control of father, husband and son
Claim that Vedas are created by Brahma, the God	Claim that 'Our' creed based on divine law: holy book coming from God himself
Golden past of religious rule is shown to be the ideal goal	Same
Demand homogeneity of Hindu culture	Abhor pluralism
Political onslaught to impose interests of elite, middle class, upper caste on whole society	Creates hysteria (against Shah of Iran, in Iran, against women in Saudi Arabia)
Creates hysteria against internal enemy, the Muslim	Hysteria against Women, Imperialism, neighboring country
Great importance to women's dress code	Same
Built around emotive appeal of religion	Same

Hindutva's Goal

Hindu Rashtra is not a religious state; it is a 'modern' phenomenon to impose the pre–modern social hierarchies on all sections of society. It is the goal of a section of society, which is the major beneficiary of current social privileges, the section of society, which have gained in the process of development of last few decades. It was the goal of section of society which was threatened by the social changes in pre–independence times (*zamindar–brahmins*) and who were champions of status quo and were allies of British at economic and political level. The Hindu Rashtra which is threatening to engulf the society from last two decades is the battle cry of the sections who again are upholder of a status quo vis-à-vis social position of women, workers, dalits and Adivasis. It is the offence of the section of society, which has benefited maximum by proliferation of middle classes—small industries, petty business and agriculture of the 'Green Revolution' type and of the professional and bureaucratic cadres. Indian Nationalism as an encompassing concept based itself on secular grounds and attempts to strive for formal liberty equality and fraternity supplemented by the liberal space to struggle to convert these formal concepts in to reality. Indian Nationalism is a positive concept, incorporating different religions, ethnicities and culture and is an integral part of world economy and emerging global village.

The response to the Hindutva politics in the decades of 1980s has multiple factors behind it. In the collapse of Nehruvian consensus—the name that best defined the post–colonial project in India. Achin Vanaik points out, "The one's related to change in the social composition of the country are accompanied by global changes also. "It is not the newness of its ideological themes or messages, but the new receptivity to older, well acquainted messages that most explains its rise...the new receptivity is grounded not in the pre-fascist preparations or seedlings of economy (The New Economic Policy, whatever else it means, does not mean that) and policy, but in the collapse of Nehruvian consensus—the name that defined best defined the post-colonial project in India." (Vanaik 1995, 274)

The chronicity, i.e. slow speed of this movement has its inherent problems. Whereas on one hand it can capture the social space, on the other it can also elicit a reaction to itself. This reaction to it from dalits, workers, women, section of middle class that is secular, is a big obstacle to the march of Hindutva. Big capital, the major industrial houses have a unique relation with Sangh Parivar. Whenever faced with crisis to their own existences the socially terrorizing atmosphere created by Sangh Parivar helps the bourgeoisie to wriggle out of the compulsions of liberal ethos. The conservative movement of Sangh Parivar helps the needs of capital to keep thriving in an uninterrupted way. Thus this, chronic, resilient, thriving fascism, expressed through the vehicle of Sangh Parivar continues to throw up different shades of its existence, sometimes terrorizing (to the poor and the minorities) sometimes aggressive (to the neighboring 'enemy' countries), and sometimes even appearing to collapse under the weight of its own contradictions. But the march, at the moment is on. The social roots of Hindutva are all for the support and continuation of the repressive capitalist regime; sustaining the bourgeoisie aspirations, while continuing to pursue its own project.

Hindutva onslaught draws some support from fundamentalist concepts also. It culls out from the past–selective values to impose them on present. It uses religious imagery, glorifies the 'golden past' of rule of Hindu kings, sees women primarily under patriarchal control dictating their way of life, dress code etc. It co-opts all and sundry religious professionals and personnel to strengthen its political base and it use religion in a very effective way to create the nationalist hysteria. At present the situation is fairly in balance. The onslaught has achieved mammoth proportions in the north, but south and east are comparatively unaffected by its paranoid aggression. The reaction of Dalits, though fragmented is definitely going to retard the march of the *rath* (Chariot) of Hindutva.

The apparent target of Sangh Parivar, the Muslims and later Christians, are in a bind. On one hand they have been battered so much by Hindutva that they cannot afford to lie quiet any more. Secondly unlike the Dalits they lie in subcritical zone of backwardness where they find it difficult to come out of the grip of their own `religious leaders', `the Muslim obscurantist's' posing to be speaking on behalf of their community. Thus they face a double attack from both Hindu fascism and Muslim fundamentalism. Probably the suffering of the `poor Muslims' is so great that they will be forced to come out and resist the `bears hug' of Sangh Parivar and by side-tracking their `obscurantist leaders' will pose definite obstacle to the march of `Trishuls of Hindutva'. How Sangh Parivar overcomes this 'problem' which new `velvet gloves' it discovers to remove this obstacle remains to be seen. The response of Christian community though mixed; to a great extent has been that of responding in a strong secular manner, to defend the Human rights of different sections in general and to defend the secular rights of minorities in particular. This is an ongoing phenomenon set into motion due to the attacks on Christians by different wings of SP directed by the ideological formulation of the RSS.

Human Rights

Concept of human rights begins with the rise of democracies. The feudal societies had a neat division between rights and duties. The landlords, kings had the right on tribute and free labor, while the peasants and deprived sections had the apportionment of duties for them. Duty to give tax, duty to serve the landlords, kings. Men had the right over the women, while women had the duties towards their husbands, fathers or sons. The concept of Liberty, Equality and Fraternity (community) brought in the era of formal equinity between all the citizens. Even the concept of citizenship begins with democratic society and accompanying social transformation.

With the rise of 'religion based nationalism', the assertion of Taliban in Afghanistan, Zia ul Haq in Pakistan and Hindutva in India the notion of rights is being sidetracked and major emphasis is on the duties. One had witnessed similar processes in US with the rise of Christian fundamentalism in the decade of 1920s, and in Germany with the rise of race based politics of fascism. Under the pressure of this politics gender and caste/class hierarchy is asserted in the newer language. Since the society began as unequal one, some of the sections like dalits and women began with a big disadvantage. Social subjugation and gender subjugation were the starting point. The constitution makers kept the provision of affirmative, protective clauses for these so that century old disadvantages are done way with and there is a march from formal equality to substantive equality. With the rise of Hindutva in India the opposition to reservation is mainly to retain the social hierarchies. The Hindutva is also opposed to equality in a subtle way.

Women and Hindu Rights

The social dominance of Hindutva ideology coming to power of BJP at places has affected the rights of women in a serious way as well. It can very well be gleaned from the interview given by Mridula Sinha, the chief of BJP Mahila Morcha. In an interview to Savvy, April 1994, she states that "(1) a woman should not work outside the home unless her family is financially very deprived. (2) I gave dowry and received dowry. (3) I oppose women's liberation, as it is another name for 'loose morals'. (4) We oppose equal rights for both sexes. (5) There is nothing wrong with domestic violence against women: very often it is women's fault. We advice women to try and adjust, as her not adjustment creates the problem. (6) Women's future lies in perpetuating the present, because no where else are women worshipped as we are in India. (7) For us women's liberation means liberation from atrocities. It does not mean they should be relieved of their duties as wives and mothers. (Sinha 1994)

One of the past presidents of BJP Mahila Morcha, Vijaya Raje Scindia, led a group of women in protest march against 'anti-sati' legislation, asserting that, 'It is the fundamental right of Hindu women to commit *sati* (burning of woman on the funeral pyre of her husband), as it is in preservation of our past glory and culture'. Women's groups in resolutions opposed this stand by Scindia, "This National Conference on Women, Religion and Family Laws denounces the recent statement of Ms. Vijaya Raje Scindia, Vice President of the B.J.P., justifying and glorifying the custom of sati. We believe that customs like sati are cruel and inhuman even though they were justified in the name of religion in earlier Indian history. We consider that this glorification is an attempt by communal forces to use women for their political purposes…We demand that the Government take immediate action under the commission of Sati (Prevention) Act. 1987, against Vijaya Raje Scindia and all those persons glorifying and reviving the practice of sati (National Convention Resolution). The communalists have propagated against women's movement for equality, which feminists have held dear. "Looked at from another angle, this appropriation is also indicative of the success of autonomous women's movements which have happened…whose potential Hindu Right is quick to seize…There are nonetheless, important differences between the two: while the women's movement challenges notion's of women's domination within the family and society, the ideology of Hindutva places women squarely within the home and propagates a patriarchal model." (Sarkar and Butalia 1995: 7)

As per Ratna Kapoor and Brenda Cossman "The discourse on women is often characterized by strikingly religious overtones defining women in the images of Hindu Goddesses and consorts—as mothers and wives, dutiful and sacrificing." (Kapoor and Cossman 1995) in this approach the BJP policy focuses on women's traditional roles in the family, which pertains to their responsibility in the health care, maternal and Natal care.

The role play between men and women is also reflected in their acts of street violence. Nearly 20,000 *'kar sevikas'* helped the *'kar sevaks'* who went to demolish the *masjid*, by cooking and cleaning for them. During demolition of the masjid, Uma Bharati and Sadhavi Ritamhara exhorted their male 'brethren' to participate in demolition. One can sum up this status of women in Hindutva, as Hindutva politics "…ultimately proposes a model for domesticated, motherly or sisterly, femininity as the overwhelming ideal, both at the symbolic and material levels." (Baccchetta 2004: 37)

Dalits and Hindutva

Hindutva politics—BJP has couched its views and attitudes towards dalits in a very clever way. It will not criticize dalits, but when faced with their movements, demands and cultural upsurge it will start beating the drum of abolishing reservations and upholding merit. This was perfected as an art when Mandal commission recommendations were implemented and later when Bahujan Samaj Party began a verbal tirade against the symbolism projected by Sangh Parivar. To counter Mandal, it did not want to be visible in opposing it. So it did not support the upper caste Hindu students doing self-immolation etc., but to side track the issue it began its Rath Yatra and later withdrew its support from the V.P. Singh government leading to its fall (1990). "But the real provocation that made the BJP wholly immerses itself in the Ramjanmbhoomi issue was V.P. Singh's decision to implement the Mandal Commission...party's rank and file were virulently opposed to it." (Chatterjee 1996: 98)

While dalit reformers have always stood for opposing the Manusmriti, Dr. Ambedkar burnt it; but the ideologues of Hindutva have always upheld it. They have devised the clever ideology of integral Humanism, which argues that every society is a balanced integral whole and any change of equations will put it in crisis. The argument is to uphold the caste equations as they prevail. The scriptures and practices of Brahmanical Hindu religion do ask for Shudra Dharma, Holy duty of dalits, to serve the upper castes, Stree dharma, to serve the lord and master: husband or the male relative controlling her life.

Multiple mechanisms, social engineering techniques are being employed to marginalize the dalits on one side and to co-opt them on the other side. At the same time a section of Dalits who have benefited due to the progress during last many decades are trying to ape the upper caste, as explained in the process of Sanskritization. "The Hindutva nationalist movement has always been known for upper caste, Brahmanical character. The Hindutva ideology relies on an organic view of society, where the castes are seen as the harmonious limbs of the same body" (Jaffrelot 1993: ch 1). The RSS has concentrated on attracting to its local branches Hindus who valued this ethos, either because they belong to the upper castes or because they want to emulate them. The technique of 'conversion' of lower caste people to Hindutva relies on the same logic as what M.N. Srinivas called 'Sanskritization' (Srinivas 1995:7, quoted in Jaffrelot 2010: 479).

Anand Teltumde points out that the Hindutva politics has dislodged the central concerns of dalit movement, the struggle against untouchability, poverty, inequality and discrimination away from the central concerns of dalits. "Along with this Hindutva seeks to replace the concepts of rights and dignity enshrined in Indian Constitution with the notion of obligations inherent in Brahmanism. They do not even remotely relate to the inhuman conditions in which the dalits live or express an iota of remorse for the social oppression that they themselves caused." (Teltumde 2003: 127.) Teltumde further points out that fascism requires violence to enforce its agenda and that it does through the foot soldiers from lower strata, "In the name of "Hindu unity" the dalits and Adivasis are brain washed and made to perform this role." (Teltumbde, 2003: 130). RSS used the dalits for Babri demolition, and the violence against minorities in Gujarat anti Muslim carnage.

Minorities

Muslim community has been the victim of different biases and prejudices propagated by the Shakhas of RSS and carried through media and school books. This demonization of Muslims minorities has resulted in the an attitude of the state and the private sector due to which they have been kept out of the government and private sector jobs. Their representation in these has been very low. Also the 'social common sense' has been against them and regular and repeated violence against them has taken a heavy toll of their psyche. After partition the elite of Muslim community left India for Pakistan, and mainly poor Muslims and only few professionals and traders were left behind further worsening the status of Muslims. Muslim fundamentalist leadership came to the fore, unconcerned about the 'real' material problems of community, and today the community remains poor, backward and in the grip of orthodox elements.

It is propagated for political goals that successive governments have pampered and appeased the community. The facts are in total contrast to this. Their status in employment and other parameters are a good index of their social status and appeasement.

This has occurred due to the biases against them. The popular myth that Muslim Kings destroyed Hindu Temples (truth is that both Hindu and Muslim kings destroyed temples and mosques sometimes in pursuit of gold and sometimes for other political motives), Islam spread on the point of sword (Islam spread mainly under the influence of Sufi saints, who were away from the seats of power, and primarily Sudra's embraced Islam to escape the tyranny of Brahmanism), Muslims are polygamous (as per the census figures the percentage of polygamy amongst Muslims and Hindus is more or less same), they produce more number of children and that shortly Muslim population will overtake the Hindu population has been the major propagation of the communal politics (the Muslim population has shown a minor increase during last nearly fifty years;1947–11.4, 2001–12.6) .

These myths have been the foundation on which the anti-Muslim violence stands. "Behind the present day tribulations of India's minorities lies an insecurity pumped into the Hindu majority by a pre-meditated five decade campaign that portrayed Muslims and Christians as disloyal, anti-national or communal and Hindus as having been enfeebled by the tolerance preached by Mahatma Gandhi and others before him, implemented by Gandhi's sentimental heir Jawaharlal Nehru." (Kidwai 1985: 227)

The Muslim minority has suffered different communal violence, carnage and pogroms. This first major impact of these is the economic marginalization. The repeated violence against this community has also reduced its political representation, the increase in the insecurity due to the communal violence particularly of Mumbai 1992 and Gujarat has increased the feeling of insecurity. The economic deprivation of the community has been recorded by Justice Sachar Committee report, which in nutshell points out the decline in the social development parameters of this community, the economic marginalization of this community has been most frightening factor of the rise of the communal politics in India. Similarly Rangnath Misra Committee points out the political and social marginalization of this community. Today due to the structural inequity of this community and the parallel feeling of insecurity the community at places has withdrawn into its shell, reduced to the status of a second class citizen.

> "...wherever the Muslim community acquires considerable and economic independence, there is invariably a Hindu Muslim communal riot that that takes place, which burns down every sign of economic investment that the community have made, having them penniless and helpless again." (Vempeny 2003: 13)

Christians

Though different types of biases were spread against Christians even earlier, from last four years the anti-Christian campaign has been accelerated to the high pitch, because of which anti-Christian violence has picked up to a great extent. The attacks on Christians have begun especially from 1997 onwards. These attacks are being orchestrated by different organizations linked to Sangh Parivar (SP) and a general hysteria is being created against the Christian Missionaries in particular. During this year (1998–99) many priests were humiliated (Fr. Christudas being paraded naked in Dumka), one of them Pastor Graham Stewart Stains, being burnt alive along with his two sons aged seven and nine, many churches have been damaged in these attacks, Bibles have been burnt and nuns have been raped in interior places.

This has occurred in the backdrop of anti-Christian propaganda as per which Christianity is a foreign religion, their missionary activities are a mere ploy for inducing people for conversions to adopt Christianity, their schools and Hospitals are mere tools for the same. The CIA is planning this process and the Pope and Christian agencies, which are out to evangelize the whole country, where by Hindus will become a minority. Most of the inquiries by social activists, National Human Rights Commission, National Minorities Commission have shown that different organizations affiliated to SP are behind these attacks, and the attacks are taking place most in the BJP ruled states Gujarat, in particular.

Christian missionaries have been setting up Churches, seminaries and schools wherever and wherever possible. They learnt Indian Languages, set up printing presses and published religious as well as secular literature, to spread literacy and their faith. In the process they adopted Indian languages for their communication and the Church adopted number of native practices. Despite 2000 years of Christian presence, and 200 years of British rule the population of Christians in 1971 was 2.6 percent, which in 1991 stood at 2.32 percent, 2001– 2.30 percent. Even in Manoharpur district, where the Bajarang Dal supports Dara Singh burnt Pastor Stains on the ground that he was converting Adivasis to Christianity, Justice Wadhava Commission did not find any evidence of conversions nor of the rise of Christian population. "Religious conversions have been used as a divisive issue in many such attacks. In December 1998, 92 Christian homes were burned in Ramgiri Udaygiri areas of Orissa. A month later, in January 1999, Graham Stains, an Australian missionary and his two sons, aged six and ten years were burnt to death in Manoharpur village in Keonjhar District by a crowd led by Dara Singh." (Grover 2010: 15)

Despite this the threat of 'their' population overtaking the Hindu population has begun only from one year or so. This anti-Christian bogey comes at a time when the anti-Muslim pogroms have more or less achieved 'the target' of permanently intimidating and ghettoizing them. Also SP realizes that if it has to break the electoral jinx to be able to come to power on its own it needs a newer vote bank and for this advises have been seen as the one's having best potential. There is also a growing realization in SP that after conversion to Christianity the advasis become more educated and aware of their rights, and this is a big threat to 'status quo', which is the base line of SP politics. These two factors seem to be the major ones in the current SP strategy of intimidating the missionaries. The calculation is that after this type of 'treatment' missionaries will be reluctant to go to the remote places and that will make the SP's job of wooing Advisis to its fold comparatively easy.

Minorities in India Today

The onslaught of communal politics is intimidating the minorities while the state is extremely insensitive towards the protection of minorities. As we have seen above the ghettoisation of Muslim community is very strong. Also the present intimidation of Christian community has reached intolerable limits. The provisions for their protection are on paper but the ground reality is something else. The rise in social power of SP has been the bane for the Human rights of weaker sections of society in general and those of minorities in particular. State as it itself is infiltrated by communal elements has been unable to protect the minorities and has been fairly insensitive to their plight. It is only through the struggles for their rights and alignment with the struggles of other weaker sections of society that they can try to preserve their democratic and Human rights.

Conclusion

Secularism is an inalienable part of democracy. The modern transformation to democracy essentially stands for the abolition of structural hierarchy of caste and gender and its replacement by formal equality. The democratic state in turn gives a liberal space which can be the ground for transforming the formal equality towards substantive equality.

The Religious right wing abolishes secular values, in the garb of 'minority problem' and its core agenda is to bring back the feudal caste and gender based structural hierarchies. While the minorities get the boot in the apparent way with the attack on secular values, the core victims of this are the deprived sections of society, whose rights get suppressed. In current times it is an attempt to abolish the liberal democratic space by rousing the hysteria of religious sentiments and use this suppression of democratic values to perpetuate the pre modern status quo of caste and gender hierarchy. Human rights are essentially a concept which can go along only with democracy, which in turn can only be secular. So in Indian context the opposition to secularism is basically an attack on the human rights of workers, women, dalits and minorities, with religious minorities bearing a direct brunt of violence, intimidation and also being relegated to being second class citizens.

References

Baccchetta, P., 2004. *Gender in the Hindu Nation.* Delhi: Women Unlimited.

Basu, T., P. Data, S. Sarkar, T.Sarkar and S. Sen, 1993. *Khaki Shorts Saffron-Flags.* Orient Longman: Hydrabad.

Casolari, M, 2000. *Hindutva's Foreign Tie Ups in 1930s: The Archival Evidence*, Communalism Combat (March): 37.

Chatterjee, M., 1996. The BJP Political Mobilization for Hindutva. *Religion, Religiosity and Communalism.* edited by Bidwai. Mukhia and Vanaik, 87–107. Delhi: Manohar.

Deshmukh, N., 1984. *Moments of Soul Searching.* Delhi: Pritipaksh.

Engineer, A.A., 2006. Muslim Minority: their Rights and Status in India. *Minorities in Indian Social System,* edited by Joseph Benjamin, 38–61. Delhi: Gyan.

Golwalkar, M.S., 1939. *We or Our Nationhood Defined.* Delhi: Bharat Publications.

Grover, V., 2010. *Kandhamal.* Marg: Delhi.

Jaffrelot, C., 1993. *The Hindu Nationalist Movement and Indian Politics,* Delhi: Viking.

Jaffrelot, C., 2010. *Religion, Caste and Politics in India.* Delhi: Primus Books.

Kapoor, R. and B. Cossman, 1995. Communalizing Gender, Engendering Community. *Women and the Hindu Right: A Collection of Essays,* edited by T. Sarkar and U. Butalia, 82–121. New Delhi: Kali for Women.

Kanungo, P., 2002. *RSS's Tryst with Politics: From Hedgewar to Sudarshan.* New Delhi: Manohar.

Kidwai, S., 1985. Mohammed Ali, a Forgotten Patriot. *Muslims and India's Freedom Movement*, edited by. B. K. Ahluwalia and S. Ahluwalia, 178-227. New Delhi: Heritage

Mathew, B. M., n.d. *An Anti-Indian Nationalist Ideology.* http://www.proxsa.org/politics/hindutva/hindutva.html (accessed on 25th April 2011).

National Conference on Women, Religion and Family Laws, 1989. https://sites.google.com/site/saheliorgsite/women-s-conferences/national-conferences-of-women-s-movements/national-conference-on-women-religion-and-family-laws (accessed January 8, 2011).

Puniyani, R., 2000. *Fascism of Sangh Parivar.* Delhi: Media House.

———. 2010. *Communalism and Anti Christian Violence.* Thiruvantpuram: Mythri.

Rangnath Mishra Commission Report, 2004. http://www.indianmuslims.info/reports_about_indian_muslims/ranganath_mishra_commission_recommendations.html (accessed January 9, 2011).

Sachar Committee Report, 2005. http://minorityaffairs.gov.in/newsite/sachar/sachar_comm.pdf (accessed January 3, 2011).

Sarkar, T. and U. Butalia, 1995. *Women and the Hindu Right.* Delhi: Tanika Sarkar Urvashi Butalia, 'Kali for Women.'

Savarkar, V.D., 1923. *Hindutva, Who is a Hindu?* Bharat Prakashan: Nagpur.

Sinha, M., 1994. An Interview on Indian Women. 'Savvy' Monthly Magazine, Mumbai April.

Srinivas M.N., 1995. *Social Change in Modern India.* New Delhi: Orient Longman.

Teltumbde, A., 2003. Gujarat Carnage: The Role of Dalits. *Lessons of Gujarat*, edited by S. Pendse, 103–111Mumbai: Vikas Adhyan Kendra.

Vanaik, A., 1995. *Communalism Contested.* Vistaar: Delhi.

Vempeny, S., 2003. *Minorities in Contemporary India*, Kanishka Publishers: Delhi.

CHAPTER 8

HUMAN RIGHTS VIOLATIONS IN INDIA: EXPLORING THE SOCIETAL ROOTS OF MARGINALITY

Debi Chatterjee

At the international level India has long been a strong votary of human rights. She is a signatory to many of the international human rights instruments. She has spoken up at various international forums in favor of human rights and strongly criticized human rights violations in different parts of the world. India is fully committed to the rights proclaimed in the Universal Declaration and is in fact a signatory to all the six core human rights documents, alongside many others.

Yet, at the same time, it remains pertinent to note that when it comes to India's own track record, her human rights scenario has not been above criticism. India has not ratified the Convention against Torture, she is not a party to the Conventions on the Rights of Migrant Workers and their families, on refugees and stateless persons, the ILO Conventions on the abolition of child labor, on the rights of indigenous and tribal people. In addition, may be noted the Indian Government's persistent refusal to cooperate with the Human Rights Council's special procedures with respect to torture, the treatment of human rights defenders, contemporary forms of racism and racial discrimination in relation to Dalits and caste discrimination, trafficking, child pornography, and arbitrary detentions (Lahiri 2008)

India has a large and variegated population. Diversities have been the source of both the curiosity of the observer and confusion of the analyst. There are differences of language, caste, religion and culture, to mention but a few. Drawing on religious traditions, complex societal norms govern the activities of the people, their interactive styles, their occupations, and in fact the entire spectrum of their day to day activities. A glance at this large, variegated population group that reveals sizeable segments of it are socially marginalized and remain excluded from the goods and services available to others. They also comprise a disproportionately large section of those who regularly suffer from a variety of atrocities and rights denial. It becomes evident on careful scrutiny that the exclusion from goods and services and rights negations of these people is anything but accidental. There is, in fact, a distinct pattern about such marginality, exclusion and violations lending a unique character to the India social scenario. Their societal marginality is both a cause and effect of human rights violations. Moreover, it is, in itself a violation of human rights. This paper seeks to unravel the roots of such marginality and human rights violations keeping note of the extraordinary vulnerability of certain sections of the population.

The Indian Social Tradition

For any understanding of the Indian social scenario, it is important to understand the centrality of the Hindu Brahminical order. Today, some eighty percent of the population of India professes the Hindu religion. While there are different sects within the Hind fold, the mainstream of the Hindu order is governed by Brahminical norms claiming to draw on the traditional Vedic heritage of antiquity. It is their texts, their interpolations and their strictures that seek to determine the parameters of societal functioning. It is against their yardstick that other social groupings are placed in order of importance and status. The minor sects within the Hindu fold remain largely obscure and in the fringes of the society, setting standards of functioning for only those within the order but having no or little impact beyond and are unable to negotiate their position in terms of the dominant Brahminical order. The latter is in turn structured along hierarchic lines of caste and gender stratification.

The early Vedic society was primarily pastoral with the presence of dominant tribal elements. It is widely believed that the existence of social classes based on exploitation of social surplus was virtually unknown in the Rig Vedic days (Sharma 1990: 314). By the sixth century, however, with iron tools being used as artifacts and large-scale field cultivation being undertaken the emergence of a full-fledged class-divided social order took place. Families came to acquire resources that they were unable to exploit on their own and hence turned to procuring labor power by force of arms and perpetuate its supply by force of law and custom. To it, were added the compulsions generated by religion and ideology (Sharma 1990: 315).

In course of time different elements of compulsion, physical and ideological, were interwoven into a social system called the Varna system to facilitate the processes of extraction of surplus. This inegalitarian social order which germinated in the late Vedic period, got firmly structured thereafter through the *dharma sutras* and the *dharma shastras*, leading to the emergence of a vast segment of socially deprived people being treated as pools of extractable cheap labor. There were different categories of people identified for exploitation of their labor. There were the people who were low down in the caste hierarchy termed the Sudras; there were also those who were outside the caste hierarchy—the tribals and those who professed other religions referred to by the derogatory term *'mlechchas'* and of course there were the women of all castes, deemed to be no superior than the Sudras.

Today, so far as India is concerned, the mainstream of Indian social tradition that we have already referred to continues to be in its very essence, inegalitarian, still firmly rooted in that past. The dominance of the Hindu Brahminical order remains sacrosanct, relegating non-Hindu groups to positions of excluded inferiority in terms of social acceptance. This includes religious minorities and tribes. Within the Hindu fold, the rules of hierarchy ensure the continued stigmatization and exclusion of the Sudra and Ati-sudra castes. Changes have been introduced now and then primarily under legal compulsions, particularly after independence. But they have hardly altered the essence of societal structuring based on *varnashrama dharma*—the governing principle of Brahminical society. Under the circumstances, large segments of the population remain extremely vulnerable to human rights violations. It becomes evident that there is a very definite pattern in that vulnerability. It is the socially 'excluded' who are stigmatized and 'violated' as will be evident in the course of the paper.

The Low Castes as Victims of Oppression

In terms of the caste hierarchy, members of the lowest rung of society—the Sudras and Ati-sudras—were traditionally stigmatized as polluting to the upper orders of society and suffered perpetual and manifold rights violations at the hands of the upper castes. They were socially ostracized, denied education and access to land and property. The products of their labor, of course, were not ostracized. In fact, their stigmatization formed the basis of the surplus extraction of their labor. Marked out as an identity group on the basis of their caste, they were doomed to perform certain demeaning jobs which were essentially labor-intensive, physically hazardous, and of low remunerative value. Aspirations for wealth, power and status were cut at the roots in the name of god and the god-stipulated caste norms, as members of the low Sudra castes were prohibited by religious stipulations from accumulating the fruits of their labor. This Brahminical order of society developed from the later Vedic period and crystallized over time into a rigid stratification system. Time and again, ritual power and state authority joined hands to ensure the smooth continuance of the order.

Though the slave mode of production was not typical of ancient India, the conditions of existence of the low castes were akin to slave-like conditions. They were relegated to perform demeaning tasks, socially humiliated, and educationally deprived, and all in the name of religion. Over and above all and subsuming all, they were denied through generations the very basis of human rights–human dignity. Members of these castes were frequently abused, insulted, beaten up, and even massacred. It may be noted that in post–independence India, despite the constitutional abolition, untouchability remains very much a reality as evident from successive Reports of the Commissioner for Scheduled Castes and Tribes.

The Hindu religious injunctions codified in the *Laws of Manu,* had explicitly placed the injunction that a servant (that is, one belonging to the Sudra category) should not amass wealth, even if he has the ability, for a servant who amasses wealth annoys the priests (that is the Brahmins) (Doniger, Wendy and Smith, Brian tr. 1991). The only recommended activity for the servant was to serve the priest, beyond that whatever he did would bear him no fruit (Doniger, Wendy and Smith, Brian tr. 1991). It is these Sudra communities who formed the mass of the labor force, working under social stigma and intense economic exploitation. Religious sanctions legitimized the exploitation. Their labor helped in the sustenance of a numerically minuscule parasitic upper caste. The scriptures sanctioned their marginalization; society endorsed and implemented it. In its crudest form this exploitation took the shape of the practice of untouchability. Pollution being seen as lasting and contagious and transferable by physical contact between the polluting individual of the untouchable caste and others, the former was prohibited from moving into the proximity of the latter. Often quoted, but not the exclusive example of this can be found in the case of the Kerala castes. There the members of the low castes were not supposed to approach closer than ninety-six paces to a person of high caste status lest their nearness pollute him. In the case of the *Nayadis*, beggars of southern Kerala, they had to keep a distance of from seventy four to one hundred feet from a local Brahmin. But it has been noted that in practice they kept themselves even beyond that stipulated minimum (Mandelbaum 1970: 193).

It is this oppressed section of the population which, in course of time, came to be characterized as '*Dalit*'; a term which was popularized by the Dalit Panthers in the nineteen seventies, signifying the oppression of the Sudras and revealing their growing consciousness of their *Dalit* status. It was open ended enough to permit of varied definitions and incorporation of different groups suffering from social oppression, but at its core remained the Sudra population. This *Dalit* population has remained at the bottom of the social hierarchy, economically poor, educationally backward and politically under-represented in the corridors of power.

The majority of child workers and victims of rights abuse come from this socially marginalized section. This is a reality indisputably substantiated by facts and widely recognized not only at the national but at the international level as well. Just as it has been taken note of by the Government of India, international rights bodies like Human Rights Watch and international organizations like the UNICEF have alluded to it.

As the children of Dalit families swell the ranks of the working children, working under extreme odds, their losses are massive. They involve the denial of basic human rights of the children. The harm suffered by these children in some of the specific industries which may be noted as follows, gives us barely a glimpse of the abhorent scenario. It has been recorded, for example, that those working in the lock industries of Aligarh and the metal industries of Moradabad, Varanasi and Delhi, have to labor from dawn to dusk on the hand presses, buffing machines, electroplating and spray-painting units. Continuous chemical fumes and the white hot flames from which they have no protection, slowly destroy their respiratory system and eyesight. In the carpet weaving industry, bent over the looms in dark sheds all day with little ventilation or seating space, the children are doomed to a lifetime of respiratory diseases, joint and finger pains and emaciation. In the glass bangle and glass blowing industries, tuberculosis is widespread and lifespan short. Children are compelled to work with furnace temperatures of 700 to 1800 degree centigrade, and often for 24 hour shifts with cyanide and silica fumes.[1] Many die young, while many others are left to lives of perpetual morbidity. For most, the future has little to promise. The laws, government schemes, court rulings touch barely the fringes. For the vast majority who are not fortunate enough to be noticed either by NGOs or the Government or both, their legal rights mean little. On a day-to-day basis, the child's income remains a critical input to the survival of the entire family.

For children of the Scheduled Caste families, educational backwardness, economic deprivation and social marginalization form a persistent vicious circle. It is pertinent to remember that most Dalits continue to live in extreme poverty, and, barring a small section, they are without land, remunerative employment options or a suitable education. Constitutional eradication of untouchability, schemes for their uplift, quotas notwithstanding, the roots of the caste system on which Dalit distress rests, are yet to be shaken. Faced with discrimination based on caste, these families are left with very limited options but to use their children as 'labor'. Understandably, thus, the problem of child labor in the Indian context is inextricably linked to the caste factor. It is simply not enough to recognize the fact that amongst other identity groups, Scheduled Castes are particularly vulnerable to the exploitation of child labor. It is also not enough to recognize the links between the multiple types of marginalities to which they are victim. Addressing the problem effectively calls for addressing the roots of the problem. And, here the roots lie in the caste system itself. The Brahminical system gets reinforced through the exploitation of child labor. The continuance of child labor ensures the continuance of the supply of a pool of cheap exploitable labor not only in terms of children, but also adults. Children, who are compelled to join the workforce at an early age and are thus denied the chances of educational attainments, are left with little choice on attaining adulthood but to work in low-paid, stigmatizing menial jobs—work which Manu had stipulated for the lowdown castes! Thus, through child labor, the socially stigmatized marginals remain marginal and their marginality remains entrenched within the modern state's discourse frame. The Brahminically-induced mind-set of people makes a vast majority of even the 'socially conscious' elite virtually oblivious to the problem. The voices of protest are thus mute. In fact, the problem hardly becomes an 'issue'—a rallying point for agitation for deep-rooted social change. Child labor, bonded labor, trafficking of children, the continued practice of untouchability and social marginalization form a vicious circle—impenetrable to the ideological influences of democracy, human rights and social justice.

Even today, after years of democratic exercises, the marginalization of the Dalit is widely visible in the social, economic and political spheres. They continue to occupy the lower ranks of society; their numbers swell the categories of agricultural labor, bonded labor and child labor; they form the bulk of domestic workers and are visible as casual, unskilled, illiterate labor in brick kilns, industries and construction sites. Atrocities against them are horrifying and mounting. Convictions for such atrocities are minimal, despite the existence of laws such as the Scheduled Castes and the Scheduled Tribes (Prevention of Atrocities) Act, 1989, etc. Beyond the obvious are the more subtle dimensions of marginalization calling for attention. Significantly, in almost all areas of major decision-making the Dalit presence is either absent or marginal. This is simultaneously the result of overall marginalization as also an instrument of further marginalization. Indoctrination and violence, both overt and covert, are important in perpetrating this marginalization and, not infrequently, over the centuries, the religious and state authorities have colluded to maintain the status quo.

Since the early 1990s, violence against the Dalits has been escalating dramatically against the backdrop of the economic reforms associated with liberalization and privatization. Dalits, who happen to be amongst the weakest sections of the population, have proved to be extremely vulnerable to the adverse impact of globalization in view of their traditional exclusion from the socio-economic and power structures. It is feared that with increasing emphasis on privatization, the growing discrimination against the rural, agricultural and informal sectors, the socio-economic exclusion of the Dalits is all set to be reinforced. Shrinkage of the public sector has as its corollary the shrinkage of the reserved zone for the Dalits. Rolling back of the subsidies that have come alongside has meant added hardships for those who were, given the social odds, already at a disadvantage. They have been particularly hard hit in terms of employment, food security, health and education.

The Tribes as Excluded Communities

Members of the low castes are not the only victims of social exclusion and resultant human rights violations. As already noted, there are several other categories of the population marginalized with reference to the dominant Brahminical order and resultantly victims of exclusion and rights violations. These include the tribal communities.

Compared to other predominantly non-tribal states, India has a rather large tribal population. About eight percent of her population is tribal, comprising of different tribal communities, belonging to different language families, spread across the country and at different levels of socio-economic development and pursuing different occupations. There are communities with very large populations of around three to seven million people, whereas there are others who are so small as to return one or two persons in the census. Among the larger tribes are the Gonds, the Santals, the Bhils the Munda and the Oraon. Among the smallest are the Haisa, Tangsa, the Hotang Tangsa and the Katim Tangsa [Singh, 1994: 3). Almost all tribal communities have their own divisions and hierarchies based on ecology, descent, ranking, status etc. (Singh 1994: 7). The caste stratification of Hindu Brahminical society was traditionally unknown to them. Yet, they have not remained free from the caste impact. The impact of the dominating Hindu Brahminical order is widely felt by them in the course of their existence. It infringes on their culture, demands an acquiescence of sorts, urges a silence of protest exerting implicit and explicit threats, legitimizes an extraction of their common property resources and labor under terms that are violative of their basic rights, and ensures via all these, their continued and persistent marginality from the different sources of power, decision making and control.

These tribal people of India have been traditionally referred to by varied names. The term *Jana* was used widely in Buddhist, Puranic and secular literature of the early or medieval period, to designate those communities whom we today refer to as the tribe. In the epics and the Puranas, they were, however, given more derogatory names and described as Asuras, Dasyus, Nishadas and Rakshashas.

The tribes were initially within a relatively egalitarian and homogeneous social order with a separate socio-cultural and ecological milieu of their own but they were gradually drawn into a position of subordination in relation to the better-off and more scheming non-tribals. Some of the tribal groups were integrated into Hindu society over the years, though in most cases where it happened they were given low status in terms of the hierarchy. Others who were not drawn within the Hindu society remained outside but were perceived as inferior in relation to the Hindus and not their equivalent in any sense of the term. Rights violations of this supposedly inferior population group were thus seen as virtually a part of the natural order of things, non-issues not fit for protest. Extraction of their labor and snatching of their lands, forest rights and common property resources became more and more common and systematized during the British period. And, not surprisingly, tribal discontent had been mounting as was evident from a series of tribal revolts that broke in different parts of India around the middle of the nineteenth century. Specially mentionable were the revolts by the Bhils (1822–1857), Koala tribesmen from 1820 to 1837, Santhal revolt from 1855-56, Rampas revolt in 1879 and the revolt of the Mundas from 1895-1901. In most of these revolts, the grievances of the tribesmen revolved around questions of loss of land and forest rights, religious rights as also their overall sense of hurt pride, dignity and tribal identity.

The Government of India's tribal policy after independence largely revolved around Nehru's policy guidelines. Laws were in place to prevent alienation of tribal lands, check acts of atrocities against them and much else. Tribal sub-plans were introduced as part of the planning process to ensure focused attention on their needs. Yet, the tribal population in India continues to suffer exclusion and marginality. Constitutional—legal provisions, professedly aimed at amelioration of their age-old sufferings have failed to wipe out their sorrows. The gains of reservations in jobs and education, financial support schemes, Tribal Development Sub-plans appear to be negated by the colossal demands of development of the big Indian state geared predominantly by non-tribal interests. It is hardly noticed that at every level of decision making the overwhelming dominance of caste Hindu decision makers prevail where tribals are either totally absent or notionally represented. This is of course not to mention of the high incidents of non-tribal encroachment on tribal lands and resources, despite the existences of laws aimed at curbing such encroachments. The net result of all this happens to be that the tribals have been progressively losing their rights to their lands, homes, forests, traditional sources of livelihood, cultural symbols and much more. Protesting it has frequently meant the perpetuation of a variety of atrocities on them. Homes razed to the ground, children abducted, women raped and men beaten up or killed continue to be regular happenings across the country—being the penalties for the tribals who dare to raise their voices.

The Law and Reality in Women's Lives

Historically viewed, women have been persistently victims of brahminical oppression. The classical Hindu scriptures had relegated them to a distinctly inferior position compared to their male counterparts. On strict control of their sexuality rested the basics of caste stratification—caste endogamy. To ensure that inter-marriage amongst different caste members did not take place, strict separation of the sexes was advocated and control over women's bodies formed the crux of it. The notion of chastity, child marriage, and perpetual supervision were some of the many devices to render them incapable of treading the path of 'sin'. Independent functioning was taboo. The tutelage first of the father, then the husband and finally the son were the destiny of women.

Over thousands of years, as women's discrimination remains sanctified by tradition, religion continues to prop up the image of the docile woman dedicated to the unstinting, selfless service of the family. Patriarchy thrives comfortably, couched in religious jargon with Brahminism propagating the notion that women are incapable of functioning as independent entities. The Brahminical system's degraded scheme of purity and pollution required as its supporting pillar the complete control over female sexuality, as Uma Chakravarti (2003: 36) writes in her pioneering work on *Gendering Caste: Through a Feminist Lens,* " it is ironical ... that Brahminical patriarchy's obsessive concern with controlling female sexuality and ensuring the reproduction of pure blood—the earliest evidence we have for an abhorrent form of genetic engineering—has survived across all caste groups, high and low, in a way that changes in legal forms and even liberal ideologies have not been able to break." Women, as a category are thus socially earmarked for discrimination and the perpetual extraction of their labor below value.

Inequality that impinges on women's lives finds reflection in crucial issue areas such as access to productive resources, right of control over their own bodies and violence that women experience virtually from conception till death. Violence in fact remains central to the reproduction of patriarchy and, in India, patriarchy is deeply shaped by caste. In rural areas, women's access to health, education, capital, technology and land continue to remain severely limited. Much of women's work continues to be unpaid family labor which hardly gets any recognition as work. In urban areas, eve teasing,[2] sexual harassment at the work place, female feticide, dowry deaths are just some of the unending pains inflicted on the woman. A brief glance at recorded data pertaining to crimes against women indicates the growing rate of violence. While in 1990 the figure of crimes against women stood at 68,317, by 1996 it had risen to 106, 723.

In independent India the Constitution granted equality to women as a fundamental right and empowered the state to adopt affirmative discrimination in favor of women. It assured equal protection of the law, equal opportunities in public employment and prohibited discrimination in public places. As universal adult suffrage added women to the electoral rolls making them politically relevant, political parties pledged their commitment to women's issues. Even though due to strong opposition from the conservatives in the Congress, the Hindu

Mahasabha and the Jan Sangh the Hindu Code Bill could not be passed as envisioned by Dr Ambedkar to improve the position of women, a series of laws passed in the nineteen fifties did succeed in bringing about certain significant changes in Hindu Personal Law aimed at greater empowerment of women in terms of property, succession and matrimonial rights. Four Acts reforming various aspects of Hindu family law were passed. These were the Hindu Marriage Act, The Hindu Succession Act, The Hindu Adoption and Maintenance Act and the Hindu Minority and Guardianship Act.

By the introduction of universal adult suffrage under the Constitution of independent India women got the right to vote on equal terms with men—a right which in many of the western countries women won after prolonged struggles. But nevertheless, women's representation in legislative bodies remained poor. While in the first Lok Sabha elections the percentage of women elected to the legislative body was barely 4.41 percent, by now it has barely crossed the ten percent mark. Even when women did manage to get portfolios in the ministries they were given what may be termed as the lesser important portfolios or the soft portfolios as they are often called. They do not get portfolios like defense, external affairs or finance!

In 1971, the Ministry of Education and Social Welfare appointed a committee under the Chairpersonship of Dr. Phulrenu Guha, the then Minister for Social Welfare at the national level, 'to examine the constitutional, legal and administrative provisions that have a bearing on the social status of women, their education and employment, ' and to assess the impact of these provisions. The move came in response to a UN request to all countries to prepare reports on the status of women for the International Women's Year scheduled for 1975. The Report of the Committee was published in 1974. The findings were startling. The Indian government's commitment to equality was seriously challenged in that Report titled *Toward Equality*. The Report was the first major work to point out the extent to which constitutional guarantees of equality and justice had not been met for women. The authors of the Report charged that women's status had not improved but had in fact declined since independence. The Report noted that social change and development in India had adversely affected women.

During the International Decade for Women there were a lot of activities on several fronts. The approach to women shifted from being 'welfare oriented' to 'development oriented'. A variety of schemes in different ministries for the advancement of women were initiated or existing schemes intensified particularly relating to skill development, education and income earning capabilities. Focal points in ministries and departments were designated as 'women's cells ' to exclusively monitor programs for women. State level Women's Development Corporations were established to finance development programs for women. In 1993 India ratified the CEDAW. In the same year an Act of Parliament established the long awaited National Commission for Women. State level commissions were also set up in course of time in several states, including West Bengal.

The Government of India made the empowerment of women one of the principal objectives of the Ninth Five Year Plan (1997–2002). The professed aim was to make efforts to bring about such an enabling socio-economic and psycho-emotional environment in which women would be able to greatly exercise their rights as equal partners of men. Also, all efforts were sought to be undertaken to empower women as agents of social change. The year of 2001 was declared by the Indian Government as the Year of Women's Empowerment.

Despite these and other legal and administrative measures adopted over more than fifty years, women still remained subject to patriarchal oppression. The fact remained that the rights guaranteed failed to ensure social justice. Rising incidence of feticide, dowry deaths, female infanticide, rape and other forms of violence against women go side by side with other different forms of domestic violence. Within the confines of the home—the eulogized space that is believed to be the area of shelter and protection—the 'private' conceals many an act of spine-chilling violence. It is here that a closer perusal of the social structure helps in understanding the depths of the problem.

It may be noted that dominance, resting on resource ownership, is intertwined with notions of ritual status of the different castes. As such, it is not uncommon to find that low caste women are sexually assaulted by land-owning, upper caste men. Sexual assault and rape manifests itself as an assertion of power. Low caste men not only fail to prevent such assaults from their economically and socially superior masters, there is almost a tacit acceptance of it in many cases as the assertion of dominance is accepted as a matter of right by the upper castes.

Moreover, violence remains impregnated in India's development policy. The strategy of industrial development with its emphasis on labor saving, skill intensive technology has displaced women from traditional occupations, self-employment, small scale and cottage industries as also from large scale industries. Increasingly, women are denied access to Common Property Resources such as forests and grazing grounds on the pretext of environmental protection while at the same time those resources are made easily available to big industries, particularly the MNCs, for purposes of commercial exploitation. Big dams and other environmental policies, India's nuclear program, all pose serious threats to women and not surprisingly some of the most vocal protests come from women themselves.

Today, in the post–90s, with the introduction of structural adjustments, the targeting of production for the global market, opening up of the economy to other states as part of globalization and with the virtual acceptance of market forces as the sole determinant of economic and other activities, and the state's withdrawal from its role of social welfare agency by the encouragement of privatization on the one hand and reduction of budget allocations on health-education and social services on the other have adversely affected Indian women. Much of what was achieved during the earlier decades appears to be under serious stress since the nineties. The alarming rise of female feticide, girl child abuse, incidents of rape and domestic violence and dowry demands signal the growing threat. Women find themselves at odds in trying to cope with the demands of new skills in the job market made necessary by globalization. The rising threat of unemployment looms large and the pressure of the market all but crushes them. Skirting the labor laws, work of the big industries gets done contractually by small home based units with total disregard to working conditions, hours of work, etc., on the one hand, and on the other the women working in the traditional small industries increasingly lose their sources of livelihood. On the whole, the implications of the Structural Adjustment Programs have been negative for most women. It has meant reduced real incomes and standards of living along with greater burden of unpaid work. In a word, under globalization, feminization of poverty takes place as never before. And, all against the backdrop of the stranglehold of traditional Brahminical values imbibed, internalized and imposed that hardly get dislodged as is evident from the reinforced vigor with which the caste panchayats, better known as *Khap Panchayats* seek to establish their writ.

The Religious Minorities

Not that in terms of the wider social order, the plight of the general population subscribing to other religions is much better. Their vulnerability is visible and their exclusion from the corridors of power and access to various forms of resources reinforces it. The mine of information that has been brought into focus recently by Sachar Committee Report (2006) in relation to the largest minority group, the Muslims, is clearly disturbing. In the field of literacy the Committee has found that the rate among Muslims is very much below than the national average. Muslim community has a representation of only 4.5 percent in Indian Railways; representation of Muslims is very low in the Universities and in Banks. Their share in police constables is only 6 percent, in health 4.4 percent, in transport 6.5 percent.

Independent India's history has been spotted by periodic events of violence against minorities. The Gujarat riots in the wake of the Godhra events of 2002 in which the victims hailed from the Muslim community were a reminder of the country-wide violence against Sikhs after the assassination of the then Prime Minister Indira Gandhi in 1984. All these make news, not the more frequent threats of vandalism and terror to which individual persons of minority communities remain vulnerable should they dare to annoy the powerful.

Dalit converts to other religions form a sizeable section of the non-Hindu population groups across the country, particularly amongst the Muslim, Buddhist and Christian communities. They are no less marginalized than the Dalit Hindus. They have persistently been struggling for their rights. The struggles have been essentially on two fronts. One, in terms of the wider social surroundings and the other is in terms of the non-Dalits within their own religious folds. That is, neither could they totally escape from the trappings of their earlier identity, nor could they find the anticipated human dignity within the new milieu. On the whole it seems that in many cases conversion to the otherwise egalitarian religions failed to assure the measure of social justice which the Dalit converts had expected. Here of course the responses to conversion have not been uniform in all instances. Sometimes, discrimination is more overt than at other times. But, the humiliation and pinch remains, not to be overlooked or ignored. Struggles of the Dalit converts thus revolve around different issues. Most importantly, they demand social justice and human rights in society at large, within their community and the necessary support from the state. It is here that the question of reservation has repeatedly come up; and, for the converts, barring the Sikhs and the neo-Buddhists, the state response has so far been negative.

The Yearnings and Struggles for Human Rights

Over the years, mounting discontent amongst these population groups and their growing awareness of marginality led to various forms of struggles—some organized, some sporadic; some at the national level, some very localized. From the last quarter of the twentieth century in particular, tribes were seen participating in large numbers in movements against displacement and land acquisitions across the country. They were prominent in the NGO-led anti-displacement movements like the Narmada Bachao Andolan, as also in the land-related Maoist led struggles in different places of Bengal, Bihar, Orissa and Andhra Pradesh. Likewise, women were increasingly becoming visible in a wide range of activism ranging from the extreme left to the extreme right of the political scale. They were seen in the Maoist mobilizations as also in the RSS/ Sangh Parivar mobilizations. The fact remains that, at the ground level, as of now, neither the tribes nor the women share amongst their respective categories any common ideological position in terms of analyses or strategy of countering their marginality.

The UN General Assembly's adoption of the Declaration on the Rights of Indigenous Peoples (UNDRIP) in 2007 brought into focus of discussions the plight of tribals in India and stimulated efforts at their mobilization, much in the same way that the Convention on the Elimination of All Forms of Discrimination Against Women had done when it came into force in 1981.

The United Nations' 1989 Convention on the Rights of the Child, or CRC, the first legally binding international instrument to incorporate the full range of human rights of children—civil, cultural, economic, political and social rights, did emerge as reference point for country—specific children's concerns. Yet, India still struggles pathetically with the situations of missing children, trafficking and child labor, not to speak of the persistent health hazards and malnutrition from which innumerable children continue to suffer.

So far as the Dalits are concerned, post–90s, have thrown up the need for major re-thinking of strategies. Against the backdrop of globalization, efforts are being made by the Dalits themselves to bring in new issues into focus in the course of their struggles, develop new tools and techniques of struggles to supplement the existing ones, and to search out new support bases in combating their marginality.

The '90s saw several major developments in the field of Dalit assertion. One of the most important developments has been the formation of the National Campaign on Dalit Human Rights (NCDHR). The National Campaign on Dalit Human Rights (NCDHR) was officially launched in India in December 1998 to act as a non-political secular forum comprising of a band of Dalit scholars and activists. The purpose was to promote solidarity, cooperation, and collective action at the national level for the promotion of Dalit human rights. Its efforts were largely directed towards demonstrating the link between Dalit issues and human rights issues. The move came against the backdrop of worldwide activities centering around the completion of fifty years of the Universal Declaration of Human Rights. When other Human rights activists and institutions in India were planning to celebrate the completion of the fiftieth year of the promulgation of Universal Declaration of Human Rights (UDHR) as a response to the call of the United Nations, seventy-eight Dalit activists and Human Rights activists from across the country, concerned about the frequent atrocities and the blatant lack of implementation of the SC/ST (Prevention of Atrocities) Act of 1989, met in Bangalore to discuss a Program of action, deliberated and resolved to make use of this opportunity to "highlight the issue of Caste and Untouchability" among the International community, international organizations including the UN Bodies and especially in UNCHRs.

Religious minority interests seem to be reflected predominantly through religious fora and more as sporadic expressions of interests rather than as consistent long-term formulations of interest against the wider backdrop of the socio-political milieu. For the mainstream political parties, their, i.e. the religious minorities issues appear more as add-ons in the context of the demands of parliamentary electoral politics, rather than as genuine concern areas.

On the whole, however, it may be said that independence and the parliamentary democratic exercises over the years have given a boost to the assertion efforts of different marginalized groups that in course of time got further impetus with the growing importance of the human rights discourse at the international level. Constitutional-legal measures and judicial activism were seen as important tools for human rights protection. Yet, somewhere down the line, they continued to fail and mobilizations of the concerned were incapable of driving them on.

Even as the human rights vulnerability of different population groups become evident and focused attention of the government, NGOs and rights bodies in India and abroad increases, it is pertinent to note that,

a) Human rights threats faced by different segments of the Indian population are deeply rooted in the Brahminical societal structuring, values and norms. While it makes for the arrogance of a social elite, caste Hindu oppressing section, it also makes for the submissive internalization of the oppression suffered by the excluded.

b) Without addressing the challenges posed to the human rights of these different, apparently disconnected sections of the population, rectification of the scenario can hardly be seriously contemplated. Hence, noting the common roots of oppression under the aegis of the Brahminical system remains vital. It is undoubtedly a formidable challenge. And, none of the concerned appears keen on, or capable of taking it on. Few dare speak of the urgent necessity of dismantling it and bringing in its place a more democratic societal system.

c) In spite of the common roots of their problems, under the circumstances cited above, it is not surprising that joint efforts of the different groups at human rights protection have hardly taken place. Movements have remained isolated and fragmented, short in vision and lacking in analytical depth. Even after acknowledging the fact that the hurdles are enormous, developing a blueprint of joint action for human rights of all excluded sections remains the urgent need of the day.

References

Chakravarti, U., 2003. *Gendering Caste: Through a Feminist Lens.* Kolkata: Stree.

Dasgupta M. and P.N. Mari Bhat, 1998. Intensified Gender Bias in India: A Consequence of Fertility Decline. *Gender, Population and Development,* edited by M. Krishnaraj, Ratna M. Sudarshan and Abusaleh Shariff, 73–93. New Delhi: Oxford University Press.

Desai, A.R. 1975. *Peasant Struggles in India.* Bombay: Popular Prakashan.

Desai, N. and Thakkar, U., 2003. *Women in Indian Society.* New Delhi: National Book Trust.

Doniger, W. and B. Smith, 1991. *The Laws of Manu.* New Delhi: Penguin.

Lahiri, D., 2008. International Human Rights Standards: How Does India Measure Up? *ORF Issue Brief* May 2008. Issue Brief#13, (May 2008): 1–4. www. orfonline.org/May 2008 (accessed May 12, 2011).

Mandelbaum, D. G., 1970. *Society in India.* Bombay: Popular Prakashan.

National Commission for Women, 1974. *Towards Equality: Report of the Commission on the Status of Women in India.* New Delhi: Government of India.

Sachar Committee Report, 2006. http://zakatindia.org/Foles/Sachar%20Report %20(Full).pdf (accessed May 12, 2011).

Sharma, R.S., 1990. *Sudras in Ancient India: A Social History of the Lower Order Down to Circa A.D. 600,* Delhi: Motilal Banarsidass.

Singh, K.S., 1994. *The Scheduled Tribes, Anthropological Survey of India, People of India Series,* Vol. III, Delhi: Oxford University Press.

Notes

1. See *The Hindu* (January 26, 2003)

2. Eve teasing is a euphemism used in South Asia for public molestation of women by men.

CHAPTER 9

Media, Cultural Rights and the Third World

Pranta Pratik Patnaik

Its aim is always that of . . . adapting the "civilization" and morality of the broadest popular masses to the necessities of the continuous development of the economic apparatus of production.

(Gramsci 1971: 242)

In reference to the modern democratic state, it was for the first time, Gramsci pointed out the significance of culture at the heart of the state's sphere of activity. The relation between the state and culture changes with a shift in the cultural relations between the popular and the dominant cultures. Such transformations have contributed to and been informed by more epochal shifts in the organization of class-cultural relationships and the associated forms and mechanisms of ruling class hegemony. A distinction between popular and dominant culture smells of a power struggle between different groups, striving for cultural autonomy, equality and originality, hence begging the question of cultural rights.

Cultural rights got worldwide recognition through the International Covenant on Economic, Social and Cultural Rights (ICESCR) was adopted by the General Assembly in 1966 and entered into force in January 1976. The Covenant embodies some of the most significant international legal provisions establishing economic, social and cultural rights, including rights relating to—work in just and favorable conditions; social protection; adequate standard of living including clothing, food and housing; the highest attainable standards of physical and mental health; education, and the enjoyment of the benefits of *'cultural freedom'* and scientific progress. Significantly, Article 2 outlines the legal obligations, which are incumbent upon State parties under the Covenant. States are required to take positive steps to implement these rights, to the maximum of their resources, in order to achieve the progressive realization of the rights recognized in the Covenant, particularly through the adoption of domestic legislation.[1]

If one talks about flow of culture taking place in 'deterritorialised' (Appadurai 1996) spaces, there could be no such real thing called 'cultural exception', but merely an idea in circulation. The UNESCO Universal Declaration on Cultural Diversity in 2001 and the UNESCO Convention on the Protection and Promotion of the Diversity of Cultural Expressions of 2005, both of which demand the protection and promotion of the diversity of cultural expressions also begs the question of sovereignty: Is cultural diversity here still premised on the sovereignty problematic as much as on the human rights treaties or does it seek to modify the sovereignty question in one or the other form? Do International Human Rights Treaties actually improve the respect for human rights and works for the enforcement of these legal entitlements? For several decades, the primary focus of human rights has been limited to issues around political prisoners, torture, refugees, and displaced persons. Decolonization and increasing demands for democratization across the developing world and Eastern Europe accelerated interest among local civil society groups, activists, academics, and human rights groups on broadening and strengthening the debate on the concept of universal human rights to include: the rights to a living income, to health, to food, housing and education, and to live in a world at peace. Thus, today, across cultures around the globe, local human rights groups are pressing demands beyond the narrow confines of human rights definitions to include: child rights; women rights and the elimination of female circumcision; the rights of indigenous populations; the rights of ethnic, religious, and linguistic minorities; the rights to shelter and development; and economic and social justice. Against this backdrop, this chapter would look into the role of media in highlighting the cultural rights of the indigenous people in Orissa allegedly threatened with the massive industrial expansion project by POSCO, a South Korean Steel Company and Vedanta, another Aluminium giant. The basic purpose of looking into the role of media is to unravel the political economy aspect of cultural rights of indigenous people as played out through the media, here television.

This chapter first examines the category of 'cultural rights' and the problems inherent in it in the section—*Understanding cultural rights*. Secondly, it discusses and contextualizes the evolved notion of cultural right in the wake of the massive industrialization process taking place in the state affecting the culture of the indigenous people and the response of media, particularly television, to such events in the following section—*Contextualizing cultural rights*. Finally, these threadbare discussions help us in understanding the lacunae of cultural rights involved in the international human rights treaties and therefore, what needs to be done about it, finds a place in the final section of the chapter—*Foreseeing Cultural Rights*.

A brief background of the research area needs to be mentioned in order to have a clear picture about the prevailing situation in Orissa, a state in the eastern part of India, which can be divided into four geographical and distinct socio-cultural regions. The northern belt comprises the districts of Mayurbhanj, Keonjhar and Sundargarh. The southern belt consists of the districts of Koraput, Malkangiri, Nabarangapur, Rayagada, Gajapati, Ganjam, and Kandhamal. The north eastern areas bordering on Bengal have been influenced in dress, food habits, languages, social customs and festivities by Bengali culture and language. The southern parts of Ganjam and Koraput districts have been influenced in language, food habits, dress and marriage customs by the Andhra culture and language and have a sizeable Telugu speaking population. The western districts of Sambalpur, Nuapada, Sonapur, Baragarh, Bolangir and Kalahandi may be said in many ways to be a cultural and to some extent, linguistic continuum with the region of Chattisgarh. The fourth region including the coastal districts of Balasore, Cuttack, Bhubaneswar, Jagatsinghpur and Puri is 'distinctive' in its cultural institutions, social customs and linguistic and literary sophistication. Industry, urbanism and development have taken place massively in these areas. During the initial days of my fieldwork, there was widespread agitation in Orissa where the people belonging to the western part of Orissa were demanding a separate state for themselves, to be named as Koshala state based on their dialect. My attempt was then to show how television can then be a potential source of conflict between these two regions within the state and how television emerges as a significant social force, and an important protagonist in the contestations over what is 'true' Oriya culture. When my research began there was only one private regional television channel in Oriya—Orissa Television (OTV), which was indulged in a politics of representation by trying not only to create and define an Oriya culture and identity but also reinforcing the prevailing stereotypes and existing power structures.

The emergence of OTV was a step towards a gigantic media revolution in the state. From a small beginning in 1997 with a few news based programs, OTV has now crossed many milestones on the road to developing itself as a niche channel. Launched in the twin cities of Bhubaneswar and Cuttack, OTV has now become synonymous with television in Orissa. It has already become the premier source of news, current affairs and entertainment. However this immensely popular television channel, having its office/studio in the coastal part of the state (Bhubaneswar) tries to define a particular Oriya culture (read: coastal Oriya culture) which leaves out the 'Other' half of the state thereby, in a sense, marginalizing their cultural rights. The chapter looks into the area of cultural diversity and the rights of marginal people where the primary objective is to reflect on the implications of the UNESCO Declaration on Cultural Diversity to various groups, ranging from marginal peoples whose cultural forms are being appropriated by music, fashion and other industries to producers and consumers of mass culture. It also attempts to identify areas of conflict between protection of cultural diversity and policies on culture industries, in a scenario where there is commoditization of culture, and a set of critical concerns with respect to existing or proposed state policies on the rights of marginal people. Before moving further into this problem in Orissa, I would like to draw attention to the category of cultural rights itself.

Understanding Cultural Rights: Issues and Perspectives

In its anthropological use, culture refers to a system of shared meanings through which collective existence becomes possible. Culture must be seen in terms of that which it eliminates as also that which it establishes. Edward Said (1983) argues that when culture is consecrated by the state, it becomes a system of discriminations and evaluations through which a series of exclusions can be legislated from above. By such legislative enactment, the state comes to be the primary giver of values. It defines anarchy, disorder, irrationality, inferiority, bad taste and immorality: these are all located outside culture and civilization by the state and its institutions. This exclusion of alternatives—other forms and ways of living—is an important device by which the hegemony of the state is established. Either certain 'others' are defined as being outside culture or are defined as domesticated. Cultural rights as a category itself, therefore, is problematic and needs close attention.

In international human rights jurisprudence, cultural rights began as an issue of minority rights. It opened up a range of contentious issues regarding the nature of minorities and minority cultures and has spawned its own history of documentation, which ultimately turned on the questions around cultural autonomy and cultural self-determination. The rights question becomes even hazier in the time of cultural markets than it ever was before and the question of what are cultural rights becomes more complicated and more important.

The Indian constitution through Article 29 and Article 30 provides special measures to protect the cultural rights of the minorities. It states that any community which has a language and script of its own has the right to conserve and develop it. This begets another set of questions—should cultural rights be confined to the preservation of one's language and script alone or does it extend beyond this?

The issue of cultural rights also brings in an equally important question of the nation versus the people or 'community'. The more the term 'cultural diversity' pops up from various official forays, the more one smells a kind of reductionism—it actually becomes the opposite of diversity and there is a kind of paring down or reduction. There is always a surgical split being made between information and entertainment or recreation, when reference is being made by the officials concerned with the cultural rights issue. The issue of diversity gets funneled into these two very easily matching and seemingly symbiotic wings.

Cultural rights, according to Veena Das (1994), include a variety of situations with different moral implications which cannot be considered to be analogous to political rights. Cultural rights are not generated solely due to preservation of culture or interests but are also guided by political passions. The preservation of cultural rights calls for the notion of a 'community', which stresses that the issue is not only of biological survival and of ensuring against discrimination towards individuals within minorities, but also that in order for individuals to be able to enjoy their culture it must be preserved in the collective conscience. The issue of cultural rights is debatable, she argues, if one divides the rights into individual rights and collective rights. Secondly, in granting individuals the right to enjoy their culture, what obligations does the state have towards ensuring the survival of that culture? Is the state simply required to abstain from interference or does it have positive obligations towards these groups? Another related issue with this question is the role of non-formal rules and sanctions imposed by the group or community which might go against the state. Finally, if we consider it necessary that right of collectivities as distinct from the collective rights of individuals be recognized, then how relations between different collectivities would on the one hand, and the collectivity and the individual on the other, be governed?

It must be noted further that culture and tradition are subject to the constant change which marks every living society. Any attempt to confine or fix cultural traditions may jeopardize their survival. In the contest between states, communities, and collectivities of different kinds on the one hand and the individual on the other, we see, what Veena Das calls, the double life of culture: its potential to give radical recognition to the humanity of its subjects, as well as its potential to keep the individual within such tight bounds that the capacity to experiment with one's self—which is equally a mark of one's humanity—comes to be severely at risk. This double definition of culture as a system of shared meanings defining the collective life and keeping the individual within strict social bounds, places the question of cultural rights squarely within the larger question of passions rather than interests.

The demand for cultural rights in contemporary times has come to be articulated in a context where cultural symbols have been appropriated by the state, which tries to establish a monopoly over ethical pronouncements. The state is thus experienced as a threat by smaller units who feel that their ways of life will be penetrated if not engulfed by this larger unit. This clearly reveals that culture and power are closely related, if not in fact almost synonymous. Culture is used as a soft power through the media in order to exercise, manipulate and persuade towards the creation of a dominant culture. This issue is discussed more in detail in the next section in the context of television in Orissa, the state politics and the economic interest, where the cultural rights of the marginalized section are in jeopardy.

Contextualizing Cultural Rights: Cultural Politics of Television in Orissa

In an era of global communication flow, culture industries need to be reconsidered through the inter linkage between culture, economy and politics or political gain. The period of 1990s in India earmarked the beginning of import of 'foreign' TV programs. Since 1990, the Indian cultural basket has been dramatically inflated by the entry of major foreign players. All the global mega-entertainment giants now have a presence through the media and the entertainment sector—whether it is fashion, or beauty contests, or even mainstream media—virtually taking over the entire sector. The state instead of being the buffer and putting in place protectionist policies has withdrawn completely, opened the doors and given a red carpet welcome to these foreign players. What one witnesses then is a new negotiation of cultural power that enables corporate multinationals to indulge themselves into the nation's economy and markets through the parliament and the Planning commission, which are in fact supposed to be the filters against this kind of development. The global market player enters the National Planning Commission discourse in a masked way where 'policing culture' is out and policy-in culture has become the norm.

India signed the Memorandum of Understanding (MoU) with South Korea for expansion of economic infrastructure of both the countries. The economic relationship gave way to the cultural expansion of Korea's media items in India. Korean TV series were shown in state owned television channels in India. This section is an evaluation of "Korean wave"[2] in Orissa during a period when there was huge protest against the Korean investment in the state in the wake of displacement of tribals due to its industrial projects. The notion of Korean wave per se might not apply to Orissa though there have been cultural imports (in the form of TV series). In an attempt to understand the basic tenets of such import, one unravels the cultural-economic-political nexus which has implications for a better understanding of culture industries and subsequently, cultural rights.

In economic terms, Korea had a huge impact for the investment it made and the number of jobs it created. The proposal of the Pohang Steel & Co. (POSCO), a steel giant of Korea, to invest around 12 billion US dollars in integrated steel plants at Paradip in Orissa is the largest ever foreign investment in India till date and the single largest overseas investment by a Korean company.[3] However the project was received with much criticism within certain sections in the state as it was alleged to ruin the source of livelihood of innumerable tribals and poor people. The state government with its pro-development agenda turned a blind eye to this problem at the initial stage. With intensification of protest against the project certain rehabilitation measures were undertaken which were inadequate and mostly remained in black and white.

The Economic Times (13th February 2009) quoted Mr. Pradip Kumar Amat, the steel and mines minister of Orissa, as saying that POSCO India has so far spent only INR 176 crore[4] of the planned INR 51,000 crore investments in the proposed mega steel plant in Orissa. Mr. Amat said that "Though Supreme Court had already cleared the forest land diversion proposal, the Forest and Environment Ministry was yet to accord its permission." Though, POSCO India signed a MoU with the state government way back in June 2005, it has so far failed to acquire the land for the project due to stiff opposition from the public until recently when the environment minister of India Jairam Ramesh showed a green flag to the project.

Local Oriya newspapers like *The Dharitri*, *The Samaja* and *The Economic Times* (12th February 2009) carried out stories of the sufferings of the Posco project hit villages of Dhinkia, Gadakujang and Nuagaon gram panchayats falling under Kujang block of Jagatsinghpur district. The health services in these areas were affected as the health officials stopped entering the villages for the last two years following the blockage of all entry points to these villages by the villagers to prevent the entry of the government officials.

The health services are in shambles in these seaside gram panchayats. The villagers were protesting against the decision of the government to acquire 4,004 acres of land in these areas for the Posco India to build a steel plant with an investment of Rs 51,000 crores.

Commenting on the anti-Posco movement, Sishir Mohapatra, Secretary, POSCO Pratirodhaka Sangram Samiti (PPSS) said, "Police filed false cases against more than five hundred anti-POSCO villagers allegedly for attacking government officials, forcefully locking the village post office, assaulting pro-POSCO villagers and blocking the roads by erecting wooden gates and committing other crimes due to which many anti-Posco villagers are not coming out of these villages - the bastion of anti-land acquisition movement".

On May 15, 2010, public protests against proposed POSCO steel plant in Jagatsinghpur district of Orissa turned violent when police *lathi*-charged people sitting on *dharna* and fired rubber bullets at them where over 100 persons were injured. The protesters had been blocking the road to the South Korean company's steel plant site since January 26, 2010. The police were helping the district administration acquire land for the project. "We saw policemen torching shops and houses. They used unjustified force to evict POSCO Pratirodh Sangram Samiti (PPSS) members protesting peacefully on Balitutha bridge," said Satyabati Swain, an activist. Kishore Kandi of Dhinkia village said police has filed false cases against all protesters. He said he did not dare to step out of the village to seek treatment for his back injury caused by a rubber bullet. Even bystanders were not spared. Alekh Chandra Sahoo, 72-year-old male, who lives next to the Balitutha Bridge, said his house was burnt along with rice stocks by the police. The police action was the second such incident in the state in a week.[5]

While on one hand, there were huge protests against the Korean Steel giant, simultaneously on the other hand, the Korean cultural expansion was manifesting itself in Oriya Television Channel as well. The first Oriya channel to show Korean TV series dubbed in Oriya was through the only channel available in the regional language, i.e., DD Oriya. DD Oriya, a state owned television channel since 1994, broadcasts serials, cultural programmes, infotainment, news produced at Doordarshan Kendras of Bhubaneswar, Sambalpur and Bhawanipatna. The weekly transmission hours for the terrestrial channel with satellite support is 37 hours and 30 minutes. DD Oriya grabs about 29 percent of the total market share in India reaching to almost 23 per cent of the total population in India.[6]

The Korean serial shown in DD Oriya titled 'Maya' was aired in 2006. Maya was the story of a girl who was famous for her brilliant farming techniques. This serial was a South Korean serial that was being dubbed in Oriya. This was something new to the Orissa Television. Unlike other Oriya television serials, this serial had all the characters that belonged to South Korea and they were showing the farming community of South Korea. Only the voices of the characters have been muted and been dubbed in Oriya language so that the people of Orissa can understand it. During my Ph.D. fieldwork, one of my respondents—Prasanta Das (name changed), a government school teacher in Bhubaneswar—did mention once in our conversation that these people are talking in Oriya but they don't look like an Oriya rather they look like 'Chinese' people. This brings home the fact that physical appearance of the characters also has a bearing on the acceptance of a TV series rather than mere dubbing of the language. Though 'Maya' was seen in families of my respondents but not on a regular basis:

> I want to hear the Oriya news which is telecasted at 7:00 p.m. Maya is shown at 6:30. I don't want to miss the news so I turn on the television either at 6:40 or 6:45 p.m. and see Maya but I generally would be either reading Newspaper or talking over phone and do not watch it on a regular basis. I do not who is who in this serial. *These are not Oriya people. They do not act the way our actors do.* (Mr.Prasanta Das, Bhubaneswar)

> When Maya was going to be aired, there were few promos of it on television. I was excited to see a new serial in Oriya. We don't have cable connection so the excitement was more. Somehow I watched the repeat telecasts of the serial in the afternoon but *it did not interest me much as the storyline was more about the farming community and farming techniques.* I didn't watch after a few episodes. (Mrs. Ira Panda, Bhubaneswar)

In my attempt to know about the serial 'Maya', I came across media personnel in the Orissa Doordarshan studio:

> Orissa is a land of farmers and people over here have little knowledge about the farming techniques. In that case, Korean serial 'Maya' is a good thing to happen to Oriya television. Farmers in the village have DD Oriya as the only source of knowledge about the farming techniques through our programme, Krushi Darshan. You might have seen on television the letters written by farmers about the problems they face. Maya is a good response to these problems. It is in a way spreading the message that women should take part in agricultural activities as well as how to choose good soil, seeds, and manure. (Mr.Mohapatra, Doordarshan Kendra Official, Bhubaneswar, name changed)

Though I had no access to the letters written by the audience to the Doordarshan Kendra in Bhubaneswar, the 'Chitthi Patra' program where letters of the audience are read was followed up by me. Surprisingly, there have never been any letter concerning the serial 'Maya' with exceptions of not to show this TV series and to extend the half an hour program 'Krushi Darshan' to one hour!

It should be noted here that 'Maya', basically a South Korean serial which has been produced by the South Korean Television Channel MBC (Munhwa Broadcasting Corporation) has found its place in Orissa Television because Mr. Naveen Patnaik (the chief minister of the state) has full support for the POSCO Company.[7] There has been a demand for his resignation by the opposition parties as the chief minister seems to be aloof with the environmental hazards and livelihood issues of the people in Orissa due to the POSCO project. Felix Padel and Samarendra Das (2006) link the exploitation of aluminum companies and the state government to a sort of 'genocide' where there might not be literally physical death of the tribals but a psychic death, which they term as 'ethnicide', that is, killing-off of culture. It is worth noting that certain sections of the government and media label the activists who fight for the rights of the tribals as 'Naxalites' or 'Maoists' to justify police brutalities against them. In the Orissa Assembly on 4 Dec. 2004 Naveen Patnaik stated (as shown on TV news): '*No one—I repeat no one—will be allowed to stand in the way of Orissa's industrial development and the people's progress'*. However what remains unanswered is who defines what is people's progress?

Furthermore, the Chief Minister has said that the demand for his resignation by the opposition parties over giving land to the steel maker POSCO is illogical and without any justification. The opposition in Orissa has been disrupting the ongoing Winter Session in State Assembly, alleging Patnaik had manipulated and bent the rules for giving the land to steel maker POSCO's proposed plant in the State. Meanwhile, the Congress party, remained adamant in its demand for the resignation of Patnaik and organized a massive rally to further press his ouster. P. Singh Deo, President of Orissa Pradesh Congress Committee said that the Patnaik government has been the only government, which has been legally malafide in its deeds. "Here is a government you voted for three times and here is a government who (which) is making a mockery of democracy, violating the Constitution, violating the law, because the High Court has indicted this present BJD (Biju Janata Dal) government that it is malafide, legally malafide, which is a very serious charge, which has never happened in 63 years of independence," he added.

The Orissa government has moved the Supreme Court challenging the Orissa High Court judgment canceling the license granted by the State to POSCO for iron ore mining in the Kandadhar mines in Sundergarh district. Acting on a petition filed by Geomin Minerals and Marketing (P) Ltd., the High Court had directed that the license recommended by the State in 2009 to be granted to POSCO be cancelled. The High Court had also held that the petitioner company should be given a preferential right of being considered for the license applied in 1991. In its Special Leave Petition (SLP) against this judgment dated July 14, Orissa prayed for quashing the impugned judgment and an interim stay of its operation, otherwise it would jeopardize POSCO's plans to set up a steel plant. The license would enable the company to explore and mine the Kandadhar hills for iron ore. In its SLP, Orissa submitted that its recommendation that the license be granted to POSCO over earlier applicants was not violating any of the Mines and Minerals (Development and Regulation) Act. It said the High Court had struck down the State's decision as violative of Section 11(5) of the Act for failing to record the special reason why POSCO, which had applied for it last, should get the license out of turn when others had applied earlier. Justifying the action, the SLP said that it had considered POSCO's application under Section 11(3) which empowered it to look into the special knowledge and experience of parties applying for licenses, financial resources, nature and quality of technical staff employed and the investment it proposed to make in the mine or industry while deciding to grant license in its favor. Contending that the High Court judgment was erroneous, the SLP sought a direction to set aside the impugned judgment.

This is a case which shows how a multi-national company has its say in the media matters of the state albeit with the full support of the ruling government in the state—indeed a case of political economy approach to study the control of media in Orissa. This reminds one of Adorno who in his work "Culture and

Administration" (1991) talks about the cultural politics of the state and not of the market wherein he states that culture and administration cannot be separated.

Though 'Maya' went off air without being noticed, OTV took centre stage in the state. On Mar 19 2008, OTV transmitted a feature film entitled *'Tamasoma Jyotirgamay'* (From Darkness lead unto light) produced by POSCO,[8] in a way implying that Orissa is in a state of darkness or underdevelopment and industrialization due to POSCO would bring light or happiness into the lives of the people. The film was made to create a mass opinion in support of the project. But certain dialogues in the film were derogatory to National Integration and also promoting regional disparity. Using few artists the film tried to convince people through some dialogues like—

> '...before the project was planned where were the outsider (other state) activists and leaders who encourage people in the project site to oppose the project?'
>
> 'Outsider activists and politicians are no way concerned with the problems of People but are envious of the development projects planned in the state of Orissa'. 'Agitating against development projects has become a fashion these days'.

It should be noted that these dialogues were intended for the creation of the 'Other' to safeguard the pride of Orissa and Oriya identity. Interestingly, the category of 'Other' includes other states in India and people within Orissa who have been raising their voice against POSCO. The 'Other' was portrayed as a threat to the developmental work undertaken by the Orissa government for the state. However, the professionals involved in the film were Oriya actors, hired on payment to make these dialogues said in the film but were no way affected by the project directly! Furthermore, there was a shift as well as a strong reinforcement and call for a pan–Oriya culture. The issue of development was made a cultural issue by persuading the people that such events are a pride for the state and Oriya culture and those who are staging a protest against such projects do not want to see Orissa as an emerging and developed state.

The film was hardly analytical about the livelihood issues of people, possible scarcity of food materials once the project stands on the lands that are used for agriculture now, and the possibility of transformation of the sustainable local market economy into one that would be controlled by outside businessmen. The culture of the tribals affected has been considered as a 'minor paying price' for the major development in their area. There was least concern about the cultural rights of the 'would be' displaced tribals and other inhabitants of the region. But instead, the film started blaming activists who are fighting for the basic livelihood rights of people in the country as envious outsiders. One might argue that there would be no problem if the film were for internal purpose of the corporate house. But when it came for transmission, how the channel could approve such remarks for public broadcasting, as these were not presented as individual viewpoints but conclusive messages of the film?

'*Tamasoma Jyotirgamay*' is, no doubt, a local production but supported by POSCO in its making. It brought along with it economic, business ties and political partnership where media becomes a play child for them? The question arises why did OTV, a private channel, made a film in support of POSCO? Is there any hidden agenda behind this? Sandeep Mishra in *The Times of India* (19th December 2010) reports that POSCO is ready for a tie-up with the Indian Metals and Ferro Alloys Limited (IMFA) to get a foothold in Orissa. It should be noted that Member of Parliament from Biju Janta Dal, the ruling political party in Orissa, Mr. B. Panda's younger brother is the managing director of IMFA. Interestingly enough, Mr. Panda's spouse is the managing director of OTV. It is the unholy alliance of state politics, economic interest and family business that has a role in the politics of representation of the Oriya culture, aligning it with the issue of development for the entire state thereby neglecting the plight of those who would be bearing the adverse effect of such developmental projects.

A fact finding team of People's Union for Democratic Rights (PUDR), Delhi in their study of parts of Rayagada and Kalahandi districts of Orissa in April 2005 found that there is a struggle between the inhabitants of the region with the paid goons of the mining companies. The peasants of the land, tribals and dalits are at the receiving end where the process of usurping their land for the project involves coercion as well as manipulation. Sadly enough, the policemen were also involved in various atrocities against the poor, especially those who protested against these companies. Orissa lacks a comprehensive policy of rehabilitation as well. The water sources to these districts would be affected due to these mining companies along with the forest cover. It is surprising that such projects are being carried out in the name of 'national interest' and 'public purpose'.

On the basis of her research and findings in Orissa, Vidhya Das (1995) comes to the conclusion that such development projects are more violent than wars which is chiefly for export purpose at the cost of displacing tribal people. Had it been for the purpose of national energy consumption, the tag of 'national interest' would have sufficed but such activities directly feeds into the corporate interests in Europe and North America. At the end, she poses the question— How does the government justify driving its own people away to make way for these neo-colonizers? One can also witness huge billboards, supposedly another form of media, of POSCO and Vedanta in major parts of Orissa claiming to have ushered happiness in the lives of millions of poor and underprivileged people. Though some of the newspapers in Orissa have been critical about such development projects being undertaken in the state, the Oriya television channels which have wider reach and are much more powerful medium have become the handmaid of the state government. The cultural divide between the different parts of the state has become more sharpened with such development agenda where three bauxite companies have been set up in the western Orissa, displacing the people without accruing the benefits of such projects.

The industrial expansion, visual exclusion and violation of cultural rights along with other human rights proves the international human rights treaty, to which India is a signatory, a mere mockery. It could not foresee that people belonging to the same region can also be denied of their cultural rights. Moreover in case of Orissa, from a cultural rights perspective, what is more problematic is what constitutes an Oriya culture? Who are the definers and upholders of such culture and who plays a major role in legitimizing it? What is the role of the state in protecting the culture of the minorities? Where does it leave an individual as a citizen? All these questions compel us to re-look and re-examine the cultural rights enshrined in the international human rights treaties.

Foreseeing Cultural Rights: From 'Here' to 'Where'?

From the above discussions, it has become clear that the relation between a community and its culture brings two distinct sets of preoccupations in creative tension with each other. These are: first, how does the culture of a community create a shared vision of the world—a resource for questioning the ideologies of the state, including an unquestioned allegiance to it, and second, does this shared culture homogenize the community to the extent that other definitions of culture and community are effectively denied or silenced? At the heart of culture there is an enormous conflict not only between state and community but also within community. Communities need to resist the encompassing claims of the state and the individuals need to develop an inner resistance to even the most vital communities as a condition of human freedom, which brings with itself another set of problems.

Citizenship and human rights are closely related in terms of their origin in liberal individualism where the state plays a major role in reinforcing and legitimizing the identity of its citizens and also ensuring their rights according to the universal norms. Cultural rights of the citizens, in the human rights laws, have been defined through their being a member of a bounded region or territory with a shared notion of historical events and memory which gives them their identity. However with the processes of globalization, migration and 'deterritorialisation', the close relationship between citizen and their national identity has been put under scrutiny. A sociological understanding of rights is not confined to their legal aspect or entitlement but also its manifestation or application in actual lives where individuals' lives are regulated by social structures, informal rules and norms. Universal Declaration of Human Rights seems to be the moral principles entrusted with the states for its implementation through legal bodies. The situation in Orissa reveals the inadequacy of the universal cultural rights and poses the question whether such laws are potential enough to fight injustice?

The social conflict prevalent in Orissa affects the mode of identity constructions and lead to what Berking (2003) terms as the *'ethnicization of cultural identities'* (Berking, 2003: 255; emphasis in original). In such a scenario, cultural relativism becomes a strong guiding force and principle for the individuals who tend to identify themselves to be separate from others, sever the previous ties with the larger group and cultivate all the feelings and strong identification of an in-group making their previous loyalties and shared collectivities fragile. Cultural differences and cultural identity are made readily available in their everyday struggle for advantages and benefits. The politics of identity provides a ground for symbolic mobilization and emancipation from the universal demands of justice and equality in favor of the particular through the 'global valorization of particular identities' (Robertson 1992: 130). Such universalization of particularities undercuts socio-structurally induced disparities and moves towards 'totalizing fictions' (Somers and Gibson 1994: 55) in which a single category (for example, tribal/western Oriya) determines all other attributes signifying identity. What remains problematic is that these totalizing fictions run contrary to the infinite processes of identity formation. Since these identities are socially constructed, they are prone to modify or changeable under certain circumstances especially in favor of chances for political mobilization through a process of 'forgetting something deliberately'. In this context, ethnicization needs to be understood as an affirmation of difference in which certain ascriptive features are (re) essentialized and the reflexive mode of constructing difference or identity is consciously abandoned, 'deliberately' forgotten'. The universalization of human rights has witnessed a growing trend of assertion of particularistic rights of the individuals who are treated as sub/quasi citizen in their own region thereby undermining the classical link between individual rights and national identity. Moreover the global institutionalization of human rights through their incorporation into the body of international law makes it possible to constitute both individual and legal subjects, regulating their relationships through rights and obligations.

What then needs to be done? As Cassel (2001) points out, the institutions of international human rights law deserve our energetic support only to the extent they contribute meaningfully to protection of rights, or at least promise eventually to do so. The chapter believes that the nonbinding Universal Declaration of Human Rights might be more effective if it takes into consideration the inherent problems in the context of cultural rights. Consequently, the human rights laws will become more meaningful in a democratic set-up like India, where the onus rests on the government, citizens and a strong civil society in ensuring cultural freedom to the citizens.

References

Adorno, T. W., 1991. Culture and Administration. *The Culture Industry*, edited by J.M. Bernstein, 107–131. London: Routledge.

Appadurai, A., 1996. *Modernity at Large: Cultural Dimensions of Globalization*. Minneaplis: University of Minnesota Press.

Berking, H., 2003. `Ethnicity is Everywhere': On Globalization and the Transformation of Cultural Identity. *Current Sociology* 51 No. 3/4: 248 - 264.

Cassel, D., 2001. Does International Human Rights Law Make a Difference? *Chicago Journal of International Law* 2:121-35.

Das, V., 1994. Cultural Rights and the Definition of Community in Oliver. *The Rights of Subordinated Peoples*, edited by Mendelsohn and Upendra Baxi, 117–158. Oxford University Press: New Delhi.

Das, V., 1995. Development or Destruction?: New Mining Projects in Orissa. *Economic and Political Weekly*, Vol. 30, no. 22: 1281-1282.

Gramsci A., 1971. *Selections from the Prison Notebooks*, edited by Q. Hoare and G. Nowell-Smith. Lawrence and Wishart: London.

Koenig, M., 2008. Institutional Change in the World Polity: International Human Rights and the Construction of Collective Identities. *International Sociology* 23, no. 1: 95–114.

Padel, F. and S. Das, 2006. Double Death: Aluminium's Links with Genocide. *Social Scientist*, 34, No. 3/4: 55-81.

People's Union for Democratic Rights, 2005. Alumina Projects in South Orissa. *Economic and Political Weekly*, 40, no. 18: 1794+1920.

Robertson, R., 1992. *Globalization*. London: Sage.

Said, E. W., 1983. *The World, the Text and the Critic*. London: Faber.

Somers, M. and G. Gibson, 1994. Reclaiming the Epistemological "Other": Narrative and the Social Constitution of Identity. *Social Theory and the Politics of Identity*, edited by C. Calhoun, 37–99. Cambridge, MA: Blackwell.

Notes

1. Monitoring the implementation of the Covenant by State Parties was the responsibility of the Economic and Social Council, which delegated this responsibility to a Committee on Economic, Social and Cultural Rights.

2. 'Hallyu' was the term coined by the Chinese media which literally meant "Korean Wave". It is a collective term used to refer to the phenomenal growth of Korean popular culture encompassing everything from music, movies, drama to online games and Korean cuisine. Korean wave was first introduced in the late 90s when exported Korean TV dramas and remakes of pop music became popular in China and Hong Kong.

3. See www.posco-india.com and also www.Korea.net/Korea/Go8_board_view.asp?board_no=63

4. Crore is a South Asian system equal to ten million.

5. Report by Ashutosh Mishra in Down to Earth, 15th June 2010 (www.downtoearth.org.in).

6. See www.ddkoriya.tv

7. The Pioneer, 20th September 2009 report–Orissa for Peaceful Industrialisation, says Naveen Patnaik.

8. Basudev Mahapatra, 2008. TV Journalism in India: Money and Sensationalism dominates News, Ethics and Principles (www.thehoot.org).

CHAPTER 10

The Fault Lines in Soviet-Style Accommodation of Minority Rights in Ethiopia

Semahagn Gashu

In the past, political theorists were assuming ethnicity, a result of lack of modernization or democratization is a marginal phenomenon that would gradually disappear once a prosperity and democracy are firmly established (Kymilcka and Opalski 2001). Marxists, too, ascertain that socialism would mean the end of the ethnic tension and consciousness that existed in pre–socialist societies(ibid). According to both assertions assimilation of minorities into a large integrated whole was viewed as the inevitable future (Spiro 2007). Recent political developments, however, indicated that such assertions are not valid. According to scholars, there is not much evidence that suggest achievement of democracy, economic prosperity and personal tolerance would lead to abatement of ethno-cultural mobilization (Kymilcka and Opalski 2001). To the contrary, the achievement of democratization, prosperity and tolerance has gone hand in hand with increased ethno cultural mobilization (ibid).

The contemporary trend seems to be accommodating multicultural pluralism rather than attempting to stifle it. Western democracies such as Belgium, Netherlands and Canada have established effective political systems that accommodate cultural pluralism. But successful protection of ethno-cultural right in the west is possible largely due to the existence of peace and individual security, democracy, protection of individual rights, rule of law and economic prosperity (Kymlicka 2006). There seems to be no clear data that suggest such multicultural accommodation can work well in a non-western context where those factors are largely non-existent (Liphart 1977). Since non-western communities and economies are predominantly based on agriculture, where large sections of populations live in the rural areas, there are no western style classes (workers and capitalists) and the ruling elite remains a minority whether it is a military or civilian (Hameso 2002).

This is principally the case in sub-Sahara Africa. Except with some notable exceptions, sub-Sahara Africa countries have problems of national integration and the absence of political legitimacy due to ethnic fragmentation (Alemante 2003). In Africa, there is a tendency for individuals to think of themselves primarily as Oromo, Hutu, or Masai rather than an Ethiopian, Rwandan or Kenyan (Spiro 2007). Ethnic heterogeneity in the countries of Africa is also exacerbated by national boundaries drawn by foreign powers, which for the most part ignored tribal cultural patterns in the subjugated societies (Jalali 1992). Despite such glaring diversity, most African states are in the practice of ignoring or suppressing this major aspect of their socio political realities:

> Believing that official recognition of ethnic diversity would foster divided loyalties and separatism, virtually all African states have avoided coming into terms with heterogeneity of their ethnic make-up. Such denial is an unwanted approach both as matter of expediency and as matter of constitutional theory. Far from helping to achieve the goals of national integration and political legitimacy, ignoring or suppressing ethnicity has led to militant ethnic nationalism, conflict and political disorder (Almante 2003: 53).

Thus, the major conflicts that have plagued the continent are primarily due to lack of an appropriate mechanisms for accommodating ethnic diversity. Unless properly addressed, ethnic tension leads to fierce competition and conflicts among the various ethnic groups for controlling state power that will directly give access to controlling of economic resources (Fukui and Markakis 1994). According to scholars, to address challenges of diversity in Africa, constitution makers need to devise mechanisms and institutions that best accommodate the interests of different ethnic groups co-habiting the same state in such a way to integrate ethnically diverse citizens in abroad and inclusive national society that shares, represents, or respects their ethnicity (Alemante 2003).

Against all the odds, some African countries have courageously under taken measures to accommodate cultural diversity through political institutions.[1] One of the countries that have undertaken such measure is Ethiopia. Since 1991, Ethiopia is experimenting with a soviet-style ethnic federal system as a mechanism to address the challenges related to ethnic diversity in the country. The experiment has posed different opportunities and challenges. The purpose of this article is thus to high light the basic features of the Ethiopian ethnic federal system and the various pitfalls this risky experiment has faced in relation to the protection of minority rights in the country.

Background of the Ethiopian Ethnic Federal System

In many respects, Ethiopia had very impressive moments in its long history. Its old history has been elevated with the discovery of *Dinknesh* as it is known by the outside world as Lucy in 1974, which is the oldest fossil of humankind as old as 3.2 million years. This discovery has proved that Ethiopia is the birthplace of mankind. It is also the only African state that was not colonized by a foreign power. In its long history, the country had also been under the rule of traditional feudal system. In addition to this, the country has diverse cultures, languages and religions.[2] Particularly, the incorporation of a large number of diverse ethnic groups which now inhabit the larger part of the state in the second half of 19th century has created a complex evolving situation fraught with potential for manifold controversy (Markakis 1973).

Though Ethiopia was deeply traditional, the expansion of modern education during the time of Emperor Haile Selassie created a new elite group that started to challenge the traditional political order. The emergence of the new elite signaled the commencement of collision between the old and the new elite group. As Messay (1999) rightly assessed, Ethiopia's problems of modernization are thus derived from the failure to equate modernity with the revival of tradition. The gap between the modern and old elite reached at irreconcilable level beginning from end of 1960s when university students began to show dissent to the age old feudal system. In their struggle against the feudal state, the students resorted to the mantra of Marxist ideology without any consideration of its relevance and consequences to a country that was deeply traditional. Especially, the students were fond of the Stalinist notion of 'the right to self-determination of nations and nationalities' to the country's eighty ethnic groups'.[3] In addition to the political questions raised by the students, the urban middle class and the military had their own economic grievances. Finally, due to mounting opposition from different sections of the society, the emperor was deposed in September 1974 paving the way to a new era of uncertainties.

After the emperor was deposed, a Provisional Military Administrative Council (PMAC) rather known as *Derg* in Amharic, assumed political power and declared socialism as its ideology. The military regime undertook fundamental reforms, particularly related to changing the exploitative land holding system. Though the *Derg* had attempted to answer the so called 'national question' on its own terms, none of the efforts were satisfying the demands of ethnic nationalists. Contrary to the expectation of many scholars and students who made the revolution a reality, the *Derg* pursued a very harsh measure against any political dissent including ethno-regional movements. The complete closure of political space by the *Derg* reinforced ethno-regional movements namely, the Tigrean Liberation Front (TPLF), Eritrean People's Liberation Front (EPLF) and the Oromo Liberation Front (OLF). According to the assessment of these ethno nationalists, the *Derg* rule was simply a continuation of the imperial period when it comes to the issue of ethnic oppression (Berhanu 2010).

Mobilization of these ethno-regional forces coupled with some military gains further strengthened and took the 'question of nationalities' beyond the scope of the Marxist view of the concept that was advocated during the student movement.[4] Among the ethno-regional movements, north-based Eritrean People Liberation Front (EPLF) and Tigrean Peoples Liberation Front (TPLF) who fought for the 'self-determination' rights of the Eritrea and Tigray regions respectively became more prominent in terms of posing threat to the military regime.[5] Finally, these two groups collaborated their forces and defeated the military regime in 1991. EPLF took control of Eritrea while TPLF controlled Ethiopia through its cover organization, the Ethiopian People's Revolutionary Democratic Front (EPRDF).

Soon after it controlled power, EPRDF called a National Conference on Peace and Reconciliation in July 1991 meant to lay the foundations for a transitional period after the regime change. A precondition for the organizations to take part in the conference was that they need to be ethnically based (Lyons 1996). Though EPRDF attempted to reach beyond its original base and include a variety of political groups, it managed the conference and kept participation, the agenda, and the eventual outcome was firmly under its careful control (ibid). The outcome of the transitional conference, the Transitional Charter, was thus an agenda predetermined by the EPRDF and partly by the OLF, rather than a pact between all the political forces that have stakes in the future restructuring of the Ethiopian state.

The Transitional Charter, in unprecedented fashion, recognized the rights of Ethiopia's nationalities to self-determination, including secession and established 'local and regional councils based on the basis of nationality'. Accordingly, the country is divided into fourteen administrative regions called *kilil*. The basis of the new language and administrative policy is ethnic identity and affiliation. EPRDF continued to dominate the political landscape during the transitional period by virtue of its military power, effective organization and leadership, and control of the agenda and rules of competition (Lyons 1996).

Later, the Transitional Government established a constitutional commission to prepare a draft constitution for submission to a specially elected Constitutional Assembly. But the constitutional drafting process was, once again, largely dominated by EPRDF's ideals. After a formal constitutional drafting process was undertaken, the drafted constitution was submitted to a Constitutional Assembly that supposed to deliberate and ratify the constitution. But the election process to the Assembly was largely flawed. As C.N. Paul (2000) noted, "There was little meaningful public participatory debate, especially debate focused on devolution versus ethnic federalism, let alone sovereignty or self-determination …Just as the EPRDF controlled the Constitutional Commission's work, so it controlled the election, and then the deliberations, of the Constitutional Assembly" (Paul 2000: 189). Finally, the constitution was ratified 1995 leading to the establishment of Federal Democratic Republic of Ethiopia (FDRE), heralding the commencement of a new ethnic federal system in Ethiopia's political discourse.

The Fault Lines in the Structure of Ethiopia's Ethnic Federal System

The most striking aspect of the Ethiopian constitution is its complete departure from the past by making transformation from strong centralized monarchical (later socialist) state to highly decentralized federal state by institutionalizing ethnic identity as organizing principle of state. The constitution addresses a wide range of issues dealing with rights of minority groups, the powers and duties of the federal and regional governments including intergovernmental relations. Ethnicity, all of a sudden, became the predominant explanation of many of the things that went wrong in the society (Hizikias, 2010).The ideological backdrop of the Ethiopian constitutional model is largely the Stalinist notion of 'self-determination rights of nationalities' that was part of the leftist political rhetoric leading up to the 1974 revolution and its aftermath in Ethiopia. As a leftist organization, the notion of 'self-determination rights of nationalities' was part of the political program of Tigrean Peoples Liberation Front (TPLF) that toppled the military regime in 1991. Since the constitutional making process was tightly controlled by TPLF, it has translated its political program into a constitutional principle without much difficulty.

In this soviet-style constitution, state sovereignty is not attributed to the 'Ethiopian people' as it is commonly stated in liberal constitutions rather to 'nations, nationalities and peoples' (Art. 8, FDRE constitution). The attribution of sovereignty to nations, nationalities and peoples means the constitution is product of consensus among the constituent ethnic groups inhibiting the Ethiopian state (Alemante, 2003). This indirectly implies that every Ethiopian should first identify herself with one of the ethnic groups in the country before she claims the Ethiopian nationality.

Based on the notion of 'self-determination of nationalities', the constitution establishes nine regional states. Despite the fact that the constitution provides regional states are to be delimited on the basis of settlement, language, identity and consent of the people, they are largely structured mainly following language and ethnic lines. All federal units are constitutionally symmetrical having the same formal relationship to the federal government. In actual reality, however, the social, economic and political situation and leverage of the constituent units is quite different. Some of the regions have millions of population while others have only tens of thousands of residents. In addition to this, all the regions are heterogeneous consisting of more than two ethnic groups. Few of them have one dominant ethnic group and different ethnic minorities,[6] few others having two or more dominant ethnic groups,[7] one is multi-ethnic[8] while city–states are considered distinct.[9]

Though the federation consists of only nine regional units that have regional autonomy; the constitution grants every 'nation, nationality and people' unconditional right to self-determination including the right to secession. Since it is only few of the ethnic groups who have full territorial self-rule, it is very ambiguous how this principle applies as many as eighty ethnic groups that have not been granted with territorial autonomy.[10] The constitution further recognizes equality of all languages while maintaining Amharic as a working language of the federal government. In relation to distribution of power between the central and federal units, the constitution expressly enumerates exclusive powers of the federal government and assumes all other residual powers are competencies of the regional government (Art. 51, 52 and 55, FDRE constitution).

The federal parliament has lower and upper houses. The upper house is composed of representatives from 'nations, nationalities and people'. This chamber has a number of roles including interpreting the constitution and deciding on any issue of self-determination or secession. Unlike the experience of other federal systems, the upper house has not any role in the law making process. The lower house is composed of up to 550 representatives elected directly by the people. Though the house is constitutionally the supreme state organ, due to the fact that the system is dominated by a single party and the members of parliament are tightly controlled by Leninist-style democratic centralism, it is merely a rubber-stump organ for the misdeeds of increasingly authoritarian executive branch.

The other Soviet-styled aspect of the Ethiopian federal system is its constitutional adjudication mechanism. Unlike democratic federations, power to adjudicate constitutional issues is granted to the second chamber of parliament. Article 83 of the Ethiopia Constitution states that all constitutional disputes shall be adjudicated by the House of Federation (HOF). The chamber is aided by the Council of Constitutional Inquiry (CCI), another organ which investigates constitutional disputes and submits recommendations to the house on cases dealing with constitutional issues. The official justification behind the granting of power of adjudicating constitutional issues to a political organ is related to the principle of sovereignty of 'nations, nationalities and peoples' envisaged under the constitution. According to the argument advanced during the proceedings of the Constitutional Assembly, 'since the constitution is a political contract made between nations, nationalities and peoples, the constitution need to be interpreted by the nations and nationalities themselves' (Minutes of Constitutional Assembly, 1994).

The most likely justification behind adoption of such constitutional adjudication mechanism is rather transplantation of constitutional adjudication approach of former socialist countries. In socialist legal system, the legislature is conceived to be the supreme expression of the will of the people and beyond the reach of judicial restraint (Hazard and Maggs, 1984). In addition to this, as Ludwikowski (1988) noted "Marxist-Leninist jurisprudence rejects the doctrine of separation of powers, but allocates State functions to three governmental authorities (the legislature, executive and judiciary). It assumes that these segments of the socialist state work together under the leadership of the party" (Ludwikow 1988: 89-90). Given the Marxist origin of TPLF where all powers are concentrated with a central vanguard party, the likely ideological backdrop of the Ethiopian model of constitutional adjudication is the soviet model that excludes any sort of separation powers and mechanisms of checks and balances. By structuring the system in a way that does not permit an independent organ responsible for interpreting the constitution, the regime has got a free ride to interpret and apply the law on its own terms that jeopardizes rights of citizens, intergovernmental relations, accountability and transparency of public officials.

Challenges of Protection of Minority Rights in Ethiopia

In terms of granting rights to minority groups, the Ethiopian constitution incorporates the most liberal provisions. According to Art. 39 of the constitution, every 'nation, nationality and people' has unconditional right to self-determination, including the right to secession. The article further elaborates other rights of 'nations and nationalities'. Accordingly, every nation, nationality and people in Ethiopia has the right to a full measure of self-government which includes the right to establish institutions of government in the territory that it inhabits and to equitable representation in state and federal governments (Art

39.3 FDRE constitution). In addition to this, the provision endows 'nations and nationalities' the right to speak, to write and to develop their own language; to express, develop and promote its culture; and to preserve its history. Furthermore, the constitution has laid down the procedures to be applicable during right to self-determination and secession.[11] The initial procedure for appropriating the right to self-administration or secession is a demand for secession to be approved by a two-thirds majority of the members of the legislative council of the nation, nationality or people concerned. Then after, the federal government has to organize a referendum which must take place within three years from the time. After such procedures are undertaken, the secession or right to self-determination will be materialized.

Though the constitution appears to be friendly and sensitive to rights of minority ethnic groups, the Ethiopian system has confronted structural and practical problems of translating constitutional promises into practice. The primary challenge to protection of minority rights in Ethiopia is the very structural deficit of the federal system that threatens state survival and social cohesion. Due to the unprecedented measures taken by the Ethiopian new rulers to define the Ethiopian political discourse in terms of institutionalizing ethnic identity in line with the Stalinist 'self-determination right of nationalities', the country's survival has been at stake and a sustainable regime for protection of minority rights has not been achieved. Primarily, the worrying aspect of ethnicity is that it is overshadowing our common humanity and sense of citizenship since people's ethnic consciousness tends to reduce their concern for human rights or public morality (Ghai 2008). In countries where ethnic identity has been institutionalized, the social bondage that was binding society has been eroded and replaced with very narrow ethnic identity.[12] Since ethnic politics assumes in differences, it does not give much attention to our common humanity and history. In his historic speech in Ghana, Obama (2009) reiterates, 'We all have many identities—of tribe and ethnicity; of religion and nationality. But defining oneself in opposition to someone who belongs to a different tribe, or who worships a different prophet, has no place in the 21st century'.

In the Ethiopian context, the application of ethnicity as the Alfa and Omega of political discourse has brought different negative implications and neither achieved efficient protection minority rights nor brought societal cohesion. Presently, ethnic identity is the normative identity on the basis of which the new state prefers to deal with its citizens in many spheres of life, especially in the political, economic and for election registration, people have to state their ethnic identity (Abbink 1997). Since the definition of ethnic groups and the distinction between people based on ethnic criteria is difficult, inconsistent, and confusing (Hizkias 2010), defining the political discourse solely on the basis of ethnicity has become increasingly risky as properly assessed by Alem (2004):

> Ethnic communities rise and fall, persist and dissolve, change and resurge. Ethnic identity is malleable and overlaps with other important social identities based on local or region, religion, gender, class, citizenship, etc. As a consequence, individuals possess multiple identities. Yet the framers of the federal system in Ethiopia who used ethnicity as their organizing principle appear to

have been unaware of the scope and complexities of ethnic pluralism and ethnic identity (Alem 2004: 108).

Though it is commendable to accommodate different ethnic related claims of minority groups in the political system, it should have considered the significance of historical ties and multiple identities among the various communities in the country. In Ethiopian context, despite the controversy of the making of modern Ethiopia and injustices that were committed in the past, there have been cultural, historical and social ties among the various ethnic groups that are binding the society in its long history. This reality in Ethiopia is consistent with the argument of scholars who contend the chances for stable democracy are enhanced if individuals have cross-cutting affiliation to a variety of groups that pull them in different directions (Liphart 1968). Contrary to the multiple identities that have been crystallized through time, the introduction of the new political dispensations in 1991 was made in a circumstance that ridicules the achievements of the past and an attempt has been made for formation of a new patterns of ethnic relations in the country. The manner ethnic politics introduced in Ethiopia invented ethnic identity consciousness afresh or as Messay puts it 'ethnic identities that used to be weak are restructured' (Messay 2009). Due to such unprecedented emphasis given to ethnicity in Ethiopian federal system, Ethiopian system, besides being imposed, is deliberately established to encourage ethnicization, whereas other countries, such as Nigeria, India used federalism as a devise to dilute ethnicity so as to safeguard national unity (Messay 2009).

The political measures taken by the new rulers of the country have created a new political reality that undermine social cohesion and has complicated the quest for appropriate regime needed for the protection of minority rights in the country. According to scholars, institutionalizing the federation along ethnic lines is more likely to promote primordial nationalism, which in politically unstable politics increases the likelihood of inter-ethnic violence and civil war (Ghai 2008, Kymlicka and Norman 2000). This is due to the fact that structuring states based solely on ethnic lines reinforces ethnicity, threat to separation and gives rise to divergent and conflicting visions of citizenship (Alemante 2003).[13]

The way 'self-determination right of nationalities' is applied in Ethiopia to each ethnic group without considering other cross-cutting and multiple identities has opened a new era of inter-ethnic relation and competitions. As Kymlicka noted, contrary to the traditional application of the principle of self-determination only to groups who clearly showed interest for such group right, the Ethiopian federal system gives the right in blanket to every ethnic group including to people who have not showed any interest for such right or who have not developed any ethnic or linguistic group identity consciousness (Kymlicka 2006)[14] or those who have no interest to express themselves in terms of ethnic identities. The emphasis on ethnicity as an absolute value, manifest in the EPRDF's commitment to ethnic federalism, traumatized those who considered themselves to be above and beyond tribal allegiances (Levine 2007). Thus, rather than paving the way for effective protection of minority rights, the unprecedented emphasis given to ethnicity has opened the door to unhealthy relation among the various ethnic groups in the country. Communities who had been attempting to find common grounds for survival and continuity of the nation in the past are now largely engaged in tracing their differences that may lead to social fragmentation.

Defining the political system solely in ethnic terms has also created new socio-economic relations in the society. This is particularly apparent in raising ethnic consciousness in social, economic and political relations among the elite. As such relations become more and more ethnic oriented, the bias and prejudice to one another's ethnic group is increasing[15] specially between previously dominant and dominated ethnic groups, as all are forced to adjust to new terms of inter-ethnic and inter-regional relationships (Alem 2004). Clear tensions are emerging for control of political power and economic resources among the elites of different ethnic groups.[16] There is also clear tension emerging between people who favor the Ethiopian nationalism and those who favor the narrower ethnic nationalism. Ethnic politics has also become instrumental for ethnic entrepreneurs to mobilize their respective groups for controlling the local resources since ethnically oriented institutional arrangement has had the effect of strengthening ethnic difference and providing resources for political entrepreneurs to play the "nationality card" (Hale 2004). In such ethnicized political discourse, the protection of minority rights appears to steer up emotional feelings rather than addressing genuine demands of minority groups.

The other challenge to protection of minority rights in ethnically defined federal system in Ethiopia is the ideological background of the federal system itself. The backdrop of the Ethiopian federal model is the Stalinist model of federalism that was responsible for the disintegration of the former USSR and Yugoslavia. The adoption of 'right of self-determination of nationalities' dogma that was used to formulate socialist federations in the past is devoid of any principle of consensus, political negotiation or political institutions that governs intergovernmental relations. Due to the absence of genuine democracy, socialist federations were used as instruments of coercion rather than protecting the aspirations of minority groups. The contradictions inherent in the systems finally dismantled the former federations who lacked the basic ingredients of genuine federation. In the same manner, the adoption of federal system that resembles the former socialist federations in Ethiopia has become increasingly instrument of oppression rather than protection of rights of minority groups. As noted by Engedayehu as cited in Kidane (1997) "following the Soviet lead, the Ethiopian government had embarked on a path bound to lead either to increased repression or to mounting ethnic conflict and the eventual disintegration of the country" (Kidane 1997: 125). Unless the country's federal system is reinvented in terms of the principles of democratic federalism based on political negotiation, consensus, protection of human rights and building up of democratic institutions, the Ethiopian federal system may eventually face disintegration when the military might of TPLF that presently control the system start to weaken.

The other challenge to the country's model of protection of minority rights is absence of consensus on the mode of accommodation of minority rights and structure of state. According to scholars, federal systems grow out of the idea that free people can freely enter into lasting political associations to achieve common ends and protect certain rights while preserving their respective integrities (Elazar 1987). This is because federal system is a function of not of constitution but of societies and it emerges out of bargain and consensus (Turton 2006).[17] In Ethiopian context, the introduction of the federal system and the constitution of 1995 itself are emerged out of revolution or as some refer it from "the barrel of the gun" (ibid). Due to the fact that the process was not result of the bargain of different political forces and all stake holders, the legitimacy of the federal structure and the constitution itself suffers from serious problem of legitimacy (Aalen 2002; Tesgaye 2008).[18] The political exercise since in 1991 has been simply institutionalizing and legitimatizing the political program of TPLF/ EPRDF which was in the making underground before the making of the constitution. The nominal peace conference that was conducted in summer of 1991 could only attract likeminded political organizations who were one way or the other against the state status quo that was in the making since late 19th century.

The lack of consensus at the dispensation of this new era has not yet been resolved. Due to lack of legitimacy of the system during its inception, the status quo has faced perpetual challenge from different directions. The most recent formidable challenge to the new status quo was manifested during the 2005 general elections. The huge support the Coalition for Unity and Democracy (CUD) party able to command during the election was largely due to the dissatisfaction of the public the way the country is ethnically structured since 1991. Despite the fact that the regime presented the movement behind CUD as forces that desire to resurrect the feudal system, there has never been any serious political or scholarly discourse from the side of CUD that totally rejects the accommodation of ethnic diversities in the country. The fierce opposition seems to be rather towards the way ethnic related claims are institutionalized or using the ethno-regional claims for 'divide and rule' strategy and the dire consequences of ethnicized political structure. The confrontation among the various political forces on issues related to ethno-regional claims is still vivid as ever. The future life span of the country's federal system, thus, seems to be dependent on the willingness of the political leaders to agree on principles and mechanisms of accommodating ethnic minority rights in state structure. In such political environment where there is no minimum consensus on modes of accommodating rights of minority groups and maintaining national integration, lasting solutions to the country's problems related to ethno-regional claims appear to be elusive.

The other major missing link in protection of minority rights in Ethiopia is the stifling of democratization process in the country. The regime claims that the federal system has built one 'political community' that fosters unity in diversity and there is consensus in the country on the policies of the regime revealed through the 99.6 percent win of EPRDF in the general election held in 2010 (Meles 2010). On the other hand, international human rights institutions, opposition groups and scholars argue that the regime is becoming increasingly authoritarian and the federal system is not properly functioning (Smith 2007,

International Crisis Group 2009, Human Rights Watch 2010). According to International Crisis Group (2009), there is fierce enmity between government and opposition, there is little space exists for non-partisan involvement and debate and freedom of expression and association has been severely undercut by the EPRDF. Freedom House (2010) has moved Ethiopia from partially free status to 'not free'. Particularly, the various measures that have been undertaken by the regime since 2005 further narrowed down the political space significantly. As one writer properly noted, Ethiopia today is in many respects a *defacto beaurocratic* authoritarian regime dressed in the garb of constitutional democracy (Harbeson 1998). Though the regime categorically rejects all these criticisms, Ethiopia's 'democracy' is characterized by extreme control, atmosphere of fear and mistrust, lack of strong institutions, problems of protecting rights of citizenship, lack of legitimacy and democratic values are largely used for propaganda purposes devoid of any significant practical application.

The stifled democratization process is apparent in different aspects of the political system. Though the constitution of the country permits the operation of opposition parties and their participations in elections, general elections that held so far are marred by harassment of the opposition parties, vote rigging, killings and violence. Particularly, the general election that was held in 2005 was considered by many the most competitive and fairer in the country's history (Abbink 2006). But the circumstances after the day of voting became so controversial that it resulted in the killing of hundreds of people, imprisonment of thousands including opposition leaders and the banning of all political demonstrations (EU EOM 2005). It seems the country is still suffering from the aftershocks of that election. During the 2010 general elections, the regime claims to have won 99.6 percent of the total parliamentary seats. On the other hand, major opposition parties had reported harassment, imprisonment of their members and closure of their offices in various parts of the country (EU EOM 2010).[19]

Though there were printed private newspapers operational since 1992, the government is largely condemned by international human rights organizations for its heavy handedness on the private press. The concern is much more serious after the introduction of the new press law recently.[20] The government's stance against civil society groups has also been intense in the last few years. The government has issued a new law that restricts the activities of civil society groups. This law requires civil society organizations that are engaged in human rights activities not to receive more than 10 percent of their budget from international sources.[21] In general, after two decades of soviet-style rule in the country, it has become clear that protection of minority rights unlikely to be realized in a political environment that seriously lacks the ingredients of genuine democracy. Unless there is genuine democracy and democratic institutions that promote democratic values, effective protection of minority rights to the various ethnic groups in the country is unlikely to be achieved.

The other serious challenge to the existing arrangement of protection of minority rights is the narrow base of the system. In the last two decades, the federal system is dominated by TPLF that claim to represent a population that constitutes only 6 percent of the Ethiopian total population. Initially, TPLF was waging warfare to liberate Tigray region and establish a state independent of Ethiopia.[22] Despite democracy is all about majority and the political power in the federal system needs to be allocated in light of size of population of the different ethnic groups, the fact that major political power is still dominated by TPLF, led people to think that the federal system is simply another form of control of the country with a minority group (Abbink 2006).[23] Clapham, too, argues:

> The EPRDF has never been able to rid itself of the sense that this is essentially a Tigray government. Though it has selected ministers from a wide range of nationalities, the core of the regime has always lain in the TPLF that created it. Tigray, with some 10% of the population, provides much too narrow a base from which to govern Ethiopia (Clapham 2005: Para. 2).

The dominance of Tigreans in the political, defense, security, police and public enterprises is so impressive that may send wrong perception about the federal system in general and the accommodation of minority rights in particular. The perceptions of the public believing the system is dominated by Tigrean minority group may create sense of marginalization on part the people that belongs to other minority groups.[24]

In addition to the challenges related to the aforementioned structural problems that prevented effective protection of minority rights, the soviet-style principle of 'self-determination right of nationalities' granted to minority groups has not been properly implemented in the last two decades. Though the constitution asserts minority groups have different rights, the country is in practice under the control of centralized government. Real powers of the regional governments that have been effective in the last two decades are those powers related to cultural and language rights. All regional governments only have been empowered to use and develop their languages and cultures including adoption of their own working language for instruction in schools and official purposes. But the achievements in relation to protection of cultural rights could not be accompanied by economic and political autonomy of ethnically defined regional governments.

Due to the interference and control of regional units by the federal government, minority groups have been subjected to imposition of policies from the central government. There are different ways the central government violates rights of minority groups. Primarily, since EPRDF is a Marxist party; it is led by strong principle of democratic centralism. A policy adopted by the central party organ has to be abiding by party apparatus at regional level rendering formal intergovernmental relations irrelevant. Policy decisions made by the Executive Committee of the vanguard party handed down to the regional government and to *woreda* and *kebele* (lower units of government) administrative structures (Berhanu 2009). This approach is clearly contrary to the principle of the constitution that envisages autonomous rights to minority groups at lower regional administrative units. As noted by Human Rights Watch report, 'Local and national government officials from opposite ends of the country all seem to speak from the same script when it comes to the partisan administration of government services, whether regarding identification cards, teacher training, university entrance, or fertilizer and the safety net' (Human Right Watch 2010).

The other mechanism used by the regime to subdue regional governments is through establishing regional parties client to the centre rather than genuine parties that represent the interests of the regional constituency. In order to fully realize rights of the various ethnic groups in the country, the minority groups need to be represented by independent political parties that may promote the need of minority groups. Contrary to this principle, regional parties that claim to represent rights of respective ethnic groups have not been evolved through regional political processes but they are organized and guided by EPRDF/TPLF at the centre. Since the TPLF/EPRDF controls the central economic and political resources, it maintains the clientelistic relation with loyal regional party leaders (Paulos 2007). Loyalty and obedience to the central TPLF leadership has been critical assets for regional leaders for their political survival (ibid). As one scholar properly noted, 'regional autonomy is not how a region is allowed to decide and control its affairs; rather, the system creates client parties that allow the centre to maintain its controls through dependent local elites' (Messay 2009).Thus, the rhetoric of the rights of minority groups outlined under the constitution are usurped indirectly by the centre through party discipline and client–patron hierarchy of the party apparatus orchestrated by the regime.

The other problem that has made protection of rights of minority groups ineffective in Ethiopia is the dependence of regional administrative units to the federal government in areas of financial expenditure. Since the federal government has monopolized important powers of taxation,[25] only tax sources which yield limited amount of revenue have been allocated to the states (Solomon 2008). Such fiscal imbalance between the centre and the states has made the autonomy of states dependent on the transfer of revenue controlled by the center (Solomon, 2008). This has greatly undermined the role of regional administrative units in the implementation of policies specifically applicable to the various ethnic groups. This in turn has affected the independence of the regions in terms of exercising self-administration rights of minority groups. To resolve such issues, and to uphold the general principle of equalization of resources and development, scholars argue, a complex scheme of taxation and revenue distribution would be required (Ghai 2008).

In addition to the control of the regional units by central government, there has never been consistent approach in relation to the limited rights granted to minority groups. In some instances, some minority groups are empowered to have more autonomous regional autonomy while others have been denied of this right. Some minority groups with relatively bigger population and geographic size are not allowed to have their own regional government while other minority groups with lower population or geographical size have more autonomous local rule.[26] Furthermore, while some of the minority groups have been endowed with their own regional government, others have been forced to share political power with different minority groups. A typical case in this regard is the case of Southern Nations, Nationalities and Peoples Regional State. In this region, there are about 56 minority groups. Though the ethnic groups in the region have various languages and historical background, the regime merged all these groups under a single regional state that has suffocated the rights of minority groups. All these ethnic groups could not enjoy self-determination rights as prescribed under the constitution while other minority groups in other parts of the country have been treated differently.

Due to such structural and policy problems in the protection of minority rights, a number of violations of the rights of minority groups including various ethnic conflicts have been recorded in the last two decades. Not only the minority groups have not been allowed to be administered by political leaders elected by the people but also their request for more independent self-rule has been met with government violence. The regime has been actively suppressing demands of minority groups in different parts of the country. One of such state violence is directed against the aspirations of the Oromo ethnic group. Oromo Liberation Front (OLF), a political organization that claims to struggle for the Oromo people, which is the largest ethnic group in the country. The organization claims that the Oromo people is under the colony of Ethiopian Empire and the people's right to self-determination need to protected.

During the imperial and military regimes, the organization was waging low level guerrilla fight against the central government. In 1991, in conjunction with EPRDF, OLF was part of the transitional government that ended the military rule. But after two years, the party withdrew from the transitional government and returned to its violent tactics of struggle. Since then, there has been confrontation between the regime and members and sympathizers of the dissident OLF. According to reports of human rights groups, there are continued human rights violations in the regions to suppress the movement towards wider regional autonomy. According to Human Rights Watch Report, since 1992 there has been arbitrary detention, torture, harassment, abuse of right of expression in Oromia regional state (Human Rights Watch 2005). Similar crackdown has also been orchestrated against the Sidama minority ethnic group that demands for more autonomous regional autonomy. Particularly, as part of continued political demand for regional autonomy, members of the group held demonstration on 24 May 2002 at Awassa town. But government forces used live bullets to disperse the demonstration killing and wounding dozens of individuals.

The other serious violation of minority rights movement has been occurring in the Ogaden region of the country. Due to the armed resistance waged by dissident political organization called Ogaden National Liberation Front (ONLF), there is continued confrontation and violation of rights in this Somali speaking region. Since the existing autonomy granted to the region is largely controlled by the central government, the organization claims that the people of the region should have right to self-determination. Due to the continued warfare in the region, both the rebellion group and the government have been implicated in the various violations of human rights in the region. According to human rights reports, in the war-affected areas, continuing abuses by both rebels and Ethiopian troops pose a direct threat to the survival and create a pervasive culture of fear forcing relocations and destruction of villages, arbitrary detentions, torture, and mistreatment in detention are continuing since 2007 (Human Rights Watch 2010).

Furthermore, in the Gambella Regional State, there had also been violence in relation to demands for more regional autonomy. In 2003, when an ethnic conflict erupted between indigenous and non-indigenous population in the area, as many as 424 people from Anuak ethnic group were killed (Human Rights Watch 2005). In addition to such serious violations of minority rights in the last two decades, there have been wide spread ethnic conflicts due to resources and border issues among the various ethnic groups.[27] Furthermore, due to ethnically modified regional system, citizens who are in the wrong region or considered to be from other ethnic groups have been increasingly marginalized. These people have never been properly represented in local political administrations and largely viewed by local administration as outsiders. Such people have been subject to displacement from their localities and sent back to their 'mother region'. Due to such ethnic related conflicts, an estimated 300,000 to 350,000 people remained internally displaced within Ethiopia in late 2010 (Norwegian Refugee Council 2011).

Thus, it is submitted that the ethnic political structure that has been adopted to protect the rights of minority groups in Ethiopia lacks the basic principles of democratic governance and has further complicated the various political demands raised by different political groupings rather than rectifying them. In addition to this, not only the regime has been violating rights of minority groups under the guise of stability but also the regional governments' that are established to further the interests of minority groups have been controlled by centralized party structure that does not allow any deviation from the official party position. Thus, the most appropriate mechanism protecting rights of minority groups in Ethiopia is abandoning soviet-style ethnic federal model and adopt democratic federal system that could allow different political groups participate in the political discourse and a system that allows real autonomy to local governments.

Conclusion

Since 1991, Ethiopia has been experimenting soviet-style ethnic federal system as a mechanism to address the challenges related to ethnic diversity and demands of minority groups in the country. The constitution that has been enacted in 1995 recognizes the right of self-determination of nation and nationalities up to secession and other related rights of minority groups. The ideological backdrop of the Ethiopian constitutional model is largely the Stalinist notion of 'self-determination of nationalities' that was part of the leftist political movement that led to the 1974 revolution and its aftermath. In addition to such problems related to Ethiopia's constitutional design, the soviet-style principle of 'self-determination right of nationalities' granted to regional units has not been properly implemented in the last two decades. Though the constitution asserts minority groups have different rights, the country is in practice under the control of a centralized government. This is primarily, due to the fact that EPRDF is a Marxist party led by strong principle of democratic centralism that controls every government apparatus in central and regional governments and as well as establishing regional parties' client to TPLF rather than genuine parties that represent the interests of the regional constituency.

In addition to this, the Ethiopian approach to protection minority rights neither achieved appropriate protection of rights of minority groups nor it has promoted national cohesion due to a political error that disregards multiple identities that exist among the various ethnic groups in the country. Contrary to the multiple identities that have been crystallized through time, the introduction of the new political dispensations in 1991 was made in a circumstance that ridicules the achievements of the past and an attempt has been made for formation of new patterns of ethnic relations in the country. Defining the political discourse solely on the basis of ethnic identity has become increasingly risky by creating new political realities that undermine social cohesion and complicated relations among the various ethnic groups.

Furthermore, due to the absence of genuine democracy in the country, the federal system has been used as instruments of coercion rather than protecting the aspirations of minority groups. Currently, the major bottleneck for the democratization process in the country is the perverted notion of democracy maintained by the regime. The conception of democracy of the regime aims at controlling all the political space by stifling multiparty system, freedom of expression and association through intimidation and harassments of any dissenting group. Due to such perverted view of democracy, the Ethiopian political discourse is characterized by the absence of genuine democracy, evidenced in the stifling of multi-party democracy, freedom of the media and association. Unless the country's federal system is reinvented in terms of the principles of democratic federalism based on political negotiation, consensus, protection of human rights and building up of democratic institutions, the Ethiopian federal system may eventually face disintegration when the military might of TPLF that presently control the system start to weaken.

The other important missing link to the country's ethnic federal experiment is absence of consensus on the mode of accommodation of minority rights and the narrow base of the system. The political exercise since in 1991 has been simply institutionalizing and legitimatizing the political program of TPLF/EPRDF which was in the making underground before the making of the constitution. In addition to this, the federal system is dominated by TPLF who claim to have represented a population that constitutes only 6 percent of the Ethiopian total population. This trend has marginalized other political forces from political participation. In conclusion, despite the measures undertaken by Ethiopian regime to recognize rights of minority rights is commendable, due to the fact that the approach used to accommodate ethno-regional claims is the undemocratic Soviet-style model of federation, the process lacks political consensus, legitimacy and devoid of genuine democratization process, effective protection of minority rights has not been achieved. Thus, to make the Ethiopian federal experiment a success story in terms of protecting rights of minority groups, concrete measures in relation to political accommodation of various political groupings, realizing genuine democracy and establishing efficient political institutions are critical.

References

Aalen, L., 2002. *Ethnic Federalism in Dominant Party State: The Ethiopian Experience 1991–2000.* Bergen: Chr. Michlsen Institute.

Abbink, J. 1997. Ethnicity and Constitutionalism in Contemporary Ethiopia. *Journal of African Law,* 41, no. 2 (1997): 159–174.

———. 2006. Discomfiture of Democracy? The 2005 Election Crisis in Ethiopia and its Aftermath. *Journal of African Affairs* 105: 173–179.

Alem, H., 2004 .Ethnic Pluralism as an Organizing Principle of the Ethiopia Federation. *Dialectical Anthropology* 28: 91–123.

Alemante, S., 2003. Ethnic Federalism: Its Promise and Pitfalls for Africa. *Yale Journal of International Law* 28: 51-107.

Balcha, B.G., 2009. *Constitutionalism in the Horn of Africa: Lesson from the new Constitution of Ethiopia.* Development, Innovation and International Political Economy Research (DIIPER). Aalborg University, Denmark.

Berhanu, B., 2009. *Constitutionalism in the Horn of Africa: Lesson from the new Constitution of Ethiopia.* Development, Innovation and International Political Economy Research (DIIPER). Aalborg University, Denmark.

Berhanu, N., 2010. *Identity Politics and the Struggle for Liberty and Democracy in Ethiopia.* Paper Prepared for the Oromo Studies Association (OSA) 24th Annual conference. Howard University, Blackburn Centre, Washington DC.

Chanie, P., 2007. Clientelism and Ethiopia's Post–1991 Decentralisation. *Journal of Modern African Studies* 45: 355–384.

Clapham, C., 2005. *Comments on Ethiopian Crisis,* 2005. http://www.african.cam.ac.uk/people/registry/subjectlist/clapham.html (accessed January 20, 2010).

Elazar, D., 1987. *Exploring Federalism.* Tuscaloosa, AL: University of Alabama Press.

Elliott, T.P., 2005. Nationalism and Federalism. *Theories of Federalism: A Reader,* edited by Damitrios Karmis and Wayne Norman, 221–226. New York: Palgrave Macmillan.

European Union Elections Observation Missions Final Report. (EU-EOM), 2005.

European Union Elections Observation Missions Final Report. (EU-EOM), 2010.

Fukui, K and J. Markakis, eds., 1994. *Ethnicity and Conflict in the Horn of Africa.* Ohio: Ohio University Press.

Ghai, Y., ed. 2008. *Creating the New Constitution: A Guide for Nepali Citizens.* International Institute for Democracy and Electoral Assistance.

Habtu, A., 2004. Ethnic Pluralism as an Organizing Principle of the Ethiopia Federation. *Dialectical Anthropology* 28: 91–123.

Hale, H. E., 2004. Divided We Stand: Institutional Sources of Ethno-federal State Survival and Collapse. *World Politics* 56: 165–93.

Hameso, S. 2002. Issues and Dilemmas of Multi-Party Democracy in Africa. *West Africa Review* 3, no. 2: 1–26.

Harbeson, W. J., 1998. Bureaucratic Authoritarian Regime: Is Ethiopia Democratic? *Journal of Democracy* 9, no. 4: 62–69.

Hazard, J. N., W. E., Butler, and. P. B. Maggs, 1984. *The Soviet Legal System: The Law in the 1980s*. Oceania publications, New York.

Hizkias, A., 2010. *Ethnic Conflict in the Horn of Africa: Myth and Reality*. http://www.unu.edu/unupress/unupbooks/uu12ee/uu12ee06.htm (accessed January 26, 2010).

House of Peoples Representatives' of Ethiopia, 1994. Minutes of Constitutional Assembly, Vol. 1–9 (Unpublished).

Human Rights Watch, 2005.. *Suppressing Dissent: Human Rights Abuses and Political Repression in Ethiopia's Oromia Region*. http://www.hrw.org (accessed February 15, 2010).

———. 2005. *Targeting the Anuak: Human Rights Violations and Crimes against Humanity in Ethiopia's Gambella Region*. http://www. hrw.org (accessed March 2, 2010).

———. 2008. *Collective Punishment : War Crimes and Crimes against Humanity in the Ogaden area of Ethiopia's Somali Region*. http://www.hrw.org (accessed April 22, 2010).

———. 2010. *Development without Freedom: How Aid Underwrites Repression in Ethiopia*. http://www.hrw.org (accessed September 10, 2011).

International Crisis Group, 2009. *Ethiopia: Ethnic Federalism and Its Discontents*. Africa Report N°:153–4.

Jalali, R. and S.M. Lipset, 1993. Racial and Ethnic Conflicts: A Global Perspective. *Political Science Quarterly* 107, No. 4: 585–60.

Kebede, M., 2009.. *In Search of Peace: Ethiopia's Ethnic Conflicts and Resolution*. http://www.ethiopianreview.com/content/10016 (accessed March 20, 2010).

———. 1999. *Survival and Modernization Ethiopia's Enigmatic Present: A philosophical Discourse*, Red Sea Press Inc: Lawrenceville.

Kidane, M., 1997. New Approaches to State Building in Africa: The Case of Ethiopia's Ethnic-Based Federalism. *African Studies Review* 40 (3): 111-132.

Kymlicka, W. 2006. Emerging Western Multinational Federalism: Are they Relevant for Africa? *Ethnic Federalism: The Ethiopian Experience in Comparative Perspective,* edited by D. Turton, 32–64. Addis Ababa: Addis Ababa University Press.

Kymilcka, W. and M. Opalski, eds. 2001. *Can Liberal Pluralism be Exported? Western Political Theory and Ethnic relations in Eastern Europe*. Oxford: Oxford University Press.

Kymlicka, W. and W. Norman, eds. 2000. *Citizenship in Diverse Societies*. Oxford University Press.

Levine, D. N., 2007. *Ethiopia's Missed Chances–1960, 1974, 1991, 1998, and 2005–and now: II an Ethiopian Dilemma: Deep Structures, Wrenching Processes*. Keynote address at the Fourth International Conference on Ethiopian Development Studies, Western Michigan University, Kalamazoo.

Liphart, A., 1977. *Democracy in Plural Societies: A Comparative Exploration*. Yale: Yale University Press.

———. 1968. *The Politics of Accommodation: Pluralism and Democracy in the Netherlands.* California: University of California Press.

Ludwikowski, R., 1988. Judicial Review in the Socialist Legal System: Current Developments. *The International and Comparative Law Quarterly* 37, no. 1: 89–108.

Lyons, T., 1996. Closing the Transition: The May 1995 Elections in Ethiopia. *The Journal of Modem African Studies* 34, no. 1: 121–142.

Markakis, J., 1973. Social Formation and Political Adaptation in Ethiopia. *The Journal of Modern African Studies* 11, no. 3: 361–81.

Meles, Z., 2010. *Keynote Addresses International Conference on Federalism.* http://www.ethiopianfederalism.org/uploads/media/keynote_HE_Meles_Zenawi_01.pdf (accessed April 11, 2011).

Messay, K., 1999. *Survival and Modernization Ethiopia's Enigmatic Present: A philosophical Discourse.* Red Sea Press Inc: Lawrenceville.

Messay, K., 2009. *In Search of Peace: Ethiopia's Ethnic Conflicts and Resolution.* http://www.ethiopianreview.com/content/10016 (accessed 20 January, 2010).

Norwegian Refugee Council, 2011. Ethiopia: Monitoring of Conflict, Human Rights Violations and Resulting Displacement Still Problematic. http://www.internal-displacement.org (accessed December 11, 2011).

Obama, B., 2009. Speech to Ghana's parliament, Saturday (July 11). http://www.usatoday.com/news/world/2009-07-11-obama-ghana-speech-text_N.htm (accessed December 29, 2010).

Paul, C.N. 2000. Ethnicity and the New Constitutional Orders of Ethiopia and Eritrea. *Autonomy and Ethnicity: Negotiating Competing Claims in Multi-ethnic Societies* edited by Yash Ghai: 173–196, Cambridge University Press.

Paulos, C., 2007. Clientelism and Ethiopia's Post-1991 Decentralization. *Journal of Modern African Studies* 45: 355-384.

Selassie, A., 2003. Ethnic Federalism: Its Promise and Pitfalls for Africa. *Yale Journal of International Law* 28: 51–107.

Smith, L., 2007. Voting for an Ethnic Identity: Procedural and Institutional Responses to Ethnic Conflict in Ethiopia. *The Journal of Modern African Studies* 45 (4): 565-594.

Solomon N., 2008. *Fiscal Federalism in the Ethiopian Ethnic based Federal System.* Addis Ababa.

Spiro, N. B. H., 2007. Can Ethnic Federalism Prevent "Recourse to Rebellion?" A Comparative Analysis of the Ethiopian and Iraqi Constitutional Structure. *Emory International Law Review* 321: 321–372.

Turton, D., ed. 2006. *Ethnic Federalism: The Ethiopian Experience in Comparative Perspective.* Addis Ababa University Press: Addis Ababa.

Notes

1. South Africa, Nigeria, Ethiopia and recently Kenya are some of the countries that are attempting to address their diversity through political institutions.

2. According to recent census the country has more than eighty ethnic groups and languages.

3. Oromo comprises the largest ethnic group with 25.4 million people followed by Amhara with 19.8 million while other ethnic groups have far less population compared to the two major ethnic groups.

4. The students' movement, as part of the main stream Marxist ideology, was largely viewing question of nationalities as part of the larger class struggle, while these ethnic organizations mobilized their forces merely to separate from the Ethiopian state.

5. Both regions belong to the same culture and language group despite the fact that the former seems to have adapted some new identities due to the occupation of the region by Italy for few decades.

6. Notably Somali, Tigray, Amhara, Afar and Oromo regional states.

7. Benshangul Gumuz and Gambella regional states.

8. Southern Nations and Nationalities Regional State with 56 ethnic groups.

9. Addis Ababa and Dire Dawa.

10. It is states of Amhara, Oromia, Tigray, Afar and Somali that have wider autonomous regional government. In the case of all other four regions, they formed coalition governments between the respective ethnic groups in the regions.

11. This is enshrined under Art 49(4) FDRE constitution.

12. Former Yugoslavia and the USSR are examples where by ethicized political atmosphere led to the down fall of the political systems.

13. That is why Swiss and Nigerian federal systems do not form regional state solely based on ethnic lines, rather other economic, geographical and historic factors are taken into consideration

14. The best example for such invented mobilization is with respect to the Amara ethnic group. The people in the present 'Amara' region had not any common psychological makeup of being 'Amara'. Rather provincialism plays an important role in terms of defining identities in the region. The new rulers are attempting to create new Amara nationalism through mechanism of bringing of Amharic speaking population under one regional state.

15. It is not nowadays uncommon to find bank, insurance or other commercial companies and association organized largely through ethnic ties.

16. Besides the common conflict for water and grazing land, during the 2005 general elections, winning or losing the election was associated with certain ethnic groups. Even the Public Prosecutor filed genocide charges against opposition leaders claiming that they attempted to commit genocide against a Tigrean ethnic group.

17. This has been, for instance, the case in the process of drafting South African constitution which is result of negotiated compromise between elements of centralism and federalism.

18. On the one hand, the regime is accused by ethno regional political organizations like OLF and ONLF for not implementing the principles of federalism provided under the constitution. On the other hand, there are groups that accuse EPRDF's ethnic project is creating deep division among the various ethnic groups of the country and it is weakening the unity of the country.

19. Since EPRDF successfully excluded the most genus elite from political participation through harassment since 2005, the opposition parties that are currently operating are disorganized, confused and some even tend to support the regime.

20. The new press law restricts activities of the private media by imposing complicated conditions that forced many of the private press resort to conduct self-censorship or being sympathizers of the regime.

21. The government's justification for such law is to restrict the meddling of foreign forces in the Ethiopian internal affairs. The bottom of the fact is rather the public awareness Civil Society Organizations created preceding to the 2005 elections was so vital for the vote gains of the opposition parties and the government was not happy about it.

22. This vision was provided under in 1976 Manifesto of TPLF.

23. That is why the most generous constitution in granting right to self-determination including secession could not satisfy ethno- regional- organizations such as OLF. By claiming that the regime is not serious about self-determination and secession demands, they are still waging armed struggle for independence.

24. It is important to note here the case of Rwanda. Before the genocide was committed in Rwanda; there had been intense real and perceived conception that Tutsi ethnic group control major economic and political structure. It was this perception that primarily triggered the deadly genocide.

25. The Federal Government has power to levy and collect custom duties, taxes and other charges on imports, collect income, profit, sales and excise taxes on enterprises and other major taxes (Art.96, FDRE constitution).

26. Smaller minority groups such Adere or Silte have granted with autonomous administrative rights while the request for regional administration from bigger minority groups such as Sidama or Wolayta has been neglected.

27. By a very conservative estimate, several thousand people were killed in inter-ethnic conflicts in Ethiopia between 1991 and 2005 (International Crisis Group 2009).

CHAPTER 11
Human Rights and the Third World Other
Subrata Sankar Bagchi

The notion of the universalistic nature of human rights is being increasingly challenged by many Third World scholars. The recent shifts in political and economic power have further intensified this argument in the Third World academia. The basic debate is between the liberal emphasis on individual rights in a society and the alternative concept of collective rights, found especially in traditional Third World societies that attach more value to the wellbeing of society as a whole. The notion of collective rights is not popular in Western thought, while the rights of the individual are not highlighted in the traditional societies particularly in the Third World. This chapter delves into this difference, and seeks a new discourse where the two positions can meet.

On the one hand, the liberal concept of individual rights does not recognize the Third World concern for the preservation and wellbeing of society as a whole. On the other, the Third World concern sometimes requires absolute conformity from individuals to the norms of society, and this has a potential of becoming oppressive. There are instances of national governments oppressing their own citizens, particularly minorities, in the Middle East, East Asia, South Asia, Africa and Latin America where scores of people were killed and traumatized by their own governments. Strict compliance with either of the above positions is unlikely to ensure the protection of human rights, particularly for the marginalized and vulnerable individuals and populations of the Third World. Thus the question of including the voice and concerns of the Other in a society becomes pertinent to human rights discourses, as perhaps the only plausible way of protecting the wellbeing of traditional societies and the rights of vulnerable and marginalized minorities in those societies. It could also point the way towards the discovery of culturally compatible models of political and economic amelioration at the micro-level for all sections of a traditional Third World society.

Study of the Other and Human Rights

The study of the Other began in the early 20th century, in the form of an ethnographic effort taken up almost exclusively by Western scholars. After Malinowski's ground breaking work 'Argonauts of the Western Pacific' in 1922, participant observation became the sine qua non of ethnographic studies of the Other. Till the Second World War, Western scholars continued writing objective accounts of field experiences, mostly from field situations in colonized countries, in which the Other was perceived as alien, strange and exotic. The rights of the Exotic Other were not the scholars' primary concern during this period; rather, they were more eager to document the 'exotic' practices in the lives of these 'Others'. Upon many occasions, they held back their personal views on native practices (cf. Malinowski's diary published by his wife in 1967). Many of these studies enjoyed colonial patronage, because the field findings proved useful for strengthening the grip of imperial rule.

For instance, the 'Sepoy Mutiny' (now called the 'First Battle of Independence') of 1857 against the British rule in India was sparked off by the introduction of a new, more accurate breech-loading Enfield rifle by the British East India Company. The loading of these rifles entailed the biting of a greased cartridge which, the sepoys (native soldiers) feared, contained either cow or pig fat—'the first, from an animal sacred to the Hindus, and the second from an animal held unclean by the Muslims. The Hindu sepoys saw this as an attempt to break their caste as a preliminary to making them all Christians. The Muslim troops were disgusted and no less insulted than the Hindus' (Edwardes 1963: 7–19). This cultural insensitivity of the British led to an unprecedented form of rebellion against the Raj in the subcontinent, almost overthrowing the colonial rule. After brutally suppressing the rebellion, the British crown started ruling the colony directly, taking charge from the East India Company in 1858. The proclamation of Direct Rule coincided with the proliferation of several studies of the Indian people by missionaries, administrators, travelers, and scholars, a practice which continued till the exit of the British rulers from the subcontinent.

Till the Second World War, many scholars studying colonized peoples believed that their efforts would help preserve local, 'exotic' cultures in the way a museum preserves its fossils and rare collections, inert and immutable. These pre–War studies, laden with colonial perceptions of native populations, were primarily concerned with documenting the cultural life of those peoples, and cared little about the rights of the 'Exotic Other'.

The Post War Study of the Other

After the Second World War, the world community (led by the West) formulated UDHR and other human rights principles, organizations, covenants etc. However, studies on the Third World Other continued without much concern about the rights of these people. Until 1970, a holistic ethnographic trend of studying the Other in the Third World comprising different aspects of their lives was formalized in the West. At the same time, a critical debate about the nature of ethnographic interpretation of the Other emerged both in the West and in the Third

World with the rise of a new breed of scholars in both domains. Holistic ethnography started right after the Second World War, i.e. immediately after the de-colonization of most Third World nations. In sharp contrast with their predecessors, most scholars of this later tradition held the task of giving voice to society's underclass as one of their central goals. Though not directly pertinent to formal human rights discourses, their activities helped them to achieve an understanding of the basic power relation existing between the privileged and the underprivileged in the society, and provided them with insights into the ways in which the voice of the latter is silenced in a majority of the discourses. It also unraveled the power relation between the Western or the West-mediated ethnographers and their Third World 'subject'.

The term 'ethnocentrism' was coined during this period to refer to the tendency of people in most cultures (mostly Western) to think of their own culture as the best and most sensible. A good ethnography, however, was one which 'sensitized' the reader to the beliefs, values, and practices of the natives of another society. Kenneth Pike (1954), at a very early stage of post–War ethnography, called for a need to develop an 'emic' approach (insiders' point of view) rather than an 'etic' approach (outsiders' point of view). Most scholars of the holistic school say that empathy and identification with the social grouping being observed is needed; they insist that an ethnographer should 'go native' and live like the local people (e.g. Evans-Pritchard 1950; Cohen 1985). The assumption is that the ethnographer has to become like a blank slate in order to understand local social and cultural practices fully. The ethnographer acts like a sponge, soaking up the language and culture of the people under study. Then they would write up on that culture and if, after reading the ethnography, actions which were previously seen as absurd, strange or irrational 'made sense', then that ethnography had achieved its purpose.

Toward the end of the 1960s, the concept of the 'flawed ethnographer' was introduced with the publication of Malinowski's diary—'Diary in the Strict Sense of the Term' (1967). This diary revealed the duality in the life of an ethnographer, showing how an ethnographer can be torn between his/her notion of civilization and the 'objective' analysis of the native practices. Though the holistic trend survived well beyond the 1970s, its influences were significantly diminished with this publication which created some serious dents in the notion of a flawless empathic ethnography. It is however undeniable that the goal of the holistic ethnographers to give voice to the Other brought them closer to the real needs of the Others in the Third World, and this may be regarded as the first steps in the process of human rights discourses becoming relevant in ethnography.

The 'Thick Description' of Clifford Geertz and Human Rights

The waning of the holistic school gave rise to a period of generic blurring of ethnography in the West. Clifford Geertz, the foremost exponent of the 'thick description' (semiotic) school, proposes that ethnographers do not need to have empathy with their subjects (Geertz 1973, 1983, 1988); rather they need to look for and analyze symbolic forms—words, images, institutions, behaviors—with respect to one another and to the whole that they comprise. According to him, ethnographers need to understand the 'webs of significance' which people weave within the cultural context, and these webs of significance can only be communicated to others by thickly describing the situation and its context.

> *Doing ethnography is like trying to read (in the sense of constructing a reading of) a manuscript – foreign, faded, full of ellipses, incoherencies, suspicious emendations, and tendentious commentaries, but written not in conventional graphs of sound but in transient examples of shaped behaviour* (Geertz 1973: 322).

Moreover, the writer/ethnographer does not have any privileged position in making interpretations on the situation and its context. Thus according to this approach, the rights discourses in the Third World can be found in the 'thick description' of the symbols which orient people with respect to the systems of meaning in any particular culture. This interpretive approach in ethnography made any universalistic generalization of principle including human rights impossible.

Crises of Representation and Legitimization

From the mid 1980's a crisis crept in the field of ethnography regarding the study of the Other, which can be called the 'crisis of representation'. *Writing Culture* (Clifford and Marcus, 1986) pioneered this crisis as it influenced more reflexive writings in ethnography and 'post-paradigm' critiques of culture. Drawing on various issues regarding race, class and gender in actual field situations, ethnographers became more and more familiar with new models of truth (i.e. multiple truths). It became increasingly difficult for these scholars to claim that they could directly capture the lived experiences. It marked the ushering in of the postmodern period of experimental ethnographic writing. It started with developing a paradigm that is an amalgam of the 'classic' approach (observation and interpretation) with the more recent trends that place the researcher within the field. The resulting new 'ethnographic ethic' is itself in a state of flux, and the next few years or so could result in other configurations of ethnographic research on the Other (Altheide and Johnson 1998). 'Who represents whom' became a central question in the study of Other in the Third World. This made the entire notion of universalism in human rights untenable, because it was accepted that only the 'Other' can represent the 'Other'. Another potential problem with classical, holistic and interpretive ethnography is the creation of 'false' cultures (Schiller, Crystal et al. 1994), and according to postmodern ethnography this must always be borne in mind to avoid stereotyping. These notions triggered another major crisis in the study of the Other, i.e. the 'crisis of legitimization' which put doubt on the legitimacy of any researcher's claims to generality, intersubjectivity or objectivity. All researchers including ethnographers are related to a particular historical and social context. The findings of the predominantly Western researchers even in ethnographic research and their claims to generality, intersubjectivity or objectivity can never be separated from the Western cultural hegemony. This crisis possibly created the deepest rift between ethnographers and human rights scholars, because the latter's claim of the generality or objectivity in the perception of human rights throughout the world was not only challenged but shaken vigorously on the ground of legitimacy.

Globalization and the Rights of the Other in the Third World

The effect of globalization on human rights in the Third World is immense, particularly because of its much discussed 'homogenizing effect' endangering the space of the Other. Globalization primarily requires a general dismantling of trade barriers and a free mobility of financial and productive capital, in the context of accelerated technological change, and to this end it advocates the opening up of nations' economies to free competition on the world market. Globalization also promotes the elimination of the regulatory functions of the state apparatus and promotes the denationalization and privatization of its goods and services. The market is supposed to determine the growth of distribution, production, technological innovation and even social needs. Observers feel that this formulation of globalization is incomplete and inadequate unless placed in the context of the power play between the core and the peripheral countries. Third World countries like India have experienced globalization as colossal arrogance and violence (Chandhoke 1999), as an instance of the West imposing its own ideas on the Third World nations regarding how their societies, cultures, economies and/or politics should be arranged. The peoples of these nations suffer a crisis of de-culturalisation, feeling oppressed by the devaluation and erosion of their cultural and identity rights. As Appadurai (1996) argues, '...globalization of culture is the same as its homogenization, but globalization involves the use of a variety of instruments of homogenization (armaments, advertising techniques, language hegemonies, clothing style and the like), which are absorbed into local political and cultural economies, only to be repatriated as heterogeneous dialogues of national sovereignty, free enterprise, fundamentalism etc.' Questions of heterogeneity arise in these 'instruments of homogenization' as core questions regarding Pacific diasporic identities/representations, for example language hegemonies sustained by terms like 'islander'. In this instance the impact is not on nation states in Appadurai's sense, but as markers of identity and representation in the determination of individual and diasporic scapes within the larger globalized hegemonies of definitions of people sustained in homogenising terms such as the 'global village'. With the growing predominance of a few languages and the emergence of fusion languages like Chiglish, Spanglish, Hinlish, Benglish, etc., a dwindling number of Third World children continue to learn the languages of their parents. According to some estimates, one language dies every fourteen days; by 2100, more than half of the 7,000 languages now spoken on Earth will have disappeared. There are steady losses of oral history and local knowledge due to language extinction and the erosion of cultural heterogeneity in the Third World. Since the beginning of globalization, transnational companies operating across borders have increasingly gained in influence and power. Corporate activity has not always benefited societies, but there are few effective tools to prevent human rights abuses or hold companies accountable in the Third World. The exploitation of natural resources and pollution of natural environments have devastating and long-term implications for the traditional cultural, land, health and property rights of the locals, leaving them powerless and vulnerable.

A pertinent example involves the German oil company Shell which began oil production in Nigeria in 1958, and worked with the government to quell factions opposed to its presence. Shell financed and assisted violent military raids against popular movements by the Ogoni people who raised concerns with respect to the widespread poverty, inequalities, human rights abuses and environmental degradation occurring in the region. Wiwa, the founder-leader of the human rights group called Movement for the Survival of the Ogoni People in Nigeria, was falsely accused, arrested, detained, convicted, and executed by hanging in 1995 by the Nigerian military regime, to safeguard the interest of Shell.

Thus we locate a duality in the West-mediated human rights approach in the age of globalization. On the one hand, it advocates individualistic and universalistic notions of human rights with little concern about the authentic voice of the Third World 'Other'. On the other, it fails to speak up for individual rights when they are threatened and violated in the Third World, as becomes evident through the above instance. Resistance against globalization, however, exists in many parts of the Third World. Certain East Asian governments, in their opposition to Western cultural models, have implemented strict adherence to more traditional values that are usually interpreted as having greater affinity with economic, social, and cultural rights than with political rights. Since political freedom, liberty and democracy are Western concepts, many Asians regard them with suspicion because they feel these ideas may facilitate the infiltration of their traditional societies with Western values. Many people in the Third World fear that globalization would result in native values being supplanted by Western values. In Saudi Arabia, there are no voting rights, and there is censorship of Western movies, alcohol and Internet access. Despite these well-known and documented instances of human rights violations, the US Army has large bases in Saudi territory, and maintains a perfectly cordial relationship with the Saudi ruling class—which is another example of Western double standards regarding human rights in the Third World.

My Dilemmas on Child Rights in a Third World Situation

During my long association with ethnographic research on child labor in the city of Kolkata, I faced several dilemmas regarding child rights in my own city. The child labor issue raises concerns about the right to food, health, and access to adequate health care (Ozar 1981; Wolstenholme and Elliott 1974) along with a host of other rights including the right to lead a decent life. These dilemmas thus ranged from legal questions like that of the efficacy of the legal provisions and constitutional safeguards, to more ethnographic dilemmas like the question of legitimacy and representation in the context of insiders' views on child labor.

National and International Safeguards and Child Labor in India

In India, there are several constitutional safeguards against child labor:
1) Article 14—Prohibition of the employment of children under 14 in any factory or mine, or in any other hazardous employment.
2) Article 23—Prohibition of traffic in human beings and forced labor
3) Article 24—Prohibition of employment of children in factories etc.
4) Article 39(e) and 39(f)—Certain relevant policy principles to be followed by the several states
5) Article 41—The right to work, to education and to public assistance in particular circumstances
6) Article 45—Provision for free and compulsory education for children
7) Article 47—Responsibility of the states to raise the nutritional levels, and standards of living of its citizens and to improve public health

Several legislations have been passed by the pre-Independent and post-Independent governments to address the child labor situation in India. Some relevant pre-independence acts are:

i) Indian Factories Act, 1881: Prohibited the employment of children below 7 years in any factory and banned a working period exceeding 9 hours a day.

ii) Indian Factories (Amendment) Act, 1891: Raised the minimum age for work to 9 years and reduced the working period to 7 hours a day with the prohibition of work at night between 8 p.m. and 5 a.m.

iii) The Mines Act, 1901: Prohibited the employment of children under 12 years in mines.

iv) The Factories Act, 1911: Prohibited the work by children in factories between 7 p.m. and 5.30 a.m. and in certain dangerous processes.

v) The Factories (Amendment) Act, 1922: Raised the minimum age to 15 years in general, fixed the working hours to a maximum of 6 hours and an interval of half an hour in between, and prohibited the employment of children below 18 in certain processes.

vi) The Indian Mines Act, 1923: Raised the minimum age from 12 to 13 years for employment in mines.

vii) The Indian Ports (Amendment) Act, 1931: Fixed 12 years as the minimum age for handling goods in ports.

viii) Children (Pledging of Labour) Act, 1933: Prohibited parents and guardians from pledging the services of a child. It was followed in quick succession by the Employment of Children Act, 1938 which has now been replaced by Child Labour (Prohibition and Regulation) Act, 1986.

ix) The Factories Act, 1934: Employment of children under 12 prohibited, of children between 12 and 15 restricted to 5 hours.

x) The Indian Mines (Amendment) Act, 1935: Prohibited the employment of children under 15 in mines.

xi) Employment of Children Act, 1938: Sought to prohibit employment of children below 14 years in occupations relating to transport of passengers by rail and in work relating to the handling of goods within the limits of any port. The Act fixed the minimum age of employment at 14 years for those engaged in *beedi* making, carpet weaving, cement manufacture, cloth printing, dyeing and weaving, match manufacture, mica cutting, tanning etc.

After independence, various legislations were made to prevent/minimize child labor.

i) Factories Act, 1948: Prohibits employment of young children under 14 in any factory employing more than 10 persons and using power or employing more than 20 persons where power is not used.

ii) The Minimum Wages Act, 1948: Provides for an institutional mechanism and procedure for fixation, review, revision, and enforcement of minimum wage rates.

iii) Plantation Act, 1951: Prohibits the employment of children under 12 to work in any plantation. Also prohibits the children (above 12 years but below 15 years) employed in a plantation to work for more than 40 hours a week.

iv) Mines Act, 1952: Prevents children under 15 in any underground or above ground mining operation.

v) Merchant Shipping Act, 1958: Prohibits children under 15 from being carried to sea to work in any capacity on ships.

vi) Motor Transport Workers Act, 1961: Prohibits children under 15 from being employed in any capacity in any motor transport undertaking.

vii) Apprentices Act, 1961: Prohibits any person from being engaged as an apprentice unless he is not less than fourteen years of age and satisfies such standards of education and physical fitness as may be prescribed.

viii) Beedi and Cigar Workers (Conditions of Employment) Act, 1961: Prohibits children under 14 from being employed in beedi and cigar making units irrespective of the number of persons employed.

ix) The Bonded Labour System (Abolition) Act, 1975: Intends to abolish age-old bonded labor system of India. Government of India has ratified the ILO Convention No. 29 on forced labor in 1954 and the corresponding act on bonded labor was passed in 1996 but made effective from 24 October 1975.

x) The Employment of Children (Amendment) Act, 1978: Includes the new clauses connected with cinder picking, clearing of ash pits, building operation or connected with the work on railway stations and moving trains.

xi) Child Labour (Prohibition and Regulation) Act, 1986: The most comprehensive act on child labor. Under this act Government of India prohibited the employment of children in dangerous and hazardous industries and services, and regulated their engagement and working conditions in non-hazardous jobs listed in Parts A and B of the Schedule of the Act. Through a Notification dated 26.05.1993, the working conditions of children were regulated in all employments not prohibited under the Act. Through subsequent notifications the Schedule of the Act prohibiting child labor in different occupations and processes has been substantially enlarged, bringing the total to 13 occupations and 57 processes. Thus in many important occupations[1] and services,[2] child labor is completely prohibited. The regulation provides that a child can work up to a maximum of 6 hours a day, and is entitled to an hour of rest after every three hours of continuous work. Any employer found in violation can be punished with 3 to 12 months of rigorous imprisonment, or a fine of up to 20,000 rupees, or both.

One major shortcoming of this act is the omission of many industries/occupations/processes that may initially appear to be harmless or non-hazardous, but turn out to be the opposite upon closer examination.[3] Another major criticism can be leveled against the provision regarding a definitional loophole which allows the possibility of a child being employed in a prohibited occupation at home along with other members of the child's family, because the home of the employed is not a 'workshop' of the 'occupier' according to the provisions of the Act. Indeed, many manufacturers of beedi or carpets exploit this loophole by handing over raw materials to the parents of the child laborer and asking them to do the manufacturing in their homes. Similar problems have been faced regarding the determination of a child's age, because the Act provides that disputes over age should be decided on the basis of a certificate of age provided by the prescribed medical authority to whom such an issue has to be referred for decision, and that such a certificate shall for the purpose of the Act be conclusive evidence of the child's age. There being no systematic recording of birth registration in India, it becomes extremely difficult to correctly determine the age of a child. The provision of determination by registered medical authority, which took away the court's power to intervene, is leading to many circumventions of the Act.

In a later gazette notification in 2008, the Indian Government, on the recommendation of the Child Labour Technical Advisory Committee, made various amendments of the 1986 Act including the banning of the employment of children in further occupations where they would be exposed to excessive heat and cold, for instance in the mechanized fishing, food processing and beverage industries etc., and exposed to free silica such as slate, pencil industry, stone grinding, etc.

Supreme Court Judgment on Child Labor: The matter of the elimination of child labor has also been deliberated by the Supreme Court of India from time to time. In its judgment dated 10th December, 1996 in the Writ Petition (Civil) No.465/1986, the Supreme Court provided certain directions regarding the manner in which children working in hazardous occupations are to be withdrawn from work and rehabilitated, and also the manner in which the working conditions of the children working in non-hazardous occupations are to be regulated and improved. These important directions also mandated completion of the survey of children working in hazardous employments within a period of six months, payment of compensation amounting to INR 20,000/- (USD 370) by the offending employer for every child employed in contravention of the provisions of the Act, providing of alternative employment to an adult member of the family in place of the child withdrawn from the hazardous occupation or payment of an amount of INR 5,000/- (USD 92) for each child employed in hazardous employment by the appropriate Government, payment of interest on the corpus of INR 25,000/- (INR 20,000/- to be paid by the employer and INR 5,000/- to be contributed by the appropriate Government) to the family of the child withdrawn from work, provision of education in a suitable institution for the child withdrawn from work, constitution of the Child Labour Rehabilitation-cum-Welfare Fund, and constitution of a separate cell in the Labor Department of the appropriate Government for the purpose of monitoring. The implementation of the directions of Supreme Court is monitored by the Ministry of Labour, and compliance with the directions reported to the Hon'ble Court on the basis of information received from the State/UT Governments from time to time.

Some Ratified ILO Conventions: Being an important member state of ILO, India has ratified many of the significant Conventions adopted by ILO at different times.

i. Convention No. 5: Minimum Age (Industry) 1919—Seeks to prohibit employment of children under 14 in any public or private industrial undertaking. Ratified by India on 09.09.1955.
ii. Convention No. 123: Minimum Age (Underground Work) 1965—Provides for banning persons under 16 years of age from working in underground mines. Ratified on 20.03.1975.
iii. Convention No. 6: Night Work for Young Persons (Industries) 1919—Seeks to abolish night work for young persons in any public or private industrial undertaking. Provisions modified for India. Ratified on 14.07.1921.
iv. Convention No. 15: Minimum Age (Trimmers & Stokers) 1921—Seeks to prohibit employment of persons under 18 as trimmers and stokers in ports. In case of unavailability of persons over 18, persons between 16 and 18 may be employed. Trimmers/stokers younger than 16 can be employed, subject to medical fitness, in the coastal trade of India. Ratified on 20.11.1922.
v. Convention No.16: Medical Examination of Young Persons (Sea) 1921—Stipulates that person younger than 18 can be employed on a vessel only on the production of a medical certificate attesting fitness for such work. Ratified on 20.11.1922.

The Indian government ratified only four of the eight core conventions known as fundamental/human rights but did not ratify the other four. The ratified four are:
i) Forced Labour Convention (Convention No. 29)
ii) Abolition of Forced Labour Convention (Convention No. 105)
iii) Equal Remuneration Convention (Convention No. 100)
iv) Discrimination (Employment Occupation) Convention (Convention No. 111).

The four non-ratified conventions are:
i) Freedom of Association and Protection of Right to Organised Convention (No. 87)
ii) Right to Organise and Collective Bargaining Convention (No. 98)
iii) Minimum Age Convention (No. 138)
iv) Worst forms of Child Labour Convention (No. 182)

Consequent to the World Summit for Social Development in 1995, the above-mentioned Conventions (Convention Nos. 29, 105, 100, 111, 87, 98, and 138) were categorized as the Fundamental Human Rights Conventions or Core Conventions by the ILO. Later, Convention No. 182 (Sl.No.8) was added to the list. According to the ILO Declaration on Fundamental Principles and Rights at

Work and its Follow-up, each Member State of the ILO is expected to give effect to the principles contained in the Core Conventions, irrespective of whether or not the Core Conventions have been ratified by them.

The Indian government's many botched attempts to prevent child labor have resulted in several legislative initiatives, but not in any significant reduction of the practice. Data from the census of 2001 puts the number of child laborers at 12.7 million. Some unofficial estimates claim that the real number is somewhere between 40 million and 110 million at present. Scholars suggest that the formulation and fulfillment of children's rights is largely dependent on the specific socio-cultural and politico-economic conditions of the individual countries of the Third World. The actual reason for child labor and allocation of lesser household resources to the children may be more complex than it seems from the Western perspective. Scholars also suggest that one must first identify the actual behaviors which result in a child being allocated fewer resources within and outside the household, leading to malnutrition, premature deaths and ill-health. Following that, the ideas behind such behaviors should be examined which might include the value of children in that society, or specific traditions like that of taking child labor as granted as we see in the subcontinent in the ancient concept of the 'Guru–Shishya Parampara' (a tradition of accepting service from pupils as a part of training) which led to the widespread practice of apprenticeship of children in this part of the Third World (Scheper-Hughes 1987, 1992; Cassidy 1980; Bagchi 2009, 2010a, 2010b, 2010c). The question of 'insiders' view' also becomes important to this analysis, because the perception of discrimination is not always culture-neutral. In fact, some scholars argue that a people should be allowed to decide whether and how to maintain their traditions and culture even if those are deemed harmful by the rest of the world. Ethnographers have always put stress on considering differential cross-cultural life stages, behavioral expectations, and educational issues (Schirmer, Renteln, Weisberg 1988) that may not conform with UNESCO's 1952 Declaration of Children's Rights which tried to adopt a universal framework for the emotional and mental development of children (UNESCO, 1953). More recently, scholars have concentrated on cross-cultural perceptions of nutritional needs, child abuse and neglect (Scheper-Hughes 1987, 1992; Cassidy, 1980). Thus we need more cross-cultural studies on this issue which now faces questions regarding representation and legitimacy.

The Questions Regarding Representation and Legitimacy

The question of representation in non-Western human rights accounts by both Western and non-Western scholars have been intensely debated. Even the most amicable routes to decolonize these accounts might involve some sort of adversarial relationship with the West, and this immediately sets up a tension, intensified by the fact that any such route must involve an erasure of colonial subjugation and the perception of equality with the erstwhile masters. The question is also a source of extreme anxiety for scholars of non-Western human rights issues, because it seems to threaten any distinctive (non-Western) identity, which can be the only proof of true equality. This anxiety has become multiplied by the debates on the effect of globalization on non-Western societies.

As an ethnographer, I have always preferred long-term association with the field and participants of my research, and to involve myself as a participant observer in the field. In my early days as a Third World ethnographer, I was not too worried about the question of representation. Especially while working on the child labor problem, I thought I was largely exempt from this particular crisis because I was raised in a poor family, and for some time after the death of my father, our sole bread-earner I myself ran the risk of becoming a child laborer.

Question 1: Who is Studying Whom?

I always thought that studying the child labor problem in Kolkata would be easier for me than for many others, that in fact it would be a kind of collaborative research effort between a 'once potential child laborer' (me) and 'virtual child laborers' where both the collaborative parties can claim co-authorship. But as I started working on this project I found that an urban middle-class identity had in the intervening years crept into my psyche, preventing the ideal co-authorship and raising the question of representation. My formal training as an ethnographer had indeed helped in effective rapport establishment with the research participants, but done little more than that. So the basic question regarding representation prevailed in my study, and the insider/outsider dichotomy remained, my position remaining that of a 'familiar' outsider.

Question 2: How are the Participants Being Represented in the Rights Discourses?

The second major question that bothers human rights researchers is how to build co-authorship with the participants so that the voices of the participants can also be incorporated in the research discourse. In my research, most of these efforts were linked with the actors' own perceptions about their reality. But the main problem that I faced in this co-authorship was language. The language I spoke with them (Bengali) was different from the language in which I wrote my research outcomes (English). My own intervention in this co-authorship in the role of translator was a serious deal-breaker, and I am afraid that none of the co-authorship in the local languages can achieve its desired goal of including the Other. For Benjamin, (1968: 69) translation is ever the 'same' as the 'original'. In other words, a translation cannot 'possibly reveal or establish this hidden relationship' (Ibid. 1968: 72). It is not the translator's task to represent the original, for such a representation is impossible: 'Even the greatest translation is destined to be part of the growth of its own language' (Ibid. 1968: 73). From Spivak's point of view, an earnest listening is the first step to translation, and to be more accurate, declaring the 'subaltern' (Spivak's term for the Other) silent is the initial stride toward an 'unsilencing' of the subaltern (Spivak 1988). In my experience, however, one can never be sure, when engaged in the rights research in the Third World countries like India, whether the authentic self-expression of the Other is properly incorporated in the rights discourse when translation is involved. This is particularly true for that part of the Third World where the major languages like English, Spanish, French and Russian are not spoken, but the research outcomes must be written in one of these languages.

Question 3: Whether the Insiders' Perceptions also favor the Rights Concerns?

Insiders' perceptions of their own situation are extremely important in the ethnographic studies now. When extended to rights discourses in a Third World milieu, it might bring forth some unprecedented revelations. My work on child labor can perhaps adequately illustrate the dilemma. Here is an excerpt from the child laborer Farah (10 years old at the time of the study) who lived in a squatters' settlement on the side of a main thoroughfare. When I asked her about the kind of education she had received and her desire for receiving further education, she said:

> I am living in this settlement since my birth... I have two brothers... one is elder to me and the other is younger... I can sign my name in Urdu... I learnt to read Kalma (Arabic verses of Koran)... I read for few days in a nearby Madrasa school but my parents withdrew me from that school. I am a girl and there is no use for me to go to the school leaving all the household works and other works unfinished. Finally, when my younger brother was born 2 years ago I stopped going to school. Yes, my elder brother still reads in a nearby school and my younger brother is yet to be grown enough to be admitted in the school... Now I act as a scrap-picker and sometimes as a scrap-sorter... After returning from work I help my mother with household activities...(Fieldnote).

I did not feel that Farah missed her school. I talked to her parents and found them least bothered about Farah's education, since girls, particularly in the Muslim community living here, are not expected to be educated. According to her parents the kind of education received in the local schools was of no use in their life, particularly for the girl child who was supposed to be involved more with domestic drudgery. The question of 'Right to Education' seemed very alien to these people, and perhaps even in conflict with their day-to-day reality.

A similar study on a slightly better off population, though still living in a slum, revealed a somewhat different picture. This story is about Sikha, an 11-year-old Hindu girl from a *Basti* (slum) reading in the fifth standard, her parents willing to continue her education till she finished school. But they were keener to educate their boy, willing to support him beyond school, because they regarded him as a future resource. Once again, 'Right to Education' had been realized only partially, and remained inextricably bound with the financial stability of the family.

> I am Sikha Adhikary, my age is 11 years. I have lived in this settlement since my birth... I read in Class V in a nearby Bengali-medium girls' school. I have an elder brother who reads in a nearby boys' school in class VII... I and my brother get (private) tuitions in the morning and then go to school... After I

> return from the school I play with my friends... Then at dusk I again prepare my lessons. Our mother keeps a strict vigil on our study... (Fieldnote)

During the same study I tried to discover the child laborers' own perceptions of the reason for their working. Most of them thought that the family's inability to continue their study was the main reason of their working. Other most cited reasons were their family needing their contribution, helping their family businesses and the necessity of money for their own survival. A few child laborers also cited boredom with studies, the importance of learning a skilled and lucrative job, and still other reasons like a prevalent tradition in the family of working early, or even destiny, etc. I found none among the child laborers who could comprehend the rights discourse, i.e. the fact that they have certain rights which can empower them to remain in school. Here is an excerpt from my field notes—

> I met Kabirul... an eleven year old boy, who used to work in a nearby garage as an apprentice. His father was a contractual worker in a nearby factory and his mother worked as a scrap-sorter in a nearby place. Kabirul had a younger brother and a sister also. His sister (elder to Kabirul) was also working in a house as domestic help. Kabirul had attended school (a non-formal school run by a local NGO) for few months and developed some reading and writing skills. Later, according to Kabirul, his father and mother began to think that Kabirul should learn motor-repairing, a skill in demand in the local market, and earn some money for the family. Thus Kabirul stopped going to school. Kabirul's father established a contract with a nearby motor garage where Kabirul has now been working for nearly a year. At about this time, Kabirul's younger brother was born. During the time of my fieldwork Kabirul's father got Rs. 200/- each month for Kabirul's work. The garage owner provided Kabirul a morning Tiffin (bread and tea), but for his lunch Kabirul had to return home, for which he was allowed an hour's break. Kabirul was learning motor-repairing works. He was hoping to learn the work quickly, and aspired to become a skilled and independent motor mechanic (Fieldnote).

It is also important to study how the parents of working children perceive the phenomenon of child labor. I have found that the responses of the parents, like those of their children, to the question of the reason why their children were working, were various. Most of them cited the family's need for the child's contribution. Other often cited reasons included the inability of the family to continue the child's education, the prudence of apprenticing the child in a skilled and lucrative job, and the child's inattentiveness to study. Still other parents said that the family had not interfered in the child's own decision to work, or cited some other reasons like spontaneous decision of working to save destitution of the family, a family tradition of working early in life, etc. These perceptions, too, were completely unrelated with the rights discourse. Here is another relevant excerpt from my field notes taken during the study among child laborers and their families living in a squatter settlement in Kolkata:

I met Nusrat Begum... who had two sons and a daughter. Her 12 year old elder son worked in a local restaurant as a helper boy. Her younger son, 10 years old, worked as a scrap-sorter. I asked her why she had let her children work so early. She replied that her husband worked as a porter in a nearby market and earned very little, which was insufficient for the family's survival. She was also engaged in some ill-paid low-skill jobs like domestic help, helper in construction works etc. But together they did not earn enough to meet the expenditure of their household, and their family had been suffering terribly because of this. Hence they had no other option but to engage their children in work. The small sum of money which the children brought was a great help for their family. They could spend that money on food, clothing, and for the costly treatment of Nusrat's chronic chest pain (possibly a heart problem). When I asked her about the education of her children, I found that she thought education was of little use in their lives. She said that she had seen many educated people who did not have any job. This had led her to realize that educating her children would not serve their purpose, which was day-to-day survival. Despite her opinion of education, she had sent her elder child to a nearby (non-formal) school for few months till boy had learnt to sign his name. Both Nusrat and her husband were of the firm opinion that their children needed to work to support the family (Fieldnote).

Nusrat Begum did not have any option but to release her children for work, and the chronic poverty of the family compounded with her persistent health impairment would not even let her think about the education of her children. The apparently low and deferred returns yielded by education made it useless for families like Nusrat's. They perceive education as the privilege of rich families that can afford to invest in an uncertain future. Child labor for these families is a natural recourse.

Finding the Voice of the Third World Other

Even the non-Western perspectives favoring collective rights for traditional societies may not readily ensure the inclusion of voice of the Other from the Third World. Even Marx argued, when he was commenting on peasantry, 'They cannot represent themselves, they must be represented'. However, the question remains—who is representing whom and with what kind of legitimacy? This question applies to all the West-mediated projects including the universalistic notion of human rights which often miss Third World concerns. After decades of denial in the post–War era, a section of human rights scholars has finally acknowledged the problem. This acknowledgement has led a part of the Western scholarship to completely withdraw from the debate, with the intention of depoliticizing these issues. However, this withdrawal hardly relieves the West from their complicity in the West–Non-West power relationship. But the core question remains. How can we incorporate the authentic self-expression of the Third World Other, something I call 'unsilencing the Other'? My first possible point of departure is with Gayatri Chakraborty Spivak, my 'native' representative in the West. In Spivak I find a benevolent West; the Other in the Third World requires such a benevolence for gaining a foothold in intellectual discourse. Spivak points out how 'progressive' Western intellectuals such as Foucault and Deleuze tend to engage in gross universalisations when they speak about the representation of the Third World 'masses', or refer to 'the workers' struggle' in a way that ignores the international division of labor (1988: 272-274). Spivak also finds both the colonial and the 'native' representations to be similarly problematic. She cites the abolition of 'sati' (widow-sacrifice) in colonial India by the British Raj. The practice was termed 'barbaric' by the 'civilized' British [an attitude that Spivak characterized as 'White men saving brown women from brown men' (1988: 297)]. On the other hand, the then Brahminical discourse argued that the widows wanted to die. Each of these representations ignored the widow's own voice: whether she wanted to be saved from dying or she wanted to commit a 'pure' and 'courageous' act which would might give her a safe passage to heaven. 'Between patriarchy and imperialism, subject-constitution and object-formation, the figure of the woman disappears, not into pristine nothingness, but into a violent shuttling which is the displaced figure of the 'third world woman' caught between tradition and modernization' (Spivak 1988: 306-307). Spivak (1988) further argues that when the subaltern speaks, his/her voice is either appropriated or not heard by the elite. She cites the case of Bhubaneshwari Bhaduri, an activist in a terrorist anti-British organization who committed suicide in 1926 to mark her voice of protest against terrorism (Spivak 1988, 1999). But the time of her suicide coincided with her menstrual period, and this resulted in a demeaning turn to the speculations about the cause of her death. Her kinswomen interpreted the act of suicide as a last resort to avoid the scandal of an unwarranted pregnancy. Thus in this case the Other did speak, but it fell into a void because people did not give ears to her voice, and her voice was appropriated.

Another possible point of departure can be Derrida's position on the 'mechanics of the constitution of the Other'. Here the subject position of the Other remains a blank space in the elite's text. Derrida might be invoked in the present research design as a much-needed benevolent West. On the other hand, Foucault's position on the 'invocations of the authenticity of the Other' has sometimes been charged as fulfilling the imperialist design to appropriate (colonize) the mind of the people living on the margin.

We have seen that with the advent of globalization, many people in different local cultures have suffered exploitation, oppression, and social injustices. This is as true in India as in various other Third World countries where individuals in oppressed situations are getting de-valued. Though people's experiences differ in different cultures and even within the same culture, one immediate and apparently overall effect of globalization on local cultures is the denigration of the Other in the Third World situation. This has had a profound effect on the authentic self-expression of the Other as the Other in margin withdraws more and more into itself. This withdrawal of the Other into solitude and silence seems to be the most visible outcome of the present order of the Third World. On the other hand, the Other on the margins of the West is not as silent as its Third World stepcousins, as is evident from Western discourses; the Western Other can at least register its discordant voices and sometimes even speak out and inscribe itself in Western human rights discourses.

It can also be argued whether the Western-style democratic institutions can ensure the realization of the rights of all individuals and groups in Third World countries. The primary reason for this failure is that a democratic institution cannot seek to represent by proxy or on the basis of any supposed 'authenticity', because both claims ignore the role of the powerful elite in political acts. A relevant instance can be found in the Shah Bano case in India. Shah Bano, an elderly Muslim woman, was thrown out of her home by her wealthy husband after 44 years of marriage, with only the original value of her dowry (less than $100) returned to her, which was nowhere near enough for her survival. She sued her husband under the Criminal Procedure Code and got an order from the Indian Supreme Court in her favor. Controversy immediately erupted, and the Islamic clergy and the Muslim Personal Law Board, among others, organized mass demonstrations against the ruling party. The resulting public furor led the then Indian government to introduce the 'Muslim Women's (Protection after Divorce) Act of 1986'. This Act was passed by an overwhelming majority of the elected representatives in the Indian parliament, and it deprived all Muslim women of the right of maintenance guaranteed under the Criminal Procedure Code.

Thus we have an example of the Third World Other speaking, its voice being heard by the highest level of the country's judiciary and then becoming smothered by the democratically elected highest body of legislatures. Western-style democracy was therefore meaningless for Shah Bano, the Third World Other. Hence I argue that the discursive space existing in the human rights discourses in this regard should be liberated which will go beyond the Spivakian contention of the deliberate act of speaking by the subaltern (Other). Instead, we should attempt to *listen* to the Third World Other, with awareness of the many ways in which they communicate, so that their authentic self-expressions can be included in human rights discourses for the Third World.

References

Altheide, D. L. and J. M. Johnson, 1998. Criteria for Assessing Interpretive Validity in Qualitative Research. *Collecting and Interpreting Qualitative Materials,* edited by Norman K. Denzin and Yvonna S. Lincoln, 283–312. Thousand Oaks, Sage.

Appadurai, A., 1996. *Modernity at Large: Cultural Dimensions of Globalization.* Minnesota: University of Minnesota.

Bagchi, S. S. and A. Das. 2004. On the Question of Urban Poverty in a Third World Context. *Journal of the Department of Anthropology; University of Calcutta,* 8–9, no. 1–2: 18–33

Bagchi, S. S., 2005. Ethnography in Urban Context. *Glimpses into Behavioural Science: Methods and Themes in Practice,* edited by J. Basu and H. N. Gupta, 25–35. Kolkata: ASC, University of Calcutta.

Bagchi, S. S., 2005. Globalisation, Informal Sector and Child Labour in a Third World Urban Situation. *Journal of the Department of Anthropology; University of Calcutta* 10 & 11: 24–57.

Bagchi, S. S., 2006. Child Labour in Kolkata. *Asian Anthropology* 5:131–144.

Bagchi, S. S., 2009. Children of Kolkata Slums. *Child Labor World Atlas: An Historical and Regional Survey,* edited by H.D. Hindman, 796–798. Armonk, NY: M. E. Sharpe.

Bagchi, S. S., ed. 2009. *Expanding Horizons of Human Rights.* New Delhi: Atlantic Publishers.

Bagchi, S. S., 2010a. *Child Labor and the Urban Third World: Toward a New Understanding.* Lanham, MD: University Press of America.

Bagchi, S. S., 2010b. Understanding Child Labour Problem in an Urban Setting: A Third Worldly Perspective. *Journal of Indian Anthropological Society* 44, no. 3: 212–219.

Bagchi, S. S., 2010. *Child Labour in a Third World Urban Situation,* New Delhi: Atlantic Publishers.

Bagchi, S. S., 2010. *Child Labor and the Urban Third World: Toward a New Understanding.* Lanham, MD: University Press of America.

Benjamin, W., 1968. *Illuminations.* New York: Schocken Books.

Cassidy C., 1980. Benign Neglect and Toddler Malnutrition. *Social and Biological Predictors of Nutritional Status, Biological Predictors of Nutritional Status, Physical Growth, And Neurological Development,* edited by L.C. Greene, F. Johnston, 109–33. New York: Academic.

Chandhoke, N., 1999. A Nation Searching for a Narrative in Times of Globalisation. *Economic and Political Weekly.* May 1–7.

Clifford, J. and G.E. Marcus, 1986. *Writing Culture: The Poetics and Politics of Ethnography,* University of California Press, Berkeley, CA.

Cohen, A.P., 1985. *The Symbolic Construction of Community,* Ellis Horwood, London.

Denzin, N. K., 2003. *Performance Ethnography: Critical Pedagogy and the Politics of Culture.* Thousand Oaks CA: Sage.

Edwardes, M., 1963. *Battles of the Indian Mutiny* London; B. T. Batsford Ltd.

Evans Pritchard, E.E. and M. Fortes, eds. 1940. *African Political Systems.* London: Oxford University Press.

Evans-Pritchard, E.E., 1950. *Witchcraft, Oracles and Magic among the Azande.* The Clarendon Press, Oxford.

Geertz, C., 1973. *The Interpretation of Cultures.* Basic Books, New York, NY.

Geertz, C., 1983. *Local Knowledge: Further Essays in Interpretive Anthropology,* Basic Books, New York, NY.

Geertz, C., 1988. *Works and Lives: The Anthropologist as Author.* Polity Press, Cambridge.

OAU, 1982. African (Banjul) Charter on Human and Peoples' Rights (Adopted 27 June 1981, OAU Doc. CAB/LEG/67/3 rev. 5, 21 I.L.M. 58 (1982), entered into force 21 October 1986) Adopted by the eighteenth Assembly of Heads of State and Government June 1981. Nairobi, Kenya.

Ozar, D., 1981. Justice and a Universal Right to Basic Health Care. *Social Science Medicine* 15f: 135–41

Pike, K. L. ed. 1967 [1954]. *Language in Relation to a Unified Theory of Structure of Human Behavior.* 2nd edition. The Hague, Netherlands: Mouton.

Scheper-Hughes, N. ed. 1987. *Child survival: Anthropological Perspectives on the Treatment and Maltreatment of Children.* Boston: Reidel.

Scheper-Hughes, N., 1992. *Death without Weeping: The Violence of Everyday Life in Brazil.* Berkeley: University of California Press.

Schiller, N. G., S. Crystal and D. Lewellen, 1994. Risky Business—The Cultural Construction of Aids Risk Groups. *Social Science & Medicine* 38, no. 10: 1337–1346.

Schirmer, J., A.D. Renteln, and L. Weisberg, 1988. Anthropology and Human Rights: A Selected Bibliography. *Human rights and Anthropology*, edited by Downing, T.E., Kushner, G., 121–97. Cambridge, Mass: Cultural Survival.

Spivak, G. C., 1988. Can the Subaltern Speak? *Marxism and the Interpretation of Culture,* edited by Cary Nelson and Larry Grossberg, 271–313. Chicago: University of Illinois Press.

Spivak, G. C., 1999. *A Critique of Post-Colonial Reason: Toward a History of the Vanishing Present.* Harvard: Harvard University Press.

Spivak, G.C., 2005. Translating Into English. *Nation, Language, and the Ethics of Translation,* eds. S. Bermann and M. Wood. Princeton: Princeton University Press.

UNESCO, 1953. *Report to the UN 1952/53.* Paris: UNESCO.

Wolstenholme, G.E.W and K. Elliott, 1974. Introduction. *Human Rights in Health*, Ciba Foundation Symposium 23, 1–2 (NS) New York: Elsevier.

Notes

1. Major child labor prohibited occupations include transport, cinder picking and clearing ash-pits in railway sideways and workshops, working in catering establishments in railway stations or as vendors or in any establishment where the work involves moving from one platform to another or within a moving train or outside, building railway stations or any work near railway stations or between the railway lines, any work inside a port area, and in any temporarily licensed explosive and fireworks shops.

2. Major child labor prohibited services include beedi making, carpet weaving, cement manufacture and bagging of cement, cloth printing, dyeing and weaving, manufacture of matches, explosives and fireworks, soap manufacturing, wool cleaning, building and construction industry, manufacture of slate pencil, shellac manufacture, tanning and manufacture of leather goods, mica-cutting and splitting, diamond cutting and gem polishing, and any manufacturing industry where poisonous substances like lead, mercury, manganese, chromium, benzene, pesticides and asbestos are used.

3. More recently, in August 2006, the Indian government included domestic work in the list of hazardous work for children and banned the employment of children in the domestic sector.

CHAPTER 12

Culture and Issues of Rights to the Eyes of the Indians with 'Other' Self-identities of Sexuality and Gender

Arnab Das and Pawan Dhall

The definition of 'sexuality'[1] according to the second report[2] resulted from the cooperation of the WHO with the Pan-American Health Organization (PAHO) and the World Association of Sexology (WAS) in 2001, focuses exhaustively on the holistic core of human individual as an interplay of all possible inherent aspects and influencing factors, including biological, psychological, socio-economic, cultural, ethical and religious/spiritual, of life-long manifest or latent experiences and expressions that "we are, what we feel, think and do". The definition of 'gender'[3] is essentially based on 'sex', the biological dimension embracing its variation of "power relations between men and women" only. The essentialism of biology similarly prevails in the definition of 'gender identity,'[4] but it appears to be an internal subjective framework of individual that identifies and performs own sex and gender constructed over time with its essence being 'same', unique and relating to everybody concerned. On the other hand the definition of 'sexual health'[5] is also centred on individuals' personal capabilities, freedom and wellbeing, but equally emphatic on its dimensions of responsibility and harmony directed to social life. Obviously, in seeking universality, the definitions, considered together, appear little ambivalent about their foundations in individual and in society or culture. They have explicit endeavour to focus on essentialism, though they cannot deny the subjugated implications of constructivist and performative dimensions. In fact, the applicability of anything, assumed to be universal, cannot go around the constructs of societies or cultures. The initial statement declaring the sexual rights, "Human rights are above cultural values. If a particular culture has a practice that contravenes a human right, the cultural value should be changed"[6] in the said draft[7] indicates the same need to understand cultures or local constructs to make rights applicable. Over the decades the scholars went for understanding the constructs of culture around sexuality that open up regularly the changing struggle with the problems of adapting the issues of rights and justice to varied societies.

The theoretical understanding of sexuality, sex and gender since last quarter of 20th century challenged essentialism and emphatically shifted to constructivism and other perspectives. The understanding of gender, sexuality and identity has been more oriented to changing and multidimensional society and culture; individuals or groups, rather being treated as foundation, are seen as the agencies of society and culture. This growing understanding problematized the previously understood co-evolving relation between cultures/societies and human rights in the hierarchic world order of states, especially in the diverse landscapes of third World countries. This paradigm shift of looking at the changing cultural diversity poses a fundamental problem relating 'other' sexuality, gendering and human rights.

This paper intends to address the interactive order of heteronormativity and 'other' emerging contexts of gender and sexuality with respect to MSM (men having sex with men) in India as a complex of diverse dimensions of culture and agencies of actions. It is a combination of surveys of literature, ethnographic studies, documents and personal experiences of both the authors dealing with the issues for more than eight years of the first author and for more than 20 years by the second author as an insider to the Indian queer community. Starting from the plurality of understanding of gender and sexuality in and across cultures, the writing focuses on the multifaceted scene of rights and justice for and inside the MSM population in India.

'Other' Sexuality, Gender and Aspects of Culture

Nearly thirty-five years back, Rubin's (1975) influential anthropological contribution on sex and gender for cultural and political analysis, Gagnon and Simon's (1973) revolutionary studies on sexuality, later Vance's (1990, 1991) anthropological reviews of the same may be associated with a series of similar anthropological confirmations of a wide diversity of same-sex issues (e.g. Callender and Kochems 1983; Herdt 1981, 1987, 1997; Herdt and Lindenbaum 1992; Parker et al. 1991; Roscoe 1991, 1998; Turner et al. 1989; Whitam 1986; Wieringa 1989; Williams 1986) that also addressed sexuality and gender as the cultural phenomena (e.g. *berdache*[8] or *xaniths*,[9] *female husbands*,[10] "boy inseminating rituals",[11] "age-structured sexuality"[12] or different other forms,[13] *Hijra*,[14] etc.). The cultural constructions of both gender and sexuality (Ortner and Whitehead 1981) had long been at the centre of attention. Herdt (1984, 1987, 1994, 1997) is outstandingly effective in dealing with the diversity of sex, gender, sexuality in different cultures. However, scholars in anthropology addressed the problems of both essentialist and constructionist (Wieringa 1989; Löfström 1992) views and all the earlier euro-centric anthropological paradigms of dealing with sexuality (Lyons and Lyons 2004). In the paradigm-shift of 'performance theory' by Judith Butler (1990), Kate Bornstein (1994) and later reiterated by Rosalind (1995) gender was gradually understood as performance. The complex relationships of contemporary issues, concepts and dimensions related to sexuality, though old but significantly revived new visions by relatively recent works (Lancaster and Micaela 1997; Parker 2007; Parker and Aggleton. 2007;[15] Robertson 2005). The gender and feminist emphasis on intersexuality, transsexuality, and transgenderism (Ferber et al. 2008) seems to be the effect of studying the central role of gender/sex in cultures around the world (Bullough and Bullough 1993; Colapinto 2000; Griggs 1998; Kessler 2000; Nardi 2000; Parker 2003; Roscoe 1998; Stryker and Whittle 2006; Valentine 2007; Whittle 2000). Most of the works of the last two decades had its primary or secondary agenda of relating culture, sexuality with HIV/AIDS (also Dowsett, Grierson and McNally 2006; Jenkins 2004; Liguori and Lamas 2003; Parker, Herdt and Carballo 1991; Turner et al. eds. 1989), other health issues (e.g. Lingiardi and Drescher 2003) and activism as unavoidable concerns of research. The scholars also paid attention to the details of the process and formation of gendered sexuality of the localities (Carrillo 2002; Chauncey 1994; McDonald 1982; Wikan 1977). The approach of joining gender with sexuality as gendered sexuality for looking into social construction, politics, culture, law and above all health in everyday lives (Heasley and Crane 2003; Holland et al. 1992; Hoogland 1999; Ragnarsson et al. 2008; Ssali 2009; Stearns 1995) are gaining both culture-specific and general appeal to academy. "Men who have sex with men" (MSM) as a behavioral phrase[16] was seen as sub-culturally contextual, otherwise hidden, hard-to-reach, or marginalized population. The works also show that MSM[17] may not necessarily hold the notion of sexual identity or of a distinct sexual community (Alonso and Koreck 1989; Carrier 1989; Parker 1987, 1991). Both issues of exclusivity and inclusivity of sex, gender and sexuality in cultures make the same-sex behavior more complex and diverse.

Men Having Sex with Men (MSM) in India

According to Bruce's work for UNAIDS at 2006,[18] around the world transmission in at least 5% to 10% of all HIV cases occurs in sex between men. The currently engaging MSM is usually estimated at 2% to 5% worldwide. In South and South East Asia 6% to 12% of men are estimated to have same sex relations at some point in their life. HIV prevalence among MSM in India ranges from 4% to17% in some areas. The same draft resonates our common understanding that the usual underestimation of the prevalence of MSM is partly because of reasons, like (a) sensitive issues of sex and gender raised by the HIV/AIDS epidemic, (b) the stigma and denial of preferring MSM behavior in cultures, (c) the diverse circumstantial diversity of the people and situation of engaging MSM practices. The wide prevalence of MSM in space and time in South Asian, including Indian context, is supported by many works, besides the recent ones (TREAT Asia 2006; Jenkins 2004, 2006; UNAIDS 2007). The aforesaid draft (Bruce for UNAIDS 2006) mentions a survey in which 57% of the respondents of MSM in India are married. In South Asia, it is common for young men to have sex with other young men before they have sex with females. The national behavioral surveillance surveys of India (NACO 2002) document that a sample of 1,387 MSM (19–35 years old) from Delhi, Kolkata, Mumbai, Chennai and Bangalore, the median age at first sex (defined as manual, oral or anal) with another male was consistently lower (15–17) than the median age at first sex with females who were usually older than they were.

In India, even starting before the first reported case of HIV, male sexual behaviour (also with same sex) related to health slowly gained the positive attitude from academy and activism since 1980s (Aggarwal, Sharma and Chhabra 2000; Ahmed 1992; Ghosh 1986; Goparaju 1993 and 1994; Gupta 1989; Rao et al. 1994; Reddy et al.1993; Row-Kavi 1993; Saha et al 1980; Savara and Sridhar 1992, 1994). The focus on MSM continued along the decade of 1990s and onwards, at times relating sexuality and gender with culture, rights and health services (Bhende and Jenkins 1998; Chakrapani et al. 2004; Chakrapani et al. 2008; Chakrapani, Newman and Shunmugam 2008; Chan et al. 1998; Dandona et al. 2005; Dhall et al. 2004; Khan et al. 2005; Nag 1996; Setia et al. 2006; Sharma et al. 2001; Thomas et al. 2009). Simultaneously there were more serious efforts to address the issues of sex, gender and sexuality in Indian contexts with or beyond the concern of health from political, activist, cultural and psychological dimensions. (Joseph and Dhall, 2000). Since the early methodological and ethical grounds related to psychological probe on homosexuality (Pradhan et al. 1982b) and psychoanalytic terrain of sexuality in culturally embedded contexts (Akhtar 2005; Kakar 1990; Vaidyanathan and Kripal 1999), the subsequent focus on proliferation of multidimensional discourses of sexuality and gender beyond western stereotypes (John and Nair 1998) converge on the detailed studies on diversity of gender and sexuality. Nanda's works (1984, 1985, 1990, 1999) on the diversity of gender and sexuality, with emphasis on *hijras* had parallels (Jaffrey 1996; Kalliat 1990; Lal 1999; Penrose 2001; Reddy 2005; Sharma 1989; Vyas and Yogesh 1987). This "third gender" consists of hermaphrodites, women who do not menstruate, as well as 'passively' homosexual and castrated men—all who proclaim they are "neither man nor woman" (Nanda 1990). Well-acclaimed studies of non-heterosexual sexuality and relationships according to varied documented narratives in the past and present in cultures of India (Devi 1977; Thadani 1996; Vanita and Kidwai 2000; Vanita 2002) found a suitable ground to proliferate. This issue of diversity related to seeking justice appears much realistically complex in TREAT Asia (2006: 1) paper,

> The most prominent feature of MSM identities in Asia is their diversity. MSM identities include transgender individuals, feminine-acting MSM, their masculine-acting partners, gay-identified men and men who have situational sex with each other. All of this diversity is in theory covered by the term MSM, which focuses on behavior rather than identity, but unfortunately in some locations even this broad term has become associated with single groups—often those that are most visible (e.g., feminine acting MSM) or most politically active (e.g., gay-identified MSM) TREAT Asia (2006: 1).

It points out the linkages among (I) backdrop of present claims of action, (II) different frameworks of understanding same-sex scenario in India, (III) the diverse categories of MSM in India, (IV) use of femininity and masculinity in MSM population of India, (V) the differentiated MSM population with respect to activism in civil society for ensuring rights, justice and legal reforms. All these issues help constituting the pivot of the problems in dealing with the rights and justice to the MSM population in India.

The reviews, data and discussion below are based on the experience of the two authors. The first author supervised two ethnographic projects and four individual dissertations on sexual health of 'high risk' population that had major concerns about the MSM population, especially in urban context of the three provinces of India, namely West Bengal, Bihar and Uttar Pradesh,. The approach was qualitative, though not devoid of quantitative data. The following account focuses on the principal and in cases much overlapping reasons that add to the scene of MSM in India more complex, specific and varied.

(A) The Expanding Scene of Action Claims Inside

With some antecedent local initiatives for organization, finally in 1994, the historic Mumbai national conference for *gay* men raised many of the key issues faced at that time, including HIV among MSM. Humsafar Trust and Naz Foundation International (NFI), as the most large-scale foundations, started to develop and support HIV programming for *gay* men and MSM, including *hijras* and *kothis*, in India and Bangladesh, and afterwards in Nepal and Sri Lanka. Many meetings at sub-regional and provincial levels began to take place from the late 1990s onwards with participatory purposes of MSM civil society. It did not exclude members from both the donor and government sectors as official participants. After in the International AIDS Conference in Bangkok, Thailand, in 2004, the idea for a pan-regional consultation on MSM and HIV initiated the INGO Naz Foundation International (NFI) to appeal for support from UNAIDS and WHO. The sponsorship of what was to become the International Consultation on Male Sexual Health and AIDS in Asia and the Pacific, Risks and Responsibilities (referred to here as the RR process). More than 20 International donor agencies with big contributors, like DFID, USAID, and INGO supported the RR[19] actions. In Asian contexts (a) Epidemiology of HIV infection and risk behaviours, (b) an overview of human rights related to health and male-to-male sex, (c) HIV programme spending, (d) same sex male sexuality and HIV, (e) prevention-based best practices, (f) a summary paper of the pre–RR in-country responses, including the above-mentioned 2006 TREAT Asia paper, came out as the key research issues. The papers were the effect of commissioning by RR with the coordination of NFI and support of UNAIDS and USAID. The subsequent response from all areas of the AIDS in Asia Pacific and other regions with over 30 different countries to the RR consultation received significant support from leading international human rights activists.[20] In addressing MSM related AIDS responses five key measures were declared as "should be regarded as non-negotiable actions for the national governments."[21]

Many of the low and middle income countries, including India, are found to share commonalities in criminalization of Male to Male Sexual Activity

(MMSA), social exclusion from mainstream healthcare systems including infection control planning and services, societal stigma and discrimination against non-mainstream same sex 'orientations', exclusion from human rights initiatives and protections, and lack of comprehensive HIV surveillance (Bayer 2008).

Simultaneously with the above development, the culture-sensitive, politically implicated and activist engagements in the emergent complexity of culture and MSM gender-sexual identities added more empirical focus on

a) situations of 'different' sexual and gender identity and 'marginalized' sexuality (Reddy 2000, 2004, 2005),
b) both the identification/visibility problem of diverse MSM practices and the related minority issues (Kala 1991, 2004),
c) diverse MSM frameworks of sexuality and gender in terms of language, culture, politics, rights issues in India (Asthana and Oostvogels 2001; Khan 2000, 2001, 2005; Cohen 2005; Purkayastha 1999; Hall 1995, 2002, 2005, 2009; Hall and O'Donovan 1996; Reddy 2000, 2004, 2005; Jenkins 2004; Das et al. 2005; Bose and Battacharyya 2007; Chakrapani et al. 2007),
d) the targeted participatory consequences of rights, empowerment, social work and activism (ABVA 1991; PUCL-K, 2003; Arvind and Bhan eds. 2005; Boyce 2007; Joseph, 2005; Lorway, Reza-Paul and Pasha, 2009) and finally,
e) The counterpart of Indian silence of health service and response of the medical world to the issues of MSM (Parekh 2003; Ranade 2009).

With all the aspects of rights and justice, ethics, empowerment, health, and other universal claims of individuals and groups of the men having sex with men in India, both for activist and academic concerns, variation and particularities of MSM practices of India might bring in some unique problems and prospects. Both variation and similarities are observed across social, ethnic and spatial positions of individuals, groups and networks with MSM behavior. Variation and similarity exist in identity of self and that ascribed by others.

(B) The Frameworks of Understanding the Diversity/ Categories of MSM in India

Either or both with emphasis on the past and the present of the local categories of 'other' genders and sexuality in India, the scholars (Cohen 1995, 2005; Hall 2005; Jenkins 2004; Khan, 2000, 2001, 2005; Nanda 1999; Purkayastha 1999; Reddy 2000, 2004, 2005 and others) differ and overlap in their frameworks in accepting any unanimous position. Cohen (1995) studies *hijras* and comments on castration as castration of desire. He introduces *jankhas* and *zenanas* (similar to *kothis*) as "men who sometimes dress like women and dance like *hijras* but do not elect castration" (Cohen 1995: 276). Hall (2005) posits *kothi* as a reference point for other sexualities and not as a distinct identity to claim a space within the sexuality continuum, as they (Hall, 1996) switch between the use of feminine and masculine gender symbols[22]. Almost in the similar vein Jenkins (2004) locates *Kothis* inside the culture, as lesser men and the most stigmatised in the patriarchal, heterosexist and homophobic framework[23]. Non-*kothi* men having sexual engagements with the *kothis* perceive about themselves that they just fool around when they have sex with *kothis,* just discharging, not really having sex, like a 'real man' (Jenkins 2004).[24] In contrast to the somewhat similar positions of Cohen, Hall, Jenkins, Naqvi and Mujtaba, Reddy's ethnographic fieldwork in Hyderabad conceptualizes that *hijras* fall under the umbrella term *kothis* referring to a multitude of identities within the spectrum of male sexuality. Reddy examines the configuration of the related male identities around the axis of act of penetration in sexual intercourse, along with doing other [gendered] works. Reddy (2004) finds out two models of sexuality and gender in male same-sex behaviours: a "gay" model[25] and a "*kothi*" model.[26] Joseph (2002, 2004) addresses complex fabric of orientation, partnership and identity in regional and national contexts. National AIDS Control Organization (NACO) (2002, 2004, 2006 and 2007) tries to reconcile a balance among the positions of health, cultural and political dimensions both in academic and activist contributions, though not achieving the necessary integration of all the nuances of reality. The consideration of high-risk group NACO (2002, 2006)[27] finally led the Union Minister of India for Health and Family Welfare, Dr Anbumani Ramadoss at the XVII International AIDS Conference (3–8 August, 2008) to the clear statement to end the discrimination against MSM population, which is either first or second in rank as high-risk group[28] in India. NACO (2007)[29] reconfirms the definition of MSM ("Men who have Sex with Men") population in terms of the major constituents of *Kothis, Panthis, Double Deckers* and *Hijras*.[30] This definition is inadequate and somewhat misleading to embrace and to understand the diverse population with "MSM" practices, the relations of their interests, their issues of rights and politics, especially of those huge hidden population besides the above identities.

Compared to the academic positions, the activist NAZ Foundation International, one of the largest non-profit organizations for civil society of South Asia working in the HIV/AIDS sector considers to pay due importance to the traditional hetero-normative framework in which all identities may sustain themselves. They consider *Kothi* a sexual minority, a community historically rooted in Indian cultural traditions, as well as a self-identifying label, more a sexual signifier than a gender in the broader framework of *Kothi-Panthi* dynamics. Their comprehension of "*kothi* framework" (Khan 2000) is realistically complex, nuanced and politically empowering for *kothis,* the most vulnerable section of MSM population. Almost similarly, Purkayastha (1999) asserts that gender is the pervasive organizing feature of sex between men in India. There is some consensus between Humsafar Trust and Naz Foundation International to accept MSM as their ground concern. John and Nair (1998) observe in India a proliferation of discourses on sexuality built on already extant and multiple frameworks. Yet, every position is not completely happy with each other.

(C) MSM Population in India Differentiated Inside
It has been already highlighted that the problematic differentiation of MSM population in India is multi-dimensional not only in terms of issues of social

stratification and ethnic identity, etc., but also with respect to identity construct of gendered sexuality. Apparently, it might be assumed that the divide between more urban, educated, more individualistic, femininity-irrespective, elitist, wealthier, 'gays', less publicly visible, more directly in western contact and less educated, group-oriented, femininity-focused, urban-suburban-rural, of lower income strata in contact with local *hijras,* more publicly visible 'kothis' may answer to the differentiation of MSM population in India. But, the divide itself is not so rigid and there is regular mobility and existence of non-*gay*, non-*kothi* MSM population across and beyond the divide. The numerous self-identified *bisexual* and *heterosexual* men are always in sexual contacts with the 'gay' and 'kothi' population. They are rarely visible or join any action for the MSM causes. The section of the 'gays' and sections of the organized 'kothis' might seek ways either to go beyond the GLBT framework or *kothi-panthi* framework respectively in order to obtain any consensual approach to the MSM population on the whole, but the real factions inside make it complex.

For example, if we consider the categories mentioned by the NACO (2007) the MSM include the *Kothis, Panthis, Double Deckers* and *Hijras* in addition to the *gays*, our recent ethnographic findings in *kothi/kothma* domains incorporate the categories as follows:

a) The 'Veli kothis' or 'Aariyal kothmas' prefer loud feminine make-up and dresses in any of their public events. The flamboyance is said to be either or both for self-satisfaction and drawing attention of the 'real men' or panthis/giriyas.

b) 'Koripeshe Kothi' or 'Kare talki kothma' do not choose feminine make-up and outfits, rather choose the masculine outfits, though they prefer to identify themselves with sexual role of insertee.

c) The 'Dupli kothi' is a situational term, principally found in West Bengal, that in spite of their preference of appearing as the Veli kothis, they possess both the desires of penetrating and to be penetrated like and by a 'real man' respectively.

d) 'Dupli Gupti' or 'Double Decker' or 'Do Paratha' is rarely any self-identified identity category, rather is mostly used by the *kothis* to label those 'straight' acting men, who may act both the roles of inserter and insertee in situational sexual performances with other men. In large number they are in individual contacts with the kothi-identified, gay-identified, self-identified heterosexual, self-identified bisexual and the identity-unsure men., but do not identify themselves as *kothi*s; they prefer to remain masculine and to have secret MSM behavior either in sex work or in sex with all the above categories.

In spite of the above categories based on sexual role performance, there is no reason to perceive that each category is homogeneous. Individual *kothis/ kothmas/Dangas/Kowdi bashai* join the network with their respective economic, education and other social-cultural positions. Their needs and aspirations vary, especially in relation to the power structure of the organizations they form or join. The educationally weak and unemployed youth are numerous among the *kothis/kothmas*. In most of the occasions the economic conditions aided by their desire to have sex with men, *kothis* choose the easy option of sex work or joining *hijra* groups and presently of joining the fund-aided organizations. The economically and educationally stronger sections prefer association of organizational power and prestige. Almost all of them are stressed with their past and present feedbacks to their identity from mainstream society. *Gupti* (closeted) is almost always indicative of their guard in the face of the heteronormative gaze on them. The marriages of the *kothis* explain their similar social guard. As the most diverse and vulnerable section of MSM population, the *kothis* are seen to remain bogged with the petty disputes of inter-personal and inter-group conflicts rather than their motivation for enactment of rights. Their everyday lives are remote from their participation in the occasions of activism for any undifferentiated goal. Their problems of differentiation are more rooted in structural differentiation of the whole society in terms of Human Development or class, rather in the top–down activism and piecemeal programs of development.

Hijras / Hijdes (or *Alis,* the south Indian variation) apart from their own identity of neither being men nor women, are also seen as intentional transformation of *kothis,* either to become members of a group under the authority of a *Guruma,* head of a group, who takes all responsibilities of the members or to introduce a self-proclaimed identity or group. The members of the *Hijra* group do not call themselves *Hijras.* The insiders of a group are known to each other as *Akua* and *Chhibri.* The *Akuas* are the non-castrated members of a group and if they castrate their genitals they are considered as *chhibris,* traditionally more respected in a group. The socially marginalized, yet considered being sacred, *hijras* live in groups, connected by networks. Each group is known by its name of settlement, termed as *daira, dera, khol, toli,* etc., according to functional priority of addressing it. The whole cycle of *hijra* life, constituted by initiation into a group, the everyday living, identity maintaining practices, the activities for earning, religious activities, death, inheritance and so on are regulated by distinct rituals and rules. The *chelas* or disciples of Guruma of a group are like sisters (*gotias*) to each other. The *hijra* groups are connected by ancestral, local, regional, even national networks. A *chela* of one group may form a new group in a new place. Some *hijra* groups are close to each other for local, ancestral and filial proximity. The member of one group might at times opt for joining another group in exchange of assets or wealth to the group one quits. In any region there is an implicit hierarchy of different *hijra* groups. Traditionally sustained distances from the mainstream society and paradoxical acceptance of *hijra* phenomenon in Indian society have culminated in forms of security in their secretive seclusion. However, only the *hijras* as less heterogeneous population and socially excluded population might go for mainstreaming and rights to participation in all walks of life. Apart from some particular instances this is not yet a phenomenon of organizational activism.

The self-identified *gays* are usually individualistic. "Coming out" in family or among friends with the identity is very difficult, though more prevalent among the *gays* belonging to the families of higher income groups with more urban–western exposure. If the immediate environment is not congenial they remain similarly closeted in the heteronormative mainstream society. "Coming out" is more a phenomenon for the *gays*. In most of the cases the closeted *gays* cannot hang out comfortably with the 'declared' *gays*. Consequently the movement for sexual partners is not restricted within *gays* themselves. There are many *gays* performing the insertee role (termed as *gay top* or *gay active*) as *parikhs* of the *kothis*. On the other hand there are many self-identified *gays* remaining lifelong closeted, isolated from any network of the *gays*, and even being married, whereas there are self-identified *gays* believing and participating in 'gay' way of life. Many self-identified *gays* believe that the identity is their choice, thus voluntarily alienable.

In sexual performance, though anal sex as the pivotal idea of power in emotional terms, differentiates three ("top", "versatile" and "bottom") or two ("active" and "passive") major individual preferences of the *gays*, there are some, who do not agree with such labels, so also the power relations in terms of roles. There are *gays*, though much lesser than the rest of closeted non-*gay*, non-*Kothi* MSM population, preferring 'no anal', at times called, 'body sex'. Their sexual intimacies are either for lasting relations or just for occasions. They represent the population, most distant from politically viable interest groups and networks. In cases among the *gays*, who are not part of any gay organization, there is an ethnic distance between the Muslim and non-Muslim *gays*. Initially the majority of *gays* were unwilling to form or join any collective goal and action, except those who already started the organizational ventures since the middle of 1990s.

The transgender practices in public are seen mainly among *hijras*, *kothis* and some *gays*. Nonetheless the practices are again differentiated by the contexts and the performers. The outfits and make-up of the *hijras* might appear feminine owing to the uses of feminine clothes, ornaments, make-up and dancing gestures, but in the eyes of the *hijras* they signify symbolically as neither manhood nor womanhood, rather the means to salvation (*nirban*) from desire in a state of third gender. The doubly symbolic transgender appearance though may be used for attracting men, but ideally, it is relegated to second order function of their beingness. This function of attracting men in transgender appearance among *kothis* becomes the priority apart from the self-satisfactory function of a right to expression like or more than women. The transgender demeanor causes a lot of discrimination, assault, stigma and harassment from the mainstream institutions. In fact, there are many *kothis*, who give up their *kothi* identity to accept the membership of a *hijra* group or publicly perform like *hijra*, because the traditional *hijra* identity saves them from more regular and severe assault by the mainstream institutions.

The rest of the MSM population is most difficult to handle and even to identify. The 'real man' (exclusively inserter in sexual performance) claimed by the *kothis* is addressed as 'Parikh' or 'Giriya' by the insiders of the MSM community. Generally this term is not used for self-identification of a 'real man'. If they are not self-identified *gays*, they usually believe themselves as 'straight' (heterosexual) and the representatives of the hetero-normative society. Apart from *gay*, *kothi* and *hijra* and very rare public appearance of self-identified *bisexuals*, the remaining huge male population in MSM practices is invisible. Either they identify themselves as heterosexuals or as unsure about sexual identity or vaguely identify themselves as *bisexuals*. This inseparable and less visible section of MSM population is connected either with the self-identified masculine *gays*, feminine *kothis* or among themselves, but they mostly deny or suppress their identity to be different from the mainstream heteronormative one. Rather they prefer to carry the guilt of having some 'wrong' or 'abnormal' or 'bad' sexual attitude, and behavior, similar to 'addiction' that might be punishable or undesirable or uncomfortably natural with respect to their own heterosexual identity. This idea of inherent personality problem of one's self around his same-sex behavior is observed to be true even among those *kothi* identified and *gay* identified persons, who are not well versed with the understanding of sexuality. A number of CBOS and other organizations dealing with issues of sexual and health rights range apart from the undifferentiated understanding about sexuality, even among their members.

(D) Altering and Using Heteronormativity inside MSM Population

Apart from the *hijras*, it is always uncertain to generalize whether any individual inside MSM population was or is or will be married with a woman, though one insider interpretation of MSM population about *kothis*, who perform transgender self-identification, is of having a woman's soul inside a man's body. It is found regularly among informants irrespective of positions in the society. The transgender performance is more embraced in public by the persons at lower positions in local social hierarchy. These transgender individuals, *kothis* as mentioned above, avail easier access to socially marginalized *hijras* and related networks of sex-work. The supportive insider terms *kothi, koti, kothma* originated from *hijra* vocabulary or the discriminating and abusive term *ladies, chhakka, gandu, mauga* used by heterosexist 'others' identify those men who adopt transgender appearances in public. It indicates an emulative use of heteronormative relationship between feminine men usually assimilating sexually insertee performance and masculine men usually performing sexually inserter role. For self-labeled feminine male persons (*kothis/ kotis/ kothmas/ Danga /Kowdi bashai*) it connotes their 'legitimate' sexual desire for all potentially masculine men able to be sexually insertees, who are termed as *panthis* and such sexually engaging specific individual men as *parikhs/ giriyas/ Kowriya*. However, the same term is not used by the masculine heteronormatively oriented sexual partners of *kothis* to identify themselves. For the latter such sexual acts or relationships might not usually be conceived to distort their heteronormative sexual and gender identity, though it might be considered a subversive from heterosexist act and not socially rewarding if it continues like a visible social bonding between two such men. In most of the cases, the *kothis/ kotis/ kothmas* seek the relationships within the heterosexist framework, whereas the 'outsider' men use it according to their convenience, rarely getting loyal to such relationship with or without any social pressure. Finally, the 'ideal type' of heteronormatively sought relation and pleasure, especially on behalf of *kothis/kotis/ kothmas* engage them in an obsessive journey of desire. Similar desire is true for the *hijras*, who unlike the *kothis/kotis/ kothmas* do not identify themselves as men or women, may seek their 'men' more as stable sexual partners with or without the ideal type of heterosexism. For many reasons, the *hijras*, living in groups and in a network of community are said to share both stable and temporary partners, either in the form of sex work or of sustainable sexual relationship.

However, the *kothi* performance of an individual might be fluid in the sense that many self-identified *kothis* perform 'masculine' inserter roles with their sexual partners, who perform as insertee *kothis* or non-*kothi*, non-*hijra* men preferring insertee role. Between two *kothis* such penetrative performance is usually secretive for getting discriminated among the *kothis* as impure *kothi* in performing both inserter and insertee roles that mark the identity of *dupli/double-decker*. The concept of purity of *kothi* identity is assumed to be originated from *hijra* construct of gendered sexuality. The *hijras* perceive the *kothis* in the first step to the journey of being *hijras*; rest of the men, who are not masculine and not solely inserter are considered as 'impure'/ bad (*bila*). The non-*kothi*, non-*gay*, non-*hijra* men, who prefers to perform the insertee roles remain very much closeted with the fear of being discriminated as feminine for their sexual role preference like women. Such genderisation (feminization/masculinisation) of sexual role is also found among the self-identified *gays* in the "top"–"bottom" and "active"–"passive" range of role preference. In the broad framework/ideal-type of heteronormativity, both sexuality is (un)consciously gendered and performative, not fixed for an individual, but the hierarchic positions of 'femininity' in relation to 'masculinity' work in the same framework, but in varied manners. For *hiras* themselves pro–feminine (but neither-man-nor-woman) and for *kothis* themselves the femininity is considered desirable for themselves. Heterosexist masculinity is conceived as ideal for their partners. Among the *gays* though ideal heteronormativity is not ideal for them, yet masculine–feminine hierarchic divide varies to operate across individuals. For the rest of the MSM population, masculinity is considered more powerful than the femininity. This positional discrimination of genders and gendered sexuality acts upon the well-being of the femininity preferring men across the MSM population. A large section of the self-identified heterosexual anal insertee population perceives their MSM behavior as pleasure-seeking activities of any heterosexual man. This behavior is defended as not more seriously than mere urge for seeking regular 'discharge' of any man, though secretively in order to avoid stigma of wrong/bad behavior.

(E) Practices and Problems of Health

To begin and end with such differently voiced perception—the 'otherness', 'queerness' and everything denying and against the 'normal' about same-sex sexuality and gender issues in the eye of heteronormatively determined universe offer a fundamentally unhealthy or health-altering lives to the MSM population—does assert the need of deep focus on the health-altering, rather than unhealthy practices of the people. The dominant heteronomative voices leave little or no space for alternative and 'secret' discourses. The silence and secrecy associated with institutional stigma and discrimination may provide ideal conditions for escalation of the AIDS epidemic (Mann 1987; Mawar et al. 2005). Even the escalation of epidemic mechanically attaches 'safer sex' to the existing practices, surely with the presumption that the HIV epidemic in India is "predominantly heterosexual" (National AIDS Control Organization [NACO] 2005). It seems better not to add fuel to further stigmatization of same-sex sexuality at the centre of the epidemic, but in other way it helps avoiding the vista of understanding same-sex practices and concerns of multidimensional health. To be little gross and brief, the most prevalent questions of health are reduced to access to communication and material supports to safer sex knowledge, behavior, attitude and practice and health services for treatments. Inside the studied scene of MSM population, the questions of health are reduced again to the (ab)use of condoms and utility of STD-STI-HIV check-ups, advice and treatments. The provisions of the health service are enjoyed by the men directly or indirectly connected to the MSM related organizations.

Except 'modernly' molded *gay-* and *bisexual-* identified men and the 'safer sex' understood as use of condoms poses some abiding constraints coercing the 'free', untamed desires of sexuality. It is difficult to delineate how far the desire is learnt from the heteronormative mainstream culture from how far it is the result of conflict with the same. Even in sex work, with desirable clients the *kothi*s choose to give and take best of pleasure that may not be derived from 'safer sex'.

> Nobody among us may live happy and peaceful like 'normal' people, because everybody cheats and lies to the partner, ... None remains loyal to his relationship for longer, except a very few couples.... We go always for more, more pleasure, more money, more chances. . . . The bisexuals and such other apparently straight men are worst, as they only use us and forget us. . . . . Society rejects us and we regularly reject each other more casually. .....You may come across several of us with numerous cut-marks on their limbs, so that we may feel and our boyfriends may see the extreme sadness and frustration our life could lead to! Ask anybody here how many suicidal attempts one has committed till now. Yet we try to make humour always, like to dress up beautifully, dance, sing, party and perform to our best, so that we may sustain our zest for life. ....But yes, what you pointed out is true; principally the kothis, and also some gays are always obsessed with their romantic and erotic desires, little focused on all the other important aspect of life.

The above excerpt from the conversation with a *gay*-identified, but leader of *kothi*-based organization speaks a lot of their social and psychological aspects of health. All the social processes of injustice resulting in some sort of both-way exclusion with the mainstream, including often their own families and relatives, their selfhood operates unrealistically leading them to helpless troubles, stresses and trauma that they cannot handle. Grossly speaking the group orientation helps many of them sublimation, but other 'defense mechanisms' lead to personality traits and types of obsessive, obsessive compulsive, histrionic, border-line. There are advocacy programs, there are counselors in the fund-aided organizational activities, but they hardly address their problems effectively regarding social and psychological aspects of health.

(F) Civil Society, Injustice, Rights, Legislature and Activism

Discrimination, stigmatisation, harassment, extortion, marginalization, exclusion, alienation, teasing, torture and so on are the phenomenal processes which almost each of which every person in MSM population had to face either concretely or potentially at any point of time of their lives. The risks and damages inherent in becoming a *kothi/hijra/gay* emerge from the above processes of injustice embedded in all the institutions of society and culture right from the family to state. In Indian context, the patriarchic heteronormativity is more active than homophobia, if compared to the West. It is really difficult to rightly apportion the responsibilities of civil society and its organization and those of the state. Both civil society and state have their power-wielding heteronormative worldviews at the centre with their structural forces of control of silencing those non-dominant views at margins. Such "structural violence is silent . . . Structural violence may be seen as about as natural as the air around us" (Galtung 1969: 173). They might not be visible as direct, but these indirect forms of oppression evolve into direct forms of oppression, such as violence and abuse, when stigmatized groups deny accepting the unequal status ascribed by the dominant voice (Link and Phelan, 2001).

The contemporary assessment may render more importance to civil society and its organizations to continue its long struggle for the rights historically connecting different societies of the world including India. MSM and other sexual minority self-help endeavors, wherever they have taken place in the world, have been about community building, celebrating sexual diversity, and gaining dignity of life—even while questioning social dogma. While the phenomena of same-sex sexual relations being lived out in various degrees of openness in different societies and cultures, as well as queer social and sexual networking are centuries old, a political revolution of sorts started in Europe in the mid-19th century with the writings of Karl Ulrichs[31] of Germany and Oscar Wilde of Britain.[32] Later, Alfred Kinsey's research on both male and female sexuality in the 1940s and Evelyn Hooker's[33] work in 1953 (both in the USA) added momentum to queer collectivization. In the *1960s and 1970s*, views on sexuality changed considerably in different parts of the world. The year 1969 saw the Stonewall Riots in New York, a seminal event just waiting to happen, in protest against long tolerated police violence and discrimination. This single event brought together several lesbian, gay, bisexual and transgender people under a common political umbrella, kicking off first efforts at an organized queer rights movement in the USA. The decades of *1970s and 1980s* saw the post Stonewall Riots queer organizing in the USA, which gradually inspired or catalyzed similar movements in other countries like the UK, Canada, Germany, Brazil, South Asian Diaspora and India. Queer movements in many countries also linked up with other social movements, particularly the women's movements. Besides, the larger queer movement also developed different strands. For instance, lesbians differed from gay men on certain principles and without breaking away entirely, developed an independent line of action. Similar trends were also seen with regard to bisexual and transgender people in later years.[34] Through the *1980s and 1990s*, an entire range of social action was undertaken by the queer movements everywhere—in the spheres of support group formation, culture, education, law, health and livelihood. Legal reform battles and advocacy in multilateral forums took centre stage in several countries. International groups like the International Lesbian and Gay Association and International Gay and Lesbian Human Rights Commission lead many of these efforts.

The decade of 1980s saw a new front open in the context of the HIV epidemic, which forced the queer movement to reprioritize its actions. Some people argue that the epidemic dissipated and distracted the gay and bisexual men's strands of the movement from its political agenda. Others feel that the epidemic, primarily fuelled through the sexual route, forced societies (like India's) to re-examine their closed-door attitudes towards gender, sex and sexuality.

In fact, today it is difficult to ignore the issue of HIV among sexual minorities in India. In recent years, HIV prevalence among males who have sex with males (including male-to-female transgender people) has been nearly 20 times higher than in the overall adult population.[35] Many activists who work to prevent and treat HIV among sexual minorities and other vulnerable groups say that this is not about catering to a special right. It is about the universal right to health and life. In the Indian scenario, queer organizing began sporadically in the *late 1970s and early 1980s*. However, from the middle of 1980s, the queer South Asian Diaspora became increasingly active in the USA and the UK. This inspired action within India, which started in several bigger cities in the early 1990s, and from the middle of that decade, there was a spread into smaller towns and rural areas. Through the 1990s and 2000s, there was greater visibility of queer people, advocacy was undertaken with a range of stakeholders, links were forged with other human rights movements, and the first steps towards legal and policy reforms were initiated. In the *early 1990s*, "Bombay Dost", India's first queer magazine started publishing. The year 1994 saw the first ever conference for gay men and other MSM in Mumbai organized by Humsafar Trust and Naz Foundation. In 1999, Kolkata in India saw its very first queer pride walk involving only 15 people. Last year, there were similar marches in six cities with the numbers running into a few thousands.

While quite similar to its western counterparts in appearance and approaches, the Indian queer movement has a crucial difference. Indian culture in the ancient and even medieval times seems to have had tacit acceptance of gender and sexual diversity (as captured remarkably well in recent works on Indian literary history). Even if there was no open acceptance, there was also little outright condemnation or criminalization of homosexuality or the transgender phenomenon. At least not till the British introduced the draconian Section 377 of the Indian Penal Code, which sought to criminalize and punish specific sexual acts (that were considered "unnatural" and "against the order of nature") with a fine and long term imprisonment. In actuality, it went far beyond and impacted on all same-sex sexual and romantic relations. This was not the case before. Thus in many ways, the Indian queer movement has not been just about modern political articulations but also about reclaiming our earlier tolerance of gender and sexual diversity. Even today places like Konark and Khajuraho show how our beautiful temple architecture from medieval times elevated sexual diversity.

The Indian queer movement's ambitions are well articulated in a charter of demands included in "Less Than Gay – A Citizens' Report on the Status of Homosexuality in India". This document, a first of its kind and an inspiration for an entire generation of queer activists in India, was published in 1991 by AIDS Bhedbhav Virodhi Andolan, India's first civil rights group to take up the cause of human rights around HIV, sexuality, sex work and substance use. In more recent times, the Indian (and worldwide) queer movements have based their demands and actions on the Yogyakarta Principles (2006), which confirm legal standards for how governments and other actors should end violence, abuse, and discrimination against sexual minorities and ensure full equality. The United Nations 2008 declaration on sexual orientation and gender identity, signed by 67 countries, clearly acknowledges that the universality of human rights includes sexual orientation and gender identity. Fortunately, the Indian legal environment has not been entirely bleak for sexual minorities, which is a redeeming feature of our Constitution as well as larger social milieu. The Indian Constitution protects the rights to equality, non-discrimination, freedom of speech, and personal life and liberty. Several provisions of the Indian Penal Code and Criminal Procedure Code and the Human Rights Protection Act of 1993 also provide support. It is on grounds of these progressive provisions that several campaigns for legal and policy reforms have been undertaken by sexual minority and other human rights initiatives. For instance, the public interest litigation filed by Naz Foundation (India) Trust in 2001 in the Delhi High Court against Section 377. This action led to the landmark ruling by the court on July 2, 2009 that Section 377 be read down to exclude sexual relations of any kind from the ambit of the law provided such relations are based on mutual consent among adults and are practiced in private. The case against Section 377 is now being heard in the Supreme Court, where several petitions have been filed both in favour and against the Delhi High Court's ruling. Interestingly, this development has taken nearly four decades since Britain dropped similar legal provisions of its own!

There are also other campaigns under way for framing of a comprehensive sexual assault law, and undertaking reforms in the Police Act. Many of these initiatives have drawn on international covenants like the International Bill of Gender Rights, Universal Declaration of Human Rights (UDHR), International Covenant on Civil and Political Rights (ICCPR) and the European Convention on Human Rights. Other changes are also visible on the ground. There is now better documentation by civil society agencies of human rights violations. More and more individuals are filing police complaints against sexuality based violence. Larger civil society protests (not confined to queer support groups) against police high-handedness and deception under the pretext of Section 377 have increased—as witnessed after the wrongful arrest of outreach workers of a sexual health NGO in 2001 in Lucknow, or harassment in a Kolkata police station of peer educators and leaders of another community based organization in

2005. Or even as recent as 2010, when first there was the shameful dismissal of a professor from a renowned university on grounds of his sexual orientation, and then when he fought back, his death under unnatural circumstances (Late Dr. Shrinivas Ramchandra Siras, Reader and Chairman of Modern Indian Languages at Aligarh Muslim University).

Several corporate and civil society agencies have introduced prohibition of discrimination on grounds of sexual orientation in their human resources policies. Gender and queer studies have made an appearance in university curricula. Gender and sexuality education for medical service providers, key stakeholders often accused of homophobia and transphobia, is increasingly gaining ground. Same-sex love has made an appearance in popular cultural expression—Hindi films, television, Indian popular music as well as print and theatre media. Although the public visibility of any sort of same-sex sexual intimacy is not rewarded, sustained friendship among men, regular sharing of lives among men, 'natural' intimacy of same sex in public domains, sanctioned choice of life-long celibacy of men, etc., may indicate the homo–sociable tolerance in Indian societies. Paradoxically it shields same-sex sexual intimacy for those MSM practices, which operate as closeted, even for a lifetime. The remarkable weakness in institutions of religion is combated by the above organizations.

Despite Indian society's general acceptance and tolerance over time in historical context, the lack of specific public knowledge and understanding of men who have sex with men (MSM) or same-sex sexual orientation is mainly due to colonially discontinued development. Illegal in India since 1861 codified by a British colonial law prohibiting anal intercourse against the order of nature with any man, woman or animal homosexuality was decriminalized by the High Court of Delhi on 2 July 2009. It ruled that the provision in Section 377 of India's Penal Code that criminalizes private consensual sex between same-sex adults violates the country's Constitution and international human rights conventions. "Consensual sex amongst adults is legal," and the rule "includes even gay sex."[36] Before that Indian and international human rights organizations have documented human rights violations against sexual minorities (People's Union for Civil Liberties, Karnataka [PUCL-K], 2003), the transgendered community (PUCL-K, 2001), and HIV/AIDS peer outreach workers from MSM and sex worker communities (Human Rights Watch, 2002) in India.

The legal battle currently under way for the revision of Section 377 of Indian Penal Code is crucial from the rights perspective. But at the most, a reading down of the law will lead to decriminalization of something that is not criminal in the first place. What about equity and positive acceptance of gender and sexual diversity as a way of life and in that context what about acceptance for issues like same-sex marriages, property inheritance by same-sex 'marital' partners or 'spouses' and child adoption by MSM?

Conclusion

The ongoing legal battles will require further legal reforms, but such legal reforms also require a groundswell of positive and supportive out-of-court public opinion. That means social inclusion of MSM in a larger sense that can contribute to such opinion building. One way for queer activists to achieve such social inclusion would be for more MSM, transgender and *Hijra* individuals to have space in the country's health and development programs. They need to tap into the social inclusion 'political' agenda of the government. Greater access for such individuals to social entitlements that others take for granted, like bank accounts, insurance, citizenship identity documents, food security, education and employment, opportunities for commercial enterprise and progressive media visibility can help 'normalize' their presence in society. But change makers inside the MSM communities, whether established activists or others, will have to tackle the fault lines across different gender and sexual identities, some of which this paper has highlighted. It needs a co-evolution of the understanding everyday dynamics of constructivist/performative order of identity in varied spaces of Indian society and their reciprocal integration with activism in the civil, legal, state, personal and other public spheres that would empower the identities from inside. Whether *Hijras* are entitled to a greater piece of the resources pie than the *Kothis*, or *Kothis* or feminized MSM are less able to negotiate the impact of discriminatory laws like Section 377 than 'straight acting' *gay* men because of socio-economic disadvantages, or whether *Duplis* are more deserving of resources support, will have to be settled 'internally' by the communities and their leaders. The rural–small–town–big city divide among MSM will also have to be taken into account (Dhall 2011).[37] Otherwise, chances are that the communities that will play into the hands of the system that perpetrates omnipresent structural violence as status quo will be only too happy to see the threat posed by gender and sexual diversity dissipated by wasteful rivalry.

Acknowledgments

This paper owes much credit to the UGC-UPE project titled "The Growing Constructs of Networks, Subcultures and other Social Differentiations of Sexuality and/ or Gender in Local Indian Contexts and Their Relationships with the Issues of Health".

References

AIDS Bhedbhav Virodhi Andolan., 1991. *Less than Gay: A Citizens' Report on the Status of Homosexuality in India.* New Delhi: ABVA Publication.

Aggarwal, O. A.K. Sharma and P. Chhabra, 2000. Study in Sexuality of Medical College Students in India. *Journal of Adolesc. Health* 26, no. 3: 226–9.

Ahmed, S. I., 1992. *Truck Drivers Are Vulnerable Group in North-East India.* An abstract published in the Second International Congress on AIDS in Asia and the Pacific. Randwick, Australia: AIDS Society of Asia and the Pacific.

Akhtar, S., ed. 2005. *Freud along the Ganges: Psychoanalytic Reflections on the People and Culture of India.* New York: Other Press.

Alonso, A. M., and Koreck, M. T. 1989. Silences: Hispanics, AIDS, and Sexual Practices. *Differences: A Journal of Feminist Cultural Studies*, 1(1): 101–124.

Arvind, N. and G. Bhan, eds. 2005. *Because I Have a Voice: Queer Politics in India*. New Delhi: Yoda Press.

Asthana, S. and R. Oostvogels, 2001. The Social Construction of Male 'Homosexuality' in India: Implications for HIV Transmission and Prevention. *Social Science and Medicine* 25: 707–721.

Baldauf, I., 1988. *Die Knabeliebe in Mittelasien*. Berlin: Das Arabische Buch.

———. 1990. Boylove, folksong, and literature in Central Asia. *Paidika* 2, no. 2: 12–31.

Bayer, R., 2008. Stigma and the Ethics of Public Health: Not can we but should we? *Social Science and Medicine* 67: 463–472.

Bhende, A.A. and C. Jenkins, 1998. Sexual Culture and the Risk Environment of HIV/AIDS. *AIDS* 12: 51–8.

Bondyopadhyay, A. and S. Khan, 2002 and 2004. *Against the Odds*. Dhaka and Delhi: Bandhu Social Welfare Society/Naz Foundation International.

Bornstein, K., 1994. *Gender Outlaw: On Men, Women, and the Rest of Us*. New York: Routledge.

Bose, B. and S. Bhattacharyya, eds. 2007. *The Phobic and the Erotic: The Politics of Sexualities in Contemporary India*. Calcutta: Seagull.

Boyce, P., 2007. Conceiving Kothis: Men who have Sex with Men in India and the Cultural Subject of HIV Prevention. *Med Anthropol* 26, no. 2: 175–203.

Bullough, V. and B. Bullough, 1993. *Cross Dressing, Sex and Gender*. Philadelphia: University of Pennsylvania Press.

Butler, J., 1990. *Gender Trouble: Feminism and the Subversion of Identity*. New York and London, Routledge.

Callender, C. and L. M. Kochems, 1983. The North American Berdache. *Current Anthropology* 24: 443–470.

Carrier, J. M., 1989. Gay liberation and coming out in Mexico. *Journal of Homosexuality* 17, no. 3–4: 225–52.

Carrillo, H., 2002. I Am Normal: Gender-Based Categories of Sexual Identity in the Night is Young. *Sexuality in Mexico in the Time of AIDS*: 37–59.

Carstairs, G. M., 1956. Hinjra and Jiryan: Two Derivatives of Hindu Attitudes to Sexuality. *British Journal of Medical Psychology* 29: 128–138.

———. 1968. *The Twice-Born: A Study of a Community of High-Caste Hindus*. London: The Hogarth Press.

Chakrapani, V., Babu, and P. T. Ebenezer, 2004. Hijras in Sex Work Face Discrimination in the Indian Health-care System. *Research for Sex Work* 7: 12–14.

Chakrapani, V., P.A. Newman, M. Shunmugam, A. McLuckie and F. Melwin, 2007. Structural Violence against Kothi-identified Men who have Sex with Men in Chennai, India: A Qualitative Investigation. *AIDS Educ Prev* 19, no. 4: 346–64.

Chakrapani, V., P.A. Newman and M. Shunmugam, 2008. Secondary HIV Prevention among Kothi-identified MSM in Chennai, India. *Cult Health Sex* 10, no. 4: 313–27.

Chan R. Kavi A. R, Carl G, Khan S, Oetomo D, Tan M. L, Brown T. 1998. HIV and Men who have Sex with Men: Perspective from Selected Asian Countries. *AIDS* 12: 559–568.

Chauncey, G., 1994. *Gay New York: Gender, Urban Culture, and the Making of the Gay Male World, 1890–1940.* New York, NY: Basic Books.

Cohen, L., 1995. The Pleasures of Castration: The Postoperative Status of *Hijras, Jankhas* and Academics. *Sexual Nature, Sexual Culture,* edited by P. R. Abramson and S. D. Pinkerton, 276–304. Chicago: University of Chicago Press.

———. 2005. The Kothi Wars: AIDS Cosmopolitanism and the Morality of Classification. *Sex in Development: Science, Sexuality, and Morality in Global Perspective,* edited by A. Vincanne and S. L. Pigg, 269–303. Durham and London: Duke University Press.

Colapinto, J., 2000. *As Nature Made Him: The Boy who was Raised as a Girl.* London: HarperCollins.

Dandona, L., R. Dandona, J.P. Gutierrez, G.A. Kumar, S. McPherson and S.M. Bertozzi, 2005. Sex Behaviour of Men who have Sex with Men and Risk of HIV in Andhra Pradesh, India. *AIDS* 19, no. 6: 611–19.

Das, A., R. Chakrabarty and A. Das Banerjee, 2005. The Genders and the Sexuality: The Categories and the Range in Contexts of the Urban Indian Constructs. In *Adaptation to Changing Environment: Studies in Anthropology,* edited by R. Roy, 38–57. Kolkata: University of Calcutta.

Delph, E. W., 1978. *The Silent Community. Public Homosexual Encounter.* Beverly Hills: Sage.

Devi, S., 1977. *The World of Homosexuals.* Delhi: Vikas.

Dhall, P., A. Hazra, G. Mohammed, R. Chakraborty, A. Ray Chaudhuri and S.S. Raghavan, 2004. Capacity Building of Agencies Working with MSM in Eastern India through an HIV/AIDS Support Centre. Paper presented at the *International Conference On AIDS* (Jul 11–16) Bangkok, Thailand.

Dowsett, G. W., J.W. Grierson, and S.P. McNally, 2006. *A Review of Knowledge about the Sexual Networks and Behaviours of Men who have Sex with Men in Asia.* La Trobe University, Melbourne, Australia: Australian Research Centre in Sex, Health and Society.

Evans-Pritchard, E.E., 1970. Sexual Inversion among the Azande. *American Anthropologist* 72: 1428–1434.

Ferber, A. L. K. Holcomb and T. Wentling, eds. 2008. *Sex, Gender, and Sexuality: The New Basics.* New York: Oxford University Press.

Foster, S. W., 1990. Afghanistan. *Encyclopedia of Homosexuality* edited by W. R. Dynes, 17–19 (1). New York and London: Garland Publication

Gagnon, J. and W. Simon, 1973. *Sexual Conduct: The Social Sources of Human Sexuality.* Chicago: Aldine,

Galtung, J., 1969. Violence, Peace and Peace Research. *Journal of Peace Research* 6: 167–191.

Ghosh, T. K., 1986. AIDS: A Serious Challenge to Public Health. *J Indian Med Assoc* 84, no. 1: 29–30.

Goode, E. and R. Troiden, eds. 1974. *Sexual Deviance and Sexual Deviants.* New York: William Morrow.

Goparaju, L., 1993. Unplanned, Unsafe: Male Students Sexual Behaviour. Paper Presented at Workshop on *Sexual Aspects of AIDS/STD Prevention in India,* Tata Institute of Social Sciences, Mumbai.

———. 1994. Discourse and Practice: Rural–Urban Differences in India. Paper presented to IUSSP seminar on *Sexual Subcultures, Migration and AIDS, Thailand* (February 27 to March 3).

Griggs, C., 1998. *S/He: Changing Sex and Changing Clothes.* New York: New York University Press.

Gupta, S.C., 1989. Editorial: Psychological Sequelae of AIDS. *Indian Journal of Clinical Psychology* 16, no. 1: v–vi.

Hall, K., 1995. Lip Service on the Fantasy Lines. *Gender Articulated: Language and the Socially Constructed Self,* edited by K. Hall and M. Bucholtz, 183–216. New York: Routledge.

———. 1996. *Hijra/Hijrin: Language and Gender Identity.* Unpublished PhD Dissertation. University of California, Berkley.

———. 1997. Go Suck your Husband's Sugarcane! Hijras and the Use of Sexual Insult. *Queerly Phrased: Language, Gender, and Sexuality,* edited by A. Livia and K. Hall. Oxford: Oxford University Press.

———. 2005. Intertextual Sexuality: Parodies of Class, Identity, and Desire in Liminal Delhi. *Journal of Linguistic Anthropology* 15, no. 1: 125–144.

———. 2009. Boys' Talk: Hindi, Moustaches, and Masculinity in New Delhi. *Gender and Spoken Interaction* edited by P. Pichler and E. Eppler, 139–162. Houndmills, Basingstoke: Palgrave Macmillan.

———. 2002. 'Unnatural' Gender in Hindi. *Gender Across Languages: The Linguistic Representation of Women and Men,* edited by M. Hellinger and H. Bussman, 133–162. Amsterdam: John Benjamins.

Hall, K. and O'Donovan, V., 1996. Shifting Gender Positions Among Hindi-speaking Hijras. *Rethinking Language and Gender Research: Theory and Practice,* edited by V. Bergvall, J. Bing, and A. Freed, 228–266. London: Longman.

Heasley, R. and B. Crane, eds. 2003. *Sexual lives: A Reader on the Theories and Realities of Human Sexualities.* New York: McGraw Hill.

Herdt, G., ed. 1984. *Ritualized Homosexuality in Melanesia.* Berkeley: University of California Press.

———. 1981. *Guardians of the Flutes. Idioms of Masculinity: A Study of Ritualized Homosexual Behavior.* New York: McGraw Hill.

———. 1987. *The Sambia. Ritual and Gender in New Guinea.* New York: Holt, Rinehart and Winston.

———. 1994. Notes and Queries on Sexual Excitement in Sambia Culture. *Etnofoor* 7, no. 2: 25–41.

———. 1997. *Same Sex, Different Cultures. Exploring Gay and Lesbian Lives.* Boulder CO: Westview Press,

Herdt G., and S. Lindenbaum, eds. 1992. *The Time of AIDS: Social Analysis, Theory and Method.* Newbury Park, CA: Sage Publications.

HIV InSite, 2000. *Gay Men and Men who have Sex with Men.* http://hivinsite.ucsf.edu/topics/gay_men_men_who_have_sex_with_men/ (accessed March 5, 2005).

Holland, J., C. Ramazanoglu, S. Sharpe and R. Thomson, 1992. Pleasure, Pressure and Power: Some Contradictions of Gendered Sexuality. *The Sociological Review* 40, no. 4: 645–74.

Hoogland, R. C., 1999. First Things First: Freud and the Question of Primacy in Gendered Sexuality. *Journal of Gender Studies* 8, no. 1: 53–56.

Human Rights Watch. 2002. *Epidemic of Abuse—Police Harassment of HIV/AIDS Outreach Workers in India.* Washington; London: Human Rights Watch.

Humphreys, L., 1970. *Tearoom Trade. Impersonal Sex in Public Places.* Chicago: Aldine.

Jaffrey, Z., 1996. *The Invisibles: A Tale of the Eunuchs of India.* New York: Pantheon Books

Jenkins, C., 2004. *Male Sexuality, Diversity and Culture: Implications for HIV Prevention and Care.* Geneva, Switzerland: UNAIDS.

———. 2006. Male Sexuality and HIV: The Case of Male-to-male Sex. *Background Paper: Risks and Responsibilities.* New Delhi: Male Sexual Health and HIV in Asia and the Pacific International Consultation.

John, M. E. and J. Nair, eds. 1998. *A Question of Silence? The Sexual Economics of Modern India.* New Delhi: Kali for Women.

Joseph, S., 2004. *Social Work Practice and Men who have Sex with Men.* New Delhi: Sage Publication

———. 2002. Sexual Orientation, Sexual Partnership and Sexual Identity of MSM in India. Paper presented in the *International Conference on AIDS* (Jul 7–12).

———. 2004. Sexual Orientation, Sexual Partnership, and Sexual Identity of MSM in Kolkata, India. Paper presented in the *International Conference on AIDS* (July 11–16). Bangkok, Thailand.

———. 2005. *Social Work Practice and Men who have Sex with Men.* New Delhi, Thousand Oaks, London: Sage Publications.

Joseph, S. and P. Dhall, 2000. 'No Silence Please, We're Indians!'—Les-Bi-Gay Voices from India. *Different Rainbows,* edited by Peter Drucker. London: Millivres Ltd.

Kakar, S., 1990. *Intimate Relations: Exploring Indian Sexuality.* Chicago: University of Chicago Press,

Kala, A., 2004. *Invisible Minority: The Unknown World of the Indian Homosexual.* New Delhi: Dynamic Books.

———. 1991. *Invisible Minority: The Unknown World of the Indian Homosexual.* New Delhi: Dynamic Books.

Kalliat, P., 1990. *Jareena: Portrait of a Hijra.* A 25-minute Documentary Exploring the Life of a Transsexual and Her Community in South India. New York: Third World Newsreel.

Kessler, S. J., 2000. *Lessons from the Intersexed.* New Brunswick, NJ: Rutgers University Press.
Khan, S. and T. Khilji, 2002. *Pakistan- Enhanced HIV/AIDS Program: Social Assessment and Mapping of Men who have Sex with Men (MSM) in Lahore, Pakistan.* Report for the World Bank. Naz Foundation International.
Khan, S., 2000. Males who have Sex with Males in South Asia: A Kothi Framework. *Pukaar (Newsletter of the NAZ Foundation International)* 31: 12–13 and 22–23.
———. 2005. *Male-to-male sex and HIV/AIDS in India: A Briefing Summary.* Naz Foundation International. http://www.nfi.net/downloads/knowledge_centre/NFI%20publications/articles%20and%20essays/2005_MSM%20and%20HIV%20in%20Indiabrief.pdf (accessed June 04, 2010).
———. 2001. Culture, Sexualities, and Identities: Men who have Sex with Men in India. *Journal of Homosex* 40, no. 3–4: 99–115.
Khan, S.I., A.T. Coghlan, P. Girault and D. Prybylski, 2005. *Bandhu Social Welfare Society.* Family Health International MSM Program Evaluation, unpubblished report.
Lal, V., 1999. The Hijras of India and the Cultural Politics of Sexuality. *Social Text* 17, no. 6: 112–38.
———. 1997. Not this, not that: The *Hijras* of India and the Cultural Politics of Sexuality. *Social Text* 17, no. 4: 119–40.
Liguori, A. L. and M. Lamas, 2003. Commentary: Gender, Sexual Citizenship and HIV/AIDS Culture. *Health and Sexuality* 5, no. 1: 87–90.
Lingiardi, V. and J. Drescher, eds. 2003. *The Mental Health Professions and Homosexuality: International Perspectives.* New York: The Haworth Medical Press.
Link, B.G. and J.C. Phelan, 2001. Conceptualizing stigma. *Annual Review of Sociology* 27: 363–385.
Löfström, J., 1992. Sexuality at Stake: The Essentialist and Constructionist Approaches to Sexuality in Anthropology. *Suomen Antropologi* 17, no. 3: 13–27.
Lorway, R., S. Reza-Paul and A. Pasha, 2009. On Becoming a Male Sex Worker in Mysore: Sexual Subjectivity, "Empowerment," and Community-Based HIV Prevention Research. *Med Anthropol Quarterly 23*, no. 2:142–60.
Harriet, D. L. and A.P. Lyons, 2004. *Irregular Connections : A History of Anthropology and Sexuality.* Lincoln: University of Nebraska Press.
Mann, J.M., 1987. AIDS—A Global Perspective. *Western Journal of Medicine* 147, no. 6: 693–95.
Mawar, N., S. Sahay, A. Pandit and U. Mahajan, 2005. The Third Phase of HIV Pandemic: Social Consequences of HIV/AIDS Stigma and Discrimination and Future Needs. *Indian Journal of Medical Research* 122: 471–484.
McDonald, G J., 1982. Individual Difference in Coming out Process for Gay Men: Implications for Theoretical Models. *Journal of Homosexuality* 8, no. 1: 47–60.

National AIDS Control Organization (NACO), 2004. *Annual report 2002–04.* New Delhi: NACO, Ministry of Health and Family Welfare, Government of India.

———. 2005. An Overview of the Spread and Prevalence of *HIV/AIDS in India.* http://www.nacoonline.org/ facts_overview.htm (accessed January 2, 2005).

———. 2006. *HIV/AIDS Epidemiological Surveillance and Estimation Report for the Year 2005.* New Delhi: NACO, Ministry of Health and Family Welfare, Government of India.

———. 2007. *Targeted Interventions under NACP-III: Volume I: Core High Risk Groups.* New Delhi: Ministry of Health and Family Welfare, Government of India.

———. 2002. *National Baseline High Risk and Bridge Population Behavioral Surveillance Survey*, Ministry of Health and Family Welfare, Government of India, New Delhi.

Nag, M., 1996. *Sexual Behaviour and AIDS in India.* New Delhi: Vikas Publishing.

Nanda, S., 1985. The Hijras of India: Cultural and Individual Dimensions of an Institutionalized Third Gender Role. *Journal of Homosex* 11, no. 3–4: 35–54.

———. 1984. The Hijras of India. A Preliminary Report. *Med Law*, 3(1): 59–75.

———. 1990. *Neither Man nor WomanL: The Hijras of India.* Belmont Calif: Wadsworth.

———. 1999. *Gender Diversity: Crosscultural Variations.* Illinois: Waveland Press, Inc.

Naqvi, N. and H. Mujtaba, 1997. Two Baluchi *Buggas,* a Sindhi *Zenana,* and the status of *Hijras* in contemporary Pakistan. *Islamic homosexualities: Culture, History and Literature,* edited by S. O. Murray and W. Roscoe. 262–266. New York and London: New York University Press,

Nardi, P.M., ed. 2000. *Gay Masculinities.* Thousand Oaks, Calif.: Sage Publications.

Opler, M.E., 1960. The Hijara (Hermaphrodites) of India and Indian National Character: A Rejoiner. *American Anthropologist* 62, no. 3: 505–511.

———. 1961. Further Comparative Notes on the Hijara of India. *American Anthropologist* 63, no. 6: 1331–1332.

Ortner S. B. and H. Whitehead, 1981. *Sexual Meanings: The Cultural Construction of Gender and Sexuality.* Cambridge, New York: Cambridge University Press.

Parekh, S., 2003. Homosexuality in India: The Light at the End of the Tunnel. *Journal of Gay and Lesbian. Psychotherapy* 7, no. 1/2: 145–63.

Parker, R. and P. Aggleton, eds. 2007. *Culture, Society and Sexuality: A Reader.* London: Routledge.

Parker, R. G., 1991. *Bodies, Pleasures and Passions: Sexual Culture in Contemporary Brazil.* Boston: Beacon Press.

———. 1987. Acquired Immunodeficiency Syndrome in Urban Brazil. *Medical Anthropology Quarterly* 1, no. 2: 155–175.

———. 2007. Sexuality, Health and Human Rights. *American Journal of Public Health* 97, no. 6: 972–973.

———. 2003. Changing Sexualities: Masculinity and Male Homosexuality in Brazil. *Changing Men and Masculinities in Latin America* edited by Matthew C. Gutmann, 307–332. Duke University Press: Chapel Hill.

Parker, R. G., G. Herdt and M. Carballo, 1991. Sexual Culture, HIV Transmission, and AIDS research. *The Journal of Sex Research* 28: 77–98.

Penrose, W., 2001. Hidden in History: Female Homoeroticism and Women of a 'Third Nature' in the South Asian Past. *Journal of the History of Sexuality* 10, no. 1: 3–39.

Pradhan P. V., K. S. Ayyar and V. N. Bagadia, 1982. Male Homosexuality: A Psychiatric Study of Thirteen Cases. *Indian J. of Clinical Psychiatry* 24, no. 2: 182–186.

People's Union for Civil Liberties, Karnataka, 2003. *Human Rights Violations Against the Transgender Community: A Study of Kothi and Hijra*. Peoples' Union for Civil Liberties, Karnataka (PUCL-K).

———. 2001. *Human rights violations against sexuality minorities in India.* http://www.pucl.org/Topics/Gender/2003/sexual-minorities.pdf (accessed March 3, 2005)

Purkayastha, D., 1999. *Networks of Men who have Sex with Men: Identity Categories Versus Identity Continuum*. Kolkata: Praajak Development Society.

Ragnarsson, A., H. E. Onya, A. Thorson, A. M. Ekstrom and L. E. Aaro, 2008. Young Males' Gendered Sexuality in the Era of HIV and AIDS in Limpopo Province. *South Africa Qual Health Res* 18, no. 6: 739–746.

Ranade, K., 2009. Medical Response to Male Same-Sex Sexuality in Western India: An Exploration of 'Conversion Treatments' for Homosexuality. *Health and Population Innovation Fellowship Programme Working Paper* 8. New Delhi: Population Council.

Rao, A., M. Nag, K. Mishra and A. Dey, 1994. Sexual Behaviour Pattern of Truck Drivers and their Helpers in Relation to Female Sex Workers. *Indian Journal of Social Work* 55, no. 4: 603–616.

Reddy, G., 2000. *With Respect to Sex: Charting Hijra Identity in Hyderabad, India*. Unpublished PhD Dissertation: Emory University.

———. 2004. Modern Subjectivities: The 'Gay' Sexual Archetype. *Sexual Sites, Seminal Attitudes Sexualities, Masculinities and Culture in South Asia,* edited by S. Srivastava, 147–164. New Delhi: Sage.

———. 2005. Geographies of Contagion: *Hijras*, Kothis, and the Politics of Sexual Marginality in Hyderabad. *Anthropology and Medicine* 12, no. 3: 255–270.

Reddy, D., S. M. Narayana and U. Ganesan, 1993. A Report on Select Urban (Madras) Sexuality with reference to Sexual Aspects of AIDS/STDs. Paper Presented at the Workshop on *Sexual Aspects of AIDS/STD Prevention in India,* Tata Institute of Social Sciences, Bombay.

Robertson, J. E., ed. 2005. *Same-sex Cultures and Sexualities: An Anthropological Reader Malden*. M.A. Oxford: Blackwell.

Rosalind, M., 1995. All Made Up: Performance Theory and the New Anthropology of Sex and Gender. *Annual Review of Anthropology* 24: 567–92.

Roscoe, W., 1991. *The Zuni Man–Woman.* Albuquerque: University of New Mexico Press.

———. 1998. *Changing Ones. Third and Fourth Genders in Native North America.* New York: St. Martin's Press.

Row-Kavi, A., 1993. HIV/AIDS Awareness in the Self-identified Gay Community and its Implications. Paper presented at Workshop on *Sexual Aspects of AIDS/STD Prevention in India,* Tata Institute of Social Sciences, Bombay.

Rubin, G., 1975. The Traffic in Women: Notes on the "Political Economy" of Sex. *Toward an Anthropology of Women,* edited by R. R. Reiter. New York: Monthly Review Press.

Saha, P.C., A.K. Dutta and B.N. Ghosh, 1980. Sexual Behaviour Pattern of the Male STD Patients Attending a Treatment Centre in Calcutta. *Indian J Public Health* 24, no. 1: 16–22.

Savara, M. and S. Sridhar, 1992. Sexual Behaviour of Urban, Educated Indian Men: Results of a Survey. *Journal of Family Welfare* 38, no. 1: 30–43.

Savara, M. and C.R. Sridhar, 1994. Sexual Behaviour amongst Different Occupational Groups in Maharashtra, India and the Implications for AIDS Education. *Indian Journal of Social Work* 55, no. 4: 617–632.

Setia, M.S., C. Lindan, H.R. Jerajani, S. Kumta, M. Ekstrand, M. Mathur and J.D. Klausner, 2006. Men who have Sex with Men and Transgenders in Mumbai, India: An Emerging Risk Group for STIs and HIV. *Indian Journal of Dermatol Venereol Leprol* 72, no. 6: 425–31.

Sharma, R., R.K. Verma, K.G. Rangaiyan, S. Singh and P.J. Pelto, 2001. A Study of Male Sexual Health Problems in a Mumbai Slum Population. *Culture, Health and Sexuality* 3, no. 3: 339–352.

Sharma, S. K., 1989. *Hijras, the Labelled Deviants.* New Delhi: Gyan Publishing House.

Ssali, S. N., 2009. Law, Circumcision and Gendered Sexuality in Eastern Uganda and Western Kenya. *East African Journal of Peace and Human Rights* 15, no. 1: 128–157.

Stearns, D. C., 1995. Gendered Sexuality: The Privileging of Sex and Gender in Sexual Orientation. *NWSA Journal* 7: 8–29

Stryker, S., and S. Whittle 2006. *The Transgender Studies Reader.* London: New York: Routledge.

Thadani, G., 1996. *Sakhiyani: Lesbian Desire in Ancient and Modern India.* London: Cassell.

Thomas, B., M.J. Mimiaga, S. Menon, V. Chandrasekaran, P. Murugesan, S. Swaminathan, K. H. Mayer, and S. A. Safren, 2009. Unseen and Unheard: Predictors of Sexual Risk Behavior and HIV Infection among Men who have Sex with Men in Chennai, India. *AIDS Educ. Prev.* 21, no. 4: 372–83.

TREAT Asia, 2006. *MSM and HIV/AIDS risk in Asia. What is Fueling the Epidemic among MSM and how can it be Stopped?* Bangkok: TREAT Asia.

Turner, C. F., H. G. Miller, and L. E. Moses, eds. 1989. *AIDS: Sexual Behavior and Intravenous Drug Use*. Washington, D.C.: National Academy Press.

UNAIDS, 2006. *Report on the global AIDS epidemic*. Geneva: UNAIDS.

———. 2007. Reference Group on HIV and Human Rights. Issue Paper for the Session: *Male Circumcision*. Seventh meeting, 12–14 February.

Vaidyanathan T.G. and J. Kripal, eds. 1999. *Vishnu on Freud's Desk: A Reader in Psychoanalysis and Hinduism*. Delhi: Oxford University Press.

Valentine, D., 2007. *Imagining Transgender: An Ethnography of a Category*. Durham: Duke University Press.

Vance, C. S., 1991. Anthropology Rediscovers Sexuality. *Social Science and Medicine*, 33(8): 875–84.

———. 1990. Negotiating Sex and Gender in the Attorney General's Commission on Pornography. *Uncertain Terms: Negotiating Gender in American Culture*, edited by Ed. F. Ginsburg and A. Tsing. Beacon Press.

Vanita, R., and S. Kidwai, 2000. *Same-sex love in India: Readings from Literature and History*. New York: St. Martin's Press.

Vanita, R., 2002. Introduction. *Queering India: Same-Sex Love and Eroticism in India culture and Society* edited by R. Vanita. 1–14 Routledge: New York and London.

Vyas, M. D. and Y. Shingala, 1987. *The Life Style of the Eunuchs*. Flushing. NY: Asia Book Corporation of America.

Whitam, F. L., 1986. *Male Homosexuality in Four Societies*. New York: Praege.

Whittle, S., 2000. *The Transgender Debate: The Crisis Surrounding* Gender *Identity*. London: South Street Press.

Wieringa, S., 1989. An Anthropological Critique of Constructionism: Berdaches and Butches. *Homosexuality, Which Homosexuality?* edited by Dennis Altman . 215–238. London: GMP.

Wikan, U., 1977. Man Becomes Woman: Transsexualism in Oman as a Key to Gender Roles. *Man*, 12: 304–319.

Williams, W., 1986. *The Spirit and the Flesh. Sexual Diversity in America Indian Culture*. Boston: Beacon Press.

Notes

1. "Sexuality refers to a core dimension of being human which includes sex, gender, sexual and gender identity, sexual orientation, eroticism, emotional attachment/love, and reproduction. It is experienced or expressed in thoughts, fantasies, desires, beliefs, attitudes, values, activities, practices, roles, relationships. Sexuality is a result of the interplay of biological, psychological, socio-economic, cultural, ethical and religious/spiritual factors. While sexuality can include all of these aspects, not all of these dimensions need to be experienced or expressed. However, in sum, our sexuality is experienced and expressed in all that we are, what we feel, think and do."

2. http://www2.hu-berlin.de/sexology/GESUND/ARCHIV/PSH.HTM

3. "Gender is the sum of cultural values, attitudes, roles, practices, and characteristics based on sex. Gender, as it has existed historically, cross-culturally, and in contempo-

rary societies, reflects and perpetuates particular power relations between men and women."

4. "Gender identity defines the degree to which each person identifies as male, female, or some combination. It is the internal framework, constructed over time, which enables an individual to organize a self-concept and to perform socially in regards to his/her perceived sex and gender. Gender identity determines the way individuals experience their gender and contributes to an individual's sense of sameness, uniqueness and belonging."

5. "Sexual health is the experience of the ongoing process of physical, psychological, and socio-cultural well being related to sexuality. Sexual health is evidenced in the free and responsible expressions of sexual capabilities that foster harmonious personal and social wellness, enriching individual and social life. It is not merely the absence of dysfunction, disease and/or infirmity. For Sexual Health to be attained and maintained it is necessary that the sexual rights of all people be recognized and upheld."

6. In Pan American Health Organization World Health Organization Recommendations for Action Proceedings of a Regional Consultation convened by Pan American Health Organization (PAHO) World Health Organization (WHO) In collaboration with the Promotion of Sexual Health World Association for Sexology (WAS) in Antigua Guatemala, Guatemala May 19-22, 2000

7. http://www2.hu-berlin.de/sexology/GESUND/ARCHIV/PSH.HTM#_Toc 490155412

8. Of the 'Native' North-America: Callender and Kochems, 1983; Williams, 1986; Roscoe, 1991, 1998; Humphreys, 1970; Goode and Troiden, 1974; Delph, 1978

9. Of Oman : Wikan,1977

10. Of Kenya: Oboler,1980

11. In New Guinea :Wirz, 1922;.Williams, 1939 van Baal, 1966; Herdt, 1994a

12. Of Australia, Indonesia, Japan, Africa, and the Arabic world: Leupp, 1995 for Japan; Evans-Pritchard, 1970, for the Azande in the Sudan; Baldauf, 1988, 1990 and Foster, 1990 for Afghanistan; Rahman, 1989 for Pakistan

13. Like Brazilian tranvestis, or 1960s drag queens in the U.S., contemporary Japanese sex workers and their clients, or even gay and lesbian kinship in the U.S.

14. Recent academic interest in the *hijra* really emerged in the late 1950s and early 1960s with an argument between G. Morris Carstairs (1956, 1957) and Morris E. Opler (1960, 1961). Many scholars have written articles on them, most notably S. Nanda, (1990), Lawrence Cohen (1995), Vinay Lal (1999), Kira Hall (1997); and Hall with O'Donovan (1996), the last of whom has written excellent reviews of the *hijra* though their use of language.

15. The thoughts regarding sexual rights in social, cultural, political and economic contexts of sexuality and relationships were significantly emphasised.

16. It was accepted by governments in the global programme on AIDS conference in Geneva (1992-93). The phrase "men who have sex with men" (MSM) is a collective social identity for all men, who have sex with other men irrespective of how they might identify themselves.

17. 'MSM's include all men who have sex with men whether or not they identify themselves as gay, thus including gay and bi-sexual men as well as straight men (as some men who are not the receptors of same sex relations do not consider themselves gay – i.e., a married men who receives oral sex from a man may not identify himself as gay or bi-sexual when asked) (HIV InSite 2000).

18. MSM: a missing link in national responses to HIV and AIDS in Asia and the Pacific, a Summary, Nicholas Cumming Bruce available at http://www.nfi.net/downloads/Risks_Responsibilities/background%20papers/Summary%20Paper_Missing_Link_20092006.pdf

19. Risks and Responsibilities – International Consultation on Male Sexual Health and HIV/AIDS in Asia and the Pacific

20. It includes the Most Reverend Archbishop Desmond Tutu, Dr. Nafis Sadik, the UN Secretary- General's Special Envoy for HIV and AIDS in Asia and the Pacific, and JVR Prasada Rao, Regional Director for UNAIDS RST Asia Pacific.

21. See Delhi Consultation offers new hope for MSM interventions, Press Release, UNAIDS India (2006), available at www.unaids.org as
a. Accord MSM and transgender interventions a priority in the national strategic plans;
b. Earmark resources directly to the MSM and transgender networks for capacity;
c. Change laws that criminalize male-to-male sex by creating a groundswell public opinion;
d. Undertake public education for halting harassment of MSM, transgender and community workers who provide services for these groups;
e. Ensure full involvement of MSM and transgendered people in the national planning process.

22. Naqvi and Mujtaba (1997: 265) confirm the comparison of *hijras* and *zenanas* in Pakistan similarly, in which *hijra* version of the *zenanas* include "We are certainly not the same. *Zenanas* are in just for the *dhanda* (business)".

23. They experience considerable violence, harassment and unless protected by higher incomes and social status, often are unable to finish school or gain an occupation (Bondyopadhyay and Khan, 2002, 2004).

24. "Still considered males, but feeling gratified in the receptive role, these men are called *kothis*, a term now widely used in India, Bangladesh and Pakistan and possibly related to the Thai term *katoey"* (Jenkins, 2004 : 17).

25. A result of knowledge of global categories having inroads to the urban elites and higher classes.

26. Encompassing *hijras* and *kothi*, the later being the umbrella term for both *hijras,* and *kothis* as well as other identities like, *panthis*.

27. According to NACO (2006), HIV Prevalence (%) among Risk Groups, percentage share of Adult HIV infections in MSM is 5.7 and 6.7 respectively with a total of 2,352,133 identified population (NACO, 2006).

28. According to Dr Anbumani Ramadoss "India's dedicated focus on HIVprevention is fetching dividends. We are seeing the beginning of the stabilization of the HIV epidemic in India. .. . . Structural discrimination against those who are vulnerable to HIV such as sex workers and MSM must be removed if our prevention, care and treatment programmers are to succeed .... Section 377 of the Indian Penal Code, which criminalises Men who have Sex with Men, must go."

29. It is estimated that India has 2.5 million MSM population. Of this group, about 100,000 are at high risk of contracting HIV and 15 percent have already become HIV positive (NACO 2007).

30. There are several sub-groups among MSM. For the purposes of TIs, these groups are defined as:
(a) Kothis: The term is used to describe males who show varying degrees of "femininity" (perhaps situational), take the "female" role in their sexual relationships with other men,

and are involved mainly – though often not exclusively – in receptive anal/oral sex with men. (b) Panthis: The term panthi is used by kothisand hijras to refer to a "masculine" insertivemale partner or anyone who is masculine and seems to be a potential sexual (insertive) partner. Equivalent terms are Gadiyo (Gujarat), Parikh (West Bengal) andGiriya (Delhi). (c) Double Deckers: Kothis and hijras label those males who both insert and receive duringpenetrative sexual encounters (anal or oral sex) with other men as Double Deckers. Equivalent terms are Double, DupliKothi (West Bengal) and DoParatha (Maharashtra). (d) Hijras: Hijras belong to a distinct socio-religious and cultural group, a "third gender". They dress in feminine attire and are organized under seven main gharanas or clans.

31. Lawyer, author and political activist; wrote 12 books on same-sex love, forwarding the idea that sexual orientation is biological in nature.

32. The presentation does not claim that this was the only stream of politically significant events to occur and lead to queer movements anywhere and every where. There were several other events in different times and places and even within Europe that can be considered worthy of providing a foundation for the modern queer rights movements.

33. Psychologist; her research concluded that there was no psychological difference between heterosexual and homosexual men.

34. The Fight for Equality and Liberation: Links between the Women's and LGBT Movements – An International Perspective", Somali Ghosh, 2004: http://saathii.org/ gensex/calcutta/images/pix/SAATHIICalPixPages/lgbt_movements.pps

35. National AIDS Control Organization figures for 2007.

36. Shah GK, Muralidhar S. Delhi High Court Judgment. Naz Foundation v. Government of National Capital Territory of Delhi. 2 July 2009.

37. Infochange News & Features, July 2011 (http://infochangeindia.org/humanrights/features/kahani-queer-india-ki.html).

CHAPTER 13

Roots and Shoots of Female Feticide in Pockets of India—Lending Voice to the Voiceless[1]

Tushar Kanti Saha

"As soon as there is life there is danger" said, Ralph Waldo Emerson. Now, there is a danger looming large on Indian horizon that life may not be allowed to be born by those who are already born, more particularly, when the gender of the born to-be is not a male. Whereas Mother Nature is reproductive, human irrationality is acting as a fundamental barrier to positive and beneficial use of technology and this climate of change has affected adversely the fate and status of female fetus in pockets of India.

"Intellectually, mentally, and spiritually, woman is equivalent to a male and she can participate in every activity" said, the 'Father of Indian Nation' M.K. Gandhi. Yet in his own early married life he too wanted to dominate over his wife as revealed in his autobiography (*The Stories of My Experiments with Truth*)[2]. With new realization dawned on him, he said that as long as we don't consider girls as natural as our boys, our nation will be in a dark eclipse. He often said that paternal society is the root cause of inequality. Indian society is patrilineal, patriarchal and patrilocal. Parents expect sons—but not daughters—to provide financial and emotional care, especially in their old age; sons add to family wealth and property while daughters drain it through dowries; sons continue the family lineage while daughters are married away to another household; sons perform important religious roles; and sons defend or exercise the family's power while daughters have to be defended and protected, creating a perceived burden on the household. This stereotype notion of women as "burden" is one of the main reasons behind female feticide and infanticide prevailing in India to date. These are signs and indicators of social and economic backwardness, e.g. if there is old age pension scheme, why the parents will look differentially to sons for insurance in old age which can whither away only with significant progress in economic status of both men and women. Section 125 of Cr.PC 1973 imposed a duty under sub-section (1)(d) that "if any person having sufficient means neglects or refuses to maintain his father or mother, unable to maintain himself or herself" and has been reinforced by Senior Citizen Act, 2007 to provide for more effective provisions for the maintenance and welfare of parents. In the absence of comprehensive social security legislation in India, this new piece of law has been necessitated by the changing attitude of the children towards their parents in a traditional society. Childless elderly people were not covered by the old law in the Cr.PC. The new legislation is designed to promote welfare of the elderly citizens since legal heirs to the childless elderly now owe a duty towards him under Section 4(1) of the Act. However, the Act has totally avoided State responsibility in the matter of welfare of senior citizens perpetuating the age-old approach to old age persons to forever look for support from their kith and kin more particularly and realistically their own sons. The State was nowhere in the picture earlier also since it is reasonable to expect a person (read 'son' for a realistic view) with sufficient means to maintain his elderly parents without means of support but the State did not care then nor does it presently in a situation where neither the children nor the parents have the means of support. It is not inconceivable to imagine that grown-up adult children who may have their own families are struggling to maintain their own children.

We just had a woman as the Head of the State but the female feticide continues to loom large in pockets of India. Interesting facets of different patriarchal societies point to the fallacy of the foregoing assumption that patriarchy is necessarily the main impediment to the recognition of female worth of a human being. We still have the same patriarchal society that we used to have yet we have changed to extend the concept of equality to women in many directions in our ongoing process towards progressive journey. Lesotho, a tiny mountain kingdom is a shining example of patriarchal society in which women enjoy better social and economic status compared to men folk. One can easily find women in positions of Police Commissioner, Auditor General, Speaker, Judges, Ministers and Vice-Chancellor and men are far behind mainly because they are doing manly job of tending the cattle (see table 1 below).

Table 1: World Economic Forum's Global Gender Gap Report 2010[3] (Rankings top 15 out of 134)

Country	2010	Score	2009	Change
Iceland	1	85.0%	1	0
Norway	2	84.0%	3	1
Finland	3	82.6%	2	-1
Sweden	4	80.2%	4	0
New Zealand	5	78.1%	5	0
Ireland	6	77.7%	8	2
Denmark	7	77.2%	7	0
Lesotho	**8**	**76.8%**	**10**	**2**
Philippines	9	76.5%	9	0
Switzerland	10	75.6%	13	3
Spain	11	75.5%	17	6

Country	2010	Score	2009	Change
South Africa	12	75.3%	6	-6
Germany	13	75.3%	12	-1
Belgium	14	75.1%	33	19
United Kingdom	15	74.6%	15	0

Socio-Religious Background

The role of women in India throughout history can be overviewed in two broad periods: 2500 B.C-1500 B.C., and 1500 B.C.-1800 A.D. These divisions are based on degree of freedom that women enjoyed and the role differentiation within the family. Throughout classic literature on the status of women, there is almost consistent opinion among great scholars that during the age of Vedas (2500-1500 B. C.) a woman's status was equivalent to that of a man. The deterioration in woman's status started with gradual changes during the age of Brahmanas, 1500 B.C. and by the age of Sutras and Epics, 500 B.C. to A.D. 500 and the age of the later *Srutis*, A.D.500 to A.D. 1800, this status had deteriorated considerably.

Swami Vivekananda, the famous Hindu philosopher, maintained that *Gita* is a bouquet of beautiful flowers of spiritual truth, which have been chosen carefully from the *Upanishadas*. In Tenth Chapter, 34th *shloka*[4] in Vibhooti yoga, Lord Krishna says, "I reside in women in the form of seven virtues, they are: *Medha, Kshama, Dhruti, Keerti, Sudhi, Shree* and *Vak*". *Medha* means intellect. This is the basic necessity of being intelligent. People called this as practical knowledge. *Kshama* (Forgiveness) is a state of mind, where one woman tolerates the trouble given to her by another woman, without saying anything and still not having any bad feeling about it. This means letting one go without having any hard feelings in mind. While accepting the mistake one must wish not to repeat the same mistake again and forgive the person. *Dhruti* means grasping power. *Keerti* means success, fame. This is something which one gets when he has done some good and noble work, such work, which is remembered even after when that person no longer exists. *Sudhi* means memory. This is the store-keeping of knowledge of things, which are recollected by memory. Remembering some past reference which had been forgotten, remembering things about the dear ones again and again is part and parcel of memory. The simple meaning of *Shree* is beauty, attraction, wealth, richness and growth. This means glaze, and also an ornament called *Bindi* to be worn by woman on their forehead. An auspicious vein in the foot is also called *Shree*. This is a word of respect which is used before names of a raga belonging to *Shadava* group, which is sung at the time of sunset. So, the wife of Vishnu is called *Shree*. The word also includes meaning like power, lotus, white sandalwood, clove, a medicine called *Ruddhi*. *Vak* means *Saraswati* (Vakdevi) which calls for inclusion of the splendor of music in speech, sentence, words, talking, discussion and so on. Literature and art are the twin templates of *Vak*. The consciousness of this paragon of virtues is for emulation and perfection by all and should serve as a model for equal respect towards each other irrespective of gender. Unfortunately, man and muscle mixed up to take over reason and renaissance over time and women's position was eclipsed. Amartya Sen pointed out that when he took up issues of women's welfare, he was accused in India of voicing "foreign concerns". "I was told Indian women don't think like that about equality. But I would like to argue that if they don't think like that they should be given a real opportunity to think like that."[5]

The Scene in New India

The adverse sex ratio has been linked with the low status of women in Indian communities, both Hindu and Muslim. The status of women in a society can be determined by their education, health, economic role, presence in the professions and management, and decision-making power within the family. It is deeply influenced by the beliefs and values of society. Islam permits polygamy and gives women fewer rights than men. Among Hindus, preference for the male child is likewise deeply enshrined in belief and practice. The very practice of *Garvadan* on an auspicious day created the ceremonial ritual expressing the desire for a son. *Putrarthe Kriyate Vargya*[6] (wife is taken for the birth of a son) is the ancient adage still being secretly accepted by many million in India. People of faith believe in this without questioning the wisdom in the statement. If a wife is meant for birth of sons only, who would be the wife next time in the absence of a daughter from the wife? Such an irrational and illogical approach resulted in misery and horrendous experience for many millions in the past. The practice of dowry has spread nationwide, to communities and castes in which it had never been the custom, fuelled by consumerism and emulation of upper caste practices. In the majority of cases, the legal system has no impact on the practice of dowry. It is estimated that a dowry death occurs in India every 93 minutes. The need for a dowry for girl children, and the ability to demand a dowry for boys exerts considerable economic pressure on families to use any means to avoid having girls, who are seen as a liability. It is reported that there are posters in Bombay advertising sex-determination tests that read, 'It is better to pay 500 Rupees now than 50,000 Rupees (in dowry) later'. Developments in Reproductive Technology Abortion were legalized in India in 1971 (Medical Termination of Pregnancy Act) to strengthen humanitarian values (pregnancy can be aborted if it is a result of sexual assault, contraceptive failure, if the baby would be severely handicapped, or if the mother is incapable of bearing a healthy child). Amniocentesis was introduced in 1975 to detect fetal abnormalities but it soon began to be used for determining the sex of the baby. Ultrasound scanning, being a non-invasive technique, quickly gained popularity and is now available in some of the most remote rural areas. Both techniques are now being used for sex determination with the intention of abortion if the fetus turns out to be female. These methods do not involve manipulation of genetic material to select the sex of a baby. Recent Preconception Gender Selection (PGS), however, includes flow cytometry, pre-implantation gender determination of the embryo, and in vitro fertilization to ensure the birth of a baby of the desired sex without undergoing abortion. In PGS, X and Y sperms are separated and the enriched sperms are used to fertilize the ovum. The method was intended to reduce the risk of diseases related to the

X chromosome, which are far more likely to occur in boys than in girls (who have two X chromosomes). Ironically, it is being used in India to avoid giving birth to girl children. Most of those in the medical profession, being part of the same gender biased society, are steeped in the same attitudes concerning women.

Feticide

The UN Universal Declaration on Human Rights, 1948 in its Article 3 upholds the right to life. Paragraph 1 of Article 6 of the International Covenant on Civil and Political Rights expressly provided that, 'every human being has the inherent right to life'. Humans, or human beings, are bipedal primates belonging to the mammalian species *Homo sapiens* (Latin: "wise man" or "knowing man") in the family *Hominidae* (the Great Apes). Compared to other living organisms on Earth, humans have a highly developed brain capable of abstract reasoning, language, and introspection. This mental capability, combined with an erect body carriage that frees their upper limbs for manipulating objects, has allowed humans to make far greater use of tools than any other species. Henry Bergson referred to it in *The Creative Evolution* (1907)[7], defining intelligence, in its original sense, as the "faculty to create artificial objects, in particular tools to make tools, and to indefinitely variate its makings". *Homo sapiens* thus transform into *Homo faber* in a fertile and favorable field of human existence and creativity.

Dinknesh ('The Wonderful' in Amharic) or 'Lucy' is the early hominid woman who walked on this planet, earth was found in 1974 in Ethiopia. She is the most complete *hominid* skeleton of the Pliocene Epoch [1.8-5.3 million years ago]. Recently, in 2003, the first ever 160,000 years old human sub-species, *Homo sapiens*-Edaltu, (old man) has been discovered. A more recent discovery revealed that our forebears underwent a previously unknown stage of evolution more than a million years before Lucy, the iconic early human ancestor specimen that walked the Earth 3.2 million years ago. The centerpiece of a treasure trove of new fossils, the skeleton—assigned to a species called *Ardipithecus ramidus*—belonged to a small-brained, 110 pound (50 kilogram) female nicknamed "Ardi"(stands for 'Earth' in Afar language).

In scientific language, an ovum is not alive and is not a human person. Similarly, a spermatozoon is not live and is not a human person. There is a near consensus that at, or shortly after conception, a zygote or pre-embryo—popularly called a fertilized ovum—is a form of human life. The zygote is biologically alive. It fulfills the four criteria needed to establish biological life: metabolism, growth, reaction to stimuli, and reproduction. In "Deciding Who is Human", Noonan argues for 'the classification of fetuses with human beings by pointing to the presence of the full genetic code, and the potential capacity for rational thought'.

Legal Status of Fetus

It is true that the fetus does not have a uniform value or character in the eyes of the law. The antiquated stand of conferring legal status on fetus dates back to seventeenth century: 'If a woman be quick with childe, and by a potion or otherwise killeth it in her wombe, or if a man beat her, whereby the childe dyeth in her body, and she is delivered of a deade childe, this is [...] no murder; but if the childe be born alive and dyeth of the potion, battery or other cause, this is murder; for in law it is accounted a reasonable creature [...] when it is born alive.'[8]

It is clear in UK law[9] that the fetus does not have any separate legal interests capable of being taken into account by a court. Although it had been suggested that the right of everyone to have their life protected by law, under Article 2 of the European Convention of Human Rights, could extend to the unborn, this was rejected in 2004 in the case of *Vo v. France*.[10] In this case the European Court of Human Rights held that Article 2 did not confer a right to life that extended to a fetus. Given the wide degree of variance on this point in the domestic law of individual states, determination of the commencement of life came within the margin of appreciation, which gives states discretion regarding interpretation where no consensus exists in Europe. From the decision of *Broadnax v. Gonzalez*[11] the question now is: Should the father of the fetus have a claim similar to the mother's? If so, what about if a mother chooses to have an abortion and the father disagrees? Presently, if the fetus is viable, no harm can be done even prospectively by the mother herself. Then, why kill simply because the gender of the fetus is female?

Moral and Ethical Judgments

Abortion is occasionally justified on the ground of self-interest as an extension of the pursuit of happiness regardless of other's interest and well being. Rand argues that self-interest is indeed the standard of morality, and selflessness is the deepest immorality. If abortion is morally and ethically justified, the next question is whether sex-selective abortion can be equally justified. Selective abortion is generally permissible but sex-selective abortion throws open the larger issue of discrimination under the roof of constitutional principle of right to equality and human rights.

Female Infanticide

The British became concerned when they saw the results of the first census of 1871 in India. In some villages, the commissioners reported, not a single female child was to be found. The authorities brought in the Female Infanticide Act, which set heavy penalties on child murder, and policemen were stationed in such places but, twenty years later, some provinces still had twice as many boys as girls. The murder of children which so shocked the British in 1871 when the practice led to a ratio of 972 women to a 1000 men. In 1991, modern science had shifted the figure to 929 females to each 1000 males. Devaluation of daughters was viewed as a purely cultural construct. It was assumed to be the outcome of free-floating minds spinning infinitely variable webs of meaning out of locally received traditions. As far as cultural anthropologists were concerned, the ideology of son preference along with the custom of paying dowries to marry off daughters sufficed to explain female infanticide in India.

Singular events of female infanticide had been highlighted in historical perspective by R. J. Rummel, as "In many cultures, government permitted, if not encouraged, the killing of handicapped or female infants or otherwise unwanted children. In the Greece of 200 B.C., for example, the murder of female infants was so common that among 6,000 families living in Delphi no more than 1 percent had two daughters. Among 79 families, there were only 28 daughters to 118 sons. But classical Greece was not unusual. In eighty-four societies spanning the Renaissance to our time, "defective" children have been killed in one-third of them. In India, for example, because of Hindu beliefs and the rigid caste system, young girls were murdered as a matter of course. When demographic statistics were first collected in the nineteenth century, it was discovered that in "some villages no girl babies were found at all; in a total of thirty others, there were 343 boys to 54 girls. ... [I]n Bombay, the number of girls alive in 1834 was 603" (Rummel 1994: 65-66).

Abortion by itself is not an issue in India either from moral angles or from religious point of view. In *Kharak Singh v. State of UP and Others*[12], the Supreme Court has certainly recognized that a person has complete rights of control over his body organs and his 'person' under Art. 21 of the Constitution. But sex-selective abortion is the central issue in ethical and legal paradigm as it affects human rights and wider humane approach to life. India is the heartland of sex-selective abortions. What was previously female infanticide has now turned into female feticide because of the new-found technology in which the technologists and technicians take part in the job of elimination with no qualms of conscience or moral bargaining. Female feticide is the relic of this atavistic past perpetuated by the moral decay associated with the consumerist capitalism and self-interest. Technology is advancing, so also is the evil mind catching up fast with it. The introduction in the United States, a patented sex determination kit called 'Baby Gender Mentor Home DNA Gender Testing Kit' raised fears about back-door fetus determination tests. The kit, priced at $275 was popularly known as *'Jantar Mantar'* in rural Punjab. It is a kind of built-in equipment for collecting and sending a finger-prick blood sample to a Massachusetts laboratory from where confidential results were sent via e-mail within 48 hours. Technology is advancing but, alas, the thinking is still barbaric.

Female Feticide

Female feticide is a practice that involves the detection of the sex of the unborn baby in the womb of the mother and the decision to abort it if the sex of the child is detected as a girl. This could be done at the behest of the mother, or father, or both or under family pressure. This detection of the sex of the baby is done through three methods: (a) amniocentesis; (b) chronic villus sampling and (c) ultra-sonography. Ironically, the families that commit female feticide love their living daughters while that passion is not extended to the female fetus because it has not been allowed to see the light of the day.

Myriad Manifestation of Maltreatment of Women

A documentary film entitled *Let Her Die*, produced for SBS on female feticide projected "India is short of 25 million women". It narrates that 'Many individuals in Indian society consider that if in the first instance they have a baby girl it would be considered bad luck, in the second a disaster and in third a catastrophe'. Female child is unwanted because of host of real life treatment faced by the parent and female child herself. In real life today, the status of women is surely changing. But this change is not purely wholesome. Technology, trafficking, torture and treatment are still continuing to afflict women in all societies throughout the world. The status of women can be measured by the extent of a woman's access to social and material resources within the family, community and society or her authority or power within the family and community and the prestige commanded from those other members, or her position in the social system distinguishable from, yet related to, other positions, or the extent to which women have access to knowledge, economic resources and political power as well as the degree of autonomy they have in decision-making and making personal choices at crucial points in their life-cycle (Mukherjee 1975, Committee on the Status of Women in India, 1974).[13] In childhood a female is subject to her father, in youth to her husband and when her lord is dead to her sons. A woman appears to be incomplete and never independent by herself. The reflection of anomaly in treating a female member of the society can be gathered from a variety of affronts notably among them is the dowry system causing heart burn.

Dowry as a Root Cause

Dowries continue to be socially required today not only in India but also in many other jurisdictions. Historically, dowry is the money or property a bride brings to her husband at marriage—was common throughout much of the ancient world, and also flourished in Medieval Europe. Romans had complicated traditions governing marriages that included specific dowry laws. An *in manum* marriage meant the bride and all her property came under the control of her husband. If the marriage was not *in manum* the bride's father controlled her and her property. Dowries were generally agreed upon at the time of betrothal, and paid after the wedding. The bride's family paid a dowry to the groom. The groom gave his bride a gift, often money, and an iron engagement ring, *anulus pronubis*.

Dowry is one of the root causes for misery of womenfolk in modern India. So, it is necessary to attack the root cause rather than symptoms and procedures alone. The dowry system in India effectively commodified women and converted them into chips which are seen as expensive, burdensome and poorly endowed in the economic exchange within the joint family system. The theory of equalizing differences is particularly suitable for the analysis of marriage markets, once price differences among grooms are recognized as equalizing differences for the alternative bundles of characteristics they possess. The prediction is that, grooms with higher educational qualifications and income earning potential are likely to get higher dowries. Consequently, dowry is a "payment for the establishment of socio-economic alliances valuable to the bride's family," where the value of these alliances to the bride's family is not balanced by a comparable value to the groom's family. However, dowry is the root cause of indebtedness among many million parents in India. In one rural sample the average cost of a daughter's marriage was six times the parents' annual income and, consequently, a cause of indebtedness and destitution (Rao 1993). The theories of why groom-prices have risen to focus on changes that may have taken place to reduce the relative worth of women in the marriage market. On this subject, economists have provided two major explanations—one demographic, and the other status based. The demographic explanation, originally proposed by the demographer Jack Caldwell and developed by Rao (1993), lays the blame on population growth.

The epicenter of the problem of bride burning and other forms of dowry-related violence on women is Delhi (the Indian capital), western and central Uttar Pradesh (cities such as Kanpur, Lucknow and Agra have witnessed the highest number of deaths), and places adjoining Delhi (Haryana, North-eastern Rajasthan, northern Madhya Pradesh, and southern Punjab), and the problem has largely been concentrated among the upper caste above-average Hindu communities. Now the problem has spread rapidly to other traditionally incidence-free areas and classes such as South Indian states like Andhra Pradesh, Tamil Nadu, and Karnataka, Western states such as Maharashtra and Gujarat, and Eastern states such as Bihar and West Bengal have witnessed rapid surge of incidents in recent years. The pockets of Punjab, Andhra Pradesh, Rajasthan, Delhi, Haryana and Maharashtra which I describe as PARADHAM States constitute the paradigm of India's female-specific holocaust. In 2001 The Tribune newspaper of Chandigarh, India reported that the estimated number of sex-selective abortions in 1996-98 was 62,000 in Haryana (81 percent of total abortions) and 51,000 in Punjab (26 percent). The paper found that the skewing of gender ratios in first-born children was stronger in Punjab, where the sex ratio at birth (SRB) was 131, than in Haryana with SRB 109. Preference for a son following the birth of a daughter was almost equally strong in Haryana and Punjab with SRB being 151 and 154, respectively. The practice is basically an urban phenomenon and practised by wealthier but orthodox families.

In India, 6,000 dowry murders are committed each year. This reality exists even though the Dowry Prohibition Act has been in existence for 33 years. A new trend is perceptible in systemic conversion from 'bride price' to 'dowry' system which is a noticeable change in the South because boys are increasingly marrying outside their traditional natal relationships. A play known as *Kanyasulkam* written by Gurazada Appa Rao in 1892[14] is one of the earliest modern works in an Indian vernacular language, and it is the first Telugu play to deal with social issues. The play portrays the practice of *Kanya-sulkam* (roughly translates to *bride price*) which was common among the priestly Brahmins in Telugu-speaking areas of southern India. The practice of parents arranging the marriages of their pre-pubescent daughters to old men for cash was very prevalent during those days, and was referred to popularly as *Kanyasulkam*, literally meaning "money in lieu for a girl", which also forms the title of the play. Despite the fact that it was the system of bride price, it did not reflect a higher status for women in those days rather their miseries of enslavement in another form. Bride price system prevails in some communities India till today, e.g. when a Mizo boy approaches his fiancée's parents for permission to get married; the first thing he has to do is to settle the bride price. If the price among other things is acceptable to the parents, the boy and the girl are allowed to get married. Thus the settlement of the bride price to be paid by the bridegroom is an essential pre-requisite to a Mizo marriage. The practice indicates desirability of a girl child but does not necessarily mean an equal status with men[15].

The prevailing system of dowry can be explained also by a strong correlation between demand for the groom at a higher level in terms of education, wealth, social standing and even the height. Rarely, not even one in a million, an educated Indian girl will marry a graduate carpenter; a carpenter has to marry a wood picker. This hypogyny approach is systemic and socially embedded psyche together put a marked up premium on the groom manifold according to his level. Although inter-caste marriages are taking place increasingly, there is no denial of the fact that the class consciousness is at its strongest pinnacle in marriage negotiation and arrangement. This connection has never been raised in literature while discussing the dowry devil. The tragic incidences of dowry death also have their roots in this demand and many a times incapable parents go overdrive undertaking the risk at the cost of life. This phenomenon cannot simply be explained by market driven pure economic analysis based on demand and supply. In many traditional societies where the number of marriageable girls outweighs the number of marriageable boys, bride price still dominates because it is essentially part of the cultural practices. *Lobola* or *bohali* (bride price) for example is necessary even for legitimization and recognition of the marriage itself under customary law in Lesotho.

The National Commission for women in India in one of its annual reports (2000) states that every day, almost every six hours, somewhere at some place in India, a young married woman is being burnt alive or beaten to death or being pushed to commit suicide. Over the past few years, the cases of bride burning have registered a sharp increase throughout India.

Advent of Modernity and Women in India

Modern education among both male and female did not change the psyche and attitude of a vast majority of men towards women though an enlightened section has emerged to fight against the roots causes of social evils affecting women's heath, education and welfare. Until passage of Marriage Act 1753, English society in recorded history witnessed inhuman cruelty towards women in relation to marriage and divorce. Women were completely subordinated to their husbands after marriage, the husband and wife becoming one legal entity, a legal status known as coverture—an adverse change of status from *feme sole* to *feme covert*. An eminent English Judge Sir William Blackstone wrote in 1753: "the very being, or legal existence of the woman, is suspended during the marriage, or at least is consolidated and incorporated into that of her husband: under whose wing, protection and cover, she performs everything" (Caine and Sluga 2002: 12-13). Married women could not own property in their own right, and were indeed themselves the property of their husbands. Wife selling by public auction was customary which provided a backdrop of Thomas Hardy's novel, *The*

Mayor of Casterbridge. Selling wives by *elkela clan* in Orissa during *mundapota* fair resonates such practices in India's dark corners. Under Hindu law the same concept prevails because marriage in a sacrament and not a contract although some changes have ushered in recent times. If marriage is converted into contract, there is a need for *quid pro quo* which should move from the bridegroom as 'bride price' in stead of 'dowry'. But brides are wrongly perceived as burden in India which is against the spirit of modernity. India is still not modern enough.

Legal Provision

In India since 1978 the USG test is being used as a sex determination or sex preselection test. Since then the test has become extremely popular and has led to a mushrooming of private clinics which perform the test all over the country. Earlier doctors employed the controversial amniocentesis test done between 14 to 18 weeks to determine the sex of the fetus. The ultrasound technique has also been improved. The sex of a fetus can be determined by more sophisticated machines within 13 to 14 weeks of pregnancy by trans-vaginal sonography and by 14 to 16 weeks through abdominal ultrasound. These methods have rendered sex determination cheap and easy. A sophisticated method like Erison method separates the X and Y Chromosomes from the sperm and then injects back only Y chromos into the womb to ensure a boy has been developed.

In September 20, 1994 the Parliament had enacted the Pre-Natal Diagnostic Techniques (Regulation & Prevention of Misuse) Act which came into force from January 1996. Rules were framed by the central government under section 32 of the Act. These rules are known as Pre-conception and Pre-natal Diagnostic Techniques (Prohibition of Sex Selection) rules 1996. Later, the Act was amended with effect from February 14, 2003, and was renamed the Pre-Conception and Pre-Natal Diagnostic Techniques (Prohibition of Sex Selection) Act, 1994 (PCPNDT Act). The Act has two aspects viz., regulatory and preventive. It seeks to regulate the use of pre-natal diagnostic techniques for legal or medical purposes and prevent misuse for illegal purposes. The Act provides for the setting up of various bodies along with their composition powers and functions. There is a central supervisory board, appropriate authorities and advisory committees.

The ban on the government hospitals and clinics at the centre and in the states, making use of pre-natal sex determination for the purpose of abortion—a penal offence presumably led to the commercialization of the technology; private clinics providing sex determination tests through amniocentesis multiplied rapidly and widely. These tests are made available in areas that do not even have potable water, with marginal farmers willing to take loans at 25 per cent interest to have the test. People used to be encouraged to abort their female fetuses through advertisements in order to save the future cost of dowry. The portable ultrasound machine has facilitated doctors to go from house to house in towns and villages.

Despite the law in force, due to lack of proper implementation, very few cases are registered. Under the two main laws viz. Medical Termination of

Pregnancy (MTP) Act 1971 and the Pre-Natal Diagnostic Techniques (PNDT) Act 1994, the Indian government has conceded that abortion may be carried out if there is
(a) Danger to the life of the mother in child birth,
(b) If the child is at risk of being born handicapped, or
(c) If the women has conceived the child as a result of rape.

Women are also allowed the right to abortion if they wish to do so in the interest of keeping the family small. PNDT Act has been designed only to focus on regulation and control over techniques of pre-natal sex determination, not the access to abortion in any form. That is, the Act does not concern itself with selective abortion of female fetuses as such, but rather, with medical procedures to detect the sex of the fetus, which can lead to femicide. However, it is often seen that the decision of abortion is taken after the detection that the unborn child is female, especially if it is the second or third female child. It must be mentioned here that abortion has entered the lexicon of feminist struggle through a very different trajectory from that followed in the West. Here, the 'right' to abortion has never been at the centre of much debate since it is seen as a measure to control population growth. Since poverty is seen as a byproduct of rising population, for developing countries like India, population control measures have been a central focus of government programs for economic development. The irony of the whole situation is that in the ten years since India enacted the Pre-Natal Diagnostic Technologies (PNDT) Act, not a single person was convicted till very recently and in the beginning of April 2006 only two people were convicted, fined and pronounced five years of rigorous imprisonment. Only 23 cases have been registered under this Act so far, according to India's Health Minister Ambumoni Ramadoss' recent statement in the Parliament.

The Medical Termination Act was passed in 1971 amidst Parliamentary rhetoric of choice and women's rights, but it was clearly intended as a population control measure, as several MPs pointed out during the debate on the Bill. Here, it is worth mentioning that a vocal and influential school of thought still justifies the selective abortion of female fetuses as a form of population control. Their argument is that to permit abortion of female fetuses would stop couples from continuing to have children until the desired son was produced which points to the defective reasoning and attitude of a class of people.

Female feticide is one extreme manifestation of violence against women. Gender specific laws like MTP Act 1971 which aims at empowering women has been grossly misused for female feticide after carrying out legally banned pre-natal sex-determination tests to meet the desire of the family to have a male child.

Judicial Response

According to figures released by the National Crime Records Bureau in Punjab, 81 cases were registered for female feticide while for Rajasthan the corresponding number was 51. Madhya Pradesh registered 21 cases, Haryana 18 and Chhattisgarh 24. In Rajasthan, the number of cases registered has shown a steady decline since the last three years with 25, 16 and 10 cases being registered in 2006, 2007 and 2008. The National Capital saw seven cases registered in 2006, four in 2007 and two in 2008. The conviction rate is dismally low. The decline in the registration of number of cases does not necessarily mean that there is a sharp fall in the practice.

In response to the petition filed by CEHAT[16], the Supreme Court of India issued notices to the central and state governments to file replies. Appropriate authorities were directed to send a quarterly report to the central supervisory board and initiate public awareness campaign against the practice of pre-natal sex determination. The Supreme Court of India's directive to the government to implement the provisions of the Pre-Natal Diagnostic Techniques (Regulation and Prevention of Misuse) Act banning sex determination tests and sex selection to prevent female feticide had salutary cascading effects. The Court directed nine companies to supply the information of the machines sold to various clinics in the last five years. Details of about 11,200 machines from all these companies and fed into a common data base. Addresses received from the manufacturers were also sent to concerned states and to launch prosecution against those bodies using ultrasound machines that had failed to get themselves registered under the Act. The court directed that the ultrasound machines/scanners be sealed and seized if they were being used without registration. Three Associations viz., The Indian Medical Association [IMA], Indian Radiologist Association [IRA], and the Federation of Obstetricians and Gynecologists Societies of India [FOGSI] were asked to furnish details of members using these machines. Since the Supreme Court directive 99 cases were registered and in 232 cases ultrasound machines, other equipments and records were seized Today, there is an estimated 25,000 ultrasound machines in the country, of these 15,000 have been registered. State governments have communicated to the central government in writing that according to official reports received, they are satisfied that sex determination services are no longer being provided in their respective states. However, it is widely believed that while these services are no longer openly available their clandestine availability and utilization are continuing all over the country. The observation of the National Inspection and Monitoring Commission confirms this situation and endorsed the need for stricter enforcement of laws.

The court has been closely monitoring the implementation of its various orders passed since May, 2001, regarding the ban on the use of ultrasound scanners for conducting such tests. Subsequently, it had sought status reports from all states and Union Territories. It had ordered compulsory registration of all diagnostic centers across the country. The Act prohibits determination and disclosure of the sex of fetus. It also prohibits any advertisements relating to pre-natal determination of sex. Following the apex court's orders earlier, appropriate authorities with powers of civil court have been appointed. These were empowered to prosecute the clinics and the doctors if they used ultrasound technique for sex determination. A committee has also been constituted at the national level to monitor the enforcement of the Act through field visits. However welcome these provisions are, legislation alone will not help check female feticide completely.

What is of utmost importance is a real change in the people's attitude and realization of the fact that it is a dangerously immoral, illegal and inhuman game.

In *Vinod Soni and Another v. Union of India*[17] constitutional validity of PNDT Act itself was challenged and it was held that right to bring into existence a life in future with a choice to determine the sex of that life cannot in itself to be a right. Reliance is placed on a Supreme Court Judgment and two earlier decisions whereby the Supreme Court has explained that Art. 21 and the rights bestowed thereby include right to food, clothing, decent environment, and even protection of cultural heritage. These rights even if further expanded to the extremes of the possible elasticity of the provisions of Art. 21 cannot include right to selection of sex whether preconception or post conception thus, not unconstitutional.

Research Findings

Dreze and Sen (1996) have termed the low sex ratio in India as a "missing women" phenomenon: on the basis of Sub-Saharan ratios, the number of "missing women" in India is estimated to be between 35-37 million (Dreze and Sen, 1996). There are two sides to the story. Sons are highly desired for their social, symbolic, and economic value. But daughter aversion, fuelled primarily by the perceived economic burden of dowry for daughter is playing a larger role in fertility decision-making than son preference. Cultural and religious practices that mandate boys play more important family roles compound the desire for sons. Son preference is attributed to patriarchal family systems. Boys are regarded as important because they look after property, care for parents when they get old and perform ritual duties when the parents die. There is a belief in Bihari society that, with the birth of a girl, the earth goes down by few yards whereas the birth of son raises its position. Simultaneously, the father is asked to take off his *pagadi* (turban) because with the birth of a girl, humiliation and misfortune have entered the house. And since the father is not only a male, but also on the top of gender hierarchy, he should prepare himself to fight this bad omen. In contrast, the moment the pregnancy is disclosed, the entire family and the community, expecting the birth of a boy sit together and sing.

Servitude

'Servitude' is mentioned in the Supplementary Convention on the Abolition of Slavery, the Slave Trade and Institutions and Practices similar to Slavery of 1956.The Convention binds the member States to outlaw slavery-type practices of economic exploitation in the form of bonded labor and serfdom. There is one major legal problem with regard to the claim that pregnancy and child bearing fall within the scope of the term 'servitude'. In South Africa there is of no such problem as its Constitution recognized the right to bodily and psychological integrity which includes the right to make decisions concerning reproduction [Section 12(20(a)] and right to control over one's body[12(20(b)]. So, the Court had no difficulty in upholding the validity of Choice on Termination of Pregnancy Act, 1996 in *Christian Lawyers Association v. National Minister of Health.*[18]

Does bearing a female child constitute servitude? Surely, there cannot be any such thing forming the basis for female child destruction.

Son Preference (Treasure)

Son preference is not an Asian Drama but a fact of life. In 2003, a study titled "The Demand for Sons: Evidence from Divorce, Fertility and Shotgun Marriage" was published by two professors of economics, Gordon Dahl and Enrico Moretti. Dahl and Moretti (2004) analyzed the U.S. Census from 1940 to 2000, and detected several subtle trends; each trend, they said, might be accounted for by some other explanation, but taken together showed a pattern of a preference for sons.

The so-called 'son-preference' is not unique to India but rooted in South Korea's Confucian philosophy, which stresses the role of the son in carrying on the family's bloodline, and in various ancestral rituals. Bearing a son is regarded as a woman's most important role. Girls are secondary since they become part of their husband's family after marriage. But these traditions have been modified to suit South Korea's embrace of capitalism. Authorities in Vietnam are preparing a law which will stop doctors from performing tests on pregnant women which will tell them whether they will have a son or daughter—aimed at stopping the abortion of females in a society where many parents prefer to have sons. Notably, highly biased sex ratios can also occur from some customary practices without necessarily implying infant mortality or abortion. A preference for sons also has been documented among Muslim and Christian populations in MENA region (Arnold, 1992 and Williamson 1976). But there is no menace of female feticide in MENA region which means there is no necessary linkage between the two but some influence cannot be ruled out in Indian context. One should not forget that there are many couples in India who regret not having a girl child in the family.

The cultural preferences for sons rather than daughters have skewed sex ratios in India. Census data as seen earlier show a consistent drop in the sex ratio (933F:1000M). The menace of female feticide started emerging and spreading all over northern and western India and later on all over the country. Today female feticide is no more an urban phenomenon; rural people are also getting more and more involved in it and come all the long way to cities to get these tests done.

Son is preferred because of his social standing, financial asset and spiritual worth. "Through a son he conquers the worlds, through a grandson he obtains immortality, but through his son's grandson he ascends to the highest heaven" (Baudhyana Sutra 2-9-16.3). A son also has the pious obligation of discharging debt incurred by his deceased father for legitimate purposes. He put fires on the mouth for burning his father's dead body on imaginary spiritual wellbeing. So, a son is more valuable and important than a daughter. All these apparent benefits are questionable. Does anybody conquer the world by reason of his sons? Can anyone conquer the world at all? How can a grandson accord immortality to his grand father? There is no guarantee of maintaining the lineage either. When someone has long gone, how a son's grandson can mount that departed soul to the highest heaven real or imaginary? Is there any heaven? What is the address of this heaven? This roadmap to the heaven was designed to befool the ignorant lot in the Dark Age and we now need to follow the precept of *Thamaso Ma Jyothirgamaya*.

Daughter Aversion (Trouble)

"Grooming a girl is like watering a neighbor's garden" (Downing, 2005: 431-433). The practice of sex-selection abortion is defined by the United Nations as the "intentional killing of unborn females due to the preference for male offspring (also known as "son preference")." The consequences from sex-selection abortion, female infanticide and the imbalance of male and female ratios include increased rape, sex trafficking and prostitution, crime, societal unrest and obstruction to the development of democracy and prosperity. Ironically, reducing the female population increases female discrimination. The practice carries with it many complicated issues that involve ethics, morals and fundamental human rights. Although it is most often discussed in the realm of medical ethics, sex-selection can easily be viewed as a breach of human rights. According to a journal report 500,000 female fetuses are sacrificed every year in India (Baldauf, 2006). A recent study suggests that "[S]ex-selective abortion-seekers were significantly more likely to come from joint families and were better off economically than women who had abortions for other reasons. However, they had less autonomy and mobility, and were less likely to play a major role in family decision-making. They were also less likely to have an independent source of personal income and even when they did earn money, a significantly lower proportion of these women were able to keep or spend their earned income" (Ganatra et. al. 2001: 113). However, girls are increasingly educated and going to work all over India. They are far more productive and valuable assets to any society. To undermine their worth is to impoverish the world and to unjustifiably downgrade their dignity as human beings and denial of human rights.

The Way Forward

Multiple attacks must be combined from all directions to protect our girl children. The educated women should stand up to the challenge. Elderly parents need be given an umbrella to cover for the old age so that their dependency on the sons gets reduced progressively.

National Plan of Action exclusively for the girl child (1991-2000) was formulated in 1992 for the "Survival, Protection and Development of the Girl Children". The Plan recognized the rights of the girl child to equal opportunity, to be free from hunger, illiteracy, ignorance and exploitation. The launching of the *Balika Samriddhi Yojana* in 1997 is a major initiative of Government to raise the overall status of the girl child. It intends to change family and community attitudes towards her and her mother. Under this scheme about 2.5 million girl children born every year in families below the poverty line are to be benefited.

The National Policy for the Empowerment of Women in India (2001) was a forward march in the history of Indian women's human rights. It refers to many aspects of women's lives, and includes assurances that: 'Measures will be adopted that take into account the reproductive rights of women to enable them to exercise informed choices.' (6.2) And 'All forms of discrimination against the girl child and violation of her rights shall be eliminated by undertaking strong measures both preventive and punitive within and outside the family. New measures relate specifically to strict enforcement of laws against prenatal sex selection and the practices of female feticide, female infanticide, child marriage, child abuse and child prostitution etc.' (8.1). Time is ripe for review of the MRTP Act itself and the whole issue should be covered by comprehensive legislation creating national data base for births and deaths with stricter inbuilt monitoring mechanism in place and insurance cover which can squarely address the issue in social perspective. Several sections notably IPC 312-316 need be revisited, although both these laws were meant to protect the childbearing function of the women and legitimize the purpose for which pre-natal tests and abortions could be carried out. However, in practice we find that these provisions have been misused and are proving against the interest of the females. The marriage registration system need be modernized and tightened to plug all possible loopholes. The new stipulation should incorporate a provision for imposition of a small levy along with registration fee providing for insurance cover to the future children of the newly married couples which may extend to the cost of marriage thereby lessening the burden on the parents.

The Indian government promises that it will reward girls from single child family with free education and other benefits. The move is intended to bolster India's dwindling female population and help promote population control. One writer summed up the dream scenario, "The day grooms are available without hefty price tag attached to them, female feticide will end."[19]

References

Arnold, F., 1992. Sex Preference and Its Demographic and Health Implications. *International Family Planning Perspectives* 18 no. 3: 93-101.

Baldauf, S., 2006. *India's "Girl Deficit" Deepest among Educated*. CHRISTIAN SCI.MONITOR, World, at 1. http://www.csmonitor.com/2006/0113/ p01s04-wosc.html (accessed August 15, 2011).

Bergson, H., 1907[1944]. *The Creative Evolution*. Tr. Arthur Mitchell, Henry Holt and Company. Modern Library: Random House.

Caine, B. and G. Sluga, 2002. *Gendering European History: 1780-1920*. London: Continuum.

Committee on the Status of Women in India, 1974. *Towards equality : report of the Committee on the Status of Women in India*. New Delhi: Government of India.

Dahl, G.B. and E. Moretti, 2004. The Demand for Sons: Evidence from Divorce, Fertility, and Shotgun Marriage. Working Paper, National Bureau of Economic Research: Cambridge (January): 10281. http://www. nber.org/papers/ w10281.

Desai, S., 1994. *Gender Inequalities and Demographic Behavior: India.* New York: The Population Council.

Downing, K. A., 2005. Feminist is a Person Who Answers "Yes" to the Question, "Are Women Human?: An Argument Against the Use of Pre-implantation Genetic Diagnosis for Gender Selection. *8 Depaul J. Health Care L*: 431-60.

Dreze, J and A. Sen, 1996. *India: Economic Development and Social Opportunity.* Oxford: Oxford University Press.

Ganatra, B., S. Hirve and V.N. Rao, 2001. Sex-Selective Abortion: Evidence from a Community-Based Study in Western India. *Asia-Pacific Pop. J.* (June): 109-124.

Gandhi, M.K., 1957. *An Autobiography: The Stories of My Experiments with Truth.* New Delhi: Beacon Press.

Klasen, S. and C. Wink, 2002. A Turning Point in Gender Bias in Mortality? *Population and Development Review*, 28, No. 2: 285-312.

Mukherjee, B.N., 1975. Awareness of Legal Rights among Married Women. *Indian Anthropologist.* Vol. 5, No. 2: 35-78

Rao, V., 1993. The Rising Price of Husbands: A Hedonic Analysis of Dowry Increases in Rural India, *The Journal of Political Economy*, Vol. 101, No. 4, August: 666-677.

Rummel, R.J., 1994. *Death by Government.* New Brunswick, N.J.: Transaction Publishers.

Williamson, N., 1976. *Sons or Daughters: A Cross-Cultural Survey of Parental Preferences.* Beverly Hills: Sage Publications.

Notes

1. The Paper is based on presentation made in Ninth International IDEA Conference, 9-11 June, 2011 at Bryn Mawr College, Philadelphia, US.

2. Referred to in the Lecture titled, 'Gandhi and Status of Women' by Jyotsna Kamat at the Gandhi Peace Foundation in December, 1998.

3. Source: WEF Report 2010.

4. *mrityuh sarva-haras ca 'ham udbhavas ca bhavisyatam kirtih srir vak ca narinam smritir medha dhrtih ksama*
(I am all-devouring Death, and I am the generating principle of all that is yet to be. Among feminine qualities I am fame, prosperity, speech, memory, intelligence, firmness and forgiveness).

5. library.thinkquest.org/C002291/high/present/social.htm accessed on August 17 2011) mentioned by Parmita Shastri, Outlook India, 1998.

6. According Vedic texts, the rite of Punsavan or Pumsavana was required to be performed after three months of impregnation by the couple praying for a male child.

7. Tr. Arthur Mitchell, Henry Holt and Company; 1944, Modern Library, Random House.

8. [1680] 3 Coke, Institutes 50.

9. Re MB (medical treatment) [1997] 2FLR 426.

10. (2005) 40 EHRR 12.

11. 2 N.Y.3d 148; 809 N.E.2d 645.
12. AIR 1963 SC 1295.
13. "Legal Rights among Married Women and Their Status", Indian Anthropologist 5(2) 1975.
14. The Book Review (2002: 272).
15. See V. Sawmveli's "Legal rights of Mizo Women" (unpublished) presented in Ninth International IDEA Conference, 9-11 June, 2011 at Bryn Mawr College, Philadelphia, Pennsylvania.
16. CEHAT (Centre for Enquiry into Health and Allied Themes) v. Union of India. AIR 2001 SC 2007.
17. 2005 CRILJ 3408: 6.
18. 2004 (10) BCLR 1086 (T).
19. Dr. Amit Sethi, The *Tribune of India* 27 June 2003.

CHAPTER 14

The Rights of People Living with Disability from a Third World Perspective: The Zimbabwean Context

Francis Machingura

The status of disabled people is an issue that has caused headaches in the broader world; developed, developing and underdeveloped world. Terms like 'health', 'normality', 'disability' and 'impairment' are highly contested as their meanings are not clear, objective, and universal across time and space and are contentious even for contemporaries in the same culture, profession and field (Asch 2001). The United Nations regards 'disability' as implying any person unable to ensure by himself or herself, wholly or partly, the necessities of a normal individual and/or social life, as a result of deficiency, either congenital or not, in his or her physical or mental capabilities (http://www.un-documents.net). Disability is a term that has been broadly defined and understood depending on cultural, economical, religious and social dynamics in a given nation. Disability in this paper refers to people with polio; amputees; people with club feet; congenital deformity; paraplegia; speech impairments; hearing impairments; visually impaired; physically impaired; hemi-paresis; mentally challenged; and albinos. As a result, the medical and social models have been used by various scholars to look at disabled persons (Solarsh and Hofman 2006). Disabled people have been characterized as incomplete or defective human beings, subjected at one extreme to neglect, persecution and death, and at other extreme to charity, social welfare and paternalism. Disadvantage and inequality despite international initiatives and covenants represent the everyday experience of disabled persons (Doyle 1995). Throughout the Zimbabwean history, persons with disabilities have been negatively viewed and to some extent leading to the blame of the family, for example, the mother being blamed for bringing to the world a disabled person. Discrimination against disabled persons is institutionalized and interwoven in the fabric of the Zimbabwean society, calling for major action beyond the international initiatives and covenants. Ranga Mupindu, the former

Executive Director of National Council of Disabled Persons in Zimbabwe, narrates that his mother was blamed for his disability and some people thought he had been bewitched yet it was polio (Chimedza 2001). The above case of 'denial' does not even respect the medical findings. The mother is usually suspected of having practiced promiscuity during the pregnancy or caused the displeasure of the ancestral spirits (Addison 1986). It is a cultural norm amongst Zimbabweans that pregnant women are encouraged to desist from looking at or associating with people with disabilities lest the curse is transferred to them and give birth to a child with disabilities (Barnatt 1992). In some cases, some people take disabled persons as individuals who require societal protection, sympathy rather than respect as normal people who can independently do their chores. According to Prudence Mabhena (2010):

> In Africa, when a child is born, people celebrate. When a baby with a disability is born, people cry. There is a lot of shouting, insults, and some believe that maybe the baby was bewitched. In such cases, there is sometimes pressure from family members to stop caring for the child, even to let the child die (The Herald April 05, 2010).

This was echoed by Minister of Media, Information and Publicity, Information and Publicity, Webster Shamu (2010), who argued that, despite of the enactment of the Disabled Persons Act in 1992:

> Zimbabwe had only paid lip service to legislative matters addressing the needs of disabled persons. It is no secret that in most African countries, Zimbabwe included, children born with disabilities are regarded as a bad omen to be quietly disposed of from the face of the earth (The Herald June 16, 2010).

It is the intention of this paper to look at the challenges that are faced by disabled people in relation to human rights particularly in Third World countries like Zimbabwe.

The disabled persons in Zimbabwe just like in other countries have struggled to have a place and identity in society hence cultural identity and individual empowerment (Chimedza and Peters 1999). This is despite the fact that most nations are signatories to the United Nations Universal Declaration of Human Rights (UDHR) of 1948. The world acknowledges achievements witnessed with the General Assembly's proclamation in 1981 as the International Year of Disabled Persons (IYDP). Its emphasis was on increased public awareness; understanding and acceptance of persons who are disabled; and encouraging persons with disabilities to form organizations through which they can express their views and promote action to improve their situation (http://www.un.org/esa/). The goal was on full and effective participation and integration of persons with disabilities in society and development. The United Nations Organization must be commended for its commitment to the full and effective participation of all human rights including persons with disabilities, an endeavor that is deeply rooted in the quest for social justice and equity in all aspects of societal development (http://www.un.org/esa). These were further strengthened by the newly adopted Convention on the Rights of Persons with Disabilities, adopted in 2006. Even though the General Assembly called for a plan of action in all parts of the world in relation to the rights of persons with disabilities; the context of disabled persons in Zimbabwe calls for an urgent attention. The image of persons with disabilities even in institutions believed to be associated with the love of God clearly show the social, economical, political and religious barriers faced by people with disabilities in national development let alone in the "equalization of opportunities". The success and failures of international covenants focusing on disabled persons need to be understood in relation to poverty and development at the level of the people, their communities and then situate it within regional, national and global structures of wealth and power (Stone 2001, Clements and Read 2008, Wasserman, Asch and Bickenbach 2008). Participation of persons living with disabilities is hindered as a result of social attitudes bred in a society whenever a disabled member joins a group, institution or family. What is interesting is that, fears and uncertainty about living together or integration of the disabled surprisingly come mostly from the able-bodied. I have seen that mostly with those who don't know how to greet somebody with shorter arms, or how to speak to someone who is mentally disabled and they try by all means to avoid situations which will make them socialize with the disabled persons, hence the "the barriers of the mind". The result of these societal fears in Zimbabwe is that the disabled live in their own different world where they are pushed to the edges of society, making it a separate world for the disabled.

People should realize that they too can become disabled at any time and there is an old Shona adage which goes "Scorn or laugh at disability after death (Seka urema wafa)". The Shona philosophy is against the discrimination of disabled persons even though there were no mechanisms to support that particularly to make the mainstream society positively socialize with disabled people. In fact the fears people have is that if you laugh at a disabled person, the curse will be transferred to the one who is laughing. The stigma, fears, myths and misconceptions associated with disabilities negatively affect the day to day lives of persons with disabilities leading to discrimination and the denial of even the most basic rights. It is not surprising that society still use terms like "blind and deaf" in bad light as noted by Farai Mukuta, Executive Director of National Association for Societies for the Care of the Handicapped, who argued that, it is common to find people saying "Don't behave like a deaf person or a blind person" (The Herald October 05, 2010). Such statements impact negatively on the dignity of disabled persons and also tend to have some negative impact on the socio-economical, political and religious rights of persons with disabilities. Mass media have an ethical problem when they contribute to the stereotyping of disabled persons by using vocabulary that puts them in bad light or make the public pitiful of them. According to Deni (1994), it is clear that the categories of stereotypes that media use to portray disabled persons are damaging to people with disabilities. Advertising warns people not to "buy blind". Sometimes media come up with feature stories that seem meant to portray disabled persons as managing to succeed despite their disability. The negative and stereotyped social attitude has not spared institutions of spirituality like Churches, Synagogues and Mosques. It is as a result of such challenges that one is forced to bluntly argue that, international covenants or initiatives on the rights of the disabled face implementation inadequacies and wholesale challenges in nations like Zimbabwe.

Poverty and Disability in Zimbabwe

Persons with disability in the world are put at 10 to 20 percent and disability is mostly associated with the poorest members of society as observed by the World Bank. The population figure of people living with disability is put at 650 million and those people lack opportunities of the mainstream population (http://www.un.org/disabilities). The United Nations Development Program (UNDP) adds that eighty per cent of persons with disabilities live in developing countries (http://www.disabled-world.com). Zimbabwe as one of the developing countries is believed to have a two percentage rate of disabled persons (http://www.realising-potential.org). The estimates might be lower considering that countries differ in terms of data collection, definition and cultural differences in relation to disability. The World Health Organisation puts the percentage rate at ten percent, which translates to 13 million people with disabilities (The Herald December 06, 2010). Of great challenge is the growth rate of unemployment and access to public services for the disabled persons. The rate of unemployment in Zimbabwe is put at eighty-five to ninety-four percent since the dollarization of the economy (http://ochaonline.un.org). The unemployment rate points to the level of poverty yet health specialists have established some interlink between poverty and disability particularly as a result of lack of access to good nutrition and healthcare. Persons with disabilities particularly the youth in Southern Africa are "among the poorest and most marginalised of the entire world's young people" (Groce 2003; Groce 2005). A lot of albinos in Zimbabwe die due to the unavailability of life-saving preventive medication and equipment, for example, radiotherapy and chemotherapy treatment is unaffordable to 99 percent of the affected (Sunday News June 21, 2010). African States through their voluntary membership of the UN Human Rights Charter (1945), the African Charter on Human and People's Rights (1981) and other international instruments upholding the human right to life with dignity have compromised their integrity by continuing to disregard the plight of persons with albinism by not enacting enabling laws (http://www.africa-union.org). The preferred action of making appropriate policies has not changed the socially constructed hostile environment against persons with disability in Africa. The situation is bad particularly in the Zimbabwean rural areas where people have no access to information about disability.

In the case of Zimbabwe, the majority (70 percent) of the population in Zimbabwe live in rural areas where there are slim opportunities as compared to those in urban areas. There is not much about the rural disabled persons making their situation much difficult for them and their families. Most of the organizations are based in urban centers making them easily accessed to disabled persons in cities. It must however, be commented that the government and non-governmental organizations are doing their best to work with rural communities in identifying disabled persons there. The effort is still very minimal leaving rural disabled persons out of social development. A delegation of Zimbabwean handicapped people once visited Prime Minister Morgan Tsvangirai in 2010 to request him to become their ambassador. According to Mr Alexander Phiri, the director-general of the Southern Africa Federation of the Disabled, "The general living conditions of disabled people in Zimbabwe are deplorable and most of whom are living in abject poverty. We hope the Government makes deliberate efforts to address issues of poverty as disabled people are the poorest of the poor" (The Herald December 06, 2010). Persons with disability are the most affected as their chances of getting employment are very slim when related to their counterparties in Zimbabwe. This is despite the fact that they have a wide array of skills, expertise and passion to work but as a result of discriminatory practices in the recruitment process, they are denied of their right to employment. This is also despite the fact that, the job performance of most persons with disabilities is as good, if not better, than the favored candidates. The fears and costs to employers that are raised in relation to hiring persons with disabilities tend to be exaggerated and based on foregone societal attitude towards disabled persons. Some employers only employ disabled persons for charity or out of pity or to get compensated for it. The discriminatory recruitment process emanates from the societal discrimination that disabled persons face in Zimbabwe.

According to Livion Nyathi (1986), the problem of seclusion starts when disabled persons are branded as "special cases" amongst their communities. The disabled end up earning a conspicuous social stigma that impedes progress in their social development. Social development cannot be achieved in societies if certain people are discriminated against as a result of their physical appearance or mental status. As it stands now in Zimbabwe, disabled persons do not want legislation that recognizes them as people with special needs, but instead outlaws and removes environmental and social barriers which prevent disabled persons from participating on equal terms with other people on daily life issues (Ken Davis, 1996). Any discrimination puts particularly women with disabilities at risk for HIV infection when forced by economical circumstances to turn to prostitution or transactional sex as a means of financial and material empowerment (Rohleder, Swartz and Philander 2009; McCarthy 1993). The 2007 report released by Tsitsi Chorumi entitled *"The Forgotten Tribe: People with Disabilities in Zimbabwe"* shares the experiences of disabled people, the discrimination they face in Zimbabwe society, and their exclusion from the usual government and civil society sources of aid. It exposed how the disabled are excluded in most of the issues to do with: policy and legislative needs; social interaction; poverty; gender; health; HIV and AIDS; education; employment; and sports and recreation (http://wecando.wordpress.com). Recently people living with disabilities have called for representation in the Zimbabwean Government, including Cabinet, as they feel that they are neglected as their issues are not adequately addressed. According to Councilor Lamel Mandiziba (2010):

> Only a Cabinet person who lives with a disability can fully understand our needs. We have been fighting for a long time to get what we want after being left out from developmental projects and funds meant to help start projects.

> Half the time politicians ignored our challenges, referring them to non-governmental organisations and embassies for assistance as if we pay our taxes to these organisations. Our tax is remitted to the Government, just like everyone else (Chronicle October 27, 2010)

In 2009 constitutional making, there have been further calls to include the rights of disabled persons in the constitution of Zimbabwe as they feel that they are deprived of economic and social rights. Zimbabwe's current constitution has no definite/clear clause for the protection of both the social and economic rights of the disabled members of its population (The Herald March 25, 2010; The Herald June 16, 2010). This clearly goes against the UN General Assembly declaration on the rights of disabled persons resolution number 3447(XXX) of December 9, 1975 which might be regarded as the most important document containing international commitment on the protection of some of the rights of disabled persons (United Nations, 1975). Yet there is need for governmental commitment to provide for disabled people at all stages of their life from childhood to adulthood. Despite the government adopting the Disabled Persons Act of 1992 as realization of the rights of the disabled, not much has been done to empower them to have equal access to education, health, employment, recreations, etc. The exclusions painfully include: social events, cultural activities, festivals making the disabled people vulnerable to poverty, emotional stress and neglect as they cannot socialize with other people. The assumption that one gets in Zimbabwe is that, people with disabilities do not love sport as most of the sporting facilities don't cater for them. It is regrettable that persons with disability in Zimbabwe have high opportunity infringement on their inalienable rights to do with all freedoms enunciated in the declared Articles (1-30) of The Universal Declaration of Human Rights. Persons with disability in Zimbabwe are also more likely to be victims of violence or rape or physical abuse particularly women and girls. Most of the victims with disability suffer silently or quiet revolution as individuals as a result of the social attitude. Most of the abuse (physical and sexual) as reported in the media comes from uncaring members of the family or even fellow able-bodied children. Zimbabweans have the memory of the harrowing experiences of recent Oscar winner Prudence Mabhena, a person living with disability, at the hands of her stepmother. Prudence suffered abuse because of her disability and largely due to the absence of a clause in the current constitution specifically designed to protect such children (UNICEF June 20, 2010; Chronicle March 23, 2010; NewZimbabwe.com March 23, 2010). The present constitution has a general non-discrimination clause that just forbids citizens from segregating others on grounds of disability; otherwise the stepmother could have been made to pay for her actions if there had been a clause making it a criminal offence to ill-treat disabled persons.

Disability and Freedom of Movement

What is interesting is that, governments in the African sub-Saharan region were instituting protocols on everything else save disability. As the world is broadly becoming technologically connected, the disabled persons are left behind in making technology become accessible to them as well making the world friendly to the disabled persons. This is clearly shown by the difficulties that people face if they want to access public and private institutions. The United Nations recently (2008) called at The Convention on the Rights of Persons with Disabilities for Accessibility of Buildings to all Persons. The convention was a major step toward changing the perception of disability particularly in ensuring that societies recognize that all people must be provided with the opportunities to live life to their fullest potential, whatever that may be. It states that "over time, new construction should incorporate designs that take into account the needs of persons with disabilities" (http://www.un.org/disabilities). The World Bank established that such designs in terms of costs at the time of construction of the buildings will be minimal and adds less than one percent to the construction costs. What is important is the commitment on the part of the government. Unfortunately, that commitment and urgency on the Zimbabwean government cannot be determined as the Zimbabwean government has not yet ratified the 2008 Convention on the Rights of Persons with Disabilities. By not ratifying a convention, it implies that, the treaty has still not come into force and the country does not have any legal obligations and implementing legislation in relation to the condition of disabled persons. And this resonates by what one finds in most of the private and public institutions that serve mainstream population. The unfriendly environment and the disregard for the disabled is most pronounced in public offices used by all government officials starting with both the Zimbabwean President and the Prime Minister. Tichaona Zindoga (2010) notes that:

> The very inaccessibility of the premier's office, housed at the second floor painted a gloomy picture of the current unfriendly scenario that faces disabled persons, which they endure for the foreseeable future. A number of wheelchair-bound members had to endure the humiliation of being lifted up the staircase to the second floor of the prime Minister's office. One could see the stoicism of the elderly members, some of whom were women, as they were carted up and down by strangers (The Herald December 06, 2010).

If the state of disabled persons in accessing public offices that are used by the head of state as well as the head of government cannot be noticed by those who are supposed to care for all citizens as shown above; it shows the task and challenges that persons with disability will have to endure in Zimbabwe for the near future. It is loud and clear that African governments are far-removed from the disabled people and are not there for them. One can safely argue that, the disabled are the most neglected people when it comes to the planning of buildings in Zimbabwe's towns. The possible and frequently asked question among the disabled now is: Do planners have their plight in mind when coming up with building structures? Do the facilities of everyday life put into consideration the condition of the physically handicapped? All public buildings in Zimbabwe do not have designs that are friendly to people with disabilities.

The Zimbabwean context exposes the daily degrading treatment (Article 15), infringement of their privacy (Article 22) and personal mobility (Article 20) that disabled persons face on daily basis. The Zimbabwe National Association for the Care of the Handicapped Chairperson, Godfrey Majonga (2010), bemoaned the situation in Zimbabwe as unacceptable. He narrated the ordeal of the disabled persons saying:

> Just looking in Harare, the capital city, we have city council's Town House which is inaccessible, so is the Harare Central Police Station, Banks (whose Bank managers or senior officials occupy offices that can only be accessed by stairs). You have most of the public hospitals, courts...the list goes on. The disabled people would like to be served when they approach the police, healthy personnel or City Council without asking someone's help to climb up the stairs. All services must be accessible to physically challenged people with hearing, seeing impairments but that is not the case (The Herald December 06, 2010).

Sidi Chitsiva narrated how he failed to get a job as a result of the venue where the interviews were carried out. According to Chitsiva "What is painful is that, I was not barred from working for that company and getting the highly paying job, but the building prevented me from getting the job I so loved. Most of the roads in Harare do not cater for the disabled people but pedestrians and those with bicycles. The roads are not for people with wheelchairs due to the potholes on the roads" (Njema 2010). Presently speaking the Zimbabwean infrastructure is hostile to people living with disabilities as a result of the ill-suited public services. The services are not user friendly to disabled persons hence compromising them on the Convention of the Rights of Persons with Disabilities in relation to: justice (Article 13), liberty and security (Article 14), their integrity (Article 17), and their participation in political and public life (Article 29). Besides buildings that save the public, the barriers are also experienced in transport, information, education.

Disability and Education

It is common that in most of the schools let alone colleges and universities, facilities that cater for the disabled persons in Zimbabwe still remain a pipe dream; which goes against Article 24 which encourages the state to recognize the rights of persons with disabilities to education. It is then clear that the daily lives of the disabled are hindered by the country's failure to provide the disabled persons with equality in daily life. Most disabled children opt to go to first grade primary school education when they are as old as 10 to 11 years, yet other non-disabled children start their educational life when they around five to six years. I cannot even mention pre-schooling meant for the disabled in Zimbabwe as I have never heard of it. The Vice-president of Zimbabwe, Joyce Mujuru, lamented that integrating disabled children into ordinary schools will help shape the Zimbabwean society as the International initiatives would want it to be. She argued further that, it would help demystify and deal with Zimbabwean society's patronizing and negative attitudes towards disabled people particularly those in rural areas where most disabled children failed to continue with their education because of a dearth in user-friendly infrastructure and learning materials (The Herald May 18, 2010). Teaching Aids usually for the disabled persons are scarce in most schools, colleges and universities. A twenty-seven old woman, Netsai Gashu, expressed great disappointment at the failure by the Government to establish both high schools and institutions of higher learning for people living with both hearing and speech impairments (The Sunday Mail April 11, 2010; The Zimbabwean June 20, 2010). Gashu said as a result most people only go as far as primary school education. Gashu (2010) lamented that:

> There is need for special schools and institutions, so that we can also advance academically. If that is too difficult a task, then the Government should make it mandatory that all schools have at least one class for students with special needs. We have been disadvantaged for far too long and I feel this needs to be rectified, because most of those people that you see begging or vending on the streets are not there because they want to be there (The Zimbabwean June 20, 2010).

The Zimbabwean Midlands Governor, Cephas Msipa showed empathy to the plight of the disabled when he highlighted a case of a paraplegic boy who passed his Ordinary levels but was denied a place for high school education because he "did not have a wheelchair" and the boy failed to proceed with his education even though he was bright enough to proceed to University as per his life dream (The Chronicle October 27, 2010). Research findings show that, 33 percent of children with disabilities in Zimbabwe have access to education (most choose to stay at home) when compared with 90 percent for the able-bodied populace (The United Nations General Assembly, July 26, 2010). When one looks at the uninspiring percentage difference, it spells the inadequacies of the international initiatives and the urgency that respective governments in Third World countries must be made to bear.

The educational sector in Zimbabwe as typified in schools is a reflection of the Zimbabwean society's failure to accept people with disabilities (Chimedza and Peters 1999). Educational transformation and renewal of society's perspective of disability is imperative as it is the prime mover of the religious, political, economical, civic and social aspects on disability in Zimbabwe. Unfriendly environments hinder the participation of disabled persons in the development of the country. The impediments besides claims on the lack of funds show the inadequacies on the International covenants and initiatives in targeting the disabled persons. This goes against the general principles (Article 3) and obligations (Article 4) of the Convention on the Rights of Persons with Disabilities particularly Article 5 which states that disabled people must be treated equally and the law must protect them against any discrimination such that countries are called to ensure that disabled persons enjoy their rights; the same with Article 9 on accessibility to services by eliminating challenges that disabled persons face in buildings, outdoors, transport and communication in cities as well the countryside and Article 12 on equal recognition before the law (http://www.un.org/disabilities). It is important to note that, the Zimbabwe government has made efforts to widen opportunities in tertiary education for people with disabilities, for example, at the University of Zimbabwe and Belvedere Technical Teachers College, there is a Disability Resource Centre which caters to blind and physically disabled students (The Ministries of Education, Sport and Culture and Higher and Tertiary

Education: The Development of Education National Report of Zimbabwe 2004). However the major problem is that there is a shortage of trained staff for the disabled and in some cases the staff or professionals don't accept the disabled person for what s/he is but become pre-occupied in remaking the disabled person into a non-disabled one (Chimedza and Peters 1999). The other case, facilities found at the above named institutions are not accessible in other tertiary institutions for example, braillers, tape recorders, ramps and appropriate toilets. This also implies that university education is not accessible to disabled persons. The coming of the Zimbabwe Open University will possibly make university education accessible to disabled persons as it is done by correspondence where students are examined based on studied modules. Political leaders must be reminded that their passionate concern for votes from all members of the Zimbabwean society, including the vote of the disabled people must be the passionate concern to improve the lives of the disabled people. The same passionate call must be made to religious leaders that, they must play a leading role in changing the social perspective of disabled people. As much as disabled people pay tithes and offerings as a sign of their support and love for God's work, religious Church leaders must reciprocate by fighting for the rights of disabled persons.

The discrimination of disabled persons is even noticed in the annual financial budgets of the country where the amount set aside for the disabled cannot be noticed as it will be peanuts. The grants of US$20 given to disabled persons are very inadequate in a situation where the cost of living for a family of six is US$437, 62; yet the neighboring South African country's cost of living is US$82 (The Herald June 09, 2009; The Herald May 07, 2009; The Herald April 09, 2009; The Standard June 11, 2009). The grants that are given to disabled persons who find it hard to get a job imply that they cannot: have food to spare, have access to water, electricity, healthy, transport, footwear, education, find anywhere to rent, clothe themselves. The Zimbabwean case on the grants and financial policies in relation to disabled persons is the tip of an iceberg on the cumulative gap between policy and practice. This is despite the fact that, many commitments have been made by the international development community to include persons with disability in all aspects of development. It is important to note that the Millennium Development Goals (MDGs) proposed by the United Nations cannot be fully achieved without the inclusion of persons with disabilities, if the current trend in Zimbabwe goes unchallenged. As nations move toward the achievement of the MDGs, there is a greater possibility that this may further increase the marginalization of disabled persons. There has been a trend in Zimbabwe where even the land reform processes carried out since independence and the touted indigenization process only benefits able-bodied people and totally excludes and has disproportionate negative impact towards disabled people. If economical reforms benefited the elite, why is it that the names of known enterprising disabled people do not feature at all? Does it mean that disabled people in Zimbabwe are not interested in owning farms and business? Persons with disabilities represent key target groups in all the MDGs, yet disability and the concerns of persons with disabilities still remains to be included in MDG processes and mechanisms (http://www.un.org/disabilities). The lack of representation of the disabled persons as shown above could negatively impact on progress in the world-wide achievement of the MDGs particularly in Zimbabwe. However, Governments, global leaders, policy-makers and other stakeholders' acknowledgement of the need for disability-inclusive development, must be persistently supported and governments reminded to keep their promises. The third world context particularly in Zimbabwe make disabled persons become destitute even in the biblical terms of poverty as they lack all the fundamentals of life such as: shelter, clothing and food. During the decade-long (1998-2008) economical crisis in Zimbabwe, people went to South Africa, Botswana, Mozambique and Zambia, to buy food stuffs but it was impossible for the disabled persons, forcing them to live a life of misery.

HIV and AIDS in Relation to Disability in Zimbabwe

The exclusion of disabled persons from health issues leaves a lot to be desired particularly in relation to HIV and AIDS related issues. As the world is crying about the number of people who are succumbing to the disease; not many of the organizations ever think of the impact of the disease on the disabled. If the disease mercilessly affects Third World countries, then it implies that the disabled persons will be exterminated by the disease, particularly the blind. It is painful to realize that the number of most of the blind with children in the streets is big implying that they engage in unprotected sex, exposing them to HIV and AIDS. Farai Mukuta (The Zimbabwean December 19, 2010), the National Association of Socities for the Care of the Handicapped (NASCOH) executive director, argues that "up to date, no research had been conducted to establish the number of disabled people who were HIV positive and those in need of the life-prolonging anti-retroviral drugs. What we only see is the increasing number of visually impaired people living on the streets in the company of children". It is also clear from Mukuta's statement that most of the disabled people in Zimbabwe lack the vital information about family planning methods, Sexually Transmitted Diseases (STI). Ellen Chanetsa aged thirty-three cannot speak or hear but claims (she said this through an interpreter) that those in her situation were not getting up to date information on HIV and AIDS and have been neglected for a long time. Ellen (2010) adds that:

> You might not believe this, but it is true, I know very little about HIV and AIDS. I had three consecutive miscarriages, but I do not know what caused it. I was once tested for HIV, but the doctor failed to communicate my results to me. I am now afraid to go for another HIV test. My mother tried her best to teach me about the use of condoms but still could not explain the subject fully (The Sunday Mail May 02, 2010).

This is confirmed by The National AIDS Council (NAC) chief executive officer, Tapuwa Magure that the current Zimbabwe National AIDS Strategic Plan (ZINASP) does not cover the Most at Risk Populations (MARPS) in which the disabled persons like the people fall (The Zimbabwean December 19, 2010). Lack of education and information about health issues and abuse increase the vulnerability of disabled persons (Rohleder, Swartz and Philander 2009; Pillay and Sergeant 2000; Brown and Turk 1994). The lack of awareness in relation to sexual and reproductive health shows that disabled persons are discriminated against hence trampling on the rights of every human being as declared in the UDHR and Article 25 on Health of The Convention of the Rights of Persons with Disabilities.

There have been calls by the human rights activists and groups to the Zimbabwe government through the Ministry of Health and Child Welfare, to use part of the Aids levy to formulate brochures and booklets in Braille, if the country is to have a sound HIV prevention strategic plan that includes all people without discrimination. This includes information relating to family planning methods and the fight against the spread of HIV and AIDS, for example, use of condoms. The National Association of Societies for the Care of the Handicapped once approached the government requesting for condoms with Braille inscriptions to be availed to the blind so as to minimize the spread of HIV and AIDS (Kwayedza January 07, 2010). If people with disability are like any other normal human beings who are sexually active, proper healthy information must be conveyed and financially supported. Tonderai Mureza (2010), an activist for people living with disabilities, is right to argue that:

> We cannot talk of a solid HIV prevention strategy when people living with disabilities are not covered and expect the HIV prevalence rate to decline. The parent health ministry should devise on establishing a system with a bias towards those with disabilities. There is need of HIV informative booklets, a massive campaign to urge all the visually impaired people living in the streets to undergo HIV counselling and testing (The Zimbabwean December 19, 2010).

The situation is bad for the disabled persons in rural areas as noted by the Zimbabwe National Association of the Deaf (ZIMNAD) where most families anecdotally have a tendency of neglecting and shunning disabled persons. On the other hand, the Zimbabwean government has not adequately provided measures to help disabled people with vital information policies and legislation relating to HIV and AIDS. The focus is biased towards those who hear, see and talk. It is important to note that, human rights of Zimbabweans with disabilities are the same as the human rights of all Zimbabweans.

The Zimbabwean government's response must not be largely in response to the pressures from disability organizations and their members. According to the World Health Organisations, the problem on the failure of International covenants or initiatives in Africa in relation to particularly disabled mental persons is that 60 percent of African nations have no national mental health policy, and many have no programs or legislation that cater for the disabled persons (www.who.nt). Zimbabwe has less than ten known centers for mentally challenged persons and these have very limited places for not more than fifty respectively due to limited resources (The Chronicle April 22, 2010). The percentage rate shows the low attention given to the mental health of disabled people. It is important to note that fear and stigma results in people with mental health problems being excluded from mainstream health education programs and lead to lower levels of knowledge about HIV transmission and prevention and misinformation (Grassi, Biancosino, Righi, Finotti and Peron 2004; Yousafzi and Edwards 2004; Milligan and Neufeldt 2001). The misinformation can be traced to stories reported anecdotally suggesting that having sex with a disabled woman can cure AIDS. Such myths may increase the risk rate of abuse and targeted rape on disabled persons. There have also been reports of traditional healers who sometimes tell their HIV and AIDS patients that having sex with a disabled individual could potentially free somebody from HIV. This is generally built on the 'virgin myths or virgin cleansing' where a disabled individual, a newly born baby girl are considered 'pure' (Groce and Trasi 2004). Most disabled persons are always assumed to be sexually passive hence virgins. It is then not surprising based on such assumptions that students with disabilities are being excluded from AIDS education in Zimbabwean educational institutions. Many HIV and AIDS service providers have not directed information towards them (Janssen 2003). On the other hand, teachers assume that disabled persons will not benefit from the information as they are unlikely to become sexually active and are therefore not at risk.

Further to that, there are religious myths about disabled persons as possessed by a spirit particularly a "shavi" spirit that is known to possess healing skills. The understanding is that by raping a disabled person, one is virtually healed from all kinds of diseases. It is as a result of such beliefs that some people in the Shona society of Zimbabwe believe that people with disabilities can never and will not become infected with HIV because they had already experienced disability in life and were protected from disease infection as a result of spirit possession. Some estimates are that people with disabilities are more than twice as likely to be assaulted as people without disabilities; however, estimates that individuals with disabilities are up to three times more likely to be victims of physical abuse, sexual abuse and rape. Abuse among women with disabilities ranges from 31 percent to 83 percent, or double to quadruple the rate found among women in general (Groce 2005). The marauding abusers take advantage of the vulnerability and isolation that disabled people in Zimbabwe experience. Findings highlight the concerns regarding the greater vulnerability of disabled girls and women to sexual abuse and rape compared with their non-disabled peers, which can lead to a higher risk of sexual transmitted diseases thereby increasing the susceptibility of disabled persons to contract the HIV and AIDS disease. The mostly cited factors about targeted rape are that a disabled girl or boy is an easier victim considering that most disabled girls or boys are considered: very weak to fight off their abusers (Kwayedza December 24, 2009); deaf or blind may not be able to conversely communicate a report to the police let alone identify the perpetrator (The H-Metro Zimbabwe December 14, 2010). A 17-year-old girl, who is deaf and mute, was saved from continuous rape by a man from her village in Chinamhora when her brother heard some noise in a nearby bush. It is said the girl's brother heard some noises coming from a nearby bush and what he saw was heart-breaking to say the least: The girl's brother found Leonard Chimusoro aged forty-eight busy on top of the girl with his pants down to knee level (The H-Metro Zimbabwe December 14, 2010) The other challenge is that, people who are visually impaired cannot identify their abuser and those with hearing impairments cannot tell the police unless there is a sign language interpreter. These impediments go against Article 16 of the Convention of the Rights of Persons with Disabilities to protect disabled persons against being exploited and abused. Forced sex, including incest and rape, is particularly risky because condoms are rarely used and, therefore, exposure to HIV/AIDS is increased (Mgalla, Wambura, deBruyn 1997). Yet most disabled persons in Zimbabwe have little or no access to the police, legal counsel and courts for protection, less access to medical interventions, including counseling, than their non-disabled peers.

Disability and the Right to Shelter

Some of them get abused and taken advantage of as a result of destitution, poverty and lack of shelter. Shelter might be a problem for most Zimbabweans as a basic human right but the number of disabled people roaming and staying in the streets due to lack of shelter is worrisome. The former president of South Africa, Nelson Mandela, once said (M Oren, http://www.fig.net/, accessed August 19, 2011):

> The right to housing goes further than the right not to be subjected to arbitrary or forced eviction. It also involves a duty on the State to take effective action to enable its people to meet their need for a safe and secure home where they can live with dignity. That is not achieved easily or overnight, but...... it is now internationally recognized that States must take appropriate steps to ensure the realisation of this right (From the Speech of Nelson Mandela 1996).

It is important to note that, insecure and inadequate shelter for the disabled in Zimbabwe threatens their human dignity, i.e., physical and mental health hence their overall quality of life. Most of the few Zimbabwe centers that help people with disabilities save the Jairos Jiri centre in Bulawayo and Danhiko Home in Harare do not offer accommodation. Most of the institutions that help disabled persons do not give any voice and job opportunities to the disabled. Ranga Mupindu (Executive Director of the National Council of Disabled Persons Zimbabwe) argues that, institutions for the disabled have an attitude that disabled persons should always remain disabled. They do not go to the next step to empower disabled people and to involve them in the planning and management of their lives and in societal issues (Chimedza and Peters 1999). People with disabilities in such institutions are only objects of either charity or fundraising that benefit elite able-bodied. This has forced a lot disabled persons to stay in the streets to become beggars without shelter or remain permanently on social welfare registers as destitute (Chimedza and Peters 1999). And for some strange reason, most of these disabled ones are often without dedicated people to take care of them. Guardians or parents have often been known to develop very negative attitudes towards disabled children or relatives to the extent of even denying them access to basic aids like wheelchairs for those who cannot walk.

The Herald paper reports that, Mrs Ethel Furai, a 57-year-old woman stays with granddaughter Bibian Chiputura who is 14 years old. Bibian Chiputura is fighting a lost war with severe cerebral palsy. Mrs Furai and another mother who has two disabled children are temporarily staying at the Masimba Mothers of Children centre for People with Disabilities in Highfield, after they were evicted from their respective lodgings. The two (Ethel Furai and Bibian Chiputura) were left homeless in November 2009 by relatives who could no longer cope with Bibian's disability. Bibian was always sick and did not have medication and would cry all the time. The crying did not go down well with the relatives who said Bibian was making too much noise leading to their eviction. Mrs Furai revealed that she sought help at the Masimba Mothers of Children centre. They are staying there temporarily as it is not designed for permanent accommodation. According to Ethel (2010):

> We are not allowed to stay here because this centre was designed for mothers and their disabled children to come and spend the day together and is not for permanently accommodating people. When we asked for temporary accommodation, they thought we would only stay for a few weeks. We have nowhere to go and the days are increasing. I do not know where to go if they also evict us from here. I have no money for rent and most people will not rent out their properties to parents with disabled children because they do not like us and also believe that we use too much water. Bibian was given the wheelchair when she was seven years old and was supposed to use it until she was 10. The wheelchair can no longer support her body as it used to and the wheelchair wheels are also old, make noise and pushing it is a problem (The Herald December 31, 2010).

There are so many reports of relatives, parents and people who disown their children as a result of disabled child joining the family. This has led to marriages breaking down and family relationships disowned owing to disabilities (The Manica Post, 04 June 2010). In another incident, Mrs Monica Mukapiko (48), a widow, also of Highfield was evicted because her two children are disabled. She said her twenty-five year old daughter Memory and her twelve year old son Farai both have cerebral palsy and they are the reason she is staying at the Masimba Mothers of Children centre now. According to Monica (2010):

> Their father died in 2008 and we started renting a house in the Highfield area. We paid off the water and electricity bills and had no problems until when the landlord started accusing my children of causing problems at the house. The landlord said other tenants were complaining that my children wasted water and were generally noisy. We were also made to pay higher rent than other tenants and this worried me (The Herald December 31, 2010).

Monica Mukapiko argues that the government has not been forthcoming in helping disabled persons in getting accommodation. The situation was worse with local authorities who fail to avail affordable housing stands for disabled people. She laments that "We have been on the City of Harare's waiting list for many years and each time we visit their offices they tell us that the stands are available, but we have to pay US$4 500. We do not have such prohibitive money figures and plead with them to revisit the figures they are asking us pay (The Herald December 31, 2010).

The situation of the disabled persons in most Third World nations when it comes to their right to housing does not resonate with the relevant international legislation, such as the Universal Declaration and the International Covenant on Economic, Social and Cultural Rights. The elements constitute the human right to housing. These elements are: security of tenure; public goods and services; environmental goods and services (water, considered an essential prerequisite to the right to housing); affordability; habitability; accessibility; location; cultural appropriateness; freedom from dispossession; information, capacity and capacity-building; participation and self-expression; resettlement; safe environment; security and privacy (http://www.choike.org). According to UN-Habitat figures, one billion urban inhabitants live in inadequate housing, mostly in slums and squatter settlements in developing countries (UN-Habitat 2007). The big culprit to such effects are the disabled persons as most African governments like Zimbabwe do not have explicit policies save the Ministry of Social Welfare that target the disabled. Vice President John Nkomo lamented the classification of disabled persons as welfare individuals in Zimbabwe who cannot survive by other means other than alms (Sunday News February 21, 2010). This has set a wrong precedence on the development and participation of disabled persons in Zimbabwe. It also feeds into the social attitude that is already towards the disabled persons. As Miloon Kothari (http://www.choike.org, accessed August 22, 2011), UN Special Rapporteur on the subject puts it:

> The deepening inequalities of income and opportunities within nations have led to an increase in the number or people without adequate and secure housing. In the year 2000, UN member states agreed to work towards achieving eight development goals detailed out in 18 specific and measurable development targets. Goal 7 Target 11 calls for a significant improvement in the lives of 100 million slum dwellers to be attained by the year 2020 (Kothari 2007).

The United Nations initiatives are so noble but they do not target the disabled persons who are already in the streets as a result of failure to secure proper housing let alone even space where can pitch a slum dwelling so that the disabled persons can have a roof over their heads.

Disability and Spirituality

There are religious beliefs that portray disabled persons in bad light. Some of the perspectives are as raised above in relation to HIV and AIDS. However there are certain people who regarded disability as a "curse" from God. The golden rule of Jesus is love of the neighbor as oneself in: Mark 12:30; Luke 10: 25-37; Matthew 5: 43-48 and John 13: 34-35 is generally ignored. The concept of neighborhood for Jesus was irrespective of one's condition but emphasized on everybody as created in the image of God including the disabled persons. Love of one's neighbor is a call to love others irrespective of the toxic dimension of the other as seen by society. Jesus' ministry targeted those who were regarded as belonging to the bottom of the societal heap. Jesus' teachings help to change the mentality of society towards the disabled persons. The behavior by certain religious groupings in Zimbabwe clearly shows the level of ignorance that is there in relation to the rights of disabled persons in Zimbabwe. This is clearly shown when the Zimbabwean government was forced to quickly move in and arrest a certain apostolic sect self-proclaimed prophet in Mashonaland Central Province who chained mentally ill patients (depriving them of the freedom of movement) as part of the healing process to cast out evil spirits and reverse "curses" of disability (Chronicle, 13 February 2010). In another case, a Church elder and businessman Chipo Chikozho of the popular and largest Pentecostal church, Zimbabwe Assemblies of God Africa (ZAOGA) had to keep his mentally challenged son Naison Chikozho chained to a pole under squalid conditions for three years so as to get rid of the purported evil spirits that were tormenting him (The Herald, 20 January 2010; The Herald, 21 January 2010; The Herald, 09 October 2009). It is possible that Chikozho was just like most parents who lack information feel shy and embarrassed to have a disabled child in society. Believers in African Traditional Religion associate disability with a curse from the ancestral spirits. The general accusation amongst the Shona people of Zimbabwe is that, it is mostly the spirit of the wife that causes the disability (Chimedza 1998). Such accusations usually result in divorces. However some beliefs lead to the physical abuse or murder of disabled persons.

There have been horrors of the genocide based on religious grounds in Botswana, Ghana, Kenya, Malawi, Senegal, Burundi, South Africa, Tanzania and Zanzibar against persons with albinism. The period between 2007 and 2009 witnessed widespread killings of persons with albinism in the Great Lakes Region that forced over 10,000 into hiding has compelled some States in eastern and southern Africa to accept the need for legal support that protect the right of persons with albinism to life with dignity (The Herald May 04, 2010). The belief is that if one manages to kill an albino there is a high possibility of getting very rich. Albino killings are done at the instigation of witch-doctors who claim that albino body parts bring luck in love, life and business. It is common to read reports about albino ladies whose breasts are cut off or albino children whose eyes are removed and tongues cut. Albinos endure extreme discrimination and die due to the fact that their situation is underplayed mainly because of ignorance and resurgent superstition (The Manica Post April 23, 2010). Zimbabwe is not entirely innocent from these atrocities as there have been reports of ritual killings involving persons with albinism, another clear sign of the failure of international covenants in protecting disabled persons particularly in Third World nations.

Conclusion

The article has clearly shown the disabling barriers in Zimbabwe which are institutional, material, ideological, religious and attitudinal in nature hence impacting badly on the rights of disabled persons in relation to national development and fulfillment of MDGs. Therefore, in order for international covenants or initiatives to have impact in Third World countries like Zimbabwe, there is need for such governments to recognize that human rights and the social justice of the disabled require more than laws. Political action is not only a civil right issue but a human right issue. The Zimbabwean society need to be holistically conscientized as the cited testimonies in this article show the social attitudes and values in institutions that barricade against the progress of the disabled persons. The restrictions are socially, economically, religiously and politically constructed such that they can be changed by social and political means if international initiatives and covenants are to be successful. When such changes take place, then development in Zimbabwe can be realized.

References

Addison, J., 1986. *Handicapped People in Zimbabwe*. Harare: NASCOH, 23.

African (Banjul) Charter on Human and Peoples' Rights, 1981. http://www.africauion.org/official_documents/Treaties_%20Conventions_%20Protocols/Banjul%20Charter.pdf (accessed September 20, 2011).

Asch, A., 2001. Disability, Bioethics and Human Rights. In *The Handbook of Disability Studies* edited by G Albrecht, K Seelman and M Bury. Thousand Oaks, CA: Sage: 297–326.

Barnatt, S. N., 1992. Policy Issues in Disability and Rehabilitation in Developing Countries. *Journal of Disability Policy Studies* 3: 45–65.

Brown, H., and V. Turk, 1994. Sexual Abuse in Adulthood: Ongoing Risks for People with Learning Disabilities. *Child Abuse Review* 3: 26–35.

Central Emergency Response Fund in Zimbabwe, 2010. New Release. http://ochaonline.un.org/CERFaroundtheWorld/Zimbabwe2010/tabid/6430/language/en-US/Default.aspx (accessed August 27, 2011).

Chimedza, R. and Peters, S. 1999. Disabled people's quest for social justice in Zimbabwe. *Disability, Human Rights and Education: Cross-Cultural Perspectives*, edited by Felicity Armstrong and Len Barton (Ed.), Philadelphia: Open University Press: 7–23.

Chimedza, R., 2001. *Disability and Special Needs Education in an African Context*. Harare: College Press Publishers Pvt Ltd.

Chimedza, R., 1998. The Cultural Politics of Integrating Deaf Students in Regular Schools in Zimbabwe. *Journal of Disability and Society* 13, no. 4: 493–502

Chorumi, T., 2007. A New Report on Disabled People in Zimbabwe. http://wecando.wordpress.com/2007/09/15/new-report-on-disabled-people-in-zimbabwe/ (accessed August 24, 2011).

Clements, L. and J. Read, 2008. Life, Disability and the Pursuit of Human Rights. *Disabled People and the Right to Life: The Protection and Violation of Disabled People's Most Basic Human Rights*, edited by C. Luke and R. Janet, 1–29. London: Routledge.

Davis, K., 1996. Disability and Legislation: Rights and Equality. *Beyond Disability: Towards an Enabling Society*, edited by Gerald Hales, 124–133. London: SAGE Publications.

Deni, E., 1994. Disability and the Media: The Ethics of the Matter. *The Disabled, the Media, and the Information Age*, edited by J. A. Nelson, 73–81. London: Greenwood Press.

Disabled People Worldwide. http://www.realising-potential.org/stakeholder-factbox/disabled-people-worldwide/ (accessed July 25, 2011).

Disabled World-Disability News and Information, 2011. World Facts and Statistics on Disabilities and Disability Issues (09 June). http://www.disabled-world.com/disability/statistics/ (accessed August, 2011)

Doyle, B., 1995. *Disability, Discrimination and Equal Opportunities: A Comparative Study of the Employment Rights of Disabled Persons.* London: Mansell Publishing Ltd.

Grassi, L., B. Biancosino, R. Righi, L. Finotti and L. Peron, 2004. Knowledge about HIV Transmission and Prevention among Italian patients with Psychiatric Disorders Psychiatric Services 2001. *Save the Children* 19: 46–48.

Groce, N. E., 2005. HIV/AIDS and Individuals with Disability. *Health and Human Rights* 8, no. 2: 215–24.

———. 2003. *HIV/AIDS and People with Disability.* New Haven: Yale University.

Groce, N. E. and R. Trasi, 2004. Rape of Individuals with Disability: AIDS and the Folk Belief of Virgin Cleansing. *The Lancet*, 363, no. 9422: 1663–4.

Janssen, M., 2003. Executive Summary. *HIV & AIDS and Disability: National Conference*, edited by L. Narib, 4–5. Windhoek: NFPDN/VSO-RAISA.

Kothari M., 2007. UN: Indigenous Peoples' Rights are finally recognized. http://www.choike.org (accessed August 22, 2011).

Kwayedza, 2010. Makondomu neVasingaoni (Condoms and the Blind) (07 January). http://www.kwayedza.co.zw, (accessed August 19, 2011).

———. 2009. (24 December). Murwere Wepfungwa akabhinywa (Mentally Challenged Woman raped) (accessed August 19, 2011).

McCarthy, M., 1993. Sexual Experiences of Women with Learning Difficulties in Long Stay Hospitals. *Sexuality and Disability* 11, no. 4: 277–286.

Mgalla, Z., L. Wambura and M. de Bruyn, 1997. Gender and HIV/AIDS/STDs. *HIV prevention and AIDS Care in Africa: A District Level Approach*, edited by J Ng'weshemi, T. Boerma, J. Bennett and D. Schapins, 85–100. Amsterdam: Royal Tropical Institute.

Milligan, M. S., and A. H. Neufeldt, 2001. The Myth of Asexuality: A Survey of Social and Empirical Evidence. *Sexuality and Disability* 19, no. 2: 91–109.

Njema, S., 2010. Studio 7-Interview with Disabled People in Zimbabwe. Harare (December, 30). http://www.voanews.com/zimbabwe/news (accessed December 30, 2010)

Nyathi, L., 1986. The Disabled and Social Development in Rural Zimbabwe. *Journal of Social Development in Africa* 1: 61–65.

Oren, M., 2009. The Right to Housing: An International Perspective (May, 3–6). http://www.fig.net/pub/fig2009/papers/ts03d/ts03d_oren_abs_3490.pdf (accessed July 29, 2011).

Pillay, A. L and C. Sergeant, 2000. Psycho-Legal Issues Affecting Rape Survivors with Mental Retardation. *South African Journal of Psychology* 30, no. 2: 9–13.

Rohleder, P., L. Swartz and J. Philander, 2009. Disability and HIV/AIDS: A Key Development Issue. *Disability and International Development: Towards Inclusive Development*, edited by M. MacLachlan and L. Swartz, 137–148. London: Springer Dordrecht Heidelberg.

Sen, J., 2009. Human Rights Evicted (March 25). http://www.countercurrents.org/sen250309.htm (accessed September 17, 2011).

Solarsh, G. and K.J. Hofman, 2006. Developmental Disabilities. *Disease and Mortality in Sun-Saharan Africa (2nd Edition)*, edited by Dean T Jamison, 125–138. Washington D C: The World Bank.

Stone, E., 2001. A Complicated Struggle: Disability, Survival and Social Change in the Majority World. *Disability and the Life Course: Global Perspectives*, edited by M. Priestly, 50–66. Cambridge: Cambridge University Press.

The Chronicle, 2010. Government Moves in to Assists Chained Madziva Patients (February 13).

The Chronicle, 2010. Ministry Secures Accommodation, Food for Homeless Psychiatric Patients (22 April).

The Chronicle, 2010. Disabled Call for Representation in Cabinet. (October 27).

The Herald, 2010. Church must take action on the Tafara Businessman (January 21).

The Chronicle, 2010. Prudence's Parents Regret Mistreating Her (March 23).

The Herald, 2010. Mentally Ill Son Kept in Chains for 3 Years (January 20).

The Herald, 2010. Enshrine Disabled People's Rights in New Constitution (March 25).

The Herald, 2010. Disabled People Deserve Respect (April 06).

The Herald, 2010. Hero's Welcome for Prudence (April 05).

The Herald, 2010. Albinos killed in Burundi (May 04).

The Herald, 2010. Integrate Disabled kids-Vice President Mujuru (May 18).

The Herald, 2010. A Look at Phenomenal Unemployment Rate (May 20).

The Herald, 2010. New Constitution must Embrace Disabled People's Needs: Shamu (June 16).

The Herald, 2010. Physically Challenged Feel Excluded (October 05).

The Herald, 2010. The Disabled Demand a Voice (December 06).

The Herald, 2010. When Disability Becomes a Curse (December 31)).

The Herald, 2009. Family Basket up to US$386 (April 09).

The Herald, 2009. Family Basket Shoots Eight Percent (May 07).

The Herald, 2009. Consumer Family Basket Rises (June 09).

The Herald, 2009. Mental Illness-A Condition, Not a Curse (October 09).

The H-Metro Zimbabwe, 2010. Silent Crime as Man Rapes Deaf and Dumb Girl (December 14).

The Manica Post, 2010. Albinos form Association in Manicaland (April 23).

The Manica Post, 2010. Father Disowns Disabled Children (June 04).

The Ministries of Education, Sport and Culture and Higher and Tertiary Education, 2004. The Development of Education National Report of Zimbabwe, National Report on the Development of Education: Ministries of Education, Sport and Culture and Higher and Tertiary Education: Zimbabwe. Presentation at the 47th Session of the International Conference on Education. Geneva: Switzerland (8–11 September).

The Social Urban Forum, 2009. The Right to Adequate Housing (23 March). http://www.choike.org/2009/eng/informes/1162.html

The Standard, 2009. Rentals Spike Family Bread Basket at Consumer Council of Zimbabwe (June 11).

The Sunday Mail, 2010) Begging is Not an Option (April 11).

The Sunday Mail, 2010. Chawasarira Bus Crew Should Respect the Visually Impaired (May 16).

The Sunday Mail, 2010. People with Disabilities being Sidelined? (May 02).

The Sunday News, 2010. Disability and the New Constitution in Zimbabwe (June 21).

The Sunday News, 2010. Disability not a Welfare Matter-Vice President Nkomo (February 21).

The United Nations General Assembly, 2010. Keeping the Promise: Realizing the Millennium Development Goals for Persons with Disabilities towards 2015 and beyond, Sixty-Fifth Session (July 26).

The Zimbabwean, 2010. Deaf and Dumb Tired of Begging (June 20).

The Zimbabwean, 2010. HIV Prevention: The Blind a Forgotten Lot (December 19).

UNICEF, 2010. Zimbabwe, 15 June: Young Zimbabwean Featured in 'Music by Prudence' Champions Disability Rights. http://www.unicef.org/esaro/children_youth_Zimbabwe_youth_champions_disability_rights.html (accessed August 19, 2011).

United Nations, 1975. Resolutions adopted by the General Assembly 3447 (XXX): Declarations on the Rights of Disabled Persons, Thirtieth Sessions, Agenda Item 12 (December 09). http://www.un-documents.net/ a30r3447.htm (accessed August 27, 2011).

United Nations, 1981. The International Year of Disabled Persons 1981. http://www.un.org/esa/socdev/enable/disiydp.htm (accessed August 27, 2011).

United Nations, 1993. The Standard Rules on Equalization of Opportunities for Persons with Disabilities (20 December). http://www.un.org/esa/socdev/enable/dissre00.htm (accessed August 27, 2011).

United Nations, 2006. Convention on the Rights of Persons with Disabilities. http://www.un.org/disabilities/convention/questions.shtm (accessed August 28, 2011).

United Nations, 2011. International Day of Persons with Disabilities (December) http://www.un.org/disabilities/default.asp?id=1540 (accessed February 27, 2012).

UN-Habitat, 2007. What are Slums and why do They Exist. Nairobi: UN-Habitat https://docs.google.com/viewer?a=v&q=cache:ziGZMU6tkgQJ:www.unhabitat.org/downloads/docs/4625_51419_GC%252021%2520What%2520are%2520slu

ms.pdf+&hl=en&gl=in&pid=bl&srcid=ADGEEShS7ivbihpPGMo4ju3whKReu2WcfUNFl_Ei0CQ0yIdSKQcadtdFu8fAQnV53P__eQhqJHnOAb-WYg0vktSkAURikRvDUNBubXdTW1ErEO2m1dMiPEA83icMUGewFXtN1MkTmcgW4& sig=AHIEtbToeF59-9kPnDA7WZSZtR1VPMvz9g (accessed February 25, 2012).

Wasserman. D., A. Asch and J. Bickenbach, 2008. Mending, Not Mending: Cost-Effectiveness Analysis, Preferences and the Right to a Life with Disabilities. *Disabled People and the Right to Life: The Protection and Violation of Disabled People's Most Basic Human Rights*, edited by Luke Clements and Janet Read, 30–56. London: Routledge.

WHO, 2002. Mental Health Policy 2002. www.who.nt (accessed August 27, 2011)

Yousafzi, A. and K. Edwards, 2004. *Double Burden: A Situation Analysis of HIV and AIDS and Young People with Disabilities in Rwanda and Uganda*. London: Save the Children.

CHAPTER 15

Disability in the Third World: A Critical Mapping of the Indian Scenario

Anuradha Saibaba Rajesh

The Westphalia framework of international law since 1648 vociferously endorsed the *States* as the primordial players and actors in the international legal landscape. Post Second World War, the consolidation of the United Nations Organization further reiterated the sovereignty and domination of States. The subsequent challenge to this State centric model of international law aroused with human rights norms essaying a centrifugal role in the global scenario. The quintessential focus of preservation, protection and promotion of human rights in the word agenda gradually resulted in *individuals* evolving as legitimate subjects of international law as well. However the recognition and affirmation of rights of individuals has not transpired in all individuals benefiting from such a scenario.

The question of subaltern groups has remained a constant and common feature across the world. The 'Persons with Disabilities' comprise such a social group that have remained at the periphery of citizenry. Their marginalization and alienation has occurred in every sphere—political, legal, social, economic, political, cultural, and familial. The invisiblization prevails to such an extent that they are often reduced to the paltry status of being 'non citizens'. The elaborate international human rights framework at the global level also echoes a similar stance of invisiblization.[1] It was only as recent as 2007 that the *United Nations Convention on Rights of Persons with Disabilities*[2] was promulgated to sanctify the status and role of the disabled community in the world.

Profiling Disability: Indian Figures

It was in 2001 that disability was introduced as a separate question in the Census questionnaire but the last minute and hurried inclusion meant a glaring lack of awareness on the issue to the common man. The Schedule of Census 2011 is a step ahead and has earmarked eight types of disabilities—*'In Seeing', 'In Hearing', 'In Speech', 'In Movement', 'Mental Retardation', 'Mental Illness', 'Any*

Other' and 'Multiple Disability'.[3] The commencement of the new millennium has placed disability figures at 21 million. This is as per the National Population Census 2001 where as in sharp contrast, the NSSO (National Sample Survey Organisation) Service estimated the differently-abled to constitute 1.8 percent that is approximately 18.5 million of the total population are disabled.[4] The information on the differently-abled is aimed to devise program, schemes, laws, policies, etc., for augmenting their protection, welfare and rights.

Disability and Definition: Perhaps a Re-Look?

What is disability? A term that showcases a complex array of reactions, responses and naturally definitions. In generic language perhaps an anomaly, an imperfect human being, a dwarfian trait, an invalid, abnormal, impaired, handicapped, disadvantaged, lack of ability or skill, etc.—all adjectives galore and synonymous with the disabled. The terminology used to address this group of individuals often varies and mostly borders on insensitivity.

The reference at times has tremendous connotations of being a slur, abuse, mockery, pity, fear, etc. and thus can impact severely on the self-worth and psyche of the individual concerned or the group in collective. In legal parlance, reference to "vulnerable" or "marginalized" groups or population is "in need of special attention". It is only in recent times that the nomenclature physically/intellectually challenged or differently-abled is being used to refer to this category of people. In reality all the terms stipulated above are used interchangeably.

Under the World Health Organisation framework, the unspecified concept of disability is replaced by three differentiated conditions labelled as *impairment, disability,* and *handicap*.[5] Impairment denotes disturbances of body structure whereas disability is the interface between the physical environment and body impairment and finally handicap is referred to as a loss or limitation of opportunities in social and community life. The *International Classification of Impairments, Disabilities and Handicaps (ICIDH)* developed by WHO in 1980 remained path-breaking for disability policy as it adopted new stance towards disability issues—it recognizes the influences of personal, social and environmental factors on people with disabilities.

It aimed preponderantly at re-invigorating the rehabilitation avenues and opportunities as well as devising social policy that facilitates economic, social opportunities to people with disabilities.[6] In 2001, the WHO re-visited the ICIDH and endorsed an improvised framework of the *International Classification of Functioning, Disability and Health (ICF)*. According to Article 1 of UNCRPD states 'Persons with disabilities include those who have long-term physical, mental, intellectual or sensory impairments which in interaction with various barriers may hinder their full and effective participation in society on an equal basis with others.' The definition does not specify types of disabilities.

The heterogeneity and diversity of the term 'disability' makes all attempts at reaching a common definition either an arduous task or a myth. Still further cross sectoral implications of disability issues and the intrinsic interface of disability with other discourse like gender, race, geriatrics, etc. and the varied and differential experiences that flow from them, eludes a definition form being attributes to the term.

The Varying Models: The Paradigmatic Transformation

Central and inherent in the disability discourse is the norm of ableism wherein power structure of the able bodied dominates over the disabled.[7] And this ableism debate manifested itself in social structures, institutions, community settings and familial life wherein the not so 'able bodied' were relegated as abnormal, marginal and useless.

Since time immemorial the 'medical model' has been the quintessential focal point of the disability discourse. The model espouses the cause and identification of disability by focusing on the person's physical impairments thus thereby necessitating clinical intervention. This approach by and large visualizes the 'disabled' as a problem.[8]

Herein the classical notion of the person being subjected to charity, welfare and protectionism remains omni-present. This model visualized the individuals to be 'fixed' and sought to rehabilitate and mainstream the disabled as per prevailing social norms without taking into cognizance the role played by the society in disabling and further victimizing the disabled[9] in the process.

In stark contradistinction, the human rights model has reinvigorated the inherent dignity of the individual to be the framework for ensuring him rights and liberties. This model places the onus on the State to combat social obstacles to facilitate full respect for dignity and equal rights of all persons. Herein the autonomy and agency of the individual is affirmed and promoted and thereby they become right holders in the truest sense.

In the third format disability remains a 'social construct' wherein the society labels the individual as disabled in relation to some other norm like the able bodied.[10] In this context the agenda remains not only to '*set people apart but also to keep people apart*'. The differentiation is visible in every sphere of life and aggravates inaccessibility—education, work, family, social interaction, etc. Herein not biological impairments but the way in which the society is designed and structured for the disabled and the non-disabled, socially alienates and marginalizes the latter.[11]

The human rights paradigm has been interwoven to moot and build inclusive societies and advocate for the mainstreaming and participation of the differently-abled wherein the societies value the differences and foster respect for the dignity and equal rights for all, differences notwithstanding and moot an equal rights language and paradigm for the disabled as well.[12] The disability rights movement often heralded as the next generation civil rights movement has been in absolute sync with this perspective.

The disability movement has evolved and transformed considerably since its inception. The different phases of disability movement are enumerated below.

Table 15.1: Disability Movement through Ages

Era	Classification	Model Perspective
Before World War I	Dependent Member of Family	Burden/Liability
Between 1950s–1960s	Patient/Clinical Intervention required	Medical Model
In 1970s	Separate Care and welfare	Welfare/Care Model
From 1980s	Persons with dignity	Self-Worth of individual
From 1990s	Person able to live independently	Autonomy Mode
2000 onwards	Person with Rights	Rights Perspective

Disability and the Third World

Even in contemporary settings across third world countries disability remains a taboo issue. The disabled remain literally invisible as apart from barriers at every level—religious tenets, societal perceptions, customs, attitudes[13] compels them to withdraw from public life and opportunities of education, socialization, and outing remain minimal as well.[14] The third world approach towards disability is extremely complicated and interwoven with religious and cultural settings. Predominantly the third world nations believe the disabled to be less contributing individuals and similar thoughts are reinforced by the disabled who themselves believe they are inferior.

Disability in third world is a reflection of the dominant cultural, social, community and familial set-up. In the disability debate the individualism versus collectivism dichotomy that shapes social behavior remains dominant. The Western, industrialized and affluent societies endorse autonomy, self-reliance and steadfast independence and thus are more inclined towards individualism.[15] In stark contrast in Asian and poorer nations the thread of collectivism denoting sacrifice, duty and conformity and primacy of group or collective goals looms large.[16] Herein the agency of the disabled is hinged more on protectionism and charity rather than rights.

The larger ideological debate that dominates the human rights discourse has been the cultural relativist paradigm. With the bulk of the Asian and African nations heralding human rights *per se* to be an off-shoot of the Western ideology as opposed to the duty based social and cultural set-up that the developing countries project, inculcating a rights framework for the disabled may posit stiff resistance.

The cultural reflection of disability is reproduced and remains complementary to the social perceptions on disability which in turn impinge not only on societal norms, relations and interactions but also influence legal language, systems and mechanisms. Popular cultural and social representation of people with disabilities as useless, inferior, deformed, abnormal, etc. often exerts tremendous bearing on the legal texts as well as its contents.[17] The legal domain further endorses, shapes and maintains such images and perceptions.

The Welfare State has in the past ravaged the status and agency of the disabled individual and community. With its overarching paternal and welfarist policy, the disabled have been left stigmatized, ostracized and patronized. Needless to say the social welfare power of the State is reminiscent of unprecedented intrusion in people's lives with the goal to normalize them, control them and discipline them.[18]

It would be a misnomer to construe disability as a uniform or homogenous term, experience or phenomenon. Disability in the third world especially remains poignant and rigorous as lack of adequate resources or unequal allocation of public funds, the disablement of the powerless and poor is substantially heightened as individuals who receive less are more socially disabled in comparison to those with similar impairments.[19] Poverty in this realm acts as a doubled edged sword and disability constitutes an added and deeper feature of impoverishment.

The disability paradigm in the Indian context has been tremendously influenced by religious and cultural dogma. Structural factors have also been considered as contributing factors like poverty, illiteracy, lack of nutrition, etc. The notion of disability as a legacy of divine retribution is commonplace, pervasive and largely unchallenged. The Hindu scriptures endorse disability as a reflection of bad deeds of the previous birth. And it is this 'Karma'[20] that ordains the family with a disabled child/person to feel ashamed and guilty and thus shun them from participating in outside world.

The disabled mostly possess low self-esteem and self-reliance as the perennial negative images portrayed by the society have been internalized by them. Unsound and irrational social and cultural construction of disability can build barriers that cannot be dislocated by law and thus possess the grave implications on positing a major challenge to eradicate prejudices and perceptions.

The disabled encounter innumerable bias, prejudices and attitudes that are not only testimonial of their basic human rights being violated but also reflect on the prevailing callousness and insensitivity of the human civilization. Exclusion is the single most significant problem that the physically challenged encounter. Exclusion could be direct as well as indirect. It might amount to a school having no policy or seats for the disabled children or something even larger like inability to access restaurants, shops and other services in the face of appropriate structures like lifts, toilets for the disabled, etc. Exclusion in any form has a destabilizing impact—physically, emotionally as well as from a development perspective. Such existing classical negative attitudes and views emerge as Herculean social barriers. In most Asian countries the disabled are deemed to be devoid of any capacity to contribute effectively.[21]

Another major area of concern has been discrimination against the disabled or the challenged. This would range from treating them unequally in terms of employment, educational opportunities[22] as well as blatant discrimination like refusing to recognize that they have rights as well and require special protection and special facilities and services to live a life with dignity and to their optimum potential.

Exploitation and abuse of varied forms is unfortunately is also extremely prevalent. It could range from physical, psychological, verbal to even sexual abuse. The vulnerability of the physically challenged makes them susceptible to abuse and exploitation of overlaying degrees and forms. It occurs within the confines of a home within a family as a unit and is often more grave when they are abandoned and depend on others for their care and needs.

The other most visible prejudice against them is the pervasive is denial of opportunities.[23] This emerges from the point it's acknowledged that the person is physically challenged. It could range from social and familial exclusion and apathy to something more pertinent like lack of opportunities to schooling, skill building, basic health care facilities, employment and avocations. Even in legitimate arenas often they are denied what is lawfully theirs. For example, with jobs reserved for the physically-challenged, the real candidates are often denied the benefit or usurped through fraudulent activities by others like producing false certificates etc. The denial of educational, vocational and employment avenues often snowball into a self-perpetuating cycle of poverty and vulnerability that is life long and inter-generational.

An absolute lack of recognition and participation is omnipresent in all domains. The physically challenged have negligible or limited say in polices that affect their rights and lives. They are more often than not only shunned by their families and relatives but also by community and society. The lack of recognition of the physically challenged as a special class of people necessitating special policies, programs, laws, rights and benefits goes a long way in their exclusion and rejection of their needs and requirements. These foster their exclusion, alienation and by virtue of lack of access to services and facilities they essentially experience a lack of role and status in the society.[24]

By erroneously depicting persons with disabilities as a-sexual, a-religious and non-functional, repressive cultural and social attributes can further harness discrimination, prejudices and repressive practices against them. With religious and cultural identities possessing insurmountable implications on one's lives at all levels—familial, communal and societal, it remains incumbent to combat these invalid customs and dubious religious injunctions to charter a course of integrating and mainstreaming persons with disabilities. The objective and subjective perceptions both require a major overhauling in this context and a rethinking and revisit to this arena by all actors is of utmost urgency. Thus the Indian model of disability is inextricably linked to the cultural and social milieu and wherein the preventive and rehabilitation model reign supreme.[25]

Constitutional Reconstruction—Reconsideration

The Constitution of India is regarded as the cornerstone as well as fundamental law of the land. The reference to human rights can be discerned from the Preamble to the length and breadth of the Constitutional text. Amidst this, both Part III and Part IV of the Constitution of India are rendered extremely pivotal with the former endorsing an impressive array of Fundamental Rights and the latter catering to Directive Principles of State Policy.

In many Asian countries, India inclusive, the 'equalizing' factor has been instrumental in acknowledging the rights language for the disabled. Article 14 of the Constitution endorses the same—equality before law and equal protection before laws. The acceptance of the disabled population as equals to the non-disabled community in centrifugal to this provision. The right to equality in Article 14 endorses both equality before laws as well as equal protection by laws and is exercisable to all persons on Indian soil. The term 'persons' includes every person in India including persons with disabilities.

This fundamental right is vital to a broad range of human rights essayed in the Constitution. Distinction between persons that is arbitrary like caste, gender, disability, etc. are irrational and illegal. Differences between people should be positively accommodated and not discriminated against. The right to equality is not static but in fact a dynamic right able to suit the evolving needs of the disadvantage people and thus constitutionally obligates the State to affirmatively ensure the disabled are on the same footing as the non-disabled.[26]

Article 15 of the Constitution of India embodies the clause of non-discrimination as a fundamental right. It is interesting to note that disability is not considered as a prohibited ground of discrimination. Still further Article 15 (3) of the Constitution authorizes the State to make special laws in favor of the marginalized section of the population and mentions women and children only specifically in this category.

Thus this provision of affirmative action for the disabled as a distinct social group is also amiss in the Constitutional framework. Article 15 (4) guarantees the prerogative of the State to make laws for the socially and educationally backward communities in India [27] and this provision would definitely be applicable to the disabled population as they remain of the periphery of every arena of life.

The fundamental right to freedom of speech and expression[28] as assured under Article 19(1) (a) places a constitutional obligation to ensure the same to all citizens irrespective of their circumstances or the class they belong to. It is this right that facilitates the citizen's right to transform into a political and social entity and thus add value to the domain his/her personality, self-worth and life. Incumbent under this is the right to receive and disseminate information so as to make the individual an informed citizen and the State is obligated to guarantee this right and ensure to people with disabilities have information in accessible formats and mediums.

Article 21 depicts the heart and soul of the Constitution by endorsing the fundamental rights to life and personal liberty to all persons in Indian Territory.[29] The right to life over the decades has been interpreted to comprise of life beyond physical and animal existence and instead encompasses the right to read, write, express oneself and live with dignity.[30] Article 21 A now makes the fundamental right to compulsory and free elementary education an intrinsic component of a human beings' political, social, cultural life. By infusing a qualitative criterion into the realm of right to life the Constitutional framework elucidates a life not of vegetative criterion but one with self-worth, participation and dignity.

All the above are a legacy of the Fundamental Rights essay in Part III of the Indian Constitution.

The Directive Principles of State Policy though classified as un-justifiable and unenforceable are nevertheless fundamental in the governance of the country. And indeed it is ironical that the only explicit reference to disability is found in this section of the Constitution. Off course it is indeed a matter of grave concern that the only space given to disability issues is in Article 41 of Part IV that places an obligation on the State to cater to old age, sickness and disablement—and this if transgressed has no enforceable remedy in law.[31] This remains the sole provision in the expansive body of the Constitutional that makes a direct reference to the issue of disability per se. The idea is also to integrate the disabled with the non-disabled community. The entire thrust is upon equal and effective enjoyment of human rights by all without discrimination

Article 38 of the Constitution[32] reaffirms the welfare function of the Indian State by obligating it to facilitate a social order for the welfare of the people. The vision of social, economic and political justice that the Constitution drafters envisaged would be fulfilled only if equality of opportunities and access to service, facilities and goods are accorded to the disabled community per se. These provisions recognized the individual rights of a person with disability as well as the rights and freedoms of the disabled population as a collective. As per Article 46 the State is under an obligation to facilitate the educational and economic interests of the Schedule Caste, Schedule tribes and other weaker section of the society.[33] Persons with disabilities unequivocally fall within the constitutional ambit of 'other weaker section' of the Indian population

With regard to constitutional duties, Article 51 A (k)[34] becomes relevant as it imposes a duty on every parent to educate his/her child and this includes a disabled child. It is incumbent on parents to provide access and opportunities to their child for education. Article 51(c) attempts to foster respect for international obligations accruing on the Government of India post ratification of a treaty and thus it proclaims a constitutional mandate on the State to domesticate the international norms in the Indian scenario.[35]

The entry No. 9 of List II (State list) of the Seventh Schedule of the constitution empowers the state government to make the laws for "Relief of the disabled and unemployable". Though the length and breadth of the Constitutional expanse can be involved to legitimize the rights of persons with disabilities in all spheres, in reality it's seldom affirmed, recognized, guaranteed or interpreted.

The Legislative Framework: Laws & Lacunae

The Indian laws boast of a dual strategy—programmatic as well as rights based legislations.[36] Though the former does not expressly grant rights to individuals they devise specific goals and measures to promote equality of the disabled persons. Couched more in the language of duties and obligations, incumbent on the States these statutes do not embody an enforceable right. On the other hand a law would qualify as rights based legislation when it confers human rights, fundamental freedoms and liberties on persons with disabilities and its transgressions would entail remedies and thus it attains the status of being justiciable and enforceable. The Indian legislative enactments addressing rights of the disabled and challenged—physical and mental inclusive have been periodically passed.

With the year 1981 being declared as the *International Year for Disabled Persons (IYDP)*, India affirmed that the education of the disabled was a human resource development. This was a paradigm shift as in the erstwhile scenario, education of the disabled, provided predominantly by special schools, fell under the ambit of the Department of Social welfare. This change of gear was path breaking as it transformed the perspective of disabled individuals as parasites or burden on the society but were, in fact, individuals with self-worth and dignity. It also generated awareness in the general education system that disabled persons were equally competent and that in actual "human resources" and had the potential to emerge as contributing members of the society.

The *Mental Health Act 1987* is the main law pertaining to the care, protection and treatment of mentally ill persons The *Rehabilitation Council Act 1992*—With rehabilitation constitution an integral part of facilitating normalcy in lives of the physically and mentally challenged implies that certain minimum standards of proficiency, qualification and training. A special category of professionals termed as 'rehabilitation professionals' were identifies herein. Another law titled the *National Trust for the Welfare of Persons with Autism, Cerebral Palsy, Mental Retardation and Multiple Disabilities Act, 1999* aims to provide total care to persons inflicted with the above and safeguard their interests, property, etc. Furthermore the *State Employment Insurance Act 1948* addresses the benefits that can be availed of in individual employed in government and public agencies.

The *Persons with Disabilities (Equal Opportunities, Full Participation and Protection of Rights) Act 1995* that is PWDA as it is commonly referred to is the central and overarching legislation on disability in India. It ushered in a new era for the disabled community as it addressed multiple needs of the disabled. The *Persons with Disabilities (Equal Opportunities, Protection of Rights and Full Participation) Act* in 1995 is the first uniform legislation on the rights and protection of the physically challenged people and those with learning disabilities. It also symbolizes the first specific legal endorsement of the government towards this category of specially-abled people. The Act endeavors improvement in educational and employment opportunities for people with disabilities and at preventing discrimination.[37]

Programmatic legislations like the The *Indian Persons with Disabilities (Equal Opportunities, Protection of Rights and Full Participation) Act, 1995* (PWDA) is comprised of not only the combination of individually enforceable guarantees of non-discrimination but also contains programmatic provisions and other provisions that moot the creation of a host of institutions to promote and protect the rights of persons with disabilities. Few other provisions in the Act exist that directly make a person with disability a rights holder and its violation can be effectively challenged in a court of law or before the Disability Commissioner.[38] The Act also endorses certain duties on establishments to advance programmatic steps and measures failing which legal action can be initiated in the courts of law.[39] Some of the glaring differences between both the documents are highlighted in the following table.

Table 15.2: Difference between PWDA 1995 and UNCRPD 2007

Issues	PWDA 1995	UNCRPD 2007
Genesis	To eliminate social and physical barrier	To recognize and affirm a whole spectrum of human rights or the disabled
Rights	Doesn't Expressly recognize it	Affirms the disabled as rights holder s and not passive recipients
Status	Overarching central law on disabled issues in India	First exclusive global human rights treaty on the disabled
Philosophy	Protectionist & Welfare	Rights language
Position of Individuals	Passive beneficiaries	Active participants
Focus	Entitlements and Protection to few categories of medically determined impairments/disabilities	Universal definition and approach of disability. No quantifying of impairments or its effects
Categories of Rights	Only second generation mainstay. No reference to first generation rights	Essays enjoyment of all rights on equal basis with non-disabled
Underlying Philosophy	Prevention, early detection for elimination of all forms of disabilities in toto	Moots social environment that facilitates equal participation and negates only the stance of a medical intervention for better quality of life
Ramifications	Stigmatizing and ostracizing	Social legitimacy and acceptance
Multi sectoral Convergence	Disability a monolithic or homogenous concept	Inter-sectionality of gender and disability recognized
Outreach	Selective. Only some forms of disability recognized	Universal

The *National Policy for Persons with Disabilities 2006* is yet another policy document endorsing the vision and commitment for entrenching a rights paradigm for the disabled community. With education being heralded as central to the overall development of an individual in the policy, the establishment of a barrier free social environment is also mooted herein. The textual content of the

Policy reverberates with the promise to fulfil a life dignity and fundamental freedoms for the persons with disabilities.

International Setting: The Global Agenda

At different points of history, attempts have been made to bring to light issues pertaining to persons with disabilities in either a welfarist connotation or in a rights framework and through a host of diversified formats—resolutions, declarations, treaties, conventions, covenants, etc.[40] Some of the extremely imperative documents with their salient features have been broadly elucidated upon

The UDHR is conspicuously silent on the agenda of disability. Though the provision of equality permeates the length and breadth of the document, it does not categorically recognize 'disability' as a protected group like race, gender, religion, sex, political opinion, etc. Article 25 is the sole provision wherein 'disability; if fleetingly referred to.[41] This is testimonial to the marginalization and stigmatization prevailing towards the disabled community. Moreover even the sporadic reference of disability in Article 25 is shrouded with paternalism and remains mute over vital issues like education, employment, access, etc.[42]

The transition of the disability debate from the medicine and welfare perspective to the human rights discourse has been gradual, painstaking and punctuated with challenges. In this regard two resolutions of the General Assembly have been instrumental in laying down the groundwork for a shift from the care to a rights based approach. The 1971 Declaration on the Rights of the Mentally Retorted Persons'[43] not only endorses the availability of rights for such persons and but also enumerates a catalogue of rights for them. The second milestone was the Declaration on the Rights of Disabled Persons in 1975[44] that mandates equal rights for the disabled community as well and elucidates the need for social integration and development of capacities so as to make the disabled self-reliant. Both the Declarations paved the path for greater endorsement of disabled rights in the global agenda.

The *International Year of the Disabled in 1981* triggered the rights based approach with the slogan 'Full participation and equality'. And this cemented the *International Decade of Disabled Persons from 1983 to 1992* with the overarching goal of prevention, rehabilitation and equalization of opportunities. The former two are a categorical reflection of the 'care model' while the latter evidences a rights based view. This notwithstanding the *Standard Rules on the Equalization of Opportunities for Persons with Disabilities*[45] that were adopted in 1993 completely abandoned the classical rehabilitation and prevention model and couched the entire document in a rights language. The normative significance of these Rules is paramount notwithstanding their declaratory effect and lack of any legal obligations that flow from it.

The UN Convention on the Rights of Persons with Disabilities: A New Rights Essay?

The *United Nations Convention on Rights of Persons with Disabilities 2007* remains a watershed instrument in the global history of the disability rights movement. It has been the first global human rights treaty of the twenty-first century.[46] It marks the commencement of a new era of disabled friendly concepts, norms, procedures and most significantly perspectives. It also remains the first ever contribution of the United Nations towards a legally enforceable instrument essaying specifically the human rights and fundamental freedoms of persons with disabilities.[47]

The UNCRPD 2007 is not only more universal in character but has also been endorsed widely due to the active participation of persons with disability in the making of the treaty. It also breaks the archaic shackles of viewing disability through the protectionist, welfares and medical prism. It endorses a paradigm shift if both approaches and attitudes. Persons with Disabilities herein are not considered as mere recipients of social protection but as active, well informed and participating individuals.

The UNCRPD 2007 has been heralded as both a development and human rights instrument. It recognizes disability as an evolving concept, affirms diversity amongst disability issues and moots the full, effective and equal enjoyment of the existing broad categories of rights by all persons with disabilities.[48] A legally binding treaty the UNCRPD stipulates obligations for the State to facilitate the process of guaranteeing and protection of human rights of persons with disabilities.[49] The UNCRPD as a policy instrument is cross-sectoral and possesses a multitude of interface and converging issues with other discourses like gender rights, etc. It advocates universal recognition of dignity of PWD beyond the classical notions of pity, sympathy, fear or diffidence. The UNCRPD 2007 elucidates the indivisibility and interdependence factor of civil, political as well as economic, social and cultural rights. The most redeeming feature of the Convention however has been the emphasis of the capability of every individual.

The UNCRPD 2007 has unimaginably altered the global and national landscape with regard to the disability discourse. Scholars have identified three core ways in which the UNCRPD 2007 can accelerate the entrenchment of a rights discourse in the disability movement world over—as an Expressive value trigger, as a National Action trigger and finally as a Social Integration trigger.[50] As an expressive value trigger the Convention undeniably couches the language of agency, autonomy and dignity of the disabled and the legal obligations that accrue from the norms stipulated in the Convention have the potential transform and overhaul existing negative images, perceptions and social attitudes towards disability.[51]

This UNCRPD 2007 against this backdrop would rekindle the social model of disability and reconstruct the barriers faced in the environmental settings as a major challenge to disability rights issue. Also the educational value of the Convention in impart icing awareness and sensitivity on issues pertaining to PWD would foster their mainstreaming and law at this juncture could be a potent tool for social engineering.[52] The UNCRPD is set to be the catalyst in triggering law reform in domestic spheres post ratification of the treaty. And address more constructively and comprehensive disability issues at both the law and policy framework.[53] The expressive value of the treaty would strengthen and would argue the process of overhauling legal social policies if it is facilitated in a broad based, transparent and participatory manner. The opportunity to equalize domestic standards with prescribed minimum standards by factoring in the country specific relevant socio-cultural milieu would sustain the movement of disability rights in the long run.

And finally the inclusive development mandate of the Convention paves the road map for the historical alienation and isolation of the PWD to be eliminated and bridge the gap between the disabled and mainstream population.[54] The social participatory approach would immensely 'visible' and integrate PWD, augur greater enjoyment of all rights and promote their identity as not the 'other' but one of the mainstream population itself.

Millennium Development Goals—A New World Order?

The domestic incorporation of the norms prescribed in the plethora of human rights treaties at the international level that the Government of India is party to, have always posited a Herculean challenge. Often the Western actors have been staunchest critiques of the ineffective or lackadaisical implementation of these provisions in third world nations. The Asian and African countries have on the other hand often emphasized human rights to be a solely western legacy with no realistic scope and advantage to the developing world.

Against such a backdrop, the Millennium Development Goals[55] have emerged as the agenda to plug the burgeoning gap between the North and the South. With collaborative partnership being the moot point to eliminate human sufferings and consolidate a human rights culture across the world; the MDGs have been heralded as the most imperative global agenda of the twenty first century.

In the *United Nations Millennium Declaration of 2000* wherein the world community with renewed vigor and commitment staunchly supported the right to survival, education, protection and participation of all especially the vulnerable. The disabled community comes within the purview of this as well. Both the MDGs and the *Millennium Declaration 2000* were endorsed and upheld in the 2005 World Summit. The eight distinct yet interrelated MDGs are premised on core human rights and reflect a blueprint of a set of intertwined and mutually reinforcing goals chartering a course of sustainable development.[56]

To classify the MDGs as goals only of the United Nations would be a misnomer, instead these are universal goals-targets that each country should strive to achieve individually and collectively. The MDGs are a reflection of the minimalist or outcome or quantitative targets to be achieved by 2015.[57] It is also a misnomer to construe the MDGs as the end in it—infect the MDGs have triggered and spearheaded the movement against poverty, human rights abuses, and bolstered the cause of security and sustainable development.

The *Millennium Development Goals (Hereinafter MDGs)* are yet another fillip in the direction of articulating and achieving human rights for all inclusive of the disabled. The eight goals that the MDGs profess to seek to internalize and make pervasive the minimum standards and human rights norms across the globe. Each of the goals has specific relevance to the disability sector. The disabled as a distinct social group constitute one of the poorest, marginalized, deprived and vulnerable communities. Each of the specified goals has a direct bearing on their status and role in the society as shown in the following table.

Table 5.3: Specific Goals and Analysis of MDGs.

Specific Goals	Analysis
Eradicate Extreme Poverty & Hunger	Disabled people have lower standards of living than people without disabilities in the same income group
Achieve Universal Primary Education	Inclusive and mainstreaming education is not widely promoted. Instead is segregation education
Promote Gender Equality & Empower Women	Double discrimination due to disability and gender
Reduce Child Mortality	Access to services or support systems restricted. Awareness also less
Improve Maternal Health	Reproductive health services or access to it is limited or minimal for the disabled women
Combat HIV/AIDS, malaria, other diseases	At equal or higher risk to infections, especially vulnerable if in institutional care to sexual abuse/assault
Ensure Environmental Sustainability	Disabled have limited/no access to services that increases their vulnerability especially during disasters etc.

In the blueprint of MDGs, the disabled have a dual role—as development agents as well as direct beneficiaries. This notwithstanding the term 'disability' or 'persons with disabilities' is amiss in the entire text of MDGs. It is also pertinent to highlight that monitoring, evaluation and implementation of MDGs also make no reference to disability. Their absence is also starkly visible in the ongoing MDG activities. The periodic reviews of MDGs within the United Nations setting is conspicuous by two element—lack of focus on disability issues and lack of participation of disabled people, both that will have severe repercussion on the disability right discourse.

The non-inclusion and ensuing alienation of the disabled persons in the MDGs would eventually question the legitimacy of these goals that have left in lurch a substantial 10 percent of the world population. Each of the indicators has a substantial bearing on the lives and issues of persons with disabilities. It is extremely imperative that disabled community are heralded as development agents as well as benefit from all development processes at macro and micro level so as to facilitate their right to equality, non-discrimination and dignity in the truest sense.

Challenges & Solutions—The Path to be Traversed

The disabled rights movement is still struggling to consolidate completely in the Indian soil. The time is however ripe for entrenching a rights culture in the disability environment and strengthen the increasing visibility of disability issues in the public sphere by various stakeholders—State, NGOs, families, media, etc. The public versus private dichotomy also need to be bridged for a pervasive human rights regime for persons with disabilities.

The Reservations Fiasco

The reservation hullabaloo did impact the interface between disability and education. The pro–reservationist argued for concessions and benefits as for decades of marginalization and disempowerment and thereby legitimizing reservations in favor of the disabled.[58] The anti–reservationists argued against reservations as it was believed that the disabled would not be in a position to do justice to the responsibilities that accompany the job/post.

However since affirmative action has been applicable to other marginalized communities it was natural that the disabled would also fall squarely under it. The primordial distinction however with regard to reservations extended to SCs and STs as compared to the disabled community hinges on the constitutional backing that the former group enjoys while the latter largely benefits from statutory and legislative enactment that is the Persons with Disability Act 1995. Therefore albeit reservations are extended to the disabled community but this protection does not flow from the constitution—the supreme law of the land— but from laws passed by the Parliament.

Limited Employment and Livelihood Avenues

For the persons with disabilities post education, opportunities of livelihood have posited a vital impediment. Job identification, retention, progress and stabilization have been some of preponderant challenges and sometimes a roadblock. The core legislation PWDA 1995 in Article 32 specifically mandates job identification and modalities yet its successful execution has been potentially abysmal.[59] Confusion exists galore with regard to self-imposed limitations of the legislation wherein the abilities of the disabled community largely ignored and overlooked.

Lack of clarity in the law, periodic updating and revisions has further hampered chances of gainful employment. The GOI is further on extremely restrictive though scholars argue that it's definitely not exhaustive and the State Government possess the discretion to open avenues of livelihood in other sectors for the disabled community.

Shoddy State of Affairs of Higher Education

With primary education only recently becoming a fundament right, the status of higher education in India is in shambles. Low rates of enrollment of disabled students in higher education remains a grave issue. The higher education system in India has not been able to keep pace with the burgeoning population and the ensuing demand and pressure. The standard and quality of higher education has also suffered a serious setback against this backdrop as higher education has now simply transformed into a certificate/degree churning mechanism. The sad state of affairs would necessarily have a tremendous impact on the status, access, quality and services for higher education opportunities for the disabled community.

Strengthen Office of Disability Commissioner

Under Section 57 of the PWDA 1995, a Disability Commissioner has been established to comprehensive secure, monitor and supervises the interest and rights of disabled persons. There is an urgent need to strengthen the working of the Office of Disability Commissioner. Also the state counterparts of such offices need to be established to provide access to putting forth concerns and grievances. More visibility to the work of the Commissioner is also required.

Inclusive Stance

The pressing need of the hour is to mainstream the physically challenged community in all spheres as far as possible. Exclusionist policies, programs and practices are detrimental to the growth and sustainability of the physically challenged community as well as to the development and progress of the country as a whole. India's aspiration of being a vibrant and participatory democracy will remain an illusion if a section of its population is denied basic rights, protection and polices. The educational and work environment should be conducive for their mobility. There should be integration with mainstream institutions that provide higher education and learning. They should have decision making powers in policies that affect the larger interest of their community. Community participation should be strengthened in the milieu of promotion and protection of rights of the physically challenged people

Multi Sectoral Partnership

A concerted, cohesive and multifaceted partnership vis-à-vis government and others are required to tackle the hurdles and problems experienced by the physically challenged community. Often the physically challenged are not aware of their rights and thus educating them and making them aware should be a vital component of government and non-government initiatives. The society and community as a whole needs to be sensitized regarding their prejudices and perceptions about the physically challenged. A sustained effort has to be launched to ensure that accessibility for this community is not denied—special toilets, special lifts, etc. for the physically challenged.

Conclusion

The approach towards this special category of people should be inclusive and rights based. The government as well as the entire country is duty bound legally and ethically to ensure that the physically challenged people live a life of dignity, self-worth, liberty and productivity. The rights of the disabled are not simply put the rights of yet another marginalized or vulnerable social group instead it forms the larger backdrop of recognizing and affirming the place of difference in all spectrums of life—family, community and society.

Moreover the norms of dignity, participation and integration should be pervasive in any disability discourse so as to facilitate their status of full and equal citizenry. Disability unfortunately is not a dichotomy but a continuum and thus it propounds and necessitates an effective and viable framework for augmenting a life of dignity and self-worth at every stage for the person with disabilities. The time is indeed ripe intellectually and politically to look beyond the shackles of paternalism and social protection and instead regard persons with disabilities as true rights holders like their other counterparts world over.

References

Bagenstos, S.R., 2004. *The Future of Disability Law, 114 Yale L.J. 1, 7,* at 3n.4.

Baldwin, J.L., 2002. *Designing Disability in Services in South Asia: Understanding the Role that Disability Organisations Play in Transforming a Rights-Based Approach to Disability.* Pittsburgh: University of Pittsburgh.

Deacon, B., 2005. From Safety Nets Back to Universal Social Provision: Is the Global Tide Turning?, *Global Social Policy* 5, no. 1:19–28.

Degener, T. and Y. Koster-Dreese, eds. 1995. *Human Rights and Disabled Persons: Essays and Relevant Human Rights Instruments.* Dordrecht: Kluwer Academic Publishers Group.

DeGeneres, T. and G. Quinn, 2002. *Human Rights Are for All: A Study on the Current Use and Future Potential of the UN Human Rights Instruments in the Context of Disability.* Geneva: UNHCHR.

Jain, M.P., 2003. *Indian Constitutional Law.* Delhi: Wadhwa and Co.

Komardjaja, I., 2001. New Cultural Geographies of Disability: Asian Values and the Accessibility Ideal. *Social and Cultural Geography*.2, no.1: 81.

Mehrortra. N., 2011. Disability Rights Movement in India: Policy and Practice. *Economic & Political Weekly* XLVI, no. 6:.66.

Michael J. O., 1996. *Understanding Disability: From Theory to Practice.* New York: St. Martin's Press.

Najman, J.M., 1993. Health and Poverty: Past, Present and Prospects for the Future. *Soc. Sci. & Med.* 36: 157.

Seigal, C. D., 1998. Fifty Years of Disability Law: The Relevance of the Universal Declaration, *ILSA Journal of International & Comparative Law*: 269.

Notes

1. DeGeneres, Theresia & Quinn, Gerard (2002), *Human Rights Are for All: A Study on the Current Use and Future Potential of the UN Human Rights Instruments in the context of Disability,* (UNHCHR002).

2. Hereinafter referred to as UNCRPD 2007

3. Census of India 2011. http://india.gov.in/spotlight/spotlight_archive.php?id=80 (accessed April 15, 2011)

4. Disability in India : A Statistical Profile, (March 2011), Central Statistics Office, Ministry of Statistics & Programme Implementation, Government of India, Essay 2:. B2. http://mospi.nic.in/Mospi_New/upload/disablity_india_statistical_profile_17mar11.htm (accessed April 4, 2011)

5. Jennifer L. Baldwin, (2002), Designing Disability in Services in South Asia : Understanding the Role that Disability Organisations Play in *Transforming a Rights-Based Approach to Disability:* 12-13

6. Metts, R. L.,(2000: 2), Disability Issues: Trends and Recommendations for the World Bank, *World Bank,* February.

7. Simi Linton, (1998: 9), *Claiming Disability: Knowledge and Identity* 185, New York University Press.

8. Simon Brisenden, (1998), Independent Living and the Medical Model of Disability, in *The Disability Studies Reader: Social Science Perspectives* 20 (Tom Shakespeare ed.,)

9. Sagit Mor, (2006: 4), Between Charity, Welfare & Warfare : A Disability ;legal Studies Analysis of the Privilege & Neglect in the Israeli Disability Policy, 18 *Yale Journal of Law & the Humanities.*

10. Michael J. Oliver, (1996: 30-42), *Understanding Disability: From Theory to Practice.*

11. David Pfeiffer (2002), The Philosophical Foundations of Disability Studies, 22 *Disabilities Stud. Quarterly.* 3

12. Samuel R. Bagenstos, The Future of Disability Law, 114 Yale L.J. 1, 7 (2004)., at 3 n.4

13. Mehrotra, Nilika (2004a): "Understanding Cultural Conceptions of Disability in Rural India: A Case from Haryana", *Journal of Indian Anthropological Society.* 39: 33-45

14. Vash,C.L,(1981: 23), Psychology of Disability, *Springer,* New York.

15. Vash,C.L,(1981: 23), Psychology of Disability, *Springer,* New York.

16. Komardjaja, (2001: 81), New Cultural Geographies of Disability : Asian values and the Accessibility Ideal, *Social and Cultural Geography*, Vol.2, No.1.

17. A disabled rights activist and himself a disabled, Neil Marcus, an artist living with dystonia states: "Disability is not a 'brave struggle' or 'courage in the face of adversity' .... [D]disability is an art. It's an ingenious way to live." Disability Social History Project, http://www.disabilityhistory.org (last visited December, 2010)

18. Jenny Morris,(1995), Creating a Space for Absent Voices: Disabled Women's Experience of Receiving Assistance with Daily Living Activities, *51 Feminist Rev. 68*

19. Jake M. Najman (1993), Health and Poverty: Past, Present and Prospects for the Future, *36 Soc. Sci. & Med.* 157

20. The Islamic faith does not endorse the theory of rebirth or reincarnation or Karma; nevertheless, Quran stipulates disability as a manifestation of sins committed by ones parents. Christianity on the other hand is premised on the doctrine of the Original Sin and our presence in the world was very much to atone and pay penance for that. Y. Takamine (2003: 21), Disability Issues in East Asia : Review and Way Forward, Report submitted to the World Bank.

21. Ibid: 20

22. Review of national progress in the implementation of the Agenda for Action for the Asian and Pacific Decade of Disabled Persons suggests that less than 10 per cent of children and youth with disabilities have access to any form of education. ESCAP, "Regional trends impacting on the situation of persons with disabilities," background paper submitted to the high-level meeting to conclude the Asian and Pacific Decade of Disabled Persons, 1993-2002, Otsu, Shiga, Japan, October 2002, p 2.

23. N.Mehrortra, (February 5th 2011: 66), Disability Rights Movement in India : Policy and Practice, *Economic & Political Weekly*, Vol. XLVI No. 6.

24. Westbrook, M.T,(1993: 25-41), How Social Expectations Become Different for Men and Women who Become Disabled, *Australian Disability Review*, 11.

25. Supra note 20:.66

26. M.P. Jain, (5th ed.: 2003: 1000-1005) Indian Constitutional Law, Wadhwa and Co..

27. Article 15 reads—Prohibition of discrimination on grounds of religion, race, caste, sex or place of birth.—(1) The State shall not discriminate against any citizen on grounds only of religion, race, caste, sex, place of birth or any of them. (4) Nothing in this article or in clause (2) of article 29 shall prevent the State from making any special provision for the advancement of any socially and educationally backward classes of citizens or for the Scheduled Castes and the Scheduled Tribes.

28. Article 19. Protection of certain rights regarding freedom of speech, etc.—(1) All citizens shall have the right—(a) to freedom of speech and expression.

29. Article 21 reads, "No person shall be deprived of his life and personal liberty except according to procedure established *by law*."

30. *Francis Coralie Mullin* v. *Administrator, Union Territory of Delhi and Ors, AIR 1976 SC 746*

31. Art 41 directs the State to make effective provisions for securing the right to work, education and public assistance in cases of unemployment, old age, sickness and disablement, within the limits of its economic capacity and development.

32. Article 38 reads- The State shall strive to promote the welfare of the people by securing and protecting as effectively as it may a social order in which justice, social, economic and political, shall inform all the institutions of the national life. The State shall, in particular, strive to minimize the inequalities in income, and endeavour to eliminate inequalities in status, facilities and opportunities, not only amongst individuals but also amongst groups of people residing in different areas or engaged in different vocations.

33. The State shall promote with special care the educational and economic interests of the weaker sections of the people, and, in particular, of the Scheduled Castes and the Scheduled Tribes, and shall protect them from social injustice and all forms of exploitation.

34. Through the 86th Amendment Article 51A(k) was introduced wherein duty exists on part of a parent or guardian to provide opportunities for education to his child, as the case may be, ward between the age of six and fourteen years.

35. Article 51(c) reads Promotion of international peace and security.—The State shall endeavour to—(c) foster respect for international law and treaty obligations in the dealings of organized peoples with one another.

36. Disability Discrimination Law & The Asia Pacific Region " Progress & Challenges In the Light of The United Nations Convention on the Rights of the Persons with Disabilities , Economic and Social Commission for Asia & the Office of the UN High Commissioner for Human Rights,Expert Group Meeting on the Harmonization of National Legislations with the Convention on the Rights of Persons with Disabilities in Asia and the Pacific 8-10 June (2009: 17) Bangkok

37. Under the PWDA 1995 children in India disabled received specific and special attention. The Act stipulates under Section 26 the Central and State Governments to ensure that all children with disabilities get free education till they are eighteen years of age. Efforts should also be made to integrate these children in the regular schools and to set up special schools with vocational training facilities in deficient areas. The PWD Act

also in Section 30 mandates that special provisions such as transport facilities, removal of architectural barriers in schools, supply of books, uniform and other materials to children with disabilities to encourage them to go to school and to pursue basic education be made available. Under the legislation in Section 39 a mandatory three percent of seats have to be reserved for children with disabilities in all the Government and government aided educational institutions.

38. Section 47 is the major example: this section provides that no (public) establishment "shall dispense with, or reduce in rank, an employee who acquires a disability during his service", but should find him another appropriate post if he or she cannot continue with current position

39. ss 32–33, s 37) or adapting forms of transport or the built environment so that they are accessible (ss 44, 45, 46)

40. Universal Declaration of Human Rights (1948) (article 3, 21, 23, 25), - International Covenant on Civil and Political Rights (1966) (article 26), - International Covenant on Economic, Social and Cultural Rights (1966) (article 2) elaborated in 1994 (article 3,6,8,9-15), - Declaration on the Rights of Mentally Retarded Persons (1971), - Declaration on the Right of Disabled Persons (1975), - Declaration on the Right of Deaf-Blind Persons (1979), - Convention on the Elimination of Discrimination against Women (1979 (article 3), - Convention on the Rights of Persons with Disabilities (2007) etc

41. Article 25 of Indian Constitution.

42. Charles.D.Seigal, (1998-1989: 269),5 Fifty Years of Disability Law : The Relevance of the Universal Declaration, *ILSA Journal of International & Comparative Law.*

43. General Assembly Resolution 2856(XXVI) of 20th December 1971

44. General Assembly Resolution 3447 (XXX) of 9 December 1975

45. General Assembly Resolution 48/96 of 20 December 1993. B.Lindqvist, Standard rules in the disability field-a United Nations Instrument; Degener & Koster-Dreese,(1995: 63), Human Rights and Disabled Persons, , eds.(Dordrecht, Kluwer Academic Publishers Group.

46. Convention on the Rights of Persons with Disabilities, G.A. Res. 61/106 (2007) [hereinafter UNCRPD].

47. Hereinafter referred to as PWD

48. The Convention notes that disability is an evolving concept and results from the interaction between a person's impairment and obstacles such as physical barriers and prevailing attitudes that prevent their participation in society.

Source: http://www.un.org/disabilities/default.asp?navid=24&pid=151

Last visited on 12/3/2011

49. Article 33 of UNCRPD covers national implementation and monitoring, which states that all State Parties have to establish a Focal Point to facilitate implementation. However, Indian Government has not yet established a Focal Point for the implementation and monitoring of UNCRPD in the country. UNCRPD further states that civil society, in particular persons with disabilities and their organizations, should be involved and participate fully in the monitoring process

50. M.A. Stein & J.E. Lord, (2008: 31), Future Prospects for the United Nations Convention on the Rights of Persons with Disabilities.

51. Lawrence Lessig, (1998), The Regulation of Social Meaning, 62 *U. Chi. L. Rev.* 943

52. Convention on the Rights of Persons with Disabilities, G.A. Res. 61/106 (2007) art. 8 (requiring States Parties "to adopt immediate, effective and appropriate measures . . [t]o raise awareness throughout society, including at the family level, regarding persons with disabilities, and to foster respect for the rights and dignity of

persons with disabilities . . .)

53. Michael Ashley Stein, (2007), Disability Human Rights, 95 *Cal. L. Rev. 75*

54. Art. 33 reads- (providing that "States Parties recognize the importance of international cooperation and its promotion, in support of national efforts for the realization of the purpose and objectives of the present Convention, and will undertake appropriate and effective measures in this regard, between and among States . . . [which] measures could include . . . [e]ensuring that international cooperation, including international development Programmes, is inclusive of and accessible to persons with disabilities.").

55. Hereinafter MDGs

56. The UN Millennium Declaration was adopted by all 189 members of the UN via General Assembly Resolution 55/2. The 8 goals are- *Eradication of Extreme Poverty and Hunger, Achievement of Universal Primary Education, Promoting Gender Equality and Empowerment of Women, Reduction of Child Mortality, maternal Health, Combating HIV/AIDS, malaria and other diseases, Ensuring Environmental Sustainability and Developing a Global Partnership for Development*

57. Deacon, B., (2005), From Safety Nets Back to Universal Social Provision: is the Global Tide Turning?, *Global Social Policy*, 5(1):19-28.

58. The Ability Debates, P.K.Pincha, India Together, February 22 2008. Website: http://www.indiatogether.org/2008/feb/hlt-debate.htm (Last visited 25/01/2011)

59. Article 32 of PWDA 1995.

CHAPTER 16
"People's Health in People's Hands"—A Goal Ever–Elusive?

Satyabrata Chakraborty[1]

Health is an intrinsic value. Long back Aristotle, the master philosopher, had considered 'health of body and mind' as 'fundamental to good life', and 'men have an absolute moral right' to good health. More intriguing was his assertion that 'society alone is able' to provide such measures as to enable man to enjoy that right. More than two millennia have passed since Aristotle. The health condition of a very large section of the population of the developing world is abysmally bad. Health occupies no place of priority in the policy agenda of most of the states in this part of the world. Nevertheless one important change has taken place, particularly since around the mid-twentieth century. Health has come to be recognized as an integral component of the intellectual discourses and political rhetoric on human rights, democracy and development.

Health as Human Right

Health and human rights linkages are now universally recognized. "Every country in the world is now party to at least one human rights treaty that addresses health-related rights. This includes the right to health as well as other rights that relate to conditions necessary for health."[2] Right to health is a composite right and should not be reduced just to provisions for medical care. The Universal Declaration of Human Rights is quite eloquent on these non-medical components of health. Article 25 of the Declaration reads:

(1) Everyone has the right to a standard of living adequate for the health and wellbeing of himself and of his family, including food, clothing, housing and medical care and necessary social services, and the right to security in the event of unemployment, sickness, disability, widowhood, old age or other lack of livelihood in circumstances beyond his control.

(2) Motherhood and childhood are entitled to special care and assistance. All children, whether born in or out of wedlock, shall enjoy the same social protection.

The human rights component of health is explicitly admitted by the World Health Organization too. The WHO does not define health just in terms of absence of disease. Far more holistic, it views health as a state of complete physical, mental and social well-being which, it further affirms, is one of the fundamental rights of every human being. The linkage between health and human rights and the fundamental importance of health for a human being as a human being is also recognized in the International Covenant on Economic, Social, and Cultural Rights (ICESCR). Article 12 of the Covenant writes: "the States Parties to the present Covenant recognize the right of everyone to the enjoyment of the highest attainable standard of physical and mental health". The ICRSCR also enjoins upon the member governments the obligation to honor right to health as a fundamental human right.[3]

According to the World Health Organisation, health and human rights are inextricably linked at least in three ways:
a) Violations or lack of attention to human rights can have serious health consequences (e.g., harmful traditional practices, slavery, torture and inhuman and degrading treatment, violence against women and children);
b) Health policies and programs can promote or violate human rights in their design or implementation (e.g., freedom from discrimination, individual autonomy, rights to participation, privacy and information); and
c) Vulnerability to ill-health can be reduced by taking steps to respect, protect and fulfill human rights (e.g., freedom from discrimination on account of race, sex and gender roles, rights to health, food and nutrition, education, housing.[4]

Health and Right to Development

Health is not just a right which the state is obliged not to compromise. It is a more positive entitlement. Today health is universally recognized as an important component of development. As an ideology development is new, and there are multiple intellectual and political discourses on development. However, if its basic spirit is rescued from such muddling multiplicity development may be taken as *attainment of conditions for self-fulfilling life*. And this is an eternal human aspiration which found universal recognition when the General Assembly of the United Nations Organisation adopted the Declaration on the Right to Development in December 1986. It defines development as 'a comprehensive economic, social, cultural and political process' for 'the constant improvement of the well-being of the entire population and of all individuals'. Equally important is the mode of this development which should be on the basis of the people's 'active, free and meaningful participation' resulting in 'the fair distribution of benefits...'. The Declaration is also explicit in recognizing health as a component of the right to development and in affixing the responsibility for the attainment of this right on the states. Article 8 of the Declaration reads: "States should undertake, at the national level, all necessary measures for the realization of the right to development and shall ensure, inter alia, equality of opportunity for all in their access to basic resources, education, health services, food, housing, employment and the fair distribution of income." It also urges: "States should encourage popular participation in all spheres as an important factor in development and in the full realization of all human rights."[5]

Health and Democracy

In our age, democracy is the most coveted political ideology. Asked by a Japanese newspaper as to how he would remember the twentieth century Professor Amartya Sen replied, not very unexpectedly, it was for democracy. Democracy, he asserts, is the most important contribution of the last century. The respectability of democracy is so high for more than half a century now that an overwhelming majority of states claim to be democratic; although some of them are ruled by manifestly authoritarian regimes. Democratic system, explains Samuel P. Huntington, has no rival in the contemporary world. Such wide appreciation from curiously different sources indicates that the concept is impregnated with disagreements as to what it means and how it is to be attained, deepened and sustained.

How is health related to democracy? Democracy demands active citizenry which presupposes public authority's commitment to some 'enabling' conditions. Health is one such enabling condition without which many of the rights remain elusive (Dreze and Sen 2002: 38). But formal rights often remain unfulfilled even in a procedural democracy. Hence democratization of health does not merely refer to an individual's capability. What is important is public participation in political decisions and social choice. Democracy is empowering because it enhances both individuals' substantive freedom and their agency to control their own life situations. (Ruger 2005) As Dreze and Sen write: "Entitlements of this type are important not only because they consolidate the bargaining power of those who are deprived of basic health and education services, but also because they shape broader notions of solidarity and citizenship." (Dreze and Sen 2002: 41–2) Citizenship entails conscious and enlightened participation in public affairs underlining the importance of deliberation—a political culture of influencing governmental institutions through debate, discussion and public reasoning. At the ground level, this otherwise inarguably sound proposition may and often does confront a number of problems. First, a 'democratic government' may not really be too keen to extend 'real' opportunities without which no meaningful deliberation can take place. This does not imply that people are or they can always be kept as 'dumb millions'. They might assert against a mighty regime at certain conjunctures. But such conjunctures are few and far between in a democratic polity which can carry on relatively undisturbed with minimum and superficial care for the large and the underprivileged people. Second, access to opportunities does not necessarily graduate to the *will* to deliberate. Third, debates and discussions have a tendency to get reduced to less consequential prolixity. Fourth, since power is intrinsically driven to exclusion, formal deliberation might be robbed of creativity turning into an agency of legitimization. This underlines the need for *public action* beyond just deliberation. This is true for development and protection of human rights too. We shall elaborate on this point in the last section of our paper.

The Indian Scenario

Indian state proclaims itself to be a democracy with its commitment to both development and human rights. Health does not figure in the list of fundamental rights guaranteed to the Indian citizens though concerned social thinkers like Amartya Sen believes that there is "a strong case for thinking about education and health in terms of fundamental rights". (Dreze and Sen, 2002: 42) However, there is explicit reference to nutrition and public health in Article 47 of the Constitution of India as obligation of the state. Health also finds indirect reference in Article 48A which directs the state to protect environment. Both the articles are part of the Directive Principles of State Policy which is important as guidelines of state action but they are not justifiable. However, J.S. Verma, former Chief Justice of India argues in the forward to the report of NHRC in collaboration with the Ministry of Health and Family Welfare (MHFW), Government of India [and] WHO (2000) on Regional consultation on public health and human rights that these two articles "have been judicially interpreted to expand the meaning and scope of 'right to life' guaranteed as a fundamental right in Article 21 of the Indian Constitution. Thus, in India the national Constitution elevates the 'right to health of the highest attainable standards' to a guaranteed fundamental right which is enforceable by virtue of the constitutional remedy under Article 32 of the Constitution" (Verma 2001: 4).[6]

Even before independence of India in 1947 two important developments regarding health system took place. In 1938, the National Planning Committee of the Indian National Congress set up a subcommittee under the chairmanship of S.S. Sokhey to study the health situation of the country. The committee found poverty as the root of health problem. It also proposed appointment of one Community Health Worker (CHW) for every 1000 population. The CHW was supposed to work as the base of rural health service (Banerjee 2005). In 1943, the Government of India appointed a committee for more or less the same purpose with Joseph Bhore as the Chairman. Its report was adopted by the Government of India after independence as the basis of the health system in the country. The Bhore Committee's focus was on preventive care, and it placed Primary Health Center at the core of the health system. In course of time, however, a major shift away from this emphasis on prevention was noticed (Antia, Dutta and Kasbekar 2000). Much later, in 1978, was held the Alma-Ata convention in Kazakhstan. India is a signatory to the declaration of the Convention jointly sponsored by the WHO and UNICEF. The Declaration accepted WHO's broader definition of health and adopted the goal of 'health for all by 2000'. Some of the highlights of the Declaration may be noted in this connection. First, it declared that 'the Government has a responsibility for the health of their people'. Second, it is the right as well as the duty of the people 'to participate in planning and implementation of their healthcare'. Third, Primary Health Care (PHC) should be brought as close to where people live and work as possible. Fourth, PHC should be grounded in 'the conditions and characteristics of the country and its communities'. Fifth, PHC addresses the main health problems in the community 'providing promotive, preventive, curative and rehabilitative services'. Sixth, the principal aspects of PHC are basic health education, ensuring adequate food, nutrition, safe drinking water and basic sanitation, providing for maternal and child health including family planning, prevention of locally endemic diseases, making treatment of common diseases with essential drugs available and relying on grassroots health workers acting as a team. Finally the Declaration called upon the states to take appropriated measures to ensure PHC for all people (Tulchinsky and Varavikova, 2000; Basu and Chakraborty, 2007).

Food and Nutrition

As we have already noted, the non-medical components are more important for understanding and improving the health scenario of a country. Among these components food security happens to be most important. Food security means availability of food, access to food and absorption of it in the body. Adequate food by itself would not ensure nutrition security. As the Report on the State of Food Insecurity in Rural India, by MS Swaminathan Research (MSSRF) and World Food Programme (WFP) (2008) notes, along with access to balanced diet nutrition security involves clean drinking water, sanitation and primary health care for every child.[7]

India's food and nutrition security situation is grim. According to the *Human Development Report 2010*, during 1990–1992, the rate of the prevalence of undernourishment in India was 24 percent of the total population. In 2004–2006, the decline was barely 2 percent. (Human Development Report 2010: 174). The HDR 2010 has also measured intensity of food deprivation by taking into account the average percentage shortfall in minimum dietary requirements. Here again the rate of decline has been 2 percent—from 17 to 15. (HDR 2010: 174) According to FAO estimates of 2008, more than 230 million people, i.e. about 21 percent of the total population of the country, are undernourished.[8] In October 2010, the International Food Policy Research Institute brought out its latest global hunger index. Out of 84 countries it rated India stands 67, below even Pakistan; and China is well ahead of India. The rating is based on three indicators—prevalence of child malnutrition, rate of child mortality and the proportion of calorie deficient people. The report also shows that 42 percent of the world's underweight children live in India.[9] Recently, the United Nations World Food Programme (WFP) and MS Swaminathan Research (MSSRF) Foundation have jointly released the *Report on the State of Food Insecurity in Rural India*. It is based on a composite index using several indicators like calorie consumption, availability of safe drinking water, access to toilet in the premises, prevalence of anemia, growth of children, etc. There has been persistent official claim of increased rate of economic growth in India. But, as the report suggests, such economic growth has not helped to improve food security of a large section of the rural people. It also says that 'the number of undernourished people is rising'. As a whole, rural economy in India is weakening due to slow 'growth in food production, rising unemployment and declining purchasing power' of the people.[10] Expectedly, the Report shows considerable variations across the country. But some of its findings are alarming. There is 'very high' level of food insecurity in Jharkhand, Chhattisgarh, Madhya Pradesh and Bihar.

> Even economically developed states like Gujarat, Maharashtra, Andhra Pradesh and Karnataka find themselves in the category of high food insecurity..... As many as eight states—Andhra Pradesh, Bihar, Gujarat, Haryana, Karnataka, Kerala, Madhya Pradesh and Rajasthan—have shown increase in the incidence of anaemia among women in the reproductive age group.12 out of 20 states under consideration have figures higher than 80 percent for proportion of rural anaemic children.[11]

In fact, the increase in the number of hungry people has been a global phenomenon in recent years.[12] The introduction of universal Public Distribution System (PDS) to provide people with food grains at affordable price is the most urgent task to fight such food insecurity. This is recommended by the MSSRF report too.[13] But the present government in spite of its election promises is keen to introduce targeted PDS instead of universalizing the program. That the present system of identifying the people below the poverty line (BPL) is erroneous is generally admitted. Moreover discrimination in matters as vital as food is unethical. The proposed targeted PDS has pushed Jean Dreze to quit the food panel of the National Advisory Council. Criticizing the government's policy Dreze has said: "When it comes to food security, "exclusion errors" are really unacceptable—everyone has a right to be protected from hunger. When it comes to corporate-friendly projects, the sky is the limit. The Planning Commission is proudly talking of "infrastructural investment" to the tune of $1 trillion in the 12th Plan, about half of that would be public money. $1 trillion! That's astronomical: nearly 10 percent of GDP, year after year. But for food security, 1 percent of GDP is considered extravagant—that's not "investment".[14]

Besides food security and adequate nourishment availability of clean toilets and access to safe drinking water are two vital requirements for good health. On both counts India's performance even after more than sixty years of independence is regrettable though these days India is considered as the second fastest growing economy of the world. According to one report India is at the top of the ten nations lacking sanitary facility.[15] A recent U.N. report writes:

> It is a tragic irony to think that in India, a country now wealthy enough that roughly half of the people own phones, about half cannot afford the basic necessity and dignity of a toilet .... India has some 545 million cell phones, enough to serve about 45 per cent of the population, but only about 366 million people or 31 per cent of the population had access to improved sanitation in 2008.[16]

With regard to safe drinking water Lizette Burgers, Chief of Water and Environmental Sanitation, UNICEF writes that 'out of 150 million, 134 million (almost 90 per cent) living in rural India have no access to safe drinking water.[17] A government survey based on NSSO study, 2008–09 gives somewhat higher figure—30 percent of rural population having access to safe drinking (tap) water. However, this enhanced figure is not at all comforting. Lack of access to clean toilets and safe drinking water causes lots of health problem affecting particularly the poorer sections of the society. According to a WHO report, "80 percent of India's diarrhoeal diseases is the result of drinking water contamination by poor sanitation."[18] Zafar Adeel, a noted UN expert says in a cautionary report: "Anyone who shirks the topic as repugnant, minimizes it as undignified, or considers unworthy those in need should let others take over for the sake of 1.5 million children and countless others killed each year by contaminated water and unhealthy sanitation."[19]

At the root of the above scarcities, especially food insecurity and malnourishment, is poverty. As the *Human Development Report 2010* (hereinafter HDR 2010) rightly points out poverty is multifaceted, and there are different dimension of poverty. As a result, it has introduced a new measure called Multidimensional Poverty Index (MPI). (HDR 2010: 94) India's MPI is 0.296 whereas that of comparable countries like Brazil, China and Egypt are respectively 0.039, 0.056 and 0.026. 55.4 percent of Indian population is included in multidimensional poverty. The percentage of population in deprivation in education, health and living standard are respectively 37.5, 56.5 and 58.5. The figures pertain to the period 2000–2008 (HDR 2010: 162).

There are wide differences among experts and different agencies as to the exact number of poor in India. There is yet to emerge any uniform measure of poverty. The poverty line even varies from state to state within India. According to one World Bank estimate, India is the home of one-third of the world's poor. Roughly 80 percent of the Indian 'live on less than $2 a day', and one-third of the Indians have less then $1 a day to survive which means they are 'extremely poor'.[20] The Government of India's estimation of poverty attracted wide criticism from different quarters as gross underestimation. That led to the setting up of the Tendulkar Committee. It worked on a new definition of poverty which considered, along with access to food, expenditure on health and education also. According to the Committee, 37 percent of the Indians live below the poverty line. Finally the Planning Commission accepted the report. It means about 10 percent rise in the number of the poor the Government had been working with. However, two other reports released by committees set up by the Government of India itself contradicted the figures cited by the Tendukar Committee. According to the Arjun Sengupta committee report, 77 percent of Indians can spend less than INR. 20.00 (less than 40 cents) a day and the report submitted by the N.C. Saxena Committee holds that 50 percent of Indian live below the poverty line. The Government rejected the Saxena Committee report on unconvincing ground. In 2009, Montek Singh Ahluwalia claimed on the basis of a calculation made by the economist Abhijit Sen that 'overall poverty has in fact fallen to 32 percent in 2009 from 37 percent estimated in 2004'.[21] However, the calculation has been criticized for using a 'thin sample data' surveying 'fewer number of households to get overall trend in their income, expenditure and other consumer behaviour'.[22]

State of Health

According to the Human Development Report (HDR) 2010, the latest in the series, with HDI value of 0.519 India ranks 119 out of 169 countries. In terms of

HDI value, this is a not an insignificant increase from 0.320 in 1980. However, it should not appear as much consoling since in terms of ranking there has been just one point rise between 2005 and 2010. Though India has done quite well on GDP growth it has not been adequately reflected in human development. India's neighbor China, another high growth economy, has gained eight marks during the same period securing 89th rank. What is more significant is that on a number of major indicators of human development like life expectancy at birth, mean years of schooling and participation of women labor India is beaten by not only China but by Pakistan, Bangladesh, and, in some respects, even Nepal (HDR 2010).

The HDR shows that in Gender Inequality Index India ranks 122. This is worse than even most of the medium and low human development states. Gender inequality, it needs no mention, has profound implications for a number of health related issues. During 2003–2008 Maternal Mortality Rate (MMR)—maternal deaths per 100,000 live births—in India was 450. This is worse than even Pakistan and most other medium human development countries. If women's presence in the national parliament is an indicator of women's empowerment, India with just 9.2 percent of the seats occupied by women presents a disheartening picture. Women's share of seats in Indian parliament is lower than many African and even Islamic countries including, again, Pakistan. (HDR 2010: 158)[23] In 2010, while 26.6 percent of Indian women of 25 years of age and older had at least secondary education, the corresponding figure for the same category of male population was 50.4 percent. The rate of female education of the same standard is much higher even in countries like Congo, Swaziland, Guyana and Egypt. (HDR 2010: 158) India's record in antenatal coverage is also quite mediocre. More alarming is the fact that only 47 percent of births in India are attended by 'skilled health personnel' (HDR 2010: 158).

Education which is again vitally linked to health situation presents a disconcerting situation. In gross terms, India is the home of largest number of non-literate people. Even after more than sixty years of independence more than 30 percent of Indian population is not literate. Even those who get enrolled in primary schools the dropout rate is quite high—34.2 percent. As far as pupil-teacher ratio is concerned India's record with 40.7 (2005–2008 figure) is poorer than most of medium human development states, the category to which India belongs. (HDR 2010: 194)

According to HDR 2010 which cites 2008 figure, infant mortality per 100 live births is 52 in India. (HDR 2010: 199) The rate of under-five mortality is even higher, i.e. 69. But there is more disquieting information. According to a Union Human Development report, in 2009 India has slipped from 128 to 134 rank in infant mortality rate. *Save the Children*, a voluntary group, reports, "...one infant dies every 15 seconds in the country. Over 4 lakh (0.4 million) newborns die in the first 24 hours of their life and 90 per cent of deaths are due to preventable diseases like pneumonia and diarrhea". There are also great variations across states, maximum neo-natal mortality being reported from Uttar Pradesh, Madhya Pradesh, Orissa and Rajasthan (Shakil 2009). In 2008, Maternal Mortality Rate (MMR) in India was 230 per one lakh (0.1 million) live births. This is a significant decline of 59 percent between 1990 and 2008. However, it means an annual decrease of 2.3 percent. If India is to attain the target of 75 percent reduction in MMR between 1990 and 2015 as set by the Millennium Development Goals, the rate of decline has to be 5.5 percent. Thus, while India's performance is not to be ignored, one has also to admit that India falls far behind the targeted rate of decline. India's population being second largest in the world, the highest number of women deaths during childbirth takes place in the country (Sinha 2010).

There are also great inequities between the rich and the poor, between urban and rural population in some vital areas of public health. For instance, the ratio of the richest 20 percent to the poorest 20 percent with regard to skilled attendant at birth during 2000–2009 was 4.6 percent. Similar ratio of underweight prevalence in children under five during 2003–2009 was 2.9 percent. The ratio of the richest to the poorest in immunization (measles) coverage during 2000–2008 was 2.1 percent. With regard to use of improved sanitation facilities the ratio of urban to rural in 2008 was 2.6 percent.

While, as Ivan Illich said long back, health has been growingly 'medicalized', Medicare facilities fall far short of the minimum requirements. India has 0.47 doctors per 1000 population. The relevant world and developed country figures are respectively 1.5 and 2.8. The respective figures for hospital bed per 1000 population for the three categories of countries are 0.8, 3.3 and 7.2. India's health expenditure is among the lowest in the world. According to one account, developed countries of Europe and North America and even some Latin American countries spends from about 15 percent to nearly 20 percent of their annual budget for health care. India's neighbor China spends 9.9 percent of its total budget as health expenses. Even for countries like Thailand and Iran the figures are respectively 11.3 and 11.5. By sharp contrast, India's health spending is 3.7 percent of its total annual spending.[24]

In 2010–11 budget of the Government of India, a total amount INR. 251.54 billion has been allocated for health which, according to Ravi Duggal, is just 0.36 percent of the projected GDP. If the estimated expenditure supposed to be incurred by the state governments is taken into account, even then overall health budget turns out to be barely 0.89 percent of GDP. This is far below the first UPA[25] government's promise of taking public health expenditure to 2–3 percent of GDP. With liberalization as the driving ideological force the government has explicitly announced its role as an enabler and facilitator. Effectively it has meant abdicating its role of directly providing even the basic minimum services like public health. Assessing the role of the two successive UPA governments Duggal writes in the cover story of Uday India (2010):

> The rural public health system continues to suffer from the same malaise as earlier—not enough doctors and nurses, inadequate medicine supplies, poor maintenance etc. What was worse is that the reasonably robust urban public health system has also begun to collapse with rapid private sector growth and expansion, including the support of private health insurance. Thus the inadequate public investment in health during the previous UPA regime actually led to the boom of private healthcare which has now jumped to 5.5% of GDP. Since pri-

vate insurance covers barely 2% of the population, most of this expenditure is out-of-pocket indicating a huge burden on households who often have to sell assets or take loans for their hospitalization needs. Thus the UPA-1 government had failed to make any significant impact in the public health domain and the current budget tells us that it is unlikely to make any impact in its current avatar.[26]

Regrettably, this insufficient arrangement also does not find optimum utilization. This is true even for Kerala which has received wide acclaim for its performance in human development sector. The major factors allegedly contributing to such state of things include bureaucratic inefficiency, widespread corruption, lack of minimum work ethic on the part of a section of health personnel including doctors, their unholy nexus with private interests and irresponsible trade unionism of the hospital staff. As a result, profit-seeking private sector has, by default, got a free hunting ground fleecing the ailing and the dying. Absolutely unregulated, these mushrooming private hospitals, nursing homes and pathological laboratories have perfected the art of commoditizing healthcare though with questionable quality of service. Interestingly, the exploitative practices of the private sector hospitals often escape the scanner of the mass media, which never relent in exposing public sector inefficiency hardly bothering to make any dispassionate analysis of its inadequacies in the face of ever-mounting problems. They are also extremely tardy in bringing to public notice some bold initiatives, some remarkable achievements, however few and far between, made in a generally indifferent atmosphere. Thanks partly to media 'crusade' the middle class has, by and large, deserted public hospitals creating a strong impression in people's mind that government hospitals are the final destination of those who cannot afford. The result is booming business for the private sector. According to one estimate, "At the time of Independence, the for-profit sector had a 5 percent–10 percent share of the total patient care. Today, it accounts for 82 percent of outpatient visits, 58 percent of hospitalisation days, 40 percent of institutional deliveries, 35 percent of antenatal care visits, and 15 percent of children immunized. The private sector's success is attributable less to its own efficiency and more to the government's failure" (Varatharajan 2004: 22). With the neo-liberal turn of the economy, government's planned withdrawal from the health sector has only intensified.[27] The UPA[28] Government's much-publicized National Rural Health Mission introduced in 18 poor-performing states is supposed to salvage the decayed public health system. It suffers from a number of serious shortcomings confirming our bureaucracy's tenacity not to learn from past mistakes. (Banerjee 2005) Nevertheless, the limited opportunities they offer should not be wasted and local self-governing institutions and people's movements might act together to extend its frontier.

Decentralization

Decentralization is the buzzword in contemporary participatory democracy and development discourses. In rural India, (Panchayati Raj Institution) PRIs are the constitutionally recognized bodies for people's representation at the grassroots level. Along with acting as delivery agencies they are supposed to garner people's initiatives for self-rule and self-development. It would be, however, misleading to assume that the institutionalization of panchayati raj is a gift from above for facilitating popular initiative. They are also the outcome of people's struggles for democratization. Kerala, Karnataka, Madhya Pradesh and West Bengal offer some of the interesting, though different, experiences of relative success of PRI intervention.

The politics of decentralization in West Bengal is an area widely commented upon by scholars across the world. Depending on respective ideological-theoretical dispositions some have found in it an advancement of democracy, while for others this is a site for neo-elite corruption and an instrument for deepening the hegemony of the ruling front, especially its dominant partner, the Communist Party of India (Marxist). We hold that as far as developmental experience is concerned, panchayat system in West Bengal deserves neither unqualified kudos nor unalloyed curse. As for democracy, thirty years of West Bengal experiment has changed the structure of rural politics. Politics today is much more a mass business rather than an exclusive elite enterprise. Politicization of the masses has not always gone to the benefit of the ruling regime and that should be read as a positive sign for democratization.

Involving the PRIs in human development initiatives is a relatively recent step. Following the 73rd Amendment of the Constitution *The West Bengal Panchayat Act 1973* empowered the State Government in 1994 to transfer as many as seventeen functions, including some health-related functions, to PRIs. The declared objective of the change is `to ensure 'people's health on people's initiative'. As for the Gram Panchayats (GP), the lowest tier of the rural self-government, the obligatory public health related duties are to provide (a) sanitation, conservancy and drainage and the prevention of public nuisances; (b) curative and promotive measures in respect of malaria, small pox, cholera or any other epidemic; (c) supply of drinking water and the cleansing and disinfecting of the sources of supply and storage of water. For the promotion of such functions the government has provided each GP with necessary funds for the construction of a Head Quarter sub-center in its premises. The sub-center will be manned by one female health assistant and one male health assistant. All the sub-centers within the GP-area will be supervised by one Health Supervisor posted in the Head Quarter sub-center. The GP is to extend cooperation in running the sub-centers. It is also required to provide rooms and infrastructure to the ICDS centers. Ensuring improved sanitation and safe drinking water to every household are among its essential functions. The GP functionaries are supposed to supervise, coordinate and monitor the functions of the health and anganwadi workers.

How active are the GPs in respect of public health related functions? In 2007, the present author and his co-researcher conducted a study in 28 GPs from seven districts from across the state under the auspices of the State Institute Panchayat and Rural Development, Government of West Bengal. Along with GP functionaries, we interviewed 2800 respondents, 100 from each GP. The investigation revealed considerable variations in terms of public health attainments in different GP areas. But we also noticed that better attainments were associated with better endowment factors like education, income and proximity to urban areas. It was therefore difficult to assess the role of the GP or the party running the GP in public health performance. We could guess that the agility, motivation and will of the Pradhan may make some difference provided the party leadership at the relevant level is not too constraining. If personality-based performance is really confirmed that does not augur well for the system introduced. In fact, our investigation reveals certain limitations of the decentralized public health system introduced in West Bengal. One of the crippling factors appears to be lack of cognition on the part of the functionaries. Since the GP is the grassroots institution of democratic governance, the basic purpose of assigning a role to it in public health was to bring government actions in this crucial area of human wellbeing under democratic accountability in the sense of day-to-day social vigilance and monitoring. As yet, such perceptual transformation is not in sight—neither among the GP functionaries, nor the staff of the line departments. As a result, the former cannot make demands and the latter cannot think of complying. For the line department staff, it is more of a new bureaucratic formality—to hold the statutory monthly meeting with GP and keep routine records. The lack of cognition is reflected in lack of coordination. When asked in the formal interview if they found any coordination problem among the different agencies involved in health related functions a good majority of the functionaries denied the occurrence of any such problem. Such no-problem attitude, we hold, comes from their non-involvement. This was confirmed in course of our discussion with the health and ICDS (Integrated Child Development Services) staff who presented a much less rosy picture. If the GP functionaries fail in coordination function, much of the problem lies with the existing framework. For a host of public health duties the GP is statutorily responsible and politically accountable but they have simply no control over those who are to perform such duties. The health and ICDS staffs are accountable only to their respective departments. Lack of control contributes to lack of initiative which was evident in most GPs with only a few exceptions. Initiative is encouraged by autonomy. An enterprising Pradhan may carve out some space even within the framework but generally little effective autonomy is contemplated at the systemic level. The GPs appear to be drowned in the proverbial GOs (Government Orders) containing specific 'guidelines' even on minute details about dos and don'ts. The problem of 'too many and too often' tends to reduce the Pradhan as non-functioning head-clerk discouraging the vision of GP as the institution for mobilizing people's energy and initiative in order to ensure their participation in governance (Basu and Chakraborty 2007).[29]

If we are unable to present a rosy picture about the GPs in human development functions, especially public health, we do not mean to suggest that GPs have no future in the process of democratization. In fact, there are many instances of inspiring performance through popular participation by the GP. In our SIPRD (State Institute of Panchayats and Rural Development)–study we have referred to some such cases. The more important point for our present purpose is that the general institutional milieu of grassroots democratic governance is not yet very conducive for whetting people's creativity. For an instance of what such creativity can dare aspire and at least partly attain, we now turn to the story of a very small non-governmental voluntary social initiative.

Sundarban Sramajibi Swasthya Prakalpa (Sundarban Working People's Health Project)

About 65 kilometres from the center of Kolkata on the gateway to the Sundarban is Sarberia, a village with less than 2500 population. It is in the Sandeshkhali I Community Development Block in the district of North 24 Parganas. The block has a total population of 140,446 (2001 census), majority of them living below poverty line mostly from different Scheduled Caste groups and Muslims. With long stretches of fisheries interrupted by some patches of urbanization the area has for long been infamous for crimes, poverty, ill health, and lack of education. Of late the face of the Sundarbans has been slowly changing with improvements in communication and some expansion of income opportunities. Nevertheless, it remains one of the poorest regions of the state. Both out-migration and trafficking in women and children are high. Agriculture and fishing are major occupations in the area. Land holding is small and the number of landless is high. The landless people live mainly by working as day laborer in agriculture, fisheries and brickfields along with any odd jobs they might procure. There is one Primary Health Center in the block along with two subsidiary centers. Nevertheless, the over all healthcare scenario in the area is in a very poor shape allowing a thriving market for the untrained village doctors commonly called quacks. True, these quacks are the only people available at any odd hours. But many of them are also quite ruthless in swindling the hapless patients compounding their financial distress as well as, in many cases, health hazards.

Amidst such a rather gloomy scenario, some young men of the area—moderately educated and with very slim or no financial resources—set up in 1989 sort of a cooperative agricultural farm, named *Krisichakra*, primarily for organic farming. Ten bighas (3.3 Acres) of land were leased out by an elderly lady of the area at a nominal rent. Her son was among the founders of the organization. About a dozen men and women from very poor families gathered around the organization to start a new experiment for frugal but dignified and collective living. Most of them were agricultural laborers with very little formal education. Meanwhile turning paddy field into more lucrative fisheries had been going on unhindered in the area adding further plight to the poor and eroding their capacity to afford even minimum medical facility which is prohibitively expensive in the private sector and extremely erratic and inadequate in the public sector. An additional disturbing problem was that many of the migrant workers from the surrounding villages were coming back with a host of communicable diseases and were getting no proper treatment. This prompted the organizers of the *Krishichakra* to make a small beginning by way of organizing medical camps once in every fortnight with the help of some sympathetic doctors who agreed to attend the camps against only the cost of traveling by car. The organizers, however, could not manage to raise even this amount and the camp ceased to operate after some time.

Some time later, on June 21, 1999, medical camps were restarted with support from the *Belur Sramajibee* (Workers') *Hospital*, which had been built from nothing by the workers of a local factory fighting against closure. The episode of struggling workers taking into constructive activities for their own welfare and empowerment had been forcefully articulated in Chattisgarh region of the Indian state of Madhya Pradesh (Chattisgarh became a state in 2000) by the Chattisgarh Mukti Morcha (CMM) under its visionary leader Shankar Guha Neogy who was murdered allegedly by an industrialist-liquor baron-politician nexus. To address the pathetic state of health of the mine workers the CMM had founded the Shaheed Hospital. The Belur experiment drew inspiration from Neogy's famous call for *Sangharsh aur Nirman* (Struggle and Construction). It was truly an effort of the subalterns, with help from a section of the civil society, for self-empowerment in the face of governmental apathy. The founding of the hospital was no smooth exercise, as it had to face severe hostility, legal and extra-legal, from the vested interests at each step.

The organizers of the Krisichakra at Sarberia soon realized that fortnightly medical camps were too inadequate to make any dent in the enormous healthcare gaps faced by the underprivileged people of the area. They started toying with the idea of setting up a hospital to render some minimum medical services including provisions for inpatient service. On 12 May 2002, they took this giant stride in four thatched huts with makeshift furniture and very basic equipment. From day one, however, they could ensure the presence of a qualified allopath, seven days a week and twenty-four hours a day—something unimaginable in such a remote village, something even the government with its ever-mounting expenditure has not been able to provide in many primary health centers in West Bengal. By the end of the year, in December 2002, the hospital was shifted to a somewhat more spacious four-room building with concrete walls and corrugated roof. Following the Belur experiment the organizers named the hospital as Sundarban Sramajibee Hospital. To comply with some legal paraphernalia, however, it was renamed as Sundarban Sramajibee Swasthya Prakalpa (SSSP). In 2007, some further extension took place with the construction of three new concrete rooms. Today, it has provisions for twenty-four beds in two wards for male and female patients respectively. In addition to the inpatient wing, the hospital has outdoor services, a small pathology wing, medicine outlet, X-ray, and 24 hours' emergency service with doctor, oxygen and some life-saving arrangements in an area notorious for snake-biting and diarrhea. At the time of writing, nine doctors, both general physicians and specialists in pediatrics, eye, gynecology and skin attend the outdoor clinic on specified days in each month. But one general physician is available all through the week—day and night. From December 29, 2002, to December 31, 2007, the hospital has provided outdoor service to 63,891 and indoor service to 1784 persons. Patients come to the hospital from villages as far as 25 kilometers. All these services are provided at a cost much lower than what the patients are normally to pay to the private providers with comparable or inferior service. It is not rare that patients cannot pay even this nominal charge but that never causes refusal.

The hospital is a good example of an experiment with people's participation. Voluntary labor was an important component in construction works, saving costs. Part of the funds was mobilized by small donations from the people of a number of adjacent villages who were given a small earthen pot (in Bengali called *ghat*) to save whatever small coins they could afford. Some villagers with better means donated more. All these, however, were not sufficient to meet the costs, and considerable help, in cash and kind, came from outside the area, particularly from the organizers of the Belur Sramajibee Hospital. However, the important point is that neither government funding nor contributions from any funding agency or corporate house, Indian or foreign, had any role in founding the hospital. It was entirely the product of hard labor of some local people high in social commitment with aid, advice and assistance from fellow doers from outside the area. The expansion works since 2002 have also been done in the same way—initiated in the area and facilitated by outsiders who contributed and collected small amounts from many people. For instance, in 2007 and 2008, some students from two departments of Calcutta University, Political Science and History, donated more than eighty-five thousand rupees to facilitate construction of a room and to install an X-ray machine. They raised the fund from hundreds of people including their parents, teachers, and fellow students.

People's initiative is relatively easy to garner in taking a new venture but far more difficult to sustain for every day mundane works. For the last five years the SSSP has somehow managed to accomplish it. Only the doctors are paid regularly. All those rendering paramedical services are members of the Krisichakra who work as health volunteers. They are young boys and girls with very modest formal education and mostly from agricultural labor families. With practical training undergone in the Belur Srmajibee Hospital these volunteers have developed reasonable expertise in pathological tests, imaging, administering injections and medicines and all other related works. All the arrangements betray frugality but they are so well maintained. The wards are always kept clean. The volunteers themselves do all these works. They are not paid staff; most of them live in the hospital premises and all eat together in a common kitchen. These expenses are met from the hospital fund. Different activities of the Krisichakra such as paddy cultivation, vegetable growing, pisciculture, poultry, bee-keeping and grinding and sale of spices are distributed among the members. They get some small maintenance allowance according to their respective needs from the revenue earned from such activities. Though 2/3 members have specific responsibility for a particular wing of the Krisichakra labour is provided by others also as such needs arise. The members sit together every evening and discuss for about an hour the next day's manpower requirements in the farm and in the hospital. On rotational basis they are also allotted duties at the night shifts in the hospital; and in case of any emergency all of them come forward.

If the volunteers manage the internal works of the hospital, its expenses are borne from user charges and donations from people. For example, in 2006–07 financial year, out of a total income of INR 1,340,911 (USD 25075) the revenue component was INR 763,520.25 (USD 14278) while donations on different heads amounted to INR 403,239 (USD 7541). Since the area is generally poor, only a small part of the donated amount can be mobilized from the villages. A large part of the donation comes from the hospital's well-wishers from Kolkata and other places. However, the organizers try to approach as many local people as possible and try to generate the feeling that the hospital is a people's property and hence it is their responsibility to nurture and maintain it. The villagers are sought to be involved for other activities as well. In surrounding 14 villages, the SSSP has either a unit or some sympathizers extending different types of help. In order to keep popular contact lively, the organizers try to associate the people of these villages in three events that they hold every year. On the last Sunday of December each year a large number of local people, well-wishers from outside, and representatives from like-minded organizations gather in hundreds in an annual fair, called *milan mela*, in the adjacent school ground where different groups from the villages as well as the volunteers of the hospital and members of other organizations present different cultural events like choir, folk songs and dances, and drama. On 21 June, the foundation day of the medical camp, a blood donation camp is organized. On the second week of September is held the Annual General Meeting. It is interesting to note that there is no restriction on attending the meeting and non-members can also ask for clarifications and advance suggestions. Both in the *milan mela* and in the Annual General Meeting several hundred people from the surrounding villages join in community lunch for which articles and money are collected by the volunteers from the villagers themselves. For about a month, boys and girls from the hospital go out to the villages for such collection and also talk with the people about the hospital and issues related to health awareness.

The SSSP and the Krisichakra are carrying out an interesting experiment in democratic participation. True, the organization is yet to come out of the influence of its key founder, in spite of his sincere efforts to project himself as a self-effacing personality and continuous emphasis on the 'collective'. They have introduced the norm of taking all decisions—even the minute ones—through discussion among the members, who as we have noted, meet every evening. Discussion often turns into prolonged debate which is not sought to be scuttled. To give a recent example, the organizers have long been feeling the need for an ambulance to carry ailing patients in emergency cases from remote villages where sometimes no vehicle can be found, especially during night. One gentleman offered to buy an ambulance for the hospital only on the condition that it should be dedicated to the memory of his deceased mother. This is nothing very unusual in philanthropic overtures. The organizers debated over the issue for several days and, finally, decided to politely refuse the offer on the grounds that it might create an inclination among them to get things done in easy ways which would mean dependence on moneyed people and would also involve maintenance costs they are unable to bear at the moment.

Conclusion

Once we asked Nabirul Islam, one of the volunteers working in the hospital since almost its inception, if he thought the hospital could run in absence of its founder-leader who has always been its guiding spirit. Nabirul did not appear very confident. There is a second persistently asked question. Can we really imagine series of Sarberia experiments as the way to bringing healthcare to all? In fact, sustainability and replicability are considered two of the major problem areas of micro-level social initiatives in participatory development discourse. Social initiatives should not be romanticized. The role of personality has often been closely related to their success and limitations. More importantly, society is no undifferentiated mass nor is 'social' a conflict-free space. Consensual intervention is extremely difficult to build up and far more difficult to sustain. Social activists are often baffled by the amazing heterogeneity of opposition beyond any simple categorization. Often the real reason for opposition is not the one cited. We guess, in some cases those who oppose an initiative do not themselves know why they are opposing. Even sometimes they do not believe that they are opponent to what they are opposing. Proneness to conflict may be as deep-seated in human psyche as compulsions for cooperation. Moreover, indifference to what happens around is more pervading than concern. Further, to convert concern to action involving some personal investment is a very rare spirit. Social initiative, thus, is perforce fragmentary; and much of its resources are expended to tide over the pricks and pangs of such fragmentation.

What, then, is the significance of experiments like the one at Sarberia? First, it helps dispel the myth that healthcare is a very expensive proposition beyond the ability of the State to ensure. Such demystification is more prominently illustrated by the Belur Hospital which, on no-profit-no-loss basis, charges just INR. 25,000 (USD 468) for cardiac bypass surgery. Even in government hospitals people are required to expend more than a lakh of rupees (0.1 million) for the same operation; and in the so-called state-of-the-art private hospitals the charge is astronomical. This is just one example. The hospital also treats many other serious ailments at a very reasonable cost with the provision for free treatment to workers of closed factories and their family members. This is possibly the only hospital in the state which charges no money in case a patient dies while under treatment in the hospital. All these notwithstanding the hospital has not only been running for more than 15 years now; it has been expanded to a nearly 100-bed hospital, often packed to its capacity, from a mere 4-bed beginning. The crucial question, therefore, both ontological and political—is health a commodity or a public good? That for the private sector it is a commodity to be traded against profit is understandable though one may reasonably assert that the fleecing operation that they are infamous for is absolutely unethical, and governmental indifference to such malpractices is unpardonable. The more important issue is if the government considers health, as a public good, should be accessible to all. Those who can afford and desire to go for the luxury of expensive hospitals need not be deterred. But there have to be sufficient and efficient public healthcare arrangements for the people without any discrimination. The experiments like in

Belur and Sarberia testify to the fact that given political will healthcare—both basic and specialty—should not remain beyond the reach of the masses. This may be an important lesson for those who are committed to democratizing governance. They must keep on mounting pressure on the state that it must provide and also enhance basic opportunities for human development without which proper democratic governance cannot even take off.

It also sensitizes us to another linkage between democracy and people's movement. The SSSP is a school of democracy where people learn to feel empowered by way of participation through debates, deliberations and, most importantly, responsibility-sharing actions. The story of Sarberia shows what people's creativity can achieve despite innumerable constraints once they feel they can help themselves. The lesson is particularly instructive in the context of the grossly poor performance of many of our democratic institutions including the grassroots ones which are steadily drifting away from the *demos*. In West Bengal, for example, as we have already noted, PRIs have ushered in some significant changes through participatory development. But their success is uneven. Most debilitating limitations are found in human development areas like public health and education which need persistent and creative association of the masses. Much of the failure of the PRIs in arousing such creativity from below may be attributed to the dominant paradigm of formal democracy which discourages diversity by denying autonomy of thought and action. The PRIs are getting rapidly initiated in the culture of complying with 'guidelines' from above. This may be a sad commentary on democracy but not so much a surprising one. After all, the institutional domain of democratic politics finds comfort in exclusion. In addition, social initiatives often confront resistance from political institutions including political parties. This, again, is not surprising. In the politically surcharged milieu of West Bengal with sharp partisan polarization any independent initiative is likely to be viewed as partisan, either explicit or hidden. Besides, non-party initiatives for social change are no less *political*. Formal political institutions naturally develop a propensity to view social assertion, especially those for the underprivileged, as intrusive to their domain.

The reticence and hostility of the institutional domain of democracy should alert micro-level people's initiatives to the urgent need for critical engagement with the former instead of wishing it away. It is illusory to seek empowerment of the masses by distancing from formal power. To shun political parties, elections and elected bodies, especially the PRIs, is to leave a vital area of struggle for democratization uncontested. After all, social initiatives have to change the context of power on which alone democracy can flourish. The struggle for changing this context involves struggle both within and outside the domain of formal political power. The compulsions of competitive electoral democracy sometimes force even pro–rich governments to adopt policies which people's movements should strive to utilize to the fullest and also to extend its frontier for the benefit of the people. As all civil society movements are not democratic and all people's movements are not pro–people, so also there are vital differences between political parties. Political institutions do not necessarily form any monolith working in fine concert on all issues. There are many cracks and fissures in the political society which people's movement can manipulate to find a space to wage its struggle in the cause of democracy. There is no point in people's movements' expressing self-righteous indignation for political parties irrespective of ideology, policies, programs and compulsions. If democracy has extended its reach in India over last sixty years—which it has definitely done—the role of the political parties and institutions in it cannot be denied. If the social context of democratic governance has at least partially changed for the better in states like West Bengal or Kerala it is largely because of protracted mass mobilization of left political parties and their mass organizations, their working within and outside governmental institutions. The Chhatisgarh Mukti Morcha we have already alluded to offers one variant of people's movements' engagement with the institutional domain of politics. (Chattopadhyay 2005) Another form may be found in the role of the Kerala Shastra Sahitya Parishad (KSSP) (Thomas and Franke 2000). Both, we hold, have helped the process of democratization. The nature of engagement cannot be generalized and will depend much on the democratic sensibility and political acumen of the forces operating in the area and beyond. What, however, is important is the realization that it is good to be ideologically charged but not blinkered. Like the civil society, the State also, on many occasions, behaves as a fragmented entity. Nor does it always enjoy ideological and programmatic homogeneity. The politics of democratization must remain alert to avail of all the cracks and fissures and also empathies—here and there—within the formal political domain. People's initiatives should realize that setting good examples is only the beginning and not an end. Its value is primarily instrumental. Martyrdom may be necessary. It should not be the goal.

Acknowledgment

I acknowledge my debt to the Jadavpur University for allowing me to reproduce a part of my article 'Democratizing Healthcare: The Story of a Social Initiative' published in Partha Pratim Basu, Purusottam Bhattacharya, Debi Chatterjee, Shibashis Chatterjee, eds. 2012. *Democracy and Democratization in the 21st Century: The South Asian Experience*, Har-Anand, New Delhi.

References

Antia, N. H., G.P. Dutta and A.B. Kasbekar, 2000. *Health and Medical Care: A People's Movement*, Bombay: FRCH.

Banerjee, D., 2005. Politics of Rural Health in India. *Economic and Political Weekly* 40, no. 30: 3253–3258.

Basu, G and S. Chakraborty, 2007. *Public Health Initiatives Undertaken by Gram Panchayats*, Unpublished Report. Kalyani, Nadia: Government of West Bengal, SIPRD.

Chandoke, N., 2003. When the Voiceless Speak: A Case Study of Chhattisgrah Mukti Morcha. *Does Civil Society Matter?: Governance in Contemporary India*, edited by Rajesh Tandon and Ranjita Mohanty, 198–242. New Delhi: Sage Publications.

Chattopadhyay, T.K., 2005. *Empowering the People: The Shankar Guha Neogy Way*. Kolkata: Department of Political Science, University of Calcutta.

Drèze, J. and A. Sen, 2002. *India: Development and participation*. New Delhi: Oxford University Press.
Duggal, R., 2010. India's Health Budget 2010–2011: The Malaise Continues. *Uday India, The Weekly that Empowers*, Cover Story (March 20). www.udayindia.org/content_20march2010/cover_story.html (accessed April 24, 2011).
Isaac, T. T. M. and W.R. Franke, 2000. *Local Democracy and. Development: People's Campaign for Decentralised Planning in Kerala*. New Delhi: LeftWord.
National Human Rights Commission in collaboration with Ministry of Health & Family Welfare, Government of India [and] World Health Organization, South East Asia Regional Office. 2001. *Regional Consultation on Public Health and Human Rights, 10–11 April, 2001*. New Delhi: Report and Recommendations. New Delhi: National Human Rights Commission. http:// www.nhrc.nic.in/Publications/publichealthText.pdf (accessed February 19, 2011).
Ruger J. P., 2005. Democracy and Health. *Quarterly Journal of Medicine* 98, no.4: 299–304.
Shakil M., 2009. Infant mortality rate highest in India. *IBNLive India* (October 5). http://ibnlive.in.com/news/infant-mortality-rate-highest-in-india-report/ 102751-3.html (accessed February 19, 2011).
Sinha K., 2010. India: Maternal Mortality Plummets, Still Highest in the World. *OneWorld South Asia* (September 17, 2010). http://southasia.oneworld.net/ todaysheadlines/india-maternal-mortality-plummets-still-highest-in-the-world (accessed February 19, 2011).
Thomas Isaac T. M. and Franke, R. W., 2000. *Local Democracy and Development*. Left Word Books: New Delhi.
Tulchinsky T. H and E.A. Varavikova, 2000. *The New Public Health: An Introduction for the 21st Century*. San. Diego: Academic Press.
United Nations, 1948. Universal Declaration of Human Rights. Adopted 10 December 1948. GA. Res. 217 AIII. United Nations Document a/810. New York: UN. http://www.un.org/en/documents/udhr/index.shtml (accessed February 19, 2011).
UNDP, 2010. Human Development Report, 2010. http://hdr.undp.org/en/media/ HDR_2010_EN_Complete_reprint.pdf (accessed February 19, 2011).
Varatharajan D., 2004. Provision of Health Care by the Government. *Ind J Med Ethics* 12, no. 4: 22–25.
Verma, J.S., 2001. Forward. Regional Consultation on Public Health and Human Rights of National Human Rights Commission, New Delhi (10–11 April).

Notes

1. Department of Political Science, University of Calcutta. Email: mumling2004 @yahoo.com.
2. "Health and Human Rights" *The World Health Organization.* http://www.who.int/ hhr/en/ (accessed February 11, 2011).
3. Health and human rights are inextricably intertwined (http://www. expresshealthcaremgmt.com/ 20031215/health01.shtml).
4. "Linkages between Health and Human Rights" *The World Health Organization.* http://www.who.int/hhr/HHR%20linkages.pdf (accessed February 19, 2011).
5. The Declaration on the Right to Development was adopted by the General Assembly in its resolution 41/128 of 4 December 1986. *See* G.A. Res. 41/128, U.N. GAOR, 41st Sess., Supp. No. 53, at 186, U.N. Doc. A/41/53 (1986).
6. http://www.nhrc.nic.in/Publications/publichealthText.pdf (accessed February 19, 2011).
7. Report on the State of Food Insecurity in Rural India, by M S Swaminathan Research Foundation (MSSRF) and the World Food Programme (WFP), December 2008 (http://s3.amazonaws.com/zanran_storage/www.mssrf.org/ContentPages/112651312.pdf accessed February 19, 2011).
8. http://documents.wfp.org/stellent/groups/public/documents/newsroom/wfp197348.pdf (accessed February 20, 2011).
9. http://articles.timesofindia.indiatimes.com/2010-10-11/india/28248911_1_global-hunger-index-ifpri-hunger-levels (accessed February 19, 2011).
10. http://southasia.oneworld.net/todaysheadlines/food-security-in-india-leaves-much-to- be-desired (accessed February 19, 2011).
11. Report on the State of Food Insecurity in Rural India, by M S Swaminathan Research Foundation (MSSRF) and the World Food Programme (WFP), December 2008 (http://s3.amazonaws.com/zanran_storage/www.mssrf.org/ContentPages/112651312.pdf accessed February 19, 2011).
12. http://articles.timesofindia.indiatimes.com/2010-10-11/india/28248911_1_global-hunger-index-ifpri-hunger-levels (accessed February 19, 2011).
13. http://southasia.oneworld.net/todaysheadlines/food-security-in-india-leaves-much-to-be-desired (accessed February 21, 2011).
14. http://www.tehelka.com/story_main47.asp?filename=Ne061110The_middle_class.asp (accessed February 19, 2011).
15. http://news.oneindia.in/2010/11/22/indiatops-list-of-nations-lackingtoilets.html (accessed April 26, 2011).
16. http://www.un.org/apps/news/story.asp?NewsID=34369&Cr=mdg&Cr1 (accessed April 26, 2011).
17. SME World: Focus: April, 2010: Almost 90 per cent rural population doesn't have access to drinking water (http://www.smeworld.org/story/focus-100/almost-per-cent-rural-population-doesnt-have-access-to-drinking-water-217.php accessed April 26, 2011).
18. 60% INDIANS ARE LIVING WITHOUT TOILETS. (http://uttamagarwalblog.wordpress.com/60-indians-are-living-without-toilets/ (accessed April 19, 2011).
19. http://www.un.org/apps/news/story.asp?NewsID=34369&Cr=mdg&Cr1 (accessed April 26, 2011).
20. Livemint.com. 80 % of Indians live on less than $2 a day. Author: Alison Granito. October 16 2007. (http://www.livemint.com/articles/2007/10/16235421/80 -of-Indians-live-on-less-th.html accessed April 29, 2011).

21. http://e.mydigitalfc.com/dcf/dcf/2011/04/21/ArticleHtmls/21_04_2011_009_028.shtml (accessed April 22, 2011).

22. Ibid.

23. Human Development Report 2010, UNDP (http://hdr.undp.org/en/media/HDR_2010_EN_Complete_reprint.pdf accessed February 19, 2011).

24. How Countries Spend Their Money – Visual Economics. http://www.visualeconomics.com/how-countries-spend-their-money/ accessed April 20, 2011).

25. United Progressive Alliance—the federal government in India led by the Congress Party.

26. www.udayindia.org/content_20march2010/cover_story.html (accessed April 24, 2011).

27. "The big squeeze" By Amit Sen Gupta. http://infochangeindia.org/index2.php?option=com_content&do_pdf=1&id=401 (accessed April 22, 2011).

28. Present ruling coalition government in New Delhi, India.

29. The Report was presented and discussed in a workshop organized by the SIPRD and attended by scholars and activists from different academic institutions and development organizations. The author takes this opportunity to acknowledge my gratitude to the Department of Panchayat and Rural Development, and the SIPRD, Government of West Bengal.

CHAPTER 17

Human Rights and Information Society: Problematizing India

Dipankar Sinha

Let us clarify at the very outset that this essay primarily attempts to situate the human rights problematic in the broader context of the Information Society. At the outset it is also important to note that while there exists prolific and ever-growing literature on the respective themes of human rights and the Information Society the effort to relate the two has been far less frequent. There are a number of reasons for such gap and one major cause could be the fact that the scholars theorizing the two vitally important themes tend to have such an 'exclusive' emphasis on one that the other is at best provided secondary role, or at worst, simply omitted from the analysis. Thus, for instance, *A Dictionary of Human Rights* (Robertson 2005), notwithstanding its vast array of entries, has none on the Information Society. Nor does *Dictionary of Media and Communications* (Danesi 2009) have an entry on human rights. The list of instances can be made longer by referring to other kinds of academic literature too but that is not exactly the objective of the current essay. There are some notable exceptions though, which would be subsequently cited here, but in their cases too, the exceptions only prove the rule. The scenario is not much different in the domain of practice either. Hamelink (2003), an ardent advocate of the communicative dimensions of human rights, puts the point in perspective in these words:

> No effective mechanisms have been established to deal with all the obstacles that hamper the realization of human rights in the field of informational developments. Moreover, current human rights provisions focus exclusively on information and ignore communication. No human rights standard has been adopted to address communication as an interactive process. Communication tends to be seen as the transfer of messages (Hamelink 2003:1).

We would discuss the communicative foundation of the Information Society but at this juncture it is necessary to point out that the first part of this essay deals with a conceptual framework and the second part focuses on the Indian scenario.

It is also worth noting that while the essay seeks to problematize the Indian context the clues that come up might be relevant for the third world societies in general. The point remains true despite the fact that the third world is not to be considered a homogenous space. As we shall find in the following discussion, insofar as the construction of the Information Society is concerned, and more specifically, as far as the perception, treatment and status of the *culture of information* are relevant, the third world societies perhaps display only a difference in degree, rather than a huge qualitative differentiation.

Information Society: The Back of the Beyond

The core of Information Society is communication, which goes much beyond the technical calculation of the quantum of raw information and Information and Communication Technologies (ICTs). Both raw information and the ICTs can facilitate communication but neither can substitute or surpass it. Yet there seems to be a rhetorical consensus particularly about the ICTs being the be-all and end-all of the Information Society. There is a political reason for such maneuvering by which the Information Society has steadily, and perhaps too subtly, acquired the status of a buzzword in the policymaking arena of the third world, India being no exception. While human rights is a 'nasty', controversial category, and even a 'threat' to them, the Information Society, because of the proclamation of its immense power of technological might, is a safe and seductive bet for the elite policymakers in the third world. Such 'specific' construction and representation of the Information Society, however, are not solely a national phenomenon. It has powerful transnational roots as well (Sinha 2010a). The ICTs are being ceaselessly publicized as the "motive force" of the Information/Communication Revolution by the developed states, the transnational organizations, the donor agencies, and no less, the transnational corporations—all promising a "better society" by the transformatory potential of new technology. But at the same time they do largely remain silent on the 'non-technical' constraints and limitations that mark the 'deployment' of the ICTs in societies in which the democratization of information is yet to be viewed in favorable light by the rulers themselves.

The transnational/global construction of a stiffly mechanistic Information Society unilaterally roots out the sources and manifestations of confusion, dilemmas, tensions and contradictions that invariably accompany the process of 'deployment'—a term, significantly enough, borrowed from the military vocabulary. It thus becomes a strategy-cum-narrative of a process of regimentation in which the specific context and the milieu are considered secondary. The policy orientation to such conceptual framework is provided not just by the western states, especially the G-8, but also by the west-controlled transnational agencies like Organization for Economic Cooperation and Development (OECD), United Nations Development Program (UNDP), United Nations Conference on Trade and Development (UNCTAD), International Labour Organization (ILO), International Telecommunication Union (ITU), the World Bank and so forth.

Amidst the construction of the transnational/global variety of the Information Society, and the plethora of recommendations relating to the 'correct' and 'sound' policy and regulatory regime, establishment of norms and principles, and the rules of internet governance, e-network readiness, e-commerce, intellectual property rights protection, taxation of goods and services delivered via the networks, issues of privacy, surveillance and security and so forth, the overwhelming attention is focused on the technicalities. Incidentally, the Okinawa Economic Summit of the G8, held in June–July, 2000, and the Okinawa Charter (2000) with its dual emphasis on the need of "everyone's inclusion in the global information society" and the "need for appropriate policy and regulatory environment", set the ball rolling for the transnational foundation of Information Society. Recognizing the revolutionary impact of the ICT in the "way people live, learn and work and the way government interacts with civil society" the Charter encourages further development of "user-friendly", "barrier-free" technologies with a simultaneous emphasis on the advancement of the Information Society "underpinned by the development of human resources capable of responding to the demands of the information age" (Provision 11). In the process, there is hardly any space and scope to ponder over the 'organic' notion of information, which should have been the fountainhead of a context-specific Information Society (or Societies).

Some hope for reducing the technocratic core of the Information Society rested with the World Summit on Information Society (WSIS) meeting, which were held in Geneva in 2003 and in Tunis in 2005. Much publicity has been attached to two major WSIS documents—the *Declaration of Principles* and the *Plan of Action*—which claim to have made breakthroughs in the construction of the Information Society and the removal of digital divide. In recognizing the importance of "our common vision of Information Society" the WSIS *Declaration of Principles* (Declaration I: 2003) mentions a number of measures for reorienting the Information Society, including cultural diversity and identity, linguistic diversity and local content. However, several critiques, including one based on an intensive ideological-discursive and content analysis-based study (Pyati 2005) of the documents, assert that both the *Declaration of Principles* and the *Plan of Action* paint a wholly utopian picture that grossly oversimplifies and generalizes a complex issue and social phenomenon. The WSIS's vision of the Information Society is based mainly on ICTs, and it is technologically deterministic in outlook. The major thrust of the critique is that the information industries and ICTs are important in today's world, but the WSIS's conceptualization of the Information Society serves to "fetishize" ICTs and technology, promoting technological determinism, simplistic answers, and perhaps even "wrong solutions". Incidentally, the *Civil Society Declaration* of the WSIS, in a unanimous resolution (WSIS Civil Society Plenary 2003), has provided "centrality" to human rights—with the Freedom of Expression at the top of the list. It states in a clear-cut manner: "Technological decisions should be taken with the goal of meeting the life-critical needs of people, not with goal of enriching companies or enabling undemocratic control by governments" [WSIS Civil Society Plenary 2003: 8]. But the question is how to go about it?

The irony is that the other side of the fence, as far as the spell of the Information Society is concerned, is no different. The third world countries too are eager to "deploy" the ICTs, led by the false belief that the new technologies have acquired such power that they would provide a sort of quick-fix solution to the deficiencies in governance that the rulers have been unable to address and remove for decades. As a result, we encounter the shrill cry announcing the arrival of the Information Society, which overwhelmingly revolves around the question of 'access', that too without referring to the need to contextualize and democratize the *culture of information*—based to a large extent on equitable access to media and other means of communication (including face-to-face communication) and the right to information—in the respective states. The concern over the Digital Divide is sought to be accompanied by the continuous promise of "access" but the vital question of control—on the basis of which *how such access is to be made* in the absence of the endeavor on the part of the rulers to privilege and prioritize the culture of information—remains hidden from deliberations. As a result, even societies in which the people are sought to be subject to incommunicado by the powers that be, the Information Society is claimed to have been established with much fanfare—with lot of implications for human rights.

With the ICTs thus unilaterally and uncritically regarded as the guiding force of the Information Society there is burgeoning literature, too many to be enumerated here, which analyze the great potential of computer-mediated communication, such as, the Internet. As a result, the impression gains ground that what matters in ensuring the efficiency and effectiveness of the Information Society is the virtual world and the integration of the virtual communities based on the extensive network of personal connectivity in it. The discourses that nurture such ideas accord greater priority to the capacity of the 'netizens', rather than the capability of citizens. In this technocratic set-up the nitty-gritty of the establishment and sustenance of human rights does not find its well-deserved place. We would submit that there are two reasons for such deliberate omission. First, for the rulers of the third world, armed with the 'new strategy' of celebration of the "revolutionary power" of the ICTs and the associated image of the Information Society as the 'magic wand', it is assumed that 'thorny' issues like human rights would not come much to the surface to disturb their peace of mind. Second, for the transnational/global sponsors and stakeholders of the Information Society of the dominant variety, human rights are supposed to constitute a separate arena of struggle, mainly because engaging human rights issues to the Information Society would hamper the market potential of the latter, thereby harming economic interests of the developed states and the quantum of profit of the non-governmental entities. Thus, in an unwritten rule, the Information Society falls in the domain of the 'rational'–'technological' while human rights are to be attached to the domain of the 'irrational'–'political'. The domains are to remain compartmentalized and the associated strategies are to run along the parallel lines.

To refer briefly to the recent history, the mechanistic construction of the Information Society has its intellectual roots in the work of scholars like Fritz Machlup (1962), Daniel Bell (1973) and Marc Porat (1977), who have played a pioneering role in familiarizing us with the conceptual categories of 'knowledge production', 'information economy', 'post–industrial society' and 'information society'. A detailed review of their formulations is beyond the purview of this essay but it can be mentioned that for all of them the vigorous indication of the 'dawn of a new era' was marked by a change in the American economy in which in 1956 the number of "information workers" reached an unforeseen and hitherto unimaginable scale. A close reading of Daniel Bell's classic *The Coming of Post–industrial Society: A Venture in Social Forecasting* (1973) would reveal that while putting information at the centre-stage of framework he was lending it an overwhelmingly technocratic character. Thus, in his schema, the culture of information holds the key to the transition to the post–industrial society, characterized by a three-fold process: i) Change from goods-producing to service society, based on the programming and processing of information; ii) Centrality of theoretical knowledge, resting on the fusion of science and technology—with high degree of predictability and elimination of trial-and-error empiricism; and iii) Intellectual technology, with technology as the instrumental mode of rational action giving rise to techno-social reality. However, Bell would somewhat balance the technocratic framework by referring to certain 'structural' constraints and problems regarding reorganization of institutions, and 'cultural' problems like the rise of adversary culture like student revolt. In a later piece Bell (1989) would go a step further in expressing apprehension about the centralization of power. But this was as far as Bell could go. In a significant development during the same period, Alain Touraine, the sociologist, would write a book with a tantalizingly close title *The Post Industrial Society* (1974), in which he would drop enough clues for the theorists and activists of human rights. In the book Touraine would rigorously explain why class struggle is not a thing of the past and why various social frictions would emerge in such society because of the new modes of power alignments.

The foregoing discussion brings us to a more fundamental question which has important bearing on human rights: what kind of economic arrangement lies behind the dominant construction of the Information Society? One does not necessarily have to be a Marxist to recognize the key role of Information Capitalism and its power-play in this regard. To elaborate, the organizational-constitutive logic of Information Capitalism has lot to do with contradictions, which, as Govindan Parayil (2005) rightly argues, always remains expunged from the dominant-mainstream discourse of the Information Society. Parayil points out that the network produced out of the marriage of the ICTs with globalization of trade, investment, business regulation, production, and consumption gives rise to two sets of contradictions: i) contrary to expectations that rising per capita income will tend to reduce wealth and wage disparities, the distribution of income and wealth both between countries and between individuals has sharply skewed in the information age; ii) knowledge production is a self-reinforcing cycle that tends to disproportionately reward some and exclude others. He adds that the so-called Digital Divide is as much a symptom as a cause of these broader techno-economic phenomena, and regarding it as a simple issue of connectivity is both simplistic and reductive. We would on our own add that in this scheme of things, characterized by the hype over connectivity, the articulation of debates and deliberations over human rights are regarded as 'noise'.

In an essay with lot of radical flavor, which conceptualizes the Information Society from a post–colonial subject position, Bhuiyan (2008) also puts information capitalism at the center-stage to analyze how the "south"—constructed as a combine of geographical space, metaphor and worldview—is "now up for grabs..."(Bhuiyan 2008: 100). But Bhuiyan at the same time focuses on a specific space and timeline, his point of departure being the colonial era, to explain the *modus operandi* of the "new imperial project" in the third world societies. His important point, at least in the context of our essay, is that the third world is both complicit and resistant to the Information Society project. As he argues: "There is both resistance to and complicity with the new imperialist ideology, the (I)nformation (S)ociety. The beneficiaries and comprador class that have been created over the years through imperial economic and cultural interventions welcome the (I)nformation (S)ociety in its existing form. The sufferers of imperial interventions resist anything that comes with the imprimatur of imperialism."(Ibid: 112). Bhuiyan qualifies the extent of resistance by adding that the incidents of resistance "are sporadic, sometimes unorganized and undocumented. They don't sustain themselves for long and cannot cross borders..." (Ibid: 112). However, what he seems to have missed out is that the forces offering resistance might be long on critiquing and targeting the capitalist policies but are short on exploring ways and means of critiquing the Information Society born out of such policies.

Human Rights: Communicative Foundation

Human rights, broadly put, are rights which all persons hold by virtue of the human condition. But how can human condition, which is in turn enmeshed with the notion of human dignity, be realized unless, as we continue to reiterate, the culture of information—its democratization for effective communication—is accorded importance in governance? If the citizens of the third world are subject to lack of information or to a more subtle venture of subversive and manipulative information, or to an even more sophisticated act of 'information overload', the 'human condition' that is entangled with the notion of human rights fails to take shape. Let us elaborate the hitherto unexplained equation of the democratization of the culture of information and its relationship with communication.

Communication to us is an out and out social process of formation, generation and exchange of meanings. The democratization of the culture of information is supposed to have information as "basic ingredient" but it goes far beyond in harnessing the mediating potential of information to transform them into the components of communication.

In ascertaining the linkage of information in the arena of human rights Charles Beitz (2009) has the following point based on contrasting vantage points:

> Human rights doctrine does not present a set of standards that can always be expected to be satisfied simultaneously and it does not include priority rules for settling conflicts when they arise. It has no clear principles and no process for assigning specific obligations to specific external agents when human rights are violated. If one were to think of claims of right as conveying information, then

one might say that, ordinarily, a valid claim of right is information rich. It conveys information about the nature and importance of the benefit that would be provided or the harm avoided by compliance with the right's requirements, the identity of the agents whose conduct is regulated by the right, the conduct required of them, and the kinds and range of circumstances in which it could be permissible not to comply. In contrast, within the practice of human rights, a valid claim of right is less information rich. It conveys information about the nature and importance of the benefit or harm, the likelihood that eligible agents will have reasons to act, and the aims at which their action should be directed, but in the general case it tells us less about the identity of the agents whose conduct is regulated and the circumstances in which it would be permissible not to comply ((Beitz 2009: 119).

Elsewhere I have advocated (Sinha 2005: 138) the 'cultural' construction of an Information Society with communication as its core: "By the cultural dimension of the information society we refer to the *awareness* of the importance of information for individual and collective development, with the idea that there is more to information than mere data and mechanical transmission of messages. Information in this case is not an end in itself but a means to facilitate communication which we define as a process articulation of social relations through making, unmaking and neutralization of meanings. Communication, to go a step further, is a process of negotiation, a struggle and contestation over meanings." Here I shall submit that in a mechanistic construction of the Information Society, which disengages it from the civil society[1], human rights remain largely unrealizable. It is mainly because in the mechanistic approach, as we have already noted, there is the celebration of the technocratic order of things—now having the most evident manifestation of the ICTs and the associated notion of 'connectivity'. This trend counters and overrides (Sinha 2010b, 2010c) the 'organic' connections that the notion of democratic governance in general and the construction of the Information Society in particular require—in terms of having its roots from the soil itself—in/by utilizing the appropriate local resource, knowledge and skill.

In the absence of the cognitive awareness and practical realization of the organic approach human rights continue to be violated everyday, and more dangerously, without much recognition of the same. When the technology-induced connectivity overwhelms and overrides the human-sourced connections that are supposed to be the 'backbone' of the Information Society, the large scale but 'non-dramatic' human rights violations—such as the displacement of huge number of low-skilled labor from the mainstream economy—goes more or less unnoticed. The roots cause of this 'hidden' trend lies in the constitutive logic of the mechanistic form of Information Society itself. To further explain, with the ICT as the primary source of information circulation and the mainstream media as the near-exclusive source of information the vital role of the interpersonal interactions—the prime component of *connections*—is no longer accorded importance. As a result, the communicative foundation of the human rights as linked with the down-to-earth grassroots level struggle for their access and sustenance is grossly undermined. The 'Information Society' in the process becomes a buzzword, a convenient political slogan, but in effect a key source of disinformation and silence insofar as the question of human rights are concerned. Let us now turn our attention to the Indian context.

The Indian Scenario: Glass Half Full or Half Empty?

To what extent has India been able to ensure human rights for the people? The two contending versions, nor surprisingly, are respectively positive and negative. The first has a statist orientation and the second has an activist core. Both overwhelmingly contribute to binary interpretations. On our part, not in any way ignoring the possible gray zone, if we takes into account the last twenty-five years of the human rights scenario in the post–colonial India one can find the completion of a circle—from the Bhopal gas tragedy (1984) to the fate of the eminent Indian human rights activist Binayak Sen. While the two incidents have many points of difference—not just in temporal locations but also in terms of the collective annihilation unleashed in the first case and the repression of a non-conformist individual in the latter—by way of a careful scrutiny one finds some common threads in both cases insofar as the gross violation of human rights and the associated culture of non-information and/or distorted information are concerned. A further clarification: our purpose here is not to provide a detailed discussion of the cases nor are we embarking on providing a chronicle of human rights cases in the post–colonial India. Here the endeavor is limited to taking up a 'representative sample' in order to analyze them—as 'symptoms' of a broader design at work—within the purview of the specific conceptual framework developed in the preceding sections.

Without doubt, human rights scenario in India is both complex and sensitive. The tussle between 'national interest" and 'rights violations' has its dramatic manifestations in Punjab, the North East, the Kashmir valley and the Maoist-dominated areas but there are less dramatic instances as well. As pointed out by Mukul Sharma (2010) in *Human Rights in a Globalized World: An Indian Diary*, the list of the 'target-groups' of the violation of human rights is fairly long: women, children, elderly, differently-abled, lesbian-gay, tribals (indigenous people), labor, farmers, minorities of various categories and so forth. Even if India was one of the early signatories of the Universal Declaration of Human Rights (1948), which came into force in less than a year after her independence, the track-record of the world's largest democracy in the arena of human rights is marked by many instances of violations.

The categories of the violation of human rights are many: first, there are the long and regular use conventional methods like killing and /or maiming by fire and physical torture of multiple kinds, Second, there are also the non-conventional methods, such as, the 'fake encounter' and the 'forced disappearance', used by the powers that be to stifle resistance, dissent and protest. Third, there are the 'fuzzy zones' created by extra-ordinary acts like The Terrorist and Disruptive Activities (Prevention) Act (TADA) and The Armed Forces Special Powers Act (AFSPA), which have a strategically blurred distinction between 'national security' and 'state repression', and no less important, between the 'right' and the 'wrong' application. Fourth, human rights violations also take place because of the failure of the state to ensure protection to its citizens—not only in terms of denial of food, clothing, shelter, health and education to a significant segment of the population—but also by ways of trafficking in women and children, dowry deaths, domestic violence and so forth. The last mentioned category may be less direct in terms of the role of the state, less visible, and henceforth, comparatively less newsworthy, but it is no less significant.

The oft-repeated arguments of the defenders of the violation of human rights, which are based on the comparison of the Indian scenario with that of her "worse performing" neighbors vis-à-vis the human rights does not hold much ground because India is supposed to have a more firmly rooted democratic system than any of her neighbors. The Constitution of India has a fairly large section on the Fundamental Rights, backed up by their justifiable base, which by itself is a testimony to the fact that its framers were committed to the establishment of a democratic political order after having come out of a protracted and repressive colonial rule. By the same logic any instance of violation of human rights in India, irrespective of the performance of her neighbors or any other country having authoritarian, autocratic and dictatorial regimes, should be of utmost concern to its citizens. At the other end of the scale, India has indeed been blessed with a strong foundation of numerous people's organizations, including a number of proactive organizations fighting for civil rights/civil liberties, and many social and civil rights movements.

However, a major weakness of human rights activists in India is that in most cases they prefer to operate on the 'case to case' basis—without having invested much effort to create avenues for dissemination of the culture of information appropriate to the growth of the communicative foundation of the Information Society. Here one can point out that India, despite being a treasure trove of various struggles—some well-publicized and some not so well-known—against human rights violations, very little attempt, if at all any, can be found in promoting information literacy. Thus, there is a 'negative edge' in the struggle for human rights in India, which is reinforced regularly by highlighting individual instances of the violation of rights. Such method is not unimportant but unless it is supplemented by a vigorous act of awareness generation of human rights such violations would continue to occur. The implications of the lack of balance in this regard are grave also because the struggle for sustenance of human rights in the face of their gross violations would be the proverbial 'flash in the pan', minimizing the dynamism and significance of the 'counter-point', if the 'prevention is better than cure' approach in undermined.

The need to encounter the acts of violation of human rights in India with a positively oriented awareness generation endeavor is needed particularly to address the subtle acts of violation. Thus, for instance, while the magnitude of the destruction caused by the Bhopal Gas Disaster was too immediate, too evident and too transparent to escape public attention the fact that the multinational Dow Chemicals, which has replaced Union Carbide as the owner of the plant, refuses to part with the toxicological data about the gas leak and denies any responsibility of medical relief to the survivors, is itself a glowing instance of the simultaneous denial and violation of human rights beyond the limelight and glare that are the immediate effects of such tragedies of mammoth proportions. The silent suffering of the survivors of the disaster goes largely unnoticed not only in the precincts of governance but also among the fellow citizens. As such, the public memory is short. The mainstream media in India facilitates such process of amnesia by gradually losing interest in an event that has gradually lost its 'follow up' value. Consequently, the victims and survivors of the disaster became a classic tragic case of 'out of sight, out of mind' syndrome. Had there been an ambience in which information creation and dissemination had a more people-centric and inter-personal orientation the lonely struggle of few human rights groups to demand medical relief and toxicological data would not have remained largely 'invisible'.

In Binayak Sen's case the travesty of justice is a combined manifestation of the lack of credible information and the dominance of distorted information. The lack of credible information has resulted from the inability to know exactly what kind of nexus in the corridors of power had worked against Sen by which, in the courtroom, an academic organization like the Indian Social Institute was made synonymous to the Inter Service Intelligence of Pakistan, when the two have nothing in common except the abbreviations. The common abbreviation came in handy to indict Sen on the ground of encouraging anti-state activities. Various instances of distorted information were circulated to brand Sen, an eminent doctor who gave up a lucrative career to serve the poor in the tribal areas, as a vicious 'anti-national'. Admittedly, Sen's case has received wide publicity and extensive consternation in India and beyond her borders by virtue of the fact that he is an eminent figure. This has also led to his release and the induction in an advisory body of the Planning Commission, a belated but wise decision. In most other cases the violation of human rights of the lesser and least known individuals (such as the bonded labor or the 'missing women') remains unheard of. Yet, eminence is not a sure guarantee of survival. Thus, when well-known activist Sankar Guha Niyogi or theatre-worker-cum-activist Safdar Hashmi were killed by the local mafia and the organized mob, in collusion with the powers that be in premeditated acts, justice was denied to them notwithstanding the fact that the Right to Life is the cornerstone of the Indian democracy. The Indian state in its post–colonial incarnation, like its counterparts in different parts of the third world, has repeatedly shown that it is highly sensitive about any critical scrutiny of its actions, particularly in the domain of human rights. Uma Chakravarti (2009: 49) aptly attributes this to the legacy of the political and cultural experiences of colonialism and the 'burdens' of nationalism, which she argues, restrict thinking within "a set of givens" and lead to the refusal on the part of the state to "engage with interrogations".

Complexities Abound

Yet there are more complexities in Indian human rights scenario than depicted above. In this context Upendra Baxi (1998) incisively analyses the "dilemmas" associated with the scenario in terms of three categories. First, he refers to the empowerment/disempowerment dialectic. As Baxi clarifies, in order to combat regressive forces one needs to enhance the powers of an interventionist state but to empower the state by activist praxis, even in pursuit of rights, is deeply disturbing. As he dramatically puts it: "surely it cannot be the project of human rights activism to empower a Leviathan!"(Ibid 1998: 349). He further clarifiers that traditionally the mission of human rights activism is to disempower the state but such an approach is unproductive of struggle against the dispersed power of people's law formations, some of which strike at the roots of rights. Second, the dilemma relates to the question: what shall we do with the "sonorous enunciation" of constitutional values? In this context Baxi not only brings in the question of the lineage of the 'language' of human rights but also the erosion of rights 'fundamentalism' to combat other kinds of—majority or minority—'fundamentalisms'. Third, as Baxi goes on to note, there is a dilemma concerning the amelioration of state institutions. He takes on the human rights communities in India for having surrendered the opportunities they have had to reform state institutions by failing to organize campaigns on several key issues like India's derogation from the civil and political rights convention for compensation to victims of torture, cruel or unusual treatment or punishment.

Baxi, significantly for our purpose here, also observes that despite repeated solicitation of attention of human rights communities no supportive public opinion/pressure group campaigns had been launched. He notes that the human rights communities in India lack similar campaigns for worker and community safety against predatory multinationals in post–Bhopal India. In his search for explanations Baxi raises certain critical hypothetical questions: is the troubled bourgeoisie in India, including the human rights communities yet insufficiently historically troubled? Or, is it due to the insufficiently formed bourgeoisie? Or, is it a situation of libidinal fascination with the pathology of power, which is seen as a germinating force for the very existence of human rights communities? Or, finally, is it shaped by a formative anxiety in nascent human rights consciousness/organization that reformation of state may pose a setback to their growth and development? In terms of the earmarked categories Baxi raises some crucial points in which he is at his provocative best. He is candid about the fact that he does not have answers to these questions but he has his apprehension—based on his experience of the "agitated reaction" of the human rights communities and the "attempt to censor" such questions—that they may begin to bear "family resemblance" to the state. It is obvious that such intricate issues do not and cannot ensure readymade answers, However, they do provide a vital guideline to the understanding of the complexities and sensitivities of the human rights scenario in India, with much implications for our central concern—the construction of the Information Society. The residual question, we propose, is: how far are the human rights communities in India prepared for a democratic and organically constituted Information Society?

The human rights activists in India can find some crucial cues from the following points (DO Channel, n.d.), originally earmarked for consideration of the WSIS by its critics, if they care to transform the technocratic construction of the Information Society into an organic one. The "right questions" are:
- Who generate(s) and own(s) information and knowledge? Is it utilized for the private benefit of a few or the public benefit of many?

- How is knowledge disseminated and distributed? Who are the gatekeepers?
- What constrains and facilitates the use of knowledge by people to achieve their goals?
- Who is/are positioned best, and who worst, to take advantage of this knowledge?

The Coming of the Market

The questions posed above are all the more important at this moment when India is undergoing a huge and complex paradigmatic shift, which began since the early 1990s. It is during this period that India opted for a paradigmatic deviation from the state-led development path to embrace market economy. Any assessment of the human rights scenario in India has to be made keeping this transition in background. In our view the most fundamental impact of such transition is to be traced to the fact that the arrow-head the human rights movement and activism was hitherto pointed overwhelmingly towards the state. The state was a familiar target and its failure to live upto its human rights commitments, constitutional and otherwise, is still treated with the opposition and protest it deserves. But because the market does not have any such 'direct' responsibility of ensuring human rights the protest against the violation of human rights in the market era has to have a different kind of strategy. In such strategy the state would very much remain a 'subject' of surveillance but not as totalistically as was done before. On the process of transition itself, Usha Ramanathan (n.d.) graphically depicts the changing scenario in terms of three developments: i) the state policy of liberalization; ii) the internationalizing of human rights and iii) the prioritizing of rights that has occurred particularly, though not exclusively, through judicial agency.

In the first case, as she argues, Liberalization, the concerted moves towards opening up the Indian market and the valorization of the market economy, and the consequent initiatives to attract foreign direct investment have resulted in a re-prioritization of a range of rights, including in the spheres of project displacement, workers' rights and the casualization of work, exclusion of local populations from forests and from livelihood access. In it she finds that the restructured role of the state as a contracting party with multinational corporations and with international financial institutions has altered the nature of the dialogue between it and those affected. On the second front, Ramanathan finds that the internationalizing of human rights has had a range of effects. International pressure, both from governments and from organizations such as the Amnesty International, led to the government establishing the National Human Rights Commission.[2] She has specific instances, such as the linkage between human rights and trade, and the 'social clause' which has become an integral part of the neo–liberal strategy. This, she adds, has resulted in "wariness"—both with the state, and among a number of human rights and development activists. This threat of intervention in the arena of human rights with the possibility of sanction has been one overt cause for hostility to international instruments which deal with human rights standards and conduct. On the third front, she refers to a process of reinterpretation of rights especially in the aftermath of the Bhopal Gas

Disaster. As she notes, the disaster which resulted in mass victim-creation, statute law and court decisions have restructured the rights of victims into one of compensation. It is not only the right to see offenders brought to trial and conviction, and the need for prioritizing of safety which has been accorded a low order of importance; even medical assistance and treatment of the victim has been relatively marginalized (this relates to our reference to the refusal of the Dow Chemicals to provide toxicological information). Ramanathan relates it to the priority of attracting multinational corporate capital, technology and foreign direct investment. She also refers to the "reoriented governmental position" with regard to the casualization of labor, and the narrowing of social security and protective provisions, including a proposal to remove the prohibition of night work for women in the face of competitiveness in a globalized, market economy. Compared to Baxi, Ramanathan's stance is more friendly towards the human rights activists, but she also raises a couple of disturbing questions—the "depoliticizing" effect of the language of human rights, and the most sensitive issue of funding which are important items for debates and deliberations on human rights at the global level, that too with special implications for the third world. Hafner-Burton and Ron (2009) deal with the issues, arguing from a methodological vantage point, that "human rights language is suffocating rival idioms of social and political protest and draining resources from other, possibly more effective social movements." On the funding issue they mention: "The discursive reach of human rights is vast, and it has displaced rival narratives of dissent worldwide. Even when ineffective, activists may still use rights talk for reasons of international legitimacy and funding. Although it is too early to know with any confidence whether this is the case, such discursive crowding out of local alternatives may eventually undermine local capacities to resist oppression in more appropriate ways."(p. 393). Ramanathan on her part is also concerned about the perceptional differences that exist among different interest groups in the human rights domain and their impact on the subject groups. Thus, she identifies a number of "systemic concerns" beyond participation and consultation: the process of acquiring an understanding of what constitutes the public interest; who speaks on whose behalf, or the appropriation, or partial taking over, of the voices of those affected; the reporting-back processes, where rights groups hold themselves answerable to the community whose rights they are negotiating.

The Indian human rights scenario is at a critical juncture; so are the Indian state and the human rights communities. For long the struggle for human rights in India has been made vis-à-vis the state and this was the obvious outcome of the fact that in independent India the state—like many other states of the third world, which came out of the long and repressive colonial bondage—became the prime custodian and harbinger of rights. For a fairly long period, despite the regime changes at the Centre, the Indian state had a gloss and the struggle for human rights—both based on the demand for protection of rights and on the protest against transgression of rights—were revolving around the state. This had resulted in an 'inflated ego' of the Indian state. However, with the passage of time the legitimacy and effectiveness of the Indian state began to experience 'depreciation' notwithstanding the fact that it would ritually reiterate its sacred duty of ensuring human rights to the citizens of the world's largest democracy. In many instances, and in the most crude and dramatic instance of the Emergency,[3] which was imposed in the mid 1970s with the resultant suspension of the Fundamental Rights, the state began to lose its credibility. This in turn gave scope to the human rights communities in India to go beyond the strategy of seeking 'favorable response' from the state and questioning its rationale. Theoretically, such a strategic turn was facilitated by the neo–liberal thrust of the minimal state and maximization of the market power.

The human rights scenario in India, however, became exceedingly complex with the coming of the market and the latter upstaging the state in various spheres. It was no longer a relatively simple question of the Indian state versus the human rights activism. The market, as elsewhere in the third world, having witnessed a steep ascendance, became a major actor in determining the contours of life for the Indians. In the process the construction of the Information Society in such times has to overwhelmingly follow the economic "conditionalities", with the market unleashing the process of commodification of information in order to determine what is 'appropriate' and 'relevant' information and what is to be left out as 'illegitimate'. A major point of distinction between the (Indian) state and the market in this regard is that in the case of the former, if not for anything else but because of the fact that it needs a periodic approval of the people in the form of election of representatives, it has to at least indulge in the show of justification for its actions, including the instances of failure to protect human rights. Thus, even the dreadful Emergency and its suspension of human rights during the period were sought to be justified by the rulers, howsoever absurd the justifications were. But in the case of the market even this compulsion wears thin as the cases of violation of human rights or their denigration either do not come to the fore at all or if they at all are visible the buck is swiftly passed to the state which is supposed to be in change of the business of governance—as distinct from the market which is supposedly vested with the governance of business. Therefore, in many instances of the forced eviction and displacement of the people in the name of industrialization-based development the brunt of protests and resistance is borne by the state even if it may be the case that it only does so to facilitate the entry of the market forces. This has been evident in many instances in India, including the 'paradigmatic' cases[4] of protest against land acquisition in Singur in West Bengal and Kalinganagar in Orissa, followed by similar cases in Jaitapur in Maharastra and Bhatta Parsol in Greater Noida in Uttar Pradesh. In another instance of a slightly different kind in the aftermath of the withdrawal of the now-discredited Enron the government in Maharastra, which had shown excessive readiness to welcome the foreign investor at the cost of the people, had to bear the brunt. What is even more remarkable is that very often the violations of the people's rights are conducted—with 'appropriate' information system—in the name of the people. Thus, in a complex spin, to contextualize a cue from Ranabir Samaddar (2009), the market in its information generation fuses 'human rights' (the rights of the people) with 'humanitarianism' pertaining to population—the target to be fed, clothed, sheltered, maintained and protected), notwithstanding the "the near impossibility of coordinating the two, the reality of their coexistence"(Ibid 2009: 21).

The complexities lead us to submit that the activists in India as well as in the third world have the responsibility to make people aware of the market-led transgressions or curtailment of human rights, but till now such efforts leave much to be desired. Baxi in calling for a creation of dialogical space makes yet another provocative remark: "Internal, friendly, co-suffering interrogation of the direction and contours of human rights movements in India is disvalued, perhaps for cogent reasons of protection of fragile emergent communities, beleaguered as most are by hostility of state and society" (Baxi 1998: 351). One may concur with Baxi or may differ in terms of degree with his contention but the need for self-examination of various shades of the human rights communities, even while acknowledging their arduous struggle and instances of success, especially at this critical juncture cannot be underestimated. The success of achieving the Right to Information (RTI) by way of an act in 2005, is itself a consequence of sustained commitment and hard work at the grassroots level. But at the same time, with its limited jurisdiction vis-à-vis the government-sourced information, that too with some 'reasonable restrictions', the RTI is indicative of the magnitude of the struggle that lies ahead in the broader arena of communication.

Conclusion

The preceding discussion confirms by way of the contextual evidence the point we have mentioned at the outset: that while the human rights scenario in India has its own specificities there are certain strands in the trajectory, which have some similarities with other third world countries. The common historical experience of the colonial rule, the transfer of leadership to the indigenous elite in control of both the state and the civil society, and the ongoing experience of the steep ascendance of the market-guided development path have in their own way contributed to an obsessive pursuit of technocratic and top-heavy Information Society. Yet the vibrancy and dynamism of the Indian society see to it that there is no dominance of the so-called culture of silence. A persistent observer of the Indian case is bound to notice that numerous information societies, as distinct from the singular hegemonic form, are being constructed and sustained by the everyday struggle of the people at the grassroots level. The 'little' information societies are based mostly on local knowledge, local resource and local skill and they have their own communities of interest, communities of practice, content, capital and in a number of cases, connectivity. They are also low cost and interaction-orientated. Thus, they can be found in a more institutionalized form in the Info Villages of the southern state of Puducherry, where the Swaminathan Foundation is successfully engaged in circulating necessary information mainly for the local coastal communities earning their livelihood from fishing. The information kiosks there do not just remain kiosks but they have become part and parcel of the society itself. Numerous 'little' information societies, with lesser visibility and lack of publicity, can be found also in various locales in which, without any external intervention, the felt needs of the local community has led to the formation of some kind of information networks with 'organic roots'—by privileging the inter-personal relations and not necessarily relying on the technological artifacts. They can be found, for instance, in the remote villages of North Indian states, among a section of the *Dalits*, who stand up against the repression of the upper castes by circulating prior information among themselves. They can also be found in the remotest villages of the Darjeeling Hills in which in the absence of any kind of governmental assistance the local inhabitants maintain regular information network, especially through the constitution of self-help groups, to devise and publicize the ways and means of managing disasters from landslides.

Such 'little' versions can have a differentiating range—from embryonic to emerging to mature—but the commonality that they share is that in their own little way they contribute to the depth and breadth of the of the idea of the Information Society by diffusion of power and differential patterns of needs and concerns. No less important, faced with the common challenge they as shared space of shared interests also tend to sustain the rights of the people concerned, thereby facilitating in their own little way to the formation of an enabling environment vis-à-vis the human rights.

One need not romanticize the 'little' information societies unnecessarily as they too are vulnerable to inequitable power game based on domination–dependency syndrome and to various forms of cooption by external forces apart from their having the limitation of lack of possible 'linkage' for greater synergy. But the crux of the matter is that in such non-mainstream 'next door' information societies there is possibility of the celebration of human dignity and human spirit itself accords much credence to the broader notion of human rights. Thus, there is a formative base in India to decentralize and democratize the mega-idea of the Information Society, by creating various versions of it, with both complementary and contending modes and nodes of information. That itself is supposed to close the 'gap' between human rights and the Information Society, and on a broader scale, that is to add to the beauty of the Indian democracy in the Information Era.

References

Baxi, U., 1998. The State and Human Rights Movements in India. *People's Rights: Social Movements and the State in the Third World*, edited by Manoranjan Mohanty, Partha Nath Mukherji and Olle Tornquist, 335–352. New Delhi: Sage Publications.

Beitz, C.R., 2009. *The Idea of Human Rights*, Oxford: Oxford University Press.

Bell, D., 1973. *The Coming of Post–Industrial Society*, London: Heinemann.

———. 1989. The Third Technological Revolution and its Possible Socio-Economic Consequences. *Dissent* 36, no. 2: 164–176.

Bhuiyan, A.J.M. S.A., 2008. Peripheral View: Conceptualizing the Information Society as a Postcolonial Subject. *The International Communication Gazette* 70, no. 2: 99–116.

Chakravarti, U., 2009. Archiving Disquiet: Feminist Praxis and the Nation-State. *Human Rights and Peace: Ideas, Laws, Institutions and Movements*, edited by Ujjwal Kumar Singh, 49–73. New Delhi: Sage Publications.

Danesi, M., 2009. *Dictionary of Media and Communications*, New York: M.E. Sharpe.

DO Channel (n.d.) "Is 'Information Society' a Useful Concept for Civil Society?" http://www.digitalopportunity.org/article/view/57775 (accessed January 3, 2007).

Hafner-Burton, E.M. and J. Ron, 2009. Seeing Double: Human Rights Impact through Qualitative and Quantitative Eyes. *World Politics* 61, no. 2 (January): 360–401.

Hamelink, C.J., 2003. Human Rights for the Information Society. *Communicating in the Information Society,* edited by B. Girard and S.O. Siochen, 122–163. Geneva: UNRISD.

Machlup, F., 1962. *The Production and Distribution of Knowledge in United States.* Princeton, NJ: Princeton University Press.

Okinawa Charter, 2000. http://www.unpan1.un.org/intradoc/groups/public/documents/apcity/unpan002263.pdf (accessed June 6, 2011).

Parayil, G., 2005. The Digital Divide and Increasing Returns: Contradictions of Informational Capitalism. *The Information Society* 21, no. 1: 41–51.

Porat, M., 1977. *The Information Economy: Definition and Measurement.* OT Special Publication 77–12 (1). Washington, DC: US Department of Commerce, Office of Telecommunications.

Pyati, A.K., 2005. WSIS: Whose Vision of an Information Society? First Monday, Special Issue #8. http://www.firstmonday.org/issues/issue 10_5/pyati/index.html (accessed April 4, 2010).

Ramanathan, U., (n.d.). *Human Rights in India: A Mapping.* http://www.ielrc.org/content/w0103.pdf (accessed April 4, 2011).

Robertson, D., 2005. *A Dictionary of Human Rights.* London: Europa Publications.

Samaddar, R., 2009. In life, in Death. *Human Rights and Peace: Ideas, Laws, Institutions and Movements,* edited by Ujjwal Kumar Singh, 19–30. New Delhi: Sage Publications.

Sharma, M., 2010. *Human Rights in a Globalized World: An Indian Diary,* New Delhi: Sage Publications.

Sinha, D., 2005. Information Society as if Communication Mattered: The Indian State Revisited. *Media and Mediation,* edited by Bernard Bel, Jan Brower, Biswajit Das, Vibodh Parthasarathy and Guy Poitevin, 135–161. Communication Process 1. New Delhi: Sage Publications.

———. 2010a.. Development and E-Governance: Reflections on India's Democratic Experience." Paper presented in 2nd National-Level Research Workshop on Development, Democracy and Governance–Lessons and Policy Implications, Kolkata: Ford Foundation India-Calcutta Research Group, especially the section on "Transnational Root of Information Society, *New Subjects and New Governance in India,* edited by Ranabir Samaddar and Suhit K. Sen, 69–108. New Delhi/Abingdon: Routledge.

———. 2010b. "Connectivity" Over "Connections": Networking Governance and Technology Down South. *Global e.* http://www.globalejournal.org/2011/01/27/%E2%80%9Cconnectivity-over-connections-networking-governance-and-technology-down-south/ (accessed December 12, 2011).

———. 2010c. (De)Politicising Development: Towards an Inclusionary Perspective. [Electronic version]. *Working Paper* 19, London: London School of Economics, Department of Media and Communication. http://www.2.lse.ac.uk/media@lse/research/mediaWorkingPapers/pdf/EWP19.pdf (accessed January 1, 2011).

Touraine, A., 1974. *The Post Industrial Society*, New York: Wildwood Press.

World Summit on the Information Society, 2003. *Declaration I. Building the Information Society: A Global Challenge in the New Millennium*, Declaration of Principles. Document No. WSIS-03/GENEVA/DOC/4-E, 12. Geneva: World Summit on the Information Society (December). http://www.itu.int/wsis/docs/geneva/official/dop.html (accessed June 6, 2005).

WSIS Civil Society Plenary, 2003. *Declaration II. Shaping Information Society for Human Needs*. Geneva: WSIS Civil Society Plenary (December).

Notes

1. Here we are using the term broadly, without intending to undermine its problematic and controversial nature.

2. Even while the Government of India denies that the Commission was set up (in 1993) because of constant international pressure and to appease the western powers the human rights activists have another 'card' up against their sleeve: that the Government has set up the Commission to avoid constant international monitoring and surveillance and to argue that adequate arrangements have been made at the national level.

3. The Emergency Peiod in India lasted for 21 months from 26 June 1975 to 21 March 1977. Then Prime Minister of India Indira Gandhi requested then President Fakhruddin Ali Ahmed to declare a state of emergency under the provision of Article 352 of the Constitution of India. As a result all civil liberties as well as the elections were suspended and the nation was ruled by decree.

4. In both cases the acquisition of land for the purpose of setting up industries stirred up strong resistance and protests in the middle of the first decade of the twenty-first century, which in a major way pitched on the twin issues of human rights protection and violation—not only pertaining to the right to livelihood and freedom of expression, but also, in the aftermath of police action and loss of lives, regarding the right to life.

CHAPTER 18
Biotechnology and Human Rights
Subhasis Mukhopadhyay

Historically, whenever a new discovery or an invention had taken place in the field of science and technology, a revisit of the human rights issues had usually been undertaken by the human rights activists. The discovery of nuclear energy, antibiotics and a whole host of modern-day household names stand as witnesses to such a proposition.

Modern-day biotechnology had not suddenly put forward uncomfortable human rights issues before the human society. Even before the subject has taken a concrete shape and had emerged as an independent scientific discipline, the entire arena of life science was riddled with human rights issues arising out of moral and ethical precept.

Historical cases of unethical research showed that it was not only Nazi German state which has undertaken unethical route to scientific research, but other European countries were no exception. When the idea of "national Socialism" of Adolf Hitler was taking its root in the German society and its body-politic at large, most of the European nations had also witnessed a resurgence of racism, eugenics and all other ideas that fostered discrimination. In the United States of America, racist groups among the professionals had embraced these ideas. Some of the very reputed university departments had seriously undertaken research projects to establish the "scientific basis" of many of the Nazi ideals.

Historical Case: Abuse in the US

Long before the life science became a subject impacting the society and molecular biology and biotechnology was in the realm of science fiction, in 1932, the Tuskegee Syphilis Study shook the world with a big bang. This was a 40-year long project spearheaded by the US Public Health Service in Macon County, Alabama. The American Government promised 400 men free treatment for "bad blood" which had become an epidemic in the county. Very unfortunately the desired and required treatment was in fact never given to these subjects and the treatment was actually withheld.

As usual, the subjects were sampled from a group of poor African-American persons who were merely told by the authority that they had "bad blood". The subjects in the study were not even informed of the research design and the attendant risks involved in such an experiment. The design of the study was such that these subjects had been denied the standard treatment for syphilis even when penicillin was available later during the study.

The Tuskegee Study is a classic case of the medical misconduct and blatant disregard for human rights issues that took place in the name of Medical Science for pushing the frontier of human knowledge. One has to remember that the investigators of this study were no mad megalomaniacs from the pages of horror science fiction, but they were reputed scientists. They were serving the government in the capacity of professional physicians, publishing their research reports of the study in peer-reviewed medical journals.

The physicians who designed the study as a government program did not obtain informed consent from the subjects. The unethical nature of this study was revealed rather late, only in 1972. By the intervening period, over one hundred of the infected men died and others suffered from serious syphilis related conditions. When a class action civil suit was filed against those who were involved in the study, the government exercised their influence and the case never came to trial. A paltry sum was offered to the surviving subjects and even a lesser sum of money was disbursed to the next of kin of the person who died because of this unethical medical study.

When molecular biology was about to be established as an independent scientific discipline and biotechnology as an independent discipline was about to emerge, the Willowbrook Study once again generated a hue and cry as a case for human rights violation (Rothman *et al.* 1984). During the period, 1963 to 1966, Willowbrook Study chose as a subject a group of children living in Willowbrook who were diagnosed with mental retardation. They were admitted in Willowbrook State Hospital in Staten Island, New York. The study involved in this case deliberately infecting the mentally retarded children with the hepatitis virus. When the study began, it was not possible to obtain purified form of the infecting agent, the hepatitis virus; hence the subjects at the beginning of the experiment were fed extracts of stools from infected individuals and subsequently, when a more purified version of virus preparation was available, the subjects had received injections of these purified virus preparations. Investigators defended the injections by pointing out that the vast majority of children (the subjects) acquired the infection anyway while at Willowbrook, and it would be better for them to be infected under carefully controlled research conditions.

And what exactly was the purpose of such a study? The purpose was to study the history of the disease, the hepatitis, particularly when it was left untreated for a period and later to assess the effects of gamma globulin as a therapeutic intervention. Gamma Globulins are proteins in human blood plasma, which are known to include most antibodies that are responsible for human immunity. The antibody substances are produced as a protective reaction of the body's immune system to the invasion of disease producing organisms. When a patient is injected with an appropriate antibody, it builds up a rapid but temporary immunity in patients who have been exposed to disease.

This study could not qualify to be a pure scientific pursuit of knowledge and it had used falsehood and deceit while gaining the confidence of the subjects. The deliberate infection to the innocent children is a case in point. The other most serious allegation was that the physicians deliberately created an artificial crisis in the in-patient admission by showing a lack of beds and then luring the guardians of the subject-children to convince them to enroll them in the study in exchange for admission to the hospital.

One of the famous cases is an experiment in the area of psychology was undertaken at none other than Yale University. When we would discuss the Asilomar Conferences, we would have to mention the name of Yale University once again. Stanley Milgram (Milgram 1963) psychologist at Yale University, designed an experimental study to establish a relation between the conflict between obedience toward authority and one's personal consciousness. He wanted to explore the justification for acts of genocide offered by those accused at the World War II, revealed in the Nuremberg War Criminal trials. Most of the accused in that Trial had offered their defense against the crimes committed by them was based on "obedience"— that is, they were just following their supervisor's orders.

The design of the experiment was of a questionable character. This experiment was to demonstrate as to how people reacted toward an authority figure while giving an apparent electrical shock. The experiment involved "teachers", who were unknown subjects of the experiment and were recruited by the scientist, Milgram (Milgram 1963). These "teachers" were required to administer an electrical shock of progressively increased intensity to a "learner" (another subject) for each mistake the "learner" subject would commit during the course of the experiment. The researcher, Stanley Milgram, cooked up a story that for a serious research purpose, he was exploring effects of punishment (for incorrect responses) on learning behavior. The "teachers" accepted the story in good faith for the sake of "science" as they were not aware that the "learner" in the study was a fake subject, actually, an actor merely mimicking the effect of discomfort as the "teacher" went on increasing the intensity of the electric shocks. For the initial response to the incorrect answer, the shock was of intensity of 15 volts and for each successive incorrect response, the intensity of electrical shock was increased by a quantum of 15 volts till it reached the maximum cut off value of 450 volts.

During the course of the experiment, the "teachers" often questioned the rationale of the design of the experiment but they continued to take part in the experiment despite being not quite at home with the state of affairs. Ethically, the study, whose design is flawed, went beyond the ambit of science. The researchers did not have the right to cheat their subjects who accepted the assignment on good faith. Also, the researcher did not have the authority and right to expose the "learner" subjects to such a high intensity electrical shock which was known to be lethal for human being. The "search for knowledge" can never preponderate over the "human cost" the "learners" were supposedly subjected to.

The atrocities inflicted on the human subjects by the German physicians under Hitler were well documented. In the Nuremburg Trial, a total of sixteen German physicians practiced unethical medical experiments on Jews, gypsies, and political prisoners.

Genetic Testing and Human Rights

Biotechnology has now become an established discipline, and the new issues emerged around the discipline merit a thorough discussion. Biotechnology enabled individuals or corporate entities to devise and actively use so called "genetic testing procedures" for which only minute amount of bodily samples are necessary and sufficient. The PCR (polymerase chain reaction) technique of genetic testing enables, in principle and in practice as well, the DNA from a single cell to be amplified to such a quantity that genetic material suitable for "genetic testing" can be performed with sufficient degree of accuracy and with a very high degree of confidence level. The automated 'DNA chip' technology has already made feasible the possibility in obtaining sufficient "private" information about numerous genetic mutations of an individual simultaneously in a single test procedure.

We may now enumerate as to why these modern developments of diagnostic techniques constitute a threat to human rights of an individual. As far as human genetic samples are concerned, they are abundantly available nearly everywhere. Human being as individual routinely leaves traces of body samples which could be used without the expressed consent of the same individual for genetic testing, resulting in a serious breach of right to privacy of one's body. Shed hairs left in a comb in a public place, traces of saliva left on a glass in a pub or cigarette in an ash-tray, cheek cells left on a toothbrush, human cells carefully harvested from an item of clothing, etc., are just few examples. We may think about a variety of such situations where one's private bodily related information can be retrieved using modern-day biotechnology for non-medical and malicious purpose which can later be used against the same individual. The techniques of molecular biology and biotechnology have given a group of individuals or any corporate entity the necessary leverage for "exploiting" one's exclusive private information as a tradable entity. This non-consensual genetic testing is a major threat to human rights which we will try to argue shortly.

The question of non-consensual genetic testing is in itself a very controversial and complex issue and involves many aspects where a possible violation of individuals' human rights can happen. No matter whether one views this non-consensual genetic testing from a "sample collectors' point of view", or "sample examiners' view point" or even from a third party who as a derivative, collates and presents this information, in every such class of activities the end result might be detrimental to the individual whose genetic sample is used for any of these purposes.

Denial of insurance coverage to individuals on the basis "genetic information" is rampant and this act in itself is a violation of a plethora of human rights normally enjoyed by every member in any sane society. The corporate entities engaged in private and public insurance providing argue very strongly that it is illogical to distinguish between genetic and other health-related information in current market scenario. In this personal insurance market, voluntary, trusted and mutually rated medical information of the insured person, if some personal prohibition toward the use of genetic information is imposed, then this prohibition would threaten the viability of that market. The market force-driven paradigm often underrates the human rights issues involved. For example, if there is no prohibition in using the non-consensual genetic information of an insured person, then these pieces of information can be utilized by corporate entities in an unlimited manner and for any uncertain period of time. If this practice is allowed to be continued then this practice would certainly create (in some countries they already have created) a 'genetic underclass' who would be denied access to insurance and other related benefits. From the public health view point (preventive, rather than curative), this denial of insurance cover would impart a negative impact as less and less facilities and resources would be allocated by the state in these sector. This denial has an added dimension. Sometimes, a genetic testing may help a person to avoid unnecessary risks. But the fear of insurance denial may discourage the person to undergo such a genetic test. One may, for example, cite a case where a test for factor 5 Leiden would have enabled a person to gain knowledge if the person is at an increased risk of developing a deep vein thrombosis while availing of a long distance non-stop flight. However, the fear of not being allowed to fly or not obtaining insurance may prevent the person from opting for the test.

The right to work has been recognized by all civilized societies as a fundamental human right. A person's ability to work empowers the person to live a quality of life, full of human dignity and becomes a contributing factor towards the person's status within the community. This community involvement, in turn, has a broader implication as the person earning a modest wage would contribute to the tax system of the country and reduce the expenses towards subsidy. When a person is excluded from employment solely on the basis of non-consensual genetic information for deciding the genetic status should be a human rights issue to be addressed seriously. Genetic screening—a subset of health screening—involves examining the genetic status of an employee or a potential job-seeker for certain inherited traits, disorders or susceptibilities for the purpose of excluding high-risk persons from the workplace. In some very special circumstances, this genetic information might be used for providing the person an alternative work that may present fewer risks.

This concern about genetic discrimination is not a hypothetical or an academic one as genetic information is becoming a form of health information largely indistinguishable from other so called "conventional" health information. Due to rapid development of the discipline Clinical Genetics, apparently unrelated health information might have a direct bearing towards one's genetic makeup. This is more so as the cost of genetic as well as other non-invasive testing is coming down very fast, the accuracy and reliability of available tests are increasing; there is every reason to believe that they would be used increasingly throughout the globe for scuttling employment.

Insurance companies, as part of their business strategy, routinely collect family medical history information and use it in deciding the degree of coverage of a potential applicant. Such collection of family information and its subsequent use is based on the accepted medical knowledge that certain diseases have a hereditary component; thus information about the medical history of family members is relevant in assessing the applicant's risk. Thus, not only an individual as an applicant for insurance coverage loses her/his private information, the applicant would be required to compromise the health information of her/his family members as well!

The collection and use of family medical history is riddled with ethical issues. The procedure raises two very important questions related to the right to individual privacy. One important question is whether it is permissible to use personal information that the insurer has already collected about an insured person in assessing the insurance application of a genetic relative of the insured person. This conduct would be in breach of the rights of an individual

The second issue is concerned about whether it is permissible for insurers, in assessing an insurance application from one person, to collect personal information from the same person about that person's genetic relatives, *without the knowledge or consent of those relatives*. This widespread practice is certainly a gross violation of the notion of human rights. From the viewpoint of better patient care, a medical practitioner is entitled to record and store the medical history from patients at regular interval. As a part of the patient care and management, the regime might include the collection of personal information about genetic relatives of the patient. This absolutely ethical and scientific protocol might give rise to a problematic situation, when in the course of a diagnosis, treatment or patient care of an individual, an organization would have to be entrusted for the collection a medical history from an individual which also reveals health information about a genetic relative. Corporate and private organizations very often do not respect the right to privacy convention.

Thus discrimination on the basis of genetic make-up is rampant, no matter whether the employer is a corporate entity or a public funded institute. In this context, two classic cases may be mentioned here.

Case Study –1

In 2002, two employer companies in the US, Burlington Northern and Santa Fe Railway Company decided to go in for a genetic test for 36 employees *without* their prior consent for undergoing such a test. Their case was later taken up by the United States Equal Employment Opportunity Commission (EEOC) (EEOC, 2002). The Commission opined that this act on the part of the employers violated the national legal instrument, the *Americans with Disabilities Act 1990* (US), which is a right-based legal instrument. The genetic test in the instant case formed a part of an extensive and comprehensive diagnostic medical examination that the company required of certain employees who had filed claims or internal reports for an occupational disease, namely, the carpal tunnel syndrome injuries. The Commission mediated on behalf of the employees and the employees were awarded a compensatory sum of US$2.2 million.

Case Study-2

The Lawrence Berkeley Laboratory in the US is a government-funded research institution. The authority of the institution, at some point of time actually tested clerical and administrative employees for syphilis, pregnancy and the sickle cell trait. This was a part of routine mandatory medical examinations. Some of the employees who had to undergo such a battery of tests contested this action on the part of the employer and alleged that

a) the genetic testing was conducted without the employees' knowledge or consent and
b) testing was irrelevant to the job description of the employees.

These allegations were sustained (Miller 2000).

Case Study-3

The family members of one lady, Victoria Grove, suffered from a genetic disease, Emphysema (a disease known which has alpha-1 antitrypsin deficiency). She was worried that she might also suffer from the same genetic disorder, the treatment of which is very costly, to the tune of $100,000 per annum perhaps. Obviously she needed health insurance, secured a good job should she be detected with emphysemia. She was worried that if the result of her genetic test is known to either a prospective employer or an insurance company, she might not be considered to be a fit candidate for enjoying the benefits.

Breach of privacy through third party diagnosis centers were known to her. Thus, she sought out a service that sent a test kit to her home and returned the results directly to her. She decided not to divulge the result even to her personal physician, when the result turned out to be positive in her case. For her, it was known clinically that she could sustain permanent lung damage without immediate treatment for her bouts of pneumonia. Knowing that this could be threatening for her, she had decided to visit her clinic at the first sign of infection.

In one such occasion, while visiting her clinic for a treatment for a chest infection, the nurse on duty diagnosed her as suffering from an ordinary infection. Ms. Grove pleaded for a chest X-ray, but the nurse on duty did not think it was necessary. As her conditions turned from bad to worse, it was finally impossible for to keep her genetic condition a secret. When she contacted her clinic, she was advised to report to the clinic so that suitable antibiotics could be prescribed for her. But very bad weather prevented her to turn up to her clinic. She knew the generic name of the antibiotic which would save her life. But to receive this much-needed clinical help, she would have to reveal to the clinic the result of the genetic test for which she was diagnosed to be positive! She described her dilemma—"I have alpha-1," she remembers sobbing into the phone. "I need this antibiotic!" The clinic finally called in the prescription and she was saved.

> "Something needs to be done so that you cannot be discriminated against when you know about these things," she said. "Otherwise you are sicker, your life is shorter and you're not doing what you need to protect yourself" (Human Genet-

ics Commission 2003).

A New Look at Human Rights: The Biotechnological View

Biotechnology offers a new challenge towards viewing human rights from the perspective of UDHR alone. In fact modern biotechnology introduces a three tier perspective which is to be incorporated within the ambit of human rights by expanding its horizon. The three perspectives can be described as one relating to individual, one relating to nation–state and its legislature and the one that relates to a global perspective. A related issue is of freedom of the researchers in enhancing the biotech products and processes for the benefit of humankind. A third issue which has emerged out of these two issues is to deal with the global impact of biotechnology which transcends far beyond the realm of individual or even a community.

It is always argued that science furthers the scope and ambit of human freedom allowing one to take into cognizance of one's necessity, which in turn, expands the domain of right and freedom. Biotechnology is no exception either. Any new technology is riddled with ethical and moral issues that go with the development of such technology. The early attempts at blood transfusion, surgical intervention, chemical pesticides, and petrochemical technology are still plagued with problems. For such a technology as biotechnology, which primarily deals with the very life processes and live subjects, such moral and ethical issues would be normally manifested in its most intense form. The concept of human rights is basically founded on moral and ethical principle; it states what is to be done even if the prevalent social and cultural practices are at variance with what is suggested. Science in that sense shares the same pedestal as that of human rights.

For biotechnology, there is always a public perception about the so called hazards of the new technology. Biotechnology and its accompanying genetic consequences can be a fitting case for such a phobia about a new technology. It is certainly true that the modern biotechnology and genetic engineering has the potential of placing a "select group of people" at a comparative disadvantage. Nevertheless, a balance would allow us to appraise this new technology from a proper perspective.

It is imperative to bring in a human rights perspective in the entire issue by separating the scientific content from its moral and ethical perspective. The moral strength of a human rights approach lies in its complete transparency in disseminating information enabling an individual to take a considered view. The human rights approach also empowers an individual towards asserting one's own and collective or community entitlement(s) opposing the mighty powers of technology-fueled society or esoteric scientific pursuit.

One may recall the Article 15 of the International Covenant on Economic Social and Cultural Rights, which mentioned the right "to enjoy the benefits of scientific progress and its applications". In other words, this Covenant tacitly assumed the fundamental freedom of scientific research capable of generating such resultant benefits. From a human rights viewpoint, this freedom cannot be treated to be a straightjacket or an absolute freedom and must be subordinated to a broader moral and ethical principle of universally shared values of dignity, liberty, right to life of any individual. Concomitant to such moral and ethical principle, one would also like to include the right of not being discriminated against and right to complete information for giving consent to some act involving self and also right to participate in taking a community decision.

Traditional view of human rights presupposes that the state must remain silent by not interfering to the autonomy of an individual. On the other hand, for progress of science and technology, translating the benefit of the resultant knowledge from lab to land depends squarely on the pro-active role played by the state. The state should also play an active role towards surveillance against any real or purported abuse of the resultant knowledge. UDHR also bestowed upon every member state such a duty through Article 28.

The Engagement of the Scientists: Singer-Soll Letter and the Asilomar I

The birth of rDNA technology and the debates surrounding it started almost simultaneously. This debate eventually focused attention from lab protocols to "control" the release of biotech product for plants, animals and finally human beings. At the global level, concerns were also expressed as to risk of such biotech products as and when they will be released, either through controlled experiments supervised by qualified scientists or by mere users of the biotech product. Not only among the intelligent lay-persons in the society, qualified scientists and policy-makers often expressed opinions that the science of biotechnology had posed such a holistic challenge to the humankind that the society is yet to grapple with the consequences that are in store for all of us.

The history of science and technology, not only in the distant past, but also in the recent past had witnessed a debate within the scientific community about the pros and cons of new a technology which would have an immediate social consequence. When the nuclear scientists discovered the ways and means of releasing the enormous amount of energy buried deep in the heart of the atomic nuclei and its attendant military consequences, they started debating about the acceptability of such a research and to devise ways and means so that the military dimension of such a research should be contained by the scientists themselves.

In the same vein, the biologists had also become aware of the social, ethical and moral consequences of their research endeavors. Molecular biologist Paul Berg, in 1971, was attempting to investigate the cell transforming properties of the tumor-producing primate virus SV-40, in order to use it as a vector to bring new genetic material into different organisms. In those early days of biotechnology, it was a very bold suggestion. Scientists became apprehensive about Berg's ideas and they decided to discuss these involved issues in a full-blown scientific conference.

In January of 1973, such a meeting was indeed held at the Asilomar Conference Center in Pacific Grove, California. This Conference was eventually referred to as Asilomar I, entitled "Biohazards in Biological Research." The basic focus of the conference was to discuss the risks and benefits of research using tumor viruses.

Michael Oxman (Oxman, 1973) of Harvard Medical School, one of the organizers of the Asilomar I, observed:

> Whereas an investigator may himself decide to assume certain risks, he does not have the right to make that decision for anyone else. In fact, it seems to me that the decision to assume a risk can only legitimately be made by the individual who will be in jeopardy... (Oxman 1973: 347).

In the Gordon Conference on Nucleic Acids, there was a debate (Wright 1994) about the uncertain possibility that moving DNA sequences from a known cancer-causing agent (SV-40 virus) to E. coli, a bacterium that is "a ubiquitous inhabitant of animal and human intestines," might "infect the laboratory workers" and *theoretically* increasing the incidence of cancer in the community.

Maxine Singer and Dieter Soll, co-chairs of the Gordon Conference, drafted an epoch-making letter on behalf of the scientists in attendance to the President of the National Academy of Sciences, USA and to the president of the National Institutes of Medicine. They had also sent the letter for publication in the widely read journal, *Science*, on September 21, 1973. (Singer *et al.* 1973) The letter expressed "a matter of deep concern" over reports at the conference which described the technical ability to transfer gene sequences between organisms. The Singer/Soll letter also suggested that the National Academy of Sciences initiate a study to frame appropriate guidelines for research with rDNA molecules. When nuclear fission turned out to be a feasible proposition, physicist Leo Szilard and others appealed to their fellow scientists to observe a "self-imposed moratorium" on certain aspect of nuclear research.

The debate relating to rDNA technology was closely following the footsteps of the debates in the late thirties in the area of nuclear science. The second "Berg letter" was also published as an open letter in *Science* on July 26, 1974. In this occasion, Berg was able to collect the signatures of most of the prominent researchers in the field of molecular biology in their capacity as members of a National Research Council Committee on Recombinant DNA. In his second letter, Berg appealed to the scientists to defer voluntarily from certain types of experiments (Berg *et al.* 1974), till the scientists were in a position to evaluate the potential hazards of the rDNA molecules and some physical and biological containment procedures can be practiced. The letter also proposed that an international meeting should be held to discuss specifically these issues. In response to such a proposal, on October 7, 1974, NIH established the Recombinant DNA Molecule Program Advisory Committee, which was later renamed the Recombinant DNA Advisory Committee, or the "RAC".

Asilomar II

In response to Berg's (second) letter, the promised conference was held in February, 1975 at the Asilomar Conference Center (Asilomar II) and recommendations for physical and biological containment of rDNA organisms were compiled in the "Summary Statement of the Asilomar Conference on Recombinant DNA Molecules" (Berg *et al.* 1975).

James Watson and John Tooze in their now famous book recounted (Watson *et al.* 1981: 26):

> [They were] as exhilarated as they were exhausted. ...They had been praised ... for their social responsibility. ...They had voted to impose upon themselves special safety precautions. ... Having demonstrated their integrity, they naively believed that they would now be free of outside intervention, supervision, and bureaucracy (Watson *et al.* 1981: 26).

The debate did not end but started with renewed vigor. The Harvard biologist, Walter Gilbert, a Nobel Prize winner in biology, in an open letter wrote (Lewin 1991):

> We are concerned that the benefits of recombinant DNA research will be denied to society by unnecessarily restrictive legislation... We feel that much of the stimulus for this legislative activity derives from exaggeration of the hypothetical hazards of recombinant DNA research that go far beyond any reasoned assessment (Lewin 1991: 206).

Gilbert (Lewin 1991) later reflected the opinion of many who considered that the safety of rDNA was the *only* legitimate issue neglecting the moral issue that was brought forth in this debate. Many of the molecular biologists did not consider "safety being the only issue."

One of the pioneers of DNA research, Erwin Chargaff, clarified his position in a comment entitled "On the Dangers of Genetic Meddling". He considered this issue to be essentially an ethical problem rather than one of public health. (Chargaff 1976: 940). He said, "[t]his world is given to us on loan" and that the "future will curse us" for our "destructive colonial warfare against nature [Ibid]. Chargaff advocated congressional action to intervene with a complete ban on the use of bacterial hosts that inhabit human organ systems (for example, E.coli) in rDNA research. George Wald, a Nobel Laureate and member of the Committee for Responsible Genetics (CRG), had also cautioned against tampering with the balance of nature. Wald described rDNA technology as one that "is all too big, and is happening too fast" (Wald 1976).

The rDNA debate was raised by the scientists themselves and they themselves recognized the need to bring in the ethical and moral dimension to this whole issue. Thus it was never a barren discussion between the informed scientists on the one hand and a scientifically illiterate public on the other. Krimsky refers to a shift of the burden of proof at this time from scientists (to show that it was safe) to the public (to show that it was dangerous). (Krimsky 1986).

In some sense, the scientists could drive home the cardinal points about the uncertain nature of this technology. They were also addressing some of the ethical questions surrounding the rDNA research. Perhaps the biggest fear of rDNA did not derive from the science behind it, but from a specter of greed. That is, biotechnology might well exacerbate the difference between the haves and the have-nots. The fear was that when the risks and benefits were tallied, the many who assumed the risks might not include the few who reaped the benefits. Thus a human rights perspective becomes important in this case.

The Flip Side of the Hype

Several of the first transgenic fruits and vegetables were "notable commercial failures". Even human gene therapy, despite all its promise, has yet to produce a cure for any disease (Langreth *et al.* 1999). These shortcomings in the promises of biotechnology may bring the risks and benefits on to a more even playing field until the question really becomes, not one of relative risk to benefit ratios, but who risks and who benefits? The biotechnology debate was, and still is, about choice; who has it, who doesn't, and under what circumstances. In medical circumstances the choices are often clear. The affected person may decide to undergo an unproven procedure, such as gene therapy. The risks may be very much higher than those of well tested, genetically modified tomatoes, but, if there is no other treatment available, the choice in this case may be between a possibility of cure on the one hand and certain death on the other.

When one is accustomed to having many choices, and one is then denied the ability to choose, trouble can be expected. The public was assured that the amount of rDNA introduced into an organism would be so small that there would be no perceptible difference between a recombinant organism and its non-recombinant cousins. Unfortunately for the agricultural community, this assurance had the opposite of its intended effect. The inability to distinguish between recombinant and non-recombinant products precludes the ability to make an informed choice between them. In the case of an individual who is desperate for a cure for a disease from which he or she is dying, an uninformed choice may be the only option, but in the case of a healthy individual choosing which foods to eat (for which there are many, many options), the knowledge that informed choice has been precluded may precipitate anxiety, fear, or anger.

The Case for Agriculture

In the month of April 1980, many decades after McClintock's documentation of what was later shown to be natural recombination in maize, the RAC received a proposal from Dr. Ronald W. Davis of Stanford University to field test corn which had been modified using rDNA techniques.

Experimentation with organisms that were once investigated freely in the fields of agricultural researchers, who collectively had centuries of experience with experimental manipulation of genetic information in food production activities, suddenly came under the suspicious eye of public scrutiny.

Somehow, mutant variants that were generated with purpose by human design were seen as potentially more dangerous to human or environmental health than those generated randomly by nature (or by researchers using traditional techniques). In other words, the process by which rDNA products were made had become more suspect than the products themselves. Genetic researchers framed the issue as one of academic freedom, while critics focused on the ethics of using the new technology.

Human Rights perspective towards rDNA technology is not anti-technology per se, nor does it fear the rDNA technology—the human rights perspective only holds that it is just to question about the control of the individual that this technology confers to wealthy corporate stockholders who are known offenders and violators of human rights.

The following Fundamental questions were very succinctly put forward by Surbone (Surbone 2001) pertaining to ethical and philosophical issues in genetics:

i) Which genetic information should be generated?
ii) Who controls its use and dissemination?
iii) Which genetic procedures are allowed?
iv) How is genetic normalcy defined and by whom?
v) How does genetics change lives?
vi) Does genetic knowledge expand our control on life? (Surbone 2001: 151)

As response towards the severe criticism, both from the society at large and from the informed and practicing scientific communities alike, most of the countries tried to evolve their own regulatory framework, based on the prevalent laws and legal and ethical instruments. As collaboration among countries became a routine affair, conflicting interests and protocols, suggested by various local instruments within nation–states, compounded the already murky scenario.

Biotechnology and the Expanding Horizon of Human Rights

The intervening period between the two World Wars, and particularly after the Second World War, the human society had witnessed a rapid development in the fields of medicine, biology, and chemistry. As a consequence of such unheard-of development as rDNA technology, the nation–states face unprecedented problems in their endeavors to safeguard and guarantee the fullest possible enjoyment of rights and fundamental freedoms to all their citizens under their political administration. The tragic experiences of the consequences of "medical experiments" in the Nazi Germany served as an impetus to formulate legal instruments and sound "Code of Conduct" to address the inherent rights of human beings—both national and international domain.

As the knowledge about the human body and mind was greatly enhanced, and the methods to be employed to adjust or change congenital qualities and physically challenged individuals had gained more importance in the society at large, the scope, form and content of some human rights had to be re-evaluated, while new categories of rights would have to be conceptualized.

The new forms of legal instruments or covenants became mostly right-based aiming at removing discrimination in social life, limiting access to social goods or services for human beings with certain traits, convictions, or characteristics. These new legal or moral instruments propagated the ideas that discrimination on the basis of traits, conviction etc., should be unjustified on moral ground and hence should be made illegal. Policy frameworks were postulated to guarantee equal access to goods and services to all citizens. Misusing power through defining the contents of an agreement to the disadvantage of a weaker party would make the contract void, as a legal basis was lacking. This process also had enormous repercussions for the health-care sector and in particular the physician–patient relationship.

The right to health care was subsumed as : "a right to a standard relevant to health" (Article 25 of the Universal Declaration of Human Rights, UDHR); "a right to the enjoyment of the highest attainable standard of health" (Article 12 of the International Covenant on Economic, Social, and Cultural Rights, ICESCR, and the Preamble to the Constitution of the World Health Organization, WHO); "a right to enjoy the best attainable state of physical and mental health" (Article 16 of the African Charter on Human and Peoples' Rights, ACHPR); "a right to the preservation of health" (Article 11 of the American Declaration of the Rights and Duties of Man, ADRDM); "a right to health protection" (Article 11 of the European Social Charter, ESC) and "a state of complete physical, mental and social well-being, and not only the absence of disease or infirmity, is a fundamental human right and ... the attainment of the highest possible level of health is a most important social goal" (Article 1 of the Declaration of Alma-Ata). As a corollary to the obligations of states, individuals can invoke several rights and freedoms, which are inherent in the right to health care.

We may recall here that broadly speaking the following human rights became particularly important and relevant for the protection of an individual's health and well-being against impairments inflicted (intentional or unintentional) by others:

a. The right to life as envisaged in Article 3 of the Universal Declaration of Human Rights, UDHR; Article 6 of the International Covenant on Civil and Political Rights, ICCPR; Article 4, the American Convention on Human Rights, ACHR; Article 4, African Charter on Human and Peoples' Rights, ACHPR; Article 2, European Convention for the Protection of Human Rights and Fundamental freedoms, ECHR.
b. The right to equality and non-discrimination—Article 2, Universal Declaration of Human Rights, UDHR; Articles 2, 3, 23, 24, and 26, International Covenant on Civil and Political Rights, ICCPR; Articles. 2 and 3, International Covenant on Economic, Social, and Cultural Rights, ICESCR; Preamble to the Constitution of the World Health Organization, WHO; Articles 2 and 18, African Charter on Human and Peoples' Rights, ACHPR; Article 1, American Convention on Human Rights, ACHR; Article 14, European Convention for the Protection of Human Rights and Fundamental freedoms, ECHR; and the Preamble to the European Social Charter, ESC).
c. The conference at Alma-Ata (1978), health was defined to be more than the absence of disease or infirmity. Thus it followed that arrangement of special services and measures should be the responsibility of the nation–state for people who are sick or in need, such as pregnant women, children, handicapped persons, and other such groups.

d. The prohibition of torture, maltreatment and medical experimentation Article 5, Universal Declaration of Human Rights, UDHR; Article 7, International Covenant on Civil and Political Rights, ICCPR; Article 2, UN Convention against Torture and other Cruel, Inhuman, and Degrading Treatment, CAT; Article 5, American Convention on Human Rights, ACHR; Article 6, Inter-American Convention to Prevent and Punish Torture, IACPPT; Article 5, African Charter on Human and People's Rights, ACHPR; Article 3, European Convention for the Protection of Human Rights and Fundamental freedoms, ECHR; and the Preamble to the European Convention for the Prevention of Torture and Inhuman or Degrading Treatment or Punishment, ECPT).

Emerging Issues in the Area of Biotechnology

At the global level, the emergence of Biotechnology, like the health care sector had given rise to a considerable number of so-called soft treaties and other entities. Most of global organizations were concerned about the various issues related to individual safety and the impact that as yet an unknown technology might have on the environment at large.

The Cartagena Protocol on Bio-safety was adopted which succinctly addressed the possible adverse effect that biotechnology might have on global biodiversity. Food and Agriculture Organization (FAO) Treaty on Plant Genetic Resources, ratified in 2001 has established a framework of international cooperation for the conservation and sustainable use of plant genetic resources for food and agriculture.

Release of genetically modified organisms into the environment may go against international covenant of a local or regional legal instrument, peculiar to the locale or the region and has had repercussions also on regional international law. EU Directive of 12th March 2001, seeks to put in place a surveillance mechanism by establishing a common system of authorization of the release of genetically modified organisms into the environment, and the distribution of such organisms or their products on the market. The impact of biotechnology on human rights was addressed by a myriad of instruments at the global level. The Human Genome Project gave rise to standards, like UNESCO legal and ethical standards applicable to the human genome, or the 1997 Universal Declaration on the Human Genome and Human Rights (UDHG) and its concomitant. Guidelines for the Implementation of such Declaration (1999), after the draft human genome sequences were made available. We had the 2003 International Declaration on Genetic Data and the 2005 Universal Declaration on Bioethics and Human Rights (UDBHR).

Organ Transplantation Issues

> "We will be able to repair some of the damage caused by aging, organ by organ …The application of nano-technology in bioengineering together with biotechnology offers a great new range of advanced biomaterials with enhanced functionality; and intertwined with tissue engineering, it has the potential to provide true organ replacement technology of the coming decade" (Draft on national

biotechnology development strategy by Ministry of science & technology Road Map, 2009: 3, 5).

Organ transplantation issues are already riddled with problem. Like blood transfusion and cornea grafting, transplanting human organ is also possible, thanks to the new development of immunology and biotechnology. Two issues are of importance here—the question of ethics and human rights surrounding organ transplantations, and raising "animals" as a source of "organ harvesting". We will concentrate more on human organ transplantation as the question of "harvesting animal organ for human usage" is a question that falls within the domain of animal rights.

Cloned animals can be used to model many human diseases. With these "artificial" life forms, scientists are now in a position to study effectively human diseases such as cystic fibrosis. These are diseases for which there is no therapeutic or management regime available as of this date and hence it is virtually impossible to cure a person suffering from such diseases.

Sometimes human-genome compatible active bio-molecules (proteins, DNAs etc.) will have less chance of being rejected by the human immune system. Carefully cloned animals may be used to produce pharmacologically useful proteins such as clotting factor, used by hemophiliacs, or insulin used by diabetics.

Farm animals, like goats, pigs and sheep, might be cloned, and used to grow organs such as hearts, livers, kidneys and fetal cells suitable for transplant into humans. This could end the long waiting period for organ transplants by seriously ill patients (Sinha 1999).

Human Rights Issues: The Case of Kidney Transplantation

If for some reasons, one is about to lose one's kidney, then an Organ Transplantation saves one's life. The entire procedure is a very complicated one, not to mention the prohibitive costs involved in such a procedure. It has a flip side that it is almost certain to leave some chronic disease in its wake even in the best of circumstances. On the other hand, since vital organs are unavailable, thousands of people in need of such organs die every year because of the scarcity of available organs. The cost escalates because first of all, a transplant patient must obtain a kidney. Secondly, for fear of rejection of the kidney by the transplant patient's immune system, the patient will have to be under a regime of immunosupressive therapy under the strict supervision of a physician. Though the procedure of renal transplant as therapeutic regime has been a seminal discovery, only very rich patients can afford this two stage (possibly multi-stage, in case of other medical complications) route. The practice of "kidney donation" fosters and encourages those poor persons (who are abundantly available in any third world countries of today's globalized world) who can hope to survive by selling their body parts.

In India, there is a case study available, in which the authors (Pande et al. 1992) carefully followed the subjects who "donated" kidneys to patients. The study showed that most of the "donors" who got paid for their "kidney donation", were not only financially ruined, (as their capacity for manual labor decreased), but also their health status deteriorated progressively over the years.

Many countries have a legal provision where organs can be harvested from the brain-dead. But this had not taken place anywhere to a significant degree, as the system through which such a procedure would have to be implemented is not a democratic one and the system would pay minimal or no respect for the human rights. A privatized medical system is predominantly driven by profit motive, thus quick profit overrides every other moral concern. This profit-driven system has its own dynamics which will foster live rather than cadaveric donation.

We may cite the case of Pakistan here. In Lahore alone, where about seven live transplantations happened in a day, the proportion of paid donors preponderated over next-kin non-paid donor. "Medical Tourism" has become a buzz word for those who had plenty. Already many countries in Asia had offered themselves as the physicians and surgeons of the world and acting as organ farms for those who are better off (Walsh 2005).

The Case of China

The trade in human organs is now a profitable venture in China. China has become the most coveted destination of "Medical Tourism" and citizens from Southeast Asia, Taiwan and far off countries like Canada used to arrive in China for kidney transplants. Shanghai has become the *de facto* center for kidney transplants. Medical practitioners of dubious repute (Bates 2011) (for example, Dr. Sonmez, had been barred from practicing medicine in Turkey's public health sector, but was engaged in a kidney transplantation clinic in Kosovo) perform these "group transplants". The human rights issue involved here is very simple—these organs were illegally obtained from the executed Chinese prisoners.

These "prisoners" ranged from ordinary criminals to those who differ from the politics of the state to religious minority groups. For example, in the six years period, 1999 through 2004, about 1,000 Falun Gong, non-violent religious practitioners were executed in China, of which about 52 percent were female, who had an average age of 44 years. Violating the human rights of these executed persons, their organs had been removed (Clearwisdom.net, 2000).

In China, the government used to overlook, and in most of the cases, simply condoned these practice of removing organs from the prisoners. A large number of Chinese policemen, judges, and doctors discuss in open forums as to how to obtain organs from dead prisoners for commercial usage! Even the accident victims are not spared from this ordeal. In the City of Huludao in Liaoning Province there was an accident in a coal mine on August 4, 2002. Many miners died. When the news of this accident came to the public domain, the family members of one such dead miner went to the hospital to collect the dead body of one Mr. Fang Yanjun. A post mortem examination was already conducted by the Nanpiao Medical Examiner and the family members found to their horror that part of the dead miner's organs were already missing. This had been done without the permission of his family members.

There is close connection between terrorist state, crony capitalism and military dictatorship with abuse of human rights using biotechnology. A case in point is the war-riddled country—Kosovo. The Council of Europe, in its recent report (December, 2010) alleged that the prime minister of Kosovo, Hashim Thaçi is actually the leader of a criminal ring that smuggles human organs throughout Eastern Europe. The prime minister used the money generated from human organ sales to maintain his questionable political power in Kosovo. Thaçi's came to power, backed by the NATO forces in the aftermath of Kosovo war of 1998–1999 (Lewis 2010).

Drug Test Fiasco

Another dimension of abuse of biotechnology leading to a compromise of human rights is in the area of drug testing. African and third world countries of Asia are becoming very fast the destination of unethical drug trials. We may cite the famous case of Pfizer in Nigeria. Pfizer International Incorporated (PII) had performed a "drug trial" for a controversial "drug", Trovafloxacin. This "clinical trial", popularly known as Trovan Clinical Trials, conducted on Nigerian citizens in Kano in 1996. Seven top officials of PII were accused of fraud and criminal breach of trust for instituting these "clinical trials:" Trovafloxacin is "dangerous to human health and life" and this fact was known to them. It was untested and unregistered by the country's regulatory agency NAFDAC, yet they had authorized and conducted such a "trial". The Pfizer executives were also accused of conducting a clinical trial without obtaining valid due certificate (Stephens, 2006)

A meningitis epidemic broke out in Nigeria in 1996 which killed many children and during the course of this outbreak, PII decided to test their untried drug on the ailing children. This unethical use of the drug resulted in about 200 deaths. These accused executives of PII had actually bribed physicians of Aminu Kano Teaching Hospital with $20,000 to procure a forged and backdated letter of approval for the "clinical trial".

TRIPS and Human Rights

TRIPs, or Trade Related Intellectual Property Rights, is an agreement between member states of the World Trade Organisation (WTO). This international instrument imposed a uniform Intellectual Property Rights (IPR) regime modeled after the US legislation. This is an omnibus agreement covering aspects of pharmaceuticals and human gene sequences and newer issues of abuse of human rights are emerging.

Since TRIPs brings under its purview drugs and pharmaceuticals (both manufacturing processes *and* product), the right to sound health for the citizens (as envisaged by UDHR) of poor countries is severely compromised. These countries, being member of the WTO, are obliged not to manufacture, or to import, cheap generic versions of patented drugs. A case in point is Brazil. Brazil wanted to import drugs curing AIDS from the international market through a competitive bidding process. The US Pharmaceutical company holding a monopoly over a range of such drugs through its range of patents tried to force on Brazil the drug with a high price tag. An Indian company, Cipla, responded to Brazil's international tender and offered a drug with proven efficacy for AIDS with a cheaper price. WTO tried to coerce Brazil to accept the offer of the US Company and wanted Brazil to reject Cipla's offer saying that such a transaction goes against the "sprit of WTO". Brazil could resist US pressure and Cipla was allowed to supply the much-needed drug to Brazil. The AIDS epidemic and other diseases are killing millions every year because people in poor countries cannot afford the exorbitant prices the pharmaceutical giants, protected by the WTO and are free to charge any amount for the patented drugs (Cohen 2005a; Cohen 2005b*)*.

Through TRIPs agreement, the US had been forcing all member countries of the WTO and the ones beyond the ambit of the WTO to make collateral changes in their national IPR instruments so as to accept questionable new biotech patents covering genes, cell lines, organisms and living processes. This step, in effect, has turned life into commodities. Countries under WTO umbrella all over the world have been persuaded into accepting these dubious 'patents on life' before anyone could fathom its scientific and ethical implications.

In fact, these "patents" should not have qualified to be called patents any way as they are based on plagiarism (expropriating public and indigenous wisdom) and "bio-piracy". We may cite here the famous case on Indian *neem* patent (which has fortunately been revoked) and the case of patents on extracts of the *bibiru* and *cunani* from the Wapixana Indians in North Brazil.

Biotech companies like Diversa Corporation, are aggressively scouring the globe, 'bio-prospecting' and accessing the biodiversity of the entire world. They are expanding their microbial genomic libraries to develop products for the pharmaceutical, agricultural, chemical and industrial markets. With muscle flexing in collusion with local mafias and exercising their economic prowess, they already secured access to the biodiversity wealth of Alaska, Costa Rica, Bermuda, Indonesia, Yellowstone National Park, and Russia, and the latest, South Africa. In South Africa, they almost have the exclusive rights to exploit for commercial purpose the world's most biologically diverse environments, which includes the famous Cape Floristic Region with 9,000 plant species, 70 percent of which are endemic (Crouch *et al.* 2008). The act of patenting life form and bio-piracy are in variance with the rights and livelihood of many people in the third world. They would be deprived of their traditional medicine as they would not be able to afford the price of patented medicine. The right to free access to the natural resources within the geographical and political boundaries of nation–state (which is a sovereign right anyway) is also compromised, not to talk of the breach of Convention on Biological Diversity, which is above the WTO. One can find several sober diatribes by several authors on this very important subject, (Kloppenberg 1988, Benbrook 2000, Boyd 2002).

To end this debate, we may quote the following passage:
[Biotech and] other industry voices ignore the crucial fact that the "improved" trait engineered into at least 73% of the transgenic crops actually being culti-

vated has been the ability to withstand applications of proprietary herbicides containing glyphosate or glucosinate... Such crops are neither more productive nor more nutritious, but they have substantially increased the sales of chemicals, particularly those patented and licensed by the Monsanto corporation. Far more than agronomic improvement it is economic gain, mainly from the sale of the herbicides that transgenic crops are designed to use, that has driven agro biotechnology research and development agendas. It is giant seed/agrochemical conglomerates, much more than farmers, that have benefited (McAfee 2003: 213)

Female Health and Human Rights

Biotechnology-derived drugs pertaining to female contraceptives are responsible for not only compromising the health of the hapless poor female subjects but also violate their basis human rights. A case in point is the two controversial female contraceptives, which had been tried to a great extent in India before being kept in abeyance.

Synthetic derivatives of progesterone, went by the commercial names such as Depo-Provera and Net-en, were supposed to suppress ovulation, make cervical mucous hostile to sperm and make the lining of the uterus unsuitable for implantation. Depo-Provera, developed and marketed by Upjohn of the United States was a three-monthly injectable, while Net-En is a product of Schering AG of Germany (Sathyamala 2000).

For "clinical trial" of this controversial "drug" Depo-Provera, Upjohn prospected a remote rural area in Thailand, named Chiang Mai. The female subjects could not read the consent form as it was in English, nobody had provided them with an authenticated translation of the content and the risk involved thereof. In fact, the entire exercise was not mentioned as a part of "drug trial" (Sathyamala 2000).

When the Indian government had become keen on introducing these contraceptives in its family welfare plan, a "Post Marketing Surveillance" (PMS) had been conducted and the PMS gave the drugs a clean chit. Later it turned out that two of the three authors of the PMS Report were from Pharmacia and Upjohn (Sathyamala 2000).

In developed countries, Depo-Provera is registered as a drug. It is meant primarily for the mentally challenged women. It was also advised for women with a problem of drug addiction. It was used rampantly for the indigenous populations such as Native Americans in the U.S. and Maoris in New Zealand, sexually active adolescents, African and South American women and women from low-income groups (ibid).

They are at double jeopardy for being a female and poor. They have lost the right to choose their own contraceptives without compromising their health. They were also used as unwilling subjects for unscientific and unethical medical experiments, in complete violation of Nuremberg Code of Conduct.

Conclusion

Modern Biotechnology had indeed opened up new frontier areas of science and had given rise to newer and newer dimensions relating to life and livelihood. The very concept, traditional or otherwise, of life would have to revisited, if one has to grapple with the human rights issues concomitant to biotechnology. The humankind, with its collective wisdom, had in the past overcome the ethical problem with science and technology; there is no reason that it would fail to do so now. Ethics and not profit that would resolve the issues those are in vogue now and ever since the dawn of "civilization" profit seemed to have dethroned ethics from its pedestal.

Acknowledgment

The wishes to acknowledge the support received from the Department of Biotechnology, Government of India (BT/BI/04/026/93 and BT/BI/010/019/99). The opinions expressed in this article are author's personal view.

References

Bates, T., 2011. Turkish Doctor Arrested in Organ Trafficking Ring. *AOL News* (Jan 12).

Benbrook, C.M., 2000. Who controls and who will benefit from plant genomics? The 2000 Genome Seminar: Genomic Revolution in the Fields. AAAS Annual Meeting, Washington, DC. (February 19). http://www.biotech-info.net/AAASgen.html (accessed on May 5, 2011).

Berg, P, D. Baltimore, H.W. Boyer and S.N. Cohen, 1974. Potential Biohazards of Recombinant DNA Molecules." *Science* (July 26): 185.

Berg, P., P. Baltimore, S. Brenner, R.O. Roblin and M.F. Singer, 1975. Asilomar Conference on Recombinant DNA Molecules. Summary Statement of the Report Submitted to the Assembly of Life Sciences of the National Academy of Sciences. *Science* 188 (July 26): 991.

Boyd, W., 2002. Wonderful Potencies? Deep Structure and the Problem of Monopoly in Agricultural Biotechnology. *Recreating the World: Genetic Engineering and its Discontents,* edited by Schurman, R.and Takahashi-Kelso, eds., *Recreating the World: Genetic Engineering and its Discontents,* 83–107. University of California Press, CA.

Bunting, M., 2001. The Profits that Kill. *The Guardian* (Feb. 12).

Chargaff, E., 1976. On the Dangers of Genetic Meddling. *Science* 192: 938–940.

Clearwisdom.net, 2000. Policemen Scheme to Sell the Organs of Jailed Falun Gong Practitioners. (December 22). http://minghui.ca/mh/articles/2000/12/22/5759.html (English version: http://www.clearwisdom.net/emh/articles/2000/12/ 31/3661.html) (accessed May 1, 2011).

———. 2001. Falun Gong Practitioner Ren Pengwu Was Murdered and All His Bodily Organs Were Removed by the Hulan County Police in Heilongjiang Province (April 19). http://minghui.ca/mh/articles/2001/4/19/10084.html (English version: http://www.clearwisdom.net/emh/articles/2001/4/21/6812.html (accessed May 1, 2011).

Cohen, J.C and K.M. Lybecker, 2005a. Patents: Brazil's Strategy to Committee on Biotechnology, Division of Agriculture, NASULGC, (1996). Emerging Biotechnologies in Agriculture: Issues and Policies. National Association of State Universities and Land Grant Colleges. November. Progress Report. 15: 3. Also in *The World Economy* 28, no. 2 (February): 211–230.

———. 2005b. *AIDS Policy and Pharmaceutical Patents: Brazil's Strategy to Safeguard Public Health.* Toronto: Blackwell Publishing. http://www.hmb.utoronto.ca/HMB303H/weekly_supp/week-08-09/Cohen_AIDS.pdf (accessed May 1, 2011).

Crouch, N.R., E. Douwes, M.M. Wolfson, F. Smith Gideon and T.J. Edwards, 2008. South Africa's Bioprospecting, Access and Benefit-Sharing Legislation: Current Realities, Future Complications, and a Proposed Alternative. *South African Journal of Science* 104 (Sept./Oct.): 9–10.

Declan, B., 1999. Patent on Umbilical-Cord Cells Rejected in Europe. *Nature* 399 (June 17): 626.

Department of Science and Technology, Ministry of Science and Technology, Government of India, 2009. Draft on National Biotechnology Development Strategy by Ministry of Science & Technology Road Map: 1–17. http://www.dst.gov.in/whats_new/press_releases05/ministry.htm (accessed March 15, 2011).

Equal Employment Opportunity Commission (US), 2002. EEOC and BNSF Settle Genetic Testing Case under Americans with Disabilities Act. (29 July) (Press Release) www.eeoc.gov/press (accessed March 15, 2011).

Human Genetics Commission, 2003. *Topics* (February 20) www.hgc.gov.uk/topics.htm (accessed March 15, 2011).

Kloppenberg Jr., J., 1988. *First the Seed: The Political Economy of Plant Biotechnology.* Cambridge, UK: Cambridge University Press.

Krimsky, S., 1986. The Regulatory Quandry over Biotechnology. *Conference Proceeding of the 1986 Washington International Conference on Biotechnology*, Washington International Conference on Biotechnology. Washington, DC, Center for Energy and Environmental Management.

Langreth, R. and S. D. Moore, 1999. Delivery Shortfall: Gene Therapy, Touted as a Breakthrough, Bogs Down in Details. *Wall Street Journal. Eastern Edition.* (October 27): A1.

Lewin, R., 1991. The Asilomar "Was the Asilomar Conference a Justified Response to the Advent of Recombinant DNA Technology, and should it Serve as a Model for Whistle-Blowing in the Future? *Bioscience and Society; Report of Schering Workshop* edited by D. J. Roy, B. E. Wynne and R. W. Old, 203. Chichester, NY: John Wiley & Sons.

Lewis, P., 2010. Kosovo PM is Head of Human Organ and Arms Ring, Council of Europe Reports. *Guardian* (December 14).

McAfee, K., 2003. Neoliberalism on the Molecular Scale. Economic and Genetic Reductionism in Biotechnology Battles. *Geoforum* 34: 203–219.

Milgram, S., 1963. Behavioral Study of Obedience. *Journal of Abnormal and Social Psychology* 67, no. 4: 371–8.

Miller, P., 2000. Is There a Pink Slip in My Genes? Genetic Discrimination in the Workplace. *Journal of Health Care Law & Policy* 225: 252–253.

Oxman, M.N., 1973. Panel V – Common Sense in the Laboratory: Recommendations and Priorities, Comments by Conference Organizers. *Biohazards in Biological Research: Proceedings of a Conference Held at Asilomar Conference Center, ("Asilomar I")*, edited by A. Hellman, M. N. Oxman and R. Pollack, 39–76. Pacific Grove, CA: Cold Spring Harbor Laboratory.

Pande G.K., P.K.Patnaik, S. Gupta and P. Sahni, 1992. Brain Death and Organ Transplantation in India. *The National Medical Journal of India* 5:142–3.

Rothman, D and S. Rothman, 1984. *The Willowbrook Wars*. Cambridge: Harper-Collins.

Sathyamala, C., 2000. *An Epidemiological Review of the Injectable Contraceptive Depo-Provera*. Published Jointly by Medico Friends' Circle (Pune, India) and Forum for Women's Health.

Singer, M. and S. Dieter, 1973. Guidelines for DNA Hybrid Molecules. *Science* 181 (September 21): 1114.

Sinha G., 1999. Organ Cowboy: Organs from Animals. *Popular Science* 255, no. 4: 68–73.

Stephens, J., 2006. Panel Faults Pfizer in '96 Clinical Trial in Nigeria Unapproved Drug Tested on Children. *Washington Post* (Sunday, May 7).

Surbone, A., 2001. Ethical Implications of Genetic Testing for Breast Cancer Susceptibility. *Critical Reviews in Oncology/Hematology* 40: 149–157. www.elsevier.com/locate/critrevonc (accessed March 15, 2011).

Wald, G., 1976. The Case against Genetic Engineering. *Science* 16 (September): 6.

Walsh, D. 2005. Transplant Tourists Flock to Pakistan, Where Poverty and Lack of Regulation Fuel Trade in Human Organs. *The Guardian* (Thursday, February 10).

Watson, J.D. and J. Tooze, 1981. *The DNA Story: A Documentary History of Gene Cloning*. San Francisco: W. H. Freeman and Company.

Wright, S., 1994. *Molecular Politics: Developing American and British Policy for Genetic Engineering, 1972–1982*. Chicago: University of Chicago Press.

INDEX

Aalen, L., 202
Aariyal kothmas, 242
Abbink, J., 199, 203, 204
Academia Sinica, Taiwan, 224
ACHPR. *See* African Charter on Human and People's Rights
ACHR. *See* American Convention on Human Rights
ACHR. *See* Asian Centre for Human Rights
ACP. *See* African, Caribbean and Pacific Group of States
Acton, L. J., 45
Addison, J., 286
ADEA. *See* Adivasi-Dalit Ektha Abhijan
Adegbit, L. O., 5
Adivasi-Dalit Ektha Abhijan (ADEA), 125, 130, 134
Adivasis, 8, 9, 50, 124, 132, 123–138, 140, 141, 142–145, 147, 154, 158, 160; and Rashtrasevika Samiti, 147
Adorno, T. W., 187–188
ADRDM. *See* American Declaration of the Rights and Duties of Man
Afiazova, R. K., 67
African-American, 370
African, Caribbean and Pacific Group of States (ACP), 27, 28
African Charter on Human and People's Rights (ACHPR), 5, 17, 384, 383
AFSPA. *See* Armed Forces Special Powers Act, India
Agarwal, A., 64, 77
Agarwal, B., 116, 117

Aggarwal, O., 238
Aggleton, P., 237
Ahmed, S. I., 238
AIDS Bhedbhav Virodhi Andolan, 250, 252
Akhand Bharat, 153
Akhtar, S., 238
Akua, 243
Albinos, 281, 288, 301, 304
Alem, H., 194, 197, 200
Alemante, S., 199, 200, 201
Alexander Phiri, 291
Alis, 243
Alliance of Taiwanese Aborigines (ATA), 105,
Allio, F., 100, 105
Alma-Ata Convention, 332, 382; Declaration, 12, 332–333, 382
Alonso, A. M., 237
Alpha-1 antitrypsin deficiency, 375
Alston, P., 32
Altheide, D. L., 218
Alvarado, M., 136
Ambedkar, B. R., 152, 158, 173
American Convention on Human Rights (ACHR), 132, 133, 138, 382, 383
American Declaration of Independence, 1
American Declaration of the Rights and Duties of Man (ADRDM), 1, 382
American Indians, 115
Americans with Disabilities Act, 368, 384
Amin, S., 125, 137
Amis, 105

Amniocentesis, 265, 266, 275
Anand Teltumde, 156
Anaya, S. J., 110, 112
Anchorage Declaration, 135
Antia, N. H., 332
Anti–Homosexuality Bill of Uganda, 6, 27–28
Anti-Sikh Pogrom, 148
Anuak, 207, 210
Anukansai, K., 81, 83, 84, 85, 86, 87, 89
Appadurai, A., 4, 180, 231
Apprentices Act, 1961 (India), 233
Ardi, 266
Armed Forces Special Powers Act (AFSPA), India, 358
Arnold, F., 279
Arvind, N., 240
Aryans, 150, 151
Asch, A., 285, 287
Asch, M., 107
Asian Centre for Human Rights (ACHR), 132, 133
Asian Values, 6, 21–24, 82, 90, 325
Asilomar Conference, 371, 377–378; Asilomar I, 377–378, 391; Asilomar II, 378
Asplund, K. D., 82, 90
Asthana, S., 240
Asuras, 171
ATA. *See* Alliance of Taiwanese Aborigines
Avatar, 106

Babri (Mosque), 148, 149, 153, 159
Baby Gender Mentor Home DNA Gender Testing Kit, 271
Bacchetta, P., 157
Bagadia, V. N., 257
Bagchi, S. S., 1, 2, 10, 19, 215, 225, 232
Bagenstos, S. R., 323
Bahati, D., 27
Bahujan Samaj Party (BSP), 158
Bajrang Dal, 8, 147, 152
Baldauf, S., 280

Baldwin, J. L., 253
Balika Samriddhi Yojana, 280
Balitutha Bridge, 185
Bandopadhya, D., 133
Banerjee, D., 332, 338
Bangkok Declaration, 20
Banjul Charter. *See* African Charter on Human and People's Rights
Bardhan, P., 88–89
Barlow, M., 61, 65
Barnatt, S. N., 286
Barnes, R., 138
Barnett, J., 69
Barsh, R., 37
Bashai, 243, 245
Basic Law on Indigenous Peoples, 8, 100, 102–103, 105, 106–107, 108, 109, 110, 111–112, 114, 115
Basmati, 65
Bastar, 50
Basti, 227
Basu, G, 333, 340
Basu, T., 147
Bates, T., 385
Baviskar, A., 123
Baxi, U., 31, 32, 33, 40, 42, 44, 45, 51, 123, 127, 128, 360, 361, 363, 365
Bayer, R., 240
Beaulieu, R., 108
Beedi and Cigar Workers (Conditions of Employment) Act, 1961 (India), 222
Beijing Platform for Action, 37, 76
Bell, D., 356, 357
Below Poverty Line (BPL), 335, 341
Belur Sramajibee (Workers') Hospital, 342
Benbrook, C. M., 387
Benjamin, W., 226
Berg, P., 377, 378, 379; letter, 378
Bergson, H., 269
Berhanu, B., 205
Berhanu, N., 195

Berking, H., 190
Bhakti (Movement), 151
Bhan, G., 240
Bharati, S., 124
Bharati, Uma, 157
Bharatiya Janata Party (BJP), 147, 148, 152, 156–158
BJP Mahila Morcha, 156, 157
Bhatta Parsol, 364
Bhedbhav Virodhi Andolan, 250
Bhende, A. A., 238
Bhil, 170, 171
Bhopal Gas Disaster, 33, 358, 359, 361, 363
Bhuiyan, A.J.M.S.A., 356
Biancosino, B., 297
Bila, 246
Bill–12300. *See* Indigenous Autonomy Bill
Binayak Sen, 358, 360
BJP. *See* Bharatiya Janata Party
Blackstone, William, 274
Blair, H., 94
Blaser, M., 128
Blasphemy Laws of Pakistan, 6, 24–25
Blue Star, 147
Bohali, 274
Bonded Labor, 278, 360
Bonded Labour System (Abolition) Act, 1975 (India), 222
Bornstein, K., 236
Boron, A., 125
Bose, B., 240
Bourchier, D., 91, 92
Boyce, P., 240
Boyd, W., 387
BPL. *See* Below Poverty Line
Brahma, 154
Brahman/Brahmin, 135, 146, 148, 152, 154, 167, 168, 175; Brahmanism, 148, 150, 152, 158, 159; Brahmanas, 150, 267; Brahminical, 9, 152, 166, 167, 169, 170, 172, 175, 177, 230; Non-, 146

Braille inscriptions, 296
Branigan, T., 24
Breton, A., 94
British Period/Colonialism/Raj/Rule, 130, 147, 151, 160, 171, 216, 230, 249, 251; Anti-, 146, 230
Brohi, A., 24
Brown, H., 296
Brown, R. A., 93
Browning, R., 51
BSP. *See* Bahujan Samaj Party
Bullough, B., 237
Bullough, V., 237
Butalia, U., 157
Butenhoff, L., 83
Butler, J., 236

Caine, B., 274
Cairo Declaration on Human Rights in Islam (CDHRI), 17
Callender, C., 236
Cameron, A., 123
Canadian First Nations, 116
Cape Floristic Region, 387
Carrier, J. M., 237
Carrillo, H., 237
Carstairs, G. M., 263
Cartagena Protocol, 383
Casolari, M., 146
Cassel, D., 191
Cassidy, C., 225
CCI. *See* Council of Constitutional Inquiry
CDHRI. *See* Cairo Declaration on Human Rights in Islam
CEDAW. *See* Convention on the Elimination of All Forms of Discrimination against Women
CEHAT. *See* Centre for Health and Allied Themes
Centre for Health and Allied Themes (CEHAT), 277
Centre for Science and Environment, New Delhi, 65
Cephas Msipa, 293

Cernea, M. M., 64
Cervical mucous, 388
CESCR. See International Covenant on Economic, Social, and Cultural Rights
CETIM. See Human Rights Program of the Europe–Third World Centre
Chakraborti, D., 63
Chakraborty, S., 12, 331, 335, 340
Chakrapani, V., 238, 240
Chakravarti, U., 172, 360
Chan, R., 238
Chandhoke, N., 219
Chang, C., 104
Chargaff, E., 379
Chartrand, Paul L. A. H., 115
Chasin, B., 4
Chatterjee, M., 148, 158
Chattisgarh Mukti Morcha (CMM), 344
Chattopadhyay, T. K., 349
Chauncey, G., 237
Chelas, 243
Chhabra, P., 238
Chhakka, 245
Chhibri, 243
Child Labor, 3, 165, 169, 176, 220–223, 225–229; Child Labour (Prohibition and Regulation) Act, 1986 (India), 221; Child Labour Technical Advisory Committee (India), 223
Children (Pledging of Labour) Act, 1933 (India), 221
Chimedza, R., 286, 293, 294, 298, 301
Chinese Nationalist Party, 104
Chipo Chikozho, 301
Choice on Termination of Pregnancy Act, 278
Chomsky, N., 93, 125
Chorionic villus sampling, 271
Chorumi, T., 289
Choudry, A., 128
Chowdhry, G., 81, 92, 93, 95

CHW. See Community Health Worker
Cimadamore, A., 123
Cipla, 387
CIPs. See Council of Indigenous Peoples, Taiwan
Civil and Political Rights (CPR), 3, 7, 19, 24, 32, 33, 60, 76, 82-83, 85, 95, 116, 132, 250, 269, 327, 361, 382, 383
Civil Society, 10, 44, 46, 91, 100, 101, 131, 180, 191, 203, 212, 239, 241, 248–251, 342, 346, 347, 353, 357, 365
Clapham, A., 60
Clapham, C., 204
Clements, L., 287
Clifford, J., 218
Clinical genetics, 373
Clinical trial, 386, 388
Cloned animals, 384
CMM. See Chattisgarh Mukti Morcha
Coalition for Unity and Democracy (CUD), 202
Cohen, A. P., 217
Cohen, J. C., 387
Cohen, L., 240, 241
Colapinto, J., 237
Cold War, 3, 6, 19, 31, 32, 33, 83
Collective Rights, 2, 10, 111, 122, 182, 215, 229
Commissioner for Scheduled Castes and Tribes, 167
Committee for Responsible Genetics (CRG), 379
Committee on the Status of Women in India, 274
Communal (Ethnic) Violence, 145, 147, 159
Communist, 130, 153; Anti-, 147; Block, 32; Regimes in Europe, 23; Party of China, 24; Party of India (Marxist) 339
Communitarianism, 90–91

Community Health Worker (CHW), 332
Confucian philosophy, 279
Congress (Party), 146, 147, 148, 150, 172, 187, 332
Conkin, P. K., 59
Constitution of Ecuador, 6, 26–27
Constitution of Ethiopia, 196–199, 202, 203, 204–205, 207; Article 83, 198
Constitution of India, 12, 127, 132–133, 136, 156, 158, 167, 169, 171, 172–173, 177, 182, 187, 220, 223, 230, 250, 251, 271, 278, 279, 312–315, 321, 332, 338, 339, 359, 361, 362; 73rd Amendment, 339; Directive Principles of State Policy, 312, 314, 332; Fundamental Rights, 12, 312, 313, 314, 330, 332, 359, 363; Seventh schedule, 314
Constitution of Indonesia, 89, 90–91
Constitution of Taiwan, 100, 102, 105, 108
Convention against Torture, 165, 383
Convention on the Elimination of All Forms of Discrimination against Women (CEDAW), 173, 176
Convention on the Rights of the Child (CRC), 176,
Conventions on the Rights of Migrant Workers, 165
Copenhagen Declaration, 37, 44
Corporate Accountability Strategy, 48
Corporate Social Responsibility (CSR), 7, 42, 48, 49, 51
Corruption, 7, 13, 60, 81–95, 338, 339
Corruption Eradication Team, 94
Cossman, B., 157
Council of Constitutional Inquiry (CCI), 198
Council of Indigenous Peoples (CIPs), Taiwan, 100, 105, 112
CPR. *See* Civil and Political Rights

Crane, B., 237
CRC. *See* Convention on the Rights of the Child
CRG. *See* Committee for Responsible Genetics
Criminal Procedure Code, India, 231, 250; Section 4(1), 266; Section 125, 265
Crouch, N. R., 387
Crystal, S., 218
CSR. See Corporate Social Responsibility
CUD. *See* Coalition for Unity and Democracy
Cultural Freedom, 179, 191
Cultural Rights, 3, 4, 9, 179, 180, 181–183, 184, 188, 189, 190, 191
Culture of information, 352, 354, 355, 356, 359
Cunani, 387
Cystic fibrosis, 384

Daes, E. A., 106, 113
Dahl, G. B., 279
Daira, 243
Dalit, 9, 124, 125, 130, 133, 137, 158–159, 162, 165, 168–170, 175–177; National Campaign on Dalit Human Rights (NCDHR), 176
Dandona, L., 238
Danesi, M., 351
Danga, 245
Daniel, S., 135
Darwin, C., 77
Das, A. 131
Das, J., 124, 133
Das, V., 131
Das, V., 182, 183
Dasar Negara (The State Basis in Indonesia), 91
Dasmann, R. F., 73
Dasyus, 171
Davis, K., 289
Davis, R. W., 380

398   Index

Davis, S., 5
DD Oriya, 185–186
DDPs. See Development-Displaced Persons
Declaration of Alma-Ata, 382
Declaration on the Right to Development, 38
Decolonization, 1, 18, 31-32, 33, 42, 128, 129, 131, 138, 180, 217
Degener, T., 327
Deleuze, 229
Delph, E. W., 262
Delphi, 273
Democracy, 3, 5, 9, 10, 12, 19, 20, 22, 61, 72, 84, 94, 148, 161, 169, 187, 193, 200, 201–204, 208, 220, 231, 280, 322, 329, 331–332, 338, 339, 346, 347, 358, 360, 364
Democratic Centralism (Leninist-style), 198, 204, 207
Democratic Progressive Party (DPP), Taiwan, 105
Deni, E., 287
Depo-Provera, 388
Dera, 243
Derg, 195
Derrida, J. 230
Deshmukh, N., 148
de Sousa Santos, B., 19, 20, 26
Deterritorialization, 190
Deva, S., 46
Development-Displaced Persons (DDPs), 124
Devi, S., 238
Dhall, P., 10, 35, 238, 252
Dharma shastras, 166
Dhruti, 269
Dias, C. J., 6, 3, 32, 33, 34, 35, 37, 42, 44, 45
Digital Divide, 353, 354, 355
Dinknesh, 194, 271
Disability, 11–12, 30, 33, 282–302; Convention on the Protection and Promotion of the Convention on the Rights of Persons with Disabilities (UNCRPD), 308, 316, 317–318; Disabled Persons Act, Zimbabwe, 286, 290; Human Rights Model of Disability, 312, 318; Movement, 309–310, 317–318, 319, 321; Medical Model, 309, 310; National Association of Societies for the Care of the Handicapped (NASCOH), Zimbabwe, 295; National Policy for Persons with Disabilities (India), 316; National Trust for the Welfare of Persons with Autism, Cerebral Palsy, Mental Retardation and Multiple Disabilities Act (India), 315; Persons with Disabilities (Equal Opportunities, Full Participation and Protection of Rights) Act, India (PWDA), 315, 316, 321, 322
Discrimination (Employment Occupation) Convention (Convention No. 111), ILO, 224
Diversa Corporation, 387
DO Channel, 361
Doniger, W., 167
Donnelly, J., 23, 24, 25, 81, 82, 83, 92, 129
Douglas, B. C., 359, 363
Downing, K. A., 280
Dowry, 11, 157, 172, 174, 231, 270, 272–275, 268, 359
Dowry Prohibition Act, 273
Dowsett, G. W., 237
Doyle, B., 285
DPP. See Democratic Progressive Party, Taiwan
Drescher, J., 237
Drug Trial, 386, 388
Duggal, R., 337
Dutta G. P., 332

East India Company, 216
East–West Divide, 6, 32, 216

Economic Social and Cultural Rights (ESCR), 3
ECPT. See European Convention for the Prevention of Torture
Edaltu, 269
Edwardes, M., 216
EEOC. See Equal Employment Opportunity Commission (US)
Eigen, P., 81, 85
Elazar, D., 202
Elliott, K., 220
Emergency, 342–344
Emerson, R. W., 265
Emic Approach, 217
Emperor Haile Selassie, 195
Emphysema, 375
Employment of Children Act, 1938 (India), 221
Employment of Children (Amendment) Act, 1978 (India), 222
Energy and Resources Institute, New Delhi, 61
Engineer, A. A., 149
Entitlement, 102, 190, 330, 376
EPLF. See Eritrean People's Liberation Front
EPRDF. See Ethiopian People's Revolutionary Democratic Front
Epstein, P. R., 68
Equal Employment Opportunity Commission (US), (EEOC), 374
Equal Remuneration Convention (Convention No. 100), ILO
Erison method, 224
Eritrean People's Liberation Front (EPLF), 195
ESC. See European Social Charter
ESCR. See Economic Social and Cultural Rights
Ethical and Philosophical Issues in Genetics, 381
Ethiopian People's Revolutionary Democratic Front (EPRDF), 195, 196, 202–208
Etic Approach, 217

European Convention for the Prevention of Torture (ECPT), 383
European Convention on Human Rights, 250
European Social Charter (ESC), 382
European Union (EU), 27, 39
Evans, T., 125, 130, 131, 132
Evans-Pritchard, E. E., 4, 130, 217
Exxon, 45

Factor 5 Leiden, 373
Factories Act, 1911 (India), 221
Factories Act, 1934 (India), 221
Factories Act, 1948 (India), 222
Factories (Amendment) Act, 1922 (India), 221
Falk, R., 81, 127
Falkenmark, M., 61
Falun Gong, 385
Fanon, F., 129, 131, 137
FAO. See Food and Agriculture Organization
Farai Mukuta, 287, 295
FCA. See Forest Conservation Act
FDRE Constitution 197, 198, 199, 212, 213
Feder, E., 33
Federation of Obstetricians and Gynecologists Societies of India (FOGSI), 277
Feit, H., 108, 128
Female Husbands, 236
Female Infanticide Act, 270
Feng, K., 82, 83, 85
Ferber, A., 237
Fernandes, W., 123, 124
FIAN, 49, 50, 51
Finotti L., 297
Firman, T., 94
First Battle of Independence, India, 216
Fisher, W., 123
Five Year Plan, India, 173
Flanagan, T., 101, 106, 115

Flawed Ethnographer, 217
FOGSI. See Federation of Obstetricians and Gynecologists Societies of India
Food and Agriculture Organization (FAO), 62, 71, 73, 333, 383
Forest Conservation Act (FCA), India, 132, 133
Forestry Act, Taiwan, 109, 110
Foucault, M., 229, 230
Fourth World Conference on Women and Development, 37, 76
Fowler, C., 72
Franke, R., 4
Franke, R. W., 347
Freedom House, 203
Freedom of Association and Protection of Right to Organize Convention (Convention No. 87), ILO, 224
French Declaration of the Rights of Man and its Citizens, 1, 6
Frick, M.-L., 6, 17, 24
Fujii, S., 103, 104
Fukui, K., 194

Gagnon, J. 236
Galtung, J., 248
Gambella Regional State, 10, 207
Gamma globulin, 370
Ganatra, B., 280
Gandhi, I., 148, 175
Gandhi, M. K., 126, 146, 147, 148, 159, 175, 265
Gandhian Socialism, 147
Gandu, 245
Garvadan, 268
Garvey, J., 66
Gathii, J. T., 81, 87, 88, 89
Gay, 27, 238-239, 241, 242, 244–252, 358; Active, 244; Top, 244
Gaya Group, Taiwan, 102
GCC. See Grand Council of the Crees
GDP. See Gross Domestic Product
Geertz, C., 217, 218
Geiger, K. F., 22

Gender, 4, 10, 60, 156, 161, 162, 165, 166, 168, 170, 199, 218, 235–238, 240–242, 244–246, 248, 249–251, 269, 270, 271, 273, 276, 278, 289, 308, 313, 316, 317, 318, 320, 330, 336
Gender Inequality Index, 336
Genetically Modified Foods (GM Foods), 71
Genetically Modified Organisms (GMOs), 71, 383
Genetic Meddling, 379
Geomin Minerals and Marketing (P) Ltd, 187
Ghai, Y., 199, 200, 205
Ghosh, D., 70
Ghosh, K., 123
Ghosh, T. K., 238
Gibson, G., 191
Gilbert, J., 110
Gilles, D., 37
Giriya, 224
Girl child, 11, 174, 227, 274, 279–281
GLBT framework, 242
Global South, 6, 17–18, 21, 27, 28
Glucosinate, 388
Glyphosate, 388
GMOs. See Genetically Modified Organisms
Godfrey Majonga, 292
Godhra, 175
Godse, Nathuram, 147
GOI (Government of India), 44, 321
Golwalkar, M. S. 146, 150, 151
Go Native, 217
Gonds, 170
Goparaju, L., 238
Gordon Conference on Nucleic Acids, 378
GP. See Gram Panchayat
Gram Panchayat (GP), 184, 339–340
Gramsci, A., 131, 179

Grand Council of the Crees (GCC), 107
Grassi, L., 297
Greig, E., 43
Grierson, J. W., 237
Griggs, C., 237
Groce, N. E., 288, 297
Gross Domestic Product (GDP), 61, 67, 69, 334, 336, 337
Grover, V., 161
Groves, R., 106
Guha, R., 131
Guidieri, R., 5
Gujarat Riots, 175
Gupta, S.C., 238
Guruma, 243
Guru–Shishya Parampara, 225
Gyeke, K., 5

Hafner-Burton, E. M., 363
Haisa, 170
Hale, H. E., 201
Hales, S. N., 68
Hall, K., 240, 241
Hamelink, C. J., 351
Hameso, S., 193
Hannum, H., 124
Harbeson, W. J., 203
Hardt, M., 125
Hardy, T., 274–275
Harrison, H., 104
Hashmi, S., 360
Hart, N. H. 90
Harvey, D., 125
Hashim Thaçi, 386
Haudensosaunee. *See* Two Row Wampum Treaty
Hazard, J. N., 198
HDR. *See* Human Development Report
HDSA (Human Development in South Asia), 44
Heasley, R., 237
Hemophiliacs, 384
Henkin, L., 125
Henry, N., 269

Hepatitis virus, 370
Herdt, G., 236, 237
Hijra, 236, 238, 239, 240–241, 242–243, 244–246, 248, 252
Himesh, S., 75
Hindu, 3, 4, 8, 142, 145–161, 166, 167, 170–173, 175, 177, 216, 227, 268, 271, 273, 275, 311; Adoption and Maintenance Act, 173; Dharma, 145; Code Bill, 173; Elite, 148, 150, 152; Mahasabha, 147, 152; Marriage Act, 173; Minority and Guardianship Act, 173; Rashtra, 145–154; Succession Act, 173
Hindutva, 8, 145–148, 149–159
Hitler, Adolf, 369, 372
HIV/AIDS, 237–238, 239, 240, 241, 247, 249, 250, 251, 289, 295–298, 300, 320
Hizkias, A., 199
HOF. *See* House of Federation
Hofman, K. J., 285
Holland, J., 237
Honda, Y., 68
House of Federation (HOF), 198
Howard, R., 5
Hoyt, K. S., 68
HRBA. *See* Human Rights Based Approach to Development
HTFCC. *See* Hunting Trapping and Fishing Coordinating Committee (HTFCC), Taiwan
Huang, S., 105
Huang, Y., 104
Human Development in South Asia, 44
Human Development Report (Human Development Report), 333, 335–336
Human gene therapy, 380
Human Rights Based Approach to Development (HRBA), 85–86
Human Rights Council, 39, 48, 165

Human Rights Program of the Europe–Third World Centre (CETIM), 38
Human Rights Watch, 57, 168, 202, 204, 206–207
Hume, D, 20
Humsafar Trust, 239, 241, 249
Huntington, S. P., 331
Hunting Trapping and Fishing Coordinating Committee (HTFCC), Taiwan, 108
Hussain, M., 124
Hutu, 4, 194
Hypogyny, 274

IACPPT. *See* Inter-American Convention to Prevent and Punish Torture
IBON, 33
Ibrahim, A., 92
ICCPR. *See* International Covenant on Civil and Political Rights
ICDS. *See* Integrated Child Development Services
ICESCR. *See* International Covenant on Economic, Social and Cultural Rights
ICF. *See* International Classification of Functioning, Disability and Health
ICHRP. *See* The International Council on Human Rights Policy)
ICIDH. *See* International Classification of Impairments, Disabilities and Handicaps
ICTs. *See* Information and Communication Technologies
IFC. *See* International Finance Corporation
IFPRI. *See* International Food Policy Research Institute
ILO. *See* International Labour Organization
IMA. *See* Indian Medical Association
IMF. *See* International Monetary Fund
IMFA. *See* Indian Metals and Ferro Alloys Limited
Immunology, 384
INCD. *See* International Network on Cultural Diversity
Indian Factories Act, 1881, 221
Indian Factories (Amendment) Act, 1891, 221
Indian Forest Act, 133
Indian Medical Association (IMA), 277
Indian Metals and Ferro Alloys Limited (IMFA), 189
Indian Mines Act, 1923, 221
Indian Mines (Amendment) Act, 1935, 221
Indian Penal Code (IPC), 249–251, 283; Section 377, 249–252
Indian Ports (Amendment) Act, 1931, 221
Indian Radiologist Association (IRA), 277
Indigenous and Tribal Peoples Convention C107, 8, 100
Indigenous Autonomy Law (Bill–12300), 8, 113–116
Indigenous People, 3, 5, 8, 66, 67, 74, 100, 104–107, 109, 110, 114, 132, 135–136, 180, 358
Indigenous People's Declaration on Climate Change, 135
Indigenous Self-government Bill, Taiwan, 113
Indonesian Constitution, 89, 91
Indonesian Identity, 92
Infant Mortality Rate, 336
Information and Communication Technologies (ICTs), 352–355, 357,
Information Capitalism, 355
Information Era, 366
Information Workers, 355
INGOs. *See* International Non-governmental Organizations
Insulin, 384

Integrated Child Development Services (ICDS), 339, 340
Intellectual Property Rights (IPR), 33, 39, 353, 386, 387
Inter-American Convention to Prevent and Punish Torture (IACPPT), 383
International Anti-corruption Conference, 366
International Classification of Functioning, Disability and Health (ICF), 308
International Classification of Impairments, Disabilities and Handicaps (ICIDH), 308
International Council on Human Rights Policy (ICHRP), 43, 84
International Covenant on Civil and Political Rights (ICCPR), 83, 116, 250, 269, 382, 383
International Covenant on Economic, Social and Cultural Rights (ICESCR), 83, 179, 300, 330, 382
International Crisis Group, 203
International Decade of Disabled Persons, 317
International Declaration on Genetic Data, 383
International Finance Corporation (IFC), 93
International Food Policy Research Institute (IFPRI), 135, 333
International Labour Organization (ILO), 100, 124, 352; Convention No. 5, 224; Convention No. 6, 224; Convention No. 15, 224; Convention No.16, 224; Convention No. 29, 222, 224; Convention No.87, 224; Convention No.98, 224; Convention No.100, 224; Convention No.105, 224; Convention No.111, 224; Convention No. 123, 224; Convention No.138, 224; Convention No. 169, 124

International Monetary Fund (IMF), 39, 45, 93
International Network on Cultural Diversity (INCD)
International Non-governmental Organizations (INGOs), 131
International Telecommunication Union (ITU), 352
International Women's Year, 173
International Work Group for Indigenous Affairs (IWGIA), 123
International Year of Disabled Persons (IYDP), 288, 315
IPC. See Indian Penal Code
IPR. See Intellectual Property Rights
IRA. See Indian Radiologist Association
Ishay, M., 126
Islamic Values, 82
ITU. See International Telecommunication Union
IWGIA. See International Work Group for Indigenous Affairs
IYDP. See International Year of Disabled Persons

Jaffrelot, C., 148, 150, 158
Jaffrey, Z., 238
Jairos Jiri Centre, 298
Jaitapur, 364
Jalali, R., 194
Jamaat-e-Islami, 25
James Bay and Northern Québec Agreement (JBNQA), 107, 108
Jamindari, 146
Janata Party, 147
Jan Sangh, 147, 173
Janssen, M., 297
Jantar Mantar, 271
JBNQA. See James Bay and Northern Québec Agreement
Jenkins, C., 237, 238, 240, 241
Jin, H., 105
John, M. E., 238, 241

Johnson, J. M., 218
Johnson, S., 65
Jordan, S., 126
Joseph, S., 238, 240, 241
Joshi, B., 4

Kabir, 151, 152
Kakar, S., 238
Kala, A., 240
Kalinga Nagar/Kalinganagar, 364
Kalliat, P., 238
Kalt, J. P., 116
Kanungo, P., 147
Kanyasulkam, 273
Kapoor, D., 8, 123, 125, 126, 130, 132, 133, 134, 135, 136
Kapoor, R., 157
Kapoor, V., 44
Karimi, F., 27
Karma, 311, 325
Kar Seva, 148, 157
Kasbekar, A. B, 332
Kashmir, 2
Katzenstein, M., 123
Kebele, 204
Keeley, J., 130
Keerti, 267
Kent, A., 23
Kepribadian Indonesia (Indonesian Identity), 92
Kerala Shastra Sahitya Parishad (KSSP), 347
Kessler, S. J., 237
Khalistani, 148
Khan, S., 241, 240
Khan, S. I., 238
Khap Panchayat, 175
Khare, R., 4
Kidane, M., 201
Kidney Donation, 384
Kidwai, S., 159, 238
Kieserling, M., 22
Kilil, 196
King, D. Y., 90
Kirchmeier, F., 39, 41
Kishore Kandi, 185

KMT (The Chinese Nationalist Party, Taiwan), 104–105, 112
Koenig, M., 236
Kojima, Y., 103
Kondh, 126, 128, 130, 132, 134, 135
Korean TV series, 184, 185
Korean Wave, 184
Koreck, M. T., 237
Kosovo War, 386
Kothari, M., 300
Kothi, 239–246, 247–248, 252
Kothma, 242–243, 245–246; Aariyal kothma, 242
Kowdi, 242, 245
Kowriyas, 245
Kripal, J., 238
Krisichakra, 341, 342–344
Kristiansen, S., 94
Kshama, 267
KSSP. *See* Kerala Shastra Sahitya Parishad
Kumar, A., 65
Kumar, C. R., 81
Kwayedza, 296, 297
Kymlicka, W., 91, 116, 193, 200

Lahiri, D., 165
Lal, M., 68
Lal, V., 236, 238
LAM. *See* Lok Adhikar Manch
Lamas, M., 237
Lancaster, R.N., 237
Land Acquisition Act, India, 127, 133
Langreth, R., 380
Legesse, A., 5
Levine, D. N., 200
Lewellyn, T. C., 5
Lewin, R., 379
Lewis, P., 386
Li, Y., 104
Liao, S., 102
Liguori, A. L., 237
Lindenbaum, S., 236
Lingiardi, V., 237

Liphart, A., 193, 200
Lobola, 274
Löfström, J., 236
Lok Adhikar Manch (LAM), 137
Lorway, R., 240
Ludan, 103
Ludwikowski, R., 198
Lumb, L., 72
Lyons, A. P., 236
Lyons, T., 196

Machlup, F., 354
MacIntyre, A., 94
Maggs, P. B., 198
Magure, T., 295
Male to Male Sexual Activity (MMSA), 239–240
Mall, R. K., 68
Mandela, Nelson, 298
Mandelbaum, D. G., 168
Mann, J. M., 247
Manu, 169; Laws of Manu, 167; Manusmriti, 158
Maoism, 50, 176, 186, 358
Maori, 43, 388
Marcus, G. E., 218
Markakis, J., 194, 195
Marks, S., 39
MARPS. *See* Most at Risk Populations
Marriage Act (1753), 274
Masai, 194
Masaw, M., 102, 103
Maslin, M., 68
Maternal Mortality Rate (MMR), 336–337
Mathew, B. M., 145
Mathur, H. B., 65
Maududi, S. A. A., 25
Mauga, 245
Mawar, N., 247
M'Baye, K., 32
McAfee, K., 388
McCarthy, M., 289
McLeod, R. H., 90, 92
McMichael, P., 123

McNally, S. P., 237
McNeish, J., 123
McRae, G., 128
MDGs. *See* Millennium Development Goals
Medical Termination of Pregnancy (MTP) Act, India, 268
Meharg, A. A., 63
Mehta, L., 123
Meles, Z., 202
Meltzer, R., 5
Menon, N., 123
Menscher, J. P., 4
Mental Health Act, India, 315
Merchant Shipping Act (India), 222
Messay, K., 195, 200, 205
Mgalla, Z., 298
MHFW. *See* Ministry of Health and Family Welfare
Mieville, C., 126
Milgram, S., 371
Millennium Development Goals (MDGs), 294, 295, 301, 319, 320
Miller, P., 375
Milligan, M. S., 297
Mines Act, (India), 201, 222
Mines and Minerals (Development and Regulation) Act (India), 187
Ministry of Health and Child Welfare, Zimbabwe, 296
Ministry of Health and Family Welfare (MHFW), 332
Minority, 3, 9, 149, 159, 160, 161, 173, 175, 177, 182, 240, 241, 248, 250, 361, 385; Anti-, 8; Minority rights, 10, 193–208
Mirza, M. M. Q., 67
Mittal, A., 135
MMR. *See* Maternal Mortality Rate
MMSA. *See* Male to Male Sexual Activity
Mohamad, Mahatir, 93
Monsanto Corporation, 388
Montek Singh Ahluwalia, 335

Mookerjea, S., 125
Mooney, P. R., 72
Moretti, E., 279
Morse, B. W., 116
Most at Risk Populations (MARPS), 295
Motor Transport Workers Act, 1961 (India), 222
Mountain Compatriot (shandi tongbao), 104, 105
MS Swaminathan Research (MSSRF), 333, 334
MSM (Men having Sex with Men), 10, 236, 252; India, 237–251
MSSRF. *See* MS Swaminathan Research
MTP. *See* Medical Termination of Pregnancy (MTP) Act, India
Mubangizi, M., 27
Mujtaba, H., 241
Mujuru, J., 292
Mukherjee, B. N., 272
Mulrennen, M. E., 108
Munda, 170, 171
Mupindu, R., 285, 298
Muslim League, 147
Muslim Personal Law Board (India), 231
Muslim Women's (Protection after Divorce) Act (India), 231
Mutua, M., 17, 19
Muzaffar, C., 22, 24, 25

NAC. *See* National AIDS Council
NACO. *See* National AIDS Control Organization
Nadasdy, P., 107, 108
NAFDAC. *See* National Agency for Food and Drug Administration and Control (NAFDAC)
Nag, M., 238
Nag, S., 124
Nair, J., 238, 241
Nair, P. S. G., 66, 67
Nair, S., 93, 94, 95
Nanak, 151, 152

Nanda, S., 238, 240
Nandy, A., 132
Naqvi, N., 241
Narain, S., 64
NASCOH. *See* National Association of Societies for the Care of the Handicapped
National Agency for Food and Drug Administration and Control (NAFDAC), 386
National AIDS Control Organization (NACO), India, 241, 247
National AIDS Council (NAC), Zimbabwe, 295
National Commission for Women, India, 173
National Commission on Scheduled Castes and Tribes, India, 133
National Conference on Women, Religion and Family Laws, India, 157
National Council of Disabled Persons (Zimbabwe), 286, 298
National Human Rights Commission (NHRC), India, 160, 332, 362
National Minorities Commission, India, 160
National Policy for the Empowerment of Women in India, 280
National Rural Employment Guarantee Scheme (NREGS), India, 133
National Sample Survey Organization (NSSO), India, 308, 334
Natural Rights, 1, 19, 101
Naxal, 50, 186
Nazi/Nazism, 146, 150, 369, 381
Negara Integralistik (Integralism idea in Indonesia), 89, 91, 92
Negri, A., 125
NEP. *See* New Economic Policy
Netsai Gashu, 293
Neufeldt, A. H., 297
New Economic Policy (NEP) in India, 123, 126, 155

NHRC. *See* National Human Rights Commission
Nickel, J. W., 83
Niezen, R., 99
Nigam, A., 123
Nishadas, 171
Niyogi, S. G., 360
Njema, S., 292
Nkomo, J., 300
Noble Peace Prize, 24
Norman, W., 200
Norwegian Nobel Committee, 24
Norwegian Refugee Council, 207
NREGS. *See* National Rural Employment Guarantee Scheme
NSSO. *See* National Sample Survey Organization
Nuremberg Code of Conduct, 388
Nuremberg War Criminal trials, 371
Nyansi, J. M., 5
Nyathi, L., 289

Obama, B., 199
ODA. *See* Official Development Assistance
OECD. *See* Organization for Economic Cooperation and Development
Office of the United Nations High Commissioner for Human Rights (OHCHR), 3, 47, 49, 85
Official Development Assistance (ODA), 6, 33,
Ogaden National Liberation Front (ONLF), 206
Ogoni People, 220
Ogaden region, 10, 206
OHCHR. *See* Office of the United Nations High Commissioner for Human Rights
Okinawa Charter, 353; Okinawa Economic Summit, 353
OLF. *See* Oromo Liberation Front
Oliver-Smith, A., 123
ONLF. *See* Ogaden National Liberation Front

Oostvogels, R., 240
Opalski, M., 193
Oraon, 170
Oren, M., 298
Organization for Economic Cooperation and Development (OECD), 45, 352
Orissa Pradesh Congress Committee, 187
Orissa Television (OTV), 181, 185, 186, 188, 189
Oromo, 194, 205
Oromo Liberation Front (OLF), 195, 205
Ortner, S. B., 236
Oscar Wilde, 248
OTV. *See* Orissa Television
Oxman, M. N., 378
Ozar, D., 220
Ozden, M., 38, 41

Padel, F., 123
Palan, R., 123
Panchayat, 44, 339; Panchayati Raj Institutions (PRIs), 338, 339, 346; Provisions of the Panchayat's Act (PESA), India, 132, 133; State Institute of Panchayats and Rural Development (SIPRD), 340; West Bengal Panchayat Act., 339
Pande, G. K., 355
Panos. *See* Dalits
Parekh, S., 240
Parikhs, 244, 245
Parker, R., 236, 237
Parry, M. L., 62, 66, 67, 69, 76
Pascual, M., 68
Pasha, A., 240
Pastor Graham Stewart Stains, 160
Patnaik, N., 186, 187
Patnaik, P., 9
Patnaik, U., 123
Paul, C. N., 196
Paulos, C., 205

PDS. *See* Public Distribution System
Pellizzi, F., 5
Penrose, W., 238
People's Republic of China (PRC), 23, 24
People's Union for Civil Liberties, 251
People's Union for Democratic Rights (PUDR), 189
Performance Theory, 237
Peron, L., 297
PHC. *See* Primary Health Care
Philander, J., 289, 296
Pike, K. L., 217
Pilapitiya, T., 85, 86, 89
Pillay, A. L., 296
Pimple, M., 134
Piron, L., 39
Planning Commission (India), 184, 334, 335, 360
Plantation Act, 1951 (India), 222
PNDT. *See* Pre-Natal Diagnostic Techniques
Pohang Steel & Co. (POSCO), 180, 184, 185, 186, 187, 188, 189; Anti-, 185
Porat, M., 354
POSCO. *See* Pohang Steel & Co.
POSCO Pratirodhaka Sangram Samiti (PPSS), 185; Pro-, 185
PPSS. *See* POSCO Pratirodhaka Sangram Samiti
Prasad, A., 123
Prasant, K., 130
Pratikno, Y., 94
PRC. *See* People's Republic of China
Preconception Gender Selection, 268
Pre-Natal Diagnostic Techniques (Regulation & Prevention of Misuse) Act, India, 275, 276, 277
Pre-natal Diagnostic Techniques (Prohibition of Sex Selection) Rules, 275
Primary Health Care (PHC), 332, 333

Principles of State, 91. *See also* Dasar Negara (Indonesia),
PRIs. *See* Panchayati Raj Institutions
Prudence Mabhena, 286, 290
Public Distribution System (PDS), 69, 334
PUDR. *See* People's Union for Democratic Rights
Puniyani, R., 8–9, 146, 148, 149
Puranas, 171
Purkayastha, D., 240, 241
Pyati, A. K., 353

Qing Dynasty, 103
Quah, J. S. T., 93, 94
Quijano, A., 125
Quit India (Movement), 149

RAC. *See* Recombinant DNA Advisory Committee
Raghavan, C., 31
Ragnarsson, A., 237
Rahman, M. M., 63
Rajagopal, B., 125, 127, 128–129, 130
Ramanathan, U., 127, 362
Ramdas, S., 133, 135
Ramli, M., 94
Ranade, K., 240
Rangnath Misra Committee, 160
Rao, A., 238
Rao, K. L., 62
Rao, V. N., 273
Rashtriya Swayam Sevak Sangh (RSS), 8, 146, 147, 148, 150, 152, 156, 158, 159, 176
Rath Yatra, 148, 158
Ratzinger, J., 18
Ray, R., 123
Read, J., 287
Recombinant DNA (rDNA), 377, 378, 379, 380, 381; National Research Council Committee on Recombinant DNA, 378

Recombinant DNA Advisory Committee (RAC), 378
Recombinant DNA Molecule Program Advisory Committee, 378
Reddy, D., 238
Reddy, G., 238, 240, 241
Reid, W. V., 74
Ren, C. Z., 68
Renteln, A. D., 225
Republic of China (ROC), 99, 100, 103, 104, 106, 107, 110, 112, 113, 114, 116
Revolt, 171, 357; Bhil Revolt, 171; Koala Revolt, 171; Santhal Revolt, 171; Rampa Revolt, 171; Munda Revolt, 171
Reza-Paul, S., 240
Righi, R., 297
Right of Nondiscrimination, 36
Right of Participation, 36
Rights of Nature, 26–27, 28
Rights of the Indigenous People, 5, 8, 66, 160
Right to Development, 6–7, 31–51, 76, 83, 124, 330
Right to Education, 66, 227
Right to Equality and Nondiscrimination, 382
Right to Food, 4, 41, 66, 72, 220, 278
Right to Health, 12, 66, 249, 329, 330, 332, 382
Right to Information (RTI), 44, 354, 365
Right to Life, 18, 269, 270, 288, 313, 332, 360, 377, 382
Right to Natural Resources and Property, 66
Right to Safe Life, 66
Right to Self-determination, 2, 4, 7, 9, 18, 19, 31, 36, 42, 51, 83, 99, 101, 104, 111, 113, 116, 123, 124, 127, 128, 182, 195, 196, 197, 199, 201, 204, 206, 207
Right to Water, 66
Right to Work, 221, 326, 373

Rio Declaration on Environment and Development, 36, 46, 60
Ritamhara, S., 157
Robertson, D., 351
Robertson, J. E., 237
Robertson, R., 191
Robie, D., 31
ROC. *See* Republic of China
Rohleder, P., 289, 296
Ron, J., 363
Rosalind, M., 236
Roscoe, W., 236, 237
Rothman, D., 370
Row-Kavi, A., 238
Roy, S., 76
RSS. *See* Rashtriya Swayam Sevak Sangh
RTI. *See* Right to Information
Rubin, G., 236
Rudolph, M., 104, 105
Ruger, J. P., 331
Ruggie, J., 48
Rummel, R. J., 270, 271

Sachar Committee Report, India, 160, 175
Saha, P. C., 238
Saha, T. K., 10, 11
Said, E. W., 182
Salisbury, R., 108
Samaddar, R., 364
Sangh Parivar (SP), 145, 147, 148, 152, 155, 156, 158, 160, 161, 176
Sanskritization, 158
Santal, 170
Sanyal, K., 123
Saora, 125, 135
Sapkota, A., 68
SAPs. *See* Structural Adjustment Programs
Sarkar, T., 157
Sathyamala, C., 388
Sati (Prevention) Act, 157
Savara, M., 238
Savarkar, V. D., 146, 148, 150

Scheduled Caste, India, 133, 167, 169, 341
Scheduled Tribe, India, 133, 167, 169
Scheinin, M., 110
Scheper-Hughes, N., 225
Schering, AG (Company), 388
Schiller, N. G., 218
Schirmer, J., 225
Scindia, V. R., 157
Scott, C. H., 108
Scott, J. C., 93
Second World War, 1, 3, 4, 17, 112, 216, 217, 307, 381
Seediq, 101, 102, 103, 105, 107
Selassie, A., 195
Sen, A., 43, 268, 278, 331, 332, 335
Sengupta, A., 40, 41, 335
Senior Citizen Act, India, 266
Sepoy Mutiny. *See also* First Battle of Independence, India
Sergeant, C., 296
Sethi, M., 134
Setia, M. S., 238
Sex Ratio, 268, 278, 279
Sex Ratio at Birth (SRB), 273
Shah Bano Case, 148, 231
Shakil, M., 336
Shankar Guha Neogy, 342
Sharma, A. K., 238
Sharma, M., 358
Sharma, R., 238
Sharma, R. S., 166
Sharma, S. K., 238
Sheil, D., 74
Shen, C., 94
Shepherd, G. W., 5
Shiva, V., 62, 64, 65, 74
Shizha, E., 125, 136
Shona, 287, 297, 301
Simon, S., 8, 100, 104, 105, 107
Simon, W., 236
Singer, M., 378
Singer-Soll Letter, 377–378
Singh, K.S., 170
Singh, R., 44
Singur, 50, 364

Sinha, D., 12, 13, 352, 357
Sinha, G., 384
Sinha, K., 337
Sinha, M., 156, 157
Sino-Japanese Treaty of Shimonoseki, 103
Sluga, G., 274
Smith, B., 167
Smith, C. A., 5
Smith, J. M., 71
Smith, L., 202
Solarsh, G., 285
Solomon, N., 205
Soll, D., 376
Somers, M., 191
Son Preference, 279–280
Southern Africa Federation of the Disabled, 279
Spiro, N. B. H., 193, 194
Spivak, G. C., 10, 226, 229, 230, 231
SRB. *See* Sex Ratio at Birth
Sridhar, C.R., 238
Sridhar, S., 238
Srinivas, M. N., 158
SRSG (Special Representative to the Secretary-General), 48, 49
Ssali, S. N., 237
SSSP. *See* Sundarban Sramajibi Swasthya Prakalpa
Stainton, M., 100
Stammers, N., 125, 126, 127
Stearns, D. C., 237
Stephens, J., 386
Stern, N., 73
Stone, E., 287
Structural Adjustment Programs/ Policies (SAPs), 43, 45, 65, 174, 175
Stryker, S., 237
Sudhi, 267
Sudras, 166, 167, 168; Ati-sudras, 167
Suharto, 7, 90, 92, 93, 94, 95; New Order, 82, 89, 92, 95
Sullivan Principles, 50

Sundarbans 12, 341
Sundarban Sramajibi Swasthya Prakalpa (SSSP), 341–344
Supomo, 91, 92
Surbone, A., 381
Sustainable Development, 7, 39, 69, 75–77, 111, 135, 319
Sutras, 166, 267
SV-40 Virus. *See* Tumor-producing Primate Virus
Swadeshi, 154
Swartz, L., 289, 296

TADA. *See* Terrorist and Disruptive Activities (Prevention) Act, India
Taliban, 156
Tamasoma Jyotirgamay (film), 188, 189
Tantra, 152
Tangsa, 170; Hotang Tangsa, 170; Katim Tangsa, 170
Tata Group, 49, 50, 129, 131
Teltumbde, A., 159
Tendulkar Committee, 335
TEPCO (Tokyo Electric Power Company), 45
Terracino, J. B., 83–84
Terrorist, 42, 230, 386
Terrorist and Disruptive Activities (Prevention) Act (TADA), India, 358
Thadani, G., 238
Tharoor, S., 2
Thio, L., 44
Thomas, B., 238
Thomas, I. T. M., 347
Tigrean, 204
Tigrean Liberation Front (TPLF), 195, 197
Toli, 243
Tooze, J., 379
Touraine, A., 355
TPLF. *See* Tigrean Liberation Front
Trade Related Intellectual Property Rights (TRIPs), 386–388

Traditional Forest Dwellers (Recognition of Forest Rights) Act, India, 133
Transgender, 251
Transparency International, 83, 85, 89
Transparency Thailand, 86
Transphobia, 251
Trasi, R., 297
TREAT Asia, 237, 238, 239
Tribal Development Sub-plan, 171
TRIPs. *See* Trade Related Intellectual Property Rights
Trovafloxacin, 386
Trovan Clinical Trials, 386
Truku, 101, 102, 103, 105, 107
Tsou tribe, 104
Tsvangirai, M., 289
Tuhiwai-Smith, L., 125
Tukaram, 151, 152
Tulchinsky, T. H., 333
Tully, J., 101, 106
Tumor-producing primate virus (SV-40 Virus), 377, 378
Turk, V., 298
Turner, C. F., 236
Turton, D., 202
Tuskegee Syphilis Study, 369
Tutsi, 4
Two Row Wampum Treaty (Haudensosaunee), 101

UDHR. *See* Universal Declaration of Human Rights
Ulrichs, K., 248
UNAIDS, 237, 239
UNCED. *See* United Nations Conference on the Environment and Development
UNCRPD. *See* United Nations Convention on the Rights of Persons with Disabilities UN Decade on Decolonization, 31, 33

UNCTAD. *See* United Nations Conference on Trade and Development
UN Declaration on the Right to Development, 7, 32–41, 76, 330
UNDP. *See* United Nations Development Program
UNDRIPs. *See* United Nations Declaration on the Rights of Indigenous Peoples
UNEP (United Nations Environnent Programme), 71
UNESCO. *See* United Nations Educational, Scientific and Cultural Organizations
UNESCO Convention on the Protection and Promotion of the Diversity of Cultural Expressions, 180
UNESCO Universal Declaration on Cultural Diversity, 180
UNFCC. *See* United Nations Framework Convention on Climate Change
UN Global Compact, 46–47, 50
UNHRC. *See* United Nations High Commissioner for Refugees
UN Human Rights Charter, 288
United Nations Conference on the Environment and Development (UNCED), 60
United Nations Conference on Trade and Development (UNCTAD), 352
United Nations Convention against Corruption, 46
United Nations Convention on Rights of Persons with Disabilities (UNCRPD), 11, 307, 308, 316, 317, 318
United Nations Declaration on the Rights of Indigenous Peoples (UNDRIPs), 8, 99, 100, 101, 106, 108, 111, 115, 116, 124, 176

United Nations Development Program (UNDP), 39, 43, 85, 288, 352
United Nations Educational, Scientific and Cultural Organizations (UNESCO), 61, 62, 63, 64, 65, 70, 180, 181, 225, 383
United Nations Framework Convention on Climate Change (UNFCC), 66
United Nations General Assembly, 3, 11, 17, 34, 37, 47, 60, 82, 99, 176, 179, 286, 287, 290, 293, 317, 330,
United States Agency for International Development (USAID), 239
Universal Declaration of Human Rights (UDHR), 1, 6, 12, 17, 19, 23, 32, 46, 47, 60, 82, 83, 126, 177, 190, 191, 216, 250, 286, 290, 296, 317, 329, 358, 376, 377, 382, 383, 386
UN Permanent Forum on Indigenous Issues, 100
UNPFII. *See* United Nations Permanent Forum on Indigenous Issues
UN Sub-Commission on Human Rights, 47, 48
Untouchability, 158, 167, 168, 169, 177
UPA Government, India, 337, 338
Upanishada, 267
USAID. *See* United States Agency for International Development
UUD (Undang-Undang Dasar Republik Indonesia). *See* Indonesian Constitution

Vaidyanathan, T.G., 238
Vak, 267
Vakdevi, 267
Valentine, D., 237
Vanaik, A., 155
Vanavasi Kalyan Ashram, 148

Vance, C. S., 236
Vanita, R., 238
Van Ness, P., 82, 83
Van Weerelt, P., 44
Varatharajan, D., 333, 338
Varnashrama, 167
VDPA. See Vienna Declaration and Plan of Action
Veda, 154, 267
Vedanta (Company), 180, 189
Vedic heritage, 166
Vedic period, 166, 167
Vedic society, 166
Vempeny, S., 160
Verma, J. S., 332
VHP. See Vishwa Hindu Parishad
Via Campesina, 136–137
Vienna Declaration and Plan of Action (VDPA), 3, 20, 37, 40, 41; Article 5, 83
Vishwa Hindu Parishad (VHP), 8, 147, 148, 152
Vyas, M. D., 238

Wadhava Commission, 160
Wai-Teng Leong, L., 21
Wald, G., 379
Walsh, D., 385
Wambura, L., 298
Wang, T., 110
Wang, X., 69
WAS. See World Association of Sexology
Wasserman, D., 287
Watson, J. D., 379
WCED. See World Commission on Environment and Development
WDR, 44
Weaver, J., 106
Wei Hwei-lin, 103
Welch, C.E., 5
WFP. See World Food Programme
Whitam, F. L., 236
Whitehead, H., 236
Whittle, S., 237
WHO. See World Health Organization
Wieringa, S., 236
Wikan, U., 237
Wild Life (Protection) Act, India, 134
Williams, R., 110, 125, 126, 129, 131, 137–138
Williams, W., 236
Williamson, J. B., 94
Williamson, N., 279
Wiwa, 220
Wolff, J., 84
Wolstenholme, G. E. W., 220
Woreda, 204
World Association of Sexology (WAS), 235
World Bank, 39, 45, 64, 67, 73, 93, 135, 288, 291, 335, 352
World Commission on Environment and Development (WCED), 69, 75
World Conference on Human Rights 1993, 3, 20, 37, 76. See Also Vienna Declaration and Plan of Action (VDPA)
World Food Programme (WFP), 333
World Health Organization (WHO), 61, 68, 69, 288, 296, 308, 330, 382
World Summit on Information Society (WSIS), 353, 361
World Summit on Social Development, 7, 44, 45, 60, 76; Programme of Action, 37
World Wildlife Federation, 65
Worst Forms of Child Labour Convention (Convention No. 182), ILO, 224
Wright, M., 45
Wright, S., 378
WSIS. See World Summit on Information Society
WTO, 39, 386, 387,

Xaniths, 236
Xianfa Yuanzhu Minzu Zhengce Zhixian Tuidong Xiaozu, 100, 105

Yamane, H., 4
Year of Women's Empowerment, 174
Yogyakarta Principles, 250

Zamindars, 148, 150, 154
ZAOGA. *See* Zimbabwe Assemblies of God Africa
Zhang, D., 24
Zia ul Haq, 156
Zimbabwe Assemblies of God Africa (ZAOGA), 301
Zimbabwe National AIDS Strategic Plan (ZINASP), 295
Zimbabwe National Association for Societies for the Care of the Handicapped, 287, 291–292
Zimbabwe National Association of the Deaf (ZIMNAD), 296
Zimbabwe Open University, 294
ZIMNAD. *See* Zimbabwe National Association of the Deaf
Ziran zhuquan, 102

NOTES ON CONTRIBUTORS

Subrata Sankar Bagchi is Associate Professor in the Department of Anthropology at Bangabasi Evening College, University of Calcutta, India. He is also teaching postgraduate courses of anthropology and human rights in the University of Calcutta, West Bengal State University and Jadavpur University. Recently he has also served as a Visiting Professor in the Department of Sociology and Anthropology of University of Ottawa. Bagchi has developed his scholarship in wide-ranging fields of human rights and anthropology during the last two decades. He has published many scholarly articles in different national as well as international journals and contributed several chapters in widely acclaimed volumes. Bagchi wrote three full-length monographs titled *Urban Marginalization in the Third World: Issues and Problems (2011)*, *Child Labor and the Urban Third World: Toward a New Understanding* (2010), *Child Labour in a Third World Urban Situation* (2010) and edited a volume on human rights titled *Expanding Horizons of Human Rights* (2009).

Sayan Bhattacharya is a faculty member in the Department of Environmental Science, Asutosh College under the University of Calcutta. For the last five years he has been engaged in his doctoral research in Environmental Biotechnology. Bhattacharya has published scholarly articles in the leading national and international journals, contributed book chapters. He has received young researcher awards from Govt. of India and IUPAC.

Satyabrata Chakraborty is Professor of Political Science at the University of Calcutta. He did his Ph.D. on working class movement in the Dooars plantation area. Author of *Identity, Autonomy and Development: A Study of the Tripura Tribal Areas Autonomous District Council*, Professor Chakraborty has edited three books on Political Science and Political Sociology. He has contributed articles in a number of books and journals of repute. His recent research works include 'City in the Meadow: West Bengal's Experiment in Urbanization – A Study of New Town Kolkata' (jointly with Professor Rakhahari Chatterji and funded by HIDCO, India), and 'Negotiating Globalization: The World of Auto-Rickshaw Operators in Kolkata' (funded by ICSSR, India). His present area of interest is politics of healthcare in India. He has co-authored an extensive survey report entitled "Public Health Initiatives Undertaken by Gram Panchayats in West Bengal' which was sponsored by the State Institute of Panchayat and Rural Development, Government of West Bengal.

Debi Chatterjee is Professor in the Department of International Relations, Jadavpur University, India and in charge of human rights courses in the same University. An eminent scholar on Dalit rights Chatterjee has published many scholarly articles in leading national and international journals. She has also published many widely acclaimed books which include *Ancient to Modern*

Times (2010), *Up Against Caste: Comparative Study of Ambedkar and Periyar* (2004), *Sociology of National Integration* (1993), *Marxist Thought in India* (1985), *Colour Volcano* (1981). She is currently the editor of the bi-annual journal, *Voice of Dalit*.

Arnab Das is Associate Professor in the Department of Anthropology, University of Calcutta. He also teaches postgraduate courses in Human Rights, Museology, Human Resource Management, Anthropology and Rural development in the different universities in West Bengal, India. He is also actively associated with the "Centre for Social Exclusion and Inclusive Policy" in the University of Calcutta where he organized various national and international seminars and executed the landmark project of "Sample Survey of Other Backward Classes in West Bengal". Das has published several scholarly papers in national and international journals. The paper in this book owes much of its credit to the UGC-UPE project titled *The Growing Constructs of Networks, Subcultures and other Social Differentiations of Sexuality and/ or Gender in Local Indian Contexts and Their Relationships with the Issues of Health*.

Clarence J. Dias is the President of the International Center for Law in Development, which is a Third World NGO concerned about human rights in the development process. He has taught at the Boston College School of Law and at the Department of Law of the University of Bombay. He has practiced law before the High Court of Bombay and has considerable public interest experience. He has published extensively and his books include: *Industrial Hazards in a Transnational World; Legal Professions in the Third World; The International Context of Rural Poverty in the Third World; and The Universal Declaration of Human Rights: Fifty Years and Beyond*. He assisted the drafting group that produced the 1986 UN Declaration on the Right to Development and was a consultant at the Global Consultation on the Right to Development convened by the UN Human Rights Centre in 1989. He has served as consultant to various UN agencies including UNDP, the Office of the High Commissioner for Human Rights, UNICEF and ILO and to various bilateral development agencies of many countries. He was Chair of the *Meeting of Experts on Economic Social and Cultural Rights,* convened by the UN Human Rights Centre. For a six-year period (1996 to 2001) he was the UN expert from the Office of the UN High Commissioner for Human Rights at the annual Asia-Pacific Intergovernmental Workshop on *Regional Human Rights Arrangements.* He was the primary author of UNDP's policy on *Integrating Human Rights with Sustainable Human Development* (adopted in 1997) and thereafter, undertook responsibility for the human rights component in five UNDP regional workshops for Resident Representatives on the human rights policy of UNDP. He has undertaken country missions for the UN in numerous countries including: Bosnia Herzegovina, Iran, Yemen, East Timor, Papua New Guinea, Nepal, Cambodia, Viet Nam, Mongolia, the Philippines, Malaysia, Indonesia, and Sri Lanka. During the period 2003 to 2009, he has been mainly working in post-conflict countries and led UNDP missions to Afghanistan (to develop an access to justice program for the Provinces); Iran (to draw up a 5 year program on Good Governance; Indonesia (access to justice and law reform); Laos (strengthening ratification and implementation of international law); Iraq (support for the High Preparatory Committee for and the National Conference); and Bahrain and Vietnam (UPR preparation).

Pawan Dhall works in an NGO called SAATHII that works to build the capacities of individuals and organizations working on HIV and associated issues in India. His primary area of work is documentation, learning resources development, training, advocacy and strategizing on realization of sexual and reproductive health and rights of people living with HIV, LGBT people, youth and women. He has over 20 years of experience in LGBT community mobilization, particularly in but not limited to eastern India. He was a founder member of Counsel Club and founder editor of 'Naya Pravartak', one of the first queer initiatives that started in the region in the early 1990s. He worked as a journalist in 'Business Standard' before focusing fully on social development work through stints in NGOs Thoughtshop Foundation, Humsafar Trust and Integration Society (which he co-founded as a sister agency of Counsel Club in 1999). He has contributed articles on queer, HIV, environment, child rights, corporate and economic affairs to a variety of newspapers, magazines, resource books, webzines and anthologies.

Marie-Luisa Frick is Assistant Professor, Department of Philosophy, University of Innsbruck, Austria. She has written and edited four books and published several scholarly articles on human rights both in German and English in various leading international journals like *American Journal of Islamic Social Sciences, Journal of the International Academy for Philosophy*. Frick has also contributed chapters in various books.

Semahagn Gashu is affiliated with Faculty of Law, University of Gottingen, Germany and pursuing his dissertation on 'Federalism and Democracy in Africa: the Ethiopian Experience'. He got his LLB degree from Addis Ababa University, Ethiopia and LLM degree from Faculty of Law, University of Amsterdam. He has published and presented many critically acclaimed papers.

Dip Kapoor is Associate Professor of International Education at the University of Alberta, Canada and Research Associate, Center for Research and Development Solidarity (CRDS), an Adivasi-Dalit people's organization in Orissa, India. His recent co-edited book collections include *Indigenous Knowledge and Learning in Asia/Pacific and Africa* (2010: Palgrave Macmillan, NY); *Learning from the Ground Up: Global Perspectives on Social Movements and Knowledge Production* (2010: Palgrave Macmillan, NY); *Education, Decolonization and Development: Perspectives from Africa, Asia and the Americas* (2009: Sense Publishers, Rotterdam); and *Participatory Action Research and Social Change: International Perspectives* (2009: Palgrave Macmillan, NY). Forthcoming collections include Globalization, *Culture and Education in South Asia: Critical Ex-*

cursions (Palgrave Macmillan, NY) and *Complicity, Contradictions and Prospects: NGOization and its Discontents* (Zed, London).

Francis Machingura is affiliated with Otto-Friedrich University, Bamberg, Germany. He holds an M.A. degree in Religious Studies and Post-Graduate Diploma in Education from the University of Zimbabwe. A well-known scholar on human rights issues in Zimbabwe, Machingura served as a lecturer at the University of Zimbabwe, teaching courses like Human Rights and Democracy in Religions and Pedagogical Issues in Religious Education. His research interests include Biblical Interpretation and Pentecostalism, African Independent Churches, Bible and society, Human rights and Democracy, Politics, HIV and AIDS. Francis has also published articles in those disciplines. He has recently published a book entitled *Can the Virgin Birth of Jesus be Explained and Understood? A Scientific Point of View* and *The Zimbabwean Concept of Virginity*.

Awi Mona (Chih-Wei Tsai) is Assistant Professor of Law and Indigenous Studies, Department of Indigenous Development & Social Work, National Dong Hwa University College of Indigenous Studies, Taiwan. He earned his Ph.D. from the University of Washington School of Law, Seattle, Washington, LL.M from the University of Arizona James E. Rogers College of Law, Tucson, Arizona and LL.B from the National Taiwan University, Taipei, Taiwan. A well-known specialist on the indigenous rights issue, Mona is associated with various rights-based bodies and organizations. He has contributed several scholarly articles in leading international journals and contributed scholarly chapters in many edited volumes.

Aniruddha Mukhopadhyay is Associate Professor and Head of the Department of Environmental Science, University of Calcutta. A gold-medalist for his top-rank in his master degree, Mukhopadhyay has done post doctoral research work in US. He has several national and international research publications and has been actively engaged in several research projects. He has edited four widely acclaimed books and is currently an active member in several academic bodies in India.

Subhasis Mukhopadhyay is an Associate Professor in Bio-Physics in the University of Calcutta. His current research interest is in the field of Environmental Management and Ecology for complex resource management, Bioethics, Bioinformatics and Computational Biology, particularly the application of Computational Linguistics to understand the code of life and Genome evolution. He writes about issues in biotechnology, the issues involved in GMO, agricultural biotechnology affecting the society, particularly the implication of rDNA technology for third world countries, the policy alternatives and citizen' advocacy for a just, equitable and inclusive approach from a participatory perspective. He is a regular contributor in the area of interface between science and many technical and semi-technical journals. He writes popular articles in the frontier areas of science and technology, both in English and Bengali, and runs columns in science and in daily and fortnightly vernacular journal. Designing teaching aid for the high school children in the area of science, mathematics and geography is his passion and he promotes such activities through the Department of Science and Technology, Government of India. He edited two books on Intellectual Property Rights pertaining to Science and technology and was an Adviser to the Patent Information Cell, Department of Science and Technology, Government of West Bengal. He has written three books on ecology, history of science and technology, several book chapters and had authored about 50 technical papers in peer reviewed journals.

Pranta Pratik Patnaik is now pursuing Ph.D. from the Department of Sociology, Delhi School of Economics, University of Delhi on – 'Television and Socio-Cultural Identity: An Ethnographic Study in Orissa'. He has published articles in the journals like *Women's Link* and *Third Concept. An International Journal of Ideas* and reviewed some books on social sciences.

Ram Puniyani is a former Professor in biomedical engineering at the renowned Indian Institute of Technology Bombay and took a voluntary retirement to work full-time for communal harmony and human rights in India. He is now acting as the Secretary of Center for Study of Society and Secularism, India. Puniyani is one of the most prominent human rights activists in India and a prolific writer against communal harmony and human rights. He has got several awards for his role in keeping national integrity and communal harmony in India. Some of his widely acclaimed books include *Fascism of Sangh Parivar, The Other Cheek, Communal Politics: an illustrated primer, Indian Democracy, Pluralism and Minorities, Communalism: India's Nemesis?, Communalism: What is False: What is True, Communalism: Illustrated Primer, Communal Politics: Facts Versus Myths, Terrorism: Facts versus Myths, Second Assassination of Gandhi, Religion Power and Violence: Expression Of Politics In Contemporary Times, Contours of Hindu Rashtra: Hindutva, Sangh Parivar And Contemporary Politics, Contemporary India: Overcoming Sectarianism: Terrorism, Hindutva Strategies And Dalit Movement, Hindu Extreme Right-Wing Groups : Ideology and Consequences* and *Mumbai Post 26/11*(Edited along with Shabnam Hashmi).

Tushar Kanti Saha is a Barrister-at-Law from Lincoln's Inn, London and holds LL.M and Ph.D. in law from the University of Calcutta. He has taught in five Universities/Institutes in India and four in Africa. He is currently serving as Professor of Law and Senate Member at the National University of Lesotho. He has written five books on law including a text book titled *Constitution of Lesotho-A Text of Comparative Research Study* (2010) and published many scholarly articles in leading international journals.

Anuradha Saibaba Rajesh is Assistant Professor in National Law School of India University, Bengaluru, Karnataka, India. An LL.B from the University of Delhi she got Chevening Scholarship to pursue LL.M in Human Rights Law from the Queen's University of Belfast. Saibaba is the Faculty Coordinator of the endowment chair National Institute on Human Rights (NIHR). She is also the Academic Coordinator of the Post Graduate Diploma Course in Human Rights Law, Distance Education Department, NLSIU. Saibaba authored three books, published several scholarly articles in leading national and international journals and contributed chapters in a couple of books.

Scott Simon is Associate Professor in the Department of Sociology and Anthropology, University of Ottawa, Canada. A prolific writer and a well-known scholar on the culture and rights of the indigenous people in Taiwan, Simon has written two widely acclaimed books titled *Tanners of Taiwan: Life Strategies and National Culture* (2005) and *Sweet and Sour: Life Worlds of Taipei Women Entrepreneurs* (2003). He has also written several scholarly articles in various leading international journals, contributed chapters in many well-known books, published many technical papers and has given numerous invited lectures throughout the world.

Dipankar Sinha is Professor of Political Science, Calcutta University. He is also an Honorary Visiting Professor at the Institute of Development Studies Kolkata, Honorary Associate of the Centre for Media History in Macquarie University, Sidney, and Nominated Member of the Association of Third World Studies, USA. Sinha specializes in communicative modes of globalization, governance, democracy and development. His essay *Strategies for a New Information Society in Brazil and India* has received an international 'best article' award. Sinha has authored *Communicating Development in the New World Order* (1999) and, in Bengali, *Media Sanskriti* (2003). His other books include *Media, Gender and Popular Culture in India* (forthcoming from Sage, co-authored), *Democratic Governance in India: Reflections and Refractions* (2007, co-edited), and *Webs of History: Information, Communication and Technology From Early to Post-Colonial India* (2005, co-edited). Sinha's most recent publications include a Working Paper of the London School of Economics on *(De)Politicizing Information Technology: Towards an Inclusive Framework*.

Agus Wahyudi is Lecturer at the International School, Faculty of Economic, Atmajaya Christian University, Yogyakarta, Indonesia. He is also the Chairman, Study Program of Political Philosophy at the Faculty of Philosophy, Gadjah Mada University, Indonesia. Wahyudi was Fulbright scholar and got many awards for his scholarly works. He has published several articles in the leading national and international journals and contributed many book chapters.